KT-500-836

God is Dead

Religion in the Modern World

Series Editors: Paul Heelas, *University of Lancaster*; Linda Woodhead, *University of Lancaster*; Editorial Advisor: David Martin, *Emeritus of the London School of Economics*; Founding Editors: John Clayton, *University of Boston*; Ninian Smart, *formerly of University of California – Santa Barbara.*

The **Religion in the Modern World** series makes accessible to a wide audience some of the most important work in the study of religion today. The series invites leading scholars to present clear and non-technical contributions to contemporary thinking about religion in the modern world. Although the series is geared primarily to the needs of college and university students, the volumes in **Religion in the Modern World** will prove invaluable to readers with some background in Religious Studies who wish to keep up with recent thinking in the subject, as well as to the general reader who is seeking to learn more about the transformations of religion in our time.

Published:

Don Cupitt – *Mysticism After Modernity*
Paul Heelas, with the assistance of David Martin and Paul Morris – *Religion, Modernity and Postmodernity*
Linda Woodhead and Paul Heelas – *Religion in Modern Times*
Paul Heelas – *Religion and Cultural Change*
David Martin – *Pentecostalism: The World Their Parish*
Steve Bruce – *God is Dead*

Forthcoming:

Juan Campo – *Pilgrimages in Modernity*
David Smith – *Hinduism and Modernity*

God is Dead

Secularization in the West

Steve Bruce

University of Aberdeen

Blackwell
Publishing

350 Main Street, Malden, MA 02148-5020, USA
108 Cowley Road, Oxford OX4 1JF, UK
550 Swanston Street, Carlton, Victoria 3053, Australia

First published 2002 by Blackwell Publishing Ltd
Reprinted 2003 (twice)

Library of Congress Cataloging-in-Publication Data

Bruce, Steve, 1954–
  God is dead : secularization in the West / Steve Bruce.
    p. cm. — (Religion in the modern world)
  Includes bibliographical references and index.
  ISBN 0-631-23274-5 (alk. paper) — ISBN 0-631-23275-3 (pbk. : alk. paper)
  1. Secularism. I. Title. II. Series.
BL2747.8 .B78 2002
200´.9182´1—dc21

                                        2001004195

A catalogue record for this title is available from the British Library.

Set in 10½ on 13 pt Meridien
by Graphicraft Ltd, Hong Kong

For further information on
Blackwell Publishing, visit our website:
http://www.blackwellpublishing.com

Dedicated to Erika Kadlecová

Contents

Figures

Tables

Preface

It might help the reader if I said something about the point of this book. It is a restatement of one particular approach to explaining the changes in the presence, popularity and status of religion in the modern world: the secularization paradigm. It aims to clarify it and answer the criticisms. Along the way it presents the evidence that leads me to believe that the liberal industrial democracies of the Western world are considerably less religious now than they were in the days of my father, my grandfather and my great-grandfather.

Although there are frequent references to other countries (and the United States merits an entire chapter), many of the examples are drawn from the British Isles. This is not (or not only) ethnocentrism. One of the abiding faults of modern social theory is that it is presented at such a level of abstraction that it is vapid and untestable. Pontificating about times and places of which one knows little is unhelpful. To give just one example from problems discussed below, it is common to find US scholars who wish to stress the religious diversity of the United States using modern Britain as the polar opposite: a country dominated by a single church. While we might reasonably view France and Sweden as religious monopolies, any detailed knowledge of the religious life of England, Wales or Scotland in, say, 1851 would show that there was not one state church but two very different state churches and that half the population worshipped in a plethora of dissenting sects outside the national churches. There are polymaths who know enough to be able to range across the globe and the centuries (Ernest Gellner and W. J. Runciman are examples from recent British social science), but I cannot pretend to such learning. Hence I build my theory on the society that I know intimately and leave it to my colleagues in other countries to apply their local knowledge to my lines of reasoning.

However, there is nothing limiting about concentrating on Britain. Much of what matters here can be found elsewhere. To the extent that Britain is unusual it is so in a manner that should be a magnet to the iron in the soul of the sociologist of religion. Britain is one of the most secular countries in the world and its evolution could reasonably be described as 'naturally occurring'. Unlike the case of the Soviet

Union or Ataturk's Turkey, a formally secular state was not imposed on an enduringly religious population. The decline in the political and social power of religious institutions has been slow and it has proceeded alongside declining popular participation. Finally, Britain has now been secular for long enough for us to be sure that this is an enduring trend worthy of sociological explanation and for it to serve as a test bed for theories about the obstinacy of secularization.

It is worth adding a general word about my approach. At a recent conference, I was berated by a Christian lady for my presentation of the sort of data found in chapter 3. Apparently I was a horrid little man and not only was Christianity not declining but, if it was, it was the fault of people like me who kept talking it down! When I pointed out that my evidence and conclusions were barely different from those presented by an ordained colleague and professor of theology, Robin Gill, I was told 'Yes, but he sounds like he regrets it. You don't!' I should probably plead guilty to the charge. Sociologists should describe and explain; they should neither regret nor rejoice.

This book aspires to be rather old-fashioned social science. It tries to clarify explanations and bring appropriate evidence to bear upon them, so that we can discard the least persuasive. At times (especially in the first chapter) there are rather too many ponderous words ending in 'ization' for good taste, but most of it is readable. If it does not persuade, it should at least make it possible for the protagonists to argue with, rather than past, each other.

Finally in this preface I would like to explain the dedication. In the research for *Choice and Religion* (Bruce 1999) I made extensive use of a marvellous volume edited by Hans Mol: *Western Religion: A Country by Country Sociological Enquiry*. Mol had invited an expert from every country in western Europe to write a brief account of that country's recent religious history and present the best available data on the nature and levels of religious participation and belief. Although not published until 1972, many of the entries had been written in 1968, the year that tanks of the Warsaw Pact crushed the liberalization of communism in Czechoslovakia. A footnote to the Czech chapter said: 'This article was written before October 1968, when Mrs Kadlecová held both high academic and governmental positions. It has proved impossible to communicate with her since that time' (Mol 1972: 117).

Reading it almost thirty years later, I found Mol's terse note revived memories of profound feelings. I had just been coming to an awareness of politics when the Prague Spring was repressed. I had distant Czech relatives and closer family in Bulgaria (at that time, the Soviet Union's most loyal ally) and I was drawn to the conflict. I can recall BBC news broadcasts of crowds of angry Czechs chanting the names of their deposed leaders – 'Dubček, Svoboda, Dubček, Svoboda' – at the Russian and Bulgarian soldiers. Thirty years on, when I read Erika Kadlecová's chapter, the Soviet empire had collapsed. I knew that Alexander Dubček had lived long enough to see communism overthrown and be returned to office as Speaker in the first free Czech parliament for half a century. I naturally wondered what had become of Ms Kadlecová. Had she survived or had she died in internal exile? With no real hope of success, I contacted the Czech branch of the human rights organization Helsinki Watch. A very helpful young woman e-mailed back that she had never heard of Ms Kadlecová but had found that name in the phone book. I wrote explaining my interest and two weeks later received a reply.

> Thank you for your letter. It evoked memories of a time that even those who lived in it have already nearly lost from their memory. I know the book by Hans Mol. An evangelical priest smuggled it at that time and brought it to me. But I could not answer as I was under police control and my correspondence usually ended at an address it was not meant to reach.
>
> You are asking about my fate. At the period of the Prague Spring I was nominated director of the Secretariate for Religious Matters. That was the highest control office over the churches. I tried to change the character of that office, to put an end to bothering the believers and to correct the senseless hardship used against the churches. After the occupation and the so-called normalization I naturally could not remain there. I was also expelled from working in the Academy of Sciences. The Department of Sociology I headed was dissolved. Nor could I work anywhere else in my profession. All my theses were listed as 'libri prohibiti'. When I refused to recognise my sins and to defend the reasons for the military invasion by the USSR, I was even forbidden to work in any job where I could come into contact with any large number of people. That is why I found a job in an accountant department.
>
> The situation became even more serious when I signed Charter 77, an open criticism of the regime . . . The worst sanction was that my daughter was not permitted to enter secondary school 'because of the bad profile of both parents'.
>
> I am afraid the above story sounds rather dramatic. But that is really not the case. It is quite possible to live without a passport, without a telephone, with a minimum income and now and then a police

interrogation and nevertheless to have an active life that really has a purpose. Apart from that I had a lot of friends whom I could respect and were in a similar situation trying to achieve similar goals. I think that many of those who disowned everything they did and swallowed the humiliation were in a psychologically much worse situation.

Apart from her forbearance, what I found particularly impressive was her enduring commitment to her values. In my letter I had described listening to demonstrations on the radio.

> Your still-semi-childish enthusiasm for 1968 is near to my heart and pleasing to me. I was 14 years old when I heard Hitler shouting that this Kleinstaaterei must be destroyed and when Mr Chamberlain pronounced his cool and indifferent words about the country nobody knows. For me that as the decisive moment in my life. When I was 17 years old I established contact with a group of young communists who attempted to develop some sort of resistance. In 1969 I left the communist party for similar reasons to those for which I had joined it 25 years earlier. But the original communist ideals of Marxism had got too deep under my skin. . . . A Christian does not repudiate the Sermon on the Mount because of the Inquisition. I am not able to accept that global neonormalization with prefabricated thinking, behaviour and tastes should be the best of all worlds.
>
> I can see that I produced a parody of 'Confession of a Child of my Age'. That is sufficient.

If I insult my colleagues in saying this I equally insult myself: what moves me about Erika Kadlecová's fate is that it is such a contrast with the comfortable and easy lives of Western academics, for whom 'being attacked' means having a colleague saying something unflattering about a journal article. On my shelves are rows of edited collections. That one of the contributors to one of those books should have had her country invaded and her career abruptly ended, and been subject to periodic police harassment, and that in a central European country, is a salutary reminder to the rest of us how fortunate we are to live in affluent stable democracies that have not been invaded for over half a century.

I would like to dedicate this book to Erika Kadlecová, a companion in sociology, in recognition of her courageous opposition to not just one, but two repressive regimes. Her life reminds us how trivial are our differences.

S. B.
Aberdeen, 2001

Acknowledgements

Many colleagues have helped me clarify my understanding of secularization. A first attempt at the figure in chapter 1 was scribbled on a Chinese restaurant menu by my mentor and friend, the late Roy Wallis, in 1988. For the last ten years I have enjoyed long and good-natured arguments with Paul Heelas and Linda Woodhead, two colleagues from the University of Lancaster, who will disagree with a lot of what I have to say but will continue to be hospitable. In 1999 Heelas and Woodhead organized a symposium at Lancaster on the influence of Peter Berger (for the papers see Woodhead 2001). Peter Berger not only attended but with patience and good grace listened to colleagues demonstrating their often inadequate understanding of his work. Thomas Luckmann was also present and contributed powerfully to the discussions. It was an enormous pleasure to meet the two men whose *Social Construction of Reality* (1973) had recruited me to the discipline and I am grateful to Heelas and Woodhead for organizing the symposium and inviting me.

In April 2000, Grace Davie of the University of Exeter took on the burden of arranging a conference to honour the work of David Martin and Bryan Wilson, both recently retired. I was honoured to be invited to speak and benefited considerably from the comments of colleagues such as Jose Casanova, as well as those of Martin and Wilson.

Chapters 2 and 3 are extensions of articles that first appeared in the *British Journal of Sociology* and *Sociology of Religion*. I would like to thank the anonymous readers and the editors of those journals for their helpful comments.

I would also like to thank Gordon Heald, formerly of Gallup and now of Opinion Research Business, for making survey data available to me.

Finally, I would like to thank Hilary Walford, who, as ever, diligently copy-edited the text.

CHAPTER ONE

The Secularization Paradigm

If argument in the social sciences is to be useful rather than merely entertaining, it must treat competing positions in their own terms and as fairly as possible. Sadly many contemporary debates about the fate of religion in the modern world are mulched in layers of caricature. One generation's misrepresentations are taken as authoritative and accurate by a younger generation that lacks the time or inclination to read the work of those they are inclined to disdain. In 1985, when Rodney Stark and William S. Bainbridge (1985: 430) wanted to represent the secularization paradigm (in order to show it false), they ignored the sociologists who had developed those ideas and instead cited a 1960s undergraduate textbook written by an anthropologist. Despite others pointing out that Anthony Wallace's view – 'the evolutionary future of religion is extinction' – might not be representative, Stark used this quotation repeatedly for the next fifteen years (see Stark and Finke 2000: 58). It became so firmly established that others (for example, Buckser 1996) saved themselves the trouble of reading old sociology by repeating it. The waters then became further clouded when scholars sympathetic to the secularization approach took such caricatures as an accurate account of what the paradigm entailed. They devised responses that they presented as 'neo-secularization theory', despite them differing little from the forgotten originals. In so doing, they made respectable the caricatures of what they sought to defend (Yamane 1997).

The point of this chapter is to clear the way for sensible debate about secularization. It presents little evidence; that can be found in later chapters. What I want to do here is lay out as clearly and as briefly as possible just what modern sociologists mean by secularization. Of course, this is a personal selection and interpretation, but I believe I am sufficiently well acquainted with the work I summarize for it to be representative and reasonable. As will become clear, there is no one secularization theory. Rather, there are clusters of descriptions and explanations that cohere reasonably well. I take my remit as summarizing *sociological* contributions from Max Weber onwards. Interesting though they are, I have no brief for defending the views of psychiatrists such as Sigmund Freud or the overambitious evolutionary models of social development popular with such nineteenth-century thinkers as Auguste Comte and Karl Marx. In the last part of the chapter I will discuss some criticisms of the paradigm that are not dealt with at length in other chapters.

The basic proposition is that modernization creates problems for religion. Modernization is itself a multifaceted notion, which encompasses the industrialization of work; the shift from villages to towns and cities; the replacement of the small community by the society; the rise of individualism; the rise of egalitarianism; and the rationalization both of thought and of social organization. It is not necessary to spend a lot of time at this point on the meanings of these terms; they will become clear as we proceed. Nor is it necessary to agonize over the meaning of 'religion' (though there is plenty of that in later chapters). For reasons considered in detail in chapter 10, I follow common usage in defining religion substantively as *beliefs, actions and institutions predicated on the existence of entities with powers of agency (that is, gods) or impersonal powers or processes possessed of moral purpose (the Hindu notion of karma, for example), which can set the conditions of, or intervene in, human affairs.* Although rather long-winded, this seems to cover most of what we mean when we talk about religion and offers a reasonable starting place.

Defining secularization in advance of offering explanations of it is less easy because scholars often conflate their definitions and explanations, but two quotations will suffice to begin the account. Berger and Luckmann (1966: 74) point to the declining social power of religion in their definition of secularization as 'the progressive autonomization of societal sectors from the domination of religious meaning and institutions'. Wilson made the same point in more detail and added explicit references to the thinking and behaviour of individuals when he said of secularization:

> Its application covers such things as the sequestration by political powers of the property and facilities of religious agencies; the shift from religious to secular control of various of the erstwhile activities and functions of religion; the decline in the proportion of their time, energy and resources which men devote to supra-empirical concerns; the decay of religious

institutions; the supplanting, in matters of behaviour, of religious precepts by demands that accord with strictly technical criteria; and the gradual replacement of a specifically religious consciousness (which might range from dependence on charms, rites, spells or prayers, to a broadly spiritually-inspired ethical concern) by an empirical, rational, instrumental orientation; the abandonment of mythical, poetic, and artistic interpretations of nature and society in favour of matter-of-fact description and, with it, the rigorous separation of evaluative and emotive dispositions from cognitive and positivistic orientations. (1982: 149)

This depiction is complex because it involves the place of religion in the social system, the social standing of religious institutions, and individual beliefs and behaviour. Although they are here presented as a package and Wilson believes them to be related, it is obvious that the societies we hope to encompass with our generalizations differ sufficiently within and between themselves that not all elements will develop in exactly the same way in every setting. Nonetheless, a degree of generalization does seem possible.

Wilson is careful to distinguish between the social significance of religion and religion as such. We should not foreclose on the possibility that religion may cease to be of any great social importance while remaining a matter of great import for those who have some. However, as I will argue, there is a very clear implication that three things are causally related: the social importance of religion, the number of people who take it seriously, and how seriously anyone takes it. It is possible that a country that is formally and publicly secular may nonetheless contain among its populace a large number of people who are deeply religious. But, in a number of these chapters, I will show ways in which the declining social significance of religion causes a decline in the number of religious people and the extent to which people are religious.[1]

In brief, I see secularization as a social condition manifest in (a) the declining importance of religion for the operation of non-religious roles and institutions such as those of the state and the economy; (b) a decline in the social standing of religious roles and institutions; and (c) a decline in the extent to which people engage in religious practices, display beliefs of a religious kind, and conduct other aspects of their lives in a manner informed by such beliefs.

As a final preliminary we may note that the secularization paradigm is very largely concerned with what it is now popular to call the 'demand' for religion. It supposes that changes in religious belief and behaviour are best explained by changes in social structure and culture

Figure 1.1   The secularization paradigm

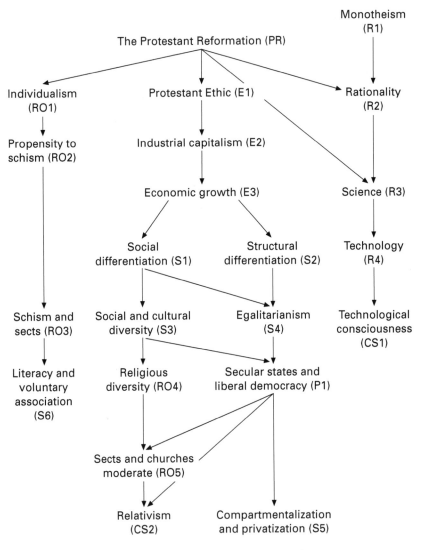

Key: R = Rationalization; RO = Religious organization; E = Economy;
S = Society; P = Polity; CS = Cognitive style

that make religion more or less plausible and more or less desirable. As we will see in the following chapters, some of the criticisms of secularization are less challenges to specific propositions and more a blanket rejection of the focus of study. Rodney Stark and his associates argue that the main determinants of religious vitality lie not in causes of varying demand but in features of the religious marketplace that affect the 'supply' of religious goods (Stark and Finke 2000). I have considered their rational-choice approach to religion at considerable length elsewhere (Bruce 1999) and will refer to it a number of times in subsequent chapters.

The paradigm

Figure 1.1 is a diagrammatic representation of the key elements and connections in the secularization paradigm. As each is well known and has its own extensive literature, in working my way through them, I will confine myself to brief elaborations.

I should stress two points about the status of the causal connections being identified. First, I am not suggesting that these causes are by themselves *sufficient* to produce their purported effects. Many other conditions, themselves deserving book-length treatment, are required. For example, the E1 to E2 link describes a change in ways of thinking about work that stimulated material changes already underway. In identifying the role of the Protestant ethic in the rise of modern capitalism, Weber is not suggesting that a Protestant culture could produce capitalism in any circumstance: the material conditions had to be right. Where they were not, Puritans simply experienced the frustration of their intentions (as in the Scottish case; see Marshall 1980). Secondly, I am not suggesting that any of these causes were enduringly *necessary*. To continue with the Weber example, once rational capitalism was well established and its virtues obvious, it could be adopted by people with very different psychologies in very different cultures (as we see in the example of Japan) – that is, many social innovations, once established, become free of their origins.

Monotheism (R1)

I will begin with the rationalization column, not because it is the most important, but because it has the earliest starting point. Rationalization largely involves changes in the way people think and consequentially in the way they act. Following Weber, Berger has plausibly argued that the rationality of the West has Jewish and Christian roots. The religion of the Old Testament differed from that of surrounding cultures in a number of important respects. The religions of Egypt and Mesopotamia were profoundly cosmological. The human world was embedded in a cosmic order that embraced the entire universe, with no sharp distinction between the human and the non-human, the empirical and the supra-empirical. Greek and Roman gods even mated with humans. Such continuity between people and the gods was broken by the religion of the Jews. As Berger puts it: 'The Old Testament posits a God who stands outside the cosmos, which is his creation but which he confronts and does not permeate' (1969: 115). He created it and he would end it, but, between start and finish, the world could be seen as having its own structure and logic. The God of Ancient Israel was a radically transcendent God. He made consistent ethical demands upon his followers and he was so remote as to be beyond magical manipulation. We could learn his laws and obey them, but we could not bribe, cajole or trick him into doing our will. There was a thoroughly demythologized universe between humankind and God.

In the myths of ancient Rome and Greece, a horde of gods or spirits, often behaving in an arbitrary fashion and at cross purposes, made the relationship of supernatural to natural worlds unpredictable. First Judaism and then Christianity were rationalizing forces. By having only one God, they simplified the supernatural and allowed the worship of God to become systematized. Pleasing God became less a matter of trying to anticipate the whims of an erratic despot and more a matter of correct ethical behaviour.

As the Christian Church evolved, the cosmos was remythologized with angels and semi-divine saints. The Virgin Mary was elevated as a mediator and co-redeemer with Jesus. The idea that God could be manipulated through ritual, confession and penance undermined the tendency to regulate behaviour with a standardized and rational ethical code. No matter how awful one's life, redemption could be bought by funding the Church. However, this trend was reversed as the Protestant Reformation in the sixteenth and seventeenth centuries again demythologized the world, eliminated the ritual and sacramental manipulation of God, and restored the process of ethical rationalization.

Making formal what was pleasing to God made it possible for morality and ethics to become detached from beliefs about the supernatural. The codes could be followed for their own sake and could even attract alternative justifications. For example, 'Do unto others as you would be done by' could be given an entirely utilitarian justification in a way that 'Placate this God or suffer' could not. In that sense, the rationalizing tendency of Christianity created space for secular alternatives.

So we can summarize these points with the links R1 to R2 (monotheism encourages rationality) and PR to R2 (the Reformation further stimulates rationality). A common red herring can be eliminated if we appreciate that no particular virtue is implied in the use of the term 'rational'. We may also note that Weber and Berger are not concerned primarily with the structure of individual thought in the sense of philosophizing. Rather, the supposed variable is the extent to which means–ends rationality is embedded in social organizations (of which the modern rule-governed bureaucracy is the clearest embodiment). As Wilson puts it: 'Men may have become more rational, and their thinking may have become more matter-of-fact, as Veblen expressed it, but perhaps even more important is their sustained involvement in rational organizations, which impose rational behaviour upon them' (1966: 7).

The Protestant Ethic (E1)

Max Weber argued that the Reformation had the unintended consequence of creating a new attitude to work. In attacking the narrow priestly notion of vocation, Martin Luther elevated all work (excluding, of course, the servicing of vanities and vices) to the status of a *calling* that glorified God. By arguing against confession, penance and absolution, the Reformers deprived people of a way of periodically wiping away their sins. They thus increased the psychological strain of trying to live a Christian life and made it all the more important to avoid temptation; hence the additional premium on work. By insisting that God had already divided all people into the saved and the unsaved, the chosen and the rejected (that is, our fate is *predestined*), John Calvin and his followers inadvertently created a climate in which the Puritans could see worldly success, provided it was achieved honestly and diligently by pious people, as proof of divine favour. These elements combined to produce a new 'ethic'. Whereas previously especially religious people had cut themselves off from the world in monasteries and in hermitages (or, in the case of Simon Stylites, on top of a column), the Puritans exemplified what Weber called 'this-worldly asceticism'.

The link E2 to E3 represents the simple fact that those countries that first adopted industrial capitalism prospered ahead of their rivals and, as we will see below, prosperity itself has contributed to the weakening of religious commitments.

Structural differentiation (S2)

Modernization entails structural and functional differentiation, by which I mean the fragmentation of social life as specialized roles and institutions are created to handle specific features or functions previously embodied in or carried out by one role or institution (Parsons 1964).[2] The family was once a unit of production as well as the social institution through which society was reproduced. With industrialization, economic activity became divorced from the home. It also became increasingly informed by its own values (that is, S2 is informed by R2). At work we are supposed to be rational, instrumental and pragmatic. We are also supposed to be universalistic: to treat customers alike, paying attention only to the matter in hand. We are not supposed to vary our prices according to the race or religion of the purchaser. The private sphere, by contrast, is taken to be expressive, indulgent and emotional.

In addition to the indirect effects described shortly, increased specialization has the direct effect of secularizing many social functions that in the Middle Ages either were the exclusive preserve of the Christian Church or were dominated by the clergy.[3] Education, health care, welfare and social control were once all in the domain of religious institutions; now we have specialist institutions for each. The shift of control was gradual and proceeded at various speeds in different settings, but religious professionals were replaced as specialist professionals were trained and new bodies of knowledge or skill were generated. Where religious institutions retain what we would now regard as secular functions, those functions are performed by lay professionals trained and accredited by secular bodies, and are exercised within an essential secular value frame. For example, the Church of England provides various forms of residential social care, but its social workers are tested in secular expertise, not piety, and they are answerable to state- rather than church-determined standards. Spiritual values may inspire the Church's involvement in social work but there is very little in the expression of that inspiration that distinguishes it from secular provision.

Social differentiation (S1)

As Marx noted in his theory of class formation (Giddens 1971: 35–45), as the functions of society become increasingly differentiated, so the people also become divided and separated from each other – that is, structural differentiation was accompanied by social differentiation. The economic growth implicit in modernization led to the emergence of an ever-greater range of occupation and life situation. The creation of new social classes often led to class conflict; it was certainly accompanied by class avoidance. In feudal societies, masters and servants lived cheek by jowl. The master might ride while the servant walked, but they travelled together. The straw given to the master might be clean, but master and servant often slept in the same room. In medieval Edinburgh all manner of people occupied the same tenements and threw their excrement into the same street. Such mixing was possible because everyone knew his or her place in the social order. 'Stations' were so firmly fixed that the gentry need not fear that allowing the lower orders to occupy the same space would give them ideas 'above their station'. As the social structure became more fluid, those who could afford to do so replaced the previously effective social distance with literal space. When Edinburgh's Georgian New Town was constructed, the bourgeoisie moved out of the old city.

The plausibility of a single moral universe in which all people have a place depends on the social structure being relatively stable. With the proliferation of new social roles and increasing social mobility, traditional integrated organic or communal conceptions of the moral and supernatural order began to fragment. When the community broke into competing social groups, the religiously sanctified vision of that community, united under its God, also broke up. As classes and social fragments became more distinctive, so they generated metaphysical and salvational systems along lines more suited to their interests (MacIntyre 1967). People came to see the supernatural world as they saw the material world. Thus feudal agricultural societies tended to have a hierarchically structured religion where the great pyramid of pope, bishops, priests and laity reflected the social pyramid of king, nobles, gentry and peasants. Independent small farmers or the rising business class preferred a more democratic religion; hence their attraction to such early Protestant sects as the Presbyterians, Baptists and Quakers.

However, modernization was not simply a matter of the religious culture responding to changes in the social, economic and political structures. Religion itself had a considerable effect on social and cultural diversity (S3). To explain this I must go back a stage to the link between the Reformation, the rise of individualism and the propensity to schism.

Individualism (RO1)

David Martin neatly summarized a major unintended consequence of the Reformation when he wrote that 'The logic of Protestantism is clearly in favour of the voluntary principle, to a degree that eventually makes it sociologically unrealistic' (1978a: 9). Belief systems differ greatly in their propensity to fragment (R. Wallis 1979; Bruce 1985). Much of the variation can be explained by the assumptions about the availability of authoritative knowledge that lie at the heart of the beliefs. To simplify the possibilities in two polar types, some religions claim a unique grasp of the truth while others allow that there are many ways to salvation. The Catholic Church claims that Christ's authority was passed to Peter, the first bishop of Rome, and was then institutionalized in the office of pope. The Church claims ultimate control of the means to salvation and the right finally to arbitrate all disputes about God's will. So long as that central assertion is not disputed, the Catholic Church is relatively immune to fission and schism. As the beliefs that one needs to abandon in order to depart from Rome go right to the heart of what one believed when one was a Catholic, such departures are difficult and are associated with extreme social upheavals, such as the French Revolution. Thus in Catholic countries the fragmentation of the religious culture that follows from structural and social differentiation tends to take the form of a sharp divide between those who remain within the religious tradition and those who openly oppose it. So Italy and Spain have conservative Catholics traditions and powerful Communist parties.

In contrast, the religion created by the Protestant Reformation was extremely vulnerable to fragmentation because it removed the institution of the church as a source of authority between God and man. Although Catholics sometimes use this as a stick with which to beat Protestants, it is a sociological, not a theological, observation. If, by reading the Scriptures, we are all able to discern God's will, then how do we settle disputes between the various discernings that are produced? Being theists who believed in one God, one Holy Spirit that dwelt in all of God's creation, and one Bible, the Reformers could hope that the righteous would readily and naturally agree, but history proved that hope false. Tradition, habit, respect for learning, or admiration for personal piety all restrained the tendency to split, but they did not prevent schism. The consequence of the Reformation was not one Christian church purified and strengthened but a large number of competing perspectives and institutions. In Protestant countries, social differentiation took the form not of a radical divide between clerical and secular elements but of a series of schisms from the dominant traditions. Rising social classes were able to express their new aspirations and ambitions by reworking the familiar religion into shapes that accorded with their self-image.

We might add a secular version of RO1. The notion of individualism, although crucially stimulated by the Reformation, gradually developed an autonomous dynamic as the egalitarianism I have located in the diagram as S4. It is placed there because I want to stress that the idea of individualism and the closely associated social reality of diversity (S3) could develop only in propitious circumstances and those where provided by structural differentiation (S2) and economic growth (E3).

The link between modernization and inequality is paradoxical. We need not explore the many differences between modern and traditional sources of power to note that, at the same time as creating classes shaped by what Marx called the forces of production, industrialization brought a basic egalitarianism. We should recognize the contribution that religious innovation made here. Although the Protestant Reformers were far from being democrats, one major unintended consequence of their religious revolution was a profound change in the relative importance of the community and the individual. By denying the special status of the priesthood and by removing the possibility that religious merit could be transferred from one person to another (by, for example, saying masses for the souls of the dead), Luther and Calvin reasserted what was implicit in early Christianity: that we are all severally (rather than jointly) equal in the eyes of God. For the Reformers, that equality lay in our sinfulness and in our obligations, but the idea could not indefinitely be confined to duty. Equality in the eyes of God laid the foundations for equality in the eyes of man and before the law. Equal obligations eventually became equal rights.

Though the details of case need not concern us here, Gellner has plausibly argued that egalitarianism is a requirement for industrialization; a society sharply divided between high and low cultures could not develop a modern economy (1983, 1991). The spread of a shared national culture required the replacement of a fixed hierarchy of stations and estates by more flexible class divisions. Economic development brought change and the expectation of further change. And it brought occupational mobility. People no longer did the job they always did because their family always did that job. As it became more common for people to better themselves, it also become more common for them to think better of themselves. However badly paid, the industrial worker did not see himself as a serf.

The medieval serf occupied just one role in a single all-embracing hierarchy and that role shaped his entire life. A tin-miner in Cornwall in 1800 might have been sore oppressed at work, but in the late evening and on Sunday he could change his clothes and his persona to become a Baptist lay preacher. As such he was a man of prestige and standing. The possibility of such alternation marks a crucial change. Once occupation became freed from an entire all-embracing hierarchy and became task specific, it was possible for people to occupy different positions in different hierarchies. In turn, that made it possible to distinguish between the role and the person who played it. Roles could still be ranked and accorded very different degrees of respect, power or status, but the people behind the roles could be seen as in some sense equal. To put it the other way round, so long as people were seen in terms of just one identity in one hierarchy, the powerful had a strong incentive to resist egalitarianism: treating alike a peasant and his feudal superior threatened to turn the world upside down. But once an occupational position could be judged apart from the person who filled it, it became possible to maintain a necessary order in the factory, for example, while operating a different system of judgements outside the work context. The mine-owner could rule his workforce but sit alongside (or even under) his foreman in the local church. Of course, power and status are often transferable. Being a force in one sphere increases the chances of influence in another. The factory-owner who built the church could expect to dominate the congregation, but he would do so only if his wealth was matched by manifest piety. If it was not, his fellow church-goers could respond to any attempt to impose his will by defecting to a neighbouring congregation.

Societalization

A number of important themes combine to produce a major change in the nature of societies that has a profound impact on the social roles and plausibility of religious belief systems. Societalization is the term given by Wilson to the way in which 'life is increasingly enmeshed and organized, not locally but societally (that society being most evidently, but not uniquely, the nation state)' (1982: 154). If social differentiation (S1) and individualism (RO1) can be seen as a blow to small-scale communities from below, societalization was the corresponding attack from above. Close-knit, integrated, communities gradually lost power and presence to large-scale industrial and commercial enterprises, to modern states coordinated through massive, impersonal bureaucracies, and to cities. This is the classic community-to-society transition delineated by Ferdinand Tönnies (1955).

Following Durkheim, Wilson argues that religion has its source in, and draws its strength from, the community. As the society rather than the community has increasingly become the locus of the individual's life, so religion has been shorn of its functions. The church of the Middle Ages baptized, christened and confirmed children, married young adults, and buried the dead. Its calendar of services mapped onto the temporal order of the seasons. It celebrated and legitimated local life. In turn, it drew considerable plausibility from being frequently reaffirmed through the participation of the local community in its activities. In 1898 almost the entire population of my local village celebrated the successful end of the harvest by bringing tokens of their produce into the church. In 1998 a very small number of people in my village (only one of them a farmer) celebrated the Harvest festival by bringing to the church vegetables and tinned goods (many of foreign provenance) bought in the local branch of an international supermarket chain. In the first case the church provided a religious interpretation of an event of vital significance to the entire community. In the second, a small self-selecting group of Christians engaged in an act of dubious symbolic value. Instead of celebrating the harvest, the service thanked God for all his creation. In listing things for which we should be grateful, one hymn mentioned 'jet planes refuelling in the sky'! By broadening the symbolism, the service solved the problem of relevance but at the cost of losing direct connection with the lives of those involved. When the total, all-embracing community of like-situated people working and playing together gives way to the dormitory town or suburb, there is little held in common left to celebrate.

The consequence of differentiation and societalization is that the plausibility of any single overarching moral and religious system declined, to be displaced by competing conceptions that, while they may have had much to say to privatized, individual experience, could have little connection to the performance of social roles or the operation of social systems. Religion retained subjective plausibility for some people, but lost its objective taken-for-grantedness. It was no longer a matter of necessity; it was a preference.

Again it is worth stressing the interaction of social and cultural forces. The fragmentation of the religious tradition (RO3) that resulted from the Reformation hastened the development of the religiously neutral state (P1). The development of a successful economy required a high degree of integration: effective communication, a shared legal code to enforce contracts, a climate of trust, and so on (Gellner 1991). And this required an integrated national culture. Where there was religious consensus, a national 'high culture' could be provided through the dominant religious tradition. The clergy could continue to be the schoolteachers, historians, propagandists, public administrators and military strategists. Where there was little consensus, the growth of the state tended to be secular. In Ireland and the Scandinavian countries, a national education system was created through the Catholic and Lutheran churches respectively. In Britain and the United States it was largely created by the state directly. However, even where a dominant church retained formal ownership of areas of activity, those still came to be informed primarily by secular values. Church schools may 'top and tail' their product with their distinctive religious traditions, but the mathematics, chemistry and economics lessons are the same in Ireland's church schools as in England's state schools.

After summarizing this case, James Beckford warned that 'the connection between religion, obligatory beliefs and community may be an historical contingency. Religion has, in the past, been primarily associated with local communities for sound sociological reasons, but it does not follow that this is the only modality in which religion can operate' (1989: 110). This is correct. I am certainly not assuming that, because religion used to be closely woven into the social life of stable communities, the decline of community must, as in a mathematical proof, logically entail the eclipse of religion. Instead I will argue for an empirical connection. In subsequent chapters, I will consider the nature of modern individualized religion and show that, first, it lacks the social significance of the communal type and, secondly, that it is difficult to reproduce. I am thus not tautologically eliding the decline of community and the decline of religion but seeking to establish causal connections between the two.

Schism and Sects (RO3)

It is useful at this point to backtrack and draw a new line of subsidiary connections between some consequences of the Reformation and the E2–E3 strand relating to industrialization. The Reformation provided a powerful stimulus to the spread of mass literacy and later the creation of voluntary associations (S6). With the power of the clergy much reduced and all of us required to answer to God individually, it became vital to give ordinary people the resources necessary to meet that new responsibility. Hence the pressure to translate the Bible from the Latin and Greek into vernacular languages; the rapid advance in printing; the spread of literacy and the movement better to educate the masses. And, as Gellner and others have argued, the spread of education was both essential to, and a consequence of, economic growth. Thus the sectarian competitive spirit of the RO line interacted with the requirements of the E line to produce a literate and educated laity, which in turn encouraged the general emphasis on the importance and rights of the individual and the growth of egalitarianism (S4) and liberal democracy (P1).

The growth of the Protestant sects also had a very direct influence on P1 in that they provided a new model for social organization. Reformed religion may have had the individual soul at its centre, but it encouraged those individuals to band together for encouragement, edification, evangelism and social control. As an alternative to the organic community in which position was largely inherited and ascribed, the sectarians established the voluntary association of like-minded individuals coming together out of choice to pursue common goals. Such associations could be thoroughly authoritarian. The Quakers sometimes exercised severe social control by shunning those who failed to live up to the required standards, even to the extent of expelling from fellowship those whose businesses had failed through no discernible fault of their own. Yet the authority of the voluntary association was firmly circumscribed because it was merely one form of association and one source of identity in an increasingly complex and differentiated society. And, unlike the organic community, participation was voluntary.

As well as creating a new form of association well suited to industrial society, the Protestant sects provided an important source of leadership skills training for the rising social classes.

Social and cultural diversity (S3)

Social and cultural diversity were central to the development of a secular state (and I include in that the secularization not just of the government but also of major public agencies and of the climate generally; what Neuhaus (1984) called 'the public square'). For the time being, I want to leave aside (a) those cases where a secular state was produced by the violent overthrow of a religious establishment by secular forces (the two obvious examples being the French Revolution of 1789–92 and the Bolshevik Revolution of 1919) and (b) those cases, such as the Lutheran Nordic countries, where the state was secularized late as a result of the autonomous appeal of the idea of liberal democracy (P1).

It is not just ethnocentrism that causes me to put Britain (and its settler-society offshoots) first. I want to argue that there is an additional charge to the secularization of the state that arises from social necessity. Modernization brought with it increased cultural diversity in three different ways. First, populations moved and brought their language, religion and social mores with them into a new setting. Secondly, the expansion of the increasingly expansive nation state meant that new groups were brought into the state. But thirdly, as I have already suggested, even without such changes in the population that had to be encompassed by the state, modernization created cultural pluralism through the proliferation of classes and class fragments with increasingly diverse interests. Especially in Protestant societies, where such class formation was accompanied by the generation of competing sects, the result was a paradox. At the same time as the nation state was attempting to create a unified national culture out of thousands of small communities, it was having to come to terms with increasing religious diversity.

As this has been misunderstood surprisingly often, I will risk losing the reader with repetition and stress that diversity need force the secularization of the state only in the context of a culture that accepts a basic egalitarianism (S4) and a polity that is more or less democratic (P1). A society in which almost everyone shares a particular religion can give that faith pride of place in its operations. The imposition of theocracy in the Iranian revolution in 1979 was possible because the vast majority of Iranians shared the same religion: the Shia strand of Islam. An authoritarian hierarchical society can ignore or suppress religious minorities (and even religious majorities): dissenters need not be tolerated, they can be oppressed (the fate of the Bahais in the

Islamic Republic of Iran) or exiled to the Gulag Archipelago (the fate of many Protestants in the Soviet Union). But a society that was becoming increasingly egalitarian and democratic and more culturally diverse had to place social harmony before the endorsement of religious orthodoxy. The result was an increasingly neutral state. Religious establishments were abandoned altogether (as with the constitution of the United States) or were neutered (the British case). As already noted, this reduced the social power and scope of organized religion. While freedom from embarrassing entanglements with secular power may have allowed churches to become more clearly 'spiritual', the removal of the churches from the centre of public life reduced their contact with, and relevance for, the general population.

The separation of church and state was one consequence of diversity. Another, equally important for understanding secularization, was the break between community and religious worldview. This is the crucial difference between popular or demotic secularization and state suppression of religion. In sixteenth-century England, every significant event in the life cycle of the individual and the community was celebrated in church and given a religious gloss. Birth, marriage and death, and the passage of the agricultural seasons, because they were managed by the church, all reaffirmed the essentially Christian worldview of the people. The church's techniques were used to bless the sick, sweeten the soil and increase animal productivity. Every significant act of testimony, every contract and every promise was reinforced by oaths sworn on the Bible and before God. But beyond the special events that saw the majority of the people in the parish troop into the church, a huge amount of credibility was given to the religious worldview simply through everyday social interaction. People commented on the weather by saying God be praised and on parting wished each other 'God speed' or 'Goodbye' (which we often forget is an abbreviation for 'God be with you').

The consequences of increasing diversity for the place of religion in the life of the state or even the local community are fairly obvious. Equally important but less often considered is the social-psychological consequence of increasing diversity: it calls into question the certainty that believers can accord their religion (Berger 1980).

Ideas are most convincing when they are universally shared. Then they are not beliefs at all; they are just an accurate account of how things are. The elaboration of alternatives provides a profound challenge. Of course, believers need not fall on their swords just because

they discover that others disagree with them. Where clashes of ideologies occur in the context of social conflict (of which more below),
or when alternatives are promoted by people who can be plausibly
described as a lower order and thus need not be seriously entertained,
the cognitive challenge can be dismissed. One may even elaborate a
coherent theory that both explains why there are a variety of religions
and reasserts the superiority of one's own. This is exactly what the
evolutionary minded Presbyterian missionaries did in the nineteenth
century. They argued that God in his wisdom had revealed himself in
different ways to different cultures. The animism of African tribes was
suitable for their stage of social development, as was the ritualistic
Catholicism of the southern Europeans. As these people evolved, they
would move up to the most fulsome understanding of God, which was
Scottish Presbyterianism! It is this ability to neutralize cognitive threats
(Berger and Luckmann 1966: 133) that explains why the secularizing
effect of diversity that results from the internal fragmentation of a
society is greater than that which results from either inward migration or the outward expansion of the state. It is easier to dismiss the
views of strangers than those of friends and kind.

When the oracle speaks with a single clear voice, it is easy to believe
it is the voice of God. When it speaks with twenty different voices, it
is tempting to look behind the screen. As Berger puts it in explaining
the title of *The Heretical Imperative* (1980), the position of the modern
believer is quite unlike that of the Christian of the Middle Ages in that,
while we may still believe, we cannot avoid the knowledge that many
people (including many people like us) believe differently.

In a final observation about the impact of pluralism, I would like
to trace a small but important connection between diversity and the
persuasive power of science and technology (between S3 and R3 and
R4). To mention this here runs the risk of confirming mistaken views
about the role of science in the decline of religion (on that see chapter
5) and I should stress that I do not see the direct contest between
scientific and religious ideas as central to the secularization process.
Rather the connection is a more subtle one about displacement and
salience. Religious pluralism is implicated in the primacy of scientific
explanations in that it weakens the plausibility of alternatives. The
rational basis of science and the social structures of training, examination and dissemination of results that protect that base mean that
there are fewer disagreements among scientists than there are among
the clergy. Or, to put it more carefully, although scientists often argue

at the front lines of their disciplines, they share a considerable body of common knowledge about the hinterland they have conquered. The basic principles of mechanics, physics, chemistry and biology are not in doubt. Except when they abandon all their specific beliefs, the clergy of competing churches and sects disagree on fundamentals. Despite the disillusionment with the authority of the secular professions commonly voiced in the last quarter of the twentieth century (see chapter 6), science still commands the sort of respect enjoyed by the medieval church. If pathologists say that forty-seven elderly people in Lanarkshire died of bacterium E. coli, almost all of us will agree with the conclusion. We may then wish to add a divine or supernatural explanation of why *those* people ate the contaminated meat. This is the logic of Zande witchcraft explanations of why a man was killed by a grainstore collapsing on him. The Zande know that termites eat wood but they can also agree on the supplementary explanation that this man was bewitched. Because we do not share a common religious culture, we will not be able to agree on whether it is even appropriate to search for such religious significance, let alone what the significance might be. While the E. coli explanation will have the support of the scientific consensus, any religious glosses will be contested minority views. Concentrating our explanations of life events on the material world brings more agreement than searching for religious messages. That the religious culture is badly fragmented thus weakens the ability of religious explanations to complement, let alone compete with, naturalistic ones. When religious explanations are sustained, it has to be in a distinct compartment; not as an equally plausible alternative but as an additional layer of interpretation. Precisely because it is additional, it can be neglected. The spread of AIDS may be God's judgement on homosexuals, as some US fundamentalists argue (though it is not clear what God has against haemophiliacs and west African heterosexuals), but as we have identified compelling and effective explanations (and treatments) for AIDS that do not involve positing divine judgement, those that do become optional.

Compartmentalization and privatization (S5)

A key element of the secularization paradigm is the individual response to differentiation, societalization and pluralism. One way for believers to reconcile their faith with the fact of variety is to seek reintegration at a higher level of abstraction by supposing that all religions are, in some sense, the same. This is discussed further in chapters 4 and 6. Another possibility (and they are not incompatible) is to confine one's faith to a particular compartment of social life. Indeed, a powerful observation about modernity introduced to the English-reading world by Berger and Luckmann's *The Social Construction of Reality* (1973) was that differentiation required us to live, not in a single world, but in a number of worlds, each informed by its own values and logics. With compartmentalization comes privatization – the sense that the reach of religion is shortened to just those who accept the teachings of this or that faith. As Luckmann puts it:

> This development reflects the dissolution of *one* hierarchy of significance in the world view. Based on the complex institutional structure and social stratification of industrial societies different 'versions' of the world view emerge. . . . With the pervasiveness of the consumer orientation and the sense of autonomy, the individual is more likely to confront the culture and the sacred cosmos as a 'buyer'. Once religion is defined as a 'private affair', the individual may choose from the assortment of 'ultimate' meanings as he sees fit. (1970: 98–9)

Daniel Bell has taken issue with Wilson's linking of privatization and a decline in the significance or popularity of religion. After agreeing that modernization has brought 'the shrinkage of institutional authority over the spheres of public life, the retreat to a private world where religions have authority only over their followers', he adds, 'there is no necessary, determinate shrinkage in the character and extent of beliefs' (1977: 427). This neatly presents us with a summary of a crucial element in the debate over the secularization paradigm. I will argue in subsequent chapters the point I have made in various places above: the privatization of religion removes much of the social support that is vital to reinforcing beliefs, makes the maintenance of distinct lifestyles very difficult, weakens the impetus to evangelize and encourages a *de facto* relativism that is fatal to shared beliefs. Of course, this is an empirical issue that must be settled by evidence. On that point it is worth noting that, although Bell's essay is entitled 'The Return of the Gods', he provides almost no evidence for his anti-Wilsonian case that privatization does not weaken religion.

Jose Casanova (1994) has made an important contribution to the debate by arguing that differentiation (which he fully accepts) has not caused privatization. His case is that the major churches, having now accepted the rules of liberal democracy and the basic principles of individual rights, are able to regain a public role. They have achieved this not by returning to the old model of a compact between a dominant church and the state, but by acting as pressure groups in civil society. This may well be true, but to present it as a counter to the secularization paradigm is to miss a number of important points. First, it is clear from the recent fate of the 'new Christian right' in the United States (on which see Garvey 1993 and Bruce 1998b) that religious interest groups have been effective in the public arena only when they have presented their case in secular terms. Hence creationism has to be presented as 'creation science', apparently every bit as compatible with the scientific record as any evolutionary model of the origins of species and open to testing in the same way. The case against abortion is made in terms of the inalienable rights of the individual. Divorce and homosexuality are damned as socially dysfunctional. That is, religious interest groups can be effective in civil society only when they accept the privatization of their distinctive religious beliefs and move on to secular ground. Secondly, even if Casanova does not exaggerate the influence of religious groups in modern societies, he does not address the social-psychological consequences of privatization.

Secular states and liberal democracy (P1)

I have been at pains to stress repeatedly the relative autonomy of many elements of this complex model. The obvious point is that social innovations, once established, can have an appeal that goes far beyond the initial motive to innovate. That is almost inevitable given that many innovations were not initially desired at all but were the unintended consequences of actions taken for quite different reasons. We can see this very clearly in the consequences of the 'Protestant Ethic'. Luther and Calvin would have been horrified to find that centuries after their reforms a secularized version of their ideas was being used to justify the pursuit of wealth (which, like most pious people, they saw as a major threat to the pursuit of godliness).

Although the creation of secular liberal democracy was initially a necessary accommodation to the egalitarianism (S4) that was made possible by structural differentiation (S2), and to the social and cultural diversity (S3) created by a combination of the fissiparousness of Protestantism (RO2) and social differentiation (S1), it became attractive in its own right and in the late nineteenth century we find societies that had no great practical necessity for them introducing the same principles as part and parcel of other political reforms. For example, in the Nordic countries we find that, despite growing religious diversity being largely contained within the Lutheran churches (or at least within the Lutheran tradition), the introduction of representative democracy and the weakening of the monarchy (or Grand Duchy) was accompanied by a gradual scaling-down of the power of the Lutheran Church (which largely retained its diverse social functions by presenting them universally as secular social services).

That similar reforms after the defeat of the Ottoman Empire in the First World War in such successor states as Turkey were at best only partial successes raises questions about the economic and social requirements for effective democracy, but they nonetheless illustrate the point that social innovations can become free of their historical roots (Robertson 1993).

Sects and churches moderate (RO5)

This element brings us close to the heart of contemporary criticisms of the secularization paradigm. Stark and a number of associates have argued on the basis of what they take to be the US experience that competition between providers of religious products increases levels of religious vitality. That argument is elaborated in subsequent chapters and elsewhere (see Bruce 1999 and Stark and Finke 2000). The secularization case is that diversity weakens religious commitments by removing the social support for any one religion and by encouraging people to confine their religious beliefs to specific compartments (S5) and to remove the specific and contested elements from their beliefs. The sect, by proliferating competing alternatives (RO3), is thus its own grave-digger.

This later case is made for one important site of secularization by H. R. Niebuhr (1962) in his extension of observations originally made by Ernst Troeltsch about the evolution of sects. Niebuhr notes that time and again what began life as a radical sect gradually evolved into a comfortable denomination on easy terms with the world around it (see chapter 4 for an elaboration of the terms 'sect' and 'denomination'). The Quaker movement began as a radical alternative to the religion of the established Church of England and its founders suffered considerable penalties for their nonconformity. Within a few generations, the movement had moderated both its demands of its members and its criticisms of alternatives. The Methodists mutated in a similar way. Isichei correctly notes that Quaker development was far more complex than Niebuhr's abbreviated account suggests, but she admits that 'in the eighteenth and nineteenth centuries Friends were coming to accept the values of their environment and respect for worldly rank and titles was often mentioned as one of their characteristics' (Isichei 1967: 162).

That such mutation has happened often suggests common social forces at work and Niebuhr attempted to elaborate these.[4] Three points are relevant to the secularization paradigm. First, Niebuhr argues that commitment is inevitably reduced because increasingly large parts of generations subsequent to that of the founders inherited rather than chose their faith. The first generation (and subsequent adult joiners) elected to be sectarians and did so in the full knowledge of the penalties that their dissent would incur. Hence they began with very high levels of commitment and, to the extent that they were victimized, their subsequent experiences of suffering for their God strengthened that commitment. Those who were born into the movement might be strenuously socialized into the tenets of the sect but they had not chosen it. Secondly, a common inadvertent consequence of sect membership was increasing wealth and upward social mobility. Partly this was merely a matter of historical accident. Despite slumps and recessions, industrial economies have grown and most people have become richer. But sectarian Protestants tended to progress ahead of the average, partly for the 'Protestant Ethic' reasons elaborated by Weber (E1) and partly because their asceticism and piety made them widely trusted. It is not an accident that almost the entire British banking system developed from family firms run by Quakers: the Barclays, Backhouses, Trittons and Gurneys. If you had to ask someone to look after your money, ask a Quaker. The problem of increasing wealth (and the social status and public acceptance that came with it) is that it proportionately increases the costs of being an ascetic Protestant. The banking Barclays who in the nineteenth century shifted from the Society of Friends to the evangelical wing of the Church of England faced far greater temptations than did the sect's founders.

A third element of the Niebuhr thesis was also elaborated by the German political scientist Robert Michels (1962) in his study of oligarchy in left-wing trade unions and political parties. Although most sects began as primitive democracies, with the equality of all believers and little or no formal organization, gradually a professional leadership cadre emerged. Especially after the founding charismatic leader died, there was a need to educate and train the preachers and teachers who would sustain the movement. If this was successful, there was a need to coordinate a growing organization. There were assets to be safeguarded and books to be published and distributed. With organization came paid officials and such people had a vested interest in reducing the degree of conflict between the sect and the wider society. They could also compare themselves to the clergy of the established church and (initially for the status of their faith rather than their own reward) desire the same levels of training, remuneration and social status. The case that Michels plausibly makes from the study of left-wing movements is that organization inevitably brings oligarchy and oligarchy subverts the initial radical impetus.

If the sect can isolate itself completely from the wider society so that its beliefs and culture form the 'taken-for-granted' backcloth to life, then it can sustain itself. The Amish, Hutterites and Doukobhors provide examples. But in most cases the sect is only slightly removed from the wider society and cannot avoid the social-psychological effects of diversity described above. Having failed to win over the majority of the population and hence having to come to terms with being only a 'saved remnant', the sect can find good reasons for moderating its claims and coming to see itself, not as the sole embodiment of God's will, but simply as one expression of what is pleasing to God.

The case of the Niebuhr and Michels theses is that the sectarian project is largely self-defeating. It sets out radically to purify a corrupt religious establishment and after a few generations moderates to become just another comfortable denomination. But, as well as failing in its own terms, it hastens secularization by weakening the dominant religious tradition and increasing the extent of diversity with all the consequences outlined above.

I might add that there are exceptions. Some sects stay sects and Wilson (1990, 1993) has elaborated the circumstances in which persistence is likely. Isichei (1967) makes the point that mutation can be paradoxical. While the English Quakers relaxed many of their behavioural standards, in terms of structure, the Society actually returned to its primitive democracy after flirting with a professional leadership. Nonetheless, the general pattern of accommodation identified by Niebuhr is found sufficiently often to be accepted as an important mediating mechanism in the secularization paradigm.

Under this heading I will add the corollary of the moderation of sects: the moderation of churches. The point has already been made under other headings. Faced with widespread defection and the loss of authority, most churches reduce the claims they make for the uniqueness of their revelation and come to view themselves as just one among others. The change is not always made willingly. For example, the Episcopal Church in Ireland bitterly resisted disestablishment, as did its counterpart in Wales. As late as the final quarter of the nineteenth century and despite representing a minority of Presbyterians, the Church of Scotland was still trying to ensure that it was the channel for the state-funded expansion of public schooling. It failed. By the start of the twentieth century most state churches were willing to cooperate with other Christian organizations. By the end of it, most were desperately trying to find a new role by presenting themselves as the senior spokesman for all religions against a largely secular climate.

Economic growth (E3)

The fate of the Protestants sects can be generalized. In one way or another very many commentators have noted that increasing prosperity reduces religious fervour (Inglehart 1990, 1997). This is partly a specific claim about the content of most religious traditions. Most of the major strands of the great religions have associated piety with asceticism, at least in theory. It is easier for a camel to pass through the eye of a needle than for a rich man to enter the kingdom of God. The more pleasant this life, the harder it is to concentrate on the next. The more satisfying being human, the harder to be mindful of God. It is also an observation about 'regression to the mean' (on which see chapter 7). Economic marginality provides one source of insulation against the world. The dispossessed often elaborate comforting theodicies that intimately connect their deprived circumstances and their religion so that what would otherwise be seen as privations are reinterpreted as signs of blessing and divine favour: blessed are the poor. Hence it is no surprise that, when material circumstances improve, the religion needs to be rewritten and in the process it may well lose much of its power. An example would be the way that the Pentecostalism of southern whites in the USA evolved over the second half of the twentieth century. Pentecostalists such as Oral Roberts (Harrell 1985) and Tammy Faye Bakker (Barnhart 1988) grew up in impoverished conditions that made it easy and satisfying to denounce flashy clothes, make-up, Hollywood movies, social dancing and television.

As they prospered and began to be able to afford what had previously been the work of the Devil, they compromised their ascetic principles. Although their morals were slower to change, fundamentalists' attitudes to sexuality have also relaxed. For example, divorce, though still regretted, is widely accepted.

Of course, this does not of itself mean that southern fundamentalists are becoming less religious. I am not cheating by defining behavioural change as evidence of secularization at the ideological level. However, I am supposing a causal connection: that the disappearance of distinctive ways of life makes the maintenance of distinctive beliefs harder.

Science (R3) and technology (R4)

For reasons I will elaborate in subsequent chapters, I have left the secularizing effects of science until this point. Various critics of the secularization paradigm misrepresent it by following popular misconceptions and elevating science to a central position. Quite erroneously, Stark says: 'implicit in all versions, and explicit in most, is the claim that of all aspects of modernization, it is science that has the most deadly implications for religion' (Stark and Finke 2000: 61). Put briefly, I assume that a starting assumption of modern sociology is that reality is socially constructed (Berger and Luckmann 1973). By this slogan we draw attention to the role of social relationships and social interests in making ideas more or less persuasive. I have already mentioned various ways in which people can seek to preserve their beliefs against what disinterested outsiders might see as overwhelming refutation. It is a mistake to assume that ideas and observations are of themselves persuasive or that, while we need to explain why people hold false beliefs, somehow the 'truth' stands in no need of explanation.

The Enlightenment zero-sum view of knowledge (with rational thought and scientific knowledge gradually conquering territory from superstition) was carried into sociology by Comte and Marx among others, but it is not part of the modern secularization paradigm. Wilson stated the position very clearly when he followed observations about the increasing influence of science and technology with: 'All of this is not to suggest . . . that the confrontation of science and religion was in itself harmful to religion. Indeed religion and science can co-exist as alternative orientations to the world' (1966: 43). The crucial connections are far more subtle and complex than those implied in some zero-sum knowledge competition.

The secularizing effects of science as seen by modern sociologists are not primarily those of a direct clash of factual claims. Rather they are the more nebulous consequences of assumptions about the orderliness of the world and our mastery over it.

One of the most powerful connections was drawn by Robert Merton (1970) in his work on Puritan scientists. Merton argues that many seventeenth-century Protestant scientists were inspired to natural science by a desire to demonstrate the glory of God's creation, by the rationalizing attitude of the Protestant ethic and by an interest in controlling the corrupt world.[5] The end result was the same irony that followed from the general rationalization of ethics. Because the Puritan scientists were able to demonstrate the fundamental rule-governed nature of the material world, they made it possible for subsequent generations to do science without topping and tailing their work with the assertion that 'This shows God's glory'. At any stage in the growth of knowledge, God could be summoned to fill a gap. Newton, for example, believed God periodically took a hand in the movement of the planets to rectify a slight irregularity. Later improved models managed without the divine corrections. Science became autonomous and generated explanatory models of the world that did not require the divine.

We can also draw causal connections between the RO line and the rise of science. The fissiparousness of Protestantism enhanced the autonomy of science by weakening the power of the Church to dominate all fields of intellectual endeavour.

More important than science was the development of effective technologies. We should not forget that in the Middle Ages (and to this day in pre-technological societies) religion was often practical. Holy water cured ailments and prayers improved crop quality. Wilson among others has argued that technology has a powerful secularizing effect by reducing the occasions on which people have recourse to religion. Again, rather than see a direct conflict, we should see the change as a matter of 'bypass'. The farmers of Buchan did not stop praying to God to save their sheep from maggots because the invention of an agri-chemical sheep dip persuaded them that God was not very well informed. The gradual accumulation of scientific knowledge gave people insight into, and mastery over, an area that had once been a mystery; the need and opportunity for recourse to the religious gradually declined. Science and technology do not create atheists; they just reduce the frequency and seriousness with which people attend to religion.

More generally, as David Martin puts it, with the growth of science and technology 'the general sense of human power is increased, the play of contingency is restricted, and the overwhelming sense of divine limits which afflicted previous generations is much diminished' (1969: 116).

Technology (R4) and technological consciousness (CS1)

Although Berger's early writings are widely associated with the secularization approach, one particular strand of his thought has been neglected. In an exploration of the social psychological effects of certain styles of modern work, Berger, Berger and Kellner (1974) argue that, irrespective of the extent to which we are aware of it, modern technology brings with it a 'technological consciousness', a certain style of thought that is difficult to reconcile with a sense of the sacred.[6] An example is 'componentiality'. The application of modern machines to production involves the assumption that the most complex entities can be broken down into their components, which are infinitely replaceable. Any 1990 Volkswagen Golf radiator will fit any 1990 Golf. The relationship between the engine and one radiator is expected to be exactly the same as that between the engine and any other matching radiator. There is nothing sacred about any particular bond. Another fundamental assumption is 'reproducibility'. Technological production takes it for granted that any creative complex of actions can be subdivided into simple acts that can be repeated infinitely and always with the same consequence. This attitude is carried over from manufacture to the management of people in manufacture (a style known after its heroic promoter as 'Fordism') and to bureaucracy generally. While there is no obvious clash between these assumptions and the teachings of most religions, there are serious incompatibilities of approach. There is little space for the eruption of the divine.

To summarize the R line, I am suggesting that the effects of science and technology on the plausibility of religious belief are often misunderstood. The clash of ideas between science and religion is less significant than the more subtle impact of naturalistic ways of thinking about the world. Science and technology have not made us atheists. Rather, the fundamental assumptions that underlie them, which we can summarily describe as 'rationality' – the material world as an amoral series of invariant relationships of cause and effect, the componentiality of objects, the reproducibility of actions, the expectation of constant change in our exploitation of the material world, the insistence on innovation – make us less likely than our forebears to entertain the notion of the divine. As Weber put it:

> The increasing intellectualization and rationalization do *not* . . . indicate an increased general knowledge of the conditions under which one lives. It means something else namely, the knowledge, or the belief, that if one but wished one *could* learn it at any time. Hence, it means that principally there are no mysterious incalculable forces that come into play, but rather that one can, in principle, master all things by calculation. This means that the world is disenchanted. One need no longer have recourse to magical means in order to master or implore the spirits, as did the savage, for whom such mysterious powers existed. Technical means and calculations perform the service. (1948: 139)

Relativism (CS2)

Relativism is perhaps the most potent and the most neglected part of the secularization paradigm. In subsequent chapters I will frequently refer to relativism in explanations of weakening religious commitment.

Finding precisely the right term is not easy; 'relativism' is perhaps misleading if it suggests an articulate philosophical attitude. I mean something closer to an operating principle or a cognitive style. I am concerned with the pragmatic concerns of what standing and what reach we accord our own ideas and how we view those who disagree with us. The Christian Church of the Middle Ages was firmly authoritarian and exclusive in its attitude to knowledge. There was a single truth and it knew what it was. Increasingly social and cultural diversity combines with egalitarianism to undermine all claims to authoritative knowledge. While compartmentalization can serve as a holding operation, it is difficult to live in a world that treats as equally valid a large number of incompatible beliefs, and that shies away from authoritative assertions, without coming to suppose that there is no one truth. While we may retain a certain preference for our worldview, we find it hard to insist that what is true for us must also be true for everyone else. The tolerance that is necessary for harmony in diverse egalitarian societies weakens religion (as it weakens most forms of knowledge and codes of behaviour) by forcing us to live as if there were no possibility of knowing the will of God.

First summary

Before turning to important qualifications to the paradigm I will very briefly summarize the case so far. In figure 1.1, I try to show the connections between a variety of changes in the industrial democracies of the West that for brevity we call 'modernization'. In different ways, elements of that package cause religion to mutate so that it loses social significance. I have gone further than some of those associated with the paradigm (though, in the case of Wilson, for example, I see that extension as merely making explicit what is already implicit) in adding that the decline of social significance and communal support causes a decline in the plausibility of religious beliefs. Changes at the structural and cultural level bring about changes in religious vitality that we see in the declining proportion of people who hold conventional religious beliefs and the commitment they bring to those beliefs. The bottom line is this: individualism, diversity and egalitarianism in the context of liberal democracy undermine the authority of religious beliefs.

Counter-tendencies

The previous sections explain what Berger described as 'the process by which sectors of society and culture are removed from the domination of religious institutions and symbols' and the associated increase in the number of people 'who look upon the world and their own lives without the benefit of religious interpretations' (1969: 107–8).

To stop there would be to create a false impression. Berger, Wilson, Martin and Wallis and many others have also written extensively about settings where religion remains seriously implicated in the central operations of economies, polities and societies, and continues to play a major part of shaping people's lives. My work on the Northern Ireland conflict (Bruce 1986, 1998b) has been much criticized for exaggerating the importance of religion. Our critics might gloss our work as predicting the imminent disappearance of religion, but this is not our view. Our case can be summarized as saying that religion diminishes in social significance, becomes increasingly privatized, and loses personal salience *except where it finds work to do other than relating individuals to the supernatural*. Such work can be described under two broad headings: cultural defence and cultural transition. To pre-empt the criticism that what follows is some recently conceived patch-up designed to preserve the secularization paradigm from refutation, I should stress that I have held what follows as long as I have held the ideas explained above. The basic framework was given by Roy Wallis in lectures in 1972 and he always attributed it to Bryan Wilson.

In previous formulations, I have simply presented these two clusters as counter-trends. Here I want to be a bit more specific about the relationship of each to modernization. One way of expressing the difference is to say that, while both sources of religious vitality involve responding to current conditions (and in that sense are modern), the cultural defence role of religion requires one 'pre-modern' element.

Cultural defence

What many settings where religion remains a powerful social force have in common is that religion is implicated in group identity, primarily of an ethnic or national character. Where culture, identity and sense of worth are challenged by a source promoting either an alien religion or rampant secularism and that source is negatively valued, secularization will be inhibited. Religion often provides resources for the defence of a national, local, ethnic or status-group culture. Poland and the Irish Republic are prime examples, but Northern Ireland can also be included, as, in more attenuated form, can other 'dual' societies, or the peripheries of secularizing societies, resistant to the alien encroachment of the centre. As David Martin put it: 'An indissoluble union of church and nation arises in those situations where the church has been the sole available vehicle of nationality against foreign domination: Greece, Poland, Belgium, Ireland, Croatia. In such countries bishops have spoken for nations and in Cyprus one actually led in the independence struggle' (1978b: 107).

I will go back over the basic elements of the secularization thesis and note how ethnic conflict can inhibit their development. Consider structural differentiation. My previous account assumed that there were no obstacles to the increasing autonomy of social functions, but clearly hostility between religio-ethnic groups can prevent or retard the process. For example, where its people have been unable to dominate a national culture, the Catholic Church has insisted on maintaining its own school system and has often generated parallel versions of secular institutions such as trade unions and professional associations. Though a minority rarely evades the state's social control systems, it may still prefer pre-emptively to exercise its own church-based controls on the behaviour of members.

In the classic model of functional differentiation, the first sphere to become freed of cultural encumbrances is the economy. Yet even in what we regard as the pre-eminent site for rational choice, ethnic identification may inhibit the 'maximizing behaviour' that is the fundamental principle of economic rationality. In Northern Ireland attempts to impose rationality on the world of work (through 'fair employment' legislation) have largely failed to prevent the exercise of religio-ethnic preferences in hiring policies (especially in small firms that do not depend on the state for contracts and thus cannot be easily controlled). People also exhibit their ethnic identity in personal consumption, which is beyond state regulation. The Northern Ireland small-business sector is irrational in that small towns often support one Protestant and one Catholic enterprise, each only marginally viable, where the market can profitably sustain only one. Especially at times of heightened tension, Protestants and Catholics boycott each others' businesses and travel considerable distances to engage in commerce with their own sort.

Consider societalization. A beleaguered minority may try to prevent the erosion of the community. Deviants who attempt to order their lives in the societal rather than the community mode may be regarded as disloyal and treacherous and punished accordingly. For example, in the ethnic conflicts in Bosnia and Northern Ireland, those who marry across the divide have been frequent targets for vigilantes keen to clarify and maintain their boundaries.

Finally, ethnic conflict mutes the cognitive consequences of pluralism because the power of invidious stereotypes allows alternative cultures to be much more thoroughly stigmatized. The gradual shift to relativism as a way of accommodating those with whom we differ depends on us taking those people seriously. If we have good reasons to hate them, such consideration is neither necessary nor desirable. Where religious differences are strongly embedded in ethnic identities, the cognitive threat of the ideas of the others is relatively weak. Thus Scottish Protestants in the nineteenth century deployed caricatures of the social vices of the immigrant Irish Catholics as a way of avoiding having to consider them as Christian.

In this sort of account, we usually treat religion as the dependent variable and look for the social roots that explain why religious and national identities remain closed tied. This is only part of the story. In his *General Theory of Secularization*, David Martin (1978b) shows that a major determinant of the different patterns found across Europe is the religious complexion of the country in question and that is not just a matter of contrasting homogenous and diverse cultures. In explaining why some religious cultures were better than others at sustaining national identity and leading nationalist opposition to communism in eastern Europe, I argued that the nature of the religion is itself a vital consideration (Bruce 1999). The differences are complex but I will mention one because it shows the observations being made here do mesh consistently with the secularization paradigm. The example thus serves against the charge that I am merely hedging my bets.

A major fault line (there are others) is between Protestantism and Catholicism. It was primarily the overwhelmingly Catholic countries that most effectively mobilized religio-ethnic identity against Communism – Poland and Lithuania being the two main cases. There are many reasons for this. For example, the international nature of Roman Catholicism provided the local Catholic Church with vital resources for resistance to incorporation. But the cause I want to draw attention to is the communal and organic nature of Catholicism. Or, to look at it from the other end, the individualism of Protestantism and its essential potential for fission encourages cultural diversity and weakens any sort of collectivist response.

Although I have repeatedly stressed that the secularization paradigm should not be taken as a universal template, it is important to note that all major cultural defence cases involve religion (or the church) *continuing* to play a role as the embodiment of collective identity. None of them is an example of a religion acquiring this role after it has been lost. Where church has become separated from state, or religion has become privatized (to put it more generally) because of the press of cultural diversity (rather than from a minority coup, as in Turkey, Russia or pre-1978 Iran), no amount of social pressure can restore the close bond. For example, the initial British hostility to Irish immigrants in the early nineteenth century was often religious. But the successful integration of that immigrant block and the secularization of the culture meant that opposition to Muslim migrants in the last quarter of the twentieth century was secular and racist and made no appeals to religious identity. The point is obvious and can be seen very clearly in comparing the resistance to communism of the three Baltic states. Lithuania, which was overwhelmingly Catholic, was better able to maintain its sense of identity vis-à-vis Russian communism than was Estonia and Latvia, which were religiously diverse. Religion can serve as a major component in cultural defence only if the people share the same religion. As there is no sign of major religious revivals reuniting religiously diverse populations, we can reasonably see the historical change as being one way. This does not mean that all religio-ethnic movements are merely survivals of pre-modern structural arrangements; they are also reactions to trouble-some aspects of modernization. We do not need to consider much detail to appreciate that the Iranian revolution of 1979, for example, was in large part a reaction to Western exploitation of Iran and to the failure of the Shah's attempts to impose Western culture. To use the terms of the theory I have advanced above, there was considerable forced differentiation and the intention of the Iranian revolution was to roll that back. In that sense, 'de-differentiation' is possible where the original change was artificially imposed. However, the crucial point is that religion could play the role of cultural defence in Iran only because the vast majority of Iranians shared the same religion and such differentiation as had occurred had been short lived, un-popular and imposed from outside, rather than emerging slowly and 'naturally' from indigenous social development (Bruce 2001b).

To put the case formally, the relative absence of the sort of differenti-ation that occurred in most parts of the stable democracies of western Europe is a necessary condition for movements of cultural defence.

Cultural transition

The other major cluster of cases of religion retaining social signi-ficance can be glossed as 'cultural transition'. Where social identity is threatened in the course of major cultural transitions, religion may provide resources for negotiating such transitions or asserting a new claim to a sense of worth. Will Herberg (1983) made this point the centre for his explanation of what he termed the American paradox. On the one hand, Americans are fond of churches; on the other, much American religion does not seem especially religious. The explanation lay in the social functions of religion for migrants to the United States: religious institutions provided resources for the assimilation of immig-rants into American society. Ethnic religious groups provided a mech-anism for easing the transition between homeland and the new identity. The church offered a supportive group that spoke one's language, shared one's assumptions and values, but that also had experience of, and contacts within, the new social and cultural milieu.

A similar pattern was evident among Irish migrants to nineteenth-century Britain. They congregated where others had gone before. They established a religious community and its appropriate institutions and roles as soon as they could, and within that community they reasserted their cultural integrity and their sense of self-worth. They often fell away from observance before families and cultural institutions were established, but they often became more observant – perhaps even more observant than they were at home – when these were in place.

There is another important manifestation of the tendency for religion to retain significance, even temporarily to grow in significance, where it comes to play a role in cultural transition, and that is in the course of modernization itself. Modernization disrupts communities, traditional employment patterns and status hierarchies. By extending the range of communication, it makes the social peripheries and hinterlands more aware of the manners and mores, life styles and values, of the centre and metropolis, and vice versa. Those at the centre of the society, the carriers of modernization, missionize the rest, seeking to assimilate them, by educating them and socializing them in 'respectable' beliefs and practices. They wish to improve and elevate the rural masses and those who move to the fringes of the cities and there form a potentially dangerous mob. Sectors of the social periphery in turn are motivated to embrace the models of respectable performance offered to them, especially when they are already in the process of upward mobility and self-improvement.

Industrialization and urbanization therefore tended to give rise to movements of revival and reform, drawing the lapsed and heterodox into the orbit of orthodoxy. The new converts and their overenthusiastic religion often offended the dominant religious organizations. They solved the awkwardness of their position by seceding (or being expelled) and forming new sects. Methodism in late-eighteenth- and nineteenth-century Britain is a prominent example. By religious dissent the formerly deferential middling and lower orders marked their withdrawal from the old system of dependency on parson and squire, asserted their autonomy, and embraced the religious values and practices that endorsed their recently acquired socio-economic and democratic aspirations. Evangelicalism gave a spiritual legitimation to the desire for improvement within these strata, while inculcating the values and habits of thrift, conscientious hard work, self-discipline, sobriety and the deferral of gratification that would assist them to realize those values. Industrialization gave people the chance to get on; evangelical religion encouraged the desire to do so.

Although industrialization and urbanization tend in the long term to undermine traditional community and thereby to subvert the basis on which religion can most readily flourish, in the short term they can be associated with an increase in attachment to religious bodies. To summarise, modernization can create a new role for religion as a socializing agent in times of rapid social change.

Second summary

It is not an accident that most modern societies are largely secular. Industrialization brought with it a series of social changes – the fragmentation of the lifeworld, the decline of community, the rise of bureaucracy, technological consciousness – that together made religion less arresting and less plausible than it had been in pre-modern societies. That is the conclusion of most social scientists, historians and church leaders in the Western world. If there is any originality in my account of these changes, it is only in the stress I give to diversity. Where others have begun their explanation for the decline of religion with the increasingly neutral state, I have drawn attention to the cause of that neutrality. Although the idea that citizens should not have their rights constrained by religious affiliation had become sufficiently well established as part of liberal and democratic discourse by the middle of the nineteenth century that it became part of democratic reform, it was born out of necessity. The cultural diversity created by the interaction of the fragmenting religious culture and structural and social differentiation pushed religious identity (and with it all but the blandest religious ideas) out of the public arena and into the private sphere.

Again it is largely a matter of emphasis, but I have also stressed the impact of diversity on the way in which people who wish to remain religious can hold their religious beliefs. The removal of support at the level of social structure has a corresponding effect on the social psychology of belief. The dogmatic certainties of the church and sect are replaced by the weak affirmations of the denomination and the cult.

However, as I have just argued, there are counter-trends that can retard or prevent secularization. The secularizing impact of diversity depends to a very great extent on an egalitarian culture and a democratic polity. In their absence, diversity may heighten racial and ethnic conflict and deepen commitment to a communal religious identity.

My observations about the role of religion in cultural defence and cultural transition are not lately added qualifications. They are part and parcel of my general approach – a necessary reflection of the fact that social development and religious history are complex. Hence any explanation must be complex.

What the paradigm does not assert

Later chapters will consider in great detail a number of objections of the secularization paradigm and will in those contexts further clarify its claims and remit. Here I want briefly to eliminate some of the objections that stem from basic misunderstanding and answer some criticisms that will not be discussed below.

Secularization is universal and inevitable

In common with many critics, Jeffrey Hadden (1987) has offered as a compelling reason to reject the secularization paradigm the importance of religion in countries such as Iran. This would be germane only if the paradigm was intended as a universal model. Anyone who had actually read Weber, Troeltsch, Niebuhr, Wilson, Berger or Martin (and Hadden cites none of them) would appreciate that they did not see themselves as discovering universal laws comparable to the basic findings of natural science.[7] Like Weber's Protestant Ethic thesis, the secularization story is an attempt to explain a historically and geographically specific cluster of changes. It is an account of what has happened to religion in western Europe (and its North American and Australasian offshoots) since the Reformation. Whether any parts of the explanation have implications for other societies is an empirical matter and must rest on the extent to which the causal variables found in the original setting are repeated elsewhere. Although careful comparative analysis, by highlighting the 'all other things' that are not equal, can shed further light on the secularization approach, of itself that religion in Iran in 1980 or Chile in 1990 is not like religion in Belgium is neither here nor there.

The secularization paradigm does not imply that the changes it describes and explains are inevitable. There is nothing inevitable about human life except death and taxes and I can think of very few social scientists who would think otherwise. After all, people are sentient beings who can change. However, it does seem reasonable to see some social changes as accumulating in a 'value-added process' (Smelser 1966) so that, once they have occurred, it is very difficult to see how their effects can be reversed in any circumstances that are at all likely. Egalitarianism is now so firmly embedded in the West that I cannot imagine the United States, for example, again restricting the franchise to white people or preventing married women taking paid employment. To use the example given above, it is difficult to see how a religiously diverse liberal democracy can again become religiously homogeneous while religion retains much substance. Proponents of competing religions can converge by gradually dropping what divides them (the general pattern of sects and churches becoming denominations) but the mass conversion required to make all US citizens Protestant fundamentalists or make all Germans Mormons is very unlikely in a diverse culture that stresses the rights of the individual. We are claiming irreversibility, rather than inevitability.

The paradigm is progressive and secularist

As far as I know, Berger, Wilson, Martin, Dobbelaere and Wallis have never cited Comte, Freud or Huxley as intellectual progenitors, but it is still common for critics to denigrate the secularizationists for the humanist arrogance of supposing that religion has declined because people have become more sophisticated, clever, mature or well informed. Peter Glassner, for example, criticizes the paradigm for being nothing more than 'generalizations from limited empirical findings used by sociologists to bolster an implicit ideology of progress' (1977: 64). In reply to the assertion of 'limited empirical findings', we could note that the twenty-five years since Glassner made that claim have seen the addition of very large amounts of data to support the paradigm and very little to undermine it. But it is the second point that concerns me here. While some secularizationists have been neutral about the changes they describe and explain, many have been anything but in favour. Weber's description of the modern ethos as 'the iron cage of rationality' hardly sounds like endorsement. In unusually predictive mode, Wilson wrote: 'Religion in modern society will remain peripheral, relatively weak, providing comfort for men in the interstices of a soulless social system of which men are the half-witting, half-restless prisoners' (1976b: 276). In case the pessimism in that assessment is not obvious, consider the following assessment of the effects of the decline of community and of secularization:

Because such developments facilitate a variety of criminal or antisocial behavior, such breakdown of moral control leads inevitably to the threat of more oppressive measures for the maintenance of public order. . . . Modern governments, even in the modern liberal states . . . contemplate or institute such devices as data retrieval systems, video monitoring of public space, the electronic tagging of offenders, 'three-strike' convictions, reimposition of visa requirements for migrants, boot camps, zero tolerance and the like. (Wilson 2000: 46)

Far from seeing modernity as liberating, Wilson believes that the erosion of shared values will make life decidedly less pleasant.

The paradigm is poor theory

In his omnibus critique, Hadden includes being 'a hodge-podge of loosely employed ideas rather than a systematic theory' (1987: 587). Remove the insulting language and I would agree but regard it as a virtue. In their concern to make sense of the relationship between the modernization of the West and the decline in the power and popularity of religion, thousands of scholars have studied cases that run from Anabaptists in eighteenth-century Germany and Freethinkers in 1920s London to Moonies in 1960s California. So large a phenomenon could be comprehended by a 'systematic theory' only if (as has been the case with both of Stark's theories of religion) it is so abstract as to be worthless. There is no secularization theory. There is a cluster of testable explanations that cohere as well as anything in the social sciences. That they are sometimes 'loosely employed' is neither here nor there. What matters is that they can be tightly employed.

Secularization must have an even trajectory

The secularization paradigm is not the sociological equivalent of synchronized swimming. It does not require or expect that all indices of religious vitality will decline at the same speed or evenly. The process is bound to be lumpy because the world is complex. In the 1970s, parts of Birmingham would have defied the expectation of declining religious vitality because the secular English were being displaced by Pakistani Muslims. Migration changed the religious complexion. That would refute the secularization paradigm only if the secular English had moved towards Pakistan's level of religious observance. The reverse is the case; as they become English in every other respect, the third generation of Muslims is also approaching the English level of religious indifference. Sociological explanation requires that all other things be equal. They very rarely are.

Unlike the laws of the material sciences, our propositions are generalities. That there has always been the maverick peer of the realm who supports anarcho-syndicalism does not invalidate the claim that the British aristocracy supports the interests of the rentier and the capitalist classes. That a few thousand people become Moonies need not defeat the secularization paradigm.

It is in the nature of sociology to seek the general social changes that explain whatever interests us. We should never forget that such perceived changes are abstractions created by colour-washing the jagged edges of events in the real world. That, on close acquaintance, the history shows that things could have been very different is not refutation of the secularization paradigm; it is merely the normal relationship between history and sociology. The jagged bits are a problem only if it can be plausibly argued that a different abstraction can be better drawn from the same material. If there are too many exceptions, then we should consider painting 'growth' or even just 'random fluctuations'. But some small reversals need not trouble the paradigm.

A further reason for lumpiness is that organizations have their own histories. It is here (rather than as a general theory of religion) that some of the supply-side observations of Stark and his colleagues have value. Whatever the general level of demand for religion, churches, sects, denominations and cults can vary their support by their actions. Or, to put it more generally, social life is not predetermined. Individuals, groups and organizations can make more or less of what is possible. By its support for Franco, the Catholic Church in Spain probably alienated a large part of the population. By virtue of his forceful personality and single-mindedness, Ian Paisley was able to create a sect of over 100 congregations.

The hard social determinist line is that such things do not affect the big picture. Had it not been Paisley, it would have been someone else. Had it not been support for Franco, it would have been something else. We do not need to take sides in this ancient quarrel between old-fashioned history and high sociology. We need only recognize that there is some freedom in the system: individuals and agencies can behave more or less competently. Hence religious change, even if following a pattern we can explain, will be uneven. Even if the social changes that strengthen or weaken the plausibility of religious beliefs were to press equally on every part of a society (and they do not), that people can respond in different ways to the same stimuli will ensure that religious change will never be even.

All of which is a long way to this point. Unevenness of itself does not refute the secularization paradigm; what matters is the overall direction of trends and their long-term stability. The religious revival in the fishing communities of Norfolk and the north-east of Scotland (Griffin 2000) does not disprove secularization, but a recurrence in any Western country of anything on the scale of John Wesley's Methodist revivals most certainly will.

The endpoint is atheism

One common misattribution is to gloss the secularization paradigm as predicting (and hence requiring for its fulfilment) that everyone becomes an atheist. Prominent US sociologist of religion Andrew Greeley frequently uses the numbers of what he calls 'hard-core atheists' as a measure of secularization (for example, Jagodzinski and Greeley 2001). Paul Heelas (2001) refers repeatedly to the small number of people who in surveys describe themselves as atheists and agnostics as a reason to be sceptical of the secularization approach. I will say more about this in chapter 10 but it seems an arrogance on the part of believers to assume that those who do not share their beliefs must nonetheless find them so important as deliberately to disavow them.

Wilson has always been quite clear about this. In one place he says the secularization approach 'does not imply . . . that all men have acquired a secularized consciousness. It does not even require that most individuals have relinquished all their interest in religion, even though that may be the case. It maintains no more than that religion ceases to be significant in the working of the social system' (1982: 149–50). In another he says 'Religion is not eliminated by the process of secularization, and only the crudest of secularist interpretations could ever have reached the conclusion that it would be' (1987: 8).

I would go further than Wilson and argue that the decline in the social significance of religion, in turn, reduces the number of people interested in religion. That is, the connection is causal rather than a matter of definition. But, even in my more radical view, there is no expectation that religion will disappear.

That many people continue to be in some sense religious could be taken as proof that the changes we see in the religious life of Britain is not 'secularization'. I do not see any major difficulty in using a term to describe a process that has no fixed destination. Take, for example, the idea of 'fragmentation'. If a political party with, say, 1,000 members divides into ten competing factions, I would describe that as 'fragmentation'; even though the process has not reached its potential endpoint of 1,000 one-person parties. Fragmentation takes it sense not from where it is going but from where it has been. In the same way, secularization can take it sense from meaning 'becoming less religious'.

In so far as I can imagine an endpoint, it would not be self-conscious irreligion; you have to care too much about religion to be irreligious. It would be widespread indifference (what Weber called being religiously unmusical); no socially significant shared religion; and religious ideas being no more common than would be the case if all minds were wiped blank and people began from scratch to think about the world and their place in it. This is an important point, because the critics often assume that the secularization paradigm supposes the human default position to be instrumental, materialist atheism. Of course, what people are 'essentially' like, stripped of their culture and history, is unknowable, because we are all products of culture and history. But, as it has a bearing on what would count as fulfilment of the paradigm, this requires some consideration.

If we imagined away all traces of previous religious traditions and started with completely blank minds, some of us would produce religious ideas and elaborate rituals. I say this not because I suppose there is an inevitable need for religion but because there is obviously the logical possibility of some religious propositions arising from any contemplation of the human situation. To say 'Ethel has died and is no more' is to imply other possibilities: Ethel has gone to another world; Ethel's body has died but we can still communicate with Ethel-ness; Ethel has not died but has gone into hiding and will reappear when we deserve her; the essence of Ethel has left her worn-out frame and reappeared in a baby born the same day as she died, and so on.

The difference between a religious and a secular world is not the possibility of imagining religious ideas. Anything can be imagined by someone. It is the likelihood of them catching on. The removal-of-supports approach to secularization does not posit secularity as an endpoint. Indeed it posits no endpoint. Rather it explains why shared ideas are no longer as persuasive as they once were. It does not rule out the possibility of someone putting together strange claims about space travel, the likelihood of life on other planets, and the unlikelihood of people having built the pyramids, marinating these with a large dose of wishful thinking, and coming up with Bo and Peep's flying saucer cult (Balch 1982), a group that hit the news in 1997 when, as Heaven's Gate, its thirty-nine members committed suicide. What it does rule out is the possibility of any such theories becoming very widely accepted, under the political, social and economic circumstances that we can presently imagine. David Martin, who has criticized clumsy secularization theories, while making some of the most important contributions to the paradigm, said of his intentions in writing *A Sociology of English Religion*: 'I hoped to show among other things that the decline of religion was followed not by rationality but by subterranean theologies and nonrational sentiments and superstitions' (2000: 35). Provided that he agrees that none of those theologies has become very popular, that the non-rational sentiments are confined to small parts of the lifeworld, and that the superstitions remain a pale shadow of those of the Middle Ages, I have no quarrel at all with Martin's judgement of what follows religion.

To restate the crucial principle, while the proportion of atheists in a population is an interesting secondary indicator (and it is steadily increasing in the West), it is not the primary test. For Wilson that would be data on the social significance of religion and the endpoint would be 'very little'. Others (I among them) would add a second consideration. As I expect that ideologies that lose relevance will also lose plausibility, I see the popularity of religious beliefs as a useful index of secularization. I expect the proportion of people who are largely indifferent to religious ideas to increase and the seriously religious to become a small minority.

Conclusion

Marxism as a political programme was killed by its dismal failure to deliver; Marxism as a social scientific theory was killed by being endlessly qualified to preserve it from refutation. Too many lifesavers may smother the drowning man. I hope the above clarifications have not saved the secularization paradigm from being disproved at the price of making it untestable. My aim is to ensure that we are testing the right things. The paradigm does not require secularization to be universal or even; it is not thinly disguised Progressivism; it is a set of associated explanations rather than a single theory, but that is no bad thing; it does not suppose the course of history to be smooth and hence is not refuted by humps and lumps; and it does not suppose that the only alternative to religion is irreligion. What the paradigm does require is a long-term decline in the power, popularity and prestige of religious beliefs and rituals.

CHAPTER TWO

The Golden Age of Faith

To talk of secularization is to suppose that the present is less religious than the past. Hence the paradigm can be challenged by asserting that whatever point in the past is taken as the start was actually less religious than we think or by asserting that the present is more religious than we believe. Richard Neuhaus has suggested that the disparity between what we know about ourselves and what we know about the past distorts our judgement. We are acutely aware that contemporary Christians often fall short of the standards they set for themselves in religious observance or in ethical behaviour. We see this as evidence of 'the church on the rocks' and miss the point that exactly the same sort of disparity was noted at various points in the past (Neuhaus 2000: 1).

An even more thoroughgoing rejection of the assumption of decline is offered by Rodney Stark and his associates, who think medieval Britons were no more religious than their modern counterparts (Stark and Iannaccone 1994; Stark et al. 1995). Their assessment of the strength of religion in Britain at the end of the twentieth century will be considered in the next chapter. Here I will try to reestablish the conventional view of the past. I will argue that nothing in the secularization paradigm requires that the religious life of premodern Britain be a 'Golden Age of Faith' (as it is so unhelpfully caricatured); what it does require is that our ancestors be patently more religious than we are.[1] The purpose of this chapter is to lay out as clearly and as honestly as possible what is known about religion in premodern Britain. Neuhaus might be right that modern Americans are ignorant of the past, but there is no reason for sociologists to remain so.

The critics

Clearly David Martin could not have written *A General Theory of Secularization* (1978b) unless he believed that there was some secularization about which to have a theory, general or otherwise. Sadly, the magisterial but complex *General Theory* is less often cited than a brief and early essay (D. Martin 1965) in which he argued that the term 'secularization' was part of a utopian intellectual project and best abandoned, advice that fortunately he did not himself take. He also began the fashion for assuming that secularization theories posited a 'Golden Age of Faith' and arguing against such an estimation of the piety of the past: 'secularist history tends to accept Catholic laments about the period when men were truly religious. In this instance the backward-looking utopia of medievalism becomes the basis for writing about secularization' (D. Martin 1969: 30).

Ten years after Martin's first sally, Martin Goodridge, in a paper entitled '"The Ages of Faith" – Romance or Reality?', insisted it was the former. He noted from the work of Le Bras that many of the rural clergy of nineteenth-century France were too poorly educated to give sermons; that many nineteenth-century Gloucestershire parishes celebrated the Eucharist only two or three times a year; that laws introduced by ninth-century German Bishops were widely resisted; and that in thirteenth-century Italy and France substantial sections of society hardly attended church (1975: 383–7).

It is worth marking the gadfly nature of these observations. Evidence from such a diversity of times and places would be refuting only if the secularization paradigm needed to suppose that expressions of religiosity were constant and uniform up to whatever point is identified as the start of decline. What is obvious from any broad reading of religious history is that the Church (or churches) changed; as complex organizations deeply embedded in the economy, society and polity of their countries, they could hardly do otherwise. They rose and fell. They became corrupt and they reformed. They were more and less popular. For example, Whiting documents a marked decline in popular support for the Church in the south-west of England during the Reformation. In some places it recovered; in others the change was less 'a transition from Catholicism to Protestantism than a decline from religious commitment into conformism and indifference' (1989: 268). As in any other grand comparative story, what matters is the generality of circumstances over the long run.

A second preliminary point, to which I will return, is that Goodridge's historians are working primarily from material that was more apologia than reportage. As Martin says, we need to be sceptical about medieval utopianism, but we need to be equally conscious of the interest many contemporary sources had in identifying and exaggerating signs of religious deviance or apathy. Many of them were produced as part of arguments about the structure of the church and state support for its activities.

The same point can be made in response to the work of Keith Thomas, the main source of Goodridge's observations about England and almost the only British historian cited by Stark in his revisionism. Keith Thomas (1978) demonstrates that the people of sixteenth- and seventeenth-century England were not all well informed, reverent and regular church-attending Christians. A major source for his work are the records of church courts and the correspondence and diaries of leading churchmen. Spufford (1985) reminds us that complaints to church courts were themselves religious acts of people trying to change the Church in this or that direction. In some places enthusiastic clergy and elders prevented people taking communion because they were judged to be unregenerate and then reported them for not communicating! This tells us a lot about struggles for the soul of the Church of England, but it means that such data as can be extracted from church court records and ecclesiastical correspondence cannot be taken as evidence of the extent or nature of lay church involvement without a degree of sophistication that is missing from most sociological uses of the historical literature. At the risk of labouring the point, would we be wise to base conclusions about the diligence in study of twentieth-century university students by examining the minutes of discipline committee meetings, the letters sent to students who fail to attend our classes, or the sometimes bitter comments of academics disappointed that their charges do not match their enthusiasm for the discipline?

If we read Thomas's observations, not as evidence of the laity falling short of the standards of religious officials and enthusiasts, but simply for what they tell us, they show his subjects to be profoundly superstitious, to believe implicitly in the supernatural, and to accept thoroughly the most basic of Christian beliefs (a creator God, heaven and hell as rewards and punishment for good and bad behaviour, the Church's control of access to salvation). The English peasants may have often disappointed the guardians of Christian orthodoxy, but they were indubitably religious.

It is noticeable that such sociological critics of the secularization thesis as Stark and Iannaccone (1994) cite Thomas without referring to the debates among historians that his work stimulated or to the huge amount of relevant material published after 1973. Margaret Spufford wrote the following, initially as a reply to Keith Thomas's claim that super-stition and magic were more important than orthodox Christianity:

> The degree of importance that religion held in the lives of non-gentle parishioners in the sixteenth and seventeenth centuries will never be established. The beliefs of such people were not normally of interest even to the ecclesiastical authorities. . . . Genuine popular devotion of a humble kind leaves very little trace upon the records of any given time. The believer, especially the conforming believer, makes less impact than the dissentient. At no periods is it possible to distinguish the conform-ing believer from the apathetic church-goer who merely wished to stay out of trouble.
>
> It is possible, therefore, for the historian to start from the very prob-able thesis that 'the hold of any kind of organized religion upon the mass of the population was never more than partial', add the complaints of puritan reforming ministers about their flocks' performance of their uncongenial duties, support these with figures of the considerable minority who were presented for absenteeism in the church courts, and point the case further with the disrespectful remarks of a further mi-nority, which was also presented in the church courts. If it is set against this background, the importance of astrology and magic . . . then seems very great. Yet the negative picture that emerges is based on the silence of the majority of witnesses.
>
> An alternative picture, illustrating the convictions of the humble, also depends on the selection of examples which may be atypical. It runs from the demonstration of bequests to the church lights, altar and fabric normally made by every parishioner who left a will before the Reformation, through the remarkably concrete fact that over half the Marian martyrs listed by Foxe whose social status is known were agri-cultural labourers. It continues by showing that the rural laity were actively involved in the complaints against scandalous ministers and in the anti-Laudian petitions of the 1640s. (1981: 194–5)

Clearly Spufford favours the second perspective she offers and it is also clear from her work that she does so because she is persuaded by the evidence, even though it cannot be supported by the sorts of measurements she would ideally like. But, as I hope to argue, the crucial point for the secularization thesis is that, even if all historians concurred with the first perspective – the Thomas case – this would still be sufficient for our purposes because, unless we are going to use an extremely narrow definition of religion, even that shows a culture considerably more religious than our own.

Martin, Goodridge and Thomas all appear as witnesses for the prosecution in one of the best-known sociological criticisms of the secularization thesis: Abercrombie, Hill and Turner's *The Dominant Ideology Thesis* (1980). Indeed, with French historian Le Roy Ladurie, they form the entire case. Abercrombie et al. are critical of the notion that the people of the Middle Ages were incorporated in a shared belief and value system. As Bottomore summarizes their case in his introduction to their study:

> the maintenance and reproduction of a given form of class society – or in other terms, its cohesion – is not to be explained by the influence of a 'dominant ideology', but principally by what Marx called the 'dull compulsion of economic relations'. . . . In feudal society, they argue, it was not religion but primogeniture which played the major part in maintaining class domination . . . (Abercrombie et al. 1980: p. ix)

This may well be the case, but it is a claim about the social consequences of a particular form of religion. It is not the same as arguing that most people in feudal societies were not religious. We can well accept the point that 'The peasantry . . . were largely untouched by the civilising role of the church throughout the Middle Ages and they remained the main vehicle of magical, irrational practices up to the Counter-Reformation and the era of the Protestant evangelical movements of the nineteenth century' (Abercrombie et al. 1980: 69–70) without, as they do, generalizing this into a critique of the secularization approach. Instead, we can note the near universality of the 'magical, irrational practices' and recognize that they were often tied to a popular interpretation of Christian themes through an instrumental attitude to shrines of saints, holy water and the like. We can then appreciate that Abercrombie et al.'s work is a challenge to the secularization approach to religious change only if one anachronistically expects the religious people of feudal societies to think and act like nineteenth-century Methodists.

It is a mark of Abercrombie et al.'s excessively narrow view of religion that they interpret witchcraft as evidence against the secularization paradigm. Because they confine religion to what the Church did (and minimize its influence), and note that witchcraft accusations were most common where the Church was weakest, they can present the obsession with witches as evidence that the people of sixteenth-century Languedoc and the Pyrenees were not very religious (1980: 77). If we can accept Durkheim's description of what aboriginal peoples thought and did as 'the religious life', we need not be deflected by Abercrombie, Hill and Turner.

What historians show: Institutional religion

The Welsh historian Glanmor Williams offers a summary of a 'Golden Age' story:

> The medieval period is generally regarded as one of outstanding achievement in the history of religion. It is looked upon as an age of universal faith, when western Christendom flourished, secure in its beliefs and united under the authority of the supra-national papacy. An age in which long strides were taken in the outward organization of the Church into provinces, dioceses, and parishes; one which raised awe-inspiring cathedrals, monasteries and many parish churches, still surviving among us as monuments to the beliefs and aspirations of medieval men and women. An age which witnessed the creation of an ordered body of Canon Law and its general acceptance and enforcement; and which saw the construction of a superb intellectual synthesis combining the testimony of faith and reason and the enthronement of theology as the queen of all knowledge. An age when the Church dominated the content and conduct of education in the universities, grammar schools and other institutions. An age which looked to the Church as the creatrix and nurse of the crowning achievements of art and civilization. (1991: 22)

Although he believes that this picture is an 'oversimplification', and goes on to detail political changes that variously strengthened or weakened the church in Wales, Williams, well enough versed in the debate to parody it, concludes the summary by saying: 'Underlying this attractive scenario there is a core of reality which cannot be gainsaid' (1991: 22).

As Williams notes, the flourishing of Christianity in medieval Wales was an achievement of a small elite. But before we follow Abercrombie et al. we need to appreciate just exactly what was expected of the laity. The unitary church of the pre-Reformation feudal society did not have members; it represented the entire people. It was financially supported primarily by the rental or produce from gifts of land given by the king and the gentry. Its offices were performed according to the Church's calendar and they were thought to be pleasing to God even if, as in the case of the daily Masses said in many churches in the fifteenth century, almost none of the common people attended. At the heart of the religious system was the implicit notion that religious merit could be transferred: the propitious ritual acts performed by the religious officials and religious virtuosi could benefit the rest of the population. People believed the religious offices to be effective even if those who performed them were lacking in some aspect of personal character. It was the ordination of the priest, not his personal piety, that gave him power. Coming behind four centuries of Protestantism, we may interpret a lack of theological education or high moral character among the clergy as evidence of a lack of religion, but this is to misunderstand the basis of religious power in the pre-Reformed Church. It is surely greater testimony to the *strength* of religion than to its weakness that people should belief that the sacraments worked even if performed by an ill-trained cleric.

Williams puts it succinctly when he says that the people of the Middle Ages were 'community Christians' – that is, they accepted that the ritual being conducted by the priest, in a language that almost none of them understood, was being undertaken on behalf of them all (1991: 23).

That the religious activity of the Middle Ages did not depend on the involvement of individual members of the laity was clear from the architecture of churches and from the forms of the services. In small parish churches, away from the high ceremonial of the cathedral, 'frequently the priest read the entire service in a low and inaudible voice with his back to the congregation throughout' (B. Hamilton 1986: 55). The laity were not discouraged from attending 'offices' in places where they were publicly sung, but 'unless they understood Latin there was little inducement for them to do so' (1986: 56). Because there were no seats in churches and most of the business was muttered away from the audience, people milled about and gossiped with their neighbours. Thomas cites many cases of people being charged before church courts with improper behaviour in church: knitting, gossiping, conducting trade, fighting and, in one case, loosing off a fowling piece.

We might find such behaviour disrespectful and see it as proof of slight commitment, but we would miss the more important point that people still felt obliged, by God as much as by social pressure, to be there even when there was so little for them to do. This point of social pressure must be addressed. It is common for the church attendance and involvement in religious rituals of the people of the Middle Ages to be dismissed as mere conformity. But, if allowed to stand unchallenged, this presents a bizarre picture of a powerful social institution. If nobody believed in it, from whence came the pressure to conform? Furthermore, it is clear from the fact that lay people used to ask church authorities which parts of the divine offices deserved particular attention that they thought certain parts of the services were a matter of great importance. Again we can refer to Keith Thomas's own evidence. He quotes a sixteenth-century source saying: 'when the vicar goeth into the pulpit to read that [he] himself hath written, then the multitude of the parish goeth straight out of the church, home to drink' (1978: 191). Leaving aside the almost certainly exaggerated claims for alcohol consumption, what does this show? First the 'multitude of the parish' were actually in church. Secondly, they stayed for the parts of the service they regarded as of divine origin and only left when the priest engaged in the innovative 'Protestant' practice of preaching a sermon. During the Elevation of the Host, which was signalled by the ringing of a bell, people stopped milling about and kneeled in reverent silence (B. Hamilton 1986: 115–18). When our present church leaders agonize about how they might make church services more interesting and exciting for young people, the fact that such large numbers of people in the Middle Ages attended church services that made almost no concessions to their presence suggests that, despite their failure to comport themselves in the manner that we now expect of churchgoers, our medieval ancestors were religious people.

A personal anecdote may illustrate the point. I once had to interview a Jewish businessman in Belfast and we arranged to meet at the synagogue. I expected to see him before or after the service and was initially shocked to find us talking about mundane matters in the very doorway of the room in which the prayers were being said. While we talked, he stood with one foot inside the room. This, he later explained, was because his presence was required to make the quorum necessary for prayers. My first reaction was to think that this was a man who did not take his religion seriously; where was the attentive posture redolent of piety? Later I realized that his attitude expressed absolute certainty, a conviction that there was a God, that God required ritual prayers, that for the prayers to be effective there had to be a quorum of male Jews, that his toe in the door met those requirements and thus glorified God, and that the prayers were sufficiently important for him to turn out.

Even allowing that the model of appropriate religious behaviour for the Middle Ages was very different from that of the nineteenth century – communal conformity rather than individual enthusiasm – and hence that we are not comparing like with like, we should get the numbers into perspective. We could cite Peter Laslett's very different observations (1983) about church attendance (that in most places, most people took communion and attended the main services), but the case is most strongly made by concentrating on those who wish to challenge the Laslett view. Keith Thomas cites a Jacobean preacher complaining that there were 'sometimes not half the people in a parish present at holy exercises upon the Sabbath day, so hard a thing is it to draw them to the means of their salvation' (1978: 191). That 'sometimes not half' clearly implies that most times there were more than half the people present. Peter Clark attempts to put a figure on what Thomas calls 'the certain proportion' who 'remained utterly ignorant of the elementary tenets of Christian dogma' (1978: 189) when he writes: 'Probably something like a fifth of the population of Kent stayed away from church on a regular basis in the later sixteenth century' (Clark 1977: 156). So four-fifths did not stay away. This is the degree of church attendance well in excess of what is now held by Stark to show that the United States is a highly churched society and well above what is cited for the 1851 Census of Religious Worship as the high point of nineteenth-century religiosity. Of Bromley in Kent, Gill notes that about 30 per cent of the population were in church in 1903 but only 10 per cent in 1993. For Kent overall, at least nine-tenths now stay away from church (Gill 2001).

We can move from church attendance to the social presence of the Church more generally. All historians, Thomas included, agree that the medieval Church was intimately involved in all major rites of passage.

> Every time a child was baptized, a couple married, or a body buried in Elizabethan and Stuart England – the figures are in the millions – the religion of protestants was both taught and tested. Routine religious observances – the weekly and seasonal round of services and the life-cycle offices of baptisms, weddings and funerals – served as primary points of contact between family and community, centre and periphery, and between men or women and God. Their rhythms and messages were made familiar through frequent reiteration. (Cressy 1997: 2)

Some rituals provoked principled opposition. In parts of England, the Puritan reformers were highly critical of the ritual of 'churching' of mothers a month after childbirth, a ceremony that marked the end of their privileged lying-in period. One reformer listed it as 'No. 55' of the serious errors of the Church of England! Nevertheless, in late Elizabethan Salisbury more than three-quarters of mothers were churched (Cressy 1993: 115).

That the Church controlled the fate of the soul after death was so widely accepted that midwives were taught a simple formula for baptizing babies who were not expected to live long enough to reach a priest. In writing of the various sacraments, Keith Thomas says: 'Before a man died . . . he was extended . . . extreme unction, whereby the recipient was anointed with holy oil and tendered the viaticum. In the eyes of everyone this was a dreadful ritual . . .' (1978: 41). Rituals that are not widely believed in hardly inspire dread.

Nor is it difficult to find other evidence of the strength of Christianity's grip on popular consciousness.[2] Despite the Church insisting that ultimate salvation was a freely given gift of God's grace, the laity of the Middle Ages was obsessed with the idea that the prayers of the living could speed the soul on its way. In 1546 Gilbert Kirk of Exeter bequeathed 4d to each householder in St Mary Arches parish 'to pray to Our Lord God to have mercy on my soul and all Christian souls'. Robert Hone donated 1d to each spectator at his burial in return for their prayers and forgave his debtors on the condition that they prayed for him. He also left 12d to each of his godchildren 'to say a *Pater Noster, Ave* and Creed, praying for my soul' (Whiting 1989: 70). The merely wealthy left large sums to pay for Masses after death, thirty days later, and on the anniversary of their demise: Joan, Lady Cobham, paid for 7,000 Masses to be said after her death. The extremely wealthy ensured an indefinite future of Masses by establishing 'chantries'. A survey of twenty English parishes in the sixteenth century found 2,118 chantries or similar foundations (Harper-Bill 1996: 68). Richard, earl of Arundel, 'left the enormous sum of 1,000 marks to maintain prayers for his soul in Arundel castle' (Keen 1990: 274). The wealthy who were philanthropic as well as devout would attach an almshouse or a school to the chantry and thus reinforce the prayers of the priests with those of the generous recipients of their charity.

Concern for the soul was widespread in every social stratum. Those who could not buy post-mortem services on their own banded together in guilds and fraternities. To quote from the rules of the guild of St George at Lynn:

Ordained it is, that what brother or sister be dead of this fraternity, the alderman shall warn . . . all the company . . . men and women, that is within the town, to come to the exequies of him or her that dead is . . . and be ready to bear them to church, and to offer for the soul as the manner is to do for the dead. . . . And also ordained it is, that what brother or sister so ever be dead of this fraternity, he shall have said for his soul 60 masses. (Keen 1990: 275)

As we will see from survey data presented in the next chapter, most Britons no longer share a dread of hell. Quite what they believe about the soul is a more difficult matter, but George Orwell made a telling point in the 1940s when, with a certain rhetorical flourish, he wrote:

Now, I find it very rare to meet anyone, of whatever background, who admits to believing in personal immortality. Still, I think it quite likely that if you asked everyone the question and put pencil and paper in his hands, a fairly large number . . . would admit the possibility that after death there might be 'something'. The point . . . is that the belief, such as it is, hasn't the actuality it had for our forefathers. Never, literally never in recent years, have I met anyone who gave me the impression of believing in the next world as firmly as he believed in the existence of, for instance, Australia. Belief in the next world does not influence conduct as it would if it were genuine. With that endless existence beyond death to look forward to, how trivial our lives here would seem! Most Christians profess to believe in Hell. Yet have you ever met a Christian who seemed as afraid of Hell as he was of cancer? Even very devout Christians will make jokes about Hell. They wouldn't make jokes about leprosy, or RAF pilots with their faces burnt away: the subject is too painful. (1998: 152)

Consider the lengths to which people went to avoid blaspheming. Or note the institution of swearing oaths on the Bible. How could those who wished to ensure that the truth was told have for centuries insisted that an oath be sworn with one hand on the Holy Book unless it was very widely believed that the Bible was not like other books and that there was a God who would punish those who lied under oath? That we are now cynical of such testimony when for centuries our ancestors were not surely shows that their attitude to the Bible was not ours.

We might also note that the habit that is often invoked as proof of the corruption of the pre-Reformation Christian Church – the sale of indulgences – actually testifies to the popular power of religion. People would not have paid considerable sums of money to be easily relieved of the burden of their sins if they had not believed, first, that there was a God who would punish them for those sins and, secondly, that the Church had the power to intervene of their behalf.

As well as dominating significant rights of passage, the Church imposed its calendrical structure on the seasons of the year. The working year was marked by festivals and feasts, many of pre-Christian origins, which the Church had taken over: Plough Monday, Candlemas, Shrovetide, Lady Day, Palm Sunday, Easter, Hocktide, May Day, Whitsuntide, Lammas, Michaelmas, All Hallows and Christmas. Rents were paid at Lady Day and Michaelmas; events were dated from the nearest saint's day (Harrison 1984: 156). Of course, as Harrison, Collinson (1982) and others note, none of this directly tells us much about what went on in the hearts and minds of ordinary people, but there are two obvious responses to such agnosticism. First, it applies as much to almost everything we as social scientists claim to know. Secondly, to shift from a humble agnosticism to the assertion that the Church's domination of the physical, social, political and economic landscape had no corresponding effect on the consciousness of the people is to deny all that we know about socialization. Can we really believe that people whose lives were organized by the calendar of the Church, whose art, music and literature were almost entirely religious, who were taught the basic prayers, who regularly attended church services, and for whom the priest was the most powerful person after their temporal lord, were untouched by religious beliefs and values?

Furthermore, we can note that the common people were sufficiently religious that they not only supported the conventions of the Church in the normal round of their lives. Religion also figured in their periodic rebellions against the established order. Most uprisings of the sixteenth and seventeenth centuries had at their core grievances over changes in the organization of agriculture, but many also included elements of religious dissent. In Devon and Cornwall in 1549, the rebels of the Western rising 'repudiated the English Prayer Book and demanded the restoration of the Roman Catholic mass and ceremonies . . . Ket's revolt later in the same summer was noticeably anti-clerical and the new Prayer Book was used in the daily services on Mousehold Heath' (Harrison 1984: 162). So Ket's rebels held daily services; the miners who struck for a year in 1984 did not.

In summary, Bernhard Hamilton's judgement of the impact of Christianity seems sensible: 'The medieval world was Christian in the sense that everybody shared a common understanding of the world in which they lived based on Christian premises. Only the very learned had full and detailed knowledge of the whole world picture, but everybody understood some part of it' (1986: 106). He goes on to note that 'Everybody knew the *Our Father*', that 'People in the Middle Ages were willing to spend considerable sums of money in payment for masses', that 'Everybody believed that man had an immortal soul' and that 'Most people seem to have accepted that it was necessary to make reparation to God for serious and wilful sins either in this life or the next' (1986: 106).

What historians show: Supernaturalism

The further point overlooked by critics of the secularization paradigm is that the challenge posed by Thomas, the only British historian cited by such revisionists as Stark and Iannaccone, is limited to an argument about the authority of the Christian Church. In showing the extent to which pre-Christian superstitions and magical practices continued alongside orthodox Christianity, Thomas amply illustrates the importance of those superstitions. Church officials may have despaired at the perversions of their teachings peddled by the laity, and at the relics peddled by pardoners (Chaucer's *Canterbury Tales* offers a fine illustration of that trade), but for the secularization paradigm what matters is that superstition was widespread and effective. Horoscopes were read, not just as a bit of fun, as a giggle or even as a cause for rumination, but as a taken-seriously guide to action. Spells were cast to ward off dangers. Amulets were worn as protection against ailments. Holy relics were venerated and used as sources of magical powers. Belief in the Devil was strong and widespread, as was the corresponding belief that the Church had the power to protect against evil: 'People wanted their houses blessed, their fields blessed, their food blessed, their weapons blessed' (K. Thomas 1978: 32). St Agatha's letters, an inscription placed on tiles, bells or amulets, was a protective against fire. 'In addition, there were exorcisms to make the fields fertile; holy candles to protect farm animals; and formal curses to drive away caterpillars and rats and to kill weeds' (K. Thomas 1978: 35).

Conclusion

I have attempted to summarize the weight of evidence about religion in Britain before and shortly after the Reformation. The domination of the Church cannot be denied. What is at issue is the extent to which its social power had corresponding resonances within the consciousness of ordinary people. While all historians necessarily admit to a degree of agnosticism, even the most sceptical document a degree of popular involvement with institutional religion far greater than anything found in contemporary Britain. It is also clear from the contemporary literature of complaint that, when the people were not practising orthodox Christianity, they were doing something else that, unless we are going to subscribe to an excessively narrow Protestant definition, we would still call religion.

To summarize my argument in a few sentences, I conclude that the new revisionists have misunderstood what is required by the secularization paradigm. The case does not require that the starting point of the comparative description be a society of theologically competent committed Christians enmeshed in a hegemonic dominant ideology. It does not require that what Peter Berger (in the US title of the book published in Britain as *The Social Reality of Religion* (1969)) called the 'sacred canopy' be particularly Christian. Nor does it require that the sacred canopy be an ideological straitjacket.

Two mistakes are commonly made by those who set up the straw man of the 'Golden Age'. First, they anachronistically import to a world in which high religion was primarily a matter of a small group of professionals glorifying God on behalf of the people, a modern Protestant vision of enthusiastic true believers and then, when they find few such believers, mistakenly conclude that premodern Britain was irreligious. Secondly, the revisionists are fond of historians (such as Thomas) who focus on the struggles of the Christian Church to dissuade the laity from their pre-Christian practices and on the tension between the official teachings of the Church and the bastardized magical and superstitious uses to which the common people put what they took from Christianity. They thus tend to be impressed by illustrations of the institutional weakness of the Church and, as well as exaggerating that weakness, miss the fact that the very same evidence shows the common people inhabiting a thoroughly supernaturalistic world.

This is what is at the heart of the paradigm. What is required in the contrast between the past and the present is that there be an identifiable difference in the popularity and salience of beliefs, actions and institutions that assume the existence of supernatural entities with powers of action, or impersonal powers or processes possessed of moral purpose. As Wilson put it: 'All that needs be asserted is that society was much more preoccupied with supernatural beliefs and practices, and accorded them more significance than it does now' (1975: 79). If, instead of thinking in terms of dominant ideologies, we think of pervasive worldviews, it seems quite proper to describe the 'world we have lost' and our world as respectively 'religious' and 'secular'.

CHAPTER THREE

God is Dead:
Christianity in Britain

Introduction

The previous chapter answered the criticism that the secularization paradigm exaggerates the importance of religion in the past. This chapter is intended to re-establish the other end of the comparison against those critics who assert that the secularization paradigm exaggerates the secularity of the present. A considerable body of evidence on church membership and church attendance shows that, unless trends that have held since at least the 1950s are soon reversed, major British denominations are only a generation from extrication. While we may legitimately argue about the causes or the exact trajectory of secularization, no amount of revisionism will change the fact that, if we can legitimately extrapolate from well-established trends, the religious culture that has dominated Britain for the last twelve centuries is in serious trouble. Furthermore, there is also considerable and consistent evidence that conventional religious beliefs are also declining in popularity. Finally, there is no sign of any new religious phenomenon to fill the space. Britain is indeed becoming secular.[1]

Stark theory

In 1966, when Bryan Wilson published *Religion in Secular Society*, it was, to borrow from Jane Austen, 'a truth universally acknowledged' that Britain was less religious than it had been 100 years earlier. That remained the consensus until the late 1970s and 1980s. In each of those decades Rodney Stark discovered a compelling reason why the consensus must be wrong.

His first reason for denying secularization came from the theory he developed with William Sims Bainbridge (Stark and Bainbridge 1987). According to their complex reasoning about the links between rewards and compensators, humankind will always need religion. Desires (if only the desire for immortality) always outstrip rewards. In the absence of rewards, people seek compensators. Religion is superior to secular providers of compensators because it can play the God trump card. Invoking the supernatural increases the attractiveness of compensators and reduces their vulnerability to refutation. In the absence of inheriting anything in this world, the meek will want to be told they will inherit the earth *in the next life*. Hence the demand for religion should be pretty well universal and stable. If one form of religion declines, another should take its place. Enduring secularization is impossible.

The second reason for Stark to deny secularization is that, in the British case, it would run counter to the expectations of the supply-side model of religious economies to which he became attached in the 1980s (Stark 1999). For a variety of reasons that sound rather like propaganda for laissez-faire capitalism, competitive free markets are supposed to be better at meeting not only material but also spiritual needs. Religious monopolies (especially state-supported ones) dampen the demand for religious products. Competitive free markets produce a wide variety of religious products (thus meeting a wide range of preferences) at low costs (thus increasing consumption). So there should be a strong positive correlation between religious diversity and religious vitality. The religious history of Britain, conventionally understood, is a problem. Before the Reformation there was one church, organized on a national parish structure, which glorified God on behalf of, and provided religious offices for, the entire people. With the Reformation, the religious cultures of Scotland, Wales and England diverged. Each national church also fragmented internally, to create a large number of competing organizations. By the middle of the nineteenth century, about half the population worshipped outside the state churches of England, Wales and Scotland. Since then pluralism has increased further with the growth of non-Trinitarian sects and Pentecostalism. There are interesting technical arguments about exactly how one measures diversity but no one questions that the last 200 years have seen a considerable increase in its extent. Few Britons are far from a major urban area and for most of the twentieth century it was possible to find almost every imaginable variant of Christianity on offer in British cities. According to Stark, the increase in diversity and the gradual removal of constraints on competition (such as supporting the state churches with public funds and denying government office to dissenters) should have created an increase in religious vitality. Britain of the 1990s should have been more religious than Britain of the 1890s or 1790s or 1690s.

To summarize, it is vital for the theoretical positions that Stark has long promoted that the conventional view of religion in Britain be wrong. He makes the case from both ends. He argues that the Britain of the past (and that could be any date before the Census of Religious Worship of 1851, which provides us with our first Britain-wide data on church attendance) was nowhere near as religious as we think. And that the present is considerably more so.

The world we have lost

In the previous chapter I answered Stark's assertion that British sociologists exaggerate the religiosity of pre-industrial Britain and there is no need to repeat my case. I will simply summarize it by saying that, to sustain Stark's judgement, we would need to accept most or all of the following sociologically implausible assumptions.

- The most powerful national institution had little or no influence on the people.
- The sums given by people of every station of life to fund Masses were a reflection of religious indifference.
- The huge sums given by rich people to build and to endow churches, chantries and chapels were not a mark of religious interest.
- Those institutions and the social practices they sustained had no impact on cosmology, theology or morality.
- The people who allowed very large proportions of the national wealth to be given to religious activities believed them to be pointless.
- The institution of swearing oaths on the Bible was used to encourage truth-telling because few people believed anything bad would come from offending God.
- Most people attended Mass at Easter just because most other people did and nobody actually believed in it.
- All rites of passage, all significant dates in the agricultural calendar, and all important community events were glossed with religious rituals because nobody believed religion mattered.
- Finally, we must conclude that the enormous intrusion of organized Christianity into social and cultural life was utterly ineffective in socializing people into the beliefs and values that organized Christianity represented.

Religion in Britain 1851–2000

I will now offer a summary description of popular involvement in organized religion by considering evidence of church attendance, church membership, Sunday school attendance, the number of full-time clergy, the popularity of religious rites of passage, the size of new religious movements and the popularity of religious beliefs.

Church attendance

Even if we accept Stark's claim that the religious vitality of pre-industrial Britain has been exaggerated, we may ask how the changes of the last 150 years fit his expectations. The best British data for the nineteenth century are to be found in the 1851 Census of Religious Worship. It is a highly complex source that is only now being analysed with appropriately sophisticated statistical techniques (Crockett 1998) and analysts differ in how they report its findings (in particular, how one deals with the fact that the original returns reported *attendances* at morning, afternoon and evening services rather than the number of *attenders*). Nonetheless, there is a consensus about the plausible upper and lower figures. Brown (1987a) reports attendances (not attenders) as 61 per cent of the adult population for Scotland and 59 per cent for England and Wales. In turning those data into an estimate for attenders, Brown almost halves the attendances and gives a Scottish figure 'in the region of 30–35 per cent' (1993: 7). Crockett, working from the original data and with better statistical techniques, comes to a higher figure: 'one can estimate that between 61.5% and 65.1% of the "potential congregation" attended worship on census Sunday' (1998: 131). Even allowing for rounding-up in the original returns, he concludes that the best estimate would be between 57 and 61 per cent. Let us, accordingly, take as our best base for evaluating the twentieth-century data the assumption that between 40 and 60 per cent of the adult population of Great Britain in 1851 attended church.

Peter Brierley, Britain's foremost collator of religious statistics, has conducted a number of censuses and surveys of church attendance in England, Wales and Scotland. As in the 1851 Census, the data come from clergy estimates of how many people come into their churches on a particular Sunday. Brierley's return rates are good, for he is well known to, and trusted by, church leaders and, moreover, has some thirty years' experience of working with such data. In short, if we can accept any survey data as reliable, Brierley's should surely rank high in confidence.

From his third English study, conducted in 1998, Brierley (2000a) concludes that 7.5 per cent of the adult population attended church. This represents a continuation of the trends previously found: the figures for his 1979 and 1989 censuses were respectively 12 and 10 per cent.

Brierley divides his results into those for institutional and for non-institutional organizations. The Catholic Church (the largest of the 'institutional' group) has seen its attendances drop markedly and at an accelerating pace. In the 1980s attendances fell by 14 per cent. In the 1990s they fell by 28 per cent. The second largest, the Church of England, saw attendances fall from 1,671,000 in 1979 to 980,000 in 1999 – a fall of 24 per cent for the 1980s and 23 per cent for the 1990s. The United Reformed Church suffered a similar fate. Only the very small Orthodox Church grew (from 10,000 to 25,000). Overall, attendance for these four churches fell over two decades from 3.9 million to 2.4 million.

Among the non-institutional churches or denominations, Methodist attendances fell dramatically: from 621,000 in 1979 to 379,700 attendances in 1999. The less numerous Baptists and Pentecostalists pretty well held their own and the 'new churches' grew over the same period from 64,000 to 230,000. However, this growth failed to compensate for the decline in the larger denominations, so that the non-institutional sector showed a decline from 1.6 million in 1979 to 1.4 million in 1999.

To summarize Brierley's data, the big organizations shrank badly; those that stayed stable or grew were the small ones. Hence the pattern for England overall was of a decline in church attendance over thirty years from 12 to 7.5 per cent of the population.

There are three good reasons why we should have confidence in these survey data. First, they fit with what we know from the institutions themselves. The Church of England's own records show that in 1997 Anglican church attendance fell below 1 million for the first time since records began in the eighteenth century and this is in the context of a population that has grown steadily from 18 million in 1850 to 52 million in 2000. Secondly, these attendance figures are consistent with the membership data (of which more below). Thirdly, the national figures are consistent with what is known from detailed area studies. Robin Gill's painstaking work (1993) on Northumberland shows that in the 1980s only 9 per cent of the population attended church. He summarizes his equally detailed work on Bromley, Kent,

Table 3.1 Age profile of church-attenders, England, 1979, 1989 and 1999

Religions identity	% aged 65 and over		
	1979	1989	1999
General population	15	15	16
Anglican	18	19	25
Baptist	18	19	23
Catholics	13	16	22
Methodist	25	30	38
Pentecostal	10	10	10
United Reformed	26	30	38
Other denominations	19	24	29

Source: Brierley (2000a: 117).

in these terms: '31% of the Bromley population were in church in 1903 but only 10.5% by 1993. Thus a threefold decline, and perhaps in reality a fourfold decline, seems to have taken place in these ninety years' (2001: 4). In November 2000, a team of researchers from Lancaster University, led by Paul Heelas, Bronislaw Szerszynski and Linda Woodhead, counted attendance at every church in the Cumbrian town of Kendal (see www.kendalproject.org.uk). Their total, at 7.9 per cent of the population, fits well with the national figures Brierley derives from estimates made by the clergy.

Brierley, not an intemperate man, entitles one chapter of his book 'Bleeding to Death'. One reason for his pessimism is that the gross figures of decline hide a trend even more worrying for the future of Christianity in Britain: age bias. For each of his three English surveys he estimates the age profile of the various groups of denominations. With the exception of the Pentecostal churches that recruit mainly from the Afro-Caribbean population, churchgoers are considerably older than non-churchgoers. Worse, as table 3.1 shows, the bias increased over the two decades.

Similar figures can be found in recent UK-wide social surveys. A study of 1,000 respondents conducted by Opinion Research Business (ORB) for the BBC in May 2000 showed a considerable difference in age between regular churchgoers and the rest of the sample. While 18 per cent of survey respondents were aged 16–29, only 15 per cent of those who said they attended worship once a month or more were in that age band. Of the regular churchgoers, 30 per cent were aged

30–49; for the sample as a whole it was 41 per cent. The relationship reversed for the 50–69 age group; 42 per cent of regular churchgoers but only 31 per cent of the total sample fell into that age group. The greatest difference was at the top end. Of the regular churchgoers, 13 per cent were aged 70 years or above; for the total sample it was only 9 per cent. Were it the case that a large proportion of the population was churchgoing or had been socialized in the Christian churches in childhood, we might suppose that, as those young people presently avoiding going to church aged, they might attend more frequently. That would be consistent with the ideas that approaching death causes us to become more attentive to our spiritual state. But, as the vast majority of young Britons have no church connection or religious socialization and hence no acquaintance with an ideology that could provide a solution to such anxiety as they might feel when they grow old, Brierley's pessimism seems well founded. Only time will tell, but it seems highly likely that the age differences in church attendance are a cohort effect rather than an effect of biological ageing.

Church membership

The picture of change in church membership over the twentieth century is clear (Brierley 1999: table 2.8). In absolute terms, the major Protestant churches grew slightly between 1900 and 1930, but the membership growth always lagged a long way behind the growth in the general population. From the 1950s onwards these churches declined in net terms. The Roman Catholic Church came close to matching population growth, not because it recruited Britons in proportion to their growing availability but because it was bolstered by large numbers of migrants from Ireland. Since the 1960s it too has experienced absolute as well as relative decline.

Brierley has helpfully aggregated the figures. As table 3.2 shows, church membership for the UK as a whole fell from 27 per cent of the population in 1900 to 10 per cent in 2000. Of course direct comparison with any period before the middle of the nineteenth century is impossible because the nature of church involvement has changed so much. Nonetheless, it is hard to imagine any serious historian arguing that less then 10 per cent of the people of 1750 or 1800 would have had any sort of church connection.

It should be stressed that Brierley is not alone in these conclusions. With the exception of Stark and his associates, every scholar who has

Table 3.2   Church membership, United Kingdom, 1900–2000

Year	Members (000)	Population (000)	Members (as % of population)
1900	8,664	32,237	27
1920	9,803	44,027	22
1940	10,017	47,769	21
1960	9,918	52,709	19
1980	7,529	56,353	13
2000	5,862	59,122	10

Source: Brierley (1999: tables 2.12 and 4.10.2).

studied British church membership has reported similar trends and come to the same conclusions. Brown (1992b) amply documents the decline of church membership in Scotland. Sawkins has studied the Methodist data (which are among the most accurate and detailed). In the late 1940s and early 1950s there were five years when there was a net and very small increase in membership. In 1985 there was a 1 per cent increase when it was decided to include various local ecumenical congregations in the Methodist figures. Apart from that one year, every year since 1957 has shown a net decline, usually of between 2 and 3 per cent. If that remarkably consistent trend continues (and Sawkins can see nothing to indicate it will not), the Methodist Church will cease to exist in 2031 (Sawkins 1998).

Let us put these figures in a longer historical context. My estimates of church membership in Britain (for the basis of calculation see Bruce 1999: 209–12) are as follows. In 1800 some 18 per cent of the adult population was in church membership. In 1850 it was around 27 per cent. In 1900 it was 26 per cent. Set against those figures, I can see no reason to describe the subsequent changes over the twentieth century (21 per cent in 1940; 10 per cent in 2000) as anything other than decline.

The relationship between attendance and membership   It is worth saying a word about the increase in church membership between 1800 and 1850. Taken on its own (and ignoring the fact that the subsequent decline has now gone on unaltered for a century), we could interpret that period of church membership growth as evidence that church adherence varies cyclically and hence that describing the overall pattern as one of decline is at worst mistaken and at best premature. However, any knowledge of the way in which the nature of church membership

Table 3.3 Sunday school scholars, United Kingdom, 1900–2000

Year	% of population
1900	55
1920	49
1940	36
1960	24
1980	9
2000	4

Source: Brierley (1999: table 2.15).

has changed would answer that point. In the eighteenth century only the dissenting congregations had 'members'. The national churches of England and Wales, and Scotland, served all those people who did not consciously dissent (and at times they insisted on serving them also!). Formal membership was not a consideration, and attendance was a better mark of adherence. At the end of the eighteenth century and during the first half of the nineteenth, as religious dissent flourished, so people came to mark their loyalty by joining as well as attending their preferred church.[2] By the end of the twentieth century, attendance had again become a better index of attachment than membership, because churches gave membership very readily and were slow to revise rolls and hence many people remained nominal members while their active involvement withered.

Sunday school attendance

One way in which the British churches dominated the culture and society was through the provision of education. Until the middle of the nineteenth century (and later in many places) most formal schooling was provided by the churches and many children (and some adults) attended Sunday schools to gain a 'secular' education. Even as a viable nationwide system of state schools was being constructed, very many non-churchgoing parents sent their children to Sunday schools. Their motives may have been secular, but the result was that most Britons gained at least an elementary knowledge of the Christian faith. Table 3.3 gives figures for UK Sunday school scholars. What it shows is that at the start of the twentieth century half of Britain's children were socialized into Christian beliefs and doctrines. By the end of the century, the number of Sunday scholars was so small that either only the children of church-attenders went to Sunday school or not even all the children of regular churchgoers were being so socialized.

Full-time professionals

Full-time clergy may be paid out of either public taxation (or some equivalent such as land rents) or the donations of their congregants. In the first case the size of the clergy is a useful indicator of the social power of religion; in the second, it is a good sign of its popularity. In 1900 there were about 45,400 clerics in the UK. That figure declined steadily, until in 2000 there were only 34,160: a fall of 25 per cent at a time when the population almost doubled. To put it another way, had the Christian churches been relatively as powerful or as popular at the end of the twentieth century as at the start, there would have been 80,000 clerics, well over twice the actual number. For the first half of the century, the Catholic Church in Britain showed considerable growth, as the small pre-Reformation population was boosted by migration from Ireland. In Scotland the number of Catholic priests rose from 475 in 1900 to peak at 1,437 in 1960. It then started to decline, so that in 2000 there were only 861 priests (Brierley 1999: table 8.6.4). Entries to training declined even faster. In 1979 there were 193 men studying for the priesthood. In 1999 there were only fifty-seven (Mackay 1999).

I might add that, were the churches dependent on their present power or popularity, there would be even fewer clerics than they are. Most of the major UK organizations now depend for almost half their income on profits from invested capital garnered during better days. Ironically, many congregations are now enjoying a windfall from rising house values and from their dependence on elderly women. As their elderly congregants die without dependant relatives, ever larger bequests are being left to ever-smaller churches.

Religious rites of passage

As I showed in the previous chapter, one way in which those outside the inner circle of the personally pious continued to retain contact with organized religion was through the use of religious offices for rites of passage. While the proportion of people coming to church to be married, baptized and buried remains higher than the number of members or regular attenders, the trends are moving in the same direction. In the nineteenth century almost all weddings were religious ceremonies. We have data for all denominations only from 1971, but these show that the proportion of English weddings that was then religious was 60 per cent. This declined fairly steadily to 31 per cent in 2000. Given its position as the national church, the Church of England's record is a good indicator of how popular church weddings are for those outside the narrow circles of committed church members. In 1900, 67 per cent of all weddings in England were celebrated in an Anglican church; in 2000, it was only 20 per cent (Brierley 1999: table 8.5).

The role of the medieval midwife in performing emergency baptism was mentioned in the previous chapter. In 1800 almost all newborns were baptized. The proportion of infants baptized in the Church of England is a good indicator of the general popularity of baptism in England, because, unlike nonconformist bodies, the Church has maintained a commitment to the population at large. Between 1895 and 1950 the Church of England baptized about 63 per cent of English babies (Bruce 1996b: 268). In 1962 it was 53 per cent. In 1993 it was 27 per cent.

New religious movements

The idea that secularization is impossible because people have an enduring need for religion, and hence that the decline of one sort of provider will be compensated for by the rise of some innovation, cannot be tested unequivocally because its proponents may always extend the timescale for its fulfilment. However, it seems reasonable to suppose that, were some such self-limiting mechanism in operation, we would by now have seen some signs of vigorous religious growth. Brierley (1999: table 10.2) estimates the total membership of non-Trinitarian churches (including the Christadelphians, Christian Scientists, Mormons and Jehovah's Witnesses) as having risen from 71,000 in 1900 to 537,000 in 2000. The Mormons and Witnesses together account for more than half that growth. But that seemingly impressive figure amounts to *only one-sixth of the members lost to the main Christian churches over the same period* and less than 1 per cent of the total number of people who do not belong to a Trinitarian Christian church.

The new religious movements of the 1970s are numerically all but irrelevant. On the most generous estimates, Brierley (2000a) can find only 14,515 members. Knowing that the Unification Church has fewer than 400 members puts the contribution of the new religious movements in its proper context.

Religious beliefs

One response to this evidence is to argue that religious belief remains strong; what has declined is faith in the traditional religious institutions as institutions. As one leading Anglican cleric put it: 'There has been a general flight from institutions. Trade union membership is down, as is that for political parties and voluntary organizations' (Petre 1999: 15).[3] Sociologist Grace Davie made a similar point when she subtitled her book on *Religion in Britain since 1945* 'believing without belonging'. It is always possible that private religious sentiment has remained strong while the form in which it has been expressed for centuries has withered (though even that would be a momentous change that should not be dismissed with a Starkian flourish). However, two points suggest that, whatever changes there may have been to our ways of expressing religious sentiments, the strength and popularity of those sentiments have also declined. First, and this is the weakness of the supply-side model, there is no shortage of varieties of Christian (and non-Christian) organization. We could imagine people losing faith in a certain institution (too sexist or insufficiently sexist; too hierarchical or too democratic; too formal or too informal; too liberal or too conservative), but if there was still a lot of demand for Christianity one would have thought that it would find some avenue of expression in the plethora of choices. And the religious market is now so 'free' that there are no obstacles to creating new churches. Given that Christianity has always laid considerable store by collective acts of worship, it is difficult to suppose that the almost universal decline of the Christian churches in Britain does not signify a decline in the demand for Christianity.

The second point is that we do have evidence of changes in the popularity of beliefs. Measuring beliefs independently of people acting on them is always difficult, but we now have fifty years of opinion polls and attitude surveys and their message is consistent. The proportion of people claiming Christian beliefs is considerably higher than the proportion of people who actively support the Christian churches, but there has been a steady decline in the popularity of Christian beliefs, which shadows the decline in church adherence. In the 1950s, 43 per cent of those surveyed said they believed in a personal creator

God. In the 1990s, it was 31 per cent. In the May 2000 ORB survey the figure was 26 per cent. The number of those explicitly saying they did not believe in God rose steadily from 2 per cent in the 1950s to 27 per cent in the 1990s. Field (2001) has provided a very useful summary of Scottish survey data for the last quarter of the twentieth century and comes to the same conclusion as Gill, Hadaway and Marler. They end their review of almost 100 surveys from 1939 to 1996 by saying that:

> these surveys show a significant erosion of belief in God. . . . Second, the most serious decline occurred in specifically Christian beliefs including belief in a personal God and belief in Jesus as the Son of God as well as traditional Christian teachings about the afterlife and the Bible. . . . Third, while traditional Christian beliefs changed markedly, non-traditional beliefs remained stable albeit among a minority of respondents. (Gill et al. 1998: 514)

That last point is worth dwelling on. Keith Thomas (1978), who is favourably cited by Stark, shows that, in certain times and places, significant sections of the laity of the Middle Ages were not orthodox and observant Christians. He does so by showing in great detail that they were believers in heretical superstitions and practitioners of deviant magic. The orthodox and the deviant together formed the vast bulk of the population. In twentieth-century Britain, the swing to 'non-traditional beliefs' fell a long way short of compensating for the decline in orthodox Christian beliefs.

If we move from cognition to experience, we might assert that, despite the decline in Christianity, religious experiences are nonetheless common. The evidence suggests otherwise. Aquaviva (1993) shows that those people who claimed religious experiences were also the most likely to be conventionally involved in the church. Ken Thompson concludes: 'Whilst some form of religious commitment appears to be widespread, it seems doubtful that there is a dimension of religiosity which varies independently of the degree of attachment to traditional beliefs' (1986: 229).

The decline of traditional Christian beliefs should be no surprise. Whether there is some essential human need to raise spiritual questions is too broad a question to be answered here, but there is no mystery about why Christian beliefs should decline when the institutions that carry them decline. Ideologies do not float in the ether. They need to be preserved; mechanisms must exist to acquaint the next generation with those beliefs. As Gill (1999) demonstrates with a very wide range of data, there is a strong connection between churchgoing and holding Christian beliefs.

In the 1850s, most people attended church. Basic Christian ideas were taught in school, legitimated by every major social institution, promoted by the social elites, reinforced by rites of passage, and pervaded every aspect of social life. Even in the 1930s, when church-going was becoming less common, a large proportion of Britain's children would have had some acquaintance with Sunday school. At the start of the twenty-first century the vast majority of people do not go to church and only the children of churchgoers go to Sunday school. Christian ideas are not taught in schools, are not promoted by social elites, are not reinforced by rights of passage, are not presented in a positive light in the mass media, and are no longer constantly affirmed in everyday interaction. Given those changes, it would indeed be a miracle if Christian ideas remained as popular as they were in the 1950s.

Conclusion

Taken in isolation, none of the data presented above would be compelling. Any one index can reasonably be challenged. Definitions of membership or attendance change, as do the ways of measuring them. Any one set of survey data can readily be contested on methodological grounds and comparisons between sets of data are always open to the challenge that the data are not properly comparable. In a multinational state with a wide variety of churches, the baselines used to construct percentages and to measure change inevitably shift. Proportions are inevitably dubious, because some sources use the entire population while others use only adults as the denominator (and the cut-off point for defining adulthood shifts). However, we need not be paralysed by such methodological concerns, because what make the data presented above compelling are their consistency and cumulative effect. All of them point the same way: declining involvement with religious organizations and declining commitment to religious ideas. And the trends in the data have been regular and consistent for between 50 and 100 years, depending on the index in question.

When Stark first articulated his revisionist depiction of religion in Britain, church attendance stood at 12 per cent. In 2001, it is below 8 per cent. Well-informed commentators sympathetic to the plight of the churches, such as Brierley, write seriously of the prospect of organized Christianity falling below the critical mass required to reproduce itself (2000a: 28). Unless it can find the secret that has eluded it for fifty years of decline or negotiate a reunion with the Church of England, the Methodist Church will finally fold around 2031. The Church of England will by then be reduced to a trivial voluntary association with a large portfolio of heritage property. Regular churchgoers will be too few to show up in representative national survey samples. Perhaps then the critics of the secularization paradigm will recognize that, however convincing our explanations of decline, decline is not a sociological myth.

CHAPTER FOUR

The Failure of the New Age

Introduction

William Bloom, one of the doyens of the New Age in Britain, offered the following review of the last quarter of the twentieth century:

> Twenty-five years ago, when I first became involved in New Age thinking, it was distinctly embarrassing to talk openly about it. It was like being a vegetarian at a rugby club dinner. . . . Twenty-five years later, however, the movement is growing in strength and is in many ways an established part of contemporary culture. . . . Cherie Blair wears a pendant to ward off bad vibes in her final days of pregnancy. Prince Charles talks to plants. Oprah Winfrey leads a television revolution in which anyone and everyone can talk about their innermost secrets and seek instant healing. (2000: 9)

This chapter will consider those features of New Age spirituality most germane to the secularization paradigm. I will try to identify its extent, nature and significance. On that last point, I will consider how the achievements of the New Age compare with those of an earlier counter-cultural religious movement: British evangelicals of the late eighteenth and nineteenth centuries. First, a word about scope. There is always a degree of artificiality in dividing diffuse cultural movements into chunks. J. Gordon Melton in the introduction to his *New Age Almanac* sets the start date as 1971 but immediately adds that the movement should be 'seen as the latest phase in occult/metaphysical religion, a persistent tradition that has been the constant companion of Christianity through the centuries' (Melton et al. 1991: 4). More proximately, there are considerable continuities between what is now termed New Age spirituality, the more world-affirming new religious movements of the 1960s, and the more spiritualized elements of that decade's interest in psychotherapy and human potential. Where the differences are significant, I will attend to them, but generally I will treat the New Age in very broad terms.

Cultic religion

It is possible to group religions by their major themes. Linda Woodhead and Paul Heelas do this admirably in their *Religion in Modern Times*, where they distinguish religions of difference, religions of humanity and spiritualities of life. The first stress the divisions between God, humanity and nature (conservative Protestantism and Catholicism would be examples), the last (Buddhism, for example) stress the essential unity of all three, and the religions of humanity aim to keep the three elements in balance (2000: 2–3). Roy Wallis also used the substance of belief in his seminal *The Elementary Forms of the New Religious Life* (1984), where he borrowed Max Weber's point about the importance of attitudes to the mundane world to divide new religions into world-affirming, world-rejecting and world-accommodating types.

Typologies are neither true nor false; they are just more or less useful. The purpose of grouping and dividing cases is to draw attention to those features that are most relevant to the matter in hand. As my argument is that much of the fate of any belief-system is explained by the way it (and its adherents) can be organized, I will arrange my material around those beliefs that have implications for access to persuasive power. Just what I mean by that will become clear shortly.

As often as not, 'cult' just means 'a religion the writer does not like', and there is a case for leaving the word to tabloid newspaper subeditors. However, I find the term useful to designate one of four contrasting ways of organizing religious beliefs and behaviour – the others being church, sect and denomination. As the terms are used often in these essays, I will briefly define them. Wallis built on the earlier work of sociologists such as Weber, Ernst Troeltsch, David Martin and Roland Robertson to produce a simple shorthand that neatly brings together much of what interests us about religious beliefs, structures, levels of commitment and relations with the wider society. He believed that, though much of value had been said about religious organizations by people using those terms, they tended to be used in an *ad hoc* way, with little attempt to construe them in consistent terms, and with too great a reliance on the history of developments within Christianity. After considering a range of characteristics of sects and eliminating those that 'appear to be contingent features of the circumstances in which sects in Christian cultures emerged' (1973: 149), he concluded: 'the criteria of sectarianism appear finally to centre around the right to exclusion, self-conception as an "elect" or elite, and totalitarianism' (1973: 150).

Figure 4.1 A typology of religious organizations

External conception

		Respectable	Deviant
Internal conception	Uniquely legitimate	CHURCH	SECT
	Pluralistically legitimate	DENOMINATION	CULT

Source: R. Wallis (1976: 13).

In his elaboration of this principle, Wallis was careful to put the *ideological possibility* of exclusion before the habit of excluding people. This is a small but significant difference between the view Wallis and I developed (Bruce 1996a: 94; 1999: 138–44) and the way that Dean Kelley, for example, deals with the characteristics of what he called 'strong' religion: strict memberships tests, distinctive lifestyles, high levels of commitment and the like (1972, 1978). Our point is that these features are not available to any ideological collectivity but can be attached only to belief-systems that start with the claim to a unique grasp of the truth. For example, much as some liberal Protestants might envy the cohesion and commitment of evangelical sects, they cannot emulate the practices that play a large part in creating those characteristics because liberal Protestantism lacks the essential foundation for authoritarianism: it is not convinced that there is a single authoritative source of divine revelation and that it has it.

Wallis's review of what was meant by 'cult' led him similarly to strip out those parts of the description that depended on a specifically Christian history and theological perspective and he concluded: 'where the sect is "epistemologically authoritarian", the cult is "epistemologically individualistic"' (1974: 304) – that is, in the sect there is an authoritative source of knowledge that stands over and against the individual believer. In the cult the individual consumer decides what he or she will accept. Wallis rightly observed that exactly the same distinction could be made between the church and the denomination (see figure 4.1). Thus, where historians had tended to concentrate on the differences between a church (the Catholic Church in nineteenth-century Ireland, for example) and dissenting sects, Wallis stressed their similarity. Because of its size and its desire to encompass an entire society, the church type of religion must tolerate considerable laxity, but the church and sect have in common the belief that they and they alone possess the truth. Again, where others had stressed the differences between denominations and cults, Wallis argued that both forms have a common attitude to the truth: they did not claim unique access to saving knowledge. Rather they suppose it widely available. Many people can reasonably claim insight into the will of God (or Gods) and hence a very wide variety of even apparently paradoxical alternatives can be similarly valuable.

What distinguishes the church and the denomination, on the one hand, from the sect and the cult, on the other, are their respectability (which is a consequence of historical presence, congruence with the values of the wider society, and elite support, among other things).

It is worth briefly eliminating some possible misunderstandings of the Wallis approach. First, when he used the term 'epistemology', he was concerned not with academic philosophy but with the practical issues of the status that believers claimed for their revelations and how widespread they think is access to those revelations. Secondly, the approach is robustly sociological. As Wallis made clear in developing the ideas of Roland Robertson, and as Robertson himself argued (1972: 120–42), we are not pursuing theological arguments but trying to highlight the sociological causes and consequences of certain types of ideas. We are certainly not taking sides and we are not even confining our attention to religion. The model works as well for secular ideological collectivities as for religious ones. Examples can be found in Jones's analysis of therapeutic groups and O'Toole's analysis of left-wing political sects (Wallis 1975).

This is an important point, because the sorts of observations I am about to make have often been misinterpreted as implying that only the epistemological authoritarian religion of the church or the sect is 'true' religion. Though postmodernists reject the possibility of social science, Wallis and I always aspired to value-free and objective sociological description and explanation. We believed it possible to describe various sorts of religion and explore their organizational consequences without engaging in theology. My arguments about the precariousness of diffuse belief-systems may well be wrong, but they are not religiously partisan.

They are also not tautological. A related version of the above objection is that I manage to 'prove' the existence of secularization by defining religion in such a way that such modern developments as New Age spirituality and the types of liberal Christianity that come close to unitarian-universalism are not really religious. Hence I depict as decline what should properly be seen only as change. Before I elaborate my argument about the problems of diffuse belief-systems, I want to be perfectly clear about what is being proposed. I have no difficulty accepting that cultic religion is indeed a form of religion. My case is that, like the denomination in its most liberal form, cultic religion lacks the *social significance* of the church and the sect. Furthermore, it is a form of religion that is particularly difficult to sustain and promote. Hence the number of adherents (if that is not too strong a term for the consumers of cultic religion) will decline. For those two reasons, cultic religion is unlikely to stem secularization. This argument may turn out to be wrong, but it is empirically testable. It is not a tautology.

One virtue of the Wallis typology is that it provides a convenient shorthand for recapping the mutation of religion with modernization that was detailed in the first three chapters of this volume. Modernization entails structural and social differentiation and geographical and social mobility. Leaving aside the cases where ethnic, national or international conflict cause social solidarity to remain the primary imperative, these social forces typically bring cultural diversity and egalitarianism, which in turn make the church form of religion impossible. The sect form can survive where, and to the extent that, the social structure permits the creation of subsocieties. That leaves the denomination and the cult. Because they have at their heart an individualistic epistemology, both types are sociologically precarious. Elsewhere I have discussed at length denominational Christianity (Bruce 1990: 119–54). In this chapter I want to highlight one aspect of secularization by examining the weaknesses of cultic religion. I will argue that the individual autonomy at the heart of the New Age will prevent this new form of religion gaining the presence or influence of the denominational, sectarian and churchly forms it replaces.

The extent of the New Age

That there appears to be considerable interest in a huge range of spiritual ideas, rituals and therapies in places such as Britain is often cited glibly as refutation of the secularization paradigm. This is a particular instance of the general claim that secularization entails people becoming self-conscious atheists. In chapter 1 I tried to answer this sort of response by clarifying what I believe the paradigm requires. Shortly I will consider the social significance of New Age religion.

Here I will try to give some estimate of its size or reach. It follows from its nature that the New Age is extremely difficult to enumerate. Because it has an obsessive interest in separating the saved from the damned, us from them, the sect normally has a very clearly demarcated membership. The religions of the cultic milieu do not. However, we must try to estimate the popularity of the New Age and my first point is that, in terms of the gross numbers of enthusiastic adherents, New Age religiosity is not terribly significant.

At first sight the growth of the New Age is impressive. The first Festival for Mind–Body–Spirit in 1977 was a one-day event; the 1993 version lasted ten days. In most bookshops the occult is now given more space than Christian titles. Popular magazines carry articles on Feng Sui, spiritual healing and shiatsu massage. New Age publishers proliferate and, a good sign of the strength of the market, most of the major commercial publishers now have a New Age imprint.

It would be easy to take all this endeavour as proof that interest in the supernatural is a constant; that we have mistaken for secularization what is merely a change in the mode of expression of that interest. It would be easy but wrong.

First we need to get the numbers in proportion. Thousands of people attend the Festival for Mind–Body–Spirit[1] but then it is an annual showcase taking place in the nation's capital. Numbers resident at the Findhorn Community, Britain's oldest New Age centre, rarely exceed 200 and many of them come from continental Europe and the United States (Riddell 1990: 132). Barker (1989) estimates the membership of some of the best-known new religions of the 1970s in the hundreds. The more exotic and attention-getting the activity, the fewer the participants. Given the press coverage one might think otherwise, but Harvey says of British Satanists that there are 'six groups who between them have less than 100 members' (1995: 284). A representative national sample of 1,000 respondents could not find one person who opted for 'Pre-Christian religions such as Druidism/Wicca/Pagan' (Opinion Research Business 2000).

As we would expect, those organizations that offer specific training programmes and events rather than try to recruit followers to a philosophy or a lifestyle can claim to have influenced much larger numbers of people. For example, *est* claims to have had 8,000 graduates during its time in Britain. A similar number may have gone through the Forum, *est*'s successor. The same again may have been trained by Exegesis and by the Rajneesh Foundation and so on (Barker 1989:

Table 4.1 New Age practices: acquaintance and salience, Great Britain, 2000 (%)

Beliefs or practices	Have tried or experienced	Important in living life
Alternative medicine	39	14
Aromatherapy	32	7
Reflexology	16	3
Crystals	6	1
Prayer	41	25
Tarot cards/fortune telling	17	2
Astrology	16	2
Meditation	22	9
Faith healing (in a church context)	3	0
Faith healing (not in a church context)	6	0
Contact with supernatural beings such as angels	4	0
Not answered	25	49

Source: Opinion Research Business (2000).

151). But, on Barker's informed estimates, the totals involved at some point in all such organizations cannot exceed 100,000 people over twenty-five years.

Such figures can be viewed in two comparative contexts. In 1985 the Christian denominations and sects in Britain could claim seven million members (Bruce 1995b: 31–42). Furthermore, the decline in the main religious traditions leaves very much larger numbers of people free to experiment – free because they are personally not tied to an older form and free because the older forms no longer have the social power effectively to stigmatize cultic alternatives. Leaving aside the aged and the infants, there must be at least twenty-five million people in the United Kingdom who have no connection with any mainstream religious organization (Brierley 1997). The Methodist figures are typical of the major denominations. In 1947 there were 743,000 Methodists in Britain. In 1995 there were 380,000. Even the most generous estimates of the New Age are unlikely to have the new spiritual seekers filling the space left by the decline of just one denomination.

Some data from a recent British survey are interesting. As table 4.1 shows, the British have little acquaintance with a number of specifically

New Age beliefs and practices. Respondents were asked 'Which of the following have you tried or experienced?' and presented with the items listed. While alternative medicine and aromatherapy are popular (with 39 and 32 per cent respectively of the respondents had sampled them), crystals, tarot cards, astrology and even meditation (which one might suppose was widespread) had been tried or experienced by only small numbers of respondents. Even more revealing is the second column, which reports the answers to the follow-up question 'And which are important in helping to live your life?' Apart from alternative medicine, only 'prayer' gets above 10 per cent and much of that popularity is due to the conventionally religious rather than to the preferences of those outside the churches. More than half of those who said prayer was important to them were regular churchgoers. Particularly important, given the ubiquity of horoscopes, astrology is regarded as important by only 2 per cent of the sample.

Clearly we could do with more and better surveys and until these become available we have to rely on impressions. In closing this brief assessment of the reach of the New Age, I will support my impression that the movement has been much exaggerated with the views of Paul Heelas, one of the best-informed students of the New Age. Heelas follows a more positive evaluation of the New Age than the one I intend to offer here by saying:

> the fact remains that it would be rash in the extreme to maintain that expressive spirituality has become the 'dominant' source of significance within religion today. Places like Totnes, Glastonbury and Findhorn are the exception; in the great majority of population centres – from Barrow-in-Furness to Worthing to south London – expressive spirituality is decidedly marginal. (2000: 243)

The nature of the New Age

However, I will suggest that the themes of the New Age are in many ways emblematic of religion in our culture. Heelas recognized the dominant characteristic of the New Age when he dubbed many of its elements 'self-religions'. New Agers believe that the self is divine or, if it is not yet, then it can become so with the right therapy, ritual or training. We need to appreciate the novelty of this idea. Christianity, like most major religions, has generally assumed a radical division between God the Creator and the people he created. In Woodhead and Heelas's terms, it is a religion of difference. God is good; since the

Fall, people are bad. People become good by subjecting themselves to God's will and God's commandments. Religion is about controlling the self and shaping it into a valuable object. The New Age does not have that division of God and his creation. Instead it supposes that we have within us the essence of holiness. The human self is basically good. If it is bad, that is a result of our environment and circumstances. The aim of many New Age belief-systems and therapies is to strip away the accumulated residues of our bad experiences and free our human potential. The point of the spiritual journey is to free the God within, to get in touch with our true centre.

Secondly, it follows that, if the self is divine, there is no authority higher than the individual self. Of course we can learn by reading books and listening to great teachers and some New Agers have an unfortunate fondness for gurus, but the final arbiter of truth is the individual. Personal experience is the acid test of truth. Whether we should accept some revelation or therapy is framed in terms of whether it 'works for you'. The final authority of the self is often expressed in a rule of social interaction: thou shalt not argue. Findhorn, one of Europe's oldest centres of New Age thought and teaching, requires of those who take part in its various forms of group work that they confine their talk to 'I statements'. The point of this is to establish that, while each participant has a right to say how he or she feels or thinks, no one has a right to claim some extrapersonal authority for his or her views.

Thirdly, individual autonomy brings eclecticism. As we differ in class, in gender, in age, in regional background, in culture, we will all have different notions of what works for us and this is reflected in the enormous cafeteria of cultural products from which New Agers select. A simple way of illustrating that range is to consider the subjects covered in a very popular series of books called 'Elements of . . .'. The nouns that follow that opening phrase include: Aborigine Tradition, Alchemy, Astronomy, Buddhism, Chakras, Christian Symbolism, Creation Myth, Crystal Healing, Dreamwork, Earth Mysteries, Feng Sui, Goddess Myths, the Grail Tradition, Herbalism, Human Potential, Meditation, Mysticism, Natural Magic, Pendulum Dowsing, Prophecy, Psychosynthesis, Qabalah, Shamanism, Sufism, Taoism, Visualization and Zen. An issue of the magazine *Planetary Linkup* chosen at random contains features on or advertisements for the following: Sogyal Rinpoche and his teachings, the Dalai Lama, Alice Bailey's The Fifth Ray of Concrete Knowledge, Channelling, Crop Circles, the Sufi tradition, Dolphin Love,

Light-Medicine, Mongolian and Tibetan overtone chanting, crystals, the Lila Dance Centre of Divine Love, Shiatsu massage, Mother Meera, clinical dowsing, self-hypnosis, flower essence therapy and the White Eagle Lodge. As Bloom says: 'A planetary culture of free-flowing information is absolutely bound to manifest new ways of enquiring into meaning. This is to be applauded. It is liberating and deeply democratic. . . . It encourages and empowers people to taste around until they find those pieces of the jigsaw that fit their character and temperament' (2000).

Individual New Age practitioners can be highly creative in their syntheses. Eleni Santoro offers what she calls a 'smudging' service to New York estate agents. She removes 'bad vibes' from hard-to-let properties by 'balancing energies'. The tools of her trade are:

> A multifarious collection of objects from all parts of the world, includ-
> ing silver Tibetan bells, a statue of Ganesh – the Hindu God of prudence
> and sagacity – an antique Chinese bell, an African necklace of yellow,
> red and green beads and a silver bowl containing three limes. . . .
> Having meditated for several minutes, shuffling a slim pack of 'angel
> cards', she picks three. Or rather, as she later explains, it is the angels
> who pick the cards – Light, Release, Humour – best suited to this
> interior. The smudging session also has a soundtrack – sounds of moun-
> tain streams or Japanese drums. (Fowler 1997: 59)

Even many of the new religious movements of the 1970s such as Scientology and Transcendental Meditation, whose cadres privately believe that they have the truth and everyone else is plain wrong, have been forced by market pressures to accept the eclecticism of the New Age milieu (that is, they are at heart sects but are forced by the attitude of most of their customers to act as cults). Instead of recruiting loyal followers, they market their services to people who will take some course, attend some events, and then move on to some other revelation or therapy.

Fourthly, New Agers are keen to be holistic. The term is very widely used and embraces a variety of meanings but among them we will find the following. New Agers do not like the reductionism of modern rationality (seen particularly in science), which breaks complex pheno-mena into their simplest constituent elements. Hence scientific medicine is bad because it treats symptoms rather than the whole person. The differentiation of modern culture (discussed in chapter 1) is bad because it separates the economy from society, treats people as commodities, and distinguishes between the material and the spiritual to the disadvantage of both. New Agers tend to be environmentalists. Many are vegetarians and most would claim an interest in animal welfare. In brief, they tend to favour Eastern views of the common essence of everything: the divine, the mundane world, human society, the human body and individual personality (see chapter 6). Holistic is good; fragmented is bad.

Fifthly, eclecticism is accompanied by an appropriate epistemology. In practice many New Agers are relativists; they generally sample a range of ideologies and therapies without noticing incompatible assumptions and truth-claims. If forced to attend to them, they resolve paradoxes by asserting integration at the level of cosmic consciousness: the Eastern notion of a fundamental unity behind apparent diversity. To quote from the biographical sketch on the web site of a transpersonal psychologist and counsellor: 'Spending a significant amount of time with Mother Nature fostered in me deep soul searching questions in regard to the meaning and purpose of life. I set out in search of the "fruit" in religions knowing intuitively that they must have a commonality where all peoples can meet.'

Sixthly, New Age spirituality is distinguished by its focus of attention or manifest purpose. All the major world religions have claimed that if we follow their teachings we will be happier and healthier people but those therapeutic benefits have generally been secondary or latent. Medieval Christians followed the instructions of the Church because that is what God required. The Church advertised certain rituals (the curative properties of a shrine, for example) as efficacious and beneficial in this life, but its ultimate selling point was the knowledge of God's will that must be obeyed. While Christians might hope for a good life, it was always possible that divine providence destined otherwise. In this scheme of things, suffering could be given spiritual significance. In much New Age spirituality, therapy is the manifest, not the latent, function. Good health, self-confidence, prosperity and warm supportive relationships are no longer the accidental by-product of worshipping God; they are the goals sought through the spiritual activity.

The appeal of the New Age

That a variety of self-religions should appear in the last quarter of the twentieth century suggests that in some sense they fit the time. If it is not simply an accident, it should be the case that those who seek spiritual expressions do so in this form because it is particularly well suited to the dominant ideas and assumptions of their society. I will suggest briefly some of the ways in which the ethos of the New Age resonates with that of the culture of modern industrial democracies at the end of the second millennium.

One of the major virtues of the epistemology of the New Age is that it solves the problem of cultural pluralism. If everyone believes the same thing and sees the world the same way, then it is possible for a society to believe that there is one God, one truth, one way of being in the world. However, when that single culture fragments into a whole series of competing visions, you have the possibility of endless argument and conflict. One resolution is to change the basic idea of knowledge so that we become relativists. We suppose that there is no longer one single truth, one single way to God, but a whole variety of equally good ways. We shift in effect to a perennialist view of reality that supposes that behind all the apparent diversity there is a single essence.

Relativism also accords well with our increasing self-assertiveness in that it allows a thoroughly democratic attitude to knowledge. As Bloom says:

> everyone has access to ideas and sources that were previously the exclusive remit of authoritarian men holding positions of status in authoritarian hierarchies. This is what you should believe. And this is how you should believe it. . . . The single field expert pontificating ceremonially is now a symbol, not of wisdom, but of emotional stupidity and communications ignorance. (2000)

We can picture the 'new science' and 'new medicine' of the New Age as the third stage in a progressive rejection of authority. Once culture was defined by experts. Now we accept the freedom of personal taste: I may not know much about art but I know what I like. In the late 1960s claims for personal autonomy moved to a second stage of matters of personal behaviour: I may not know much about ethics and morals but I know what I like to do and claim my right to do it. In the third stage the same attitude is applied to areas of expert knowledge: I may not know much about the nervous system but I know what I like to believe in and I believe in chakras and Shiatsu massage and acupuncture.

But such individualism would bring social conflict if it was framed within the traditional notion that there is one true version of reality.

The solution is relativism. Though the term 'hermeneutic' is still foreign to most people, the general notion that different sorts of people will see the world in different ways has become deeply embedded in our culture.

There is no space here fully to explain the rise of relativism. Bloom implies that no longer deferring to experts is a natural response to a communications revolution that has given all of us the sort of access to a plethora of ideas that was previously restricted to only small numbers. For reasons given elsewhere (see chapter 6) I am not persuaded that the simple widening of access to information is enough to carry the weight of explanation. It leaves unexplained why more people now feel they are competent to decide what is information and what are the mad ramblings of the deranged. Or, to put it another way, that web sites and cheap printing allow us to become aware that there are alternatives to the explanations of the Pyramids or AIDS offered by the professionals does not explain why more of us are willing to bypass the experts. There is not scope here to pursue a fully sociological explanation of that change but the following suggests other components of an explanation.

I suspect that our increasing unwillingness to accept the authority of professionals is part of a general decline, not in class differences (which remain salient) but in the deference that used to accompany them. In the early 1960s sociologists used to distinguish professions from other occupations by accepting at face value the justification that professions made for their high status. Professionals asserted that they were motivated not by a desire for money and power but by a commitment to serve fundamental social values. Professional autonomy (including the power to maintain lucrative closed shops) was defended as essential to preserving some social good (such as justice or health). Sociologists are now much more sceptical. More to the point, so is the general public, which readily assumes that everyone is self-interested and is deeply suspicious of claims to altruism (especially from people who are well paid). The assumption that most of us have motives baser than the ones we assert is accompanied by an implicit epistemological premiss. People's perceptions will be influenced by their backgrounds. Hence objective or authoritative descriptions of the world are not possible; hence there can be only partial understandings.

Claims to professional expertise have also been undermined by the growth of the natural sciences. When scientific knowledge was not extensive and relatively undifferentiated, widespread social respect for those who carried it was common. The 'professor', the man in the white coat who saved the planet from space invaders in those early 1950s science-fiction films, was just a 'scientist'. Now biology, physics and chemistry are subdivided into hundreds of highly specialized subfields. The number of practitioners has vastly expanded and their social status has been reduced. What is now done by scientists is too esoteric for us to understand, let alone admire, while those who do it are too numerous and too ordinary to command respect.

The mass media have played an important part in devaluing the status of science. As has become very obvious in the reporting of such 1990s health scares as the links between bovine spongiform encephalopathy (BSE) and Creutzfeldt–Jakob disease or the outbreak of E. coli food poisoning, most journalists are simply not equipped to evaluate competing positions and so reporting very easily slips into the conventional confrontational mode of aiming for balance rather than accuracy.

A further explanation for the decline in deference to experts is the increased level of education of the general population. In 1900 there were 25,000 people in full-time higher education in Great Britain (Halsey 1972: 206). In 1991 there were 400,000, which represented a doubling of the number for 1970 (Church 1994: 47). Whether this means that we are better educated than our grandparents is neither here nor there. What is important is that more of us are at least superficially closer in status to the experts than was previously the case.[2]

These observations deserve to be explored further, but it is enough to note here that the high place accorded to the self in the New Age fits well with the class background of most New Agers. A survey of 908 readers of the magazine *Kindred Spirit* noted: 'almost without exception, participants are middle class' (Rose 1998: 11). The point can be reversed. We can ask why it is that the unemployed and the poorly paid workers, those who would most benefit from increased mastery over their fate, are least likely to be interested in New Age techniques for empowerment. We might suppose the costs of many programmes would be prohibitive until we compare them to the costs of smoking, drinking alcohol, attending dance clubs, taking drugs or attending major football matches. A more fruitful line of explanation is to be found in ideas about self-confidence and cultural capital. A basic requirement for an active interest in 'new science' or 'new medicine' is the belief that one is intellectually on a par with the experts in the old science and old medicine. A basic requirement for the endless introspection that is the stock in trade of the New Age is the belief that your self and your relationships are worth talking about at length.

The point can be extended from class to race. Race is trebly absent from the New Age. It is firstly absent in the sense that racial and ethnic minorities are patently under-represented among New Agers consumers. Considering how much the New Age borrow from Africa, Asia and the indigenous peoples of the Americas and the Antipodes, that almost all the popular New Age teachers and therapists are white, as is almost all of their audience and their market, is worthy of note. Race is also absent in the sense that New Agers do not talk or write about it. The twin foci are the very short and the very long: the individual self and the cosmos. Although there is some attention to gender stereotypes (presumably because of the preponderance of women in the milieu), social identities based on race, ethnicity and nationality are ignored. The third sense in which race is overlooked is that expert commentators do not refer to it. It does not rate a mention in the indexes of two major British books on the New Age (Heelas 1996; Sutcliffe and Bowman 2000) and I cannot recall anyone previously commenting on the fact that the New Age is lily white.[3]

I am guessing here, and for the sake of brevity there must be an element of caricature, but I suspect the explanation parallels that for the absence of the working class. First, there is a culture block. In many black British circles, as in the working class, group hugging, talking to angels, spiritual dancing and Tibetan overtone chanting is just too feminine. A West Indian acquaintance reacted to my account of a Findhorn 'Experience Week' with: 'Sounds to me like something for poofs.' Secondly, the attitude of disdain towards the material world and towards economic striving (which is not the same as renunciation) is fine for those born into comfortable circumstances but unattractive either for those who have yet to find security or for those who have just achieved it through hard work and deferred gratification.

Finally, the assumptions of the New Age fit well with a society that is short on authority and long on consumer rights. In the free market for fridges, autonomous individuals maximize their returns by exercising choice. In the free market for ideas, New Agers maximize their returns by choosing what suits them best and synthesizing their preferred combination.[4]

In this context it is worth drawing attention to the role of 'commodification' in the New Age. Traditionally, suppliers and consumers of religious goods have been linked by moral persuasion and loyalty.

The officials perform their tasks because that is what God requires. The laity supports the officials because that is what God requires. Although there are connections between how much one pays and what one receives (the rich medieval Christian, for example, would endow a chapel to ensure that Masses were said for his soul after death), too direct and mechanical a connection would be rejected as impious; hence the objections to the Church selling indulgences and holy artefacts. The New Age movement operates on a very different basis. Products, be they objects (such as crystals) or services (such as a weekend's training or a tarot reading), are sold for a fee. One might, like the Protestant reformers, see such commerce as unspiritual, but it is perfectly acceptable to New Agers because it fits with the general consumerist ethos of their world and because it reinforces the autonomy of the consumers. They are not locked into open-ended commitments of reciprocal obligation; they buy the book, tape or training session, and are free to make of it what they will.

The precariousness of diffuse beliefs

As the consequences of an individualistic epistemology for the organizing of beliefs are central to my assessment of the power of the cultic milieu, I will briefly address a possible source of confusion in Wallis's initial distinctions. He sensibly describes the church and sect forms of religion as epistemologically authoritarian and contrasts that condition with the epistemological individualism of the denomination and cult. The confusion comes about because Protestantism (the main source of the sects he and I use as examples) is, compared to other strands of Christianity, a highly individualistic faith.

Protestant sects, like most left-wing movements, have a practical epistemology that almost guarantees factionalism and schism. On the one hand, they have a view of knowledge that encourages authoritarianism. They suppose that there is a single source of truth (usually the Bible) and that they and perhaps a few others correctly understand it. On the other hand, they allow that anyone (with the right attitude) can interpret that source. There are, of course, many non-essential sources of cohesion (such as a respect for formal theological training or similar cultural backgrounds), but these are not legitimated by any core theological propositions. The Free Church of Scotland, for example, has a complex structure of assemblies and an elaborate legal code that would appear to be similar to the bureaucracy of the Catholic Church, but when major disagreements arise (as they did in the 1990s over the liberal views of one of the Free Church's leading clergymen), such constraints do not prevent schism. They merely enrich the lawyers who argue about dividing the family silver. The consequence of this combination of authoritarianism and individualism is that competing interpretations are generated and their proponents fight about which is the right one. Hence conservative Protestant (and Marxist) movements repeatedly split. Within each sect there tend to be great certainty and high levels of commitment but there are also frequent conflict and division.

In the denominational and cultic type of ideological orientation we have the very different phenomenon of an individualistic epistemology that is openly relativistic. There are many Gods and many ways to God and hence no need to argue about which is right. Members of one denomination or followers of one New Age school of thought may suppose that what they have now is better (for them) than what others have, but, because the crucial test is personal experience, there can be few rational grounds for argument and postulating some cosmic consciousness can save diversity from the strongest anti-relativist arguments. I am concerned here with that type of ideological belief-system where an individualistic epistemology produces tolerance and relativism rather than the older sectarian Protestant form where individualism produces fission and schism. For the sake of brevity I will call this *diffuse religion*.

What makes diffuse religion precarious? I want to suggest that lack of obedience to a central authority (be that an organization as in Catholicism, a text as in Protestantism, or a body of religiously sanctioned law as in Islam) produces various closely related problems of social organization. Diffuse religion elicits only slight commitment and little agreement about detail. It thus makes a shared life unlikely. Diffuse religion has little social impact. It has little effect even on its adherents. It does not drive its believers to evangelize. Finally, it is vulnerable to being diluted and trivialized. I will now consider each of these problems in some detail.

Commitment and consensus

Most religions, for most of their history, have supposed that we the believers are subordinate to the God or Gods in which we believe. In Judaism, Christianity, Islam, Hinduism and the more theistic versions of Buddhism, there is a God or Gods who tells us what to do. Although all these religions have produced deviant strands in which the believer to varying extents may manipulate the deity, essentially we worship and obey the deity, not the other way round.

The increasing power given to the individual in cultic religion has important social psychological consequences. It is unlikely that such a religion will attract the high levels of commitment found in other forms of religion. Sectarian Protestants often give a tenth or more of their income to religious activities. Conservative Catholics and Protestants often give up a great deal for their faith: witness the asceticism of such communitarian sects as the Amish or of Catholic monasteries. There may be exceptions but there seems a fairly obvious connection between ideological certainty and commitment. We make sacrifices because we believe that something vital follows from having the correct religion.

Getting people to agree (especially about making sacrifices) is always difficult. Consensus is never the default position, even for people who inhabit similar social circumstances and are faced with a common threat. It must be engineered. If one doubts that, just consider the enormous apparatus of repressive legislation and propaganda that was erected by the UK government during the two world wars, when one might have thought the grave threat to the nation's survival enough to produce a spontaneous pulling-together.

For any belief-system to survive intact there must be control mechanisms. These may be formal and bureaucratic, as they are in the Catholic Church, where officials deliberate slowly before announcing the Church's position. They may be informal and 'charismatic', as they are in many branches of Protestantism: the minister who preaches a gospel unacceptable to the audience finds himself without an audience. But in either case there are controls. To put it starkly, consensus requires coercion. In the church and sect types of religion, coercion is possible because it is legitimated by the claim to have unique access to the will of God. We constrain freedom because the Lord tells us to do that. As the denomination and the cult do not claim a monopoly of salvational knowledge, they are severely limited in what they can do to maintain discipline. Indeed, many relish their freedom from such oppressive notions.

Of course New Agers share much in common. However, the consensus is greater the more abstract or procedural the proposition. Thus there is near unanimity on the principle of individual autonomy.

There is considerable agreement on a variety of inclusive social principles: racism and sexism are bad, egalitarianism is good, everyone should be treated with dignity, and those principles should be extended to non-humans. However, when we get to the specific application of these we find little agreement, precisely because the things on which they agree encourage autonomy and diversity. The death of Peter Caddy, one of the three founders of the Findhorn Community, was marked by *One Earth* (Summer 1994) publishing a series of memories and reflections. It is clear that, though the various contributors had great respect for Caddy, they almost all disagreed with him about some central aspect of his teachings. In illustrating the diversity of paganism (hardly a large movement), Marion Bowman said:

> Contemporary pagans might be anarchic, left-wing, liberal conservative, monarchist, right-wing, apolitical; individualistic, communistic, tribal, egalitarian, authoritarian, hierarchical; gender-aware, sexist; pacifistic, militaristic; universalist, fundamentalist; smoker, non-smoker, 'stimulant' user, drinker, abstainer; vegan, vegetarian, semi-vegetarian (meat is murder, fish is justifiable piscicide), organic/compassionate farming, carnivorous, omnivorous. (2000)

To make the contrast, we can note that, at their ordination, ministers and elders of Ian Paisley's Free Presbyterian Church (a classic Protestant sect) are asked a long series of very specific questions about their beliefs. This is itself a quite deliberate expansion of the practice in most Presbyterian churches, where the minister or elder is asked only to subscribe to the church's standards and hence can do so with various forms of mental reservation (such as accepting that the Westminister Confession is an important element of Presbyterian history but is no longer binding in its specific details). No comparable mechanism for ensuring doctrinal cohesion is possible in the diffuse cultic forms of religion.

Individual autonomy, the freedom to choose, competes with the power of the community. To the extent that the former is stressed, the latter is necessarily weakened. In so far as New Agers are bound to each other at all (and many associate only in the sense of coincidentally consuming the same product), those bonds are weak because they are entirely voluntary and their voluntary nature is repeatedly asserted. Transcendental Meditation advertises itself with the slogan 'No change of belief is required'! The residents of Findhorn can pack up and leave any time they find the company of their fellows uncongenial and their wills thwarted (Sutcliffe 2000). Indeed, New Agers pride themselves on constantly growing out of whatever 'school' or therapy they are presently exploring.

Commitment and community are closely related. Because there is no binding believing community, New Agers determine for themselves the extent of their involvement, which is 'temporary, occasional and segmentary' (R. Wallis 1974: 308). Only a handful modify their working lives or make great breaks with their previous patterns of behaviour. And when they do, it is in disparate directions. For a handful the pursuit of self-actualization and growth may lead to a repudiation of previous ways of life and personas, but in the process they do not come to form a viable alternative community or society.

Diffuse religion cannot sustain a distinctive way of life. When there is no power beyond the individual to decide what should be the behavioural consequences of any set of spiritual beliefs, then it is very unlikely that a group will come to agree on how the righteous should behave. Although the specific behavioural consequences of the Protestant ideal of 'getting saved' vary from one time and movement to another, sectarians believe there must be some. Evangelicals in the tobacco-growing counties of the Carolinas might be keener to give up drinking than smoking, but they gave things up. Little specific need follow from involvement in the New Age. The language of discovering yourself and getting in touch with the God within can, and is, used to justify almost any sort of behaviour. To give the most obvious example, for all the talk of radicalism, many male New Age gurus have thoroughly patriarchal and exploitative relationships with their female followers. This is not an accident and is not comparable to the common incidence of sexual exploitation in conservative Protestant sects. There 'free love' (always freer for men than for women) arose against the grain and only with considerable reinterpretation of the tradition. In New Age circles it occurs easily because the absence of any source of authority other than the actor (who is divine after all) means that there is no justification for external constraint. If my friend's child within and my wife's Goddess within say that they should discover each other's sexuality, there are no agreed higher grounds that I can invoke to oppose such selfish betrayal of our marriage vows. Even with all its circumlocutions, the following recollection of Peter Caddy by his wife Eileen shows that what to an outsider would seem like callous neglect and sexual promiscuity can be justified in terms of self-growth:

We worked closely together . . . for twenty-six years. It was a fruitful relationship although not balanced in itself. The will and power he had developed was so strong that I often felt it suppressed my emotions and feelings. The structure of our relationship also didn't allow him to show his emotions and love. He was not able to open his heart in our relationship but after our time together he did make the tremendous leap to do this through other women. . . . My love for Peter has never faltered. I shall always love him despite everything. This has been the vitally important lesson I have needed to learn in this life, to Love Unconditionally. The sadness in my relationship with Peter has allowed me to learn this lesson. (1994: 9)

Sacrifice, commitment and community are intimately related. Shared beliefs sustain the community, which in turn extracts commitment and sacrifice from the individual. Sacrifice reinforces the sense of commitment and of belonging to a community, which strengthens the beliefs. In summarizing what has been traditionally expected of the Christian, Wilson very clearly expressed the point:

Whether the idealized role model was the martyred saint of medieval myth or the ascetic Calvinist of the seventeenth-century mercantile classes, self-denial and self-sacrifice in one form or another were the demands made of the faithful Christian. All of which is not to say that men generally lived up to such models. Clearly they did not. It is rather to emphasise the importance of a given value consensus which set community at a premium, and individual self-interest at a discount. (2000: 49)

Social impact

Many New Age providers claim to be counter-cultural and alternative. They are critical both of specific features of the modern world (such as the consumption of natural resources at an unsustainable rate) and of the general tenor and ethos of modern life (in particular, bureaucratic rationality). As one contributor to *Kindred Spirit* (Autumn 1990: 4) put it: 'We watched as the world became consumed by greed. A greed where values changed and the "material" was given greater precedence than the "human"'. Some of these concerns, such as the lack of authenticity in lives integrated through social roles, are properly tackled at the level of the individual (of which more later), but many require concerted social action. Although a very few New Agers have become active in environmental protests, in anti-capitalist rallies, or in developing alternative technologies, the impact has at best been slight.

One way to illustrate the point is to compare the impact of the New Age with that of another counter-cultural religious movement. In the late eighteenth and throughout the nineteenth centuries groups of British evangelicals banded together to campaign against what they believed to be un-Christian aspects of industrialization (Smith 1998). The religious motives of William Wilberforce MP and fellow reformers were so obvious that they were known (both derisively and affectionately) as the 'Clapham sect'. There were two aspects to the evangelical improvement of industrial society. One was philanthropic. Evangelicals gave large amounts of money and time to voluntary activity. Dr Barnado founded a network of children's homes. The Quaker Elizabeth Fry led in penal reform and prison visiting. Octavia Hill and George Peasbody promoted improvements in working-class housing. Hannah More pioneered free schools for the poor. The second strand was legislative. Although the evangelical temperament was in favour of personal philanthropy (which was held to benefit the giver as much as the recipient), Wilberforce and his colleagues appreciated that the grossest abuses of the industrial age could be prevented only by legislation. Hence their campaign to ban slavery. Hence their promotion of factory acts. Some idea of the character and consequences of the reforming evangelicals can be gained from this brief description of Anthony Ashley (Earl of Shaftesbury from 1851). This successor to Wilberforce was:

> a puritanical, narrow-minded gloomily devout Evangelical, tough, determined, courageous and indefatigably energetic. . . . In the course of a long life of feverish activity he promoted dozens of good causes . . . sweeps' climbing boys, shoe blacks, crossing sweepers, Ragged School children, factory children and those in the mines and workshops all received his attention. He investigated the situation of milliners and others, mostly women, working in the sweated trades, as well as the treatment of lunatics, burglars and pickpockets. He inspected sewers and cottages, attended parliament, chaired meetings and committees, supported philanthropic societies of all kinds, and personally wrote hundreds of letters seeking support for his reforms. (Stiles 1995: 32–3)

Against considerable opposition from industrialists, evangelical reformers stopped women and children working in the mines, gradually increased the minimum age at which children could be employed in hard and dangerous work, ended the payment of wages in kind, restricted the length of the working day, humanized the prisons and stopped men being paid their wages in pubs. In an attempt to reduce the debilitating amounts of alcohol drunk by the urban working class,

Quakers promoted drinking chocolate as an alternative to gin and beer and found ways of making tea affordable. Evangelicals also founded schools, lending libraries, penny savings banks, housing associations and mutual insurance societies. It is not much of an exaggeration to say that most of the constraints on the right of employers to exploit ruthlessly their workers were the work of evangelicals, inspired by a shared vision of a better society.

Of course there are many differences between the eighteenth and the twenty-first centuries. Life (in Britain at least) is no longer as nasty, brutish and short. Nor is such a large part of the population so powerless that it depends on an enlightened elite to advance its interests. With the introduction of popular democracy and the rise of the trade-union movement, the working classes could be expected to exercise the right for which they had fought: the right to take care of themselves rather than be the recipients of paternalistic philanthropy. Nonetheless we have a strong contrast. New Agers and Victorian evangelicals alike condemn their worlds. But the latter were able to unite around very specific goals and devoted vast amounts of time and money to promote them. Their value-consensus meant that the movement organizations they formed exerted influence beyond that of their number as individuals. New Agers are highly critical of many aspects of the modern world but make little or no effort to change it and such efforts as they do make are not amplified by being concerted. Or, to put it rhetorically, where are the New Age schools, nurseries, communes, colleges, ecological housing associations, subsistence farming centres, criminal resettlement houses, women's refuges, practical anti-racism projects and urban renewal programmes? Writing out such a list strengthens the force of the critique, because it reminds us that a large proportion of those apparently interested in the New Age work in just these fields. It is where the creative arts overlap with social work and education that one finds the greatest interest in the New Age, but that interest does not seem to generate powerful social innovations and experimental social institutions. Unlike the Victorian evangelical interest in social reform, the New Age never becomes more than the sum of its transient and relatively uncommitted parts.

Individual impact

Where we most clearly see the impotence of the New Age is in the shallowness of much of the rhetoric about taking control of one's own life, being the person you want to be and such like. Some elements

of the New Age (those closest to the secular human potential movement) do not aspire to radical social change. Exegesis courses did not
turn stock traders and bankers into trade-union activists, community
workers or subsistence farmers; they just made them happier and
more effective stock-traders and bankers. However, even those therapies that claim to be life transforming often do more to *reconcile* people
to their place in the world than to change it. In Zen Buddhism the
secular man peels potatoes, the religious man thinks of God while
peeling the potatoes, and the truly enlightened man just peels the
potatoes. The point of this paradox is that, for the Buddhist, the final
stage of seeking detachment from the material world requires becoming
detached even from the search for detachment. Final liberation means
liberation even from the spiritual quest. Thus the life of the saint may
look unremarkable; he just peels the potatoes. Much New Age thinking
follows this logic but reduces to a few trivial exercises the intervening
ascetic period of monastic discipline. It allows novices to become adepts
without the difficult bits in between. There really is no difference
between the secular man and the saint. What is advertised as personal
transformation is little more than acquiring a new vocabulary. What
the Brahma Kumaris advertise as 'insights and methods to enable us
to take full control of our destiny' (*Press and Journal*, advert, 5 Oct.
1998) turns out to be more a way of accepting one's fate.

This should not be scorned. There is doubtless much to be said for
accepting one's self and circumstances. However, transformations of
the personality that do not much change behaviour should not be
confused with those that do. Methodism profoundly changed those
people who adopted it and it profoundly changed their society. The
New Age has changed very little.

I might add here that my argument does not suppose that the
adherents to sectarian and cultic religion initially or enduringly differ
in their moral fibre. In many instances it does seem proper to impute
a degree of hypocrisy to those New Agers who use the language of
being 'alternative' and 'counter-cultural' while continuing to enjoy all
the material benefits of bureaucratically rational consumerist capitalism. But, even without making any imputations about the character of
individuals, we can see the effect of differing notions of authority. In
the case of the sect, the authority of the group shapes the individual
and thus permits something other than self-interest to take priority.
The Victorian evangelical who is fed up with having to subscribe to
yet another good work, take round yet another petition, or organize

yet another public meeting to denounce another crime against God, can be pressed by the authority of the group's shared definition of what God requires yet again to fight the good fight. There will be some breaking point at which the potential dissident is driven from the group, but a considerable degree of commitment may be exacted before that point is reached. There is no corresponding power in the cultic milieu to override individual preferences.

Reproduction

To put it succinctly, coherent ideologies can be transmitted intact but diffuse ideologies must always be reinvented. In essence there are two problems: the transmission of diffuse beliefs is unnecessary and it is impossible.

The first point is obvious because it is recognized in the logic of the New Age. There can be general agreement that all of us should change but, as we are required to get in touch with ourselves, there is no justification for requiring that any particular person change in any particular way. No particular set of ideas or patterns of behaviour is required and none is specifically outlawed. New Agers may object that sexism or racism or consumerism is agreed to be bad, but, in practice, the enormous ideological flexibility of the milieu allows all of these things to be defended in some guise or another. In the final analysis the injunction to be true to yourself subverts the possibility of effectively asserting that *these* people would be better if they became like *those* people. In contrast, sectarians are certain that their beliefs are superior and must be propagated. Ian Paisley's Free Presbyterians devote enormous effort to trying to socialize and convert their children, friends and even strangers because they know that unbelievers will go to hell. It is possible to moderate that claim considerably – by supposing, for example, that the unbeliever will linger in limbo or will simply fail to be reunited with loved ones after death – and still have a compelling interest in ensuring that others share one's beliefs. Sectarian socialists devote enormous energy to trying to persuade the rest of us that their understanding of the course of history is correct and that we must embrace it and the actions that are held to follow from it.

This is not to say that New Agers do not want to see others (their children especially) come to share their views. They naturally seek the confirmation of rectitude that comes from being surrounded by like-minded people. My vegetarian wife will be as distressed if our

children become meat-eaters as sectarian Protestants will be if their
children go over to Rome. But the central place given to individual
autonomy means that New Age persuasion must be confined to encouraging one's children to discover for themselves the same truths as
you have discovered. The procedure takes precedence over the outcome. For the cultist good child rearing means encouraging children
to think for themselves; for the sectarian it means ensuring that your
children think as you do.

I might add here that the socialization of children is vital, because
it accounts for most of the variation in the fates of different religions.
Obviously any new religion must recruit adults and well-established
religions sometimes spread to new territories or enjoy waves of adult
converts. But for most of the time religious organizations grow or
decline according to life expectancy and success in keeping the children
of members in the faith. At first sight, this may seem to make redundant
my above comments on the differential propensity of sects and cults
to evangelize, but evangelism remains central, even when it is barely
effective outside the home. First, the impetus to convert strangers
strengthens the will to convert one's children. Only where a religion
is particular to an ethnic group (Judaism, for example) or is regarded
as so deviant by the surrounding society that evangelism is almost
impossible do we find groups that work hard to convert their children
but make no effort to convert others. The political career of its leader
means that Ian Paisley's Free Presbyterian Church of Ulster has very
little chance of converting Catholics, but it still runs missions in the
Irish Republic. Secondly, evangelistic work provides important tests of
the faith of members and often reinforces it; Mormon missionary
work, for example, while it recruits few new members relative to the
effort invested, seems to do a great deal for the commitment of existing Mormons.

But there is a less obvious difficulty in reproduction that stems
from the difference between a cluster of coincidentally somewhat
similar individuals and a community. The adherents of cultic religion
cannot form combinations to promote specific agreed beliefs. They
can cooperate in joint marketing, as in London's long-running Festival
for Mind–Body–Spirit, where hundreds of purveyors of various forms
of cultic religion rent stalls in a large hall and mount a week-long
programme of New Age events. They can provide a general location
for the promotion of New Age ideas. These may range from the large
and internationally known (for example, the Osho Multiversity in

Holland and the Findhorn Foundation) to the very small (for example, the Beacon Centre at Cutteridge Farm where Wendy and Basil Webber run a 'transformational centre for personal, inter-personal and planetary healing'). They can organize regular presentations on the model of adult education evening classes. But in each of these sites for reproduction, a wide variety of revelations and therapies, that can be reconciled only at a fairly high level of abstraction, are presented. The appeal or persuasive force of any one approach is not reinforced by its coincidence with another. Cultists cannot add momentum to their persuasive efforts because their diffuse beliefs prevent them agreeing in sufficient detail on what is to be promoted.

I might add here that the two advantages of commodification mentioned above (that it leaves the consumer in command and resonates with the general ethos of the modern world) have a corresponding weakness. While the individual New Ager may have an enduring commitment to the culture as a whole, he or she will have very little commitment to any particular element or expression of it. Like any other consumer-oriented market, the New Age has constantly to produce new products. For example, the organizers of the Mind–Body–Spirit Festival have annually to find new attractions to draw in the crowds: 'Fashions that have been noticeable in the past have included Aromatherapy, colour therapy, crystals, and more recently Reiki' (M. Hamilton 2000: 193). Of course, more conventional religions are also affected by short fashion waves (the brief flurry of the Toronto Blessing in evangelical Protestant churches would be an example), but, because those fashions operate within a solid consensus of essential beliefs, they do not do much to hinder the consolidation of commitment. The New Age lacks that solid base and thus constantly has to market itself anew.

We should note that the above is not a solution looking for a problem. My explanation may be unconvincing, but we can be confident of the problem it seeks to address. On the basis of his survey of *Kindred Spirit* readers and his extensive knowledge of the milieu, Rose notes: 'the majority of participants in the New Age are in the middle-age groups. . . . whether or not significant numbers of younger people will adopt New Age ideas and activities as they get older cannot be foretold, although, judging on the basis of my findings, this does not appear to be happening to any great degree'. He adds 'the New Age could very well have an ageing, and therefore diminishing population in the years to come' (1998: 10).

Dilution and compromise

Underlying my argument is the assumption (pursued in chapter 7) that cultural products, and in particular belief-systems, have a tendency to dissolve. Unless one constantly works to preserve a body of doctrine, the ideas will gradually accommodate to the cultural norms. Deliberate social control is required to preserve a distinctive body of ideas and practices and the associated sense of shared identity. However, even once such social control has been abandoned, there will be a lapse of time before all sense of coherent distinctiveness has disappeared. An abandoned garden takes many years to lose all traces of deliberate selection. I raise this point because it alerts us to an important difference between two forms of religion that are similar in their diffuseness: liberal Christianity and New Age spirituality.

Although both are similar in their rejection of authority, the denomination continues to enjoy some cohesion from its more sectarian or churchly past. For example, many contemporary Methodists would not subscribe to the theology of the Wesley brothers but the fact that they still sing the hymns of Charles Wesley at least gives them an identity and a language that masks the extent of their failure to agree. Ordinands of the Church of Scotland still subscribe to the Westminster Confession of Faith. Most of them believe very little of it, but the fact that their forefathers once did gives Scottish Presbyterian a degree of cohesion. The architecture and the sung offices of the ancient cathedrals give the Church of England some sort of identity. Like the financial resources that the major denominations inherited from a more religious time, this ideological heritage is a wasting asset but it nonetheless gives the denominations a cohesion that is missing from the individualistic forms of religion in the cultic milieu. Particular New Age insights and therapies are often marketed as 'traditional', but the tradition is not ours; it is Chinese or Egyptian or Tibetan. It has no magnetic pull in our culture.

One consequence of this is that particular elements of the New Age easily lose their essence, through either the selective attention of the consumers or the cynical marketing strategies of commercial enterprises. As an example of the former, we can note the way that meditation, taken out of its Hindu monastic context, is now used widely simply as a form of relaxation. As an example of the latter, we can note that in 1999 the Glasgow branch of Texstyle World, a British chain of textile warehouses, offered 'An Introduction to Feng Sui' (with 10 per cent off throughout the evening!) at which the Director of Feng Sui Scotland 'will be talking about how the use of colour, texture and design can be used to create a harmonising environment in your home' (*Herald*, 16 Apr. 1999). Ayurvedic medicine is trivialized into a range of supposedly therapeutic beauty products. 'Instead of employing gnarly medicine men to stand in their stores and assess the dosha of prospective customers, The Body Shop has place a helpful quiz beside their Ayurvedic products. Presented in the *Jackie* magazine style, it uses colour coding and avoids the more probing queries about bowel movements which feature in more clinical consultations' (Burnside 2000) *Woman's Own* magazine offers a profit-making 'Ask the Runes' telephone service, which it advertises with the following:

> The magic of the Runes can be your guide. The power of the Runes can help you control your destiny by giving you mystical insight into your heartfelt feelings and desires. They can act as a touchstone to help you chose the right course of action. Now you can let the Runes speak to you by ringing *Woman's Own*'s Runes mistress Rebecca Hart. When you dial the number . . . their force will be with you. Concentrate on your question – such as 'Should I take this new job?' or 'Should I change my man?'. As you think, providence will draw your three Runes for you (if you have a push-button phone, you may choose your first Rune). You'll be given your personal Runes reading. (*Woman's Own*, May 1997)

Conclusion

Before concluding I want to remove one possible misunderstanding of the above argument. In exploring the precariousness of diffuse belief-systems, I am not suggesting that tightly defined belief-systems are invulnerable. They have their own problems, which I have discussed at length elsewhere (Bruce 1999: 148–58). Two of the most pressing are the high costs of separation from the mainstream and the vulnerability to demographic changes. Sectarian beliefs are often sustained by subcultures that, as well as seeking to inoculate adherents against the disease of worldliness by intense socialization, also try to isolate them from secular society. Naturally sectarians work to persuade themselves and their children that they gain rather than lose, but such persuasion often fails. The young are seduced by the bright lights. As many sectarian subcultures have been created by traditionalists responding to the increasing secularity of places closer to the metropolis, they are often found in relatively isolated regions (in Britain, the Welsh valleys, the Yorkshire dales and the Scottish highlands and islands). If such regions prosper and grow (as was the case with the southern states of the USA from the 1960s on), the sectarian subculture, though faced with new and more immediate challenges, may also grow in size and confidence. But, more commonly, the population ages and shrinks and with it the subculture.

I am not suggesting that the potential of belief-systems to be protected, preserved, elaborated and transmitted intact to others is the only consideration in secularization. However, it is important for the general question of the likelihood of a reversal of the decline of religion in the West. In a 1957 Gallup survey, 73 per cent of Britons said they had attended Sunday school regularly as children (Gallup 1976). At the start of the twenty-first century, British Sunday school attendance is no greater than that of adult church attendance: around 8 per cent. Combine that with the fact that other institutions such as the school system and the mass media do little or nothing to socialize children into Christianity and we have an explanation for what all of us whose work requires us to explain religion know very well from our own experience: the bulk of the British people (and I see no reason not to extend this to other European societies) have little or no knowledge of what was once their dominant religion. To use the apt phrase introduced by David Voas in a symposium discussion, the levels of 'ambient religion' are at an all-time low. In this context, the arguments about a pre-modern Golden Age of Faith (discussed in chapter 2) are irrelevant. However much evidence of ritual laxity or ignorance of doctriness one may find in the sixteenth century, it is obviously the case that religion had a far greater presence then than it has now.

Rodney Stark, in his various theories of religion, has argued that, as humans have an enduring need for religion, secularization can only be temporary and that a new religion will arise to fill the gap. Although she does not elaborate the same functionalist theoretical underpinning, Davie has suggested that secularization has been limited to organizational structures and shared rituals. Despite the decline in churchgoing, we remain believers. My response is that the nature of cultic religion shows why Stark's hope is impossible and Davie's is irrelevant.

In essence both positions are unsociological. Even if Stark is right that we have some enduring need for religion, it is obviously possible for needs not to be met. Animals need food, but sometimes they do not get it and they die. I begin from the sociological position that all but the most basic needs require social interpretation. It may well be that the fact of death forces all of us to consider what might follow the here and now, but there seems little else about our biological condition that inevitably raises the sorts of existential and ontological questions that religion has traditionally answered. This is the crucial and usually neglected point: human culture not only provides the answers; it also teaches people to ask the questions in a way that makes any particular set of answers plausible.

That all hitherto known cultures have provided religious frameworks for interpreting our condition does not mean that all future cultures will do the same. What those, such as Davie and Heelas, who point to evidence of enduring interest in matters spiritual do not seem to consider is that such interest will not be sustained or form the basis for any sort of enduring shared culture so long as the possibility of shared beliefs and common reinforcing patterns of behaviour is subverted by the stress on individual autonomy.

The New Age is eclectic to an unprecedented degree and it is so dominated by the principle that the sovereign consumer will decide what to believe that, even if it were the case that we have some innate propensity to spirituality, we will not get from where we are now to any sort of religious revival. The principle of individual choice seems so firmly established in our culture that, while I see every possibility that some sections of the population will continue to be interested in spirituality, I cannot see how a shared faith can be created from a low-salience world of pick-and-mix religion. Furthermore, I suspect that the New Age, weak as it always has been, will weaken further as the children of the New Age prove indifferent to the spiritual questing of their parents.

In one of his periodic criticisms of the secularization paradigm, David Martin asked the following rhetorical question: 'Does the fact that religion is embedded less in the institutions of the state and the economy and more in the hearts and sentiments of people mean that it is literally inconsequential?' (1991: 467). Martin obviously answers in the negative and I agree with him. I am not suggesting that only communal religion, supported by a majority of the people, legitimated by the state and constantly reinforced by everyday interaction is 'real' religion and that, by definition, individualized privatized religion is something inferior. My case is one of causal connection. Diffuse religion is not *literally* inconsequential. It is, for the reasons I have outlined here, *practically* of less consequence than either the church or sect types it has largely replaced in the West.

CHAPTER FIVE

Science and Secularization

Many of the misunderstandings of the secularization case stem from the views of liberal Christians being mistakenly imputed to sociologists. Many more stem from a failure to appreciate the nature of much sociological explanation. Both errors combine in thinking about the links between science and religion. In 1973 a leading liberal Protestant theologian James Barr wrote *The Bible in the Modern World*, just one of thousands of works that took it for granted that people who can generate electricity, understand genetics and travel beyond the pull of the earth's gravity will not believe in the supernatural. The assumption that scientific advances have made religion (or at least a certain kind of religion) impossible is very widely shared. Every year, at the start of my sociology of religion course, I ask a fresh cohort of students what they believe causes secularization; science always figures high on their list of answers.

There are certainly enough well-known battles (the early church and the movements of the planets; Victorian church-leaders and evolution) to sustain the impression that science and religion confront each other in a zero-sum contest and hence that it is the growth of the former that has diminished the latter. Sociologists are not immune to this mistake. Rodney Stark, for example, who should know better, says of the secularization paradigm: 'implicit in all versions, and explicit in most, is the claim that of all aspects of modernization, it is science that has the most deadly implications for religion (Stark and Finke 2000: 61).

If we go back far enough, we can find sociologists who subscribe to the zero-sum model. It is certainly the case that nineteenth-century Frenchman Auguste Comte thought science the enemy of primitive superstition and Herbert Spencer probably agreed. Sigmund Freud certainly did but then he was not a sociologist. The position of Emile

Durkheim, Max Weber and Ernst Troeltsch is less clear, but there is no doubt about the views of post-1960 theorists of secularization. Peter Berger talks a great deal about technological consciousness and bureaucracy; he barely discusses science. Bryan Wilson's two major expositions of the secularization paradigm – *Contemporary Transformations of Religion* (1976a) and *Religion in Secular Society* (1966) – hardly mention science and in neither is it important enough to merit a subheading or an entry in the index. David Martin does not blame science for secularization nor does Roy Wallis (who wrote extensively on the sociology of science and consistently argued that scientific and religious beliefs should be treated in the same way by the social scientist). In my *Religion in the Modern World* I leave science to the end of my explanation and introduce the topic by saying: 'I do not actually think that science has directly contributed much to secularization' (Bruce 1996a: 48). Mature reflection causes me to recoil at the spurious 'actually' but I stand over the judgement.

As chapter 1 shows, sociological explanations rarely rest on the direct competition of ideas, because we are well aware that the intrinsic merits (or otherwise) of any idea, perspective or ideology are usually only a small part of their success or failure. Their plausibility is a complex social construction in which social relations with the person, group or institution promoting the idea is a major consideration, as are the wider resonances of the idea. Darwinism convinced many Americans, not because, having examined the case in detail, they found it well supported by the weight of evidence, but because the very idea of evolution resonated with the self-confidence and growing prosperity of the era. Also relevant is the role of repetition. Ideas that are endlessly represented in communal rituals and ceremonies are more persuasive than those that are not. Modern sociological explanations, in so far as they treat science as an important variable, suppose its effects to be mediated by many other factors; the embodiment of rationality in bureaucratic organization, for example, or the role of technology in reducing our sense of being at the mercy of fate. And most sociological explanations also suppose that some separate explanation of the weakening address of religion is required, because we know that people who have a powerful desire to believe, who are thoroughly socialized into a particular worldview, and who can construct appropriate sustaining social institutions, are well able to maintain their faith despite what an outsider might take to be overwhelming refutation. A simple example is the persistence of millenarian movements such as the Seventh-Day Adventists and the Jehovah's Witnesses after the world failed to end on cue.

The paradox

Were it the case that science and religion compete in a zero-sum game, it should also be the case that those most exposed to the former, natural scientists, should be less conventionally religious than those not so exposed. There is some evidence for that. Stark (1963) and Vaughan et al. (1966) show that when scientists are religious they tend to be members of liberal denominations rather than conservative sects. In 1996 Larson and Witham repeated a landmark survey of the religious beliefs of two groups of US scientists. In 1914 James H. Leuba surveyed 1,000 natural scientists, randomly selected. He found that 58 per cent expressed disbelief or doubt in the existence of God. As we see in table 5.1, the figure rose to 74 per cent for a subsample of 400 'greater scientists' (Larson and Witham 1998: 313). Leuba repeated the survey twenty years later and found that the percentages had risen to 67 for the larger sample and 85 for the more eminent scientists. In 1998 Larson and Witham repeated the elite part of the original study by surveying all 517 members of the National Academy of Sciences. Their results are presented alongside Leuba's in table 5.1. Only 7 per cent of this elite group of US scientists said they believed in God. The comparable figure for the population at large is over 90 per cent (Inglehart et al. 1998: V166). Only 8 per cent said they believed in human immortality. A British study describes 34 per cent of a sample of scientists as atheistic, which is at least in line with and probably significantly higher than the national average (see tables 10.1 and 10.2).

The second half of my paradox is not supported by any survey evidence. It rests solely on my impressions of thirty years of research with a wide variety of conservative evangelical Protestant groups, particularly those formed by students. Medical and science students played some part in the first wave of evangelistic activity in British universities at the end of the nineteenth century but they were particularly prominent in recreating a national organization in the 1920s, after the Student Christian Movement (SCM) abandoned its initial conservative evangelical basis and became liberal and ecumenical. The evangelistic Christian Unions created in Bristol, Edinburgh, the Queen's University of Belfast, Aberdeen, Glasgow, Liverpool, Newcastle

Table 5.1 The religious beliefs of US 'greater' scientists, 1914, 1933 and 1998 (%)

Religious belief	1914	1933	1998
Belief in personal God			
Personal belief	28	15	7
Doubt or agnosticism	21	17	21
Personal disbelief	53	68	72
Belief in human immortality			
Personal belief	35	18	8
Doubt or agnosticism	44	29	23
Personal disbelief	25	53	77

Source: adapted from Larson and Witham (1998).

and London were all started up by medical students. Even in Oxford and Cambridge, where there were proportionately fewer medical students, they were influential. When the patrons of such student bodies were not ordained clergymen or professional evangelists, they were almost invariably medical men or natural scientists. When the Cambridge Christian Union celebrated its fiftieth anniversary in 1927, the Jubilee Breakfast was chaired by the Master of Trinity College, the celebrated physicist J. J. Thomson. Douglas Johnson, a medical student who became the first full-time secretary of the Inter-Varsity Fellowship (IVF, as the evangelical alternative to the SCM was later known), said: 'It remained something of an enigma to the SCM leaders that some of the distinguished seniors were sympathetic to the Evangelicals. They, however, would pass it off with the comment that scientists and medicals, however well trained, would not know any better theologically' (1979: 153). Three of the first eight pamphlets published by the IVF were written by Sir Ambrose Fleming, Professor of Electrical Engineering at University College; three were the work of Professor Albert Carless, a leading surgeon. A. Rendle Short (Professor of Surgery at Bristol) was a tireless speaker for the IVF, as were Duncan McCallum Blair (Regius Professor of Anatomy, Glasgow) and Frederick W. Price (a cardiologist and editor of a well-known medical textbook). The one theologian whom Johnson can claim as a supporter of the IVF in the inter-war period was the Very Revd Prof. Daniel Lamont of New College. Edinburgh. Before his call to the ministry, Lamont had trained as a physicist and had worked in Lord Kelvin's Glasgow laboratory.

Science and Secularization

Table 5.2   Religion by academic discipline, USA, 1969 (%)

Academic discipline	Attendance		Religious identity	
	Regularly attend	Never attend	Religious conservative	No religion
Mathematics/statistics	47	35	40	27
Physical sciences	43	38	34	27
Life sciences	42	36	36	29
Social sciences	31	48	19	36
Economics	38	42	26	30
Political science	32	43	18	30
Sociology	38	43	16	36
Psychology	20	62	12	48
Anthropology	15	67	11	57

Source: Stark and Finke (2000: 53).

Dr Martyn Lloyd-Jones, a staunch supporter of the IVF, and one of Britain's leading evangelical preachers, had trained as a doctor before becoming a minister. Oliver R. Barclay, who succeeded Johnson as general secretary of the IVF, was a biologist.

In reflecting on the inter-war period in British universities, Johnson wrote: 'there had been a marked preponderance of students from the faculties of theology, science, medicine and sometimes engineering. The faculty of arts was poorly represented, as were also the more philosophical aspects of Western culture' (1979: 248). With the addition of the social sciences to that last sentence, the relationship has remained to this day. Although there are many graduates and professional people in British evangelical circles, there are very few social scientists and academics in the arts and humanities.

Some US data suggest a similar relationship. In 1969 the Carnegie Commission conducted a survey of the religious beliefs of 60,000 US academics. The results are summarized in table 5.2.

The figures show a strong connection between academic discipline and orthodoxy. Natural scientists are considerably more likely than social scientists to be regular churchgoers and to describe themselves as religiously conservative. And within the social sciences those whose methods most closely mirror those of the natural sciences – economists – are more conservative than sociologists or anthropologists (Stark and Finke 2000: 53).

So, if we summarize the above and simplify, we have two propositions. Most scientists are not religious. Among one major group of conservative Christians, scientists are much more common than social scientists. I might add that others have found a similar relationship for Islam. Dekmejian notes: 'university students and graduates with specializations in science and technical fields are more prone to be attracted to fundamentalism than those with humanistic backgrounds' (1995: 47).

In his history of the IVF, Johnson offers three sorts of explanation for the over-representation of scientists and medical students (1979: 111–13). The first is practical. The extended career required to qualify as a doctor meant that medical students tended to be more mature and self-confident. They also stayed students for longer, which meant that they had greater opportunity for such involvement and were more likely to be invited to take on leadership roles by the other students who were only too well aware of the practical difficulties of maintaining organizational continuity in a field where a third of members left every year.

Johnson's second explanation concerns socialization and motive. Many medical students were committed evangelicals before going to university; they were studying medicine because they wanted to engage in some sort of Christian service, either at home or in a mission field. For such students, evangelical identity came before choice of academic discipline. At first sight, this might seem to make the subject of this chapter redundant. If religious faith comes before academic socialization, then there is no need to consider the role of science in shaping religious beliefs, but, of course, the question remains, even if it can now be rephrased as follows: if it is the case that science is a threat to Christian faith (especially of a conservative variety), how were a sufficient number of young evangelicals able to survive their medical training without losing that faith? The presence of so many medics (and the relative absence of students and graduates of the arts, humanities and social sciences) in British evangelical circles remains an interesting intellectual problem.

Although he does not address this question directly, in commenting on other aspects of the formation of the IVF, Johnson does suggest a third answer.

The resolution

The explanation of the paradox can be found if we move from the apparent clash between certain scientific findings (such as the age of the earth, the origins of species and so on) and the traditional teachings of the Christian tradition and concentrate instead on more abstract assumptions about the nature of knowledge or what we might call cognitive styles.

Johnson's account of debates within what became the Inter-Varsity Fellowship about the organization's ideological foundations is inadvertently revealing: 'The future medical missionaries in most of the universities were always in the vanguard of evangelistic activity and advocacy of a crystal clear basis of belief and principle for Christian action' (1979: 112). Leading the movement 'to enshrine the essentials of Christian doctrine – biblical theology – in their official documents' were the students of the London medical schools, who 'repeatedly put on the spot' some of the leading clergy and ministers of London and their theological student colleagues. The medics were 'suspicious of any ambiguity when reference was made to the authority of the Bible or the central facts of the gospel. They wanted no stone left unturned in order to find what was *essential*' (1979: 122; emphasis in the original).

It is first necessary to distinguish between the epistemologies of liberal and conservative Protestantism. For the conservative Protestant, the Bible is the authoritative source of all knowledge and we must begin by grasping how conservatives view the Bible. Although it is crude we can contrast empiricist and interpretative perspectives. The empiricist sees the mind as 'the initially empty and passive receptor of impressions or "ideas" through the organs of sense' (Benton 1977: 22). The world simply flows into the head of the observer, who perhaps selects by attention but adds nothing by way of interpretation. The meaning of sense data inhere in those data themselves. Trees are trees by virtue of their treeness.

An interpretative view of perception would argue that such naive reception of sense data is not possible. For American pragmatists such as Mead, James and Dewey, meaning was something we conferred on objects as we made sense of them in terms of some scheme or plan of action involving those data (Rock 1979: 59–82). What things mean depends on what we may intend to do with them and thus the same object may have different meanings for different people. To borrow Blumer's example (1966: 10–12), a tree is not the same thing to a lumberjack, a botanist, a painter and a fugitive from a search party.

These alternative views of perception illuminate the central division between conservative and liberal Protestantism (and can be extended to conservative and liberal wings of most major religious traditions).

The conservative view of the Bible and how it is to be read is classically empiricist. Conservatives do not see themselves as adding anything by way of interpretation. Though not always an easy task, interpretation is simply a matter of finding the correct meaning. Biblical literalists believe that 'the semantic effect of these words as directly formed in the mind of an English reader formed a direct and not a mediated transcript of God's intention' (Barr 1977: 210). The reader does not confer meaning on the words and phrases; they simply leave impressions on the mind like animal prints on sand. This view of reading explains the common conservative concern for a particular interpretation of the Bible: the King James or Authorized version. Conservative intellectuals would offer a more sophisticated defence and argue that translation is a creative process; that the men who produced the King James version were more completely filled with the Holy Spirit and hence better minded in their work and that they were better linguists and hence more likely to be accurate. The point about the spirit in which the work was done is often given a negative twist so that the errors of other translations are explained by the malign motives of their producers. So the Jerusalem Bible is dismissed as a papist plot and some American fundamentalists regard the Revised Standard Version as the product of a Jewish conspiracy (Gasper 1963: 72). But the attitude of many conservatives is far simpler – the King James version is correct – and is humorously expressed in the apocryphal story of the man who said that, if the King James version of the Old Testament was good enough for Jesus to quote, it was good enough for him.

Such a preservationist attitude towards a particular translation is not shared by liberals, because they are already committed to an interpretative epistemology. Given that meaning is at least partly the produce of the reader's activity, meaning can change. What the gospel meant to Reformation divines and what it means to us will differ. Indeed, it must, if we are to find it plausible. Hence the supposed unchanging core of the faith must be 'represented' anew for each generation.

To say that conservatives have an empiricist epistemology does not, of course, mean that they take every part of the Bible literally. No fundamentalist thinks that the 'Lamb of God' would be good with mint sauce. Conservatives understand metaphor and allegory. The difference is that the conservative asserts that the text itself tells us what is metaphorical; the liberal supposes that all texts are in some senses metaphorical.

On some occasions the conservative notion of the non-interpreting reader is taken to the point where it is assumed that the right response follows entirely automatically from the mechanical fact of reading. In one sermon US evangelist Billy Graham challenged the audience to sit down with the Gospel of John, read it through five times and then ask for salvation. Understanding is not a problem. Reading is all. It is only a short step to supposing that even reading is not necessary. Anita Bryant, a leading American gospel singer of the 1970s and anti-Gay Rights campaigner, said: 'I've heard weird stories all over the world about where people have gone to some weird places and people have been saved just by seeing a torn page of the Bible on the floor' (1978: 92).

Further vital differences can be found in the conservative and liberal views of discovering patterns. How do we know, when we sense an orderliness to what we perceive, if the pattern is actually there outside us or if it is a function of our ordering what we see? I sense that a series of events shows my colleagues are conspiring against me. Is that an accurate reading of the signs or is it paranoia? The conservative Protestant with his belief in divine creation and divinely ordained providence supposes that the patterns are real and external. In contrast, the liberal sees a lot of orderliness as a function of the ordering mind. This is all of a part with the general liberal Christian rewriting of Christianity to make what were once taken to be external realities into psychological states. Heaven and hell are reworked as 'peace of mind' and 'alienation'. The white-bearded patriarchal God is put inside us as some variant of Tillich's 'ground of our being'.

A major advantage of an empiricist epistemology is that it allows arithmetic. If the meaning and significance of any object or sense datum varied with the perceiver, then it would not be possible meaningfully to treat objects as things that could be added up. Billy Graham demonstrated the importance of 'bread' by telling his audience that the word is used nineteen times in just one chapter of the Book of John. In another sermon he said 'the end is coming. Jesus predicted it 318 times in the New Testament' (Coomes 1973: 76). The fascinating feature of this is the use of exact numbers.

The fondness for arithmetic combines with the belief that the patterns we perceive are external realities to produce the sort of literature common to evangelical Christian organizations. A Campus Crusade for Christ pamphlet tells us that there are four (not three or five) spiritual laws. There are four (not three or five) steps to being filled with the Holy Spirit. Of course, dividing complex realities into neat and memorable packages is something that all of us engaged in persuasion do frequently, but my reading of evangelical literature and thirty years of listening to fundamentalist preaching convinces me that this mode of thought is, for evangelicals, not merely a pedagogic convenience. While the liberal sees himself as sorting material for persuasive purposes, the conservative thinks he is discovering innate orderliness.

This account of the cognitive style of conservative Protestantism suggests a reconciliation with a certain sort of science: the inductionism pioneered by Francis Bacon and described by Karl Popper in his *Logic of Scientific Discovery* (1978) as the 'bucket' theory of science. Facts are collected up and when you have enough of them you have an explanation. Historians, philosophers and sociologists of science have done much to weaken faith in inductionism, but, I suspect, it is still at the heart of most views of science held by science undergraduates, lay people and those working in the 'applied' sciences. For brevity let us distinguish mundane from advanced science. With few exceptions (for example, J. J. Thomson), most British conservative Protestants have acquired their science at the peripheries of the enterprise: Ambrose Fleming was an electrical engineer and most IVF patrons were doctors. Although he does not accept the critical spirit in which it was intended, and goes on to show the shallowness of much liberal rhetoric, Johnson reports the liberal Christian view that: 'IVF supporters were mostly drawn from what were really the applied sciences in which the student was never compelled to think at the deeper levels of the true intellectual' and adds 'There may have been some truth in that' (1979: 248).

The conservative Protestant inhabits a world of hard empirical reality – a world where facts are separate from interpretations. There is thus a basic resonance between the cognitive styles or operating assumptions of evangelicalism and Baconian mundane science. We can see this very clearly in the teaching styles associated with each. Evangelicals see themselves as transmitting a body of facts. The laws of God and the evidences for those laws are passed from one generation to the next by instruction. There are no better illustrations than the catechisms that were once standard in Catholic and Protestant churches but are now used only by the most conservative elements of those confessions. Ian Paisley's Free Presbyterian Church, for example, still encourages its young people to memorize the questions and answers of the *Shorter Catechism*, the document developed by British Presbyterians in the seventeenth century as a handy breval. In the same way, the fundamental laws of physics and chemistry are taught to schoolchildren. Both evangelicals and geographers can test knowledge with multiple-choice exam questions.

It is worth saying a few words about creationism and creation science. In chapter 11 I treat the creation science now popular with the religious right in the USA as a rebranding of traditional Christian beliefs in a language designed to win advantages in the courts. When William Jennings Bryan fought with Clarence Darrow over Darwinian evolution in the courtroom of Little Rock, Arkansas, in 1925, he said bluntly that, if science and the Bible were in conflict, he would believe the Bible every time: 'It is better to trust in the Rock of Ages than to know the age of rocks; it is better to know he is close to the heavenly father than to know how far the stars in heaven are apart' (Marsden 1980: 212). In the 1970s, evangelicals presented their case in a very different way. They argued that the Genesis 1–12 account of the origins of the world and species by 'special creation' was every bit as compatible with the scientific evidence (properly understood) as Darwinian evolution. With good reason I argue that creationists changed their presentational style when they realized that theocratic claims would not work in US courts. Current US interpretations of the separation of church and state prevent any public policy being justified on the grounds that God requires it. This story could be read as cynicism on the part of the creationists but that would be inappropriate. Although the rebranding of creation science was consciously undertaken for presentational reasons, it was possible because the creationists really do believe that the biblical account of creation is compatible with the best science.

Conclusion

Much more could be said, but the central point is simple and need not be laboured. That science and religion may clash over specific propositions about the nature of the world should not cause us to miss the similarities of cognitive style and epistemology. As Marsden put it: 'Far from emphasizing the irrational, fundamentalists characteristically presented their faith as being the exact representation of biblically revealed matters of fact for which could be claimed the highest positive standards of scientific objectivity' (1980: 138). In explaining the over-representation of science and technical students among Islamic fundamentalists, Dekmejian made a similar connection when he pointed to 'the attractiveness of the certainty inherent in the exact sciences as opposed to the analytical and speculative nature of the humanities and social sciences' (1995: 47).

This chapter has been intended as part of an attempt to correct a common misunderstanding of the secularization paradigm. As I said in the introduction, no contemporary sociologist of religion argues that Christianity has been fatally undermined by science. In chapter 1 I suggested that the primary secularizing effects of science came not from its direct refutation of religious ideas but through the general encouragement to a rationalistic orientation to the world that science has given; the embodiment of that rationalistic outlook in bureaucracy as the dominant form of social organization; and the role of technology in increasing our sense of mastery over our own fate. That some people are quite capable of sustaining beliefs long after the point where the impartial observer might suppose those beliefs refuted by the evidence (creationism, for example) suggests that, whatever the persuasiveness of science, we need a complementary explanation of the declining plausibility of the alternatives it is supposed to have displaced.

It is worth looking again at the figures in table 5.2. It would be useful to see such surveys repeated, not just in the USA but also in other countries. But, if we take these data as food for thought, the most striking line is that for Anthropology. Here is the discipline that most obviously confronts its students with the fact of cultural diversity. If it does nothing else, anthropological fieldwork forces the student to appreciate that other people do it differently. It is also the social science that in the second half of the twentieth century led the way in arguing that all accounts and explanations were partial, the product of interpretation. That the anthropologists should be the least religious of various groups of academics seems entirely consistent with the case I have advanced in this chapter and with the thrust of the whole book. At the risk of trying the reader's patience with repetition, I will again stress that the greatest damage to religion has been caused, not by competing secular ideas, but by the general relativism that supposes that all ideologies are equally true (and hence equally false).

CHAPTER SIX

The Easternization of the West

Introduction

The last twenty years of the twentieth century saw a paradoxical change in the power of the West. It won the economic argument. Communism, the major alternative to Western capitalism, collapsed in the 1980s. Most of the world has been integrated into a global market for Western consumer goods. McDonald's and Coca-Cola are now genuinely global brands. The West has also won the political argument. The reality may often fall short of the rhetoric, but almost all states now have liberal democratic polities. But, at the same time, the West has suffered a crisis of confidence in one aspect of its culture: religion. In the nineteenth century Britain sent out Christian missionaries to convert the world; it was a net exporter of its religious goods, which it took to be self-evidently superior. Although evangelical Protestants in the United States still confidently try to convert the rest of the world, most European societies have become net importers of religious innovations and even the United States has been considerably influenced by the trends I will describe.

By 'the Easternization of the West', I do not mean the migration of Hindus and Buddhists to Europe and the United States. Though there has been some of that, the religion brought by such migrants is generally too closely associated with their ethnic identity to appeal to Europeans and Americans. Nor am I mainly concerned with the insignificant numbers of Westerners who join Hindu or Buddhist movements. What I want to consider are two related phenomena: the importance of Eastern religious themes in what is usually called 'New Age spirituality' and their general spread into the wider culture.

I will first describe what seem the major themes, explain their popularity, note the way that key ideas have been transformed in the borrowing, and then suggest that what we see is not a single social change but two quite different things coinciding. While the core of

New Agers are consciously attracted to Eastern ideas (in part because they are not Western), some of the apparent easternization of the West has very different origins: some Britons are becoming what we might call 'Buddhist by default'. The erosion of specifically Christian ideas has left a vague spirituality that is coincidentally similar to the more philosophical and less ritualistic traditions in Hinduism and Buddhism.

Eastern themes

One of the major changes of recent decades has been the decline of Christian notions of time as having a beginning and an end. In the beginning God created the world. Sometime he will end it. Until relatively recently, Christian thinkers tried to work out, from a combination of secular history and biblical exegesis, when exactly the serpent tempted Eve and apocalypse-minded fundamentalists still try to predict the battle of Armageddon. For the Christian, the life of creation is, in the biggest sense, linear and directional. So too is the life of the individual. We are born and we die. And at the point of death we go to heaven or hell. All of those views have largely been discarded, even by mainstream Christian denominations. They are now largely the preserve of fundamentalist Protestant sects (though we should recall that in the United States fundamentalism is popular). People are now more likely to think of time as having origins so far back as to be beyond contemplation. And, unless human stupidity creates an ecological disaster, time has no end.

The traditional Christian ideas of what becomes of the self after death are no longer binding and the stark alternative of heaven or hell has come apart. Surveys show that only a quarter of Britons say they believe in hell but twice as many say they believe in heaven (Gill et al. 1998). However, belief in personal immortality has not declined because people have consciously embraced a purely materialist conception of the self. A lot of people believe in some sort of essence that endures. Recent surveys show between 40 and 50 per cent of respondents saying they believe in life after death and between 50 and 60 per cent say they believe in a soul. A survey conducted by Opinion Research Business (ORB) in May 2000 asked very pointedly: 'Do you consider yourself solely to be a biological organism, which ceases to exist at death, or is there another existence after death?' Only 31 per cent chose the first option and 52 per cent chose the latter.

According to a 1947 Mass Observation study, only 4 per cent of Britons said they believed in reincarnation. The 1990 European Values Survey found 24 per cent; the 2000 ORB survey reported 25 per cent. Some of this apparent increase may represent confusion about terms. Some Christians may be taking reincarnation to mean being born again in heaven, but that itself would be significant as a sign of a decline in well-informed Christian orthodoxy. Waterhouse's detailed study (1999) and my own impressions lead me to conclude that this is rarely a full-scale endorsement of the karmic model of rebirth reflecting the moral quality of previous lives. It seems more a consequence of (a) experiences of having lived before; (b) some sense of contact with the dead; and (c) a vague hope that there is something about us that endures after death. Campbell notes:

> That proportion of the population prepared to say that they believe in the standard Christian beliefs concerning heaven and hell has declined considerably . . . However, belief in reincarnation (which is not, of course, officially part of the creed of any mainstream Christian Church), has actually been going up. About one-fifth of Britons subscribe to this belief, which is even more marked among the young. (1999: 36)

Instead of the Christian's clear division between God and his creation, and between us and the animal and material worlds, there is a fondness for ecological notions of the interconnectedness of everything. Where the Christian view stresses the divisions of life forms and worlds, the Eastern perspective argues for a fundamental unity beneath the surface differences. That may be a dog, but it embodies the same cosmic consciousness as the farmer.

If we put together all of the above, we arrive at what is perhaps the core notion of New Age spirituality. God is not an external entity, 'out there'. Rather, the divine is within us. In the Christian vision, the self, since the expulsion of Adam and Eve from the Garden of Eden, has been bad and only becomes good by a combination of God's gracious forgiveness and external discipline. The more the self is controlled and constrained, the better it becomes. The New Age view is almost the opposite. The self is essentially good (or divine or perfect). Our experiences – repressive parents, materialistic society, stifling bureaucracies, competitive school system – make us bad. We can become good again and release our innate power by learning to strip away the layers and get down to the 'real' me, the child or God or Goddess within.

Related to this idea of an inner core of perfection, waiting to be liberated, is a particular view of knowledge. New Agers have a very high opinion of intuition and tend to disdain rational thought. This is often put in such terms as 'trust your feelings', 'put your heart before your head' and 'Accept only what rings true to you'.

Associated with the idea of the divine within, the interconnectedness of everything and the value of intuition is the frequently made claim that appreciation of these three principles can give access to considerable power. This can be thought of in the purely secular terms employed by some psychotherapists. By removing various sources of psychological problems, we can release previously constrained psychic energy and become more effective people. But in New Age circles this is often augmented by claims to supernatural or magical powers. The old Protestant Ethic idea of striving diligently as the route to material success has for some people been superseded. Soka Gakkai (or Nicheren Shoshu) promises that those who desire something (and that thing can be as abstract as affection or as material as a new car) can gain it by thinking of it while chanting a simple form of words to a piece of parchment with some characters drawn on it (Wilson and Dobbelaere 1994). Prior to the 1970s, 'training' meant working hard to acquire new skills. Now promoters of such organizations as Werner Erhard's *est*, Insight, Exegesis and the like argue that the way to material success is not through rational striving but through getting in touch with your inner self and aligning it with the rhythms of cosmic consciousness (Heelas 1996).

Campbell (1999: 42–3) provides a helpful summary of the Eastern and Western perspectives, which, adapted slightly, I present as figure 6.1. With good reason, Campbell believes that the principles of the first list are becoming popular at the expense of the principles of the second list, not just in New Age circles but in our culture more widely.

Explaining the changes

In the final part of this chapter, I will suggest an alternative explanation of some of the above changes. It may well be that two analytically separate things are coinciding; that at the same time as Eastern ideas are becoming influential, indigenous changes in the nature of Western religious thinking are producing attitudes and beliefs that appear similar to the more philosophical strands of Hinduism and Buddhism. That point will be reserved for the time being and I will

---

Figure 6.1   East and West compared

Eastern

- Humans and nature are one.
- Spiritual and physical are one.
- Mind and body are one.
- Humans should recognize their basic oneness with nature, the spiritual and the mental rather than attempt to analyse, label, categorize, manipulate, control or consume the things of the world.
- Because of their oneness with all existence, humans should feel 'at home' in any place and with any person.
- Science and technology, at best, create an illusion of progress; enlightenment involves achieving a sense of oneness with the universal; it is a state where all dichotomies vanish.
- Meditation, a special state of quiet contemplation, is essential to achieving enlightenment.

Western

- Humans have characteristics that set them apart from nature and the spiritual.
- Humans are divided into a body, a spirit and a mind.
- There is a personal God who is over humans.
- Humans must control and manipulate nature to ensure their survival.
- Rational thought and an analytical approach to problem solving should be emphasized.
- Science and technology have given us a good life and provide our main hope for an even better future.
- Action and the competitive spirit should be rewarded.

Source: adapted from Campbell (1999: 42–3).

---

first consider how we might explain a preference for the oriental over the occidental.

We might suppose it results simply from greater contact with, and hence better knowledge about, these alternatives to the Christian tradition. That is certainly the implication of Bloom's point (2000: 9) about global communication. But there are two problems with a simple contact model of the diffusion of innovation. The first is logical. There is no reason why knowing about something should lead to taking it seriously or adopting it. I know about exercise and its virtues but do not do much of it. I know about Islam but have not become a Muslim. Indeed, if knowledge was sufficient for belief, then there would not have been any secularization, because each generation that is less Christian than its predecessor grew up in a world shaped by the culture of its parents.

The second is factual. To suppose that recent improvements in international communication and travel explain the popularity of Eastern themes in the West is also to suppose that such contact is novel. But it is not. Perhaps because it is a small island, Britain has never been short of contact with the rest of the world. In the fifteenth century, Scots fought alongside the Teutonic Knights in Prussia, Lithuania and Russia. In the sixteenth century, 'when Ivan the Terrible was on the rampage in the Baltic, he picked up hundreds of Scots in Stockholm, who later fought for him in his campaigns against the Crimean Tatars' (White 1996: 29). In the 1660s General Tam Dalyell of the Binns commanded a Russian army and fought against the Turks. Patrick Gordon, Thomas Gordon and Samuel Greig served as admirals in the Tsarist navy. A century later, James Bruce, a member of the same Masonic Lodge as James Boswell, explored the source of the Nile and became an Abyssinian Captain of Horse. His five-volume *Travels* was a bestseller of its day, as were many tales of foreign parts with titles such as *Travels from St Petersburg in Russia to Diverse Parts of Asia* (Bredin 2000). Robert Brown of Montrose (best known for discovering the 'Brownian motion' of particles) became an army surgeon in 1794. He was the naturalist on the ship *Investigator* in the Flinders expedition, where he gathered data for a widely read book on flora.

This sort of luminary apart, men in maritime communities have long sailed the world and returned with tales of the exotic. Daniel Defoe's fictional castaway Robinson Crusoe was based on the real character of Alexander Selkirk of Largo in Fife. Most importantly for my concerns, in the late nineteenth century British Christians went to Asia and Africa as missionaries. They not only observed other religions but they learnt enough about them to engage in apologetic and persuasive work (for example, translating the Bible into languages for which they first had to construct a script). And missionaries on leave toured the country delivering fund-raising lectures that made very many Britons aware of the heathenism and paganism to be found elsewhere in the world. In brief, many people in Britain have long known about alternatives to Christianity.

This suggests that it is not contact as such that has changed but the attitudes that people have brought to such contact. What matters is receptivity. Before I consider the intrinsic appeal of Eastern religious ideas, I will explain why we have become more receptive to such notions by considering two clusters of causes of a loss of confidence in the Christian tradition.

Declining confidence in the Christian heritage

The first cluster is obvious. It is hard to remain sure that our own religious heritage is superior to the alternatives when those who have been privileged to be raised in it are giving it up. The confidence that produced the bulk of British missionary activity rested on a society that was thoroughly Christian in the general sense and was stimulated by the evangelical and High Church revivals of the nineteenth century. It was far less easy to be bullish when the British churches had begun visibly to shrink. We can explain a lot of the loss of missionary confidence by the general social changes that undermined the power and popularity of the Christian churches at home.

The second cluster is perhaps more complex. It involves both the new attitudes to the heathen that resulted from the intimate connections established in the mission field and the later revulsion against the whole project of imperialism. This simplifies, but we can distinguish two populations that are relevant to the overall argument: the committed Christians and the middle classes outside the churches. As we will see, the effect of missionary work was often the opposite of what was initially intended. Christians went out to change the heathen but themselves became changed by the experience and in turn influenced the attitudes of British Christian churches in a more liberal direction. I will consider the thinking of such people in a moment. There is also a quite different population that is central to my thesis: the New Agers. By and large such people are either deliberately opposed to imperialism or at least disdainful of the British Empire and its achievements.

The attitudes of British imperialists to the cultures of the people they conquered and administered were never simple. There were at least two clear principles in tension and there are neatly encapsulated in the opening sentences of a declaration made to her Indian subjects by Queen Victoria in 1858. After the Sepoy rebellion, she said: 'Firmly relying ourselves on the truth of Christianity, and acknowledging with gratitude the solace of religion, we disclaim alike the right and desire to impose our convictions on any of our subjects' (Embree 1992: 151). The second part of the sentence was written by civil servants and reflects the professional imperial administrator's desire for a quiet life. Victoria herself added the first two phrases as a personal declaration of her commitment to evangelical Protestantism.

From their first involvement in India, the officials of the East India Company had taken the view that their primary concern was trade and disclaimed any great interest in trying to change religious culture (or much else about) those parts of India they came to control. Robert Dundas, who as President of the Board of Control oversaw the operations of the Company on behalf of the British government, said in 1808 that we had 'virtually contracted an obligation . . . to support . . . those establishments which have immemorially been held in reverence and deemed sacred by their subjects' (Embree 1992: 156). William Wilberforce and the British evangelicals hated this laissez-faire attitude towards what they saw as barbarism and savagery. William Gladstone (himself an evangelical) was horrified when he discovered that for forty years the Company had been managing Hindu festivals such as that at Jagganath (the origins of our word 'Juggernaut'). The Company's position was pragmatic. Very large numbers of people gathered for religious festivals. The Company had a responsibility to manage large public gatherings so as to reduce the dangers of accidents. In so doing it was not countenancing or legitimating but merely accommodating.

The division over the propriety of missions was not simply between the religious zealots and the religiously indifferent. Even those who had no doubt at all about the superiority of the Christian faith could have reservations. In 1796 the General Assembly of the Church of Scotland was invited to endorse the recent foundation of the Glasgow and Edinburgh Missionary Societies. It now seems remarkable that the majority declined to do so. It seems even more remarkable that they did so because they thought missionary work among the heathen was 'highly preposterous, in so far as it anticipates, nay, reverses, the order of nature. Men must be polished and refined in their manners before they can be properly enlightened in religious truths. Philosophy and learning must, in the nature of things, take the precedence.' The Moderates were also concerned (rightly as I will argue) that evangelizing the heathen would disrupt social relations; hence missionary societies were 'highly dangerous in their tendency to the good order of society at large' (Morrison 1927: 36). The second largest Presbyterian organization had a further reason for disparaging missionary work: it would involve a 'lowering of denominational testimony by promiscuous association' (Morrison 1927: 37) and, again, it was proved right. What were at home profound differences in the interpretation of Christianity often seemed rather shallow in India or Africa.

Concerns about good order were partly fed by the example of the recent revolution in France. With increased distance from the events of 1792, fear that permitting subordinate peoples to get ideas above their station would encourage anarchy subsided and the evangelicals eventually won the argument. In 1824 the Church of Scotland reversed its position. Alexander Duff arrived in Calcutta in 1830 and founded a college that in little over a decade would grow to have 900 students.

At the same time as churches were becoming more active in missionary work, the second pincer of the evangelical attack, pressure on the British government, was also working. In 1813, when it faced opposition in parliament to having its charter renewed, the East India Company agreed to pay for a Church of England Bishop and three archdeacons. In 1838 it was prevented from supervising native religious ceremonies. Restrictions on missionary work were removed. Gradually what was a religious establishment for the benefit of British civil servants was expanded through missionary recruitment and became a state-funded Church of India. In an interesting act of toleration the government also funded dissenting Protestant and Catholic clergy.

The Scottish Presbyterian Moderates who in 1796 opposed missionary work were certain that they had the true faith. They hesitated only because they perceived that, once the heathen became Christian, an important line of social demarcation would be removed. The English evangelicals were absolutely sure that they had the true religion. This does not mean they were blind to the faults of their own country. Contrary to the view we now have of Christian missionaries as uncritical promoters of Western civilization, the evangelicals were only too well aware of the defects of the West; after all, William Wilberforce and his 'Clapham sect' spent a lot of their time trying to reform industrial urban Britain (Howse 1971). The author of a 1920s promotional review of Scottish missionary work began by noting that Christendom could be criticized for 'its drunkenness and prostitution, its white slave trade, its war spirit, its mad race for riches and pleasure', and adds: 'We are not concerned to deny these charges, nor do we hold a brief for the defence of western civilization', but this is just a preliminary to asserting that: 'The vital element of difference between Christendom and the heathen world lies in this, that in the former the powerful leaven of the gospel is at work . . . In Christendom the Gospel is at war with vice and wickedness in every form; in heathenism abominable evils are wrought under the sanction of religion' (Morrison 1927: 14–15).

Inspired by the 1874 missions of the American evangelists Moody and Sankey and by the decision in the late 1880s of seven prominent Cambridge students to dedicate themselves to the mission field, the Student Volunteer Missionary Union (SVMU) was founded in Britain in 1892 with the aim of recruiting young middle-class men and women for foreign mission. Its high point came between 1893 and 1898. At the same time, student Christian groups with a wider remit formed what was first called the British Colleges Christian Union and then the Student Christian Movement (SCM) and the two organizations merged, with the SVMU becoming the 'foreign' department of the SCM. In 1896 the SVMU recorded 1,038 student volunteers (832 men and 206 women); with reference to the subject of the previous chapter, we might note that almost 300 of them were medical students. That year the SVMU adopted the slogan 'The evangelization of the world in this generation' (Tatlow 1933: 97). Evangelization was not taken to mean conversion (for that was the work of the Holy Spirit) nor did it mean the hurried proclamation of the gospel.

> We understand it to mean that the Gospel should be preached intelligibly and intelligently to every soul in such a manner that the responsibility for its acceptance shall no longer rest upon the Christian Church, but upon each man for himself. Hence the Watchword is perfectly in harmony with the leavening influences, educational, medical and pastoral, now in operation in the mission-field. (Tatlow 1933: 98)

Such qualifications were written into the resolution of the Liverpool Conference because (for quite the opposite of the reasons given by the reluctant Presbyterians in 1786) some students argued that evangelism should take second place to general betterment. Nonetheless, all were unanimous that Christianity was superior to alternatives, that Christians had a duty to evangelize the world, and that the conversion of the whole world was perfectly possible if Western Christians would only accept their responsibilities.

Such confidence was short lived. A 1916 conference reported that, while the number of full-time students in Britain had increased considerably over the previous two decades, membership of the SCM had grown only slightly, and the number of missionary Volunteers had remained static. Already the explanation was being given that 'many who do not suspect themselves of any disloyalty to Christ have unconsciously or half-consciously drifted into the position where they do not really believe in the final and universal message of the gospel of Christ' (Jackson 1980: 52). The American Robert Wilder, one of the most influential promoters of missionary work, said: 'Change has come over the evangelical world in the past few decades. To the generation of which few now remain there was no question that souls without Christ were perishing. Now, however, some hesitate' (Broomhall 1966: 17).

Ironically one of the main causes of such hesitation was the experience of working in the mission field. Alexander Duff said: 'We need to be wary how we thrust upon our Eastern converts anything that is solely of ourselves and not of Christ, for it is their own Christ they must find' (Jackson 1980: 87). A leading ideologue of missions, J. W. Farquhar, went so far as to consider replacing the Old Testament with selections of Hindu scriptures, a clever idea that flattered the Indians by accepting that Hinduism could be as good a preparation for the true gospel as the religion of the ancient Jews, while nonetheless presenting Christianity as trumping Hinduism. When it was first published in 1915 his *Crown of Hinduism* was regarded as dangerously avant-garde, because it found virtues in Hinduism and described it not as a damnable heresy but as an incomplete perception of the truth (Jackson 1980: 94).

Christian missionaries could not remain indifferent to the social and material conditions of the heathen. Inevitably they were drawn into providing education, medical help, trade networks, technical expertise and social work. Such peripheral activities may initially have been promoted in an instrumental spirit (show the heathen the Christian God could deliver), but they developed their own impetus and came to be viewed as virtuous in their own right.

Two things happened in that process. The first is that, merely by educating Indians, the missionaries reduced the social distance between them and the objects of their evangelical activity and came to think better of them: hence the increasing appeal of Farquhar's respectful approach to Hinduism. At the same time, the educational work took on a life of its own. It was necessary to improve the natives so that they could appreciate the true religion. To win the confidence of high caste Hindus, who thought themselves second to no one, the conversionist ethos had to be toned down. Educating became an end in itself. That tendency was amplified by the rapid growth of the Christian colleges, which become popular so quickly that they had to recruit non-Christian staff. When this was coupled with a growing sense of national consciousness among even those Indians who were sympathetic to Christianity, it undermined the certainty that was once the spur to missionary work. Indians ceased to be viewed as the objects of Christian endeavour and became partners in a collaborative enterprise that outgrew its evangelistic roots.

The extent of the change can be seen in W. E. Hocking's *Rethinking Missions: A Layman's Enquiry after One Hundred Years*, which represented the thinking of the 1930s. As Neill summarizes it:

> The task of the missionary today . . . is to see the best in other religions, to help the adherents of those religions to discover, or rediscover, all that is best in their own traditions, to cooperate with the most active and vigorous elements in the other traditions in social reform and in the purification of religious expression. The aim should not be conversion . . . Cooperation is to replace aggression. (1975: 456)

The end result of a century of Christian missionary activity was a return to a position not all that different from the pragmatic laissez-faire of the East India Company. One difference, of course, was that the missionary work had succeeded to the extent of establishing viable Christian churches in foreign fields, and, as I have noted, the close ties between the clergy of such churches and those of the home churches undermined the easy division between the Christian British and the heathen foreigners, a division already fatally weakened by the decline in the membership and confidence of the churches in Britain.

The loss of Empire

Our current hostility to the British Empire leads to inaccurate stereotyping. In particular, it causes us mistakenly to see Christian missions as simply the cultural justification for commercial and military exploitation. As I have noted, missionaries were often vocal critics of imperialism and by the time the fabric of the Empire started to unravel there was little regret in the churches, which were usually ahead of the government in granting autonomy to the native enterprises they had helped found.

India gained its independence in 1947 and other British possessions followed quickly thereafter. By 1965, when Rhodesia unilaterally declared its independence, the Empire was over and few Britons mourned its passing. The political left was opposed on principle, as by and large were the young. The growing doubts about the propriety of managing other peoples were exacerbated by the Suez crisis of 1956, in which British and French troops invaded Egypt in response to Egypt's decision to nationalize the Suez Canal and were then forced by UN and US pressure to withdraw.

Even before the student radicalism of the late 1960s and the opposition to the US war in Vietnam made support for liberation movements popular, attitudes were turning against imperialism. In many parts of the world British rule had been markedly more liberal, efficient and honest than what preceded or followed it, but that was largely forgotten in a blanket rejection of the idea that any one people had a right to rule over another. And, for the left-leaning sections of the middle classes at least, with the disdain for the Empire came a widespread general dislike for missionary activity and by implication for Christianity as a whole. This is where we come to our second distinct population. The above explains the gradual change in attitude of British Christians towards other religions. Coupled with secularization, that explains much of the decline in self-confidence of the Christian tradition. The views of the non-churchgoing middle classes, from which the New Age recruits, were affected not just by this general loss of certainty in the superiority of Christianity but also by a very specific dislike for imperialism. As we will see shortly, the widespread notion that the West had been wrong to impose its culture on the rest of the world provided an implicit justification for the obverse: an uncritical and romantic preference for the cultures of the underdeveloped world.

To summarize thus far, I am suggesting that, in order to understand the Easternization of the West, we should begin with some appreciation of how the West lost faith in its own religious traditions. Part of that is described in chapter 3 and explained in chapter 1: in common with that of most other industrial democracies, religion in Britain was severely affected by the changes we gloss by the term 'modernization'. To that general background I have added the specific problem of imperialism. The close historical association of missionary endeavour and the Empire gave the British churches a brief boost in allowing them to link the promotion of the gospel with the betterment of the human race, but the long-term effects were corrosive. Although by no means the sole cause of the decline in dogmatic certainty in the British churches (a combination of increasing diversity and increasing individualism were more corrosive), the cooperative and ecumenical attitudes of later generations of missionaries played an important part in undermining the conviction that Christianity was the complete and only true religion.

Those who admired the Empire had their confidence in the culture it promoted dented by its rapid demise. Those who did not, and that was a significant part of the university-educated middle classes, continued to associate Christianity with cultural oppression and hence were receptive to alternatives.

Adapting the East

Before we can appreciate the implications for the secularization paradigm of the popularity of Eastern religious and philosophical ideas, we must consider how such themes have been adapted in the borrowing.

As a preliminary, it is important to note that in giving up Christianity we have not become drawn to the other great monotheisms. The growth of Islam in the West is due almost entirely to the migration of Muslims; conversion to Islam is so rare that we need not mention it again. Similarly with Judaism. In so far as we have taken anything from these two traditions, it has been the most mystical, unorthodox and ambiguous strands. So there is some interest in Sufism (in its pacifist rather than its fighting Dervish forms) and the Kabbalah, but there is almost no interest in adopting Islamic law, the behavioural requirements of Orthodox Judaism, or the ritual aspects of either religion. What has been borrowed has either been so abstract (the notion of cosmic consciousness, for example) or so thoroughly lifted out of its cultural context (Chinese notions of ying and yang, for example) that it has proved readily susceptible to mutation. And, as I will argue, the mutations are so firmly in the direction of according with key Western ideas that this chapter might have been titled 'The Westernization of the Easternization of the West'.

One example is the way that cosmic consciousness (and, more generally, the idea of 'holism') now serves to flatter the New Ager. In its original Eastern setting it stressed the *smallness* of the individual self. The impermanence of appearances was typically offered as a solace to people whose lives were hard and miserable. It was a theodicy of insignificance and unimportance. Westernizers impressed by the calmness of the people of the Himalayas (see p. 136) are missing the point that stoicism is necessary for a people that has a great deal of suffering to be stoical about. Believing that 'This too must pass' is a way of coming to terms with a short and unpleasant life. In the Western version, the relative weight of the two alternatives – me and everything else – has been reversed so that, far from diminishing the importance of the self, it inflates it. Instead of thinking 'I am no better than, no different from, everything else', the Westerner thinks 'I contain within me the essence of all things. I am God.'

Another example can be found in Western notions of reincarnation. While the Hindu idea is doubtless comforting in providing a sense of continuity beyond the death of the body, it is also explanatory and judgemental. A problem for any religion is to explain the lack of apparent fit between fate and morality. Why do bad things happen to good people? The fact of rebirth in Hinduism restores moral order by allowing a carry-over from one life to the next. If misfortune in this life is seemingly undeserved, then it can be explained by bad action in a previous incarnation. However, this jars with most Western uses of reincarnation, because it supposes only limited continuity across rebirths. Although some sense of spirit is carried over from one life to the next, the evil man who is reborn as a horse has clearly lost a great deal if not all of his personality in the change. When the Western New Ager thinks of reincarnation, she (and it is usually 'she') sees it as a process in which her self survives intact. Indeed, one of the most common forms of evidence offered for reincarnation is the memory of having lived a previous life and in those accounts the person 'that I once was' is usually very similar to the person 'I now am'. The Western notion of reincarnation also differs from that of the East in its forward aspect. It is very rare to find among even committed New Agers any idea that one's future rebirths will be determined by the quality of one's moral life or one's ritual performances in this life. There is certainly no sense of fear that rebirth may be a punishment rather than a reward.

Another mutation that reflects the self-confidence and assertiveness of the Westerner is the disappearance of discipline. As I noted in chapter 4, in the more meditative forms of Hinduism and Buddhism enlightenment comes only at the end of a very long struggle against the temptations of the flesh. Severe disciplines were designed to free the seeker from all attachments, including attachment to the vision of yourself as a highly spiritual religious seeker. The Zen archer who can hit the target blindfold can do so because he has learnt to let go of every form of this-worldly striving (including striving to hit the target) and to get in tune with the fundamental rhythms of the cosmos. But he attains that degree of harmony only at the end of a lifetime of self-discipline (often in a monastic setting). In the Western reworking the hard bit is missed out. Where the old sannyasin (or monk) followed a regime of self-denial, the 'neo-sannyasins' of the Rajneesh movement learn what the Bhagwan called 'dynamic meditation' in a matter of weeks (usually during the holidays so as not to interfere with their careers), wear Orange, and on the basis of that truncated and trivialized monastic career claim to be enlightened. It is no accident that one of the most popular forms of Buddhism in the West is Nichiren Shoshu (also known as Soka Gakkai), the central disciplines of which can be performed in a few minutes each day. The most popular form of Hinduism in the West is Transcendental Meditation, which requires only twenty minutes of meditation each day and boasts in its advertisements that no change of belief or lifestyle is necessary.

The same point can be seen in adaptions of the priority of intuition over rational thought. In both Hinduism and Buddhism there are schools that extol the superiority of intuition and inner wisdom over logic and rationality, but they generally see the latter as an essential precondition for the former. The novice acquires the knowledge and then transcends it (again, usually by years of effort and often by the regular performance of arduous ritual actions). In much New Age thought, intuition is presented as an *alternative* to knowledge and thought, a short cut to wisdom and saintliness. Enlightenment is no longer something to be achieved by discipline; it is something you discover (through a week-long workshop or an intensive weekend) that you always possessed.

A further observation about the mutation of Eastern traditions can be illustrated with this advertisement from the web site of 'One Star in Site Inc.':

> One-day workshops allow people with busy lifestyles to learn 'the bottom line' about topics such as healing techniques, various forms of divination, how to chose an energy healer, how to spot a fake etc. That way, the individual's free time can be spent focussing on those activities that will deeply affect their spirituality rather than wasting days away in long classes only to learn that 'it wasn't for them'. (www.onestar-insite.com)

The preference for the East over the West stems from a desire to compensate. As an advertisement for Tchaé® ('available in three delicious flavours – Jasmine, Citrus and Oriental Spice – and in convenient tea bags') says:

> Modern life! Of course, it's great to work hard and play hard, but sometimes all that rushing around can get you down a bit. That's when you need to bring a little eastern balance into your western way of life. For me, taking time out to enjoy new Tchaé® flavoured green teas is the perfect eastern antidote to western stress! (*Independent*, 16 Nov. 2000)

The West is good at rationality and efficiency; it is bad because technological consciousness has pervaded non-work areas of life. What we look for in the East is authenticity, spirituality and holism. But salves for anomie must be fitted into the modern lifestyle. They must not disrupt it. The key theme is accommodation. The banker who follows Rajneesh practises his Dynamic Meditation during his summer holiday in Poona and at occasional weekend retreats. Transcendental Meditation presents itself not as a critique of materialism and consumerism but as a therapy for 'recharging your batteries' so you compete and consume even more vigorously. And, because learning about the vast range of available spiritual alternatives is time-consuming, the busy modern executive can avoid 'wasting days away in long classes' by signing up for One Star in Site's pocket guides to enlightenment.

In brief, a close look at much borrowing from the East suggests that the rejection of Western values and beliefs is only partial and superficial. Specific themes of Western Christianity have been rejected, but the deeper assumption remains in place. The self is autonomous and very important. The individual consumer decides. The busy seeker after enlightenment adopts the same efficiency-seeking attitude to compensating for the ills of modernization as he or she does to getting on in the modern world. For all but a handful of core practitioners, Eastern spirituality does not provide a challenge to the secular world: it is slotted into the same leisure-and-family-preference compartment to which Christianity is largely confined.

To summarize thus far, Western interest in Eastern spirituality would refute the secularization paradigm only if we supposed that religion had declined in popularity because Westerners had all become atheists and rationalists. As I sought to show in the last section of chapter 1, that was never part of the paradigm. My point here is that a closer look at what we have borrowed from the East, and how we have changed it in the borrowing, suggests that the Easternization of the West, such as it is, has been on our terms.

Romanticizing the underdog

All of the above suggests ways in which Eastern religious themes fit well with the culture of European societies at the start of the twenty-first century. But the intrinsic qualities of the East do not seem to provide a full explanation of their appeal. Or, to turn the question round, why do our spiritual seekers not do more with their own religion tradition?

One obvious answer is that, though the Christian churches are in decline in the West, they are still there. Christianity still has specific beliefs that constrain reinterpretation and those constraints are hard to ignore entirely when the institutions that exemplify them are still a presence. We still have an archbishop of Canterbury, a pope, and an Ian Paisley to remind us what Christians used to believe. It is easier to be creative with remote (or reinvented) traditions such as those of the Tibetans, Chinese, Celts or Native Americans than with the ones on your doorstep. Secondly, as I noted above, there is considerable embarrassment about the supposed political and social associations of Christianity: Western imperialism, sexism, racism, authoritarianism, dogmatism and puritanism.

The third point is the most general one: the New Age movement has at its heart a popularized and moralized version of the sociological distinction between community and society, between traditional and modern societies. It assumes a Faustian contract: the price the West paid for technological mastery of the material world was the loss of its soul.

When New Agers do find something positive about Christianity it is in its prehistorical forms. So Celtic Christianity (about which we know very little and hence into which we can insert what we wish to find) is held to be liberal, inclusive, earth-loving and rather pagan. More often they prefer even older traditions, such as those of the pre-Christian Celts (Bowman 1993). The ancient Egyptians are held up as possessors of great wisdom, as are the Incas and Aztecs and native Americans. And there is nothing to prevent creative combining. Ceridwen, the 'Celtic Seer and Shaman' who offers 'Help on all life problems and disorders', describes herself thus in an advertisement: 'I am from an old tradition of seers and I work shamanically with the highest spiritual laws in accordance with the craft of the wise. The Celts who saw the spiritual with the natural shared essentially the same vision as the Ancient Egyptians. For external reality is but a projection of internal consciousness . . .'(*Kindred Spirit* (1992), 3: 33).

David Carson, who designed for use in divination and healing a set of Tarot-like cards with native American animal images, is described as 'blending traditional Native American Medicine with Celtic Heritage, within the standing stones and sacred sites of Britain' (*Kindred Spirit* (1992), 3: 18).

Some New Agers prefer Chinese medicine to Western scientific medicine because it is ancient. Most of those who are interested in Reiki, Shiatsu massage, acupuncture and the like rather more cautiously accept the value of scientific medicine, fault it for being too concerned with symptoms and for being insufficiently holistic, and then experiment with their options as *complementary* rather than *alternative*.

The ways in which Western medicine is criticized and the justifications for alternatives make very clear a supposed East–West division of virtue. Our doctors know how to perform triple heart bypass operations, eradicate polio and save AIDS patients, but they treat their patients as passive objects. The aura healers ('working shamanically . . . with the craft of the wise', etc.) help the human self-mobilize its energies to heal itself. This contrast is just the latest form of a tradition that is as old as industrialization itself: romanticizing the underdeveloped and claiming to find true humanity and spirituality in the rural peripheries of the urbanizing world. It is revealing that Carson, the animal medicine man featured in *Kindred Spirit*, was 'en route from Cornwall to Scotland' – the two parts of the British Isles most favoured by New Agers. Rousseau praised the Noble Savage. Wordsworth and Coleridge condemned the cities and sought beauty in England's peripheries. The modern romantics find virtue in the few remote places as yet untouched by modernization. The following comes from a recent trekker's account of visiting Mustang, in northern Tibet: 'For me . . . the robust earthiness of the Himalayan people is the magnet. The reality of a medieval farmyard life that we have exchanged for modern urban sprawl still echoes in our hearts. Ordinary Tibetan peasants or nomads put daily spiritual practice at the centre of life, and in so doing radiate tangible inner calm and self-sufficiency' (Ravensdale 1992: 12). We can be sure that Ravensdale flew into Tibet on an aeroplane, that potent symbol of Western technological advance. He may even have arranged his travel so that he could fly on planes operated by a Western airline and serviced by Western mechanics. That preference would have shown an implicit understanding that Western bureaucracy (in this case exhibited in pilot training and plane maintenance certification systems) has very tangible benefits. But when he wants spirituality he goes to Tibet.

Buddhist by default

When I first began to think about the impact of Eastern ideas on the West I rather naively took many elements of the modern interest in spirituality as reflecting a conscious preference for the ways of the Orient over those of mundane and all-too-familiar Christianity. I now suspect that I was confusing two things that, although intimately entangled, are nonetheless quite different in origin. The difficulty is to separate a positive attraction to the Eastern philosophical positions listed in figure 6.1 from a vague commitment to remain spiritual after the content of Christianity has been given up.

The point can be made clear if we consider closely some of the evidence of ideological change. Consider the enduring nature of the self. As noted above, recent surveys show that many people are reluctant to accept a purely material view of the self, but it is also clear that people are not adopting the Eastern alternative (C. Davies 1999). Much of the preference for an enduring soul comes from a combination of uncertainty and wishful thinking. Many of us are simply not sure. It would be nice to think we lived on in some way. For centuries our culture has taught us that we have a soul that survives death in either heaven or hell. But we can no longer believe in that account. So we suppose our souls endure but we have no shared or clear idea of how that might be (and, I might add, most of us show very little interest in trying to resolve the problem). This line of reasoning suggests that what we see in responses to survey questions about the soul is not a conscious and informed commitment to a particular religious position but a residue of a more religious time now past. We have lost faith in what we used to believe but are unwilling to assert categorically that we do not believe and settle for weakly assenting to the most general and vague positions offered us in surveys.

This logic would explain survey data on belief in God. Table 6.1 shows the answers given in a number of surveys to a question along the lines of 'Which of the following comes closest to your beliefs?' As well as an increase in those who either do not believe in any sort of God or who are unable to voice an opinion, there has been a shift from the first option – the Christian notion of a personal God – to the second: a vague higher power, spirit or life force. Then, when an even vaguer formulation – 'There is something there' – is introduced, it attracts almost a quarter of preferences and the numbers choosing 'higher power, spirit or life force' drop dramatically. We could see this as a shift between equally consciously held alternatives. However, an

Table 6.1 Belief in God, Great Britain, 1940s–2000 (%)

Beliefs	1940s	1947	1981	1990	2000
There is a personal God	43	45	41	32	26
There is some sort of higher power, spirit or life force	38	39	37	41	21
There is something there		n.a.	n.a.	n.a.	23
I don't really know what to think		16	16	15	12
I don't really think there is any sort of God, spirit or life force		n.a.	6	10	15
None of these		n.a.	n.a.	1	3

Note: n.a. = not asked.
Sources: Gill et al. (1998); Opinion Research Business (2000).

equally plausible alternative is that a growing number of people are no longer sufficiently interested in religion to give the matter much thought. When confronted with the need to make a choice, they pick the least specific response. They select the item that leaves them with the greatest freedom.

Conclusion

In its own right it is fascinating that Western dominance of the increasing global economy and polity has been achieved with little of the conscious commitment to engineered cultural change that accompanied nineteenth-century imperialism. However, what concerns me here is the plausibility of the secularization paradigm. My main purpose in examining the influence of Eastern religious themes on the West is to consider to what extent the phenomenon supports or refutes the ideas outlined in chapter 1. My pertinent conclusions can be simply stated.

The appeal of Eastern religious philosophies could be presented as a counter to the claim that Western societies are increasingly secular. While it is certainly evidence that we have not all become committed materialists who think there is nothing to life but our biology, a closer look at the phenomena suggests a rather different conclusion. First, the self-conscious promoters of Eastern spirituality are few and far between. Active membership of such groups as Soka Gakkai, Hare Krishna, Transcendental Meditation, Friends of the Western Buddhist

Order and the like, even taken together, is not likely to be much above 10,000 – fewer than the numbers lost to the Christian churches in a month. While many more people have been influenced by popularized versions of the beliefs such groups represent, it would still be a small population. We can only talk about *widespread cultural influence* at a point where the substance of the Eastern innovation has been almost completely eroded. An example would be Feng Sui. This Chinese geomancy is, in its original setting, a complex set of beliefs about the presence of spirits on the material world and our ability to influence them to our benefit by rearranging the material environment. In the 1990s Feng Sui became popular in Britain but only after it had lost almost all but the vaguest references to spirits and been reduced to a novel interior-decorating style. Interest in Feng Sui is no more evidence of a spiritual revival than the fashion for 'Shaker' furniture is evidence that Londoners want to revive the nineteenth-century American Protestant sect that originated the minimalist style. That Westerners now adorn their homes with Buddhas is no more evidence of Buddhist influence than the Victorian fondness for Persian carpets was a sign that British evangelicals were attracted to Islam.

Secondly, it is clear that the non-Christian traditions that have been most influential are those that are least demanding, most pliable and easiest to reinterpret. Britons are not becoming Muslims and what they are borrowing from Hinduism and Buddhism are the least theocratic and ritualistic elements. They are not worshipping Shiva or Vishnu or Ganesh. They are not following the paths of Buddhist monasticism. They are adopting the most plastic philosophical strands and then adapting them. Central to those adaptations is the Western stress on the authority of the autonomous individual consumer.

Finally, even with these qualifications, it may still be a mistake to see the 'Easternization of the West' as a significant counter-trend to secularization. I initially coined the phrase 'Buddhist by default' in a slightly flippant spirit, but it is intended to convey a serious point. A lot of the evidence can be read, not as showing a deliberate commitment to Eastern spiritual themes at all, but as indicating a set of residual positions. The point I made about the gradual drift in survey responses from the specific to the vague can be generalized. It may well be that what we are observing is not a change in religious ethos but simply a decline in interest in matters religious.

CHAPTER SEVEN

Regression to the Mean

Introduction

Whatever a society's level of ambient religion, some people will stand out as especially godly, observant and pious. The fate of such exemplary carriers of religion is important for understanding any culture, but it becomes crucial when religion is increasingly a matter of individuals rather than for the society as a whole. This sort of contrast inevitably exaggerates, but we can reasonably describe most parts of western Europe in the Middle Ages as societies that were religious and the same places today as societies that are largely secular but contain some religious people. Britain in the thirteenth century was a Christian society. The cosmology supposed a divine creator and heaven and hell as alternative destinations for the godly and the ungodly. The Church was an immensely powerful social institution that played a significant role in every aspect of public life. People lived their lives to the rhythm of the Christian calendar and were reminded of that when the Church intervened at points that were significant for the individual (birth, marriage and death) or for the community (the changes of the seasons, the crowning of a new monarch or the blessing of a new commercial enterprise). Although not always Christian in a manner the Church desired, most people were religious to an extent and in a taken-for-granted manner now difficult to imagine. But their piety was *secondary*; a symptom of the community's culture rather than the cause of it. All the changes described in chapter 1 shift the onus for maintaining the momentum of religion from the economy, the polity and the society to the families and voluntary associations of pious individuals.

In an increasingly secular world the vitality of religion comes to rest very directly on the commitments of individuals and, as I argued in chapter 4, those commitments are a social matter. Hence, in trying to understand secularization we need to attend to a consideration that is often neglected and that is specifically rejected as significant by the rational choice or 'supply-side' approach to religion promoted by Rodney Stark and his associates. That model uses two focal lengths. One concentrates on the structure of the religious market and asserts that religious vitality depends on the degree of regulation of producers of religious goods and the extent to which one firm dominates; it is too long. The other views religious behaviour as the outcome of choices made by unconstrained autonomous individuals seeking to maximize utility; it is too short. Though each illuminates interesting aspects of the picture, even when they are combined they distort because they lead us to overlook the role of *social interaction* and *social organization*.

The theme of this chapter appears frequently elsewhere in this book. It has been separated out and presented here for a number of reasons. First, it is central to my understanding of the secularization paradigm. Secondly, it is often the root cause of differences with my colleagues over just how secular are such countries as Britain or Holland. Thirdly, it is also a major cause of my unusually pessimistic views of the future of religion in modern societies. By treating it as a topic in its own right, I hope to clarify the argument and thus make it more likely that, instead of talking past each other, the proponents of the secularization paradigm and their critics can concentrate on an issue that will divide them to some useful purpose.

Vignettes

What I plan to do is present a number of very brief vignettes (some from examples discussed elsewhere in this book) and then draw out the underlying principle.

Church schools

When the Church of Scotland handed control of its schools to the state in 1872, it did not insist on legal safeguards for their religious ethos and settled for an assurance that religious education would continue on the basis of locally determined 'want and usage'. The minority Catholic Church refused to accept that settlement and did not accept state funding until the 1918 Education Act gave it a framework that ensured church control over staff appointments and school management. The majority Presbyterians did not demand such safeguards because they assumed that their schools would continue to reflect the religious ethos of their surrounding environments. Unfortunately, they did: as the general climate became more and more secular, so did the schools.

The New Churches

The British 'house-church' movement, which is considered in detail in chapter 9, began in the 1970s as a radical alternative to the perceived laxity of the mainstream churches and the dull conformity of the evangelical alternatives. Thirty years later, many strands of the movement had become indistinguishable from the churches that its founding members abandoned.

Signs and symbols

The schism of Scottish Presbyterianism in 1843 led to the creation of two vigorously competing national organizations. A very large part of the population took sides. The ferocity of the dispute and the considerable sacrifices entailed encouraged the striking of clear ideological postures. As that generation passed away, interest in doctrinal differences declined rapidly and by the end of the century fragmentation had given way to merger and reunion. Once doctrine ceased to be an effective source of identity, two small but significant compromises started to become popular with Presbyterian clergy. To demonstrate to an increasingly indifferent population that they were 'religious', ministers started to wear clerical collars and they added the names of saints to the mundane geographical labels of their congregations.

Commerce and tradition

When Eastern religious themes and therapies were introduced into Britain at the end of the twentieth century, they were quickly simplified, secularized and commodified (see chapter 6). When Ayurvedic medicine attracted the attention of some celebrities and hence the mass media, a national chain of shops selling cosmetics and toiletries produced its own brand of Ayurvedic products.

The Gay Quakers

In the late eighteenth century, the Barclay banking family were pious Quakers. David Barclay, the founder, was the great-grandson of Robert Barclay, the famous Quaker apologist. David's grandson, Robert Barclay of Clapham (1758–1816), was active in Wilberforce's philanthropic enterprises (see chapter 4). The family's evangelical Quakerism was reinforced by marriage and business alliances with other Quaker bankers (the Gurneys, Trittons and Backhouses), and in the nineteenth century three generations of banking Barclays served as treasurers of missionary societies and assorted agencies for religious causes. As they prospered, their social circle expanded and their commitment to the Society of Friends shrank. Robert Barclay (1843–1921) was expelled for 'marrying out'. His wife was Elizabeth Buxton. Her grandfather, Thomas Fowell Buxton, was an associate of Wilberforce who acted as treasurer for a host of evangelical and philanthropic agencies, including the British and Foreign Bible Society and the London City Mission. He was knighted for his services to philanthropy. Elizabeth's nephew, the 4th baronet, was President of the Anti-Slavery Society and treasurer of the Church Missionary Society and the YMCA.

Some lines of the family continued to be committed evangelicals, even after their shift to the Church of England. Elizabeth Buxton's brother was 'born again' at a Keswick holiness convention in 1885 and his four sons all became missionaries. But her children were much more conventional in their Christianity. Robert Leatham Barclay (1869–1937) inherited the position of treasurer of the Church Missionary Society along with the bank job, but he was a firm supporter of those who led the Student Christian Movement away from its evangelical roots. Her daughter married an evangelical Anglican cleric, a grandson of the great Quaker prison reformer Elizabeth Fry. Their son, Robin Woods, was a liberal Anglican who became a bishop in 1971.

A substantial minority

In the 1950s English Catholics were distinctly more observant than Protestants. They were also distinctive. Now they are indistinguishable from everyone else. They no longer have to forgo eating and drinking on Christmas Eve in order to receive Holy Communion at midnight Mass. They no longer have to decline meat on Fridays. Holy days of obligation are no longer disruptive. There has been 'a large measure of convergence to the norms of the wider society in such matters as contraception and divorce, though to a lesser extent abortion' (Hornsby-Smith 1999: 294). Catholics are now much more likely to make friends with non-Catholics; only a third of marriages that involve one Catholic involve two.

Table 7.1   Indicators of English Catholic vitality, 1960s and 1990s

Indices	1960s	1990s
Mass attendances (000)	2,000	1,100
Child baptisms (000)	134	75
Receptions/conversions (000)	15	6
Confirmations (000)	81	46
Marriages (000)	46	17
Proportion of Catholic marriages that involve two Catholics (%)	50	33

Source: Hornsby-Smith (1999: 294).

Catholic attitudes to their Church have changed. Up to the 1950s 'Catholics differentiated relatively little between creedal beliefs, non-creedal beliefs such as papal infallibility, teaching on moral issues, and disciplinary rules in a strongly rule-bound and guilt-ridden Church' (Hornsby-Smith 1999: 297). Now they make up their own minds about non-creedal matters and show an increasingly selective attitude to the creed also.

Largely as a result of Irish migration, the number of Catholics in England grew steadily and peaked in the 1960s, as did all indicators of religious vitality. Table 7.1 summarizes a number of changes and the message is clear. Four things coincide: English Catholics became more like their neighbours in their behaviour; they mixed with and married outside the confession; they rejected the authority of the Church; and their church attendance declined to the English norm.

A communitarian sect

The Amish are descendants of the Swiss Anabaptists of the sixteenth century (Hostetler and Huntington 1971). Between 1693 and 1697 one wing of the Mennonite movement, led by Jacob Amman, developed a number of distinctive ritual practices (such as foot-washing before communion services) and became more and more socially exclusive, gradually separating itself off from those who did not share its beliefs and behaviour in every detail. The Amish moved to Pennsylvania in the middle of the eighteenth century, where they formed isolated residential farming communities. Those communities have survived to this day. Although Amish families regularly lose a few of their children (often in a two-stage process: first to less rigorously separated

Mennonite congregations and then to the mainstream), their large family size and the various social devices for remaining isolated (such as continuing to use their original language and dress styles) have allowed them to sustain their communities and prosper. Their 'teaching forbids the Amishman from marrying a non-Amish person or from entering into a business partnership with persons outside the ceremonial community' (Hostetler and Huntington 1971: 5). At the heart of their social reproduction is the shunning of members who transgress.

> The practice of shunning among the Swiss Mennonites was to exclude the offender from communion. A more emphatic practice was advanced by Jacob Amman. His interpretation required shunning excommunicated persons not only at communion but also in social and economic life. Shunning means that members may receive no favors from an excommunicated person, that they may not buy or sell to an excommunicated person, and that no member shall eat at the same table with an excommunicated person. If the person under a ban is a husband or wife, the couple is to suspend their marital relations until the erring member is restored to the church fellowship. (Hostetler and Huntington 1971: 7)

The moral

There is nothing terribly subtle or original about the point being made with the above snapshots. Belief systems exist within a wider culture and society. They compete for attention with other beliefs. The people who carry them have other lives and other interests. Distinctive beliefs are sometimes directly challenged – as, for example, when pacifists are required to serve in the armed forces or when sectarians who object to blood transfusions find the courts supporting doctors who wish to impose treatment on their children. But a much bigger problem is that they are constantly threatened with being submerged by the surrounding culture.

There is push and pull. With motives ranging from sincere admiration to a cynical desire to exploit for profit, agents outside the culture can take elements of the belief-system, free them from the context that made them arduous or implausible, and present them to a wider audience. Just as Elvis Presley and Eric Clapton took black music, watered it down, and sold it to white people, so a cosmetics retailer can turn a complex Indian healing tradition into a soap range and interior design shops can sell ceramic Buddhas and Hindu Gods.

There is also push from within. The integrity of cultural packages is threatened by the desire of adherents to accommodate to the wider society. As with the Gay Quakers, ordinary adherents may dilute their witness to win greater social acceptance. The Niebuhr and Michels theses (see pp. 23–5) point to the particular tensions that cause officials of radical movements to wish to reduce the degree of tension between their organization and the wider society. I should stress that, in both cases, people can act for the best of motives. Although the accommodation story is usually told with a hint of cynicism, the advocates of compromise may be driven primarily by a desire to expand the audience for their distinctive revelation. What to the outsider may seem like 'sell out' may to the actor be an honest desire to preserve what can be saved. In the 1850s, the English Quakers offered a prize for the best essay on the decline in their numbers. It was won by Joseph Rowntree (of the York chocolate family) for his *Quakerism: Past and Present*, which repeated the case he made eloquently to the Yearly Meeting: peculiarities that were not essential to the faith were driving away members. He was particularly critical of 'unreasonable requirements respecting matters of behaviour and attire' that 'had alienated the affections of many young persons from the Society of Friends, and induced them to leave on attaining years of maturity' (in D. M. Thompson 1972: 165). But his diagnosis of decline had a special place for the Society's marriage regulations, which required the removal of members who 'married out': 'Within a considerable portion of the present century, the Society of Friends in England has disowned nearly one-third of all its members who have married, a total of not less than four thousand persons!' (in D. M. Thompson 1972: 165). And as Rowntree pointed out, that meant the loss of their children also. Rowntree eventually won the argument. Requirements were relaxed. But the decline continued.

When the medium first became available, US pentecostalists denounced television as the work of Satan, but pentecostal preachers soon realized its value to evangelism. In his first series of programmes in the late 1950s, the well-known faith healer Oral Roberts delivered a short sermon direct to the camera and then showed footage of his tent rallies. In the mid-1960s, after a few years' absence from television, Roberts returned with a new kind of show designed to make the most of the medium. Filmed in the NBC studios in Burbank, California, it used the same crew as the extremely popular *Rowan and Martin's Laugh-In* and an announcer from the cast of *Bonanza*. It featured light breezy music, a roster of well-known celebrity guests and choirs of attractive young people. Many pentecostalists denounced this as supping with the Devil, but Roberts had the audience figures to prove that imitating the secular world was allowing him to address millions of people with the saving message of Jesus.

We need not impute self-interest or greed to those who moderate the faith in which they were raised. Indeed, the principle stands perfectly well without making any judgements about the motives of the individuals involved. We need appreciate only that any distinctive belief-system and associated cultural package are vulnerable to being sucked into the mainstream.

If a metaphor would help, perhaps the most apposite is of a garden. To be kept free of weeds, for its plants to retain their shape and character, and for the original planting pattern to remain visible, a domestic garden must be regularly tended. Left to its own devices, it will quickly revert to a state of nature. It must also be protected against admirers who lift the plants out of their native soil and take them home.

A religion is a distinctive cultural product. To be sustained and kept intact, it must be cultivated and guarded. When it is very widely shared and thoroughly embedded in everyday life and in powerful social institutions, there is little danger it will disappear (though, to pursue the garden metaphor, gardeners may argue about which plants to favour and what layouts to adopt). The problem arises when the surrounding society is becoming secular.

We can see four things in the vignettes: religious observance decaying, unusual beliefs being abandoned, once-important behavioural marks of membership being dropped, and the boundary between the community of the faithful and the rest of the world being eroded. Notice my reluctance to specify the direction of cause. Did the Gay Quakers lose their faith because their pleasure in the company of worldly people caused them to adopt their manners, or were they able to mix with the worldly only because they had already lost conviction in their distinctive beliefs? Did English Catholics reject the rule of the Catholic Church because, as David Lodge supposes, they ceased to believe in a hell to which the Church could condemn them for disobedience or did the more frequent mixing on equal terms with non-Catholics erode their commitment to the Church and thus give them the confidence to reject one of its central doctrines? The correct answer of course is 'both'.

Deep socialization and constant reaffirmation are required to sustain distinctive beliefs. When these are not provided by the community or the society, then they must be provided by the family and the faithful must form supportive associations to ensure that the basic requirements for a pleasant life are provided within a context that strengthens the bonds between the godly and prevents them being drawn into positive relationships with those outside the tent. In addition, there must be mechanisms to resolve the tensions that inevitably arise in the life of any group and to prevent the particular quarrels that arise when the faithful come to differing interpretations of God's will leading to fragmentation and schism.

Any belief-system at odds with the prevailing culture is in the position of a cultivated garden in the midst of a wilderness. It requires fences and it requires gardeners. As the wilderness grows and the size of the cultivated area shrinks, the gardeners need to work harder and the fences need to be made higher and stronger.

However, as I argued in chapter 4, we cannot think of the social requirements for maintaining deviant belief-systems in isolation from the belief-system itself. Beliefs differ systematically in their potential to justify mechanisms of social control. The human capacity for selective attention, inconsistency and hypocrisy allows the individual liberal to be dogmatic and authoritarian, but belief-systems that rest on such foundations as 'There is more than one way to God' and 'We cannot be sure what is right' cannot for long sustain effective control mechanisms. Hence certain sorts of belief (in particular those that are most influenced by modern notions of egalitarianism and toleration) are bound to regress to the mean, to be absorbed into the surrounding culture.

A further vital consideration can be seen if we consider the limits to the garden-versus-wilderness metaphor and the example of the Old Order Amish of Pennsylvania. The metaphor assumes that the threat to the cultivated area is only that of the natural forces of proliferation and cross-breeding. Of course, a more apt elaboration of the metaphor would suppose that the wilderness has its own promoters who loosen the nails of the fences and insert their own species into the cultivated areas.

Societies vary in their willingness to allow minorities to sustain their deviant beliefs. Such communitarian sects as the Amish, the Hutterites and the Doukobhors were able to survive in the New World because the wide-open spaces gave them literal space while the federalism of the emerging polity allowed them the social space in which to continue to live by rules not shared by the majority. Many other societies were and would be considerably less hospitable. Even where there is no conscious commitment to obliterate diversity, smallness, population density and the political ethos of a state may combine to make life difficult for ideological minorities. Britain, for example, has for a very long time been indifferent to religious deviation, but for a variety of very different reasons (its size, population density, mass mobilization in two world wars) it has evolved a highly centralized polity and system of public administration. With little conscious desire to do so, it very effectively prevents minorities creating the subsocieties that could sustain distinctive subcultures.

It is important not to be misled on this point by the important observation already made in chapters 1, 4, and 6 (and made again at the very end of the book) about the increasing individualism of modern societies. That a society operates increasingly on the assumption of the autonomy of the individual and that its culture stresses lifestyles and choices and options and preferences does not necessarily mean that it will permit groups of people to withdraw sufficiently to sustain a distinctive collective way of life. On the contrary, promoting the rights of individuals is often at odds with allowing freedom to subcultures. When Western education systems teach that in matters of religion children have a right to make up their own minds about what they will believe, they are denying to communities the right to impose their beliefs upon their offspring. When Western laws insist that women and men must enjoy equal rights, they are denying to communities that wish to maintain traditional gender divisions of labour the right to sustain their notion of what God requires. When Western governments prefer freedom of speech to blasphemy laws, they are putting individual rights before the right of faith communities not to have their beliefs insulted.

To summarize, I am suggesting that to understand fully the fate of religion in the liberal democracies of the modern societies we must appreciate the power of the tendency to regress to the mean. The various snapshots of success and failure presented above offer powerful and instructive examples of the importance of social organization in maintaining distinctive belief-systems and ways of life. The colleagues with whom I differ about the future of religion in the West are, I believe, being misled by their failure to appreciate two things. First, diffuse beliefs of the sort we see in liberal Christianity and New

Age spirituality (the denominational and cultic forms of religion) cannot sustain the forms of social organization that can act as a bulwark against secularization. Secondly, the ethos of the modern society (individual autonomy, social and cultural diversity, practical relativism) is a uniquely hostile environment for any minority belief-system.

CHAPTER EIGHT

Subsistence Religion

Introduction

Most attempts to explain differences in the power, presence and popularity of religion between and within societies have concentrated on variations in demand. Some elements of the secularization paradigm (the Niebuhr and Michels theses, for example) concern the behaviour of religious organizations, but most try to explain why people differ in their desire, need or willingness to believe. Since the 1970s there has been an alternative that eschews talk of demand in favour of observations about supply. In their theory of religion, Rodney Stark and William Bainbridge (1985, 1987) argue that there are aspects of the human condition (essentially the scarcity of 'rewards') that mean people are always in the market for 'compensators'. As religion is able to invoke the supernatural, it is superior to secular philosophies and therapies in the supply of such compensators. The meek can be promised the earth in the next life. Hence the demand for religion should be high and stable. If that is the case, then the large variations we see in the rates of church attendance, church membership and other indices of interest in religion must reflect differences in the supply side of the equation.

In his association with Roger Finke and Laurence Iannaccone, Stark has since gone further in elaborating a supply-side theory of religious behaviour. Taking as his paradigm the supposed virtues of the free market in meeting and stimulating needs for such consumer goods as cars, Stark argues that differences in religious vitality (usually measured by church membership or church attendance) can be explained by features of the structure of the religious 'economy'. Where there is a free and competitive market, religion will flourish. Where one supplier of religious goods dominates the market, religious vitality will be low. This will especially be the case if the unevenness in market share is a result of state regulation (Iannaccone 1991; Finke and Stark 1992; Finke and Iannaccone 1993).

The supply-side model has been subject to considerable testing. Finke, Stark and Iannaccone find much evidence to support it; most sociologists remain unpersuaded. Chaves and Gorski (2001) summarize all the published responses and conclude that the approach is not well founded. In *Choice and Religion* (Bruce 1999), I offer a very detailed critique of the application of economistic approaches to human behaviour to religion. Here I want to consider just one element of the supply-side logic: the purported passivity of the laity. For a lack of supply to explain low levels of involvement and participation, it must be the case that people cannot engage in 'subsistence' religion by meeting their own demands. I hope to show that this assumption is mistaken. Furthermore, to explain why the incidence of subsistence religion varies, we must consider three things that are largely absent from the economistic sociology of the supply-siders: the nature of the religious tradition in question, the level of social development and the extent of freedom in the most general sense.

The defects of state churches

At the heart of the supply-side approach is the belief that lack of competition (especially when it results from the state regulation of religion) depresses religious vitality for a variety of reasons: scarcity, unpopularity, and clerical sloth.

Whether it can sustain a general explanation of variations in piety is another matter, but there is an obvious connection between the provision of religious offices and their uptake. Crockett's work (1998) on the England and Wales Census of Religious Worship of 1851, pioneering in its statistical sophistication, shows the lowest rates of church attendance in the most urban and the most remote rural parishes. The first finding fits secularization expectations. The second is explained by the paucity of population and the great distance from churches. Where churches are few and very far between, many people will be unable to attend. If new churches are built between the existing ones (rather, than as often happens with inter-sect competition, right next to them), more people can become involved in church life. The same point can be accepted for particular classes of events. If people wish to take communion more often than it is presently offered, increasing the frequency of communion will increase the uptake. Hence competition between churches may raise the levels of church involvement.

A second general class of problem for a dominant or state church is the unpopularity that may come from association with the ruling class. The nineteenth-century French traveller Alexis de Toqueville noted the contrast between the vitality of religious life in America's competing sects and the stagnation of the Catholic Church in France, and supposed that the Catholic Church was unpopular because it was associated with the politics of the *Ancien Régime* (de Toqueville 1945). David Martin has made the same point about the Church of England in the eighteenth and nineteenth century (1969: 122). In both cases the close association between the clergy and the ruling class caused large sections of the laity to attach their dislike of their rulers to the clergy they controlled and then generalize it into a dislike of religion as such.

Although the unpopular regime is very different, we can see something similar with a variety of churches under twentieth-century communist regimes. The Russian Orthodox Church, the Lutheran Church in the German Democratic Republic, and the Georgian Orthodox Church were largely co-opted by unpopular states and themselves became unpopular by association.

A third set of defects can be grouped under the heading of clerical sloth. The security of tenure and income enjoyed by state-funded clergy may reduce any incentive to attract a congregation, or having got one, to keep it. Stark says 'the German clergy are better off with empty churches, which place little demand on their time, than with full ones' (1997: 185). Before its nineteenth-century reforms, the Church of England had many 'pluralists' who took the income attached to several jobs and did none of them, instead paying curates to do their work for them.

All of these observations have a certain intuitive appeal, but detailed knowledge of the histories of particular churches and particular regulatory regimes should lead us to question their limits. For example, a near-complete absence of competition does not seem to have harmed the Catholic Church in Poland, Lithuania or Ireland. A more subtle point is that Protestant state churches differ in important details of their establishment. It is not enough to contrast those clergy dependent on their congregations for income from those not. We would also want to know how clergy are appointed, how remuneration is fixed and how occupational status is determined. We have plenty of evidence that the eighteenth-century Church of England was stuffed with placemen and that toadying to the gentry who controlled the lucrative livings and to the senior church officials who controlled cathedral posts was common. The following description is partisan but nonetheless widely applicable:

> Unbelieving bishops and a slothful clergy had succeeded in driving from the Church the faith and zeal of Methodism. . . . That was the age when jobbery and corruption, long supreme in the State, had triumphed over the virtue of the Church; when the money changers not only entered the temple but drove out the worshippers; when ecclesiastical revenues were monopolised by wealthy pluralists; when the name of curate lost its legal meaning and instead of denoting the incumbent of a benefice came to signify the deputy of an absentee; when church services were discontinued; when university exercises were turned into a farce; when the holders of ancient endowments vied with one another in avoiding the intentions of their founders. . . . In their preaching nineteen clergy-men out of twenty carefully abstained from dwelling upon Christian doctrines. Such topics exposed the preacher to the charge of fanaticism.
> (Coneybeare 1853: 274)

George Eliot's Mr Gilfil, who preached short sermons and smoked long pipes, performing his spiritual functions 'with an undeviating attention to brevity and dispatch', seems to have been an example of the better sort of Anglican cleric (Wolff 1977: 227). But the influences on the clergy may be more complex. The Presbyterian Church of Scotland was (and still is in name, though not in funding) a state church. However, for most of its history the clergy were selected by their congregation and thus should have been responsive to their interests. Also, since the early eighteenth century many urban Church of Scotland churches charged pew rent and the clergy and church managers thus had an interest in being popular: the more pews rented out, the greater the income (Brown 1987b). Yet, for the same organization and within the same formal structure of state regulation, many clergy had a good reason to mollify the local lairds because, as the 'heritors', they paid most of the costs and made decisions about the erection and mainten-ance of churches, manses and schoolhouses. In principle, church bodies such as presbyteries could compel heritors to meet their obligations, but, as such disputes could drag on for decades, the heritors were better woed than coerced. At some times and in some places, the heritors also had the major say in selecting the minister. So it is no surprise that we find many rural ministers supporting unpopular landlords (such as those who evicted the surplus peasantry from their highlands estates to make way for sheep during the late-eighteenth- and early-nineteenth-century 'clearances'). However, and this is the sort of detail

Stark overlooks, security of tenure gave some protection to those ministers who were willing to criticize the lairds.

In brief, there is considerable sense in many supply-side observations, and they are as likely to be made by secularization theorists. But it does not follow that they can provide the basis for a coherent theory of religion. Apart from the particular problems raised above, there is one very large difficulty: the assumption that ordinary people are unable to compensate for deficiencies of supply. The latent demand for religion is taken to be constant. State regulatory regimes control supply. Failures of supply lead to demand being unmet and explain why some societies are less religious than others. But, if latent demand is not met because the dominant church fails to provide the opportunity, is loathed, or is staffed by sloths, why do people not make their own provision?

The supply-side explanation of inactivity

The supply-side model contains a number of answers to that question. First, what the state provides may be good enough partially to meet need but not good enough to generate enthusiastic commitment. Or, to put it the other way round, we may suppose some implicit threshold of dissatisfaction: the state church may not be so bad as to trigger lay initiatives while not being so good as to create a vibrant religious culture. Secondly, that many people will already have paid for the state's provision through taxes discourages them from paying a second time to do it themselves. Thirdly, as well as having raised the costs of auto-provision (by making people pay for the state church through taxes), the state may impose further penalties on those who dissent.

I will illustrate the above three observations with the case of independent Christian schools in Northern Ireland. Northern Ireland has a state school system and a Catholic school system. As it did in England and Scotland, the Catholic Church refused to accept the state schools because they were Protestant. Since the 1970s a number of ministers of the Free Presbyterian Church of Ulster, impressed by the US example, have established their own independent Christian schools. Being committed evangelicals they reject the state system because, though it may be 'Protestant' in the ethnic sense, it is certainly not evangelical and arguably not Christian.

However, although Free Presbyterians are thoroughly sectarian in their religion and entirely accept the argument that the state schools either are secular or, worse, actively promote liberal ecumenism, relatively few Free Presbyterian families send their children to the church's schools. My interviews with Free Presbyterians on both sides of the debate suggest that their reasoning is influenced by the three considerations listed above. The state schools are not what they would wish but they are not so bad that their deficiencies cannot be compensated for by a pious culture at home. Parents have already paid for the state schools through their taxes and do not wish to incur the additional costs of supporting a parallel system; they would rather spend the money on other sorts of church work. Thirdly, although the state does not imprison parents who do not send their children to state schools, it sets and enforces high standards for private provision that inflate its costs.

At first sight this seems strong support for the supply-side model. But if we look more closely we see a number of problems in applying this to the auto-provision of religion. Consider costs. At least since the professionalization of education in the nineteenth century, it has been considerably more expensive to provide schooling than to create a dissenting religion. I will say more about different sorts of religion below, but within the radical Protestant tradition subsistence religion is virtually free. If you do not require a professional full-time clergy and consecrated buildings, the costs of meeting your own demands for religion are negligible. Consider legal constraints on auto-provision. Since the second half of the nineteenth century, most European countries have codified standards for public schooling and enforced them. At the same time, most countries have abandoned the legal harassment of religious dissenters. In Britain there have been very few effective restrictions on religious dissent since the eighteenth century. But, as this allows us to raise the question again, even when there were penal codes, they did little to deter the radical sects of the Civil War period, the Quakers in the eighteenth, or the Methodists in the nineteenth centuries.

The conclusion must be that the answers given by the supply-side model to the problem of why latent demand is not met by auto-provision are insufficient. The fact is that the history of Christianity in Europe shows frequent lay challenges to the dominant churches. Regimes differed in their responses. In some countries dissenters were put to the sword or exiled (the French Huguenots). In some they were merely driven from the state churches (the English Methodists). In others, they were tolerated as factions within the state churches (the Awakened, the Laestadians and the Supplicationists in Finland).

That in 1851 about half of those people who attended worship in Britain did so in organizations other than the state churches shows that dissent was commonplace. Once we appreciate that, we can re-phrase our problem in comparative terms. Why is auto-provision more common in some places than in others, even when the regime of state regulation of religion is apparently similar?

The explanation lies in two areas neglected by the supply-side model: the nature of the religious tradition in question and general levels of social development.

The religion in question

One of the weaknesses of the rational-choice approach is that it is so taken with the contrast between state religion (bad) and free market (good) that it gives little or no attention to differences within the former. The nature of religion rarely features in the considerations of Stark, Finke and Iannaccone and when it does it is almost always as a subsidiary observation intruded to explain why their predications have not been met by their evidence. Thus Finke (1992: 160) ex-plains the unexpected success of the Catholic Church in US cities by noting that the Church is internally diverse. Even more damaging for what purports to be a universally applicable theory of human beha-viour, Iannaccone admits that 'Protestant church attendance rates are strongly related to market structure but Catholic rates are largely independent of it' (1991: 169). But beyond these *ad hoc* intrusions there is no systematic consideration of confessional, denominational and sectarian differences.

Yet, as soon as we ask what stops people who feel remote from the state-supported church making their own provision, it becomes obvi-ous that confession is the major consideration. Ease of dissent de-pends on two core considerations: how one gains access to the truth and what one must do to attain life after death.

Within Christianity there is a major difference between, at the two extremes, the democratic epistemology of radical Protestantism and the exclusive epistemology of the Catholic Church. Protestants believe that with the aid of the Holy Spirit anyone can, by reading the Bible, discern the will of God. Even within those Protestant traditions that maintain a professional trained clergy, ordination is not held to give any particularly privileged access to the will of God. A lack of confidence may prevent the typical Presbyterian layman from asserting that his understanding of scripture is as good as his minister's, but there is nothing in the core of Protestant theology that socializes Protestants into passivity. The open access to the truth explains why Protestantism has so often fragmented into competing factions and schismatic groups. The ability of the Catholic to dissent is far more constrained. Any form of Christianity that holds to some notion of an apostolic succession, that there is some crucial property that was bequeathed by Christ to one or more of his disciples and then passed down in orderly fashion, is relatively immune to fragmentation. Of course, it remains possible for large numbers of Catholics to depart from Rome and to insist that they possess that quality; hence the divisions in the Middle Ages, and the national departures from Vatican authority. But these have generally involved large numbers of Catholics with some plausible element of hierarchical support and have had more to do with national politics and international relations than with the individual's lack of satisfaction that lies at the heart of the supply-side model.

The second major variable is the religion's beliefs about what one must do to be saved. Those religions that stress right belief and a correct 'walk with the Lord' – orthodoxy and ethical discipline – lack the constraint on dissent provided in more ritualistic religions by the need to have a properly ordained official to perform the required rituals in the correct manner. The belief that only certain people can provide what is needed to ensure access to heaven or early release from limbo is a serious obstacle to auto-supply.

Social development

The second element of the explanation for variation in auto-provision can be found simply by considering, from any number of times and places, which countries had the greatest amount of dissent and, within any country, which social groups remained within the national or hegemonic church and which became religious dissidents. Of course the relationship is not simple (in part because it involves the previous point about the nature of religion), but we can note some connection between industrialization and dissent. It was common in England and rare in France, Spain or Greece. Despite the Old Believer movement (which in places was closer to the ethnic and national schisms of Catholicism than to the class-based dissent of England), the Russian Orthodox Church remained hegemonic.

We can consider patterns of dissent within particular countries. In the north-east of Ireland in the eighteenth and nineteenth centuries,

Protestants divided between the Episcopal and state-established Church of Ireland and the Presbyterian Church and they did so on lines that had much to do with class. The rising middle class and the skilled working class of Belfast and the independent small farmers of North Antrim and East Londonderry were likely to be Presbyterians. The farm servants and small tenants of the big estates were Church of Ireland – the religion of their masters. Of sixteenth-century France, Houston has written: 'Protestantism was a minority faith, concentrated in towns such as Toulouse and La Rochelle, drawing its adherents disproportionately from the middling ranks of society' (1988: 149). He goes on to cite Davis's even more specific connection of occupational status and dissent: 'A printer, a goldsmith, or a barber-surgeon was more likely to disobey a priest and doctors of theology than a boot-maker, a butcher or a baker' (in Houston 1988: 149).

The same point can be made about the rise of religious dissent in eighteenth-century Scotland. As the foremost historians of Presbyterianism put it, the Seceders recruited 'the responsible and the convinced while the parish churches drew the poor and dependent' (Drummond and Bulloch 1973: 118). In pre-Reformation England, Lollardy appears to have been more common in London and the affluent south-east than in the rest of England. Among the Lollards, 'tradesmen and craftsmen seem to have been more numerous than husbandmen, and there was a handful of merchants and professional men from the towns, especially London. Their social background was similar to the dissenters of the seventeenth century' (Harrison 1984: 159). The Puritan divine Richard Baxter noted that his supporters contained a high number of master weavers, men whose trade 'allowed them time enough to read or talk of holy things . . . and as they stand in their loom they can set a book before them or edify one another' (Harrison 1984: 192).

It would be unwise to suppose that most chose sides in the English Civil War on religious preferences (or even that many chose as distinct from simply being enlisted by their masters), but there was an obvious social basis to allegiances. Of the Levellers, one of the most radical groups on the Parliament side, it is said 'socially they were the small men, economically they were the typical independent producers' (Harrison 1984: 198).

Obelkevitch says of Methodism: 'Though winning few converts among the rich or the very poor, it was attractive to the cottagers, miners, artisans, small tradesmen and shopkeepers who were becoming more numerous in the early stages of industrial growth' (1990: 324). Part of the appeal of Methodism was that it allowed social protest: it 'enabled the common people to declare their independence of squire and parson, to show that as far as fervour, morality and self-respect were concerned, they were the equal or superior of any gentleman' (1990: 325).

The point hardly needs to be laboured. In eleventh-century England the bulk of the population were peasants and most of them were 'villeins': unfree or servile tenants. They literally belonged to their lord. They had no right of migration and could be sold with the land. At death, the lord could claim the villein's best beast as 'heriot', a death duty that was often 50 per cent of capital. As the villein and his offspring (usually referred to with the Latin for 'litter' rather than 'family') were the property of the lord, there was an array of penalties for the lord's loss of future labour. If a girl married without permission, the father could be fined. Marriages off the manor were originally viewed as null by the Church. Later they were accepted as legitimate but a fine had to be paid to recompense the lord for the loss of his possession. Widows could be compelled to marry at the lord's will and fined for marrying without it. Where peasants were not allowed to own their own bodies, it is no surprise that they were not permitted religious liberty. In eighteenth-century Poland, where serfs could be sold, some sales 'were made on the condition, insisted upon by the church, that the serfs had to remain Catholic. If they did not, the seller had the right to demand back his serfs' (Blum 1978: 42).

Economic oppression had its corollary in the psyche. The mental state of the oppressed peasantry of Europe east of the Elbe in the eighteenth and early nineteenth centuries is well described by the wide variety of contemporary commentators cited by Blum. An English diplomat said of the peasants of the Danube Principalities in 1820: 'Accustomed to the state of servitude which to others might appear intolerable, they are unable to form hopes for a better condition; the habitual depression of their minds has become a sort of national stupor and apathy, which render them equally indifferent to the enjoyment of life, and insensible to happiness, as to the pangs of anguish and affliction' (Blum 1978: 47–8). When servile peasants did revolt, as they periodically did, their concerns were always material rather than ideological and had at their heart some very specific economic grievance. The most common form of resistances, however, were sloth and alcoholism.

In the context of Europe as a whole, the English peasants were among the first to gain their freedom. Whereas in 1300 the majority of peasants were villeins, by 1500 very few were still servile. Of course, restrictions remained, which is why, 300 years later, the Methodist movement recruited better from free villages than from villages that were owned by a single estate. Nonetheless we can see the contrast if we appreciate that the Russian serfs were not granted the same formal freedoms under 1861.

An important cause and indicator of individual autonomy was literacy – an essential requirement for independence of mind and dissenting political action. Estimates vary, but as late as the seventeenth century 65 per cent of English yeoman farmers and 56 per cent of tradesmen and craftsmen could read but only 21 per cent of husbandmen and 15 per cent of labourers could write their names (Harrison 1984: 164). Even in the second half of the nineteenth century, the bulk of the peasantry of southern and eastern Europe were illiterate.

The Men

The Scottish highlands in the late eighteenth and nineteenth centuries offer an interesting case study in the links between social status and religious dissent. The Reformation in Scotland was popular and thoroughgoing in the lowlands, but its impact on the highlands was patchy. The Scottish clan system was the English feudal manor with the added element of military service. Where the chief remained Catholic or Episcopalian, his people followed. There was a supply-side element to the slow conversion of the highlands. The terrain made provision of any service difficult and costly. Although the national parish structure nominally encompassed the entire country, the difficulty of serving the highlands can be simply illustrated by observing that the parish of Ardnamurchan was ninety miles wide and possessed no metalled roads. The national Church had the further difficulty of providing enough trained clergy who could speak Gaelic. We can also find many examples of inattentive and slothful clergy. Many 'regarded the difficulties of their situation not as spurs to action but as convenient excuses for doing nothing' (J. Hunter 1978: 29). Many ministers depended on farming their glebe lands for income, but some took the injunction to be shepherds rather too literally. John Skeldoch, the Minster of Farr (1732–1751) who rented three large farms, repeatedly ignored injunctions from the Presbytery of Tongue to attend more to his spiritual duties. The Synod of Caithness judged that he 'seems to be obstinately determined to entangle himself with worldly

affairs and to have no regard to the command of the [Presbytery]'
(McInnes 1951: 107). The minister of Applecross celebrated communion only four times in twenty years, kept a boat for his fishing, and
'has a considerable land property and money stocked otherwise' (McKay
1980: 4). It is said of the minister of Duthill that he had only two
sermons but for variety changed the passages of scripture that were
a pretext for them. As an aside, we might note from the Caithness
Synod's criticism of Skeldoch that, however common was inattentive-
ness to duty, it was not tolerated by the clergy in general.

Yet between 1700 and 1850 the religious culture of the highlands
was so transformed that in all the theological schisms of the nineteenth century the highlands came out on the Calvinist evangelical
side. By the middle of the twentieth century, when the lowlands were
either secular or liberal in their Presbyterianism, the highlands and
islands were the strongholds of conservative orthodoxy.

That transformation had clear social and economic roots. The conversion of the highlands coincided with the collapse of the old social
order. The failure of the Jacobite project to restore the Stewarts to the
throne and the imposition of Hanoverian law and order made it
pointless to maintain large armies of dependent clansmen. Clan chiefs
started to see themselves as landlords and their lands as estates to be
managed for personal profit. The result was the clearance of the
peasants to make way first for sheep, later for deer walks. With their
physical dislocation, the peasants also suffered a socio-psychological
dislocation very similar to that of the twentieth-century Latin Americans leaving their haciendas for the cities (D. Martin 1990). The collapse
of their old world put the highland peasants in the market for a new
worldview, one that would make sense of their sufferings and allow
them to blame their masters, but that would also equip them with the
persona required to survive in the new circumstances. For Latin
Americans in the 1970s, Pentecostalism provided the solution. For the
highlanders of the late eighteenth century, it was a Calvinist evangelicalism tinged with heavy millenarian expectations.

We can find a de Toquevillian theme in this story. Many Church of
Scotland ministers in highland parishes made themselves extremely
unpopular with their congregations by supporting the clearing landlords and their land agents. Indeed, some were themselves the hated
tacksmen who rented the cleared land. But, and this is where the
supply-side account fails, alienation from particular ministers resulted
not in a decline in religious vitality but in the rise of a powerful lay

movement led by 'the Men', so-called not because they were not women, but because they were not ordained. Some of the Men enjoyed official status as teachers employed by the Gaelic School Society and others were appointed as catechists by the Church, but many had no formal status. All owed their popularity to their personal piety and their ability to preach and expound scripture in an informal but forceful manner. Most laced their sermons with direct criticisms of clearing lairds and Moderate ministers. Although communion was often held only once a year or less in highland parishes, the communion season lasted a full five days and people travelled considerable distances to attend and to hear the Men speak at the Friday fellowship meetings, where anxious enquirers would put forward a passage of scripture and ask what marks of the true believer could be discerned in it. Although the Men were enthusiastic promoters of evangelical ministers, they did not hesitate to criticize Moderates, even to their faces. One memorably insulted his minister by crying out in extempore prayer for the Lord to tell his people for which of their sins this man had been sent to minister to them!

The social background of the Men is suggestive. The first point is that they were not servile peasants. The lairds had abruptly broken the reciprocal bonds of feudalism by clearing them off the land and settling them on plots of land that were deliberately kept so small as to force the crofters into wage labour (usually fishing; for a short time kelping). They were literate, articulate, opinionated self-reliant people whose close ties with their fellows were as part of a community of equals rather than as the lowest layer of an hierarchically organized organic whole. The second is that they were generally of slightly higher occupational status than most of their audience. They derived their persuasive power from a delicate balance of being sufficiently like their audience for class differences to provide no obstacle to plausibility but sufficiently superior to carry authority and to exemplify the claim that the true religion would lead also to this-worldly improvement. Macfarlane's *The Men of the Lews* (1924) contains a large number of detailed biographies that show, in addition to crofters and fishers, teachers, craftsmen (such as rope-makers, master weavers and boat makers) and even small merchants. There is also evidence of upward social mobility among the Men over the nineteenth century. In the second generation one finds a doctor, a few large merchants and a chemist. And we also find that many of the sons of the first generation had become ordained evangelical clergy.

In summary we find in the conversion of the Scottish highlands (and I could have as easily used the example of the English Quakers or Methodists) a clear illustration of the phenomenon missing from the supply-side model of religious behaviour. Latent demand was not being met by the state church or was being met by clergy whose sloth and indifference to the suffering of their people alienated those people from the Church. But, instead of religious vitality declining, a section of those alienated people took it upon themselves to provide lay leadership and did so to such effect that the Presbyterian Church in the highlands was itself fundamentally reformed and became a byword for Calvinist evangelicalism.

The explanation of why such movements occurred in Scotland, Wales and England far more frequently and with greater effect than in France, Spain or Italy can be summarized in the following two observations: the religious traditions were radical Protestant and the people in question had greater freedom and autonomy.

It is important to note that in specifying those two conditions separately I am not suggesting that they were unconnected. Far from it. Without needing to repeat the details of Weber's Protestant Ethic thesis or the subsequent reappearances of the causal connections he traces – in the Latin American Pentecostalism case, for example (see D. Martin 1990) – I would stress that the cultural and social changes go closely together. The spread of Protestantism was made possible by, and reinforced, economic and social development. Within any one region, the more radical Protestant ideas appealed most to the most advanced sections of the subordinate social classes in large part because they reinforced and legitimated the claims to autonomy and independence that such social and economic changes had awakened in those groups.

At this point it is important to distinguish my argument from the supply-side claims. There are essentially two points of difference: the first concerns the preconditions for autonomous action; the second concerns the causal status of state penalties against dissenters.

The rational-choice model supposes that people are able to consider alternative courses of action and weigh the costs and rewards. To say that potential religious entrepreneurs are put off by the artificially high 'start-up' costs imposed by a state regime presupposes a level of self-awareness and deliberation that is clearly not characteristic of many subordinate and oppressed populations. When the Church in Poland insisted that a change of their religion would void the sale of serfs and allow them to be reclaimed by the seller, it was not supposing that the serfs would themselves convert. That was unthinkable. The issue was the right of a buyer to change the religion of his property. The Catholic Church feared Lutheran lords forcibly converting Catholic serfs. When the supply-siders think of constraints on desired action, they miss the point badly by concentrating on secondary and often trivial matters of cost. My point is that, at the level of social development of the Russian serfs, there was a much bigger and more important constraint than state support for the Orthodox Church: the inability even to imagine that one might be free to have a view.

Price differentials and economizing opportunities may influence the choice of car. There is no evidence that people choose the cheapest religion or are put off by the prospect of sacrifice. On the contrary, the survival of the Amish, Hutterites, Doukhobors, English Puritans, Mormons, Jehovah's Witnesses and the like shows that persecution can stimulate dissent as much as discourage it. What is clear from the example of John Bunyan or George Fox or any number of nonconformists who were punished by the state for their disobedience is that, *once people can conceive of themselves as actors* and consider costs and rewards, the penalties that the state can impose are largely shown to be empty. What matters is confidence and power. The Quaker farmers of Lancashire who incurred considerable hardship by refusing to pay tithes to the Church of England were educated articulate people who fought their cases through the courts. They often lost but they were rarely cowed (Morgan 1988). Whether penalties are effective depends on issues of democracy and social development. This simplifies, of course, but we can recognize the difference between modernizing economies that are coming to accept egalitarianism and thoroughly oppressive and authoritarian regimes. George Fox was mercilessly persecuted by local magistrates in some parts of England and welcomed as a hero in others. Some magnates used their power to harass him, while others, either out of sympathy for his beliefs or, more commonly, out of a clear sense that to attempt to use force to produce religious conformity was no longer viable, left him in peace. In contrast, the absolutist Czarist state of late-eighteenth-century Russia used its power to crush many sections of the Old Believer movement.

We could express that as the state using its power artificially to raise start-up costs, but to focus on the state regime for the regulation of religion is to miss the point. When they were minded so to do (which was very rarely), the Russian serfs were dissuaded from dissent, not because the state supported the Orthodox Church (though it did) but because the state supported the repression of serfs in all matters.

Conclusion

One of the problems of scholarly argument is that it often polarizes unnecessarily. Although my introduction was framed in terms of supply and demand as two alternative sources of causes of religious change, I hope the above has demonstrated that someone who is widely taken to exemplify demand explanations can, where appropriate, invoke supply features of the religious environment.

For all the detail that could be presented, my point is remarkably simple. Whether we compare across or within societies, and at every point in time, we find that the likelihood of religious dissent is closely related to two things: the opportunities that the dominant religious tradition gives for self-expression and the degree of social and political autonomy among the potential dissidents. The former theme is neglected almost entirely by the supply-siders and the latter is misunderstood. They wish to treat religion as a unitary phenomenon. Their concentration on the freedom of the religious market has caused the supply-siders to miss the much greater consideration of freedom in general. The mistake is understandable. Close church–state relations tend to be characteristic of feudal societies, but the laws that oppressed religious liberties were weak symbols of a much greater oppression. It was not the state support for the Russian Orthodox Church that muted religious dissent; it was state support for feudalism that prevented the Russian serfs engaging in any kind of autonomous action. We might go further and argue that formal state support for feudalism was merely the legislative confirmation of the economic and political reality. This we can see from the failure of the Czar's liberation of the serfs in 1861 to make much difference to their lives. Perhaps this is the final criticism that should be made of the supply-side model. In the way that it operationalizes and measures its central concerns, it gives far too great a weight to the formal legal position. The presence of a battery of penal laws to suppress religious dissent hardly discouraged British dissenters, and their liberation in 1861 hardly changed the position of Russian serfs.

CHAPTER NINE

The Charismatic Movement and Secularization

Introduction

It is inevitable that journalists will view the world through a distorting lens that makes everything that attracts their attention radical, sensational and mould breaking. As they know very little about any one thing, they are constantly surprised and their exaggerated responses fit well the task in hand. They must sell stories to their editors, who must sell papers to a jaded public. Hence the hysterical tone of what little reporting of religion we now have in Britain. The churches are alternatively dying and thriving; religion is doomed and there is a great revival under way. Since the 1970s a series of stories about the decline of the mainstream denominations has been punctuated with breathless reports of outbreaks of charismatic enthusiasm.

In a much less shrill fashion, Peter Berger added his weight to criticisms of a secularization view of religion in Britain when he repeated Grace Davie's view that: 'despite the dramatic decline in church participation and expressed orthodox beliefs, a lively religious scene exists. Much of it is very loosely organized (for instance in private gatherings of people) and has odd do-it-yourself characteristics' and added 'the presence of these phenomena cast doubt on any flat assertion to the effect that Western Europe is secular territory' (Berger 1998: 796). I hope the previous chapters clear me of the charge of 'flat assertions' about secularity.[1] In this chapter I want to look closely at the primary location of loosely organized and do-it-yourself Christianity: the charismatic movement. I will begin with a brief history and then consider the challenge the movement presents to the secularization paradigm.

Renewal and restoration

The Christian churches have regularly and periodically been affected by movements of criticism and revival. In the twentieth century, the most successful of these involved the rediscovery of various 'charismata'. Christians disappointed with stagnation in their institutions or their personal religious lives were drawn to the idea that the various gifts of the Holy Spirit described in the Acts of the Apostles (such as speaking in the tongues of men and angels, prophesying and healing) were not confined to the age of the original Apostles but were enduringly available. Such interest was usually accompanied by a desire to replace the formal bureaucratic structures of churches, sects and denominations with what was taken to be the structure of the authentic early Christian church.

The modern British charismatic movement came in four waves. In the first quarter of the twentieth century the interest in charismata gave rise to various Pentecostal sects (such as the Elim Pentecostal Church, the Assemblies of God and the Apostolic Church). The second wave, coming in the second half of the twentieth century, was of charismatic renewal within the major English denominations. There was some interest among Catholics, but the greatest impact was on the Church of England. Michael Harper, who founded the Fountain Trust in 1964 to promote charismata, was committed to the Church of England and saw the renewed interest in the gifts of the spirit as a way of enlivening all organizations (especially his own). A similar view was taken by Revd David Watson of St Michael-le-Belfry in York, who became an extremely popular conference speaker, especially with young audiences. Although the involvement of Catholics such as Cardinal Suenans tested the tolerance of the more conservative Protestants, 'the emphasis was on co-operation, ecumenism and being one in the spirit' (Walker 1998: 59). But there was also a separatist strand being incubated in Baptist, Brethren, Pentecostal and independent evangelical circles.

One of the things that persuaded separatist leaders that they were about to see God's blessing was the apparently providential appearance of the Nationwide Festival of Light. A young evangelical Christian, Peter Hill, returning from several years of distributing Christian literature in India, was horrified by the open display in bookshops and newsagents of magazines and advertisements 'selling sex in a way that he thought four or five years ago would surely have been carefully hidden out of sight' (Capon 1972: 6). He had a vision of mobilizing popular support against this tide of filth with a march of thousands on London. Hill met Eddie Stride, an Anglican vicar who had organized small demonstrations against pornography. In turn, Stride introduced him to Mary Whitehouse, whose National Viewers' and Listeners' Association was already engaged in public protests and in lobbying the BBC over sexual explicitness in the mass media. A prominent journalist and moral critic, Malcolm Muggeridge, suggested the 'Festival of Light' name.

The Festival of Light had two ambitions that attracted distinct but overlapping constituencies. First, it intended to 'alert and inform Christians and others like-minded to the dangers of moral pollution'. Secondly, it intended 'to witness to the Good News about Jesus Christ' (R. Wallis 1979: 133). Apart from tapping personal contacts, its main method of enlisting support was to advertise in evangelical publications. On 25 September 1971 Hill's vision was fulfilled with a rally of some 30,000 people in Trafalgar Square. A range of prominent personalities and civic leaders castigated the churches, the government and the mass media and enjoined them to mend their ways. After the speeches in Trafalgar Square, the crowd moved to Hyde Park, where the event became an gospel rally. All the speakers, notable among them the American Arthur Blessitt (who was famous for towing a full-size cross everywhere he went), were evangelical preachers, and 'The talk was of Jesus, Christ, the Holy Spirit, repentance and conversion, rather than of "moral pollution"' (R. Wallis 1979: 136). The success of the first rally persuaded the executive committee to plan a five-day London festival for Jesus and eventually to create a permanent bureaucracy to maintain the work.

The direct effects of the Festival of Light were negligible, in part because the movement could not decide whether evangelizing or campaigning against pornography should be its main goal. It is certainly hard to see that it did anything to retard the growing acceptability of sex in the media. But the brief flurry of publicity did encourage a small group of charismatics to think that God was about to send revival rain on the nation. One such was Arthur Wallis, an evangelical critic of the mainstream churches who believed that the purification of the Church would herald the restoration of God's righteous kingdom on this earth: 'God has a grander and greater purpose for this age than simply saving souls from hell; he is bringing 'sons unto glory'.... He is forging an instrument, glorious and holy, that shall rule and administer the world in the coming age . . .' (A. Wallis 1956: 215).

In February 1972 Wallis called together a small group of like-minded evangelicals to discuss eschatology. Wallis was convinced not only that Christ was returning soon but 'that he wanted to establish the foundations of his kingdom before he arrived. . . . there soon emerged the conviction that God had separated the group to be leaders and apostles in his end-time church' (Walker 1998: 75–6). They believed that they exemplified the various forms of leadership listed in *Ephesians* 4: 11: apostles, prophets, evangelists, pastors and teachers.

The 'Restoration' leaders, to use the name of one of their publications, had a complex message. They were prophetic in the sense of teaching that God was about to intervene dramatically in the world. They were also prophetic in the sense of being critical of existing sects and denominations. John Noble made his views clear in a phrase he frequently used: forgive us our denominations. They were also highly critical of established conventions (especially those of the evangelical circles from which they all came). Clerical dress, the ceremony of communion taking, pedestrian styles of worship, Sabbath keeping and total abstinence from what Ian Paisley called 'the Devil's buttermilk' were all attacked as man-made contrivances that distracted people from the gospel message. They taught that the truly saved person was 'free from the Law' (a doctrine that in unwary hands led to licentiousness).[2] But they countered this release from one form of authority with a firm belief in their own authority to impose and to lead. One of the distinctive features of the Restoration movement was its view of discipline. Everyone should be under authority. Every small cell of Christians should be directed by a leader who in turn should be under the authority of another and so on.

> House church fellowships did not seem to want to resist this leadership. On the contrary, scores of independent groups now began to align themselves with the merging apostles. They wanted to be 'in' on the new thing that God was doing. The discipling and submission doctrines were couched in the language of biblical imagery as 'shepherding' or 'covering'. To be under authority was seen to be in 'relatedness' to apostles and their appointed elders. Both the emerging leadership and the rank and file thought in terms of being 'bound by cords of love', and being released from the bondage of wilful independence. (Walker 1998: 78–9)

Pyramid structures were established in many new fellowships. The sheep were required to obey in all things and at all times. Wives were to obey their husbands; men were to obey their elders. Inevitably this led to some abuses. The press reported stories of Christians being commanded by their shepherds to move house, to get married or to change their jobs.

The Restorationists were convinced of their divinely ordained role in creating a new church: 'The leaders were to be bound together in covenant relationships . . . catalysts of a coming together of the Body of Christ, joined and knit together in a way that would supersede the broken and compromised state of the denominational churches' (Wright 1997: 65). Although each succeeded in building a considerable following, their union was short lived. The initial covenant did not long survive disagreements about particular doctrines, matters of style and, particularly, matters of structure. If everyone should be under an apostle, then whose authority should the apostles respect? The result was division. Or, to be more precise, the leaders failed in their initial intention to turn their growing networks of influence into a single unitary movement. Maurice Smith, Gerald Coates, Roger Forster, Graham Perrins, Bryn Jones and others stimulated the creation of many small groups. They toured extensively, wrote a great deal, and became known through weekend and week-long Bible conferences. Notable among these was the Dales Bible Week organized by Jones at the Great Yorkshire Showground in Harrogate. In the early 1980s, some 8,000 people would assemble with their tents and caravans for a week of rallies, services and workshops. The magazine *Fullness* was an important vehicle for the dissemination of their views, as was *Restoration*, published by Jones from Bradford. As particular Apostles became well known, they attracted to their leadership existing independent congregations. The net result was not the purification of the churches or the creation of one new radical church but the creation of what were in effect new sects.

As the Restoration movement aged, so it moderated. The social and political aspects of the movement largely disappeared as the expectation of the imminent return of Christ receded. The Apostles came to accept that they would not take over the world. Their own history of persisting divisions and the failure of some of their enterprises (the Jones work in Bradford, for example, withered away) deflated their expectations. As they were forced to realize that they had just added to the divisions of the Church, many toned down their criticisms of longer-established denominations and sects. Charismatics (in the New Frontiers International network, in particular) sought better working relations with other local churches. The distinctive 'shepherding' model of organization was relaxed or abandoned. Although the Bible retained central place in the movement's rhetoric, many congregations gave up the distinctive behavioural standards that had traditionally been expected of 'Bible Christians'. Speaking in tongues became less frequent and expectations of the Holy Spirit moved from world reformation to personal healing.

Although the period of rapid growth was over by the end of the 1980s, the movement had an enduring impact on British church life more generally. Many congregations of existing denominations adopted (albeit in a modified form) the 'happy-clappy' style of the charismatics. Some Roman Catholic and Anglican congregations tried to create a sense of community by having congregations embrace or kiss. With the greater restraint we would expect from Presbyterians, Ian Paisley's congregation adopted a routine of mass handshaking. In many denominations and sects, services became less routinized and formal. There was a marked change to the interior of many church buildings, with informal expressive decorations (often produced by children) taking the place of the professional and restrained decor that had been the style of the Protestant churches. Although it usually concerned psychological rather than physical states, there was a greater emphasis on personal healing. Charismatic hymns such as 'Bind us together, Lord' and 'Majesty' became popular even in churches that did not share the Restorationist theology they expressed. A personal relationship with Jesus became a more prominent motif of British Christianity generally.

The fourth wave of charismatic enthusiasm was the 'Toronto Blessing', so-called because it first appeared in a Vineyard Ministries church near Toronto airport in January 1994 (Richter 1997). During a revival meeting, a number of members of the congregation fell to the floor and began to laugh hysterically. Such bodily signs of being 'slain in the Spirit' were not new. In the eighteenth century, John Wesley and George Whitfield had seen their preaching greeted with similar hysteria. US fundamentalists acquired the tag 'holy rollers' because nineteenth-century tent meetings had often produced prostrations.

Reports of this new outbreak of hysteria spread rapidly and charismatic churches throughout the English-speaking world (and particularly in England) were soon experiencing it. The British papers had a field day with their tongue-in-cheek accounts of fainting, uncontrollable laughter and animal utterances. With an eye to the approaching end of the millennium, some charismatics took the Toronto Blessing as proof that Christ was about to return. One leading Baptist rather incautiously mused that 'We could be on the brink of the greatest revival in the history of the Church, the revival that precedes the return of Christ' (D. Thompson 1996).

Of course, the great revival failed to materialize. A rally in London's Docklands intended to herald its start was a damp squib. Encouraged by the Blessing, the Pentecostal churches organized a joint missionary campaign that aimed to recruit 250,000 new souls for Christ. In the end recruitment was probably no more than 10 per cent of the target and most of the recruits were the children of existing members. A sympathetic commentator concluded: 'the Toronto Blessing does not appear to have dramatically expanded a church's market share or resulted in many new conversions; indeed it is typically referred to as a time of "refreshing" rather than "revival"' (Richter 1997: 108).

The scale of the movement

That there is any sign of life in the body religious is sometimes taken to refute the secularization paradigm. As I was at pains to show in chapter 1, there is actually nothing in the secularization approach that rules out occasional signs of revival. What would threaten the paradigm is sustained and widespread growth in places that were previously secular. Hence what matters is the scale of the movement and the source of recruits.

It is easy to be impressed by signs of religious vitality. The success of the Dales Bible Week in the early 1980s was reported in a number of breathless television and radio programmes. At a time when the general trend in church involvement was downwards, the growth of some networks was indeed impressive. The Pioneer network led by Gerald Coates grew to include about seventy congregations in 1998. Terry Virgo's New Frontiers International Network by 1998 had 112 congregations. The Icthus Fellowship had thirty-eight churches (Love 1998: 4). Although it was potentially misleading (because some observers took it as representative rather than rare), the growth of a small number of very large congregations was striking. Pastor James McConnell's congregation on the Whitewell Road in north Belfast grew so much that its second home, built in the early 1980s to accommodate just over 1,000 people, had to be replaced a decade later with the Metropolitan Tabernacle, which in 2001 had 2,000 members.

St Andrews in Chorley Wood, the New Life Christian Centre in Croydon and the Basingstoke Community Church all had over 1,000 members. A less dramatic but more widely distributed sign of growth was the reoccupation of neglected Victorian red-brick nonconformist chapels. As fellowships outgrew front rooms, sad old buildings in town centres were given new leases of life. What were once Unitarian and Congregational chapels became the homes of the 'New Life Fellowship' or the 'Community Church'.

However, it is always likely that much apparent growth was actually relocation. Pastor McConnell's Tabernacle has a fleet of buses that collects its members from all over Northern Ireland. To form a sensible judgement of overall impact we must take the national figures. According to the *UK Christian Handbook*, there were in the 1990s some 2,000 New Churches, mostly charismatic, pastored by a slightly smaller number of clergy. Brierley and Wraight (1995) guess about 170,000 members. How does this compare with the losses to the major churches? The Church of England alone lost a million members between 1970 and 1990. The Methodists, Baptist and Brethren between them lost 213,000 members in that period. On the most generous evaluation, recruits to the New Churches were no more than a tenth of those lost to other Trinitarian churches. Together the Church of England and the Methodists lost 5,000 full-time clergymen between 1970 and 1990 – five times the number of clergy being supported by the new charismatic congregations and networks.

Of course, we need to be careful with such figures. The reliability, validity and comparability of such data vary considerably. Though Brierley and his associates have done their best to make accurate estimates of the scale of the New Church phenomenon, because the congregations are only loosely federated (if not entirely independent) and are often small, they can easily be overlooked in censuses and surveys. On the other side of the equation, there is evidence of double-counting. *The Body Book* (Love 1998) lists a number of Baptist, Pentecostal and Methodist congregations that, I presume, still appear on the rolls of their parent denominations. In any case, it is unlikely that the estimates are so far off as to much change the basic relationship between the scale of this growth and the extent of decline elsewhere.

We might also add that the power of the New Churches is greater than their numbers would imply because their members are more committed than the average British Christian. We can see statistical evidence of that if we compare success in replacing members and in replacing full-time officials. The ratio of New Church members to those lost elsewhere is around 1:10 but the ratio of full-time clergy is about 17:120. Even if some of this is explained by it being easier to count clergy than members, it still suggests that charismatics are spending more on the ministry than are other Christians.[3]

If relative size is one important consideration for testing the secularization paradigm, another is the source of members. Although we do not have national survey data that bear on this point, we do have a very large number of institutional histories and personal biographies that show that most of the growth in the charismatic movement was a result of Christians moving spiritual home. Wallis was ex-Open Brethren, as was Coates. Jones was formerly in the Assemblies of God. And it was not just the leaders who were defectors from other evangelical organizations. Walker says: 'The members of these [house] churches were primarily from sectarian backgrounds. . . . dissenters from Brethren, classical Pentecostal, Evangelical Free Baptist, Salvation Army, and various non-aligned churches' (1998: 59). Jones's Bradford work, for example, began by bringing together a Holiness assembly, a former Brethren assembly and a charismatic house church. It is, as Richter (1997: 108) put it, 'refreshing' rather than 'revival'.

Trajectory

Even with an appropriate sense of proportion, one may take the view that any resurgence of interest in religion (even one failing to compensate for losses elsewhere in the religious economy) challenges the secularization paradigm. This would be the case if one expected decline to be uniform and linear. For reasons made clear in chapter 1, this is not my expectation.

Decline will be anything but uniform. I have already suggested that we need to consider separately denominational and sectarian responses to the collapse of the church form of religion. I would also stress that secularization will be filtered through various prisms that give it very different forms in different sorts of societies and cultures. Precisely because it is a social process, it cannot be uniform.

There is no reason to suppose the decline of religion to be linear. In posing new problems, modernization also provides new resources for coping with them. The decline of the feudal agricultural world and the growth of the cities undermined the plausibility that being all-pervasive and deeply embedded in the life of a stable community gave to religion, but it also encouraged the formation of voluntary associations and created a culture in which the persona of the pious believer had valuable secondary social consequences.

Far from supposing linearity, my model of secularization is *cyclical*. For the sake of brevity I often describe the changes that accompany modernization and that create problems for religion as if they were evenly progressive (or regressive!), but I also attend to elements that repeat and mutations that run counter to the overall direction. Perhaps a suitable metaphor is that of the progress of any point on the circumference of a wheel on a vehicle running down a gentle slope. As the wheel turns the point rises and falls but after each turn it is lower than it was before.

From the Reformation to the present the religious life of western Europe changes as follows. We start with a society dominated by a single religious institution whose professionals worshipped God on behalf of the general population. The laity was expected to accept the authority of the church, fund its professionals, behave morally and actively participate in major festivals and periodic acts of worship. Though most lay people were not terribly well-informed or committed Christians, they inhabited a world dominated by an all-pervasive supernaturalism and decorated with religious rituals (see chapter 2). Modernization wrought a gradual change in the background cultural climate, which at the same time strengthened the explicitly 'Christian' and created secular components, with the secular eventually coming to dominate. The proportion of well-informed pious Christians first increased and then declined drastically. The crucial point, which I made in chapter 3, is this. Although we can find some superficial similarity between our present and the pre-industrial past in the proportion of the population that is educated and articulate in its Christianity, there is a huge difference in the extent to which our present and past are and were informed by religious beliefs and sustained by frequent low-intensity affirmations of those beliefs. Glanmor Williams could say of medieval Wales: 'the people were, as far as can be judged, "collective Christians". That is to say, they reposed their trust in the prowess of the saints and in the ritual performed by their clergy on their behalf to do all that was necessary to safeguard them from evil and ensure their salvation in the world to come' (Williams 1991: 23). I do not believe any future historian will say that of us.

Specific changes trigger radical breaks from the religious mainstream. These fail to take over the church and become sects. Some sects survive in that form (shrinking in the process). Most become increasingly liberal and tolerant and denominational (as does the church), which in turn triggers another wave of sectarian religion, which in turn becomes more denominational and so on. I describe the overall consequences of such oscillation as secularization because (a) the influence of religious institutions is less at the end of every cycle; (b) the numbers involved at every stage are smaller than at the previous one; and (c) the total stock of shared religious beliefs (and the word 'shared' is central to the argument), and hence the amount of 'ambient religion', are markedly less.

Furthermore, although I have just described even that addition to the general secular trend in general terms, we cannot ignore the histories of particular individuals and organizations. Churches, sects and denominations are not just the carriers of social forces. The larger the organization, the less vulnerable it is to idiosyncratic problems, but no organization ever escapes the play of what Harold Macmillan, on being asked what he most feared in politics, called 'events, dear boy, events'.

This is a long way round to saying that there is nothing in my view of secularization that makes periodic resurgences of interest in enthusiastic or sectarian religion unexpected. They would refute my approach only if (a) the totals remaining at the end of any of these cycles were greater than those lost or (b) those recruited in any resurgence had previously been outside the churches. Neither is true of the charismatic movement.

The nature of the movement

If not its size or source, does the *nature* of the movement contain anything that defies the expectations of the secularization paradigm? It has been suggested by a number of critics of the paradigm that the resurgence of particularly supernaturalistic forms of religion refutes the approach. Peter Berger makes that case the other way round when he offers the relative failure of the more liberal versions of Christianity as evidence that his earlier view was mistaken: 'If we really lived in a highly secularized world, then religious institutions could be expected to survive to the degree that they manage to adapt to secularism' (1997: 33). This is a curious argument, because it is not at all clear why adapting to secularism should mean imitating it and there is nothing about Berger's original arguments for secularization that requires such a link. Although committed to the same core ideas as the young Berger,

I have always thought that liberal religion was precarious, because the tolerance and individualism at the heart of its ideology undermined the cohesion that is required for the large variety of organizational tasks vital to the survival of any shared belief-system (Bruce 1982, 1999). Some aspects of liberal religion (such as the unfortunate fondness for claiming that aspects of secular culture are more Christian than Christianity) are conscious attempts to regain relevance by aping the secular world and are doomed to failure. But the root of liberal Christianity's problems lies not in specific innovations but in the diffuseness that permits such innovations, and diffuseness is a result of secularization, not a deliberate attempt to adapt to it.

My reading of the secularization paradigm leads me to expect that, as the West becomes more secular, those people who wish to remain religious will increasingly be found embracing the highly individualistic and consumerist spirituality of the cultic type, exemplified by the New Age. Within Christianity, the conservative varieties will become increasingly dominant, not because they are growing in absolute terms but because the alternatives are declining faster. Hence I am not at all surprised that the most vital form of British Christianity in the last quarter of the twentieth century came from the conservative wing of Protestantism (or that the same pattern can be found in the USA and elsewhere).

Once we move beyond the initial observation that the charismatic movement is deeply religious (in the sense of being concerned with the supernatural and the miraculous) to consider its beliefs and ethos in detail, we see that, far from refuting the secularization paradigm, the movement fits well with what Wilson expected in 1966.

The point to grasp is that the modern charismatic movement differs from traditional evangelical Protestantism in ways that fit with the general cultural direction posited by the secularization paradigm. Douglas Davies has suggested a very specific connection between the new style of religion and the requirements of late capitalism: 'The contemporary charismatic ethic is rooted in a personal fulfilment in supporting relationships in this life within a potentially alienating and atomising world of partial personal relations within the service industries. An interest in personal salvation remains but its realisation has been brought forward from the hereafter to the here and now' (1984: 144). I am not sure I would want to draw so tight a line between the shift from a manufacturing to a service economy as a stimulus to the charismatic movement, but this summary, from a committed Christian who knows the movement intimately, contains within it many of the points I would now like to elaborate.

First, the charismatic movement differs from traditional conservative Protestantism in giving a much higher place to personal experience than to shared doctrines. Both the 'personal' and the 'experience' are important and I will take the latter first. This puts it very crudely, but if we accept that what people will find plausible will be influenced to some extent by their existing beliefs and expectations, by their social psychology, and by their social status, then, as the secularization paradigm argues, social and cultural diversity will be obstacles to the spread of any ideological innovation. The more detailed and specific the innovation, the more it is limited in its appeal. The more diffuse or procedural the shared beliefs, the wider the possible audience. As I argued in chapter 4, the success of the New Age, such as it is, depends on its core beliefs being so vague and general that people from a wide variety of backgrounds can read into it what they wish. The same point can be made about the charismatic movement (in contrast to, say, orthodox Presbyterianism or Catholicism). Some aspects are specific: for example, the beliefs about the imminent end times or the shepherding structure. And we should note that these were the first to be compromised or abandoned. The experience of being filled with the Holy Spirit and the significance of that experience offer considerable scope for diverse interpretation. Clearly the fact that most charismatics were raised in more conventional evangelical backgrounds means that there is a considerable reservoir of shared doctrine that informs the interpretation of utterances in tongues and prophecies, but nonetheless there is an unusual degree of flexibility in the charismatic movement. It would be impossible to quantify this impression, but I am struck by how quickly some elements of the charismatic movement can change. For example, in the early 1970s Jones's views of gender relations were at the conservative end of the spectrum: women had no place in Christian leadership. Less than twenty years later his views had changed and a close associate was arguing 'against the inherited patriarchalism of the movement' (Wright 1997: 69). Dave Tomlinson went from being a significant figure on the conservative Jones wing of Restorationism through social action in Brixton to giving up church leadership altogether and organizing 'Holy Joe's', a group that met in a pub. Of course, all sources of authority need to be interpreted, but the direct revelations of the Holy Spirit offer far more flexibility than the written texts of Holy Scripture (which come with an established body of interpretation), and the freedom so created may well explain the speed with which the movement has changed.

The novel stress on experience can be seen in the way that many strands of the movement deal with the second person of the Trinity: Jesus. Traditionally Jesus has been important for two reasons. First his death is the sacrifice that atones for our sins. God freed us from the burden of sin acquired at the expulsion from the Garden of Eden by sending his only son to die for us on the Cross. Believing that to be the case is a crucial part of the Christian faith. The second role of Jesus is to serve as a role model of obedience to God and ethical behaviour. From the stories of his life we learn how to live as Christians. What is new about the charismatic movement is the place it gives to an emotional relationship with Jesus. Many of the most popular charismatic hymns talk of loving Christ and being loved by him in a manner that suggests a relationship between two humans, rather than the more distant respect for the Son of God found in Methodism or Presbyterianism. This development is very much in line with the emphasis in the wider culture on authentic personal relationships rather than conformity to roles defined by the social system. As Douglas Davies says: 'it is . . . telling to observe that the concepts of sin, the Bible, heaven, grace and salvation are less frequently dealt with, whilst notions of love for fellow men have increased' (1984: 145).

A second major theme of the charismatic movement that chimes well with the secular climate is its attitude towards the individual self. Although there is much talk of the 'majesty' of God and the need to live as if his kingdom had been established (in order to hasten its arrival), the sense of smallness in the presence of God that previously offset the individualism of conservative Protestantism has been much moderated. As Walker puts it: 'People in the Renewal were in touch with themselves as well as with God. As the Hobbessian and hedon-istic individual replaced ascetic individualism in the larger culture so the Renewal reflected these changes in its style or worship and ex-perientially driven theology' (1997: 30). A leading Baptist who is sym-pathetic to the movement warned: 'If the movement ends up as a form of inverted narcissism, then the long hoped for revival will tarry' (McBain 1997: 57). It may be that McBain, when he talks of *inverted* narcissism, wishes to imply that the claim to be especially under divine discipline betrays an improper degree of self-importance. That may well be true. I would add that we can also see more straightforward narcissism in the modern charismatic movement's claim to offer access to divine power.

I return here to a point I made in chapter 6 about the mutation of the notion of cosmic consciousness in the Western borrowings from the East. The majority of those recruited to the Pentecostalism in Britain of the first half of the twentieth century (in such organizations as the Elim Pentecostal Church and the Assemblies of God) were working class and lower middle class. Many of those subsequently recruited to that older style of Pentecostalism were West Indian immigrants. In the United States old-time Pentecostalism also recruited most heavily from the poor and dispossessed. The wave of interest in the Spirit that began in the last quarter of the twentieth century has a markedly different class profile. Many adherents are prosperous well-educated professional people. That change in class base is reflected in a subtle difference in the role of the Holy Spirit. In Pentecostalism, being filled with the Spirit was *compensation for deprivation*: out there 'in the world', you are worthless but here in the assembly you are a healer or a prophet. It offered a promise of a better life to come in the next world. Just sometimes, it gave believers a magical device for levering some benefits from an unforthcoming world. For the modern charismatics, being filled with the Holy Spirit is proof that they are actually pretty marvellous, divine confirmation of the very positive image they already have of themselves.

We see this sense of being very much at home in the world in the absence of asceticism. Unlike most British evangelicals of the first half of the twentieth century and some today, most charismatics renounce very little. In the mid-1970s, the Restorationists divided over aspects of what was a 'proper walk with the Lord'. What did it mean to say that the true Christian was free from the dispensation of the Old Testament law and living in grace?

> None of the London Brothers ever claimed that Christians could murder, steal or commit adultery. However, John Noble and Gerald Coates did think that masturbation could be a neutral act, and not necessarily a sin. . . . Drinking alcohol was also a major bone of contention. Most of the brothers drank alcohol, but Gerald [Coates] and John [Noble] counted it as a virtue to declare it openly. Bryan [Jones] and Arthur [Wallis] were not exactly secret drinkers, but neither did they declare it from the rooftops. Gerald and a number of the London brothers liked the cinema, theatre and pop music. Others thought this worldly. (Walker 1998: 104–5)

The Coates view won out to the extent that 'worldly' as a term of criticism is rarely heard in charismatic circles. Indeed, it is hard to think of much in the lifestyle of the typical right-of-centre middle-class British person that would be rejected by charismatics.

There is an interesting divergence among charismatics around class and race. In the USA there is a popular and important strand of Pentecostalism known to its detractors as 'Name it and claim it' and to more neutral observers as the Health and Wealth gospel. It is less popular in Britain, where it is found largely in black Pentecostal circles. It offers a thoroughly materialistic interpretation of the benefits of salvation. Get right with the Lord and he will give you a well-paid job, a nice house and a new car. Not surprisingly, British charismatics, most of whom are white and already have well-paid jobs, nice houses and new cars, tend to stress more nebulous and therapeutic benefits of getting saved and being filled with the Holy Spirit.

Had the charismatic movement remained committed to Arthur Wallis's original vision (shared by some Festival of Light enthusiasts) of transforming the world and had it grown on those terms, it would have raised some difficult questions for the secularization paradigm. As I noted in chapter 1, the paradigm asserts the related claims that religion in modern societies is becoming increasing privatized and divorced from the public world, and that the focus of religious think-ing is shifting from the next life to this one. These two apparently paradoxical claims are reconciled in the proposition that modern re-ligion is increasingly therapeutic for the individual rather than for the society. As I noted, all major religions have offered this-worldly bene-fits, but these have normally been tangential to the principal enter-prise of pleasing God, and, as Job found out, God may not choose to make your life here on earth more pleasant. One of the characteristic transformations of religion in the modern world is that it turns down-ward and inward. And this is what we see in the New Churches: 'Salvation means wholeness and embraces integrity of self and healing of ailments' (D. Davies 1984: 146). A further sign of the movement's accommodation to the prevailing culture is that, unlike 1920s Pente-costalism or the preaching of Morris Cerullo (which attracts largely black audiences), the New Churches downplay the healing of *physical* ailments (claims for which are strongly contested by health profes-sionals in Britain and forbidden by the Advertising Standards Authority) and stress instead psychological benefits and improvements in per-sonal relationships.[4]

In summary I see nothing in the nature of the modern charismatic movement that refutes the secularization paradigm. 'Despite the persistence of external church structures, the privatization of religion and the demand for contemporary this-worldly salvation can be seen powerfully in charismatic renewal, in the house church movement, and in the new concern with healing and the enhancement of personal competence' (Wilson 1988: 204).

Denominationalism

Finally, I want to return to another theme of chapter 1: Niebuhr's observation that radical sects almost invariably become denominations. I have already illustrated the changes that affected many of the house churches in the three decades of the Restoration movement. Andrew Walker has studied the movement closely since its earliest days. In the conclusion to his revised edition of *Restoring the Kingdom* he says: 'Gradually Restorationists adapted to the larger cultural milieu and were domesticated by it. They did not merely slow down; they settled down to a regular church life and a principled charismatic evangelicalism' (1998: 23). In that edition, Walker also added an epilogue that very successfully conveys the extent to which the movement had changed and it is worth quoting from at length. In the early 1980s, Dales Bible Week had been one of the main showcases for Restorationism. In 1989 Walker returned to the Great Yorkshire showground in Harrogate for a successor event ('Harry') organized by Dave Tomlinson:

> Dales was replete with massive crowds of some 8,000 or more; Harry attracted some 800 people, most of them young. The Dales was ordered with military precision; Harry was cosily shambolic and anarchic. Evening celebrations and apostolic ministry dominated the Dales Bible Weeks; at Harry, the worship services were morning events and distinctly low-key. . . . everything at Dales reflected Restorationist teachings, from the seminars to children's fun-time. Harry did have seminars on the 'gifts of the Spirit', but these were tucked away between workshops on religion and science, sexual relationships, capitalism and the exploitation of the Third World.
> Everything for sale and on display at Dales reflected Restorationist concerns. At Harry, there were stalls representing Christian CND . . . Amnesty International and environmental organizations . . . Dales represented the arts in the sense that art was used for propaganda purposes,

to extend the kingdom message. At Harry, the artists – whether Christian street poets or the sculptors and painters – seemed content to promote 'art for art's sake'.

The bands and artists at Harry, ranging from the country and western style 'Country Potatoes' to the avant-garde 'The Revolutionary Army of the Infant Jesus', seemed to be there primarily for fun and honest revelry, rather than for specifically religious reasons. . . . The Dales bristled with kingdom directives and military metaphors. Harry was decidedly pacifistic and conciliatory in tone.

The young of Harry, some with punk and gelled hairstyles, rocker or romantic clothes, seemed to be excited, yet relaxed. These teenagers were not, on the whole, the 'unsaved' or the waifs of the inner cities – they were the second generation of Restorationists and their friends. No longer interested in the revivalist stories of their parents, they were bored or irritated with charismatic worship and wanted some hard answers to tough questions about love, life and, in Woody Allen's phrase, 'the whole damn thing'.

What has to be said, as a matter of fact, is that Harry's hard-working team diligently tried not to go for the easy-answers approach. This was probably just as well, for it was quite obvious that many of the teenagers were in no mood for answers that always fell into the category, 'the Bible says that . . .'. Indeed when Josh McDowell, one of the most polished performers on the American campus circuit, dropped in for a night and a day, he was, if not exactly heckled from the floor, given a run for his money. (Walker 1998: 373–4)

Conclusion

One of the few benefits of growing old is perspective. When I first became interested in the sociology of religion in the early 1970s, the house-church movement was being hailed as dramatic proof that the British were really religious after all and I was frequently contacted by journalists who wanted me to explain this powerful revival. Like Andrew Walker, I was taken as an expert commentator to the Dales Bible Week by a BBC team. In the 1990s the journalists were again phoning, this time for a sociological explanation of the Toronto Blessing. In 1999 the phones rang again and now it was in anticipation (frustrated as it turned out) of end-of-millennium madness.

In this chapter I have presented the sociological version of that sense of having seen it all before. I have tried to counter the view that the charismatic movement offers convincing evidence against the secularization paradigm. In concluding, I want to present a quite different evaluation of the movement. Let us go back to two observations made by all the commentators: it has mostly recruited from older evangelical organizations and it has accommodated considerably to the secular world. Combined, these suggest that, far from representing a radical religious alternative to the secularization of the wider society, the charismatic movement has been the route by which many previously conservative evangelical Protestants have become increasingly liberal and denominational. It is not a powerful example of a previously secular people rejecting modernity: it is an illustration of the staged way in which religion in Protestant cultures declines. People raised in Baptist and Brethren churches in the 1950s used the language of religious revitalization and reform to move out of their stifling orthodoxy and into a setting that offered much more flexible interpretations of Protestant doctrines. In turn, some of their children will abandon Christianity altogether, some will continue in the New Churches and make them ever more liberal, and others will reject that trend and break away to form new sects. Those new organizations will be smaller than those founded by their parents and will gradually evolve in the same way, and so on. The charismatic movement does not refute secularization; it shows how it works.

CHAPTER TEN

Discovering Religion: Mistakes of Method

Introduction

The secularization paradigm is a cluster of related claims about the nature, extent and cause of religious change. To be of any value those claims must be clearly articulated, be internally consistent and consistent with each other, and they must rest on evidence. Almost all commentators agree that Christianity is markedly less popular now in most Western societies than it was one, two or three hundred years ago. If we accept that, there are two good reasons to try to identify and measure the extent of religion 'beyond church and chapel'. First, conclusions will be important for testing competing explanations of secularization. For example, the greater the evidence of enduring religious sentiment among the unchurched, the less persuasive is any explanation that concentrates on changes in the plausibility of religious beliefs and ideas. If the British are really 'believing without belonging', in Grace Davie's phrase (1994), then we can eliminate a very large part of the explanation presented in chapter 1. Secondly, the extent to which we can discover religious sentiment in a society that offers it little encouragement is important for the debate between those who see religiosity as an enduring human characteristic and those who see it is a cultural product.

This chapter will not address directly those questions of substance. Instead, through criticisms of previous attempts, it will consider the prior matter of how we identify and measure religion at the margins. The background is this. I frequently find myself at odds with other sociologists of religion (such as Berger, Stark, Heelas, Bailey and Davie) about the extent of what is variously called 'non-organized' religion, religious potential, receptivity to religion, spirituality, implicit religion and the like. They find a lot of it; I see little. Much of my scepticism stems from the conclusion that current work in this area is methodologically inadequate.

Given the current popularity of post-modernism and other forms of relativism, I will begin by saying that I confine my attention to empirical studies within a conventional notion of social science. Although defining, identifying, measuring and comparing types and levels of religiosity are never easy, I assume that such are indeed our tasks. If we are to talk sensibly about changes in patterns of religious beliefs and behaviour, whether we favour interpretative or quantitative methodologies (and this chapter considers examples of both), we are doing social science. Using roughly the order in which they will be introduced, I want to suggest that some scholars invent considerable latent religiosity because (1) they use vague and leading questions in generating their data; (2) they use contestable cut-off points in sorting data; (3) they unwarrantedly interpret possibly secular responses as religious; and (4) they are unfortunately tolerant of the evasions of their respondents. Slightly apart from those errors, much of the discovery of latent religion rests on definitional fiat.

Questions and answers

The first three problems are all illustrated in two pages of Canadian sociologist Reginald Bibby's *Unknown Gods*. As a compendium of statistical information about religion in Canada, it is excellent, but, as serious social science, it is less impressive. The first part of the book details all the signs of decline of religiosity in Canada. Bibby then looks for evidence that Canadians remain enduringly religious. To set the scene for his presentation, he approvingly quotes two clergymen (1993: 147). The first says that he believes students 'need more than just education. They need spiritual and emotional support.' The second says people outside the church are among those 'seriously seeking a better life for themselves and others. They want love, justice, peace and freedom in the here and now.' The cleric adds that, where preaching and prayer 'prove relevant to such goals, they will listen'. To which pious hope, Bibby adds 'I agree'.

Bibby's reason for supposing that Canadians might return to the churches, if the churches could just become 'relevant', is that his surveys show 'that people over their lifetimes are asking questions about meaning and purpose and they are doing so with some urgency. . . . We asked Canadians about the extent to which wondering about the purpose of life is a current concern for them' (1993: 146). Apparently 9 per cent said 'a great deal' and a further 16 per cent said 'quite a bit'. Bibby describes this interest as urgent because, when he combines these two groups, he gets 25 per cent of the sample expressing concern about the meaning of life while only 30 per cent are similarly concerned about health. He adds: 'Moreover, a further 25% of the population say that they are "somewhat" concerned about the purpose of life, bringing the total percentage of Canadians troubled about purpose to around 50%' (1993: 146). Note the inflation. The survey question asked rather mildly about 'concern'. But the accompanying text inflates this to talk of 'trouble'.

My first problem with Bibby's data is that it was elicited with a question designed to maximize the evidence of existential concern. The possible answers set a curiously low threshold: what sort of person would not be 'somewhat' concerned about the meaning of life? There is a similar difficulty with some data in Ronald Inglehart's impressive body of social analysis (1997) built on the recurrent World Values Survey. Inglehart shows that, for a very large number of interestingly different societies, there is a common and statistically significant connection between increasing prosperity and *'diminishing* faith in the established religious institutions and traditional religious beliefs' (1997: 284). However, he identifies a counter-trend. An increasing number of people are responding positively to the question: 'How often, if at all, do you think about the meaning and purpose of life?' (1997: 285). What Bibby treats in terms of levels of concern, Inglehart tries to access through frequency. Inglehart's explanation is that science has undermined the previously orthodox answer to the questions without removing the causes of the questioning; hence 'Our prediction is that interest in the meaning and purpose of life will be a rising concern' (1997: 285).

As an aside, we might note that the adjective 'rising' is potentially misleading. Agreement with this specific survey item is rising, but, as Inglehart views it as a 'functional equivalent' of conventional religion (which he says is declining), what should have been presented is the combination of the two.

Inglehart may well be right, but I have trouble being confident about the data because, as with Bibby's, the question used to generate it is not terribly incisive. Inglehart's questionnaire asks: 'How often, if at all, do you think about the meaning and purpose of life?' The answer 'Never' could be interpreted by respondents as shorthand for 'I never think about the meaning and purpose of life because I am crass'. Some macho working-class lad might feel obliged to assert 'never' in case anyone thought he was an art-lover, but I suspect many people will claim some interest in the meaning of life, just because the implied opposite could be seen as insulting.

Contentious cut-offs

So we begin with data generated by unfortunately broad and potentially leading questions. In the Bibby analysis, we then have a second problem: the contestable cut-off point. It is common for survey questions to offer a range of answers. These might indicate different states (as in 'religious', 'spiritual', 'agnostic' and 'atheist') or they might be different degrees of a single property. In both cases, interpreting the data may well involve grouping them into fewer divisions or dichotomizing them. The analyst has to decide where to put the cut-off point. That judgement may be contestable. Repeated over a number of survey items, small differences in how we interpret the answers to questions can lead to vastly different conclusions. Sigelmann and Presser (1988) illustrate this very neatly by taking attitudinal data from a large US survey and showing that, by varying how one groups and divides the responses, one could equally reasonably conclude that the vast majority of US citizens are likely supporters of the new Christian right and that very few are.

Let us go back to Bibby's question about concern over the meaning of life. There were five possible responses. Only 9 per cent were concerned 'a great deal' and 16 per cent 'quite a bit' – the two most positive responses. This second position already seems rather thin ground for supposing great existential concern. But he then adds in the further 25 per cent who were 'somewhat' concerned and, instead of the conclusion that fewer than 10 per cent of Canadians are troubled by the meaning of life, we have every second Canadian in an existential froth.

Another example of the way that contentious questions and contestable grouping of responses can create a misleading impression is provided by an anonymous paper I reviewed for a sociology of religion journal. As the paper was not published, it may seem a poor example, but it does raise the sorts of methodological issues that concern me here in a particularly clear way and it is those, rather than the conclusions of the paper, that are important. The study was concerned with the religious attitudes of professional natural scientists. The abstract summarized thus: 'the results suggest that scientific training affected their religious behaviour and reduced the number of believers. The

Table 10.1   'Religious sensitivity' of scientists at a British university

Stage 1		Stage 2		Stage 3	
	%		%		%
Conventionally Religious	29 ⎫	Belief	45		
Vaguely Theistic	16 ⎬			Religious sensitivity	66
Agnostic	6 ⎫				
Wavering	14 ⎬	Open-mindedness	21		
Superstitious	1 ⎭				
Atheistic	34	Atheistic	34	Atheistic	34

index of religious sensitivity, however, remained at a significant level; thus for about forty per cent of the professionally established scientists the supernatural was not an absurd possibility.'

This conclusion was arrived at by the following route. In extended conversations, 140 university scientists were invited to say if they were involved in any particular religious organization, if they believed in God, if they were superstitious and so on. The author sorted the responses three times, as shown in table 10.1.

In the first sorting of the responses, the author divided them into six groups. The six groups were compressed into three and finally into just two. The author concluded that almost two-thirds of the scientists were 'religiously sensitive', which gives a very different impression from the one created by, for example, describing the data as showing that atheists outnumbered the conventionally religious.

Many aspects of the grouping of responses could be criticized; one problem that recurs in many surveys is how to deal with agnostics. The author wishes to place the big divide between those who said such things as 'There is no way of knowing if there is a God' and the avowed atheists. But should he? And should he then regard the former as being 'open to religion'? His subjects are intelligent and articulate people. If the quotations from the interviews are anything to go by, many had given considerable thought to their beliefs. For such people the deliberately agnostic position could be every bit as unsympathetic to most forms of religion as is atheism.

Equally problematic is the author's allocation of the waverers and doubters to the class of people who are 'sensitive' to religion. We can see the difficulty if we consider a parallel from political preferences.

In describing political choices we would not readily describe as 'sensitive to socialism' people who said they did not entirely rule out the possibility of ever supporting a socialist, or who could not make up their mind about socialism, or did not think it possible to find rational grounds for political choices.

Imperialistic interpretation

This brings me to the third methodological problem: a casual habit of assuming that, because we are studying religion, when our respondents show evidence of considering anything more precious or abstract than the dishwasher they are being religious. In his introduction to the data presented above, Bibby says: 'it's not just religious folk who are trying to work out theological details . . .' (1993: 146). Without any justification, Bibby takes being concerned about the purpose of life to mean 'trying to work out theological details'. Inglehart does the same when he bridges his presentation of data on declining traditional religious faith and his data on the question about the 'meaning and purpose of life' by saying 'But spiritual needs have not disappeared . . .' (1997: 285). No justification is offered for describing an interest in the meaning of life as 'spiritual'.

The data may well show spiritual needs, but there are at least three other possible interpretations. The first is general: all these figures were generated by surveyors asking people to state an opinion. Although surveyors allow respondents to say 'Don't know', most people claim a view and we do not know if they really have what we might call *salient* opinions of any significant strength outside the social act of giving answers or whether they are just being polite and compliant. A second possibility is that people may indeed question the purpose of life and conclude that the question is unanswerable. Though they had come to no useful conclusion, because such people had thought about it at all allows Bibby to claim them as 'spiritual'. Yet, unless we knew that such people were troubled by their inability to find an answer, it would seem inappropriate to count them among those 'trying to work out the theological details'. A third possibility is that people find a perfectly satisfying secular answer to the meaning of life. Serving your country or community, succeeding in your chosen profession, enjoying a hedonistic lifestyle, finding a cure for cancer, raising your children to be good citizens – these and many others are presumably purposes to life that can be entirely secular. That, until the twentieth century, organized religions had a near monopoly of defining the purpose of life does not give us a warrant for claiming all interest in large abstract questions as religious or spiritual.

Implied trajectories

The above raises one particularly difficult question in thinking about the margins of conventional religion. What we should or could make of people's present views depends to an extent on the direction of change. If the United Kingdom had been created last week and had no cultural history, then it would be sensible to regard those who were not certain atheists as potential theists. However, the United Kingdom was not invented last week and it does have a cultural history. Despite the rapid secularization of the second half of the twentieth century, church buildings still dominate our towns and villages. Religious functionaries are given privileged access to the air waves and religious services are widely advertised and reported. Thousands of enthusiasts work door-to-door trying to persuade people to go to church, to take a book and read it, or at least listen for ten minutes to an advertising talk. Classical music constantly reminds us of our Christian heritage. Especially in the case of professional scientists employed in a university setting, we are dealing with well-educated literate and cultured adults who will have had every opportunity to pursue nascent religious interests. If they are over 45, there is a good chance they will have had some personal involvement with organized religion in childhood. That most people have had ample opportunity to become or remain involved in conventional religion surely means that we cannot view all positions between conventional commitment and avowed atheism as demonstrating religious sensitivity or a high likelihood of becoming more religious in the future. Signs of spiritual interest among people who have had no previous encounter with, or acquaintance of, organized religion must mean something different from signs of spiritual interest among people who are very well acquainted with the many forms of organized religion that are on offer in Western societies and have chosen not to follow any of them.

The bias of the starting assumption

The 'Soul of Britain' survey conducted in May 2000 by Opinion Research Business asked 'Independently of whether you go to church

Table 10.2   Self-designation, Great Britain, 2000

Label	%
A spiritual person	31
A religious person	27
An agnostic person	10
Not a spiritual person	7
Not a religious person	21
A convinced atheist	8
Don't know	5

Source: Opinion Research Business (2000).

or not, which of these would you say you are?' and offered the labels listed in table 10.2. Taken together, the figures for agnostics and atheists, at 18 per cent, seem far higher than anything we would have got a century ago, had such polls been conducted then. It is certainly higher than the 2.9 per cent reported in a National Opinion Poll survey in 1965 (Foster 1972: 159). Nonetheless, we could present this as evidence that the remaining 82 per cent are really religious or spiritual (Heelas 2001). However, the method for generating these data is slightly suspect. Consider first the proffered labels. While we can see that the adjective 'convinced' is placed in front of 'atheist' in order to distinguish the category clearly from that of agnostic, it remains the case that this is the only label that is augmented and the augmentation seems likely to minimize the frequency with which it is chosen. There is no 'really' in front of 'spiritual' or 'religious'. It may be different in other cultures, but there is a danger that to British ears 'convinced atheist' will suggest cranks in sandals. 'Agnostic' does not have the same offputting quality, but it may well be obscure to a lot of people.

The lack of symmetry in the choice of labels is problem enough, but there is an even greater source of error built into this very type of question: it supposes that being religious is the norm and then asks people to position themselves relative to that norm. In effect, it asks 'If you are not religious, what are you?' It asks those who decline the first position nonetheless to strike an attitude towards it. It thus excludes the very thing that most secularization theorists argue to be the case: that the decline of organized religion in the West is largely a result of people losing interest in religion rather than becoming consciously anti-clerical.

What is implicit in the ORB question (and in many others) is the notion that being spiritual or religious is, like height, a unitary and universal property. Everyone should fall somewhere on a scale that runs from spiritual and religious at one end, through the uncertainty of agnosticism, to the certainty that one is not religious at the other end of the scale. Anyone who does not choose the extreme atheist position can then be claimed to be really or potentially religious. But if, as I argue, the major symptom of secularization is massive indifference, then to insist that people accept either a religious or an anti-religious designation is to fail to address the point.

Evasion and collusion

What follows is necessarily speculative because I am not aware of colleagues having raised this issue in quite this form. After thirty years in the trade, I have a strong impression that studies of religious behaviour and belief take at face value what people say about themselves in a way that one does not find in political sociology, for example.

It is common for there to be a clash between the descriptions used by analysts and the self-descriptions of those being analysed. For example, recent studies of social class show that many Scots in white-collar middle-class occupations describe themselves as 'working class'. The response of students of class is not to accept that designation but to explore why those people misdescribe their position. The explanation (loyalty to their parents, combined with a desire to distinguish themselves from the English) is less important than the attitude of the researcher. Political sociologists do not take the initial description at face value but pursue the issue of what people are doing when they describe themselves in certain ways. In contrast, especially in studies of religion by church people, there seems to be an uncritical attitude to the explanations that people give for their lack of involvement in organized religion. That, in turn, gives a misleading impression of the latent or potential interest in religion in the population at large.

Consider a recent survey of non-churchgoers commissioned by the Church of England's Oxford diocese (R. Thomas 1999). Those who proposed the research wanted to know why churchgoing had become unpopular. In particular, they wanted to understand why a 1997 Gallup poll of the area could show 54 per cent of the population claiming affiliation with the Church of England but only 10 per cent attending church even occasionally. The researchers began by asking twenty-six

Table 10.3 Reasons for not going to church, Oxford, 1999 (%)

Reason	Total	Regular churchgoers	Occasional churchgoers	Non-churchgoers
Too busy	37	35	34	44
Not interested	30	6	18	41
Boring	27	17	22	35
Old-fashioned	22	13	22	24
Unfriendly	12	5	10	16
Put off as a child	12	13	12	13
Physically cold	11	10	11	11
Services hard to follow	9	14	10	8
Unknown hymns	9	10	10	8

Source: R. Thomas (1999).

clerics to guess why people did not go to church. Those explanations were merged into questions and put to a sample of the general public. So that the study would concentrate on the non-attending Anglican identifiers, the proportion of regular churchgoers was kept to 10 per cent of the sample, which was confined to those who claimed to be 'Church of England'. The responses are given in table 10.3.

One thing that is immediately striking is that the clergy guesses proliferated a variety of what we might call 'peripheral explanations'. For example, they suggested such banalities as 'The youth are deeply spiritual and searching but what they see on offer is nowhere near where they are at' and 'People want to know God but they feel the church is hard and judgemental and they don't think its fun and you can't drink'. The survey offered respondents many opportunities to present themselves as 'really' churchgoers at heart who were prevented by a variety of contingencies and institutional failures from acting out this underlying preference. Yet, if we look at the results, the obvious point on which to concentrate is 'not interested'. Of the popular categories of response, this shows the greatest difference between the faithful and the non-attenders: respectively 6 and 41 per cent say they are not interested.

I title this section 'evasion and collusion' because three of the four most popular explanations given by the non-attenders seem inadequate to the task. After all, being too busy is not an incurable illness; it is a matter of priorities and preferences. That the churches are boring and old-fashioned would only be independently persuasive if it was the case that the respondents had tried to find a satisfactory outlet for their unsatisfied religious desires. Despite the decline in churchgoing, England is still served by a range of organizations that between them represent pretty well every conceivable theology, organizational structure, polity and liturgical style. Except for those who live in the deep rural areas (and there are few of those in England) every form of religion is on offer. Hence, when people point to specific presentational features of organized religion – boring, old-fashioned, unfriendly – to explain their lack of involvement, it seems reasonable to suppose that they have not tried very hard to find a form of religion that is not crippled by such deficiencies. We know that most churches are in financial difficulties, but can we really believe the 10 per cent of the Oxford sample who said they didn't go to church because churches were too cold?

Clearly there is some limited value for the churches in such a concentration on institutional shortcomings if it points to ways in which their operations can be improved (turn up the thermostat!), but I cannot help concluding that many of the respondents are deceiving themselves or the researchers. If the very occasional attenders and those who did not attend were really interested in the religion to which they professed some sort of lip-service service, they could have reorganized their other commitments so as to be free on Sunday morning and they could have found a church that was not cold, boring, old-fashioned and unfriendly. If the researchers were really interested in understanding their respondents, they could have pressed them to be more explicit and honest. Even the one set of responses that clearly point to a lack of faith was reinterpreted by the Diocese's Director of Communications so as to avoid accepting that supernatural belief-systems may have lost their plausibility.

> A large number were not interested in the church . . . But if you look deeper at the figures from other parts of the survey, this disinterest is coupled with a feeling that church is no longer relevant. In short, people are not engaged by a church that talks a lot about beliefs, but appears to do little to show how these beliefs can make a practical difference to individuals and communities. (R. Thomas 1999: 147)

No doubt conviction is related to relevance, but to avoid addressing at all what people believe seems strange, especially when we appreciate that many of the reason for non-attendance are only persuasive explanations for those who do not much believe in the tenets of the Christian faith. Those who know there is a God who has sent his only son to die for our sins will find an hour on a Sunday. Those who believe there is 'power in the blood' will not find the worship of their God boring or old-fashioned. If the particular venue they first happen upon is those things, they can try another or they can follow the example of the house-church leaders and start their own congregation. This is speculation, but I suspect that the researchers are distracted by wishful thinking: if the churches just adjust this or that aspect of their operations, those who have turned their back on religion may return to some fold or another.

Another unreasonably optimistic study of non-churchgoing also concludes that decline could be arrested by reform of some aspects of the churches' operations. *Gone but not Forgotten* identified 400 Londoners who had once attended church more than six times a year (not counting rights of passage) but who had since given up. They completed questionnaires and twenty-seven were interviewed at length (Richter and Francis 1998). The explanations for defection were many and varied. One person said: 'The church's teaching did not give the certainty I was looking for' while another offered the opposite fault: 'I grew up and started making decisions on my own' (1998: 64). As with the Oxford responses, my first reaction on reading the explanations was that the defectors had given up rather easily. The two above would have been satisfied if they had just swapped places. Unfortunately the study did not press respondents on just how hard they had searched for an appropriate outlet for their supposedly unsatisfied faith.

The respondents claim a degree of sympathy for organized religion so much at odds with actual levels of church attendance that we must suppose that something other than the obvious is going on in the research process. Just over half the sample said they would not go back to church, but the rest 'were leaving the possibility of returning open' (1998: 138). The authors then compare the reasons for leaving of those most and least likely to return. But such comparisons are meaningful only if the stated likelihood of return is the honest expression of seriously held views. It is hard to resist the conclusion that the responses were shaded by politeness and guilt.

Such studies do throw up fascinating questions. If, as I suspect, many people who are in every practical sense indifferent to organized religion nonetheless feel obliged to suggest otherwise, what does this reluctance signify? It could be evidence of a general spiritual interest, but we could conclude that only after some other alternatives had been eliminated. An obvious possibility is that we are seeing compliance effects. Most people wish to be agreeable. Those who do not will decline to take part in such surveys. Respondents may consciously or unconsciously shade their responses towards what they think the interviewer wishes to hear. In discussing answers to survey questions about belief in God (see chapter 6), I suggested that, once people have agreed to take part in a survey and have embarked on the business of giving answers, they may well feel subconsciously constrained to avoid giving offence and hence will tend to pick the least brutal of the options on offer. That many outside the churches appear to be sympathetic to religion may be at least in part a reflection of politeness rather than enduring religious sentiment.

Another possible explanation is that people are reluctant to challenge what they suppose is (or ought to be) a 'good thing', even though they do not believe in it or really wish it for themselves. It is not hard to think of other examples: healthy eating, taking more exercise, raising taxes, reducing car use. In September 2000 I took part in a focus-group study of religious broadcasting. The Independent Television Commission was researching public attitudes to the legal requirement presently placed on British broadcasters to devote air time to religion. To balance the church representatives appearing before the group, I had been encouraged to argue the case for letting the market decide. If there was a demand for religious television, the companies would provide it. They should not be forced to provide a service for which there was insufficient demand. I repeatedly pointed out that religion was the only topic thus privileged.

The focus-group members were not impressed. All twenty thought religion was socially useful and, although none felt very strongly about it, all were in favour of the present regulatory requirement. Yet it was obvious from the questions and comments that they were quite unfamiliar with current religious programmes. When pressed, none claimed to watch any of the material that they thought should be aired, presumably for the benefit or moral edification of someone else.

Another possible explanation for evasive responses is nostalgia. Given that the most rapid decline in church involvement has occurred in the last forty years, many survey respondents will have had a church connection in childhood and since lost it. Their parents will have been church people. Though not all memories will be fond, there may still be a reluctance to say out loud that the past is indeed past.

The key point is this. Without much effort we can generate a number of plausible explanations for the disparity between the very low levels of actual church involvement and the stated sympathy for religion. Until the others have been eliminated, there is no warrant for assuming that the gulf represents latent religious sentiment.

Discovery by definition

Thus far I have been examining instances of incipient religion being discovered by questionable research methods. There is a simpler way of finding great reservoirs of religious sentiment in an apparently secular society: just rename the secular as religious! The broader the definition of religion, the more of it you will find. Thomas Luckmann, for example, says: 'It is in keeping with an elementary sense of the concept of religion to call the transcendence of biological nature by the human individual a religious phenomenon' (1970: 49). Later he describes ' "self-realization", personal autonomy, and self-expression' as 'modern religious themes' (1970: 107). For Heelas, expressive spirituality differs from traditional Christianity in being concerned with

> that which lies 'within' us all rather than that which lies over-and-above the self or whatever the world might have to offer. This is the spirituality which is integral to what it is to be truly oneself; which is integral to the natural order as a whole. This is the spirituality which serves as the font of wisdom and judgement, rejecting authoritative sources emanating from some transcendent, tradition-articulated, source. This is the spiritual which informs . . . authenticity, creativity, love, vitality. (2000: 243)

Heelas describes further what he calls 'humanistic expressivism' and then asserts, with italics to emphasis his point, that 'Both *substantively and functionally* this source belongs to the religious order of things' (2000: 247). He admits in the next line that expressivist discourse generally takes a humanistic rather than an explicitly religious form. But he goes on to make the case that to be

> True to *oneself*, trust one's *sui generis* authenticity . . . is to be informed by (ultimately) irreducible and inexplicable consciousness-cum-agency of a kind which clearly has characteristics which do not belong to secular (rationalistic, constructivisitic, etc.) accounts of the nature (biological or socialised) and operation (calculative, hedonistic, or tradition-informed) of the person. (2000: 247)

While I have some sympathy with Luckmann and Heelas, I believe they create a misleading impression by putting the dividing line between the secular and the religious in slightly the wrong place. I have no objection to describing a certain sort of concern with self-realization as religious. In chapter 4, I happily used Heelas's depiction of the New Age as 'self-religion' because, even without the angels and cosmic consciousness that often attend such beliefs, the claims that New Agers make for the self (that it endures beyond death and that it is potentially powerful enough to defy material and social forces) seem religious in a conventional sense. But here he and Luckmann inappropriately broaden the religious by narrowing the secular to a concern with fitted kitchen units and grouting. I have no difficulty imagining ways of being 'true to oneself' and of 'transcending biological nature' that have nothing to do with gods or the supernatural.

Naturally, defining religion very broadly allows us to discover a great deal of it. But even more compelling refutation of the secularization paradigm can be produced by defining religion not by its substance but by its *function*. Because the number of important social functions is few (maintaining cohesion, eliciting compliance, keeping cheerful) and the ways in which we can do these things are legion, we normally define social phenomena by their substance. Football is that game with two teams, eleven players a side, a round ball, and an injunction against anyone except the goalkeeper handling the ball. We know what football is. With ever-greater abstraction we have no trouble defining sport, and then leisure. Though some students of religion like to make a fuss about its uniquely ineffable qualities, I see no great difficulty in defining religion as 'beliefs, actions and institutions that assume the existence of supernatural entities with powers of action, or impersonal powers or processes possessed of moral purpose'. Such a form would encompass everything we normally mean by religion and would accord with almost all common uses of the term.

An alternative approach is to note that religion often performs important social roles. For Durkheim, it provides a social group with cohesion. For Weber, it provides people with explanations and justifications of their success or failure. For Marx, it justifies oppression. We then move from identifying common consequences of religion to defining religion as that thing that has those social consequences. If we make 'providing social cohesion', for example, the constitutive feature of religion, then, wherever we find cohesion, we find religion, even when the source of cohesion seems to be a thoroughly secular ethnic identity, gender interest or class-based coincidence of material interests.

Definition by function is taken to the extreme by Edward Bailey in his claims for what he calls 'implicit religion'. In his manifesto for the

Centre for the Study of Implicit Religion and Contemporary Spirituality, he offers three definitions of implicit religion (the emphases and
punctuation are as in the original text):

(1) *commitment*. . . . it directs our initial attention towards the empirical human *experience* (of *being* committed), which has the
merit of placing the 'content' or 'object' of the experience,
within the wider context, of experience-*ing*. It is concerned,
you might say, with 'religion' as such, before turning to its
'theological' component'.

(2) The second definition is *integrating foci*. Just as Commitment
covers the whole 'ladder' of levels of consciousness, so *integrating foci* covers the various 'sizes' of society, the individual
and the social, the face-to-face group and the societal . . .

(3) *intensive concerns with extensive effects*. (Bailey 1997: 1)

In so far as I can understand him, Bailey is saying that commitment,
social belonging and feeling strongly are implicitly religious. The obvious problem is that the idea becomes pointless because it excludes
very little. Indeed, I find it very hard to think of anything that would
not be encompassed.

Depicting gardening as religious seems rather pointless. It does not
help us talk about religion and, paradoxically, it hinders functional
analysis. It is perfectly proper to be interested in the social functions
of some activity, attitude or institution. We can understand eighteenth-
century patronage, for example, if we consider it not as a bad habit
but as a form of resource allocation that well suits a hierarchical social
structure based on birth rather than achievement. The notion of functional equivalent is an important one. We learn a great deal about social
evolution and social mutation if we compare the different ways that
societies can allocate resources. But, in order to demonstrate that some
social institution has the functions imputed to it (rather than, for
example, being counterproductive or a waste of space – that is, dysfunctional or afunctional), we have to be able to define the institution
independent of its supposed functions. If not, we are merely renaming.
To say that any social activity (for Bailey, 'integrating foci') is implicitly
religious tells us no more about the world than does 'this three-sided
object is a triangle'.

If, instead of renaming parts of the world and without warrant
imputing social functions to them, we try to develop testable empirical
claims about functional equivalents, we must begin with substantive
differences. To say that football may share some features of a religion

is to raise interesting research questions about the resources fans devote to football, the psychological states they attach to success and failure, the attitudes of some fans to the arenas in which their teams play and so on. Put in those terms, the identification of parallels also raises the important counterbalance of the *differences*. Few football fans marry only women who support the same team or whose fathers support the same team. Few shun those who do not share their allegiance. Few suffer debilitating trauma when they lose faith, or construct elaborate moral and social codes around their footballing interests. Few will found political parties that claim a distinctive moral and social agenda based on the principles of Scumchester City FC. Few believe that the world was created by the directors of Scumchester City FC or kept in its orbit by the club groundsman. Even those who like a bit of aggro will not seek to destroy the citadels of the Bundesliga in the belief that German football offends their God. Examining the parallels between football and religion can be interesting and illuminating but it is not helped at all by defining football as a religion. To do so is to establish by definitional fiat what should be demonstrated factually.

The notion of *implicit* religion seems particularly unhelpful. It should not be confused with the very important point that phenomena can be religious to varying degrees. At one extreme we have the self-consciously religious: praying, attending worship services, reading sacred texts, contemplating the life of the Buddha, and so on. At the other extreme we can imagine actions and states of mind that are influenced very slightly by religious ideas and motifs and we can even imagine that the people in question may be largely unaware of those religious influences. For example, a father may take pride in the effort he puts into his parenting role and implicitly suppose that there is some obscure moral order to the universe that means that good actions will be rewarded, even where there is no obvious this-worldly mechanism for such a result and where the reality seems otherwise. Someone who supposes that a cheat will 'get his comeuppance' may be relying on an unconsidered or 'implicit' hope for a supernatural karmic order. We may reasonably want to say that such a view is implicitly religious. However, we should also want to distinguish such views from thoroughly secular alternatives. It is quite possible to have a biological and secular model of the long-term rewards of good parenting. It is quite possible to suppose a thoroughly secular and mundane model of how cheats may get their just desserts.

My point is that, if the category of implicit religion is to be useful, it must be used sparingly and only where elements of religion substantively defined can be identified. There is no justification for using the term to label as religious anything that people take seriously or that makes them feel good. There is certainly no warrant for following the logic offered by a contributor to a 1999 discussion on a sociology of religion mailing list who said that anything 'not explicitly religious was implicitly religious'. By that token, bald men are implicitly hairy and fat people are implicitly thin. Such corruption of language destroys any possibility of fruitful analysis.

Conclusion

For the reasons I gave at the start of this chapter, I have every sympathy with attempts to study latent religiosity, religion 'beyond church and chapel', spirituality, religious sensitivity and the like. What I have less sympathy with are contributions to the secularization debate that use questionable methods to inflate the numbers of the unconventionally religious.

Some scholars wish to find evidence of widespread religious sentiment because they suppose that religiosity is in some sense 'hardwired' into human beings, an innate part of our constitutions. Many sociologists of religion are also Christians who seek some sign of hope that the decline of a once-dominant religion might be reversed. For whatever reason, much sociology of religion seems unusually eager to find signs of robust health in the religious life of the contemporary West. Perhaps the simplest way of expressing my reservations about this approach is to reverse the 'football-is-really-a-religion' argument. Sociologists of sport have no difficulty accepting that people may have no interest at all in sport, either as participants or spectators. They do not count as 'sporty' people who take no part in any sport, who never read the sports pages of newspapers, and who never watch sport on television but who say, when prompted in a survey, that they are 'somewhat' sporty. They do not assert that all people are latently sporty and are prevented from playing Sunday League football only by the need to go to church. Sociologists of sport do not assert that, because sport and religion share some common features, religion is really a sport. And they do not try to annex other spheres of social life to their territory by looking for 'implicit sport'.

CHAPTER ELEVEN

Religion in the United States

Introduction

If we leave aside the social, moral and political behaviour of its citizens, the United States has every appearance of being unusually godly. Americans are more likely than their European counterparts to go to church, for example, and American politicians routinely invoke God and lay claim to religious identities. Hence it is no surprise that some of the most vigorous criticisms of the secularization paradigm come from US scholars (such as Rodney Stark and Andrew Greeley), who take the US experience as refutation of any link between modernization and the decline of religion. If the paradigm is to deserve our support, it must be the case that there is evidence of secularization that is being overlooked by Stark and Greeley, that, to the extent that the USA is exceptional, the differences can be explained by principles consistent with the paradigm, or both.

This chapter will make four points. First, there is ample evidence of Christianity in the USA losing power, prestige and popularity. Secondly, there is ample evidence that Christianity in the USA has changed in ways expected by the secularization paradigm: greater emphasis on individual choice, a shift from other-worldly to this-worldly salvation, and an increasing therapeutic orientation to religion. Thirdly, for all the sound and fury that accompanied the 'new Christian right' (NCR), as a cluster of religious right organizations that mobilized in the late 1970s were known, there has been no significant reversal of the major trend of religion becoming marginal to the operation of the social system.[1] Finally, to the extent that the USA does differ from Europe, the differences can be explained in ways that are perfectly consistent with the secularization paradigm. The key point is that the federal and diffuse structure of the USA allows conservative Christians the freedom to construct distinct subcultures in which their faith retains some of the hegemony that Christianity once had in pre-industrial Europe.

Patterns of church adherence

The starting point for most claims about the vitality of religion in the USA is the enduringly high rate of church involvement. Andrew Greeley presented survey data from 1939 to 1984. Before the Second World War, 41 per cent of US adults said they had attended church 'in the last seven days'. The figure rose to a high of 49 per cent in the late 1950s and then fell to 42 per cent in 1969. He concluded that, apart from a sharp dip in Catholic attendance between 1868 and 1975, 'patterns of American church attendance are remarkably stable . . . Secularization that is not' (1989: 56). Figures for the 1980s and 1990s were around 40 per cent (Barna 2000a).

However, a certain degree of scepticism about these data seems appropriate. Considering how sceptical social scientists normally are, it is remarkable that such figures were reported for forty years before anyone pointed out that they were based on what people said about themselves. In the early 1990s, C. Kirk Hadaway, a sociologist employed by one of the major denominations, became aware that the rates of church attendance claimed in social surveys were incompatible with what the churches knew about their congregations. As Hadaway and his colleagues put it: 'If Americans are going to church at the rate they report, the churches would be full on Sunday mornings and denominations would be growing. Yet they are not' (Hadaway et al. 1993: 742). The Gallup Organization's own data contain an enigma: the proportion of Americans claiming to have attended church in the previous week has remained stable, but when people have been asked how their churchgoing has changed, the number saying they attend 'less frequently' has always been greater than the those who now attend 'more frequently' (Bezilla 1993: 44).

The apparent inconsistency between survey data and church reports is not resolved by claiming that shrinkage in the old mainstream denominations is made up for by growing evangelical denominations (although evangelical churches are indeed growing). First, the conservative churches are not growing fast enough to explain the discrepancy. Secondly, even those Americans who say they are members of denominations that we know to be contracting claim levels of church involvement that are impossible to reconcile with their churches' own estimates. Consider the example of the American Episcopal Church. Given the proportion of Americans who tell pollsters they are Episcopalians, the denomination should have grown by more than 13 per cent between 1967 and 1990. Instead, membership declined by 28 per cent: 'Moreover, attendance figures from Episcopal parishes are far below what would be expected if self-defined Episcopalians attended church in the numbers they claim' (Hadaway et al. 1993: 742). In surveys conducted by Gallup and other competent organizations, about 35 per cent of self-defined Episcopalians said they had been to church in the previous seven days. But the Church's own figures suggest that only 16 per cent actually did so.

To test their suspicion that self-reported rates of church attendance were inflated, Hadaway and his colleagues went to painstaking lengths to estimate accurately attendance at all known churches in Ashtabula County, Ohio. They not only took lists of congregations from registers and church yearbooks, but they also searched the county for unlisted churches. Where they could not get estimates of attendance from clergymen, they counted cars in the car parks during services and adjusted the figure for the probable number of passengers. Having constructed a reasonable estimate of how many people attended services from the clergy returns[2] and from their own counts, the researchers used a standard telephone survey to ask a sample of Ashtabulans if they went to church. They discovered that the observance claimed by their respondents was 83 per cent higher than their best estimates of actual attendance.

Hadaway and Marler then repeated the study with one particular congregation: a Baptist church in a metropolitan area of Alabama. They found that 984 people were at worship on a particular Sunday (about 40 per cent of the congregation's membership). During the following week a sample of 300 adult members of the congregation were interviewed about various matters, including their church attendance in the previous week; 70 per cent said they had attended. If that were generalized to the whole membership, there should have been 1,710 people in church – almost twice as many as actually were!

Even more compelling evidence of over-claiming was produced by comparing actual attendance at the adult Sunday school (where the names of those present were recorded) with what members said when asked in a telephone poll the following week. 'Sunday school attendance at this church was over-reported by 58.8%' (Marler and Hadaway 1997: 4).

It could be that Americans have always exaggerated their church-going, but the good reason for thinking it is relatively recent is that until the 1970s the claimed attendance figures were consonant with what the churches knew about their members. Such historical data as Hadaway and his colleagues could find supported their belief that the attendance gap was recent and growing. They summarize their study of Catholic church attendance in San Francisco as follows:

> The 1972 poll-based Catholic attendance rate represented a 47% over-reporting of attendance, but by 1996 over-reporting had increased to 101%. During the 24-year period aggregate Mass attendance in San Francisco declined, but the population of Roman Catholics increased slightly – as did the self-reported rate of church attendance among Roman Catholic affiliates. The net result was an increasing attendance gap. A stable rate of self-reported attendance among Roman Catholics in San Francisco masks an actual decline in Mass attendance. This is what we believe has occurred more generally in the United States. (Marler and Hadaway 1997: 6)

One good mark of the importance of some social institution is how much money people give to it. As part of a critique of the secularization paradigm, Roger Finke (1992) made much of the fact that Americans gave as generously to the church in the late 1980s as they did fifty years previously. What he failed to point out was that over that period the amount they spent on everything had more than doubled. In 1963 Catholics gave 2.2 per cent of their income to the Church. By 1983 it was only 1.6 per cent (Greeley 1989: 24). While financial contributions to the churches have in net terms remained fairly high, they have declined markedly as a proportion of disposable income.

In brief, while we can be sure that US churches remain more popular than their European counterparts, there is good reason to suppose that church adherence in the USA is declining.

Changes in the nature of US religion

Opponents of the secularization paradigm have repeatedly mocked the case made by Bryan Wilson in the 1960s that the American churches had remained popular by giving up much of their religion (Wilson 1966: 122; Brown 1992a: 36). Wilson is accused of making his position untestable by claiming both church decline (in Britain) and church growth or stability (in the USA) as evidence of the same change. Is Wilson's case so silly? In other contexts we find it quite sensible to argue that the growing popularity of an ideological organization has been bought by shedding unpopular baggage. No one would claim the British Labour Party's 1997 election victory (after three

consecutive defeats) was won on a socialist platform or that François
Mitterrand became the first French Socialist President by remaining
true to his principles. In both cases political parties responded to long
periods in the wilderness by ditching their socialism. Whether those
judgements are reasonable can be left to political scientists. My point
is this: if we can make such assertions about political parties, why
should we not at least ask the Wilsonian question? Have the churches
in the USA retained support by losing a lot of their specifically 'religious' beliefs and behavioural requirements? Or, to put it a little more
generally, did American Christianity over the twentieth century change
in ways compatible with the secularization paradigm?

Describing the faith of millions of people over a century clearly
requires considerable simplification. I will begin with some illustrative
data from social surveys and then consider the recent history of US
Christianity.

Although the change has been nowhere near as great as in Britain
or Australia, there has been a decline in commitment to what were
once orthodox Christian beliefs. For example, in 1984 Gallup reported that the percentage of those asked who believed that the Bible
is 'literally true' had fallen from 65 per cent in 1964 to just 37 per
cent (Wuthnow 1988: 165). Although heaven remains popular, belief
in hell has also declined. As I will argue shortly, the change has
actually been greater than a simple report of survey data would
suggest, because what the churches (and, we have to presume, their
members) mean by these terms has itself undergone a considerable
reinterpretation.

The simplest way of describing the changes in content is to say that
the supernatural has been diminished and it has been psychologized
or subjectivized. Religion used to be about the divine and our relationship to it. God was a real force external to us. The Bible was his
revealed word. Miracles actually occurred. Christ really was the son
of God and he did actually die to atone for our sins. Heaven and hell
were real places. Gradually over the last hundred years a quite different interpretation of these things has affected much of mainstream
Christianity. God is no longer seen as an actual person but as some sort
of vague power or, in the final reduction, our own consciences. The
Bible is no longer the word of God but a historical book with some
useful ethical and moral guidelines for living. Miracles are explained
away; either they did not really happen or they were natural phenomena misunderstand by ignorant peasants. Christ was not actually

God's son but an exemplary prophet and teacher. Heaven and hell are not real places but psychological states.

These changes have two obvious values in adjusting Christianity to the modern world. First, they save most of the specific content from clashing with secular knowledge. Secondly, they remove the necessity for arguing with other religions. If hell is a psychological state, there is less necessity to argue about its nature and how to avoid it. If religion is a matter of subjective states, there is no need for friends and neighbours all to have the same one.

Harry Fosdick Emerson, a leading liberal Protestant clergyman of the 1930s, said that the starting point of Christianity was not an objective faith but faith in human personality. The consequence of increasing irreligion was not that people were going to go to hell but that 'multitudes of people are living not bad but frittered lives – split, scattered, uncoordinated'. The solution was a religion that would 'furnish an inward spiritual dynamic for radiant and triumphant living' (Bruce 1990: 84). Religion was no longer about glorifying God but about personal growth.

This fundamental shift in American Protestantism began in the 1930s and reached its zenith in the popularity of Norman Vincent Peale. Peale was a liberal Presbyterian minister, pastor of one of the biggest churches in New York (which he built from just forty souls to over 900) and the originator of what he called 'the power of positive thinking' (George 1994). In the first two years after its publication, the book of the same name sold over two million copies. For Peale the Christian message was reduced to a battle between good and evil, but these were no longer realities external to us. Evil was a lack of self-confidence; good was positive thinking. Those people who think positively (while conforming to the norms of suburban middle-class 1950s America) will be successful; this is salvation. Those who do not will be damned – that is, they will be unhappy. The spirit of Peale lives on in the theology of Robert Schuler, who in the 1950s started preaching at a drive-in cinema in Garden Grove, California. He stood on the roof of the snack bar; his congregation sat in their cars. Televising the service as *The Hour of Power* brought a growing congregation and in 1980 the Garden Grove Community Church abandoned the drive-in for the $16 million Crystal Cathedral, a modernist edifice walled and roofed in glass. Schuler did not forget his roots: one end of the building was designed to slide open and the car park was fitted with headphones so that those who wanted to stay in their cars could still enjoy the service. In the mid-1980s, *The Hour of Power* was the most popular religious programme on US television. Schuler preaches a Pealean gospel that he called 'possibility theology'. The extent to which this differs from traditional Christianity is very neatly symbolized in the title of his most popular book. The Beatitudes (so-called from the Greek word for 'blessed') are the promises given by Christ in the Sermon on the Mount: 'Blessed are the poor in spirit: for theirs is the kingdom of heaven. Blessed are they that mourn: for they shall be comforted' and so on (Matt. 5: 3–11). The contract is clear (and it has for centuries been recited as a central part of the liturgy of most Christian churches). Christ promised the poor, the mournful, the meek, the righteous, the merciful, the pure in heart, the peacemakers and the oppressed that they will attain the kingdom of heaven. With no trace of irony, Robert Schuler's *The Be-Happy-Attitudes* promises that those who 'believe in Christ' will be rewarded with health, prosperity and happiness in this world.

At the same time as the faith was being stripped of its traditional supernaturalism, it was also losing its behavioural distinctiveness. Asceticism was out. Churchgoers no longer gave up smoking, drinking, dancing or going to the theatre. They wore the same clothes as other people, lived in the same kinds of houses, and had the same increasingly liberal moral and ethical standards. They got divorced.

Conservative Protestants stayed out of this round of change. Indeed, they defined themselves by their refusal to modernize their faith. They were able to resist new ideas and attitudes for a long time because they did not so immediately benefit from the social changes that encouraged the innovations. Their puritanism helped reconcile them to their poverty. Televisions were unacceptable because they carried Satanic messages, but then most fundamentalists could not afford a television anyway. When the prosperity of industrial America began to seep down to the communities in which fundamentalism and Pentecostalism were strong, puritanism waned. As more could afford televisions, the injunction against watching TV weakened. Fancy clothes and personal adornment were sinful until Pentecostalists could afford them and then the lines shifted. In 1988 the General Assembly of the Church of God, the USA's oldest Pentecostal sect, reconciled itself to the status quo and voted to change its moral code. 'The revised code is more flexible on some worldly issues such as personal appearance: "It is not displeasing to God for us to dress well and be well-groomed"' (Tamney and Johnson 1998: 219). So long as Pentecostalists were so poor that the break-up of the family would have pushed them into destitution, divorce was entirely unacceptable. As they became better off, so too that line was moved. A Barna survey in 2000 showed that born-again adults were more likely than others to have experienced a divorce (Barna 2000b: 3).

As part of a rich and insightful examination of how evangelicalism was evolving, James Hunter in 1982 surveyed a large number of young evangelical students in a variety of colleges with a series of questions that had been used in studies in the 1950s and 1960s (1987: 59). In 1951 almost all of those asked thought that 'social' dancing (tangos, waltzes and the like) were 'morally wrong all the time' and most were similarly opposed to folk dancing. In 1982 none of the young evangelicals objected to either. A similar proportion of the first generation (98 per cent) regarded drinking alcohol as sinful; in 1982 only 17 per cent thought it morally wrong. In 1951 almost half thought watching 'Hollywood-type' movies was morally wrong; in 1982 none did. The responses to questions about sex are interesting. The evangelical consensus against 'petting' and sexual intercourse was so strong in 1951 that the questions were not asked. In the early 1960s, 81 per cent of evangelicals thought 'heavy petting' morally wrong all the time. Twenty years later, less than half Hunter's sample took that view.

Beyond this sort of survey evidence there is a vast body of impressionistic data that we can draw from biographies, histories and social commentaries.[3] In my many visits to fundamentalist families in Virginia and South Carolina in the early 1980s I was struck by how little their lives and homes differed in appearance from those of other Americans I met. They may well have given their possessions, their occupations and their hobbies a particular significance, but they were no longer a people visibly set apart by either their poverty or their patterns of consumption. Evangelicals were no longer plain. The young men and women who made up the gospel choirs and audiences on televangelism shows were as glamorously coiffured and dressed as their secular counterparts.

An important element of Peale's psychologizing of religion was its positive valuation of the self. Conservatives were bitterly critical of liberals for abandoning the idea of sin and for turning salvation from an other-worldly destination to therapeutic improvement in this life. Yet, a generation later, evangelicals were rewriting the gospel in precisely the same way. Hunter makes the point economically by listing the titles of best-selling evangelical books of the 1980s: *You can Become the Person You Want to Be, The Healthy Personality and the Christian Life, How to Become your own Best Self* and *Self-Esteem: The New Reformation* (J. D. Hunter 1987: 69–70). God is still there, but he is no longer the strict father who crushes our pride and brings us to see our worthlessness. He is the psychotherapist who can help us to be more fulfilled and to achieve more in this life.

In my explanation of secularization I drew attention to what we might call 'practical relativism'. One vital feature of any belief-system is its supposed reach and a common feature of religions in modern culturally diverse egalitarian democracies is a shortening of that reach, so that injunctions that were once thought to be binding on all of God's creation are now thought to apply only to 'us', to those who voluntarily accept them. There are clear signs of such practical relativism becoming more common among American Christians. In the 1920s Robert and Helen Lynd studied life in a representative small American city (Muncie, Indiana), which they called Middletown. Since then there have been a series of follow-up studies and we can chart important changes. In 1924 the Lynds asked for responses to the statement that 'Christianity is the one true religion and all people should be converted to it' (Lynd and Lynd 1929: 316). Ninety-four per cent of those asked – that is, nearly everyone – agreed. When the same question was put in 1977 to a sample of *churchgoing* young people, only 41 per cent agreed. The authors of the restudy summarized that section of their book by saying: 'half of Middletown's adolescents who belong to and attend church and who believe in Jesus, the Bible and the here-after do not claim any universal validity for the Christian beliefs they hold and have no zeal for the conversion of non-Christians' (Caplow et al. 1983: 98). Hunter's study of young evangelicals suggested similar changes in even that constituency. While their views on what *they* had to do and believe in order to attain salvation remained orthodox, they had softened considerably their views of other people's chances of being saved. There was no longer the sectarian certainty that there was only one way to heaven.

A series of surveys conducted by the Barna organization (2000a, b) made the same point. Barna found clear evidence of declining ideological cohesion. Only 1 per cent of adults who described themselves as 'born again' agreed with all of thirteen statements of what was once orthodox Christian belief. Desiring to have a close personal relationship with God ranked just sixth among twenty-one life goals tested on born-again adults, 'trailing such desires as "living a comfortable life"'. Less than half of born-again teenagers surveyed claimed to be 'absolutely committed to the Christian faith', two-thirds rejected the existence of Satan, three-fifths rejected the existence of the Holy Spirit and half believed that Jesus sinned during his lifetime. Most telling, less than half of a sample of born-again adults and only 9 per cent of born-again teenagers were 'certain of the existence of absolute moral truth' (Barna 2000b: 1–3).

Americans are shifting from the church and sect certainty that their organization is the one true faith to the liberal denominational position of supposing that it is right for them but that it might not be right for others and that there is nothing wrong with people who are not Baptists or whatever. For the reasons I presented in chapter 4, as toleration increases, interest in maintaining and spreading the faith will decline. If the faith is not essential, then why put a great deal of effort into preserving it?

The Middletown restudy also contains one fascinating little observation that accords well with Wilson's view that there has been a significant change in the reasons for church adherence. The Lynds asked why people went to church and the most popular answer was that obedience to God required it. In the 1977 restudy, the most popular reason given for churchgoing was 'pleasure'.

To summarize thus far, I see no reason to deride Wilson's belief that the enduring popularity of churchgoing in the USA may well reflect important changes in the substance of American religion. It is impossible in this brief discussion to do any more than illustrate the argument, but I will rely on the conclusion of my US colleague, Wade Clark Roof, who has spent thirty years documenting shifts in American religious life. At the end of a broad survey of changes, he concluded: 'the religious stance today is more internal than external, more individual than institutional, more experiential than cerebral, more private than public' (1996: 153).

The constraints on fundamentalism

Those who believe they have the entire divine truth often try to orient their entire life around it. As chapter 1 explained, one of the features of modernization is the increasing division of the lifeworld into a variety of relatively separate compartments. In particular, modern societies operate with a significant divide between the public and the private sphere. We are increasingly prevented from exercising our prejudices in the public arena (witness the expanding body of anti-discrimination law) while being given ever greater freedom to do and believe what we like in the private leisure world of family and friends. One way of diffusing the potential for social conflict inherent in religious diversity is to prohibit everything in public and permit everything in private, which is what the US Constitution, with its prohibition on the state supporting or inhibiting religion, recommends.

Conservative religion is generally opposed to such differentiation on principle (it is a bad idea) and on substance (it has bad consequences). It is insulting to God to obey him in only a small part of our lives and ignore him the rest of the time. And, if the true faith is excluded from the public sphere, the space will be filled with sin and vice, which is bad enough in itself, but it will make it all the harder for the righteous to raise their children in righteousness.

Modern states differ in the extent to which they permit minorities the right to create their own subsocieties. Sects differ in how they respond to the state. Communitarian sects such as the Amish and the Hutterites became such when they gave up trying to impose God's will on their central European neighbours and set out for the empty lands of the United States and Canada where they could build their own godly societies free from interference. Those sectarians who do not so completely isolate themselves live in constant tension with the wide society. US fundamentalists have a history of oscillating between pious retreat and theocratic assault. For a while they sit in their rocking chairs on their porches and concentrate on their 'walk with the Lord' while the country goes to the dogs. Periodically (temperance crusades at the start of the twentieth century and anti-communism in the 1950s) they get motivated to fight to regain control of the public sphere. That fundamentalists could become politically active in the last quarter of the twentieth century is often cited as proof that the secularization paradigm is mistaken (Hadden and Shupe 1988). Elsewhere I have analysed the NCR at length (Bruce 1988, 1998b, 2001b); here I will very briefly summarize the NCR's record.

For all the noise it generated, the NCR has failed to achieve any of its specific goals. It has reinforced the secular conservative wing of the Republican Party but it has not reduced the number of abortions, cut the proportion of mothers working outside the home, restored male hegemony, made divorce more difficult, put religious ceremonies back into state schools, required biology classes to teach 'creation science', or forced homosexuals back into the closet.

One strand of NCR activity has involved trying to shape legislatures, either by helping candidates who share its goals to win seats or by running negative campaigns against liberals. Since televangelist Jerry Falwell formed the Moral Majority in 1978, NCR organizations have had some limited impact on elections where the electorate is small (party primaries to select candidates and school boards, for example), but have rarely managed to make an enduring impression on large constituencies. The NCR has the advantage of being able to mobilize a small number of highly committed supporters, but it tends to attract as much opposition as support. A good example is the 1987 campaign by Pat Robertson, a leading televangelist and founder of the Christian Broadcasting Network, to win the Republican nomination to succeed Ronald Reagan. Robertson won the Iowa caucuses, where the electorate was tiny, but thereafter failed to win a single primary election, despite spending an unprecedented sum. Subsequent favourites of the religious right such as Pat Buchanan and Gary Bauer have fared even less well. In 1994 the Christian Coalition managed to deliver the Republican Party's state convention nomination for the governorship of Minnesota to Allen Quist, an anti-abortion activist, rather than to the incumbent Arne Carlson. When the choice was put to all registered Republicans in the primary election, Carlson easily beat Quist (Stains 1994).

The legislative record parallels the electoral one: initial success in small arenas followed by defeat in larger ones. Despite conservative Republican influence in Congress in the last two decades of the twentieth century, the NCR has signally failed to make progress on its agenda. Many legislators find it advantageous to make supportive noises but then fail to commit their political capital to the cause.

Because much of the NCR wish list relates either to very basic human values or to the constitutional question of the relationship between religion and the state, court judgments are central to evaluating the NCR, and here the same 'centripetal' pattern emerges. NCR groups have often enjoyed brief victories in the lower courts and then seen those judgments overturned as the cases are appealed upwards. Despite Ronald Reagan and George Bush Senior appointing a very large number of conservative jurists to the federal courts, there has not yet been any major shift in favour of the NCR's agenda.

A detailed examination of the NCR's fate would mention tensions within the movement, problems of maintaining commitment, difficulties in keeping NCR issues high up the public agenda, the danger of having 'Back to Basics' campaigns led by all-too human politicians, the greater influence of other pressure groups, the reluctance of the Catholic Church to support campaigns it does not control, and the very successful liberal counter-attacks. But behind all these lies the simple fact that, with varying degrees of consciousness, most Americans seem to appreciate the practical benefits of liberalism and toleration. Some have a conscious commitment to the separation of church and state; others just have a vague sense that preachers should not be telling people what they cannot do. A major survey sponsored by an organization in favour of greater religious influence on public life found that 58 per cent of the public thought it wrong for voters 'to seriously consider the religious affiliation of candidates'. When asked what they thought of faith-based charities receiving government funding for welfare programmes, 44 per cent were in favour but a quarter of the sample thought it a good idea only if such programmes stayed away from religious messages.[4] Nearly a third thought it a bad idea for the state to fund religious organizations for any purpose. Most telling were the responses to questions about public prayer in schools. Only 12 per cent of evangelicals thought that such prayers should be specifically Christian and 53 per cent of evangelicals (the same as for the general public) thought that a moment of shared silence was the best solution to the problem (Pew Forum 2001).

Perhaps the most compelling evidence that theocracy is not an option in a religiously diverse liberal democracy is the fact that NCR organizations accept the need to present their causes in secular language. They cannot say that Creation should be taught in schools because God requires it. They have to accept the primacy of secular science and argue that the Genesis account of the origins of the world and species is as consistent with the scientific evidence as any other explanation. They cannot assert that their God dislikes divorce. They have to argue that divorce is socially dysfunctional. Legal battles over abortion are fought on the entirely secular principle that abortion infringes the universal right to life. Most conservative Christians accept that they cannot plausibly demand a privileged position for their culture on the ground that God is on their side. They have to accept the principle of equality and argue that they form a legitimate minority that should be treated no worse than any other interest group.

It is not just in the public presentations of their agenda that religious rightists have to accept the principles of their liberal opponents. To have any hope of being politically effective outside small areas of conservative Protestant domination, they need to compromise a key element of their identity. At its most abstract, what defines evangelicals and fundamentalists is their refusal to accept the compartmentalization and differentiation of modern society. Seriously religious people refuse to confine their God to the private sphere. Yet successful political action requires precisely that alternation between Sunday and the rest of the week. Jerry Falwell called his organization the Moral Majority. Politically involved sectarians might be 'Moral' but they are not a 'Majority'. Hence the need for coalitions with Jewish, Catholic, Muslim and secular conservatives. Successful coalition requires the sectarian to switch between two frames. On a Sunday evening Baptist fundamentalism is the only way to God and the Vatican is the anti-Christ. On a Monday morning the NCR activist sits down with his Catholic colleague to plan a campaign for the state funding of religious schools.[5]

Opportunity structure

What one makes of any social phenomenon depends rather on what one expects. I suspect that some of the more extravagant assessments of the significance of the NCR result from failing to appreciate just how open to well-organized minorities are aspects of the US political system. If we ask why socio-moral issues have not become as politicized in, say, Britain or Australia as they have in the USA, we can answer that there are far more conservative Christians in the USA; that is, it is a less secular country. But we can also note that the political structure of the USA makes it considerably easier for conservative Christians to have a public impact. In comparison with most European countries, the USA offers considerable opportunity for minorities to enter the political arena. Far more offices are elected rather than appointed.

> It is not uncommon for the electors to face a 'long ballot' containing the names of from fifty to one hundred candidates – to elect half a dozen state officers apart from the governor, to elect state commissioners and judges, state treasurer and state attorney, as well as their mayor, their councillors, the members of the local school board, the city court judges, their tax collectors and many more. (Finer 1982: 227–8)

When the turn-out for the Congressional elections that fall between the four-yearly presidential elections is often as low as 35 per cent, there is clearly ample opportunity for any committed interest group either to win seats or to exercise considerable influence on those running for office.

US politics is also unusual in the lack of party cohesion. Although most elections are nominally fought between Republicans and Democrats, party is rarely the force that it is in the UK or France. In the UK, the party selects candidates, meets their election expenses, determines policy, sets the legislative agenda, and controls the voting of elected representatives. Party domination is recognized by the electorate, which votes according to the national standing of the parties and not according to characteristics of candidates. In the USA candidates need not even be loyal members of the party they purport to represent. They are chosen by those members of the electorate who wish to register as a Republican or a Democrat, and who are willing to turn out for a caucus or a primary election.

> Consequently, the decision as to who is – and hence what is – a Republican ... has been taken from the hands of the party bosses, whether at local or at state level or at federal level, and vested in local population: and this means that Democratic or Republican means just what this or that locality, in this or that year or set of circumstances, has decided they shall mean. And that varies all over the country from election to election. (Finer 1982: 228–9)

At local, state and federal level, US politicians have considerable opportunities to initiate legislation. Though bills will become law only if widely supported, the ability to table proposals and ensure votes on them allows zealots to publicize their issues and to force others to take a position on them. Legislators who refuse to support some ill-drafted piece of pet legislation can then be depicted come the next election as people who vote 'against God and the American family'.

To summarize, it is perfectly proper to point to the NCR as a challenge for the secularization paradigm. When set against the impotence of conservative Christians in Britain or France, it is indeed remarkable that groups such as the Moral Majority and Christian Coalition can become powerful political actors. But there is no need to lose all sense of proportion and, as sociologists Hadden and Shupe did, conclude that 'In time the conservative Christian movement has the potential to become solidified enough to "take over the country"' (1988: 286). In this section I have tried to establish two important points. First, the structure of American politics makes it relatively easy for zealots to acquire some leverage. Secondly, the track record of the NCR shows enormous resistance to theocracy.

Finally, by way of getting the NCR in proportion, I will report an interesting observation about pressure group power. In the 2000 elections, nearly $250 million were spent on television advertising. Researchers estimate that about 60 per cent of that was spent by political parties; the rest came from special-interest groups. The biggest spender was Citizens for Better Medicare, a group funded by the pharmaceuticals industry. The next eight top-spending organizations were, in order, the trade-union organization AFL-CIO, Planned Parenthood (which supports the provision of contraception and abortion), Chamber of Commerce, Business Roundtable, League of Conservation Voters, Americans for Job Security, Emily's List (which raises money to promote women candidates) and the Coalition to Protect America's Healthcare (Associated Press 2001).

Why the USA is different

Even allowing for the corrections suggested above, it is undoubtedly the case that the USA remains more religious than other industrial societies. If the secularization paradigm is to stand, it must be able to explain that difference in ways that are consistent with the way it explains decline elsewhere. I think it can.

Migrants and cultural transition

One obvious cause of US religious vitality is mentioned surprisingly rarely: the last three decades of the twentieth century saw a steady increase in the number of migrants from non-industrial countries with powerful conservative religious traditions. In 1998 the number of immigrants in the USA was 26.3 million, almost one in ten of the population, and the highest figure in seventy years. The largest proportion of these, almost a third, were from Mexico (Camarota 1999). The Caribbean and Asia came next. Very few migrants were from Europe. Unless the migrants are quite untypical of their native religious cultures, they will be considerably more devout than the typical US-born American. In chapter 1 I was at pains to make clear that the secularization paradigm is in the first instance a series of related explanations of changes *within industrial democracies* that erode the power and popularity of traditional religion there. As much in those explanations relates to the experience of growing up in such cultures, they are not tested by the greater religiosity of migrants. If large numbers of Nepalese people now migrate *en masse* to England, England will in one sense become a more religious country. But increasing overall levels of religious vitality by importing a more religious people refutes the secularization treatment of England's past no more than the subsequent reduction in average height (the Nepalese typically being shorter than the English) would refute the claimed links between increasing prosperity and height among the English.

So one explanation for US exceptionalism is that what is measured in surveys is not just the experiences and beliefs of those who have grown up and been socialized in the United States; those have been augmented by the experiences and beliefs of people raised in Mexico, Cuba and Haiti.

But the impact of immigration is not limited to the transfer of existing religious 'capital'. As I suggested in chapter 1, one of the important social functions of organized religion is to aid migrants to make the transition from old to new world. Churches form important linkage points in allowing migrants to retain contact with elements of their old culture – their religion and their language – while allowing them to mix with earlier migrants who are better established in the new territory. Immigrants may be drawn to churches not just by the social and practical benefits they can provide; religion in the more abstract sense may gain in importance as it provides solutions to the anomie or sense of loss that many migrants suffer.

To complete the comparison with the UK and Europe, we need note only that most European societies have seen little immigration and such as they have experienced has been of Muslims and Hindus, who, while they add religious capital in the sense described above, do not strengthen the local religious tradition.

Local consensus and national diversity

The second major difference between the USA and other industrial democracies has already been mentioned: the federal and diffuse structure of its polity. I would now like to draw out the consequences of that for the preservation of distinctive religious subcultures and I will begin by briefly considering an approach to US diversity that fundamentally misses the important point.

The supply-side theories of Rodney Stark and his associates have already been mentioned a number of times in this book. The basic ideas were first introduced by Alexis de Toqueville in his observations about religion in colonial America (de Toqueville 1945). Drawing a contrast with the rather moribund nature of the Catholic Church in his native France, de Toqueville noted an apparent connection between the number of competing Protestant sects and the vitality of religious life. However, those who have revived de Toqueville have failed to notice that his impression of variety was formed while *travelling* around the colonies. Considerable diversity at the national level was actually a consequence of high degrees of concentration in particular places of different religions. This distinction is vital. Elements of the supply-side story operate on different geographical and social planes. Diversity at the level of the nation state may determine issues of state subsidy and regulation, but, unless there is also considerable diversity lower down, in the places where ordinary people live and purportedly engage in maximizing behaviour, then we can hardly say that the typical American has any greater opportunity to choose a religion than has the typical Briton. Gaustad's geography of religious affiliation in the United States shows that many parts of America were remarkably homogenous. There were in 1950 'very few counties that were not dominated by one or another ecclesiastical bodies . . . in approximately one-half of the counties of the nation, a single religious body accounts for at least 50% of all the membership in the county' (Gaustad 1962: 159). This unity was reinforced by the clustering of similar counties: almost all of the many southern counties dominated by Baptists were bordered by other Baptist counties. Britain is often the implied contrast, but even in 1851, the year of the Census of Religious Worship, England and Wales looked remarkably like Gaustad's America. Just over half the counties were dominated by one religious organization. To put it no more strongly than this, the de Toqueville contrast is rather superficial and ill informed.

Better evidence for the link between pluralism and vitality was presented by Finke and Stark (1988) when they used the 1906 US Census of Religious Bodies to examine the relationship between church membership and religious diversity in the 150 largest towns and cities of the United States. The results were claimed as strong evidence that competition in religion, as in car production, increased rather than undermined consumption. However, as commentators were quick to point out, Finke and Stark's own statistics cast doubts on their claims: the link between diversity and vitality was very strongly negative. The more diverse places had the lower rates of church membership. There was a very strong link between the proportion of Catholics and church membership (but that may well have been because all baptized Catholics were counted as 'members'). Finke and Stark only managed to produce statistics that suited their argument by 'controlling' for the percentage Catholic in their regression equations. The experts will understand the problem of multi-collinearity (Olson 1999). The rest of us can simply note that the procedures come close to cooking the books. When others tried to replicate Finke and Stark's work, they failed. Land and colleagues analysed county-level data for over 700 counties and for a subset of counties that contained the 150 cities studied by Finke and Stark (Land et al. 1991). In both cases they came to quite the opposite conclusion. For the large sample they found that diversity was associated with low rates of church adherence, even when 'percentage Catholic' was figured into the regression equation. On the smaller sample of just the counties containing the big cities, they found that the direct effect of diversity was negative, until they entered the percentage Catholic into the equation, when it became positive but only very weakly so. When they added data from the 1920s and 1930s so that they could see the effects of diversity on church membership over time, they found that the negative effect of diversity was even greater. Only for a small sample containing the big cities could anything like the relationship posited by Finke and Stark be found and that was so weak as to be statistically insignificant. As the team put it: 'Our conclusion is that religious monopoly – not diversity – fuels religious expansion . . . [and] ethnic homogeneity is also conducive to religious expansion' (Blau et al. 1991: 329).

Breault applied the Finke and Stark model to 1980 data and found that religious diversity had a persistent, negative and statistically significant effect on the rate of adherence. After exploring a number of other possible explanations, Breault (1989a, b) concluded that the difference between his results and those of the supply-siders was simply that they had used a biased and limited sample and allowed their results to be distorted by the presence (and greater than average religious activity) of Irish and southern European Catholics.

In subsequent exchanges, the supply-siders have tried to answer these criticisms, but they have failed to satisfy other scholars that the statistical manipulation of the data that produced their confirming results was justified.[6] Without such sleight of hand, studies of the relationship between pluralism and religious vitality in the United States have found either no connection or the negative effect I would expect. Rather than going through all the contested studies, I will defer to my colleagues Chaves and Gorski, who have evaluated twenty-six published articles or chapters that analyse the links between religious pluralism and religious participation. Ten of those (seven of them authored by some combination of Stark, Finke and Iannaccone) found a positive relationship. Eleven found a negative relationship. Five found null effects. Within these publications, Chaves and Gorski found a total of 193 separate analyses and of these only 24 (12 per cent) yielded results that appear to support the new paradigm. After painstaking secondary analysis, Chaves and Gorski conclude: 'The empirical evidence contradicts the claim that religious pluralism is positively associated with religious participation in any general sense'. (2001: 279).

If, as most scholars believe, there is a strong connection between religious monopoly and the strength of religion as measured by indices of personal religious involvement, we can consider how the structure of the USA might make it easier for sectarian religious subcultures to survive. The sensible observation of the supply-siders is that the environment in which any religious organization operates has a marked effect on it; their mistake is that, in concentrating on the structure of the religious 'market' and the state's regulatory regime for religion, they take too narrow a view of what matters about the environment. There are aspects of the structure of public administration and the operations of the state (other than the regulation of religion) that have considerable consequences for the survival or growth of the sect. If a degree of distance from the wider society is beneficial, then it ought to be the case that the sectarian form of religion does best in those societies that make such distancing easier. This does indeed seem to be the case and goes a long way to explaining the different fates of conservative Protestantism in the USA and the UK.

In order to cope with its size and internal diversity, the United States has evolved a system of regulation of such matters as education and public broadcasting, two fields that are vital to the preservation of a deviant worldview, that is considerably more open and diffuse than the heavily centralized structures of the United Kingdom. In the USA it is relatively easy and inexpensive for people to start their own schools. Private schools may teach pretty much what they like and even state schools have considerable autonomy. With the exception of the schools run by the Catholic Church and the Church of England (and the latter are not numerous), the United Kingdom has only a very small and expensive elite private-school sector. Moreover, teachers are trained in public universities, accredited by public agencies and paid at national wage rates. State-funded schools (which includes the church-managed ones) are constrained by a national curriculum and

even private schools are kept similar by the common class and educational background of their staff and the requirements of the examination boards that validate their qualifications.

The point can be illustrated with a recent dispute in Kansas. The
arguments began in October 1998 when a committee of twenty-seven
science teachers appointed by the Kansas Commissioner of Education
drew up a science curriculum. The ten members of the elected Kansas
Board of Education split 5–5 over two pages of proposals for the
teaching of evolutionary biology. The board created a three-man subcommittee to draft alternative proposals; all three were Republicans
and two were vocal supporters of creation science. Having removed
the references to evolution, the subcommittee tried to insert mention
of an 'intelligent designer' of the universe. This too was removed.
After much argument, the board voted 6–4 for a set of proposals that
avoided the subject entirely. Professional scientific opinion was out-
raged. The presidents of the six state universities in Kansas had sent
a letter to the board arguing that to reject evolution from the curriculum 'will set Kansas back a century and give hard-to-find science
teachers no choice but to pursue other career fields or assignments
outside Kansas' (Benen 1999: 2).

The curriculum was not binding on state schools but it would have
had an indirect effect in that it would have set the content for statewide
assessment tests, performance on which determines the standing of
schools. Republican Governor Bill Graves tried to downplay the significance of the outcome by saying 'There are 304 locally elected
school boards who have the option to tell the state board to go jump
in the lake' (Benen 1999: 4). And some did. The superintendent and
board president in Auburn-Washburn, one of five districts in Topeka,
announced that evolution would be taught in the district's science
classes. On the other side of the debate, the president of the Pratt
school board welcomed the outcome and said she hoped creationism
would soon be taught in her district's schools.

Three points about this are significant. First, that each of 304 elected
school boards may decide what counts as good science contrasts dramatically with the UK situation (typical of that in most European
countries) where schools follow a common curriculum designed by
professional educators. Secondly, the dispute arose after religious right
groups failed to oust Governor Graves (who defeated their candidate
by 73 to 27 per cent in the primary) but claimed enough seats on the
state Board of Education, where the smallness of the vote allowed a

small group of committed activists to elect their candidates. Thirdly, the point I made in considering the NCR generally: the initial local victory was reversed once a wider audience had become involved. The controversy ensured a much larger turn-out and the two members of the board most associated with the creationist line lost their seats.

Vital to any group's preservation of a distinctive worldview and way of life is its ability to control information and ideas. Until the technical innovations of the 1980s that brought satellite and cable television and the liberalization introduced by the Conservative government led by Margaret Thatcher from 1979 to 1994, the British mass media were heavily constrained. There were only four national radio channels, all controlled by the state British Broadcasting Corporation (BBC). Until 1982, when a fourth was licensed, Britain had only three television channels, two of them run by the BBC. Even the two commercial channels were heavily controlled. Individuals and organizations could not purchase air time to show their own programmes and ideological advertising was not permitted. The BBC and the commercial companies were required to provide religious broadcasting but its content was heavily regulated so that it encompassed the broad consensus of Christian churches. As Britain has become more culturally diverse, that consensus has been broadened. Opportunities to broadcast on BBC Radio Four's *Thought for the Day* or *Songs of Praise*, for example, are rotated around the varying religious organizations and traditions roughly in proportion to their presence in the population at large and there is a very clear understanding that spokesmen will not be provocative, will not criticize other religions, and will not proselytize. Since the 1970s, the space given to religion has diminished and the broadcasters now fulfil their statutory obligation to produce religious programming by having secular programme-makers make programmes *about* religion. To summarize, for most of the twentieth century British television and radio produced common-denominator religious programmes of an essentially ecumenical character. What they did not do was allow particular religious organizations or communities to produce programmes that represented their views.

We can see the importance of these different regulatory regimes if we consider the ability of US sectarians to construct their own world. The following is a composite sketch of a fundamentalist family in Lynchburg, Virginia, constructed by mixing together three such families that I got to know well in the early 1980s. Call them Fred and Wilma. Fred was an assistant pastor in Jerry Falwell's Liberty Baptist Church;

Wilma taught in the independent Christian school that was attached to the church. Their two children attended that school. On graduation one child went to Falwell's Liberty University; the other went to another religious institution, Oral Roberts University in Tulsa, Oklahoma. During the holidays the students of Liberty University helped run a fundamentalist summer camp. The church also supported a maternity home and adoption agency for unmarried mothers, a programme for reformed alcoholics, and a prison visiting programme. Wilma's mother had an apartment in a church-run complex for 'senior saints'. She and her elderly friends helped out with the church bookstore and with the huge mailing operation that was attached to Falwell's television show *The Old Time Gospel Hour*. The family watched programmes on Pat Robertson's Christian Broadcasting Network (now the Family Channel) or the Trinity network and listened to Christian radio channels and programmes. The kids listened to Christian rock and country music. The family did not take a secular newspaper but subscribed to a range of weekly and monthly Christian magazines. Fred had a publication called *Christian Yellow Pages* that allowed him to make sure he purchased goods and services from like-minded fundamentalists. The family typically took their holidays at a leisure complex on the South Carolina coast run by fundamentalists.

What struck me forcefully about this life was not that committed Christians should spend a lot of time in church-related activities (though they did). It was that, even when they wanted to do mundane things such as enjoy a watersports holiday, they did it in a fundamentalist environment. If they chose to, fundamentalists in Lynchburg could inhabit a world that was fundamentalist in almost the sense that England in the Middle Ages was Christian. They had constructed for themselves a culturally homogenous society to support their fundamentalist subculture. They had managed to ensure that most representations of the outside world came filtered through fundamentalist media. They had provided themselves with fundamentalist alternatives to secular institutions. Although they were extremely hospitable to me, whom they treated as a visitor from another world (one lady asked me what it was like living under communism!), they had a social life that ensured almost no positive social interaction with people who were not fundamentalists.

This is the paradox that is overlooked by the rational-choice theorists. Diversity, if it produces a pluralistic structure for public administration and government, allows people considerable freedom to *avoid* diversity.

Where British Christians are offered an almost unavoidable diet of programming that insidiously undermines their particular beliefs, US evangelicals have been able to create a system that allows them to avoid what they do not like and produce what they do like. The parallel world of US fundamentalist institutions allows a young fundamentalist to study law at a good quality conservative Protestant institution. The Scottish evangelical who wishes a career in law will be taught by unbelievers in a secular institution.

Of course, there is a degree of circularity involved in this account. US fundamentalists have the facilities to construct their own minority world because there are a lot of them. There are now so few conservative Protestants in Britain that, even when broadcasting regulations were relaxed in the 1990s, they could not take advantage of them. Although the regulations now permit the establishment of a Christian cable television channel, there is too small a market to make it viable.

To summarize: to the extent that a nation state or a society is prepared to allow people to create their own subcultures, the sect form can prosper by socializing its children in the faith. If the nation state or the society does not allow autonomous institution building, then sectarians will find it difficult and expensive to insulate themselves from the wider secular society.

Conclusion

I have no wish to protect the secularization paradigm from refutation. Its core ideas are of any value only if they can survive rigorous testing, not avoid it. Hence it is important that we consider the case of the United States.

Scholars such as Stark and Greeley have made much of the apparent stability of religious belief and behaviour in the USA. The case I have made here is that, while organized religion remains much more vigorous in the USA than in any other industrial democracy of the 'First World', there are very clear signs that the mainstream Christian churches are declining in popularity and that the conservative Protestant churches are losing their doctrinal and behavioural distinctiveness. Privatization, individualism and relativism are now affecting the US churches in the way they did the British churches in the middle of the twentieth century. In chapters 1 and 4, I argued that those three forces weakened religion by undermining the cohesion of religious

organizations, reducing the degree of background affirmation provided for any worldview in the flow of everyday life, and weakening
the commitment of individuals to ensuring the successful transmission of their religious culture intact to their children. At present this
must stand as something of a prediction but, to return to the data
presented at the start of the chapter, I think we can already see the
effects of increased liberalism in the figures for church adherence.

CHAPTER TWELVE

Postmodernism and Religious Revival

Introduction

The last two centuries have not been kind to the Christian churches in Western societies. With what sounds like more than a trace of desperation, church leaders are left having to make such spurious claims for importance as asserting that more people go to church than attend football matches – a far cry from the days when almost everyone accepted a Christian cosmology, when prelates and preachers were figures of stature, and when at least half the people attended church regularly. Not surprisingly, those who regret the secularization of the West search for signs that the cultural tide might be turning again in their favour. Some have recently seen an opportunity for hope in the social scientist's depiction of our present condition as being in some sense 'postmodern'. I will very briefly explain postmodernism, explain why some Christians hope the future will be more fruitful than the recent past, and consider whether their hopes are likely to be realized. In so doing, I will clarify just what the secularization paradigm asserts and expects.

Postmodernism

The notion of postmodernism is unfortunately popular. It is the intellectual equivalent of velcro: everything sticks to it. James Beckford's brief summary, however, captures most of what is meant by the term.

1 A refusal to regard positivistic, rationalistic, instrumental criteria as the sole or exclusive standard of worthwhile knowledge.
2 A willingness to combine symbols from disparate codes or frameworks of meaning, even at the cost of disjunctions and eclecticism.
3 A celebration of spontaneity, fragmentation, superficiality, irony and playfulness.

4   A willingness to abandon the search for over-arching or triumphalist myths, narratives or frameworks of knowledge. (1992: 19)

Before we can go further, we need to distinguish between being postmodern and, from the standpoint of conventional notions about knowledge, asserting that the world has become postmodern. Postmodernists regularly betray their own principles by engaging in the second activity: trying to persuade us that their account of the world is an accurate one supported by rational argument and compelling evidence. Beyer expresses the irony neatly when he says 'postmodern critique and analysis usually has a Phoenix-like quality in that it tends to suggest a new authoritative narrative after having deconstructed the old ones' (1996: 1). In order to evaluate the claims postmodernists make about the world, we must follow their common practise and decline to be postmodern ourselves.

The sorts of things meant by social scientists when they use the term can be reasonably summarized in two clusters. First, the term suggests that a variety of beliefs and hopes often summarized as 'the Enlightenment project' have lost credibility. The term 'project' is unhelpful on two counts. First, it suggests a closeness and deliberate cooperation among the thinkers of the Enlightenment period (the second half of the eighteenth century) that was rarely in evidence. Secondly, it gives too great a weight to philosophy. I do not want to dismiss the work of intellectuals as being of no account, but, if social science has taught us anything, it is that there is often a huge gulf between what the 'chattering classes' think and do and the lives and worldviews of ordinary people. But, with those reservations in mind, we can proceed. The general idea is that, throughout the nineteenth century and for most of the twentieth, we in the West had a rather naive and touching faith in our ability to advance human progress by applying reason (most perfectly embodied in science) and by rejecting the dark superstitions of religion. According to the postmodernists, this has changed: we have lost faith in the possibility of arriving at a single truth, be that in science, politics, culture or ethics. And we have lost faith in the notion of progress; we are no longer sure that science, technology and industrial growth do represent movement towards a better future.

The term 'postmodern' is also used to suggest significant changes in the sources of social identity. The most powerful attempts to conceptualize industrial societies in the twentieth century concentrated on the role in shaping our identities and behaviour of such social agents and institutions as the nation, the state, class, gender and race. The modern was seen as offering more freedom and variation than the premodern or traditional society. For example, in a class society people could achieve upward social mobility to an extent that was almost impossible in a feudal agrarian society: the children of manual workers could become professionals far more easily than the children of serfs could rise above their 'station'. But people in postmodern societies are even freer because what were once powerful group ties have weakened, as has the ability of the economy or polity to define us. Industrial work used to fill so much of our time and create such marked divisions between classes that what Marx called our 'relationship to the means of production' was a powerful determinant of much else about us. With the decline of 'metal-bashing' manufacture, the rise in service industries, the shortening of the working day, the increase in flexible working practices, and the increasing importance of cultural production in wealth generation, consumption has become more important than production. How we spend our money says far more about us than how we earn it. Who we are and what we do is no longer largely determined by class (or race or gender) but is selected by us, the autonomous consumers, as a 'lifestyle' choice. In that sense, the postmodernists argue that culture has become divorced from the economy, the polity and the society. The 'post-modern turn is . . . a turn away from assuming that modernity, with its typical foci on work as economic activity and on calculation as the acme of reason, will continue to form the matrix for social interaction' (Lyon 1996: 19).

One supposed consequence of our loss of faith in progress and our inflated sense of personal liberty is the relativism I discussed in chapters 1, 4 and 6. If we no longer have faith in the authority of some elite to tell us what is progress, truth, fine art or the best model for personal or social life, and if we believe that we have unprecedented freedom from external constraints, then we proliferate alternative cultures, visions and modes of behaviour at the same time as removing the grounds for setting any one above any other.

My general response to this depiction of twenty-first century Britain or the USA is to accept that it has some value; to an extent it is simply what sociologists have seen as the dominant features of the modern world. However, the extent of the changes is exaggerated. In part this is probably because the cosmopolitan middle-class intellectuals who promote the notion are blind to the extent to which they are unusual. On one late-night television chat show discussing fashion, a glamorous London journalist said: 'Of course, everyone's got a pashmina these days.' It may well be that this particular type of Eastern shawl is common in Hampstead, but it is hard to believe it has displaced the bri-nylon housecoat in Workington, Cardiff and Inverness!

A second source of exaggeration is mistaking surface appearance for reality. In advertising their products, manufacturers like to flatter us their customers by appealing to our individuality (while, somewhat inconsistently, claiming that we can all express it by consuming the same product). Doubtless we have a far greater variety of products from which to choose than had our grandparents (though, like the ten different coloured covers you can fit on your Nokia mobile phone, much of the variation may be superficial). When I was young shampoo came in just two brands. Now my supermarket stocks over 300 varieties. Doubtless many of us do use our wealth and freedom to create what we believe to be our own idiosyncratic sense of identity. When I choose coal tar soap while my vegetarian wife chooses tea tree oil, we are both making small statements about our views of the natural versus the synthetic, and the industrial versus the agrarian. But we should not underestimate the continued power of group identities; teenage schoolchildren reject school uniforms but elect to impose upon themselves a rigid dress code defined by fashion. Nor should we ignore the continued importance of social forces in the creation of group identities. We may think of ourselves as autonomous individuals, but studies of attitudes and beliefs (for example, political preferences) show that we can still predict a considerable amount about people if we know their social class. Educational performance, health and even length of life are still largely determined by class.

A third problem with many applications of the idea of postmodernity is that it is too blunt an instrument. The assertion of two distinct epochs exaggerates. Consider the supposed death of the Enlightenment project. It is certainly true that we are far more thoughtful about the consequences of science than we were fifty years ago and many of us are wary of specific scientific developments (gene therapy or nuclear power, for example), but this is a very long way from saying that thought has become so thoroughly relativized that most of us cannot see a difference in kind between astronomy and astrology, or between surgery and aura healing. To put it simply, that we are no longer as enthusiastic cheerleaders for science, technology, social planning and economic growth as the Victorians does not mean that all ways of viewing the world have become equally attractive or plausible.

The return of the gods?

But let us assume for a moment that the world has indeed changed enough to make the label 'postmodern' appropriate and consider what might be the consequences for religion. First, the promoters of religion might hope that the decline of confidence in science and technology and rational thought would relativize what they took to have been the main challenge to religious ideas. Hufford believes that the postmodern condition creates possibilities for religion that modernity denied it (Beyer 1996: 1). This claim is not all that novel. In the 1960s Peter Berger's work was seminal in drawing attention to the difficulties of maintaining high levels of commitment to a body of ideas that changed from being the taken-for-granted worldview of most people to being just one among many alternatives. In *The Social Reality of Religion* (1969) and *The Heretical Imperative* (1980) he examined the relativizing effects of religious pluralism. But alongside that strand of work he also developed a counterpoint. If pluralism relativizes, then it presumably relativizes the alternatives to religion as much as religion. Hence there is space to revive religious beliefs. They cannot be set on the same sure basis as they were in 'pre-hermeneutic' cultures. As the title of *The Heretical Imperative* says, all believers are now 'heretics' in the sense that they must be aware they have chosen God, rather than the other way round. But, with once-arrogant rationalism cut down to size by the relativizing forces it unleashed, the choice to believe can again be a respectable one. Although Berger avoided the periodizing language of the modern and the postmodern, he was making the case that others later presented under that general heading.

In a 1991 essay that repeated many of his early reservations about applications of the notion of secularization, David Martin also pointed to the possibility of new scope for religious belief. He summarizes as follows his comments on the decline of what he takes to be the two main causes of secularization: the establishment politics of religion and the rationalism of the Enlightenment.

> The two supports of that [secular] dynamic are now in terminal dissolution. On the one side, the establishments of religion which gave it a negative association with power and particular elite styles are either things of the past or ineffective facades of the kind remaining in England and

Scandinavia. On the other side, the rationalistic passions unleashed by the French Revolution have now diminished to the status of a puppet show . . . The issue is, therefore, whether this situation begins to allow a new kind of space for religiosity as old alignments become remote memories, or stimulates a total fragmentation of all belief systems. (1991: 473)

It is important to note (and I will return to this) that, unlike the more naive postmodern religious optimists, Martin sees an alternative to religious revival. But staying with his depiction of what has changed recently, I want to add some reservations. The disestablishment of religion has indeed weakened the ties between the churches and the ruling classes. However, possibly stigmatizing connections remain. In most countries (especially in those European states with Christian Democrat parties) the Christian mainstream remains associated with the political right. The past when the two were more firmly entwined is not so far past as to be beyond recall. Spaniards do not need long memories to remember Franco, nor the British to remember the Empire. Although the very specific links between the dominant church in any polity and its ruling class may have been weakened, there is still a widespread perception in the West that Christianity is on the side of imperialism (witness left-wing criticisms of Pentecostal missionaries in the Third World). As I pointed out in chapters 4 and 6, very many of the university-educated middle-class people outside the Christian churches who seek some form of spiritual enlightenment do so by exploring the religious traditions of every civilization bar their own. Christianity is bad; aboriginal traditions are good. More generally, in most European countries there is still a strong link between being conventionally Christian and being on the conservative side of many socio-moral arguments. But what is most germane to my argument is Martin's second point: a more historically fixed version of the postmodernist claim about the death of the Enlightenment.

Martin may well be right that 'the rationalistic passions unleashed by the French Revolution' are now a puppet show, if we confine those passions to their political embodiment in scientific Marxism or to the self-consciously rationalistic philosophies of humanist and rationalist associations. As I have repeatedly noted, secularism and rationalism were most popular at the same time as the evangelical and high church movements they so vehemently opposed (Campbell 1971; Budd 1977). We can even accept that beating the drum for science (in the manner of, for example, Richard Dawkins) is now rarer than it was in the 1950s. What we need not accept is that the declining social status of science has turned the competition to produce convincing explanations of the nature of the world into a handicap race, with all the competitors variously weighed down so that they start with an equal chance of finishing first. There is considerable difference between saying that we are now sceptical about some aspects of science and that we have become complete relativists. Even most practitioners of spiritual medicine defer to conventional doctors for most serious ailments and the playfulness and irony that Beckford lists in postmodern traits tends to dissolve in the fact of such obdurate realities as AIDS, falling share values and urban crime.

The idea that loss of confidence in science makes religion more plausible would be more compelling if it were the case that science played a major part in the displacement of religious beliefs and ideas. But, as I have repeatedly argued, scientific ideas were not on their own a major source of secularization. What was much more important was the general sense of mastery over fate and it is not clear that the relativizing of knowledge claimed by the postmodernists has brought about much change in that respect. Or at least, the claims are not entirely consistent. It may be that the citizens of a postmodern world will feel alienated and lost, but one element of the postmodern depiction suggests that we now reject authoritative views because we have sufficient self-confidence to 'make up our own minds' and choose our own destinies.

The claim that we have lost faith in rationality may also be a little misplaced, because this too misunderstands the causal claims made by the secularization paradigm. It does not argue that rationalism, as a positive commitment to a particular philosophy, was significant in eroding the plausibility and salience of religion. Rather it asserts that the embodiment of rational procedures in bureaucratic organizations created the underlying impression of inhabiting an orderly world; which in turn reduced the scope of religion. Whatever the standing of rationalism, it is hard to see that the industrial societies of 2001 are any less dominated by bureaucratic rationality than were those of 1901.

The general problem I have with the idea that the future of religion is closely related to standing of science or rationalism is that it rests on a basic mistake about secularization. Most people did not give up being committed Christians because they became convinced that religion was *false*. It simply ceased to be of any great importance to them; they became indifferent.

Choice and belief

Let us return now to David Martin's expectation for the future. As I noted, he offers two possibilities: 'a new kind of space for religiosity' and 'a total fragmentation of all belief systems' (1991: 473). I know he would prefer the former, but I am not sure which he believes more likely. I am convinced that it is the latter.

My grounds for supposing a revival of religion unlikely are as follows. Let us adopt a neutral position on the question of whether people are in some sense programmed to ask the sort of meaning-of-life questions that have traditionally been answered by religions. What we know is that biological needs do not automatically produce a single cultural solution. We might suppose that there is a universal sexual impulse. Yet societies vary enormously in how that impulse is exhibited and in what counts as acceptable (or even pleasurable) sexual activity. We might suppose that there is a universal reproductive impulse. Yet societies vary enormously in the way that reproduction is organized. In some societies people have many children; in others few. In some cultures, a child is raised by its mother and father; in others by its mother and uncles. Some cultures value male and female babies equally; others prefer one over the other. The same tension can be noted with the matter of instincts. There may well be a will to survive, but people can commit suicide. There may well be a sexual urge, but people can remain celibate.

The point does not need to be laboured. Even if we accept that a common human biology creates common concerns, cross-cultural comparison shows us that how those concerns are addressed is a matter of *social organization*. Even if it is the case that the declining persuasiveness of alternative worldviews has created a new space of religion in the postmodern world, it does not follow that the space will be filled. Consensus does not emerge spontaneously, especially in a field that is uniquely open to speculation.

This is an important point about religion that is insufficiently noticed. In many areas of life the options are relatively few. They are constrained by material realities and social institutions. We may argue about which of road, rail, sea and air offers the fastest, most environmentally friendly or cost-effective modes of travel, but most people have only those options for long-distance travel, and, if you live in a landlocked county that has no airport and no railway line, then road it is. More abstract fields, such as polities, obviously offer greater choice.

Political parties may present quite different possible state structures. But here too we are dealing with a small hand of cards. Monarchy or no monarchy, oligarchy or democracy, federal or centralized; it does not take long to run through the options. Furthermore, most of us confine our preferences to what seems possible. Few of us entertain the possibility of feudalism or anarcho-syndicalism. We are constrained by history and by the distribution of power. Not so in the field of religious speculation. Now that we have access to the entire world's repertoire of religious beliefs and behaviour and our previously dominant tradition is now too weak to stigmatize all but a few of them as unthinkable, in this field we have an almost unlimited range of possibilities.

All of which brings me to this point: in a world where it is possible to imagine almost any sort of supernatural power and impute to it almost any characteristics, what are the chances that people will naturally imagine the *same* religion? Very slight, I would have thought. Or, to put it the other way round, even if we were all spiritual seekers (and the evidence shows that, in secular societies such as Britain, the majority of us are not), what are the chances that we would seek in the same place and find a common answer? Again, very slight. Will consensus be produced by the weight of our religious tradition? Obviously not, or we would not have achieved our current degree of cultural pluralism.

It is this logic that causes me to doubt that the characteristics imputed by postmodernists to Western societies at the start of the twenty-first century will produce in them any marked revival of religion. There is nothing about increasing choice and a new stress on lifestyles and options that makes it any more likely that people will choose to believe similar things.

The fate of religion then turns on the difficult notion of the extent to which religious ideas need to be shared for them to be socially significant and to be sustainable. I would like to return to Berger's recantation of his early commitment to the secularization paradigm. It is clear that Berger remains committed to one of his original observations: the role that pluralism plays in undermining certainty. For example, in 1998 he wrote: 'whether we like it or not, if we are honest, religion for us cannot be based on knowledge, only on belief. The question is how we cope with this situation. Can we live with it?' (1998: 782).

The crux of the matter can be put either in terms of belief-systems or in terms of forms of association. In chapter 4 I described some belief-systems as 'strong' and others as 'weak' or 'diffuse'. Because it is misunderstood, I should stress again that this is a sociological consideration and involves no suggestion that strong beliefs are better than weak ones or that 'true religion' must be 'strong'. The strong–weak characterization was popularized by Dean Kelley in his explanation of *Why the Conservative Churches are Growing* (1972). In Hoge's summary:

> Strong churches are characterized by a demand for high commitment from their members. They exact discipline over both beliefs and life-style. They have missionary zeal with an eagerness to tell the good news to all persons. They are absolutistic about beliefs. Their beliefs are a total closed system, sufficient for all purposes, needing no revision and permitting none. They require conformity in life-style, often involving certain avoidances of non-members or use of distinctive visible marks or uniforms. (1979: 179)

The behavioural characteristics in the first four sentences and the last sentence follow from the characteristics of the beliefs given in the fifth sentence. In order to be strict and maintain zeal, believers must view their beliefs as authoritative. If they allow that there are a variety of sources of truth and a variety of equally legitimate sources of interpretation, the result is diversity and a generally tolerant attitude to most of those with whom they differ.

Allowing for some slippage, we can describe conservative Catholicism and evangelical or fundamentalism Protestantism as 'strong' and the liberal variants of Christianity and New Age spirituality as 'weak'. Elsewhere I have explored the problems of strong religion (Bruce 1999) and will say here only that the sacrifices it requires (primarily of social isolation and the forgoing of individual liberty) seem willingly made by large numbers only in circumstances that are relatively rare in the West: for example, where the believers are geographically isolated or otherwise already excluded from the social mainstream. But we can let that pass because what is at issue in Berger's revision is the future of liberal religion. He believes that it is possible for people to sustain indefinitely a loose and amorphous faith that accepts uncertainty. I doubt that.

My empirical ground for disagreeing is simply that, as Berger notes, secularization seems to have had the greatest impact on religions that are denominational rather than sectarian. In the UK, for example, the rare incidents of net growth or stability are to be found among the sects; the mainstream churches have been declining for fifty years and continue to do so.

My theoretical grounds are extensive (see Bruce 1999), but the basic disagreements can be readily conveyed. First, I believe Berger exaggerates the stability of liberal Christianity because he fails to appreciate the extent to which its cohesion is a historical contingency. The essential diffuseness of liberal religion is a constant: as soon as one permits that the truth can take a variety of forms, the epistemological basis for discipline is removed and proliferation of permissible interpretations is possible. However, the degree of cohesion in liberal religion is variable and currently mainstream churches retain some coherence from their more orthodox past. All the major denominations began life as churches or sects. This is often repeated in the biographies of individuals. Most of those responsible for the development of liberal Christianity, either as an intellectual force or in its organizational form in the ecumenical movement, were raised in conservative homes. They found it possible to be undogmatic about their faith because they had been thoroughly socialized in the dogmas. The problem is that, unless it is wisely invested, cultural capital is a wasting asset. With each generation that passes, commitment to the core beliefs (and even knowledge of them) becomes weaker and weaker.

A further sense in which denominational Christianity is precarious is that much of its appeal rested on a contrast with sectarian Christianity. Many liberals of Berger's generation were attracted to their present faith because it was a liberation from the stifling orthodoxies of their upbringing. So long as sectarian religion was popular, the liberal alternative had a pool from which it could recruit. For the ever-larger number of people who have not been socialized in a sectarian version of the Christian faith, the liberal alternative has very little appeal.

Finally I would like to repeat the observations made about the reproduction of beliefs in chapter 4. Crucial to the fate of liberal, diffuse, denominational religion is success in transmitting it to the next generation. Let us put the problem in a contrast of two imaginary couples. The liberal Protestant, because he does not have a hard line between the saved and the unregenerate, marries a non-practising Jew. He continues in his faith but what does that couple transmit to its children? How can they insist that the children go regularly to Sunday school, read their Bibles every night, and have family prayers before meals? If their children develop any interest in religion at all, it is likely to be the autonomous open seeking perspective of those who end up creating their own mixture from a wide variety of religious traditions. Now imagine an evangelical Baptist. He spends a lot of time in church-related activities and marries another evangelical Baptist. They send their children to an independent Christian school, have family prayers and Bible studies, and intensively socialize their children in their faith. Of three children one may fall away, but there is a good chance at least one will continue in that faith.

This then is the core of my disagreement with Berger's view of liberal religion. He believes that its appeal will allow it to survive the organizational problems inherent in having a diffuse belief-system. I think not. The unrelenting decline of British Methodism suggests that when levels of ambient Christianity are already low, liberal Christianity will not be able to reproduce itself. If we wish to identify a model in our days of what religion beyond the sects will look like in fifty years time, we should look not at the liberal Christian denominations, which are doomed, but at the world of New Age spirituality: a world in which individuals select from a global cafeteria of ideas, rituals and therapies that appeal to them. As I argued in chapter 4, precisely because they are so thoroughly individualized, diffuse beliefs will have very little impact even on those who carry them, let alone on their wider societies.

Conclusion

An old Chinese maxim says you should always leave a house by the door through which you entered. I have left this brief discussion of postmodernity until the end of this volume because it allows me to return to the place I started: the core principles of the secularization paradigm. We may want to explain the secularity of some elite groups (such as professional scientists) by the impact of science and rationalism, but to understand the mass of the population it is not self-conscious irreligion that is important. It is indifference. The primary cause of indifference is the lack of religious socialization and the lack of constant background affirmation of beliefs. The point stands whether we are entering some new postmodern society or merely seeing a continuation of the dominant features of the modern world. On the matters germane to understanding the key causes of secularization, the postmodernists see the same things as the modernists. The combination of cultural diversity and egalitarianism prevent our children being raised in a common faith, stop our beliefs being constantly reaffirmed by religious celebrations of the turning of the seasons and the key events in the life cycle, and remove from everyday interaction the 'conversational' reaffirmation of a shared faith. I have been at pains to make clear that nothing in the secularization paradigm requires that this be the fate of all societies. However, where diversity and egalitarianism have become deeply embedded in the public consciousness and embodied in liberal democracy, where states remain sufficiently prosperous and stable that the fact of diversity and the attitude of egalitarianism are not swept away by some currently unimaginable cataclysm, I see no grounds to expect secularization to be reversed.

Notes

Chapter 1: The Secularization Paradigm

1   Although Wilson usually confines his definition of secularization to the declining social significance of religion, it is clear from the frequent use he makes of data on individual religious beliefs and behaviour (e.g. 1966: 21) that he regards personal religiosity as both an index of the social significance of religion and an effect of it.

2   Parsons (1960) himself thought secularization in the largest sense impossible because societies needed the integration that shared values provided. Although he identified the increasing separation of church and state as a distinctive feature of modern societies, he believed that it was possible only because Christian values had been generalized to the wider society.

3   It should be noted that I am concerned with the consequences of differentiation for the plausibility and salience of religious beliefs and institutions. Though the problem of social control and social integration fascinated most of those who originally wrote on the subject, the effect of differentiation on social regulation is not my interest.

4   In line with the policy of confining myself to social science, I am concentrating on those elements of Niebuhr's work that are primarily sociological. He was a theologian as well as a historian and he has other interests that are none of our business.

5   Later historians of science have challenged some of Merton's work, but the general link between Puritanism and science has been sustained; see Klaaran (1977).

6   This is mainly a problem for theistic belief systems. It is easier for the more philosophical strands of Buddhism and Hinduism to effect a reconciliation by arguing that the natural and spiritual worlds all obey the same 'higher' laws. Transcendental Meditation's Natural Law Party frequently borrows language from subatomic physics to describe its beliefs.

7   In his early work Berger (1969: 108–9) comes close to suggesting that the 'Westernization' of the Third World would inevitably be accompanied by secularization. However, he does distinguish between social-structural secularization and the secularization of consciousness, which, though he does not develop the point, would have allowed him to see only the former as inevitable. As Berger became more interested in the Third World, he developed much more nuanced views of modernization. He also recanted his earlier views of secularization in the West. I wonder if his desire to

correct his earlier views on the Third World has led him to over-correct his stance on the secularization of the First World.

Chapter 2: The Golden Age of Faith

1 It is an unfortunate feature of Stark's style that he often misrepresents those with whom he disagrees. On this point he says of me: 'Recently, even he admitted (Bruce 1999) that, in terms of organized participation, the Golden Age of Faith never existed. Indeed, Bruce now proposes that . . .' (Stark and Finke 2000: 71). He could more accurately have said: 'Bruce has recently clarified what he believes the secularization paradigm requires of the past.' The words used suggest that at some time in the past I believed in some Golden Age of Faith and have only recently been forced to admit the error of my ways. As far as I am aware, what I say in this chapter is what I have always believed and is what I learnt from Wilson and Wallis in the early 1970s.

2 For a general review of recent historical scholarship, see Marsh (1998). A first-rate and extremely detailed study of attitudes to death (Houlbrooke 1998) also provides a good indicator of the strength of popular religion.

Chapter 3: God is Dead: Christianity in Britain

1 It is worth adding a note about non-Christian religion. It is not racism that causes me to overlook it in this analysis. Rather it is that, on three grounds, it is not yet central to the argument about the secularity or otherwise of Britain. First, despite our quite proper concern to recognize that Britain is now in some sense a 'multi-faith' society, Muslims, Hindus and Buddhists form only a small part of the population. Out of a total population of some fifty-seven million, there are around one million Muslims, 300,000 Hindus, 300,000 Jews, 300,000 Sikhs and 120,000 Buddhists. These are figures for imputed or communal identity. In national surveys, generally less than 2 per cent claim a non-Christian identity. Secondly, there is no evidence of significant numbers of native Britons joining any of these religions; they are so closely associated with ethnic identities that they do not form part of the religious expressions that the former Christians who concern us in these debates could take up. Thirdly, we are concerned with changes in the religious climate of Britain; hence the religious beliefs and behaviour of people who have recently migrated from very different countries can be left aside. It is of no consequence for the debate that the overall religious vitality of a country may be increased by importing population from a more religious country. The only point that might be worth further thought is the consequence for the meaning of data on religious beliefs. Especially in England, where British Muslims are concentrated,

their presence probably increases slightly the popularity of a number of religious items in attitudinal surveys. Finally, I might add that the evidence suggests that, as immigrants become established and they and their children become upwardly mobile, commitment to their faith is weakened.

2   This is one very limited sense in which the supply-side claims about competition are valid. Competition between dissenting sects did not make the people of Britain more religious, but it did cause them to demonstrate more obviously their allegiances by formally joining churches that previously they would simply have attended. This was particularly the case in Scotland after the major Free Church schism in 1843. The bitter controversy over the division of assets forced most Scots to take sides (Bruce 1999: 83–8).

3   This sort of remark is frequently made and deserves to be examined closely: an ideal doctoral topic. I suspect the point about trade unions is misleading. They have declined, not because workers who were trade unionists lost interest in associating, but because eighteen years of Conservative government killed off the industries with unionized labour forces, introduced penal anti-union legislation, forced many large organizations such as the BBC to contract out work to small independent firms, and encouraged the growth of freelance working. I am also suspicious of the parallel with political parties. The Conservative Party has never had a mass membership and the Labour Party has very deliberately reduced the role and influence of local branches, thus removing most of the reasons for membership. It remains the case that the majority of British people still vote but they no longer go to church.

Chapter 4: The Failure of the New Age

1   Because it is relevant to my argument about the sustainability of the movement, it is worth noting that the stability and growth of the Mind–Body–Spirit Festival conceal a considerable turnover of individual providers of therapies, ideas and products. Malcolm Hamilton (2000: 195) shows similar numbers of exhibitors in 1987, 1992 and 1997 (83, 98 and 97 respectively), but only two of the 1987 exhibitors were still there in 1997. As Hamilton says, most of those who have disappeared over the past years have probably done so 'as a result of changing fashions, loss of interest and economic unviability' (2000: 194).

2   A brief but caustic letter published in a Scottish daily paper made an interesting observation about holism that, if it can be stripped of the implied insults, deserves to be investigated: another doctoral thesis. The writer suggested that the 'middling educated' are attracted to the idea of a holistic approach to complex phenomena because it allows them to

claim to be well informed on the basis of superficial and easily gained knowledge. For example, the two ideas of 'energy lines' in the body and 'ley lines' on the ground, and the parallel between them, are easy to grasp with little study beyond reading a few thin paperbacks. Serious study of the human nervous, circulatory and lymphatic systems is extremely arduous, as is conventional archaeology.

3 Rose's *Kindred Spirit* reader survey (1998) asked for and reports social class, age and income level. That race or ethnicity is not mentioned suggests such questions were not asked and I presume that Dr Rose omitted this issue because he knew it was not a variable. Jorgensen and Russell (1999) report that 89 per cent of their sample of US neo-pagans were white but do not discuss it further.

4 In case this use of an economistic model of behaviour is thought to be at odds with my repeated rejection of such a model elsewhere, I should stress that I accept there is a place for explaining human behaviour with the assumption of a basic desire to maximize utility. As I argue at length (Bruce 1999), rational-choice approaches fail to explain conventional religious attachments and behaviour because for most people religion is not a choice in the sense that car purchase is a choice. The one field of religion where it might well work is in the cultic milieu where the individual acts autonomously (rather than continuing in the religion of birth and community) and has very low levels of commitment to any particular brand.

Chapter 9: The Charismatic Movement and Secularization

1 I have argued that Berger is similarly free of the charge and that there is very little in his early work that he need repudiate (Bruce 2001a).

2 The logic of mutation is this. The saved Christian is no longer under the old dispensation of the Jewish law. Because he is saved and filled with the Holy Spirit, he does not sin. Therefore what he does is not sin. And he can demonstrate just how free of sin he is by doing what, if it were done by less holy people, would count as serious sin indeed.

3 An alternative explanation that may account for some of the variation is that newly formed religious organizations can fund a higher number of officials than long-established ones because they are not burdened with the high costs of supporting retired clergy and maintaining old properties.

4 Britain is perhaps unusual in the extent to which it controls the claims that can be made for religious beliefs in public broadcasts and advertisements. For example, in April 1999 the Advertising Standards Authority upheld a complaint against newspaper advertisements for the Peniel Pentecostal Church that claimed the church could offer physical healing.

Chapter 11: Religion in the United States

1   For broad general studies of the NCR, see Bruce (1988), Bates (1995, 2000), Wilcox (1996), Jelen (1991) and Moen (1992).

2   We might be tempted to criticize the research for taking the estimates of clergy as the measure of actual attendance, with which self-reported attendance is compared. But I can think of no obvious reason why clergy should systematically *underestimate* attendance and no serious sociologist has suggested it. As I report (p. 65), the one recent count of actual attendances in a British town fits very well with clergy estimates. Furthermore, as I show, Hadaway and Marler subsequently devised other tests of the gap between claimed and actual involvement that were not susceptible to that criticism.

3   Balmer (1989) is an excellent ethnographic study of the evangelical subculture. Barnhart (1988) has some telling references to the biography of Tammy Faye Bakker and her initial difficulties in coming to terms with the relaxation of prohibitions in the fundamentalist world in which she grew up. Harrell's biography (1985) of Oral Roberts and William Martin's biography (1991) of Billy Graham give a good picture both of life in the rural south in the 1930s and of the subsequent changes in that world as it prospered.

4   This issue is a good illustration of why many justices have been reluctant to shift far from what is a forty-year-long judicial consensus on the separation of church and state. NCR groups have been keen to promote legislation to allow church-based agencies to receive public funds for secular good works. There is considerable sympathy across the political spectrum for anything that will encourage community activism and the importance of the churches in black communities makes it hard for liberals to oppose it on principle. However, there are a number of unpopular religious organizations – Scientology, the Unification Church and the Nation of Islam, for example – that could make strong claims for their social and psychological programmes to be so funded and it is very difficult to see how any legislation could be drafted that would allow public money to go to evangelical or Catholic agencies but not to such deviant groups, and survive the legal battles that would be sure to follow.

5   The fact that he was a pragmatist explains why Ralph Reed, who led Pat Robertson's Christian Coalition in the 1990s, was viewed with suspicion by many grass-roots NCR activists. Robertson himself lost a great deal of support in 2001 when he struck an astonishingly pragmatic attitude to forced abortion in China. When pressed in a CNN interview, he said that Beijing's leaders were 'doing what they have to do'. 'They've got 1.2 billion people and they don't know what to do. If every family over there was allowed to have three or four children, the population would be

completely unsustainable. . . . I don't agree with the forced abortion but I don't think the United States needs to interfere with what they're doing internally in this regard.' Other NCR leaders were quick to condemn Robertson and point to his business interests in China as an explanation for his about-turn (Harnden 2001).

6 Finke and Stark offered a typically rude response in which they claimed that Iannaccone had replicated Breault's research and come to quite the opposite conclusion: that there was a strong positive connection between diversity and religious vitality. When Olson tried to reconcile the two competing interpretations, he discovered that the statistical package used by Iannaccone contained a small but fatal mistake. In calculating the Herfindahl Index of Diversity, it failed to subtract the final calculated value from 1. It thus produced inverted results. What the supply-siders reported as a strong positive correlation was actually a strong negative connection; Breault was right! (Finke and Stark 1988; Olson 1998.) When Olson published that finding and made further criticisms of their handling of the collinearity problems, Finke and Stark reacted in their customary way by ignoring the criticisms, again claiming that every other bit of research supported them, and restating their hypotheses (Finke and Stark 1998).

References

Abercrombie, N., Hill, S., and Turner, B. S. 1980: *The Dominant Ideology Thesis*. London: George Allen & Unwin.

Anon. 2001: Scientific activity together with religious beliefs. Why not? Paper submitted to *Journal of Contemporary Religion*.

Aquaviva, S. 1993: Some reflections on the parallel decline of religious experience and religious practice. In E. Barker, J. A. Beckford, and K. Dobbelaere (eds), *Secularization, Rationalism and Sectarianism: Essays in Honour of Bryan R. Wilson*, Oxford: Clarendon Press, 47–58.

Associated Press 2001: Issue ad spending hit $250 million. *USA Today*, 2 January.

Bailey, E. 1997: Implicit religion: what might it be? Professorial lecture, Middlesex University, November.

Balch, R. W. 1982: Bo and Peep: a case study of the origins of messianic leadership. In R. Wallis (ed.), *Millennialism and Charisma*, Belfast: The Queen's University of Belfast, 13–72.

Balmer, R. 1989: *Mine Eyes Have Seen the Glory: A Journey into the Evangelical Subculture in America*. Oxford: Oxford University Press.

Barbour, I. M. 1968: *Science and Religion: New Perspectives on the Dialogue*. London: SCM Press.

Barker, E. 1984: *The Making of a Moonie*. Oxford: Blackwell.

Barker, E. 1989: *New Religious Movements: A Practical Introduction*. London: HMSO Books.

Barna, G. 1996: Church attendance drops again: baby boomers cut church from schedule. *Barna Research Online*: www.barna.org.

Barna, G. 1999: One out of three adults is now unchurched. *Barna Research Online*: www.barna.org.

Barna, G. 2000a: Church attendance. *Barna Research Online*: www.barna.org.

Barna, G. 2000b: The year's most intriguing findings, from Barna research studies. *Barna Research Online*: www.barna.org.

Barnhart, J. E. 1988: *Jim and Tammy: Charismatic Intrigue inside PTL*. Buffalo, NY: Promotheus Books.

Barr, J. A. 1973: *The Bible in the Modern World*. London: SCM Press.

Barr, J. A. 1977: *Fundamentalism*. London: SCM Press.

Bates, V. L. 1995: Rhetorical pluralism and secularization in the New Christian Right: the Oregon Citizens Alliance. *Review of Religious Research*, 37: 46–64.

Bates, V. L. 2000: The decline of a New Christian Right organization. Social movement organization: opportunities and constraints. *Review of Religious Research*, 42: 19–40.

Beckford, J. A. 1989: *Religion and Advanced Industrial Society*. London: Unwin Hyman.

Beckford, J. A. 1992: Religion, modernity, and post-modernity. In B. R. Wilson (ed.), *Religion: Contemporary Issues*, London: Bellew, 11–27.

Bell, D. 1977: The return of the sacred? *British Journal of Sociology*, 28: 419–49.

Bellah, R. 1970: *Beyond Belief: Essays on Religion in a Post-Traditional World*. New York: Harper & Row.

Benen, S. 1999: Evolution evasion. *Church and State*, October. Americans United for Separation of Church and State web site: www.au.org.

Benton, T. 1977: *Philosophical Foundations of the Three Sociologies*. London: Routledge & Kegan Paul.

Berger, P. L. 1969: *The Social Reality of Religion*. London: Faber & Faber.

Berger, P. L. 1980: *The Heretical Imperative: Contemporary Possibilities of Religious Affirmations*. London: Collins.

Berger, P. L. 1983: From the crisis of religion to the crisis of modernity. In M. Douglas and S. Tipton (eds), *Religion and America: Spiritual Life in a Secular Age*, Boston: Beacon Press, 14–24.

Berger, P. L. 1987: *The Capitalist Revolution*. Aldershot: Gower.

Berger, P. L. 1997: Against the current. *Prospect*, March, 32–6.

Berger, P. L. 1998: Protestantism and the quest for certainty. *The Christian Century*, August–September, 782–96.

Berger, P. L., and Luckmann, T. 1966: Secularization and pluralism. *International Yearbook for the Sociology of Religion*, 2: 73–84.

Berger, P. L., and Luckmann, T. 1973: *The Social Construction of Reality*. Harmondsworth: Penguin.

Berger, P. L., Berger, B., and Kellner, H. 1974: *The Homeless Mind*. Harmondsworth: Penguin.

Beyer, P. 1996: Postmodernism and religion: discussant's comments from 1996 ASR conference. *Catholic Issues* web site: www.adelphi.edu/-catissue/articles.

Bezilla, R. (ed.) 1993: *Religion in America 1992–93*. Princeton: Princeton Religion Research Centre.

Bibby, R. 1993: *Unknown Gods*. Toronto: Stoddard.

Blau, J. R., Land, K. C., and Rudding, J. 1991: The expansion of religious affiliation: an explanation of the growth of church participation in the United States, 1850–1930. *Social Science Research*, 21: 329–52.

Bloom, W. 2000: New Age is perfect remedy for modern ills. *Sunday Herald*, 14 May, 9.

Blum, Jerome 1978: *The End of the Old Order in Rural Europe*. Princeton: Princeton University Press.

Blumer, H. 1966: *Symbolic Interactionism*. Englewood Cliffs, NJ: Prentice-Hall.

Boice, Judith L. 1989: *At One with All Life: A Personal Journey in Gaian Communities*. Findhorn: Findhorn Press.

Bowman, M. 1993: Reinventing the Celts. *Religion*, 23: 147–56.

Bowman, M. 2000: Nature, the natural and pagan identity. *Diskus: An On-Line Journal*, 6.

Braithwaite, R. B. 1927: *The State of Religious Belief: An Inquiry Based on 'The Nation and Athenaeum' Questionnaire*. London: Hogarth Press.

Breault, K. D. 1989a: New evidence on religious pluralism, urbanism and religious participation. *American Sociological Review*, 54: 1048–53.

Breault, K. D. 1989b: A re-examination of the relationship between religious diversity and religious adherents: a reply to Finke and Stark. *American Sociological Review*, 54: 1056–9.

Bredin, M. 2000: *The Pale Abyssinian: A Life of James Bruce, African Explorer and Adventurer*. London: HarperCollins.

Brierley, P. 1989: *A Century of British Christianity: Historical Statistics 1900–1985 with Projections to 2000*. London: MARC Europe.

Brierley, P. 1999: *Religious Trends No. 1: 1999/2000*. London: Christian Research Association.

Brierley, P. 2000a: *The Tide is Running out*. London: Christian Research Association.

Brierley, P. 2000b: *Religious Trends No. 2: 2000/01*. London: Christian Research Association.

Brierley, P., and Hiscock, V. 1993: *UK Christian Handbook 1994/95 Edition*. London: Christian Research Association.

Brierley, P., and Macdonald, F. 1985: *Prospects for Scotland: From a Census of Churches in 1984*. London: MARC Europe.

Brierley, P., and Wraight, H. 1995: *UK Christian Handbook 1996/97 Edition*. London: Christian Research Association

Brierley, P., Butt, P., Selvon, S., and Noble, C. 1993: *The Body Book*, 4th edn. Romford: Team Spirit Publications.

Broomhall, A. J. 1966: *Time for Action*. London: Lutterworth.

Brown, C. 1987a: *The Social History of Religion in Scotland since 1730*. London: Methuen.

Brown, C. 1987b: The costs of pew-renting: church management, churchgoing and social class in nineteenth-century Scotland. *Journal of Ecclesiastical History*, 38: 347–61.

Brown, C. 1992a: A revisionist approach to religious change. In S. Bruce (ed.), *Religion and Modernization*, Oxford: Oxford University Press, 31–58.

Brown, C. 1992b: Religion and Secularisation. In A. Dickson and J. H. Treble (eds), *People and Scotland in Scotland*, iii. *1914–1990*, Edinburgh: John Donald, 48–79.

Brown, C. 1993: *The People in the Pews: Religion and Society in Scotland since 1780*. Glasgow: Economic and Social History Society of Scotland.

Brown, C. 2001: *The Death of Christian Britain*. London: Routledge.

Bruce, S. 1980: The Student Christian Movement and the Inter-Varsity Fellowship: a sociological study of two student movements. Ph.D. thesis; University of Stirling.

Bruce, S. 1982: The Student Christian Movement: a nineteenth century new religious movement and its vicissitudes. *International Journal of Sociology and Social Policy*, 2: 67–82.

Bruce, S. 1985: Authority and fission: the Protestants' divisions. *British Journal of Sociology*, 36: 592–603.

Bruce, S. 1986: *God Save Ulster! The Religion and Politics of Paisleyism*. Oxford: Oxford University Press.

Bruce, S. 1988: *The Rise and Fall of the New Christian Right: Conservative Protestant Politics in America 1978–1988*. Oxford: Oxford University Press.

Bruce, S. 1990: *A House Divided: Protestantism, Schism and Secularization*. London: Routledge.

Bruce, S. 1993: Religion and rational choice: a critique of economic explanations of religious behavior. *Sociology of Religion*, 54: 193–205.

Bruce, S. 1995a: The truth about religion in Britain. *Journal for the Scientific Study of Religion*, 34: 417–430.

Bruce, S. 1995b: *Religion in Modern Britain*. Oxford: Oxford University Press.

Bruce, S. 1996a: *Religion in the Modern World: From Cathedrals to Cults*. Oxford: Oxford University Press.

Bruce, S. 1996b: Religion in Britain at the close of the 20th century: a challenge to the silver lining perspective. *Journal of Contemporary Religion*, 11: 261–75.

Bruce, S. 1998a: Good intentions and bad sociology: New Age authenticity and social roles. *Journal of Contemporary Religion*, 13: 23–36.

Bruce, S. 1998b: *Conservative Protestant Politics*. Oxford: Oxford University Press.

Bruce, S. 1999: *Choice and Religion: A Critique of Rational Choice Theory*. Oxford: Oxford University Press.

Bruce, S. 2000: The supply-side model of religion: the Nordic and Baltic states. *Journal for the Scientific Study of Religion*, 39: 32–46.

Bruce, S. 2001a: The curious case of the unnecessary recantation: Berger and secularization. In L. Woodhead (ed.), *Berger on Religion*. London: Routledge, 87–100.

Bruce, S. 2001b: *Fundamentalism*. Oxford: Polity Press.

Bruce, S., and Wright, C. 1995: Law, religious toleration and social change. *Journal of Church and State*, 37: 103–20.

Bryant, A. 1978: The *Playboy* interview, *Playboy*, May, 73–6, 232–50.

Buckser, A. 1996: Religion, science and secularization theory. *Journal for the Scientific Study of Religion*, 35: 432–41.

Budd, S. 1977: *Varieties of Unbelief: Atheists and Agnostics in English Society 1850–1960*. London: Heinemann.

Burnside, A. 2000: A holistic jewel for the boudoirs of suburbia. *Sunday Herald*, 11 June.

Caddy, E. 1994: Memories of Peter. *One Earth*, Summer, 9.

Caddy, E., and Hollingshead, L. 1988: *Flight into Freedom: The Autobiography of the Co-Founder of the Findhorn Community*. Longmead: Element.

Camarota, S. A. 1999: Immigrants in the United States 1999: a snapshot of America's foreign-born population. Center for Immigration Studies web site: www.cis.org.

Campbell, C. 1971: *Toward a Sociology of Irreligion*. London: Macmillan.

Campbell, C. 1999: The easternization of the West. In B. R. Wilson and J. Cresswell (eds), *New Religious Movements: Challenge and Response*, London: Routledge, 35–48.

Caplow, T., Bahr, H. M., and Chadwick, B. A. 1983: *All Faithful People: Change and Continuity in Middletown's Religion*. Minneapolis: University of Minnesota Press.

Capon, J. 1972: *And Then There Was Light!* London: Lutterworth.

Casanova, J. 1994: *Public Religions in the Modern World*. Chicago: University of Chicago Press.

Chaves, M. 1995: On the rational choice approach to religion. *Journal for the Scientific Study of Religion*, 34: 98–104.

Chaves, M., and Cann, D. E. 1992: Regulation, pluralism and religious market structure. *Rationality and Society*, 4: 272–90.

Chaves, M., and Gorski, P. S. 2001: Religious pluralism and religious participation. *Annual Review of Sociology*, 27: 261–81.

Church, J. 1994: *Social Trends 1994 Edition*. London: HMSO.

Clark, P. 1977: *English Provincial Society from the Reformation to the Revolution: Religion, Politics and Society in Kent: 1500–1640*. Hassocks: Harvester.

Collinson, P. 1982: *The Religion of Protestants: The Church in English Society, 1559–1625*. Oxford: Oxford University Press.

Conway, M. 1966: *The Undivided Vision*. London: SCM Press.

Coneybeare, W. J. 1853: Church parties. *Edinburgh Review*, 48: 273–342.

Coomes, D. 1973: *Spree-73*. London: Coverdale.

Cressy, D. 1993: Purification, thanksgiving and the churching of women in post-Reformation England. *Past and Present*, 141: 106–46.

Cressy, D. 1997: *Birth, Marriage and Death: Ritual, Religion and the Life-Cycle in Tudor and Stuart England*. Oxford: Oxford University Press.

Crockett, A. 1998: A Secularising Geography? Patterns and Processes of Religious Change in England and Wales, 1676–1851. Ph.D. thesis; University of Leicester.

Currie, R., Gilbert, A. D., and Horsley, L. 1977: *Churches and Churchgoers: Patterns of Church Growth in the British Isles since 1700*. Oxford: Oxford University Press.

Davie, G. 1994: *Religion in Britain since 1945: Believing without Belonging*. Oxford: Blackwell.

Davies, C. 1999: The fragmentation of the religious tradition on the creation, after-life and morality: modernity and post-modernity. *Journal of Contemporary Religion*, 14: 339–60.

Davies, D. 1984: The charismatic ethic and post-industrialism. In D. Martin and P. Mullen (eds), *Strange Gifts? A Guide to Charismatic Renewal*, Oxford: Blackwell, 137–50.

Davis, N. 1975: *Society and Culture in Early Modern France*. London: Duckworth.

De Toqueville, A. 1945: *Democracy in America*. New York: Alfred A. Knopf.

Dekmejian, R. H. 1995: *Islam in Revolution: Fundamentalism in the Arab World*. Syracuse, NY: Syracuse University Press.

Dobbelaere, K. 1981: Secularization: a multi-dimensional concept. *Current Sociology*, 29: 1–216.

Drummond, A. L., and Bulloch, J. 1973: *The Scottish Church 1688–1843*. Edinburgh: St Andrew Press.

Durkheim, E. 1964: *The Division of Labor in Society*. New York: Free Press.

Durkheim, E. 1971: *The Elementary Forms of the Religious Life*. London: George Allen & Unwin.

Embree, A. T. 1992: Christianity and the state in Victorian India: confrontation and collaboration. In R. W. Davis and R. J. Helmstadler (eds), *Religion and Irreligion in Victorian Society*, London: Routledge, 151–65.

Field, C. 2001: 'The haemorrhage of faith'? Opinion polls as sources for religious practices, beliefs and attitudes in Scotland since the 1970s. *Journal of Contemporary Religion*, 157–76.

Finer, S. E. 1982: *Comparative Government*. Harmondsworth: Penguin.

Finke, R. 1989: How the upstart sects won America: 1776–1850. *Journal for the Scientific Study of Religion*, 28: 27–44.

Finke, R. 1990: Religious de-regulation: origins and consequences. *Journal of Church and State*, 32: 609–26.

Finke, R. 1992: An unsecular America. In S. Bruce (ed.), *Religion and Modernization: Sociologists and Historians Debate the Secularization Thesis*, Oxford: Oxford University Press, 145–69.

Finke, R., and Iannaccone, L. R. 1993: Supply-side explanations for religious change. *Annals of the American Academy of Political and Social Science*, 527: 27–39.

Finke, R., and Stark, R. 1988: Evaluating the evidence: religious economies and sacred canopies, *American Sociological Review*, 54: 1054–6.

Finke, R., and Stark, R. 1992: *The Churching of America, 1776–1990: Winners and Losers in our Religious Economy*. New Brunswick: Rutgers University Press.

Finke, R., and Stark, R. 1998: Religious choice and competition. *American Sociological Review*, 63: 761–6.

Foster, P. G. 1972: Secularization in the English context. *Sociological Review*, 20: 153–68.

Fowler, D. 1997: Positive vibrations. *Independent Saturday Magazine*, 6 December, 59–60.

Gallup, G. H. 1976: *The Gallup International Public Opinion Polls, Great Britain 1937–75*. New York: Random House.

Garvey, J. 1993: Fundamentalism and American Law. In M. Marty and R. S. Appleby (eds), *Fundamentalisms and the State,* Chicago: University of Chicago Press, 28–48.

Gasper, L. 1963: *The Fundamentalist Movement.* The Hague: Mouton.

Gaustad, E. S. 1962: *Historical Atlas of Religion in America.* New York: Harper & Row.

Gellner, E. 1983: *Nations and Nationalism.* Oxford: Basil Blackwell.

Gellner, E. 1991: *Plough, Sword and Book: The Structure of Human History.* London: Paladin.

George, C. V. R. 1994: *God's Salesman: Norman Vincent Peale and the Power of Positive Thinking.* Oxford: Oxford University Press.

Giddens, A. 1971: *Capitalism and Modern Social Theory: An Analysis of the Writings of Marx, Durkheim and Weber.* Cambridge: Cambridge University Press.

Gill, R. 1993: *The Myth of the Empty Church.* London: SPCK.

Gill, R. 1999: *Churchgoing and Christian Ethics.* Cambridge: Cambridge University Press.

Gill, R. 2001: Religion in twentieth century Kent. In N. Yates (ed.), *Kent in the Twentieth Century,* Woodbridge: Boydell Press, 321–33.

Gill, R., Hadaway, C. K., and Marler, P. L. 1998: Is religious belief declining in Britain? *Journal for the Scientific Study of Religion,* 37: 507–16.

Glassner, P. E. 1975: Idealisation and the social myth of secularization. In M. Hill (ed.), *Sociological Yearbook of Religion Vol. 8,* London: SCM Press, 7–14.

Glassner, P. E. 1977: *The Sociology of Secularisation: A Critique of a Concept.* London: Routledge & Kegan Paul.

Goodridge, R. M. 1975: 'The Ages of Faith' – Romance or Reality? *Sociological Review,* 23: 381–96.

Greer, P. 1995: The Aquarian confusion: conflicting theologies of the New Age. *Journal of Contemporary Religion,* 10: 151–66.

Greeley, A. M. 1989: *Religious Change in America.* Cambridge, Mass.: Harvard University Press.

Griffin, S. C. 2000: *A Forgotten Revival: East Anglia and NE Scotland 1921.* Bromley: Day One Publications.

Hadaway, C. K., Marler, P. L., and Chaves, M. 1993: What the polls don't show: a closer look at US church attendance. *American Sociological Review,* 58: 741–52.

Hadden, J. K. 1987: Toward desacralizing secularization theory. *Social Forces,* 65: 587–611.

Hadden, J. K., and Shupe, A. D. 1988: *Televangelism: Power and Politics on God's Frontier.* New York: Henry Holt.

Halsey, A. H. 1972: *Trends in British Society since 1900.* London: Macmillan.

Hammond, P. E. 1992: *Religion and Personal Autonomy.* Columbia, SC: University of South Carolina Press.

Hamilton, B. 1986: *Religion in the Medieval West.* London: Edward Arnold.

Hamilton, M. 2000: An analysis of the Festival for Mind–Body–Spirit, London. In S. Sutcliffe and M. Bowman (eds), *Beyond New Age: Exploring Alternative Spirituality*, Edinburgh: Edinburgh University Press, 188–200.

Harnden, T. 2001: Outrage as preacher refuses to condemn Chinese abortions. *Daily Telegraph*, 20 April.

Harper, C. L., and LeBeau, B. F. 2001: Social change and religion in America: thinking beyond secularization. *American Religious Experience* web site: www.as.wvu.edu.

Harper-Bill, C. 1996: *The Pre-Reformation Church in England 1400–1530*. London: Longman.

Harrell, D. E. 1985: *Oral Roberts: An American Life*. Bloomington, Ind.: Indiana University Press.

Harrison, J. F. C. 1984: *The Common People: A History from the Norman Conquest to the Present*. London: Flamingo.

Harvey, G. 1995: Satanism in Britain today. *Journal of Contemporary Religion*, 10: 283–96.

Heelas, P. 1996: *The New Age Movement: The Celebration of the Self and the Sacralization of Modernity*. Oxford: Blackwell.

Heelas, P. 2000: Expressive spirituality and humanistic expressivism: sources of significance beyond church and chapel. In S. Sutcliffe and M. Bowman (eds), *Beyond New Age: Exploring Alternative Spirituality*, Edinburgh: Edinburgh University Press, 237–54.

Heelas, P. 2001: The spiritual revolution: from 'religion' to 'spirituality'. In L. Woodhead, P. Fletcher, K. Kawanami and D. Smith (eds), *Religions in the Modern World: Traditions and Transformations*, London: Routledge, 361–81.

Herberg, W. 1983: *Protestant–Catholic–Jew: An Essay in American Religious Sociology*. Chicago: University of Chicago Press.

Hoge, D. R. 1979: A test of theories of denominational growth and decline. In D. R. Hoge and D. A. Roozen (eds), *Understanding Church Growth and Decline 1950–1978*, New York: Pilgrim Press, 179–223.

Hornsby-Smith, M. P. (ed.) 1999: English Catholics at the New Millennium. In M. P. Hornsby-Smith (ed.), *Catholics in England 1950–2000: Historical and Sociological Perspectives*, London: Cassell, 291–306.

Hostetler, J. A., and Huntington, G. E. 1971: *Children in Amish Society: Socialization and Community Education*. New York: Holt, Rinehart & Winston.

Houlbrooke, R. 1998: *Death, Religion and the Family in England, 1480–1750*. Oxford: Oxford University Press.

Houston, R. A. 1988: *Literacy in Early Modern Europe: Culture and Education 1500–1800*. London: Longman.

Howse, E. M. 1971: *Saints in Politics: The 'Clapham Sect' and the Growth of Freedom*. London: George Allen & Unwin.

Hunt, S. 1995: The Toronto Blessing: a 'Rumour of Angels'? *Journal of Contemporary Religion*, 10: 257–72.

Hunter, J. 1978: *The Making of a Crofting Community*. Edinburgh: John Donald.

Hunter, J. D. 1987: *Evangelicalism: The Coming Generation*. Chicago: University of Chicago Press.

Iannaccone, L. R. 1991: The consequences of religious market structure. *Rationality and Society*, 3: 156–77.

Inglehart, R. 1990: *Culture Shift in Advanced Industrial Societies*. Princeton: Princeton University Press.

Inglehart, R. 1997: *Modernization and Postmodernization: Cultural, Political and Economic Change in 43 Societies*. Princeton: Princeton University Press.

Inglehart, R., Basanez, M., and Moreno, A. 1998: *Human Values and Beliefs: A Cross-Cultural Sourcebook*. Ann Arbor: University of Michigan Press.

Isichei, E. 1967: From sect to denomination among English Quakers. In B. R. Wilson (ed.), *Patterns of Sectarianism*, London: Heinemann, 161–81.

Jackson, E. M. 1980: *Red Tape and the Gospel: A Study of William Paton 1886–1943*. Birmingham: Phlogiston.

Jagodzinski, W., and Greeley, A. 2001: The demand for religion: hard-core atheism and 'supply-side' theory. Greeley web site: www.agreeley.com.

Jelen, T. G. 1991: *The Political Mobilization of Religious Beliefs*. New York: Praeger.

Johnson, D. 1979: *Contending for the Faith: A History of the Evangelical Movement in the Universities and Colleges*. Leicester: Inter-Varsity Press.

Jorgensen, D. L., and Russell, S. E. 1999: American neo-paganism: the participants' social identities. *Journal for the Scientific Study of Religion*, 38: 325–38.

Kamen, H. 1967: *The Rise of Toleration*. London: Weidenfeld & Nicolson.

Kanter, R. M. 1972: *Commitment and Community: Communes and Utopias in Sociological Perspective*. Cambridge, Mass.: Harvard University Press.

Keen, M. 1990: *English Society in the Later Middle Ages 1348–1500*. Harmondsworth: Penguin.

Kelley, D. 1972: *Why the Conservative Churches are Growing*. New York: Harper & Row.

Kelley, D. 1978: Why the conservative churches are still growing. *Journal for the Scientific Study of Religion*, 17: 129–37.

Klaaren, E. M. 1977: *Religious Origins of Modern Science*. Grand Rapids, Mich.: Eerdmans.

Kuhn, T. 1972: *The Structure of Scientific Revolutions*. Chicago: University of Chicago Press.

Land, K. C., Deane, G., and Blau, J. R. 1991: Religious pluralism and church membership. *American Sociological Review*, 56: 237–49.

Larson, E. J., and Witham, L. 1998: Leading scientists still reject God. *Nature*, 394: 313.

Laslett, P. 1983: *The World we have Lost*. London: Methuen.

Lawrence, B. B. 1990: *Defenders of God: The Fundamentalist Revolt against the Modern Age*. London: I. B. Tauris.

Love, M. 1998: *The Body Book: A Directory of Christian Fellowships*, 7th edn. Walton-on-Thames: Pioneer Publications.

Luckmann, T. 1970: *The Invisible Religion: The Problem of Religion in Modern Society*. New York: Macmillan.

Luhmann, N. 1977: *Funktion der Religion*. Frankhurt am Main: Suhrkamp.

Lynd, R. S., and Lynd, H. J. 1929: *Middletown: A Study of Contemporary American Culture*. New York: Harcourt, Brace & Co.

Lyon, D. 1996: Religion and the postmodern: old problems, new prospects. In K. Flanagan and P. C. Judd (eds), *Postmodernity, Sociology and Religion*, London: Macmillan, 14–29.

Lyons, G. 1982: Repealing the enlightenment. *Harpers*, April, 38–42, 73–8.

McBain, D. 1997: Mainstream charismatics: some observations of Baptist renewal. In S. Hunt, M. Hamilton and T. Walter (eds), *Charismatic Christianity: Sociological Perspectives*, London: Macmillan, 43–59.

McConnell, D. L. 1988: *A Different Gospel: A Historical and Biblical Analysis of the Modern Faith Movement*. Peabody, Mass.: Hendrickson.

Macfarlane, N. 1924: *The Men of the Lews*. Stornoway: Gazette Office.

McInnes, J. 1951: *The Evangelical Movement in the Highlands of Scotland 1688–1800*. Aberdeen: University Press.

MacIntyre, A. 1967: *Secularization and Moral Change*. London: Oxford University Press.

McKay, M. 1980: *The Revd John Walker's Report on the Hebrides of 1764 and 1771*. Edinburgh: John Donald.

Mackay, N. 1999: The Catholic crisis. *Sunday Herald*, 25 July, 11.

Marler, P. L., and Hadaway, C. K. 1997: Testing the attendance gap in a conservative church. *Sociology of Religion*, 60: 174–86.

Marsden, G. M. 1977: Fundamentalism as an American phenomenon: a comparison with English evangelicalism. *Church History*, 46: 215–32.

Marsden, G. M. 1980: *Fundamentalism and American Culture: The Shaping of Twentieth Century Evangelicalism 1870–1925*. New York: Oxford University Press.

Marsh, C. 1998: *Popular Religion in Sixteenth-Century England*. London: Macmillan.

Marshall, G. 1980: *Presbyteries and Profits: Calvinism and the Development of Capitalism in Scotland, 1560–1707*. Oxford: Clarendon Press.

Martin, D. 1965: Towards eliminating the concept of secularization. In J. Gould (ed.), *The Penguin Survey of the Social Sciences*, Harmondsworth: Penguin, 169–82.

Martin, D. 1967: *A Sociology of English Religion*. London: Heinemann.

Martin, D. 1969: *The Religious and the Secular*. London: Routledge & Kegan Paul.

Martin, D. 1978a: *The Dilemmas of Contemporary Religion*. Oxford: Blackwell.

Martin, D. 1978b: *A General Theory of Secularization*. Oxford: Blackwell.

Martin, D. 1990: *Tongues of Fire: The Explosion of Protestantism in Latin America*. Oxford: Blackwell.

Martin, D. 1991: The secularization issue: prospect and retrospect. *British Journal of Sociology*, 42: 465–74.

Martin, D. 1997: *Does Christianity Cause War?* Oxford: Clarendon Press.

Martin, D. 2000: Personal reflections in the mirror of Halévy and Weber. In R. Fenn (ed.), *The Blackwell Companion to the Sociology of Religion*, Oxford: Blackwell, 23–38.

Martin, W. 1991: *Billy Graham: Prophet with Honour*. New York: William Morrow.

Marty, M. 1993: Churches as winners, losers. *Christian Century*, 27 January, 88–9.

Melton, J. G., Clark, J., and Kelly, A. A. 1991: *New Age Almanac*. Detroit: Visible Ink.

Merton, R. K. 1970: *Science, Technology and Society in the 17th Century*. New York: Fettig.

Michels, R. 1962: *Political Parties: A Sociological Study of the Oligarchic Tendencies of Modern Democracy*. New York: Free Press.

Moen, M. C. 1992: *The Transformation of the Christian Right*. Tuscaloosa, Ala.: University of Alabama Press.

Mol, H. 1972: *Western Religion: A Country-by-Country Sociological Inquiry*. The Hague: Mouton.

Morgan, N. J. 1988: Lancashire Quakers and the tithe 1660–1730. *Bulletin of the John Rylands University Library of Manchester*, 70/3: 61–76.

Morrison, J. H. 1927: *The Scottish Churches Work Abroad*. Edinburgh: T. and T. Clark.

Neal, F. 1988: *Sectarian Violence: The Liverpool Experience 1819–1914*. Manchester: Manchester University Press.

Neuhaus, R. J. 1984: *The Naked Public Square: Religion and Democracy in America*. Grand Rapids, Mich.: Eerdmans.

Neuhaus, R. J. 2000: The public square. *First Things*, 105: 73–100.

Niebuhr, H. R. 1962: *The Social Sources of Denominationalism*. New York: Meridian.

Neill, S. 1975: *A History of Christian Missions*. Harmondsworth: Penguin.

Obelkevitch, J. 1990: Religion. In F. M. L. Thompson (ed.), *The Cambridge Social History of Britain 1750–1950*, iii. *Social Agencies and Institutions*, Cambridge: Cambridge University Press, 311–56.

Olson, D. V. A. 1998: Religious pluralism in contemporary US counties. *American Sociological Review*, 63: 757–61.

Olson, D. V. A. 1999: Religious pluralism and US church membership: a reassessment. *Sociology of Religion*, 60: 149–73.

Olson, D. V. A., and Hadaway, C. K. 1999: Religious pluralism and affiliation among Canadian counties and cities. *Journal for the Scientific Study of Religion*, 38: 490–508.

Orwell, G. 1998: *Complete Works*, xvi. *I Have Tried to Tell the Truth*. London: Secker & Warburg.

Opinion Research Business 2000: The 'Soul of Britain' survey. London: Opinion Research Business.

Parsons, T. 1960: *Structure and Process in Modern Society.* New York: Free Press.

Parsons, T. 1963: Christianity and modern industrial society. In E. A. Tiryakin (ed.), *Sociological Theory, Values, and Sociocultural Change,* London: Collier-Macmillan, 33–70.

Parsons, T. 1964: Evolutionary universals in society. *American Journal of Sociology,* 29: 339–57.

Petre, J. 1999: Christianity 'in crisis' as pews empty. *Sunday Telegraph,* 28 November, 15.

Pew Forum on Religion and Public Life 2001: It's wrong to base voting on religion, say most Americans. Pew Trust's web site: www. pewtrusts.com.

Popper, K. 1978: *The Logic of Scientific Discovery.* London: Hutchinson.

Richter, P. 1997: The Toronto Blessing: charismatic evangelical global warming. In S. Hunt, M. Hamilton and T. Walter (eds), *Charismatic Christianity: Sociological Perspectives,* London: Macmillan, 97–119.

Richter, P., and Francis, L. J. 1998: *Gone but not Forgotten: Church Leaving and Returning.* London: Dartman, Longman & Todd.

Riddell, C. 1990: *The Findhorn Community: Creating a Human Identity for the 21st Century.* Forres: Findhorn Press.

Riesebrodt, M. 1993: *Pious Passion: The Emergence of Modern Fundamentalism in the United States and Iran.* Berkeley and Los Angeles: University of California Press.

Robertson, R. 1972: *The Sociological Interpretation of Religion.* Oxford: Blackwell.

Robertson, R. 1985: The sacred and the world system. In P. E. Hammond (ed.), *The Sacred in a Secular Age,* Berkeley and Los Angeles: University of California Press, 347–58.

Robertson, R. 1993: Community, society, globality and the category of religion. In E. Barker, J. Beckford and K. Dobbelaere (eds), *Secularization, Rationalism and Sectarianism: Essays in Honour of Bryan R. Wilson,* Oxford: Oxford University Press, 1–18.

Rock, P. 1979: *The Making of Symbolic Interactionism.* London: Macmillan.

Roof, W. C. 1996: God is in the details: reflections on religion's public presence in the United States in the mid-1990s. *Sociology of Religion,* 57: 149–62.

Rose, S. 1998: An examination of the New Age movement: who is involved and what constitutes spirituality. *Journal of Contemporary Religion,* 13: 5–22.

Sawkins, J. 1998: Church affiliation statistics: counting Methodist sheep. Edinburgh: Heriot-Watt University School of Management.

Sigelmann, L., and Presser, S. 1988: Measuring public support for the New Christian Right: the perils of points estimation. *Public Opinion Quarterly,* 52: 325–37.

Smelser, N. 1966: *Theory of Collective Behavior.* London: Routledge & Kegan Paul.

Smith, D. 1998: *Transforming the World? The Social Impact of British Evangelicalism.* Carlisle: Paternoster Press.

Spufford, M. 1981: *Small Books and Pleasant Histories.* London: Methuen.

Spufford, M. 1985: Can we count the 'godly' and the 'conformable' in the seventeenth century? *Journal of Ecclesiastical History*, 36: 428–38.

Stains, L. R. 1994: Religion as politics. *USA Weekend*, 16–18 September.

Stark, R. 1963: On the incompatibility of religion and science. *Journal for the Scientific Study of Religion*, 3: 3–20.

Stark, R. 1973: On the incompatibility of religion and science: a survey of American graduate students. *Journal for the Scientific Study of Religion*, 3: 3–20.

Stark, R. 1997: German and German-American religiousness. *Journal for the Scientific Study of Religion*, 36: 182–93.

Stark, R. 1999: Secularization RIP. *Sociology of Religion*, 60: 249–73.

Stark, R., and Bainbridge, W. S. 1985: *The Future of Religion*. Berkeley and Los Angeles: University of California Press.

Stark, R., and Bainbridge, W. S. 1987: *A Theory of Religion*. New York: Peter Lang.

Stark, R., and Finke, R. 2000: *Acts of Faith: Explaining the Human Side of Religion*. Berkeley and Los Angeles: University of California Press.

Stark, R., and Iannaccone, L. R., 1994: A supply-side reinterpretation of the 'secularization' of Europe. *Journal for the Scientific Study of Religion*, 33: 230–52.

Stark, R., and Iannaccone, L. R. 1995: Truth and the status of religion in Britain today: a reply to Bruce. *Journal for the Scientific Study of Religion*, 34: 516–19.

Stark, R., Finke, R., and Iannacconne, L. R. 1995: Pluralism and piety: England and Wales 1851. *Journal for the Scientific Study of Religion*, 34: 431–44.

Stiles, A. 1995: *Religion, Society and Reform 1800–1914*. London: Hodder & Stoughton.

Sutcliffe, S. 2000: A colony of seekers: Findhorn in the 1990s. *Journal of Contemporary Religion*, 15: 215–46.

Tamaru, N. 1987: The concept of secularization and its relevance in Japanese society. *Journal of Oriental Studies*, 26: 51–61.

Tamney, J. B., and Johnson, S. D. 1998: The popularity of strict churches. *Review of Religious Research*, 39: 209–23.

Tatlow, T. 1933: *The Story of the Student Christian Movement*. London: SCM Press.

Thomas, K. 1978: *Religion and the Decline of Magic*. Harmondsworth: Penguin.

Thomas, R. 1999: Too busy for God. *The Door*, May, 10–11.

Thompson, D. M. 1972: *Nonconformity in the Nineteenth Century*. London: Routledge & Kegan Paul.

Thompson, D. 1996. *The End of Time*. London: Sinclair-Stevenson.

Thompson, K. 1986: How religious are the British? In T. Thomas (ed.), *The British: Their Religious Beliefs and Practices 1800–1986*, London: Routledge, 211–39.

Till, B. 1977: *The Churches' Search for Unity*. Harmondsworth: Penguin.

Tönnies, F. 1955: *Community and Association*. London: Routledge & Kegan Paul.

Vaughan, T. R., Smith, D. H., and Sjoberg, G. 1966: The religious orientation of American natural scientists. *Social Forces*, 44: 519–26.

Walker, A. 1997: Thoroughly modern: sociological reflections on the charismatic movement from the end of the twentieth century. In S. Hunt, M. Hamilton and T. Walter (eds), *Charismatic Christianity: Sociological Perspectives*, London: Macmillan, 17–42.

Walker, A. 1998: *Restoring the Kingdom: The Radical Christianity of the House Church Movement*. Guildford: Eagle.

Waller, P. J. 1981: *Democracy and Sectarianism: A Political and Social History of Liverpool 1868–1939*. Liverpool: Liverpool University Press.

Wallis, A. 1956: *In the Day of thy Power*. London: CLC Publications.

Wallis, R. 1973: The sectarianism of Scientology. In M. Hill (ed.), *A Sociological Yearbook of Religion Vol. 6*, London: SCM Press, 136–55.

Wallis, R. 1974: Ideology, authority and the development of cultic movements. *Social Research*, 41: 299–327.

Wallis, R. (ed.) 1975: *Sectarianism: Analyses of Religious and Non-Religious Sects*. London: Peter Owen.

Wallis, R. 1976: *The Road to Total Freedom: A Sociological Analysis of Scientology*. London: Heinemann.

Wallis, R. 1979: *Salvation and Protest: Studies of Social and Religious Movements*. London: Francis Pinter.

Wallis, R. 1984: *The Elementary Forms of the New Religious Life*. London: Routledge & Kegan Paul.

Wallis, R. 1986: Figuring out cult receptivity. *Journal for the Scientific Study of Religion*, 25: 494–503.

Wallis, R., and Bruce, S. 1991: Secularization: trends, data, and theory. *Research in the Social Scientific Study of Religion*, 3: 1–31.

Walter, T., and Waterhouse, H. 1999: A very private belief: reincarnation in contemporary England. *Sociology of Religion*, 60: 187–97.

Warner, R. S. 1993: Work in progress toward a new paradigm for the sociological study of religion in the United States. *American Journal of Sociology*, 98: 1044–93.

Waterhouse, H. 1999: Reincarnation belief in Britain: New Age orientation or mainstream opinion. *Journal of Contemporary Religion*, 14: 97–109.

Watts, S. J. 1984: *A Social History of Western Europe 1450–1720*. London: Hutchinson.

Weber, M. 1948: *From Max Weber: Essays in Sociology*, trans. ed. and with an introduction by H. H. Gerth and C. Wright Mills. London: Routledge & Kegan Paul.

Weber, M. 1976: *The Protestant Ethic and the Spirit of Capitalism*. London: George Allen & Unwin.

White, K. 1996: Wanderlust. *Scottish Review*, 6: 27–49.

Whiting, R. 1989: *The Blind Devotion of the People: Popular Religion and the English Reformation*. Cambridge: Cambridge University Press.

Wilcox, C. 1992: *God's Warriors*. Baltimore: Johns Hopkins University Press.

Wilcox, 1996: *Onward Christian Soldiers? The Religious Right in American Politics*. Boulder, Colo.: Westview Press.

Williams, G. 1991: *The Welsh and their Religion*. Cardiff: University of Wales Press.

Wilson, B. R. 1959: An analysis of sect development. *American Journal of Sociology*, 24: 3–15.

Wilson, B. R. 1966: *Religion in Secular Society*. London: C.A. Watts.

Wilson, B. R. 1968: Religion and the churches in America. In W. McLoughlin and R. N. Bellah (eds), *Religion in America*, Boston: Houghton Mifflin, 73–110.

Wilson, B. R. 1975: The debate over 'secularization'. *Encounter*, 45: 77–83.

Wilson, B. R. 1976a: *Contemporary Transformations of Religion*. Oxford: Oxford University Press.

Wilson, B. R. 1976b: Aspects of secularization in the West. *Japanese Journal of Religious Studies*, 3: 329–76.

Wilson, B. R. 1982: *Religion in Sociological Perspective*. Oxford: Oxford University Press.

Wilson, B. R. 1987: Secularization and the survival of the sociology of religion. *Journal of Oriental Studies*, 26: 5–10.

Wilson, B. R. 1988: The functions of religion: a re-appraisal. *Religion*, 18: 199–216.

Wilson, B. R. 1990: *The Social Dimensions of Sectarianism: Sects and New Religious Movements in Contemporary Society*. Oxford: Oxford University Press.

Wilson, B. R. 1992: Reflections on a many-sided controversy. In S. Bruce (ed.), *Religion and Modernization: Sociologists and Historians Debate the Secularization Thesis*, Oxford: Oxford University Press, 195–210.

Wilson, B. R. 1993: The persistence of sects. *Diskus: An On-Line Journal*, 1: 1–12.

Wilson, B. R. 2000: Salvation, secularization and de-moralization. In R. Fenn (ed.), *The Blackwell Companion to the Sociology of Religion*, Oxford: Blackwell, 39–51.

Wilson, B. R., and Dobbelaere, K. 1994: *A Time to Chant: The Soka Gakkai Buddhists in Britain*. Oxford: Oxford University Press.

Wolff, R. L. 1977: *Gains and Losses: Novels of Faith and Doubt in Victorian England*. London: John Murray.

Wolffe, J. 1994: *God and Greater Britain: Religion and National Life in Britain and Ireland 1843–1945*. London: Routledge.

Woodhead, L. (ed.) 2001: *Berger on Religion*. London: Routledge.

Woodhead, L., and Heelas, P. (eds) 2000: *Religion in Modern Times*. Oxford: Blackwell.

Wright, N. 1997. The nature and variety of Restorationism and the 'House Church' movement. In S. Hunt, M. Hamilton and T. Walter (eds), *Charismatic Christianity: Sociological Perspectives*, London: Macmillan, 60–76.

Wuthnow, R. 1988. *The Restructuring of American Religion*. Princeton: Princeton University Press.

Yamane, D. 1997: Secularization on trial: in defense of a neosecularization paradigm. *Journal for the Scientific Study of Religion*, 37: 109–22.

Young, L. A. (ed.) 1997: *Rational Choice Theory and Religion*. New York: Routledge.

Index

5484640R00160

Printed in Great Britain
by Amazon.co.uk, Ltd.,
Marston Gate.

MERCHANT FLEETS
in profile ①

Duncan Haws

Additional research by Stephen Rabson
P&O Group Librarian

With drawings to 1:1800 scale

Patrick Stephens, Cambridge

First published in 1978

British Library Cataloguing in Publication Data

Haws, Duncan
    Merchant fleets in profile.
    1: The ships of the P&O, Orient and Blue Anchor
    lines.
    1. Merchant marine
    I. Title
    387.5   HE735

ISBN 0 85059 319 0

Text photoset in 9 on 10pt English 49
by Stevenage Printing Limited, Stevenage.
Printed in Great Britain (on 90 gsm Supreme Book Wove)
and bound by The Garden City Press, Letchworth,
for the publishers, Patrick Stephens Limited,
Bar Hill, Cambridge, CB3 8EL.

Contents

Introduction

Out of some twenty thousand companies of all nationalities that have owned mechanically driven ships during the past one hundred and fifty years, less than one hundred are familiar to the public at large, and of these possibly only fifty have become a part of everyday knowledge. Almost everyone with even the merest passing interest in things nautical will react with pleasure and even affection to ship-owning names like P&O, Cunard, United States Line, Union-Castle, Hamburg-America Line, The White Star Line, and possibly several more. But in the past there were also other names, now sometimes forgotten, that were equally illustrious as leaders and admired with national pride wherever their ships could be seen; names such as Collins, Money Wigram, Guion, Allan, Inman, American Line and Atlantic Transport to mention but a few. Even the ships that they owned sometimes acquired a place in history in their own right. *Great Britain*, *Leviathan*, *Titanic*, *Lusitania*, and *Great Eastern* will serve to illustrate the evocative power of such vessels.

With the passing of the years a comprehensive history of these celebrated companies and their ships is becoming steadily more difficult to achieve. Records have become dispersed and references are often thinly spread over a large number of books, many of which are out of print and hard to find. But like a philatelist collects individually different stamps, I collect 'ships'. More precisely, what they looked like and what happened to them during their twenty to thirty years of normal life. Nothing can be more exciting to me than finding, in an old book, an illustration of a ship which completes a gap in my collection.

In this book each company forms a chapter comprising a chronological history followed by an index of all the ships which have been owned. The numbered fleet list itself is illustrated with scale profile line drawings, although there are still gaps which one day, hopefully, will be filled. Because many ships have been altered or rebuilt during their careers two illustrations appear on a 'before' and 'after' basis where possible, but all too often my identification bears no date and is difficult to pinpoint. Friends of mine from all over the world pass me identification details and these are most welcome at all times.

Though the drawings are here reproduced to a scale of 1:1800 (150 ft = 1 in), I actually draw to a scale of 1:1200 (100 ft = 1 in), which has two distorting effects. One is vertical exaggeration and the other is thick rigging. A single pen stroke to my scale is, alas, 12 inches (30.48 cm) thick. The effect on rigging needs no further comment but on a ship's superstructure it adds a height of something like two feet (61 cm) per deck.

Duncan Haws
Cuckfield, Sussex

Explanatory notes

1 Company histories are arranged chronologically.
2 The ships owned are listed virtually chronologically except that sister ships are grouped together even when the period of their building covers more than one year.
3 Tonnage: the method of calculating tonnage has changed several times since 1830 and very few ships kept their initial tonnage. The gross and net tonnages shown are generally those recorded when the ship first entered service.
4 Dimensions: unless recorded as 'overall' the figures given are the registered dimensions between perpendiculars.
5 The speed given is service speed. This could vary according to route and ports of call.
6 Abbreviations: to assist all readers as few as possible have been used—

Apr	*April*
Aug	*August*
BHP	*Brake horse power*
Bt	*Built*
cm	*Centimetres*
cu m	*Cubic metres*
cu ft	*Cubic feet*
Cyl(s)	*Cylinder(s)*
dbl	*Double*
Dec	*December*
Dft	*Draught/draft*
diam	*Diameter*
Dim	*Dimensions*
dwt	*Dead weight*
E	*East*
Eng	*Engine*
exp	*Expansion*
fcsle	*Forecastle*
Feb	*February*
ft	*Feet*
fwd	*Forward*
g	*Gross*
GRT	*Gross registered tonnage*
H	*Hull*
HP	*Horse power/High pressure*
IHP	*Indicated horse power*
in	*Inch(es)*
Jan	*January*
kts	*Knots*
lb	*Pound(s)*
LP	*Low pressure*
m	*Metre*
Mar	*March*
mm	*Millimetres*
MP	*Medium pressure*
mph	*Miles per hour*
n	*Net*
N	*North*
NHP	*Nominal horse power*
Nov	*November*
oa	*Overall*
Oct	*October*
Pad	*Paddle*
Pass	*Passengers*
quad	*Quadruple/four*
refrig	*Refrigerated*
reg	*Registered*
RHP	*Registered horse power*
S	*South*
scr	*screw*
Sept	*September*
sgl	*Single*
Stm	*Steam*
Stm P	*Steam pressure*
SV	*Sailing vessel*
T	*Tons*
tpl	*Triple/three*
tst	*Tourist*
tw	*Twin/two*
W	*West*

7 The technical data follows the same pattern throughout—
Bt (built); *T:* (tons), g (gross), n (net), dwt (dead weight). **Dim** (dimensions) oa (overall), length × breadth × depth; *Dft:* (draught). **Eng** (engine) Pad (paddle), sgl (single), dbl (double), scr (screw); *Cyls:* (cylinders); *Stroke;* IHP, NHP, SHP, BHP, RHP, HP; Boilers; *Stm P:* (steam pressure) lb (pounds); kts (knots); By (engine builder). **H** (hull details); *Coal; Cargo; Pass:* (passengers) 1st (first class), 2nd (second class), 3rd (third class), tst (tourist class); *Crew*.

Funnels

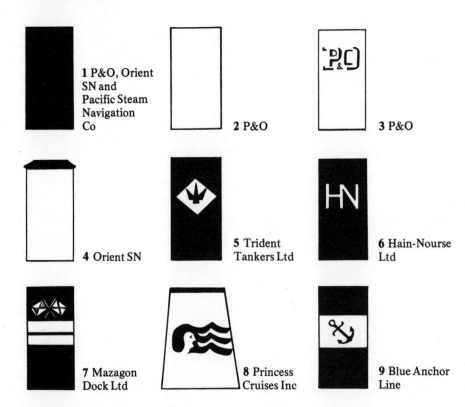

1 P&O, Orient SN and Pacific Steam Navigation Co

2 P&O

3 P&O

4 Orient SN

5 Trident Tankers Ltd

6 Hain-Nourse Ltd

7 Mazagon Dock Ltd

8 Princess Cruises Inc

9 Blue Anchor Line

1 Black.
2 Yellow.
3 Blue. The black drawn areas are white to silhouette the letters.
4 Yellow. Black Admiralty cowl.
5 Black and white.
6 Black and white.
7 Black. Two white bands. P&O and British India flags crossed.
8 White, blue device.
9 Black, white band. Blue anchor.

P&O Line

History

1815 It was in this year that the young and aspiring Brodie McGhie Willcox opened his shipbroking office in Lime Street, London. He engaged as his clerk a Scot, Arthur Anderson, who hailed from near Lerwick in the Shetlands. Brodie Wilcox was not himself a native Scot. His father was English and his mother a McGhie and although brought up and educated in Newcastle-upon-Tyne he was born in Ostend, Belgium. For seven years both men worked to develop their trade to the Iberian Peninsula. acting only as voyage brokers.

1822 Brodie Willcox and Arthur Anderson became partners and the firm took the title of Willcox and Anderson. Their main business expanded into operating a series of small sailing vessels to Spain and Portugal as agents for the owners. Regularity of departure was a prime facet.

1824-6 The Portuguese Royal Family were engaged in dealing with insurrectionists, who almost halted Willcox and Anderson's trade to Portugal. The partners gave their support to the queen and ran guns to Lisbon using a schooner which they purchased for the purpose. To ensure delivery and payment Arthur Anderson travelled on the first voyage. Discreetly he used the rather obvious alias 'Mr Smith'.

1832 The wisdom of their move to support the Crown was justified when the British Admiral, Sir Charles ('Mad Charlie') Napier, was given command of the Portuguese Naval Squadron. By 1833 the rebellion had collapsed and the partners resumed their trade with the flourish that comes from royal recognition and gratitude.

1833 But Portugal's troubles spread into Spain and Don Carlos, pretender to the Spanish throne, led the Carlist rising. Once again, Willcox and Anderson sided with royalty in the shape of the Queen Regent. During the eight short years since General Steam's *James Watt* became the first steam entry in Lloyds Register, steamships had begun to appear on the shorter Continental routes. Amongst the foremost innovators of the period was Captain Richard Bourne's Dublin and London Steam Packet Company and it was from this firm that Willcox and Anderson first chartered steamers. The earliest vessels, *William Fawcett* and *Royal Tar*, were both Bourne owned.

1835 July 10: *Royal Tar* landed at San Sebastian the first troops of the British Regiment, recruited in England.

When the revolt finally collapsed the Court of Spain encouraged the Dublin and London Steam Packet Co to inaugurate regular steamer services to the Peninsula, and the company came to an arrangement whereby Willcox and Anderson would run the service. They did so with the knowledge that the Royal Houses of both Spain and Portugal looked upon them with favour, and Captain Bourne and one of his staff, James Allan, both joined the London company.

Their early vessels were *William Fawcett*, although clearly too small, *Royal Tar* blessed with an extremely stout hull, and the chartered *City of Londonderry* and *Liverpool*.

1836 The newly built *Iberia* (I) and *Braganza* (I) really initiated 'Peninsular Steam' ownership (though the former was registered in the names of Willcox and

Anderson, the latter Richard Bourne and others) and led directly to the founding of the Peninsular & Oriental Steam Navigation Company, although at this stage in the Company's history the word 'Oriental' had yet to appear.

1837 Sept 1: The company announced weekly sailings on Fridays from London via Falmouth (the main port) to Vigo (54 hours)-Oporto-Lisbon (84 hours)-Cadiz-Gibraltar (seventh day). Every alternate week there was a connection to Malta, a voyage of five days. This inter-linked with a two day voyage from Malta to Corfu. *Iberia* (I) inaugurated the mail sailings.

Each month Malta was connected with Alexandria (four days) and from there the company introduced an overland journey to Port Suez with a connection to India. The monthly 'Indian' sailings left London on the 1st and 29th of the month but the sailings beyond Egypt were not then operated by the Peninsular Steam Navigation Co.

On the same day services were started from Liverpool under the name Liverpool Branch Line, the fares from Liverpool being the same as those from London. Once again steamers were chartered from the Dublin and London Steam Packet Co, the initial vessels being their *Manchester* and *City of Londonderry*.

Two classes were introduced: 'chief cabin' and 'second cabin'. Specimen fares were:

London or Liverpool to Vigo, Oporto or Lisbon	£15 and	£9.50
Falmouth to Vigo, Oporto or Lisbon	£13 and	£7.50
London to Cadiz or Gibraltar	£18 and	£12.00
Falmouth to Cadiz or Gibraltar	£16 and	£10.00

Such was the mutual involvement between the two organisations that Captain Bourne now joined the board of Willcox and Anderson.

1838 *William Fawcett* sold and replaced by *Achilles*. The commitments which followed the mail contract led to the chartering of several additional vessels. Names mentioned in the sailing lists were *City of Hamburgh*, *Emerald Isle*, *Glasgow*, *Juno*, *Neptune*, *Ocean*, *Royal Adelaide*, *Soho*, *Vivid* and *Wilberforce*.

An interesting development was that the British Government became so impressed with the effectiveness of the granting of a mail contract to one company that they asked for tenders to operate a North Atlantic mailship service. The Cunard company stems from this development.

1839 A serious problem arose for the Peninsular Steam Navigation Co when the British Government entered into an agreement with the French postal authorities for the carriage of mail, by rail, overland to Marseilles and thence by British Government packet to Malta and by simultaneous connection to Alexandria. But the new service turned out to be slower and less reliable than that operated by Peninsular and was quickly abandoned. In the same year Lord William Bentinck, Governor General of India, insisted upon a satisfactory solution to the erratic communications that then existed with the sub-continent. Willcox and Anderson were approached but declined to become interested, although they made available all their knowledge and information concerning the Indian route. To overcome the economic reluctance of ship owners to invest in India a Government mail contract was put out to tender. The Willcox and Anderson partnership put in a bid of £34,200 and with it secured the contract. With both the Iberian and Indian mail contracts to operate the whole complexion of their trading was altered. No longer a modest concern they needed newer and bigger ships as well as increased capital. *India* (I) was built for the Indian route.

1840 Apr 23: The Board of Peninsular Steam Navigation agreed to change the name of the company to Peninsular and Oriental Steam Navigation Co Ltd and to increase the capital to £1,000,000 divided into 200,000 shares. Immediately it became known as the P&O line.

Dec 1: The new company was incorporated by Royal Charter and its articles now included India and the Far East within its trading boundaries. The India route needed careful attention. The P&O's contract called for the introduction, within two years, of a suitable mail service between Egypt and India. In an effort to stimulate P&O the East India Company offered an annual payment of £20,000 provided four voyages were made in the first twelve months, six in the second year and twelve in the third year. The offer had to be refused, simply because each new steamer intended for the route cost more than the sum offered. Furthermore, to service the route an Egyptian organisation would have to be set up. The East India Company were also aware of the paucity of their offer: between 1829 and 1836 they had lost much more than the sum offered on the single annual round voyage of their steamer *Hugh Lindsay* between Bombay and Suez. P&O tackled the Indian Mail contract in two halves: West of Egypt and East of Egypt. For the latter they ordered two brand new vessels for the Suez-Bombay route, delivery to be made within two years.

To provide commensurate vessels for the West of Egypt's London-Alexandria connection they used the five year old *Great Liverpool* and the brand new *United States* of Sir John Tobin's Transatlantic Steam Ship Co. This company was part of the Dublin and London Steam Packet Co group, and Sir John was also involved in the City of Cork Steam Packet Co whose *Sirius* had been chartered, in 1838, for the first commercial transatlantic crossing. The connection between Tobin and Willcox & Anderson went back to 1838 when all three had seriously considered bidding for the North Atlantic mail contract.

Initially both vessels were chartered and *United States* was renamed *Oriental* (I) to mark the advent of the word in the P&O company's title. For two years they were to maintain the Alexandria service whilst preparations were also being made for the Alexandria-Port Suez overland connection. Other ships transferred were *Braganza* (I), *Iberia* (I), *Liverpool*, *Royal Tar* and *Tagus*.

Perhaps before leaving the momentous year of 1840 it is worth mentioning the personalities involved. P&O's Chairman was the city financier Sir John Larpent. The company had three managing directors: Brodie Willcox, Arthur Anderson and Francis Carleton of the Transatlantic SS Co. Richard Bourne of the Dublin and London SP Co was on the Board as was Peter de Zulueta who, as the agent for the Spanish Government during the Carlist revolt, had been instrumental in encouraging the start of regular steamer

services back in 1835. Sir John Tobin's involvement was £80,000 in P&O shares and the company took over his liabilities for *Oriental*, which had cost £60,000 to build. **1842** Jan 19: *Lady Mary Wood* delivered. Sept 24: The first of the two sisters ordered in late 1840, *Hindostan* (I), left Southampton to become the company's first vessel on the Bombay-Suez run. Her passage via Capetown to Bombay took 91 days. Her sister was named *Bentinck* (1843) after the Governor General. Both had white funnels with black tops and were deliberately identical in build. With the successful start of the new route to India the British Government awarded a new contract to P&O covering the developing area of Suez-Ceylon-Madras-Calcutta. The annual subvention was £115,000. The other bidder for the new contract had been the Eastern Steam Navigation Co which had been formed by a group of P&O share-holders whose aspirations caused them to be nicknamed 'The Precursors'. Their vessel, named *Precursor*, was acquired by P&O (in 1844) to operate the new route.

The overland route to India was to become the quickest way to travel for the next quarter century. Passengers disembarked at Alexandria and journeyed for 12 hours up the Nile to Cairo. The special shallow draft vessels *Lotus* (1838) and *Cairo* (1841) then conveyed them to Cosseir, where the desert journey to Suez began in mule-drawn carriages. The distance was 250 miles and the scheduled transit time was 88 hours for passengers.

During this year the Malta-Corfu route was withdrawn. Although stipulated in the Government mail contract this service received little support compared with the overland service by rail to Venice and thence by connecting coastal steamer down the Adriatic. However, P&O continued their Malta-Athens-Smyrna-Constantinople route. Another service which they found profitable was the connecting Alexandria-Jaffa-Beirut (Beyrouth) feeder service.

Pacha built, the first P&O vessel with an iron hull.
1843 *Tagus* and *Oriental* (I) acquired.
1844 The author William Makepeace Thackeray took the Mediterranean round

13

voyage. His experiences were duly recorded in *The Irish Sketch Book* and *From Cornhill to Cairo*.

The mail contract between Suez and Bombay, held by the East India Company, came up for tender. P&O put in a bid of £80,000 per annum against the existing fee of £110,000. However, the British Government was more interested in developing routes beyond India. So, instead of receiving the Bombay Mail contract, P&O were asked to tender for a new route from Ceylon to Penang, Singapore and Hong Kong. This was duly awarded to them and plans were implemented to tranship the mail at Galle in Ceylon and carry it on by a monthly service.

Dec 12: *Delta* (I) entered service.

1845 June 24: The new Far East mail service was inaugurated by *Lady Mary Wood* and when she arrived at Singapore on Aug 4 she brought the mails 41 days out from London. Singapore became, for P&O, the new transhipment port for the Far East. Furthermore it was logical to consider a branch service southwards to Australia as well as similar feeder services northwards to Japan.

On her return voyage *Lady Mary Wood* was loaded with no less than 4,757 packages, clearly demonstrating the viability of the service. When *Braganza* (I) took the second sailing she carried over 1,400 letters, parcels and newspapers.

Liverpool sold. *Delta* (I) sold and replaced by the larger *Madrid*.

1846 Feb 24: *Great Liverpool* wrecked near Cape Finisterre. *Ariel* and *Erin* placed on Marseilles-Alexandria service, with *Haddington* joining *Pottinger* on the Suez-India service. *Ripon* entered service.

1847 *Royal Tar* sold. *Tiber* lost on Feb 21. *Pekin* (I), *Sultan*, *Indus* (I) and *Euxine* entered service.

1848 The Sicilian Government purchased the brand new *Vectis* (I), *Bombay* (I) and *Ganges* (I). Replacement vessels were ordered at once.

Canton (I), the smallest vessel in the fleet, arrived at Hong Kong to open a feeder service with Macao. The vessel was so well armed against pirates that she resembled a miniature warship.

Rebellion broke out in Ceylon. *Lady Mary Wood* was sent from Pointe de Galle to Madras with urgent orders to return with troops. This she did and the rebellion was quelled. For this exploit *Lady Mary Wood* can claim to have been the first steam troopship.

Mar 13: *Malta* (I) delivered.

May 28: *Ariel* lost near Livorno.

1849 P&O commenced its own ship insurance scheme, mainly by allocating a percentage of all revenues to the fund.

An experimental service was started between Hong Kong and Shanghai. The vessel which inaugurated the service was *Lady Mary Wood*.

Early in the year the company offered to take over the British mail contract between Suez and Bombay from the East India Company. They would, they said, extend the service to Australia for the same sum as now applied to Bombay. However the offer was not accepted, but P&O had ordered no fewer than seven paddle steamers capable of maintaining an extended service from Singapore. One outcome of the whole affair was that a Parliamentary Committee was set up to make recommendations. They urged a formal Singapore-Australia link as soon as feasible.

Sept: *Canton* (I), going about her lawful business, came upon HMS *Columbine* becalmed off Hong Kong in the midst of a group of pirate junks who were outside of cannon range and, with their long sweeps, were slowly escaping. The steamer *Canton* was able to tow *Columbine* into range and the notorious junks were destroyed. From thence onward *Canton* was never molested and safely carried many valuable cargoes.

India (I) sold and hulked.

1850 *Ganges* (II), *Singapore* (I) and *Boulac* delivered.

1851 *Pacha* lost on July 21. *Shanghai* (I) placed on Hong Kong-Shanghai route.

Work commenced on the Alexandria to Suez railway. At home tenders were invited from interested parties for the Singapore-Australia service recommended to Parliament by the 1849 Committee.

1852 The dispute between the East India Company and P&O over the Suez-Indian routes had continued ever since the transfer to P&O of the Calcutta sector from Ceylon. The East India Company claimed that its Indian Marine should be preferred, as a necessity for the maintenance of a potential Indian navy for use in times of war east of Suez. The opposition view was that the Indian Marine was not only inefficient but also expensive, to the tune of £100,000 a year.

The East India Company's credibility was finally demolished in a spectacular way—they lost a whole ship-load of mail. When no steamer was available at Suez they foolishly entrusted the consignment to an Arab dhow, which set off down the Red Sea for Bombay and was never heard of again.

Jupiter, Montrose and *Braganza* (I) sold. *Chusan* (I), *Bombay* (II) and *Madras* (II) commissioned.

Feb 26: P&O's tender for a service to Australia was accepted at £119,600 per annum subsidy for a bi-monthly service: Singapore-King George's Sound-Adelaide-Melbourne-Sydney. The eight year contract was to be reduced to £20,000 per annum when the Alexandria to Suez railway was completed. The size of vessels to be used was not to be less than 600 customs measured tons and they had to be capable of a service speed of not less than 8½ knots. The result of this contract was that P&O now operated the following Royal Mail routes:

Fortnightly: Southampton-Gibraltar-Malta-Alexandria (overland), operated by *Great Liverpool* and *Oriental* (I). Suez-Point de Galle-Madras-Calcutta, operated by *Bentinck*, *Hindostan* (I), *India* (I) and *Precursor*. Marseilles-Malta; this accelerated overland service was operated by the fast steamer *Ariel*. P&O's agents in Marseilles became Estrine & Co.

Monthly: Bombay-Point de Galle-Penang-Singapore-Hong Kong-Calcutta-Penang-Singapore-Hong Kong. This gave a fortnightly Penang-Singapore-Hong Kong service, but more importantly the Southampton service to Hong Kong was now fortnightly via either Ceylon or Calcutta.

Bi-Monthly: The Singapore-Australia route.

In preparation for the main service to Australia, which was due to be inaugurated no later than Jan 11 1853, P&O commenced preliminary sailings.

May 15: *Chusan* (I) left Southampton via the Cape for Adelaide-Melbourne-Sydney,

where she arrived on Aug 3 amidst great excitement. Her consort for the route was to be *Shanghai* (I); in the event *Formosa* (I) had to take the sailing, *Shanghai* being unavailable, and she left Southampton for Australia on Aug 7 with 90 passengers aboard. The Sydney-Singapore fare was £50.

P&O's commencement of their experimental service ahead of the contract date was misunderstood. 'Why', the question was asked, 'did they need a subsidy when, quite unaided, they could of their own volition operate two steamers?' A Parliamentary enquiry was initiated based on the accusation that the company was making too much out of the mail subsidies. The official findings were that the profits were to be described as moderate.

Aug 31: *Chusan* left Sydney to inaugurate the Singapore branch service.

1853 Like other lines the mail contract companies, Cunard and Royal Mail, were now building iron-hulled steamers. This was notwithstanding the adamance of the Post Office that the mails should be carried in the supposedly safer wooden-walled vessels. P&O, like the others, actually operated better and faster iron-hulled ships whilst the mail went in wooden steamers. The ordinance was only changed when the Royal Mail Line's *Amazon* was lost by fire on June 2 with the loss of 115 lives as well as the mails she carried. New ships were *Norna* and *Colombo*.

The Trans-Isthmus railway from Alexandria was completed as far as the Nile.

Sept: The Australian service had, in less than a year, become so popular that the company announced that the larger ships *Bombay* (II) and *Madras* (II) would replace *Chusan* (I) and *Shanghai* (I). Their cargo capacity at 600 tons was virtually twice that of their predecessors.

Paralleling the expansion of P&O's activities came a sharp increase in the price of coal which, in turn, led to a scarcity of colliers. Whereas other firms were able to reduce the number of sailings P&O were tied to mail contracts. Their appeals for temporary subsidies were turned down and for a time bankruptcy stared them in the face.

Rajah, Valetta (I), *Vectis* (II), *Cadiz,*

15

Bengal (I), *Douro* and *Tartar* all entered service.

1854 The coal shortage of 1853 was severely aggravated by the Australian gold rush, spare shipping capacity disappearing overnight. But new coal fields were discovered and developed at Labuan and Formosa. P&O operated two colliers, *Rajah* and the new *Manilla*, ferrying coal to their Far East coaling station. Even so, the situation deteriorated further when war broke out in the Crimea between France, England and Russia. The price of coal rocketted, escalating by 50 per cent. The British Government urgently needed troop transport and requisitioned a considerable number of ships; P&O saw *Candia* (I), *Nubia* (I) and *Ripon* taken over immediately, and when further demands were made the Australian service was rather thankfully suspended in November. *Colombo*, *Malta* (I), *Manilla* and *Pottinger* all saw war service. The new *Himalaya* (I), the world's largest ship, also became hopelessly uneconomic and was sold to the Government for her building price of £130,000.

In 1854 the company, for the first time, paid no dividend to its shareholders. Both Brodie Willcox and Arthur Anderson assisted the coffers of the company by foregoing their percentage participation which was based on gross trading not net profits.

Norna replaced *Bombay* (II) on the Australia-Singapore route and the one year old *Douro* was wrecked at Hong Kong. *Simla* (I) entered service together with *Candia* (I), *Nubia* (I) and *Alma*.

1855 To augment the company's cash problems the capital was increased by £1,000,000 in £50 shares. In a matter of days the new issue was fully taken up.

New ships were *Alhambra*, *Pera* (I) and *Ava*.

1856 *Aden* (I) commissioned. *Azof* replaced *Douro*.

When the Crimean war ended P&O anticipated that the now-cancelled Australian contract would be re-awarded to them. But, much to P&O's chagrin, in March new tenders were invited. When the terms of these were announced P&O rejected them as onerous but nevertheless submitted a bid, based on their previous

experience of the route. A newcomer, the Royal Mail Steam Packet Co, put in a bid via the Cape and Robert Henderson's European & Columbian Steam Navigation Co suggested a route via the Isthmus of Panama. To the surprise of all, including Robert Henderson, the contract went to the European & Columbian SN Co (renamed The European & Australian Royal Mail Co), but for the Suez route and not via Panama. The annual rate of subsidy was so low that it was openly predicted that the novice concern would run into financial trouble. P&O were angered at the Government's comment that the award took into account the fact that their vessels were still on trooping duties and could not be made available to initiate a service. Strangely enough the people of Australia welcomed the news of a newcomer because they blamed the suspension of the service on P&O rather than the Crimean War. Perhaps correctly, they pointed out that a reduced P&O Far East service had continued throughout the hostilities. The Australian service, they said, had been cut because it was unprofitable on account of coal prices. The new contract was the cause of many and varied events culminating in the fact that the European & Australian Royal Mail Co had no vessel to take their maiden sailing, and P&O's new *Simla* (I) took the first voyage on charter.

The service between Marseilles and Malta was extended to Alexandria to give a fast overland connection for those who preferred to avoid the Bay of Biscay, which had a reputation for rough seas.

1857 *Madrid* and *Erin* lost. *Iberia* (I) and *Achilles* were sold. *Nemesis* and *Granada* commissioned.

The outbreak of the Indian Mutiny necessitated additional P&O vessels being used as troopships. Between Sept 1857 and June 1858 P&O's Egyptian overland route carried 5,400 men. At this time the railway between Alexandria and Suez still had a gap in it of 25 miles. The troops travelled on donkeys whilst the passengers travelled in vans drawn by mules. The 25-mile gap took eight hours to cross.

As predicted, the European & Australian Royal Mail Co had to cease operations, having lost its subscribed capital of £400,000 and incurring additional debts of £300,000. In July a merger with the Royal Mail Line was mooted but did not materialise. Instead Royal Mail and Cunard more or less ran the concern until its demise in 1858.

Meanwhile P&O obtained an additional contract to operate a mail service between Hong Kong and Manilla, but this was to last only two years.

1858 With the end of the European & Australian Royal Mail Co saga P&O tendered in September for the new Australian mail contract which, in due course, they obtained for a figure of £118,000 per annum and a passage time to Sydney of 55 days. The route from Suez was new, being Suez-Aden-Mauritius-King George's Sound (now Albany)-Adelaide (Kangaroo Island)-Melbourne-Sydney. This route proved unpopular compared with the India-Ceylon and Singapore routes mainly due to the enormous amount of coal needed, and lasted only one year although the branch service from Aden to Mauritius was maintained until 1866.

Dec: The Trans-Isthmus railway was completed. To meet the heavy additional passenger service needs P&O purchased four John Laird sisters from French owners. They became *Behar* (I), *Ellora*, *Orissa* (I) and *China* (I). A fifth, *Northam*, was built for P&O by Day Summers of Northam, after whom she was named. *Emeu* was taken over from the European & Australian Royal Mail Co whilst the new *Ceylon* (I) and *Nepaul* (I) took the Marseilles-Alexandria route.

1859 Feb 12: *Salsette* left to position at Sydney for the Australia-Suez sector.
Mar 12: *Pera* left Southampton to inaugurate the United Kingdom-Alexandria leg. The sailings east of Suez were taken by *Benares*, *Jeddo*, *Malta* (I) and *Northam*, *Columbian* joined *Emeu* on the Australian run. Marseilles-Malta-Alexandria was operated by *Valetta* (I), *Vectis* (II), *Euxine* and *Ellora*.

Japan was thought to be a source of future trade. P&O's General Administration Manager, Thomas Sutherland, made the company's first reconnaissance. He visited the Dutch colony there and recorded that there were less than ten Europeans in residence.

Valetta (I) and *Vectis* (II) dismantled.

Oct: P&O asked that the Australian contract be changed to link Ceylon as an offshoot of the Calcutta service. This change was eventually accepted but the subsidy was reduced because combined sailings from Suez onwards were now said to be feasible. *Benares* was placed on the route.

Lady Mary Wood sold and *Alma* lost. *Delta* (II) commissioned.

1860 Aug 20: *Pera* took the first sailing from Southampton on the revised Australian mail service. Beyond Ceylon *Behar* (I), *Jeddo* and *Salsette* were employed, the Suez-Ceylon portion being served by *Colombo*, *Nemesis*, *Nubia* (I) and *Simla* (I).

The Red Sea passage was the most trying of all P&O's journeys. Intense humidity, a blazing sun and only the faintest of breezes combined to produce a devastating heat. Frequently when the breeze came from astern ships were put about and steamed into the wind in an effort to ventilate the below decks accommodation.

This Red Sea voyage is said to have introduced the word 'posh' into the English language. The coolest cabins were those away from the sun. Outbound these were on the port or lefthand side of the ship and homeward they were on the opposite or starboard side. Thus the order for a cabin became 'port out starboard home' which became abbreviated in P&O parlance to POSH or 'travelling posh'.

Malabar lost and *Mooltan* (I) delivered.
1862 *Shanghai* (I) sold as being too small and *Colombo* wrecked on the Laccadive Islands. *Poonah* entered service.
1863 Coaling was an immense task. It is recorded that on average 170 sailing ships were on constant charter to P&O for supplying coal to the various coaling points located along their network of routes.

Golconda, *Syria* (I), *Rangoon* and *Carnatic* (I) delivered.
1864 *Corea* inaugurated a service from Shanghai to Yokohama.

The Australian mail contract came up for renewal. P&O were the only tenderers and monthly sailings together with an annual payment of £120,000 were agreed. P&O actually offered twice-monthly sailings for an extra £50,000 but this was declined.

Oct 5: *Hindostan* (I) lost by cyclone at Calcutta. During the year *Delhi* (II), *Baroda*, *Nyanza* (I) and *Corea* were delivered.

1865 *Corea* lost. *Mongolia* (I), *Niphon* and *Tanjore* entered service.

1866 *Jeddo* lost two miles from Bombay. *Ava*, *Malacca* (I), *Surat* (I) and *Sunda* (I) delivered.

1867 *Pottinger* scrapped. The sisters *Bangalore* (I) and *Sumatra* (I) entered service.

Aug 20: *Singapore* (I) lost in Japanese waters.

1868 Arthur Anderson died and Thomas Sutherland was appointed an Assistant Manager. *Euxine* and *Precursor* went for scrap. *Niphon* lost whilst *Travancore* and *Deccan* arrived.

1869 *Sultan* and *Northam* sold, the latter to the Union SS Co. *Carnatic* wrecked in the Red Sea. *Hindostan* (II) delivered. Nov 17: The opening of the Suez Canal. P&O's *Delta* (III) carried the official guests in a procession of 68 ships headed by the French Royal Yacht *Aigle* with the Empress Eugenie aboard.

Within two years, the opening of the canal would cause severe financial hardship for P&O. They had designed their services beyond Africa on the basis of the overland connection from Alexandria to Suez. Two types of ship existed: Mediterranean and Eastern. In Egypt the company owned its own transhipment wharves, at both ports, together with tugs, barges and Nile river steamers. In addition they maintained supply stores, farms for fresh produce, a water distillery and even a large ice-making plant. Now, at a stroke, the majority of their vessels were outdated and the Egyptian investment greatly reduced in value.

Before Suez, because of the necessity of transhipment, freight rates were so high that only premium cargoes could be carried profitably. The rates to Calcutta ranged from £10-£12 per ton. Australia and China reached £25-£30 a ton whilst Shanghai or Japan cost £28-£33. These tariffs and their curbing effect on cargo had resulted in P&O owning ships which averaged a mere 2,000 gross tons. With the removal of the enormous cost of the overland transhipment the rates could and would

drop substantially and by so doing boost trade with the East. This in turn would make the P&O fleet obsolete, and worse still would also make them uneconomical to operate.

This, then, was the prospect P&O faced when *Delta* headed through the canal that day. To add one final twist to the screw the Post Office insisted upon the letter of their mail contract and obliged P&O to unload the mails at Alexandria then to transport them overland to Suez and there to re-embark them. To modify the contract the Government asked for an unacceptable £30,000 a year reduction in the subsidy. It was not until the 1874 renewal of the contract that this clause was deleted.

1870 Brindisi replaced Marseilles as the Mediterranean overland port. *Australia* (I) introduced the two cylinder compound inverted engine to the fleet. *Cadiz*, *Syria* (I) and *Chusan* (I) sold.

1871 Initially few ships used the Suez Canal for reasons similar to P&O's dilemma. They were wrongly designed and supplies beyond Suez were scarce. By 1871 the Compagnie Universelle du Canal de Suez faced bankruptcy and attempts to raise capital failed. But the value of the concept of a canal was irrefutable and slowly the transits increased in volume. P&O decided not to attempt to modify their older ships but to build anew, but in the interim several ships were remodelled to take advantage of the Suez Canal. *Mirzapore* (I) took the first through sailing to the Far East via Suez.

Jan: *Haddington* broken up. *Ganges* (II) and *Norna* sold. *Indus* (I), *Khedive*, *Mirzapore* (I), *Pekin* (II) and *Peshawur* (I) all entered service during the year.

1872 Thomas Sutherland was appointed Managing Director at the age of 34. *Ottawa* (I) and *Nyanza* (I) sold. *Hydaspes* and *Cathay* (I) delivered.

1873 Whilst *Delta* (II) was disposed of a host of newly built ships arrived in service, reflecting Thomas Sutherland's bold and most necessary move to rebuild the fleet so as to take advantage of the effect of the Suez Canal. *Timsah* was built for Canal service, and together with *Malwa* (I), *Bokhara*, *Venetzia*, *Lombardy*, *Gwalior*, *Nizam*, *Assam*, *Zambesi*, *Adria* and *Khiva* made up a total of 11 new vessels introduced in a single year.

1874 The mail contracts to the Far East and India were renewed for twenty years. The land transhipment clause was dropped but the subsidy was reduced by £20,000. The Australian mail contract was not modified until 1888. *Candia* (I), *Behar* (I) and *Madras* (II) sold for further trading.

P&O moved its head office from Southampton to London. Until now their ships terminated at Southampton and all onward freight and mail went by rail. The introduction of through sea rates to London made the rail link uneconomic. The mail, however, remained based on Southampton and a pick-up call was added.

1876 *Ellora* sold.

1877 *Nubia* (I) became the boys training ship *Shaftesbury*.

1878 *Orissa* (I) sold. *Kaisar-I-Hind* (I) entered service.

1879 *Hindostan* (II) became P&O's first loss for ten years. *Ancona*, *Verona* and *Rosetta* were commissioned.

1880 Thomas Sutherland, now aged 46, was appointed Chairman.

Bombay (II) destroyed by fire and *Travancore* wrecked off Cape Otranto. *Pera* (I) sold for further trading. *Rosetta* became P&O's first vessel built in Northern Ireland; her sister *Ravenna* came from Denny's at Dumbarton.

1881 *Baroda* scrapped. Two important new ships delivered were the 5,000 ton *Rome* and *Carthage* (I), but *Clyde* and *Shannon* of the 'River' class were also delivered.

1882 Unrest in Egypt led to the Post Authorities decreeing that all mail, heavy and first class, should go by ship through the Suez Canal. Alexandria became the focus of the troubles and *Tanjore* lay off the port as a refugee ship. *Ancona* and *Surat* (I) were present in the port after the bombardment of the city by a British Naval squadron, *Surat* being sent post haste to Brindisi with dispatches for the Admiralty. A total of eight P&O vessels were used to transport the Egyptian Expeditionary Force.

Malta (I) and *China* (I) were broken up whilst *Avoca* and *Malacca* (I) both went to Zanzibar owners. New ships were *Thames*, *Ganges* (III), *Sutlej*, *Ballaarat* and *Parramatta*.

1883 British ships were being badly affected by the Suez Sanitary Board, which declared most eastern ports as being endemic for infectious illnesses which warranted quarantining for 14 days. Only when the British threatened to build a second canal on British controlled soil were the regulations modified.

Valetta (II), sister to *Ballaarat*, delivered.

1884 *Simla* (I) collided with *City of Lucknow* and sank. *Massilia* (II), last of the *Ballaarat* class, entered service. *Tasmania* and *Chusan* (II) were delivered for the Calcutta service.

1885 Friction with Russia led to *Massilia* (at Sydney) and *Rosetta* (at Hong Kong) being temporarily converted into armed merchant cruisers. They remained as such for six months at a charter rate of £7,000 each per month. The contract reduced the price to £5,000 each if Royal Navy personnel took them over.

Bengal (I) wrecked on the coast of Java. *Coromandel* (I) was delivered.

1887 To mark the twin Golden Jubilees of Queen Victoria and P&O the famous jubilee ships *Victoria*, *Britannia*, *Arcadia* (1888) and *Oceana* (1888) were built.

Tasmania, only three years old, was wrecked on the coast of Corsica.

1888 *Ava* lost and *Mongolia* (I) sold for breaking up. *Zambesi* sold. New P&O ships were *Oriental* (II) and her sister *Peninsular* (II).

1889 Jan: An 'intermediate' service to Australia was introduced by *Ravenna* and *Brindisi*. Their route was Antwerp-London-Teneriffe-Capetown-Melbourne-Sydney. The competition from the established Union and Castle companies made the venture unsuccessful and it was speedily withdrawn. But P&O still felt the need for an Australian service via the Cape and bided their time.

Caird built the four sister cargo vessels *Bombay* (III), *Hong Kong*, *Shanghai* (II) and *Canton* (II). *Sumatra* (I) burnt at sea.

1890 *Tanjore* sold and *Khiva* was disposed of for further trading. At Yokohama *Kashgar* (I) was broken up. *Nepaul* was wrecked off Plymouth.

1891 The *Formosa* (I) was hulked at Hong Kong and *Geelong* (I) had the misfortune to be lost at sea.

1892 *Bokhara* was lost when her boilers were swamped during a typhoon off Formosa. New ships to enter P&O service were *Aden* (II), *Malacca* (II), *Formosa* (II), *Manila* and *Java*, plus two large passenger liners *Himalaya* (II) and *Australia* (II).
1893 Two ships, *Venetia* and *Nizam*, were broken up but *Japan* was delivered as a replacement.
1894 *Victoria* and *Britannia* were both chartered for six months to act as troopships. The regular Naval troopships *Crocodile*, *Jumna*, *Malabar* and *Serapis* were old and inefficient. Between them the P&O pair accomplished more than the other four, with the result that the old Naval troopers were disposed of in 1896 and thereafter merchant ships were chartered. This in due course led to P&O, British India and Bibby designing ships for trooping duties.

Caledonia came into P&O service with white hull and yellow funnels. This new innovation did not last long due to the cost and time involved in maintaining her appearance up to P&O standards. *Mazagon* (I) and *Ceylon* (II) also entered company service.
1895 Additions to the fleet were *Sumatra* (II), *Borneo*, *Palawan*, *Simla* (II), *Nubia* (II), *Malta* (II) and the little coastal steamer *Harlington* (I).
1896 Only two new ships were delivered, these being *India* (II) and her sister *China* (II), the first pair of a class of five which were then P&O's largest ships.
1897 *Khedive* was sold, then had the singular misfortune to be wrecked only ten days later. *Aden* (II) was lost on Socotra Island, in the Gulf after which she was named; coincidentally a new delivery was named *Socotra* (I) to complete a strange double. The remainder of the *India* class, the *Egypt* and *Persia*, came into service.
1898 *Isis* and *Osiris* were built as express liners for the first class service from Brindisi to Alexandria. Three Hall Line ships were purchased and they became *Tientsin*, *Nankin* (I) and *Pekin* (III).
1899 *Assaye* was commissioned.
1900-1902 The South African war, popularly known as the Boer War, saw some nine P&O liners employed as troopships. They transported over 150,000 war service personnel.

1900 *Malwa* (I) was broken up in Japan. *Sobraon* and *Plassy* delivered. P&O also took delivery of *Banca*, their only turret-hulled ship.
1901 Misfortune struck when the year old *Sobraon* was lost off Foochow in dense fog on a pitch black night. But 1901 also saw the beginning of P&O's greatest ever building programme, the 'S', 'N' and 'M' class era. Lead vessel was *Sicilia*, followed by *Syria* (II), *Somali* (I) and *Soudan* (I).
1902 *Sardinia*, fifth of the 'S' class, entered service.
1903 *Massilia* (I) and *Parramatta* were both broken up. *Palermo*, *Pera* (II) and *Palma* of the 'P' class, and *Moldavia* (I), *Mongolia* (II) and *Marmora* of the 'M' class, were delivered.
1904 During the war between Russia and Japan many incidents took place. One involved *Persia*, when Russian warships stopped and searched her. *Ballaarat* was broken up while *Australia* (II) was lost by fire a few days after becoming fast on the rocks at the entrance to Port Phillip.
1905 *Bangalore* (I) foundered off the Azores and *Peshawur* (I) was wrecked on Madagascar. Two ships, *Carthage* (I) and *Valetta* (II), were broken up at Bombay. *Poona*, *Peshawur* (II), *Mooltan* (II), *Delta* (III), *Dongola* (I) and *Delhi* (III) delivered.
1906 The 'N' class of eight vessels was introduced by the delivery of *Nile* and *Namur*, both of which were to be lost during the First World War.
1907 The old *Ceylon* of 1858 finally went to the scrap yard. The 'N' class *Nyanza* (II) and *Nore* were delivered.
1908 *Salsette* (II) was commissioned for the Aden-Bombay ferry. She entered service with yellow funnels and a white hull. Her entry into service brought the number of ocean-going vessels owned by P&O up to 65. *Chusan* (II) and *Bengal* (II) broken up at Bombay.
1909 *Victoria* and *Britannia* broken up. *Malwa* (II) and *Mantua* (I) delivered.
1910 The fleet and goodwill (but not the actual company) of Lund's Blue Anchor Line was acquired for £275,000. This sum was made up of £25,000 for goodwill plus five ships at cost price less five per cent for each year of service. The vessels acquired were *Commonwealth*, *Geelong* (II), *Narrung*, *Wakool* and *Wilcannia* and they

came into P&O ownership upon completion of their then current voyages. The purchase gave P&O entry into the Australian service via the Cape which they had attempted in 1889. This new service they called the P&O Branch Line and it was operated separately because South African regulations called for the vessels to carry all white crews. Because of the age and assorted nature of the Lund ships P&O immediately ordered five replacement vessels; all were to be given names beginning with 'B' for Branch. The new ships were *Ballarat* (spelt with 3 a's), *Beltana, Benalla, Berrima* and *Borda*.
1911 *Maloja* (I), *Medina* and *Ballarat* (I) handed over. Prior to entering commercial service *Medina* was used as the Royal Yacht for King George V's journey to the Delhi Durbar. *Delhi* (III) lost on Cape Spartel.
1912 The five Branch Line vessels were planned to enter service with Lund funnels (black funnel, white band and blue anchor) but P&O livery was introduced two years later.

Nankin (II) and *Novara* of the 'N' class were delivered together with *Beltana*, the first Branch liner.
1913 *Nagoya* and *Nellore*, the last of the 'N' class, were commissioned and *Benalla* joined the Branch service. *Khiva* (II) was the first of the 'K' class. *Rome* was broken up appropriately enough in Italy.
1914 The Australasian United SN Co was acquired.
May: An amalgamation was agreed between P&O and British India, with whom there had been a good trading relationship stretching back over many years. The absence of specific P&O feeder vessels beyond Suez reflects the fact that British India (known as BI) acted satisfactorily in this capacity. The formula was the exchange by each company of £700,000 of preference stock, and P&O transferred £638,123 of deferred stock for one million BI shares. The new joint Board of Directors comprised 12 P&O members and eight from British India.
Aug 4: The outbreak of the First World War. At the time *Mantua* (I) was cruising in the Baltic and was instructed to make a dash for home. No port of call could be made and furniture and other wooden fittings were burnt as fuel. By Aug 13

Mantua had become the first P&O armed merchant cruiser, together with her sister *Macedonia*.
Dec 2: The small feeder vessel *Harlington* (I) was wrecked off the east coast of England.

Berrima and *Borda* were delivered during the year together with five 'K' class vessels, *Khyber* (I), *Kashgar* (II), *Karmala*, *Kashmir* and *Kalyan*. But the most notable addition to the fleet was the sleek 11,500 ton *Kaisar-I-Hind* (II).
1915 Dec 30: The torpedoing of *Persia* by *U-38* led to the submarine's captain, Commander Valentiner, being branded as a war criminal.

Both *Socotra* (I) and *Nile* had also become casualties. *Harlington* (II) replaced the lost *Harlington* (I).
1916 July 1: The New Zealand Shipping Company, together with its subsidiary the Federal Steam Navigation Co, was acquired by means of a mutual exchange of shares. There was, however, no other visible change in the organisations involved and Mr W. C. Dawes remained Chairman of NZSC. With Federal SN Co came the London shipbroking firm of Birt, Potter & Hughes.

Six losses occurred during the year.
Jan 1: *Geelong* (II) was sunk by collision off Alexandria.
Feb 27: *Maloja* (I) was torpedoed in the English Channel.
Apr 2: In the Mediterranean *Simla* (II) was also lost to a torpedo.
June 20: *Nubia* (II), sister of *Simla* (II), was wrecked near Colombo, Ceylon.
Nov 6: *Arabia*'s torpedoing off Cape Matapan sparked off a diplomatic flurry.
Dec 9: *Harlington* (II) was mined off Harwich.
1917 The British Government introduced its Liner Requisition Scheme whereby it now controlled all seaborne trade in the interests of the war effort.

During the year the group suffered no fewer than 41 losses. P&O bore its share with ten lost.
Feb 5: *Narrung* was sunk by torpedo off Holyhead, North Wales.
Apr 25: *Ballarat* (I) was torpedoed by *U-32* in the English Channel.
Apr 28: *Medina* was caught by a submarine off Plymouth.

June 23: *Mongolia* (II) fell victim to a mine laid by the German raider *Wolf* off Bombay.

July 20: *Salsette* (II) was torpedoed off Portland Bill in the English Channel.

July 26: This was the day that saw two P&O ships torpedoed. *Candia* (II) went near the Owers Light off the English coast, while *Mooltan* (II) was lost off the Sardinian coast.

Oct 9: *Peshawur* (II) was off South Rock, Northern Ireland, when a submarine got her.

Oct 19: *Pera* (III) became a torpedo victim 400 miles off Alexandria.

Oct 29: *Namur* was the last of the vessels to be torpedoed, this time off Gibraltar.

1917 Aug: The Union Steamship Company of New Zealand joined the P&O group by the latter's acquisition of the majority of the ordinary shares. Once again no outward manifestation took place. The company retained its separate identity and continued to be directed by its own Board of Directors in Wellington, New Zealand.

During 1917 both the Nourse and Hain companies also came into the P&O group. The Hain SS Co shares were purchased for cash following the death of Sir Edward Hain.

1918 *Naldera*, commenced in 1913, was finally completed during May. She became the first three-funneller owned by the company.

14 group ships were sunk in the fourth year of the war. Two of these were registered with P&O.

May 23: *Moldavia* (I) was torpedoed off Beachy Head.

July 23: *Marmora*, sister of *Moldavia*, was hit and sunk off the South of Ireland.

Nov 11: The First World War ended. At the end of the war there were 44 P&O ships still afloat, of which *Kaisar-I-Hind* (II) (11,430 tons gross) was the largest. War losses had accounted for 19 vessels and the company placed orders for 19 replacements, although the two ex-Blue Anchor ships lost had already been replaced by the 'B' class.

1919 Lord Inchcape personally negotiated and recommended the acquisition of a majority shareholding in the Khedivial Mail Line. After the war the unsettled conditions in the Middle East caused this concern to trade at a loss, and in 1924, at the end of five years of control, Lord Inchcape paid P&O their original purchase price for the line, thereby himself carrying the loss on the transaction.

A much better move was the buying in 1919 of a large but minority interest in the Orient Steam Navigation Co through their managers, Anderson, Green & Co.

British India SN Co acquired control of the Eastern & Australian Mail SS Co which thereby became a part of the P&O group. *Eston* and *Peshawur* (III) both joined the fleet in December.

Oct 7: *Morea* took the first P&O post-war passenger sailing under the company's own auspices.

1920 P&O had always been, essentially, deep sea traders. To strengthen their North European short-sea trading they now acquired one of the oldest steamship owning companies, the General Steam Navigation Co—GSNC. Their vessels already carried black hulls and funnels. P&O merely had to add a white band to the hull.

Five new 'B' class Branch Liners were ordered. *Narkunda* and *Redcar* were delivered, as were the first of P&O's replacement programme ships. These were *Nagpore*, *Lahore* (II), *Kidderpore*, *Alipore* and *Jeypore*, all sisters. As stopgaps two ex-German ships were handed over by the Shipping Controller and renamed *Padua* and *Perim* (I).

1921 *Mirzapore* (III) delivered. The first two of the replacement 'B' class were delivered and placed on the Suez rather than the Cape route to Australia. They were *Ballarat* (II) and *Baradine* (I).

1922 May 20: *Egypt* was sunk in collision with *Seine* and took with her to the bottom over £1 million in bullion. The subsequent salvaging of the gold was an epic feat.

Himalaya (II) and *Isis* were broken up. *Balranald* (I), *Bendigo* (II) and *Moldavia* (I) were delivered.

1923 Because of the exorbitant costs of shipbuilding P&O postponed its rebuilding programme, although the planned disposal of *Commonwealth* and *Wakool* went ahead. The feeder vessel *Frodingham* was also sold.

Barrabool and *Mongolia* (III) were completed, but the notable addition to the fleet was *Mooltan* (III), the first P&O ship to exceed 20,000 tons.

1924 Lord Inchcape purchased, and later sold, the P&O investment in Khedivial Mail.

Plassy, *Nore*, *Palermo* and *Poona* broken up. *Mata Hari* was transferred from British India for Far East feeder service, to join the new vessel *Bulan*. *Maloja* (II), sister of *Mooltan* (II), was completed.

1925 *Razmak* was delivered to replace *Salsette* (II) on the Aden-Bombay route, but she only saw service on this route for two years before being transferred to other duties.

The post-war passenger replacement programme recommenced with the arrival from the builders of *Cathay* (II), *Comorin* (I) and *Chitral* (I), plus *Ranpura*, *Ranchi*, *Rawalpindi* and *Rajputana*.

1926 *Dongola* (I) and *Wilcannia* (II) broken up.

1928 *China* (II), *Devanha* (I) and *Assaye* sold for scrapping. Four ships ordered by Hain SS were delivered in P&O colours and operated by them throughout their career. *Bangalore* (II), *Burdwan* and *Behar* (II) were delivered.

1929 *Viceroy of India* was delivered. She was the first large British passenger ship to have turbo-electric propulsion. *Bhutan*, the fourth Hain vessel, was commissioned. *Delta* (III) sold.

Dec: The service to Australia via the Cape of Good Hope was discontinued and the 'B' class ships transferred to the Suez Canal route. By now the emigrant traffic had declined and the Aberdeen and Commonwealth 'Bay's' outclassed the P&O vessels in speed and luxury.

1930 *Morea*, *Berrima* and *Borda* scrapped. *Razmak* was transferred to the Union SS Co of New Zealand to replace the lost *Tahiti*. *Somali* (II) delivered.

1931 *Macedonia*, *Khiva* (II), *Khyber* (I), *Kalyan* and *Benalla* were broken up and replaced by *Carthage* (II) and *Corfu*. The cargo vessel *Soudan* (II) was handed over.

Oct 2: The new-era passenger ship *Strathnaver* (I) commenced her maiden voyage to Australia.

1932 Lord Inchcape, Chairman and Managing Director, died. *Novara*, *Nagoya*, *Malwa* (II), *Karmala* (I), *Kashmir* and *Kashgar* (II) were broken up. *Soudan* (II) and *Strathaird* (I), sister of *Strathnaver* (I),

entered service.

1933 *Beltana* and *Padua* scrapped.

1935 The Moss-Hutchison Line was purchased. The Moss Line of Liverpool had only amalgamated with Hutchison of Glasgow in the previous year. Once again P&O left the management of the company to its incumbents.

Mantua (I) was broken up in Japan, the last of the famous 'M' class. *Perim* (I) and *Ballarat* (II) were also scrapped. *Strathmore* (I), a single-funnelled version of *Strathaird* (I), entered service.

1936 The General Steam Navigation division strengthened its Thames pleasure steamer holiday business by the acquisition of the fleet of the New Medway Steam Packet Co.

Baradine (I), *Barrabool*, *Balranald* (I), *Bendigo* and *Moldavia* (I) broken up.

1937 By the addition of Bombay to the Australian route ports of call P&O were able to plan two passenger fleets, one based in Australia and the other on the Far East route. *Stratheden* was placed on the Australian route.

1938 *Kaisar-I-Hind* (II) broken up at Blyth, and *Naldera* at Bo'ness. New ships were *Strathallan*, *Ettrick* and *Canton* (IV) for the passenger routes, whilst *Surat* (II) joined the cargo fleet.

1939 *Shillong* (I), sister of *Surat*, was delivered.

Sept 3: The Second World War commenced.

Nov 23: *Rawalpindi* fought the German battleships *Scharnhorst* and *Gneisenau* to the end.

1940 The hulk *Himalaya* (I) of 1853 was sunk at Portland by German bombers.

Feb 28: *Eston* was lost by mine off Blyth.

1941 Mar 8: *Lahore* (II) torpedoed off Freetown in convoy.

Mar 26: *Somali* (II) bombed and sunk off Blyth, Northumberland.

Apr 6: The troopship *Comorin* (I) caught fire in a gale off Freetown and had to be abandoned.

Apr 13: *Rajputana* lost to *U-108* west of Ireland.

May 6: *Surat* (II) torpedoed west of Freetown.

1942 Feb 28: *Mata Hari* was captured by the Japanese at Banka in the Dutch East Indies.

23

May 15: *Soudan* (II) mined off Capetown.
Sept 30: *Alipore* caught by a submarine off British Guiana.
Oct 28: *Nagpore* torpedoed off the Canary Islands.
Nov 3: *Jeypore* torpedoed in mid-Atlantic.
Nov 11: *Cathay* (II) bombed and sunk off Bougie. *Viceroy of India* torpedoed off Oran after landing troops in North Africa.
Nov 14: *Narkunda* bombed and sunk off Bougie, Algeria.
Nov 15: *Ettrick* was lost to a submarine on her homeward voyage from Azeu after the North African landings.
Dec 21: *Strathallan* torpedoed off Oran.
1943 Apr 5: *Shillong* (I) torpedoed in the North Atlantic.
Dec 23: *Peshawur* (II) was hit by an acoustic torpedo near Madras.

    Socotra (II) was managed for the Government by P&O and they later acquired her.
1944 June 29: *Nellore* became the company's last wartime victim when she was torpedoed in the Indian Ocean.
Nov 24: *Behar* (II), operated by P&O for Hain SS Co, sunk by the Japanese cruiser *Tone* and sixty-five of the crew deliberately killed. The *Tone*'s captain became a war criminal.
1945 With the end of the war plans were made to replenish the fleet and, as in 1919, to replace the ageing passenger fleet. But this time new criteria had to be considered. Commercial aviation was beginning to transport increasing numbers of passengers over greater distances, and the world's sea routes were flooded with redundant wartime standard ships like the tramping 'Liberty', 'Ocean' and 'Empire' ships, and the faster 'Victory' type. P&O carried out a number of inter-company transfers and acquired several ships built during the war which were being managed by them.

    Perim (II) acquired.
1946 *Socotra* (II), *Palana* and *Pinjarra* entered P&O service.
1947 New ships or transfers from the group of companies included *Paringa*, *Dongola* (II), *Devanha* (II), *Karmala* (II) and *Khyber* (II).
1948 *Somali* (III), *Surat* (III) and *Shillong* (II) delivered.
1949 *Soudan* (III), *Coromandel* (II) and

Cannanore handed over. The replacement 27,955 grt *Himalaya* (III) began the company's new post-war liner programme.
1950 *Mongolia* (III) was sold for further trading as a cruise liner; she lasted another fifteen years. *Chusan* (III) entered service.
1951 *Chitral* (I) scrapped at Dalmuir and *Ranchi* at Newport. *Patonga*, *Ballarat* (III) and *Bendigo* (II) handed over.
1954 *Mooltan* (III) broken up at Faslane, and her sister *Maloja* (II) at Inverkeithing. *Arcadia* (II) and *Iberia* (III) replaced the two faithful sisters on the Australian route.
1958 Jan 20: A new transpacific service was announced named the 'Orient & Pacific Line', the route being Sydney-Auckland-Suva-Honolulu-Vancouver-San Francisco. March 21: *Himalaya* (III) took the first sailing.
1960 May 2: P&O-Orient Lines (Passenger Services) Ltd was formed to manage the P&O and Orient passenger fleets. The unpopular 'Orient & Pacific Line' name was dropped.
1961 June: *Canberra* entered P&O service; she became the largest passenger ship ever built for the Australian route. She relieved *Strathaird* (I), which went to Hong Kong for scrapping. *Stratheden* (I) and *Strathmore* (I) were then re-classified as one class vessels for the remainder of their P&O careers.

    Carthage (II) and *Corfu* were both sold for breaking up in Japan and two ships from Cie Maritime Belge, *Chitral* (II) and *Cathay* (III), replaced them.
1962 *Strathnaver* (I) broken up at Hong Kong.
1963 *Strathmore* (I) and *Stratheden* were sold for further passenger service to John Latsis of Piraeus.
1964 British India's *Nyanza* was transferred and renamed *Balranald* (II).
1965 P&O finally acquired the remaining minority shareholdings in the Orient Line and were then able to proceed with the full integration of the two fleets.
1966 Oct 1: P&O-Orient Line Ltd was changed to P&O. The managing company P&O-Orient Management Ltd was renamed P&O Lines Management Ltd. This was the end of the Orient Line as a name.
1967 *Strathaird* (I) was broken up at Hong Kong. Three new 'Straths' were delivered,

Strathardle, *Strathbrora* and *Strathconan*. They began the new phase of renaming the General Cargo Division fleet with 'Strath' names.

1967-75 Following the sequestration and nationalisation of the Suez Canal by Egypt local military actions led to the blocking of the Canal. The later war with Israel caused the Canal to be closed for eight years.

1968 Seven P&O ships were given names beginning with the word 'Pando' (P and O). This new nomenclature lasted only three years.

1971 The P&O General Cargo and the P&O Bulk Shipping Divisions were formed. The new concerns adopted a powder blue funnel with a white P&O monogram.

1972 The new cruise liner *Spirit of London* delivered.

March: The minority shareholders in Frank C. Strick were bought out and the company's 17 vessels were transferred to the newly-formed P&O General Cargo Division, which now began to adopt the corn-coloured hulls originally introduced by Orient SN Co. Ships of P&O, British India, Nourse, Federal and New Zealand SS Co were steadily transferred into this new operating division.

1973 *Chusan* (III) and *Iberia* (III) were broken up.

1974 Princess Cruises was acquired from the industrialist, Stan McDonald. Their two 20,000 ton cruise liners were renamed *Pacific Princess* and *Island Princess*, whilst P&O's *Spirit of London* became *Sun Princess*.

Himalaya (III) broken up.

1975 By this time P&O operated through five basic shipping divisions, the Bulk Shipping Division (BSD), General Cargo Division (GCD), Passenger Division (Pass Div), European & Air Transportation Division (E&AT) and Energy Division (ED). The owning companies varied, and it is no longer possible to associate the name of the ship with her owners' traditional nomenclature. For example, the liquified gas carrier *Garinda* is owned by the Orient SN Co.

P&O Group shipping companies included in the latest Annual Report to the shareholders

1   Anglo-Nordic (50%)
2   Associated Bulk Carriers (50%)
3   Australia Japan Container Line
4   Australian Off Shore Services (Australia)
5   Australind SS Co (38%)
6   Belfast SS Co
7   Bovis South East Asia (68½%)
8   British India Steam Navigation Co
9   Charter Shipping Co (Bermuda)
10 Crusader Squire Container Services
11 Falmouth Towage Co
12 Federal Steam Navigation Co
13 Hain-Nourse
14 Kwinana Towage Services (Australia)
15 LNG Carriers Ltd (33 ⅓%)
16 Mackinnon Mackenzie & Co Private Ltd (40%)
17 Mandogas SA (43%)
18 Mauritius SN Co (28%)
19 MH Corporation (Panama)
20 North of Scotland, Orkney & Shetland S Co
21 North Sea Ferries (90%)
22 Overseas Containers (30%)
23 P&O Ferries (General European Ltd)
24 P&O Inc (USA)
25 P&O Normandy Ferries (50%)
26 Panocean Shipping & Terminals (50%)
27 The New Medway Steam Packet Co

Livery

Funnel
1835-1972 Black for cargo vessels and passenger ships.

1844-c.1850 White with black top; carried by Indian based vessels only.
1894 onwards (intermittently) Yellow for passenger ships with white hulls.
1931 onwards Yellow for all passenger ships.

1966-1971 Yellow for cargo vessels with Strath names.

1971 onwards Light blue with white P&O monogram.

Hull

1835-1971 Black, white band added in the 1840's, red waterline.

1931-1966 Passenger ships had white hulls red waterline.

1966 onwards Passenger ships given Orient green waterline.

1966-1967 For a period some Strath's had Orient Line corn coloured hulls; others retained Strick Line grey hulls.

Uppers

1835-1937 Brown.

1937-1938 Lighter brown (stone colour) and stone paintwork lowered to include fcsle poop and bridge deck, white band lowered proportionately.

Masts Brown, stone and yellow to match hulls.

Lifeboats

1835-c.1865 White.

c.1865-1888 Mahogany.

1888-c.1898 White.

1898 onwards Lifeboats matched the upperwork colouring.

Fleet index

This index lists all vessels above 100 gross tons owned and operated by the P&O Group, comprising: Willcox & Anderson, Peninsular Steam Navigation Co, Peninsular & Oriental Steam Navigation Co, P&O General Cargo Division, P&O Passenger Division, P&O Bulk Shipping Division and Princess Cruises Inc.

Morea	236	Pekin (I)	25	Singapore (III)	333
Mysore	92	Pekin (II)	122	Sir Jamsetjee Jeejebhoy	47
		Pekin (III)	206	Sobraon	210
Nagoya	224	Peninsula	3	Socotra (I)	203
Nagpore	272	Peninsular	171	Socotra (II)	318
Naldera	267	Pera (I)	67	Somali (I)	215
Namur	219	Pera (II)	69	Somali (II)	305
Nankin (I)	205	Pera (III)	227	Somali (III)	329
Nankin (II)	222	Perim (I)	278	Soudan (I)	216
Narkunda	268	Perim (II)	322	Soudan (II)	306
Narrung	249	Persia	201	Soudan (III)	328
Nellore	225	Peshawur (I)	123	Spirit of London	355
Nemesis	79	Peshawur (II)	230	Strathaddie	373
Nepaul (I)	85	Peshawur (III)	269	Strathaird (I)	308
Nepaul (II)	141	Pinjarra	321	Strathaird (II)	381
Nile	218	Plassy	211	Strathairlie	371
Niphon	103	Poona	229	Strathallan	313
Nizam	132	Poonah	91	Strathalvie	383
Nore	221	Pottinger	30	Strathangus	384
Norna	52	Precursor	20	Strathanna	385
Northam	76			Strathappin	382
Novara	223	Rajah	59	Strathardle	356
Nubia (I)	64	Rajputana	298	Stratharlick	380
Nubia (II)	194	Ranchi	296	Stratharos	372
Nyanza (I)	100	Rangoon	93	Strathaslak	375
Nyanza (II)	220	Ranpura	295	Strathassynt	376
		Ravenna	147	Strathatlow	374
Oceana	167	Rawalpindi	297	Strathavoch	377
Opawa	421	Razmak	291	Strathbrora	357
Orama	415	Redcar	271	Strathcarol	379
Oriental (I)	19	Rhoda	100	Strathcarron	378
Oriental (II)	170	Ripon	32	Strathconan	358
Orissa (I)	73	Rohilla	145	Strathdare	390
Orissa (II)	416	Rome	149	Strathdevon	391
Osiris	208	Rosetta	146	Strathdirk	392
Ottawa (I)	62	Royal Tar	2	Strathdoon	393
Ottawa (II)	417			Strathduns	394
		Salmara	346	Strathdyce	395
Pacha	12	Salsette (I)	83	Stratheden	312
Pacific Princess	430	Salsette (II)	245	Strathelgin	437
Padua	277	Salsette (III)	347	Stratherrol	438
Palana	320	Sardinia	217	Strathesk	435
Palawan	190	Scindia	95	Strathettrick	439
Palermo	226	Sewree	113	Strathewe	436
Palma	228	Shanghai (I)	45	Strathfife	440
Pando Cape	339	Shanghai (II)	174	Strathfyne	441
Pando Cove	333	Shannon	152	Strathinch	360
Pando Gulf	353	Shillong (I)	317	Strathinver	361
Pando Head	331	Shillong (II)	332	Strathirvine	359
Pando Point	354	Siam	134	Strathlairg	370
Pando Sound	340	Sicilia	213	Strathlauder	338
Pando Strait	334	Simla (I)	61	Strathleven	369
Paringa	319	Simla (II)	193	Strathlomond	346
Parramatta	157	Singapore (I)	41	Strathloyal	347
Patonga	338	Singapore (II)	194	Strathmay	386

Strathmeigle	387	Teheran	139	*P&O Australia Ltd*	
Strathmore (I)	311	Thames	153		
Strathmore (II)	388	Thibet	140	Cockburn	451
Strathmuir	389	Tiber	26		
Strathnairn	364	Tientsin	204	Lady Ann	453
Strathnaver (I)	307	Timsah	128	Lady Cynthia	447
Strathnaver (II)	368	Trafalgar	29	Lady Gay	449
Strathnevis	363	Travancore	115	Lady Jane	450
Strathnewton	362			Lady Laurie	443
Strathtay	366	Union	66	Lady Lorna	442
Strathteviot	365	United Kingdom	4a	Lady Rachel	446
Strathtruim	367			Lady Sarah	444
Sultan	29	Valetta (I)	42	Lady Vera	448
Sumatra (I)	111	Valetta (II)	158	Lady Vilma	445
Sumatra (II)	187	Vectis (I)	36		
Sun Princess	358	Vectis (II)	43	Parmelia	452
Sunda (I)	109	Vectis (III)	149		
Sunda (II)	189	Vendee	396	*P&O Offshore*	
Sunda (III)	334	Venetia	129	*Services Ltd*	
Surat (I)	108	Verona	144		
Surat (II)	316	Viceroy of India	300	Lady Alison	454
Surat (III)	331	Victoria	165	Lady Brigid	455
Sutlej	155	Vosges	397	Lady Claudine	457
Syria (I)	95			Lady Delia	458
Syria (II)	214	Wakool	250	Lady Edwina	456
		Wilcannia	251	Lady Fiona	459
Tagus	15	William Fawcett	1		
Taj Mahal	300			*P&O Subsea Ltd*	
Talamba	420	Zaida	396		
Tanjore	104	Zambesi	135	Subsea I	460
Tartar	57	Zeila	397		
Tasmania	160				

Illustrated fleet list

There are many other vessels listed under P&O ownership whose nautical history more properly belongs to their original parent company, such ships as those of the British India SN Co, the Federal SN Co and the New Zealand Shipping Co. These are not covered here but will be included in a later volume.

1 WILLIAM FAWCETT

Bt 1829 Caleb Smith, Liverpool; *T*: 206 burthen. **Dim** 82 ft (24.99 m) oa, 74 ft (22.56 m) × 16 ft (4.88 m). **Eng** Pad, sgl cyl; 60 IHP; 6 kts; By Fawcett Preston & Co, Liverpool. **H** Wood; *Coal*: 65 tons; *Cargo*: 70 tons.

1829 Built for Mersey ferry services between Liverpool and Runcorn.
Feb: Advertised on London-Portsmouth-Plymouth-Cork route.
1831 Sold to Dublin and London Steam Packet Co. Owned by Captain Bourne. Belfast-Dublin-London service.
1835 Chartered to Peninsular Steam. Placed on Lisbon-Madeira route. Not recorded as being owned by Peninsular Steam. Illustrations give her the traditional red funnel and black top of the Birkenhead Ferries. Some details imply that she was lengthened for her Madeira service, a third mast being added.
1838 Oct 4: Last known advertised sailing, Madeira branch service.

2 ROYAL TAR

Bt 1832 John Duffus & Co, Aberdeen; *T*: 308 burthen. **Dim** 165 ft (50.29 m) oa, 154 ft (46.94 m) × 27 ft 8 in (8.43 m) × 6 ft 6 in (1.98 m); *Dft*: 9 ft (2.74 m). **Eng** Pad, 2 cyls; 260 IHP; 8 kts; By builders. **H** Wood; *Coal*: 100 tons.

'Royal Tar' was the nickname of King William IV, who had served in the Royal Navy.

1832 Chartered for Don Pedro and later the Queen Regent of Spain from Dublin and London Steam Packet Co.
1835 Landed troops recruited in Britain at San Sebastian during the Carlist Revolt. Named *Reyna Governadera* for this operation.
1839 Re-engined at a cost of £16,000 and tonnage raised to 681 g.
1840 Transferred to P&O ownership. Continued on Southampton-Peninsula-Gibraltar run.
1847 Sold to Portuguese Government. Troopship.

3 PENINSULA

Bt 1836 John Duffus & Co, Aberdeen. **Eng** Pad, 2 cycls, direct acting; 9 kts.

1836 Built for Arthur Anderson. Initially intended for an Aberdeen-Lerwick service which failed to materialise. Chartered to Peninsular Steam and used as branch steamer between Gibraltar-Cadiz-Seville.

3

1840 Apr: Not listed with vessels transferred to P&O but may still have been on charter. Her two sisters *Glasgow* and *Manchester* were also on charter.

4

4 GREAT LIVERPOOL

Bt 1838 Humble & Milcrest, Liverpool; *T*: 1,312 g. **Dim** 213 ft 7 in (65.1 m) × 28 ft 5 in (8.66 m) × 19 ft 3 in (5.87 m). **Eng** Pad, 2 cyls, side lever; *Cyls*: 75 in (190.5 cm); *Stroke*: 84 in (213.36 cm); 464 IHP; 9 kts; By Forrester & Co, Vauxhall. **H** Wood, fitted with hot and cold baths; *Pass*: 98 1st.

Built for Sir John Tobin's Transatlantic Steam Ship Co, as Liverpool.

1838 Oct 20: Maiden voyage Liverpool-New York.
1839 Sept: Rebuilt, new boilers.
1840 Transferred to P&O. Renamed *Great Liverpool*. Made first Alexandria sailing from Liverpool.
1843 Feb: Sailed with first through-bookings to link with *Hindostan* (*21*).
Dec: Lost port paddle en route Marseilles-Malta-Alexandria.
1846 Feb 24: Lost near Cape Finisterre when homeward bound. Ran aground on reef, then beached on Spanish coast south of Corcubion. Captain A. M'Leod. 145 aboard but only three lost, all passengers. The vessel was insured for £30,000.

4a

4a UNITED KINGDOM

Bt 1837; *T*: 335 g. **Dim** 156 ft 9 in (47.78 m) × 26 ft 5 in (8.05 m) × 16 ft 3 in (4.95 m).

Eng Pad, 2 cyls, direct acting; 8 kts. **H** Wood.

1837 Although mentioned in P&O records there is no proof that she was ever owned by the company. Probably only chartered.

5

5 LADY MARY WOOD

Bt 1842 Thomas Wilson & Co, Liverpool; *T*: 533 g. **Dim** 160 ft 8 in (48.97 m) × 25 ft 5 in (7.75 m) × 16 ft 6 in (5.03 m). **Eng** Pad, 2 cyls; *Cyls*: 60¼ in (153.04 cm); *Stroke*: 66 in (167.64 cm); 250 IHP; 12 kts; By Fawcett Preston & Co, Liverpool. **H** Wood; *Coal*: 170 tons; *Cargo*: 200 tons; *Pass*: 60 1st, 50 3rd.

Hull cost £9,500, engines £12,209.

1841 Sept 16: Launched.
1842 Jan 19: Delivered for Mediterranean service. Her speed of 12 kts was very fast.
1845 Sent out to commence Ceylon-Singapore-Hong Kong service.
1848 Rebellion broke out in Ceylon. *Lady Mary Wood* steamed to Madras and returned with sufficient troops the quell the revolt. She thus became the first steam-propelled troopship.
1850 Inaugurated an experimental Hong Kong-Shanghai service but the scheme was dropped due to the high cost of Customs dues at Shanghai, these being 'rigged' by local sailing ship interests to counter the threat from the steamer.
1859 Sold in Hong Kong to Indo-Netherlands company. Ran between East Indies and China.

6-9

6 IBERIA (I)

Bt 1836 Curling & Young, Limehouse, London; *T*: 516 g. **Dim** 155 ft (47.24 m) × 24 ft (7.32 m) × 15 ft 3 in (4.65 m). **Eng** Pad, 2 cyls, side lever direct acting; *Cyls*: 5 in (129.54 cm); *Stroke*: 54 in (137.16 cm); 180 IHP; 1 boiler; *Stm P*: 7 lb; 7 kts; By

Miller Ravenhill & Co, Blackwall, London. **H** Wood; *Coal*: 129 tons; *Cargo:* 290 tons; *Pass*: 37 1st, 16 2nd.

Recorded as being the finest ship afloat.

1836 Sept 28: Registered as owned by Willcox, Anderson and others.
1837 Sept 1: Inaugurated the monthly mail contract London-Oporto-Lisbon-Gibraltar. Oporto passage time 66 hours.
1841 Malta-Cephalonia-Zante-Petras-Corfu service, twice a month.
1842 Peninsular service. 1848 and 1850 on Italian run.
1848 Under Admiralty orders, sailed Southampton-Cherbourg to bring out refugees from Revolution in France.
1856 Mar: Sold to North Europe Steam Nav Co, but the company collapsed and *Iberia* was broken up.

7 MONTROSE

Bt 1837 John Scott & Sons, Cartsdyke, Greenock; *T*: 603 g. **Dim** 156 ft 1 in (47.57 m) × 24 ft (7.32 m) × 16 ft 7 in (5.05 m). **Eng** Pad, 2 cyls, direct acting; 250 IHP; 1 boiler; *Stm P*: 9 lb; 9 kts. **H** Wood; *Coal*: 180 tons; *Cargo*: 250 tons.

1840 Purchased from Scottish owners.
1842 July 12: Registered as P&O owned. Mostly on Peninsular run.
1846 Lengthened to 166 ft 5 in (50.72 m); *T*: 606 g.
1852 Oct 8: Sold to Portuguese Government via the Duke of Saldanha, to establish mail service between Lisbon and Portuguese possessions in Africa.

8a

8 BRAGANZA (I)

Bt 1836 Fletcher Son & Fearnall, Poplar, London. **Dim** 156 ft 8 in (47.75 m) × 24 ft 6 in (7.47 m) × 18 ft 6 in (5.64 m); *Dft*: 13 ft 6 in (4.11 m) fwd, 14 ft 6 in (4.42 m) aft. **Eng** Pad, 2 cyls, side lever direct acting; *Cyls*: 62 in (157.48 cm); *Stroke*: 66 in (167.64 cm); 260 IHP; *Stm P*: 9 lb; 9 kts; By Scott, Sinclair & Co. **H** Wood; *Cargo*: 300 tons.

1836 Purchased whilst being built for Captain Bourne's Dublin and London Steam Packet Co and named *Braganza*. Peninsular service (Braganza was the name of the Royal House of Portugal).
1843 Constantinople service.
1844 Lengthened to 188 ft 5 in (57.43 m) by White's of Cowes; *T*: 855 g, 570 reg. Cost £15,000. Forward funnel added and passenger accommodation aft increased. Introduced what people called the P&O look (*8a*). 40 passengers.
Oct 25: Registered as owned by P&O. (Previous owners Richard & Frederick Bourne, James Hartley, Simeon Barteau and Henry Fortescue.)
1845 Sent out to Bombay for the Hong Kong service.
1852 Oct 25: Sold for breaking up in Bombay.

9 JUPITER

Bt 1835 John Scott & Sons, Cartsdyke, Greenock; *T*: 610 g. **Dim** 175 ft (53.34 m) oa, 158 ft (48.16 m) × 25 ft (7.62 m) × 15 ft (4.57 m). **Eng** Pad, 2 cyls; 210 IHP; 1 boiler; *Stm P*: 7 lb; 9 kts; By Robert Napier. **H** Wood; *Coal*: 150 tons; *Cargo*: 290 tons.

1835 Built for St George SP Company.
1847 June 17: Began service on Peninsular run, under charter to P&O. Remained on run all her career.
1848 Jan 8: Acquired by P&O.
1852 June 21: Sold. Broken up.

10-14

10 DON JUAN

Bt 1837 Fletcher Son & Fearnall, Liverpool; *T*: 800 g. **Dim** 148 ft 5 in (45.24 m) × 24 ft (7.32 m) × 16 ft 3 in (4.95 m). **Eng** Pad, 2 cyls, direct acting; *Cyls*: 62 in (157.48 cm); *Stroke*: 69 in (175.26 cm); 300 IHP; 7 kts. **H** Wood; *Pass*: 24.

1837 Sept 1: When built she was the largest steamer afloat. Carried the first mails under the new Mail Contract on the London-Oporto-Lisbon-Gibraltar service. Cost £40,000.
Sept 15: Grounded on the inbound leg of

her maiden voyage in thick fog 20 miles from Gibraltar at Tarifa Point. Captain J. R. Engledue. Peninsular Steam's co-partner Arthur Anderson and his wife were aboard. All were saved and made the journey to Gibraltar by land, after Anderson had gone by sea to obtain Navy assistance to counter unhelpful local authorities.

11 LIVERPOOL

Bt 1830 Robert Steele, Greenock; *T*: 450 g. **Dim** 137 ft 5 in (41.88 m) × 22 ft (6.71 m) × 14 ft 8 in (4.47 m). **Eng** Pad, 2 cyls, direct acting; 7 kts; By builders. **H** Wood.

1830 Built as a barque for Glasgow & Liverpool Shipping Co.
1835 Purchased for service with the City of Dublin SP Co and engines installed. Operated by Peninsular Steam from 1838. With the advent of *Great Liverpool* (*4*) in 1840 this vessel was nicknamed 'Little Liverpool', or 'Liverpool No 2'.
1840 Carried British troops to the Ionian Islands.
1841 New engines fitted in London.
1845 Ran aground off Tarifa; salvaged and returned to Southampton, where she was condemned and broken up.

12 PACHA

Bt 1842 Tod & McGregor, Partick, Glasgow; *T*: 548 g. **Dim** 160 ft (48.78 m) × 26 ft (7.92 m) × 15 ft 4 in (4.67 m). **Eng** Pad, 2 cyls; *Cyls*: 54 in (137.16 cm); *Stroke*: 60 in (152.4 cm); 210 IHP; *Stm P*: 6 lb; 9 kts; By John Duffus & Co, Aberdeen, originally from *Royal Tar* (*2*) but with new boilers. **H** Iron; *Coal*: 165 tons; *Cargo*: 200 tons; *Pass*: 55.

1842 P&O's first iron hull, apart from the Nile steamers *Lotus* (*16*) and *Cairo* (*17*) and the tug *Atfeh* (*18*). Gave increased passenger and cargo capacities.
1843 Apr 28: Registered as owned by P&O. Peninsular and Italian services. First ship to use Outer Dock at Southampton.
1847 Tonnage increased to 590 g.
Apr: Arrived Galle for Calcutta-Hong Kong run.
1851 July 21: Lost on voyage China-Calcutta when collided with *Erin* (*28*) off Formosa Head, Straits of Malacca.

Captain Miller. Four passengers, 12 crew, specie and cargo lost.

13 ACHILLES

Bt 1838 Robert Steele, Greenock; *T*: 992 g. **Dim** 205 ft 9 in (62.71 m) × 27 ft (8.23 m) × 21 ft (6.4 m); *Dft*: 10 ft 6 in (3.2 m). **Eng** Pad, pair of beam engines; *Cyls*: 74 in (187.96 cm); *Stroke*: 84 in (213.36 cm); 420 IHP; 1 boiler; *Stm P*: 7 lb; 9 kts; By Caird & Co, Greenock. **H** Wood; *Coal*: 280 tons; *Cargo*: 300 tons; *Pass*: 24.

1838 Built for J&G Burns for Irish Sea routes.
1845 Sept 22: Purchased by P&O. Peninsular and Black Sea services.
1848 Sent out for Galle-Hong Kong service.
1851 Bombay-Aden run.
1856 Mar: Sold.

14 INDIA (I)

Bt 1839 John Scott & Sons, Cartsdyke, Greenock; *T*: 871 g. **Dim** 183 ft (55.78 m) × 26 ft 5 in (8.05 m) × 19 ft 8 in (5.99 m). **Eng** Pad, 2 cyls, direct acting; 300 IHP; *Stm P*: 8 lb; 9 kts. **H** Wood; *Coal*: 250 tons; *Cargo*: 250 tons; *Pass*: 80.

1839 Built for service to India, with extra ventilation and an iron bulkhead fore and aft of the engine room space to contain the heat. Hall's new patent surface and jet condensers were installed to conserve fresh water and reduce the need to de-salt the boiler.
1845 May 16: Officially transferred to P&O for their London-Madras-Calcutta service, becoming the first P&O vessel on the route.
1847 At Calcutta hull repairs to dry rot were needed but it was deemed unsafe to bring *India* back to London.
1849 Sold and reduced to a hulk.

15

15 TAGUS

Bt 1837 John Scott & Sons, Cartsdyke, Greenock; *T*: 783 g, 900 dwt. **Dim** 193 ft (58.83 m) oa, 182 ft (55.47 m) × 26 ft

(7.92 m) × 17 ft 4 in (5.28 m). **Eng** Pad, 2 cyls, side lever at 19 rpm; *Cyls*: 62 in (157.48 cm); *Stroke*: 69 in (175.26 cm); 286 IHP; 3 boilers; *Stm P*: 10 lb; 9½ kts; By Scott, Sinclair & Co. **H** Wood; *Coal*: 265 tons, 10 days supply; *Cargo*: 300 tons; *Pass*: 86; *Crew*: 36.

1837 When built for Captain Bourne she was the largest vessel yet built on the River Clyde.
1843 Inaugurated the London-Constantinople passenger route.
To give her a consort *Braganza* was rebuilt and given passenger accommodation (*8a*).
1847 Chartered to Turkish Government for trooping Constantinople-Salonika.
1862 After Peninsular mail service ceased, chartered to T. Hill, Southampton; remained on run to Lisbon.
1864 Broken up by Swan, Thompson & Moore.

16 LOTUS

Bt 1838 Deptford; *T*: 40 g. **Dim** 83 ft 2 in (25.35 m) × 13 ft 2 in (4.01 m) × 2 ft dft (0.61 m). **Eng** Pad; 30 HP; 12 kts. **H** Iron; *Pass*: 100.

1840 Aug: Purchased as *Dahlia* from Mr Mitchell of Newcastle, and renamed.
1841 Apr: Arrived in Egypt, towed part of way by *Oriental* (*19*). Used for the Nile service between Cairo-Atfeh. 15 hour journey.
1847 Apr: Taken over by Egyptian Government.

17 CAIRO

Bt 1841 Ditchburn & Mare, Blackwall, London; *T*: 55 g. **Dim** 100 ft (30.48 m) × 14 ft (4.27 m) × 2 ft dft (0.61 m). **Eng** Pad; 40 IHP; 15 mph; By John Penn & Co, Greenwich. **H** Iron.

Passenger accommodation and engines below decks. Ladies were accommodated in a 16 berth dormitory.

1841 Sept: Sent out to Egypt. Used for the Nile service between Cairo-Atfeh.
1847 Apr: Taken over by Egyptian Government.

18 ATFEH

Bt 1842 John Penn & Co, Greenwich; *T*: 40 burthen. **Eng** Tw scr, 2 engines, 10 HP each. **H** Iron.

For her trials she was assembled with lead rivets, which were then melted out so she could be shipped to Egypt on the Oriental (19) *and there reassembled.*

1843 Entered service towing barges on the Mahmoudieh Canal between Alexandria and the Nile.
1847 Apr: Taken over by Egyptian Government.

19 ORIENTAL (I)

Bt 1840 Thomas Wilson & Co, Liverpool; *T*: 1,787 g. **Dim** 202 ft (61.57 m) × 33 ft 5 in (10.19 m) × 28 ft 5 in (8.66 m). **Eng** Pad, 2 cyls, side lever; *Cyls*: 73 in (185.42 cm); *Stroke*: 84 in (213.36 cm); *Stm P*: 7 lb; 11 kts; By Fawcett Preston & Co, Liverpool. **H** Wood; *Coal*: 450 tons; *Cargo*: 350 tons; *Pass*: 60 1st, 40 3rd.

1840 Built as *United States* for Transatlantic Steam Ship Co at a cost of £60,000, with the most powerful engine to date.
Sept: Chartered to P&O with *Great Liverpool* (*4*). Renamed *Oriental*. Opened the London-Alexandria direct service. The vessel was named in honour of the addition of Oriental to the Company name.
1843 Apr: Registered as being owned by P&O.
1848 Lengthened by 20 ft (6.1 m). Used on Suez-Calcutta service. Also employed in trooping.
1850 The company's store and receiving ship at Bombay.
1861 Oct: Arrived at Hong Kong for breaking up.

20

20 PRECURSOR

Bt 1841 J. Wood, Helvenhaugh, Glasgow; *T*: 1,817 g. **Dim** 229 ft 6 in (69.95 m) × 33 ft 5 in (10.19 m) × 24 ft 4 in (7.42 m). **Eng** Pad, 2 cyls, side lever; *Cyls*: 80 in (203.2 cm); *Stroke*: 84 in (213.36 cm); 500 IHP; 10 kts. **H** Wood; *Coal*: 550 tons; *Cargo*: 200 tons; *Pass*: 140.

1841 Built for Eastern Steam Navigation Co.
1844 June 4: Entered P&O service on London-Calcutta route. Carried white funnel with black top.
1845 Bombay-Suez service.
1846 Ceylon-Penang-Singapore-China route.
1858 Reduced to a hulk.
1869 Dec 4: Sold for breaking up.

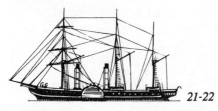

21-22

21 HINDOSTAN (I)

Bt 1842 Thomas Wilson & Co, Liverpool; *T*: 2,018 g. **Dim** 217 ft 6 in (66.29 m) × 35 ft 8 in (10.87 m) × 30 ft 7 in (9.32 m); *Dft*: 18 ft 8 in (5.69 m) fwd, 17 ft 10 in (5.44 m) aft. **Eng** Pad, pair direct acting; *Cyls*: 78½ in (199.39 cm); *Stroke*: 96 in (243.84 cm); 520 IHP; flue boilers; *Stm P*: 7 lb; 10 kts; By Fawcett & Preston, Liverpool. **H** Wood, fitted to carry 5 guns; *Coal*: 600 tons at 6½ tons per hour; *Cargo*: 300 tons; *Pass*: 102 in 60 cabins, 20 singles.

1842 Sept 3: Trials.
Sept 8: Registered to P&O.
Sept 24: Left Southampton, the first vessel to be placed on the India station. Via Gibraltar, Cape Verde, Ascension, St Helena, Cape, Mauritius and Galle to Calcutta.
1843 Opened Calcutta-Madras-Galle (Ceylon)-Suez service.
1849 July 16: Visited by Queen Victoria and Prince Albert when moored off Osborne, Isle of Wight.
1850 Returned to Calcutta-Suez run.
1860 Chartered to Madras Government for trooping to China.
1862 Withdrawn from service to be store ship at Calcutta.
1864 Oct 5: Sunk in the Great Cyclone at Calcutta.

22 BENTINCK

Details as *Hindostan* (*21*) except: **Bt** 1843; *T*: 1,974 g. **Eng** Side lever. *Coal*: 680 tons at 30 tons per day.

Both vessels were identical in appearance and wore white funnels with black tops 40 ft (12.19 m) apart. The passenger saloon was located at the stern. The cabins, built along the centre line, were reached by corridors 170 ft (51.82 m) long on either side of the vessel. The bathrooms included hot and cold showers. The vessels were designed by Mr C. W. Williams, P&O's marine architect. Fares for the 90 day voyage were £40.

1843 June 24: Registered.
July: Left for Indian Station. Calcutta-Suez service.
1851 Speed greatly increased by fitting of feathering paddles.
1860 May 11: Sold to Calcutta Government as an armed merchantman.

23 DELTA (I)

Bt 1844 Miller Ravenhill & Co, Blackwall, London; *T*: 240 g. **Dim** 149 ft (45.42 m) × 19 ft 5 in (5.92 m) × 8 ft (2.44 m). **Eng** Pad, direct acting; 120 IHP. **H** Wood.

1844 Aug 20: Launched. Delivered about two weeks later. Built for Nile service Cairo-Atfeh.
1846 Taken over by Egyptian Government, having done little if any commercial service.

24-25

24 MADRID

Bt 1845 Miller Ravenhill & Co, Blackwall, London; *T*: 479 g. **Dim** 163 ft (49.68 m) × 23 ft 5 in (7.14 m) × 15 ft 2 in (4.62 m). **Eng** Pad, 2 cyls, side lever; 160 IHP; *Stm P*: 7 lb; 10 kts; By builders. **H** Iron; *Coal*: 120 tons; *Cargo*: 150 tons.

1845 Nov 5: Registered. Iberian Peninsula service. Speed given as 13 miles per hour. Also used on Italian run.
1857 Feb 20: Lost. Hit sunken rock at entrance to Vigo harbour and beached. Passengers, crew, mails, specie and baggage saved but ship broke up. Captain Bradshaw.

25 PEKIN (I)

Bt 1847 Tod & McGregor, Partick, Glasgow; *T*: 1,182 g. **Dim** 214 ft 7 in (65.41 m) × 29 ft 7 in (9.02 m) × 18 ft 6 in (5.64 m). **Eng** Pad, 2 cyls, direct acting; *Cyls*: 73 in (185.42 cm); *Stroke*: 78 in (198.12 cm); 430 IHP; 9 kts. **H** Iron; *Pass*: 70 1st, 22 2nd.

Although not true sisters Madrid (24) *and* Pekin *had virtually identical profiles.*

1847 Entered service as a seasonal vessel for use when a larger ship was uneconomical. India-Hong Kong routes. Feb 15: Left Southampton for Galle.
1866 Mar: Sale authorised. Sold to Hong Kong breakers.

26-29

26 TIBER

Bt 1846 Caird & Co, Greenock; *T*: 763 g. **Dim** 184 ft 8 in (56.29 m) × 26 ft 9 in (8.15 m) × 17 ft 3 in (5.26 m). **Eng** Pad, 2 cyls; 280 IHP; 9 kts. **H** Iron; *Coal*: 225 tons.

Originally to have been named Ceylon.

1846 Oct 26: Arrived at Southampton from builders. Peninsular, Italian and Black Sea routes.
1847 Feb 21: Lost. Homeward bound from Gibraltar in fog, hit rock off Vila de Cupa and sank in minutes in deep water. Captain Bingham. No casualties but mails and cargo lost.

27 ARIEL

Bt 1846 Ditchburn & Mare, Blackwall, London; *T*: 709 g. **Dim** 194 ft (59.13m) × 28 ft 4 in (8.64 m) × 16 ft (4.88 m). **Eng** Pad, 2 cyls, oscillating; *Cyls*: 65 in (165.1 cm); *Stroke*: 69 in (175.26 cm); 300 IHP; *Stm P*: 7 lb; 9 kts; By John Penn & Co, Greenwich. **H** Iron; *Coal*: 220 tons; *Cargo*: 250 tons.

1846 Mar 3: Launched.
July 10: Registered.
Sept 26: Maiden voyage. Placed on Malta-Alexandria route.
1848 May 28: Wrecked 13 miles south of Livorno (Leghorn) off Vado en route Malta-Civatavecchia-Livorno-Genoa-Gibraltar-Southampton. Captain Caldbeck. No lives lost. Survivors taken off by HMS *Sidon*. Being of iron she stood up well to the weather and salvage was considered, but she broke up some time later in heavy weather.

28 ERIN

Bt 1846 Ditchburn & Mare, Blackwall, London; *T*: 797 g. **Dim** 199 ft (60.66 m) × 27 ft 6 in (8.38 m) × 17 ft 2 in (5.23 m). **Eng** Pad, 2 cyls; 280 IHP; By Maudsley, Son & Field, Lambeth. **H** Iron; *Coal*: 220 tons; *Cargo*: 350 tons.
Originally to have been named Erin-go-Bragh.

1846 June 6: Launched.
Aug 19: Registered. Consort to *Ariel* (*27*) on the Malta-Alexandria route.
1847 Southampton-Black Sea route.
1851 Sent out to Indian station.
July 22: Collided with, and sank, *Pacha* (*12*) in Straits of Malacca.
1857 June 6: Lost. Bound for China from Bombay she ran aground at Caltura, 34 miles N of Galle on W coast of Ceylon. Captain Bayley. Passengers, crew and mails saved, plus 400 out of 1,200 cases of opium she was carrying.

29 SULTAN

Bt 1847 Tod & McGregor, Partick, Glasgow; *T*: 1,090 g. **Dim** 224 ft 2 in (68.33 m) × 29 ft 1 in (8.86 m) × 17 ft 8 in (5.38 m). **Eng** Pad, 2 cyls, cross headed; *Cyls*: 74½ in (189.23 cm); *Stroke*: 72 in (182.88 cm); 400 IHP; *Stm P*: 8 lb; 9½ kts. **H** Iron.
Originally to have been named Trafalgar.

1847 June 1: Launched.
July 28: Registered.
Aug 3: Maiden voyage, Constantinople service. Larger cargo capacity than Alexandria ships.
1848 Dec 29: Under Captain G. Brookes, Commodore P&O, she made the then fastest passage to Constantinople, in 9 days 22 hours including a stop at Gibraltar.
1855 Mar 31: Converted at Southampton to single screw, powered by a direct acting horizontal trunk beam engine; *Cyls*: 42 in (106.68 cm); *Stroke*: 48 in (121.92 cm); 806 IHP. *T*: 1,125 g. *Dim*: Length 231 ft

(70.41 m), beam 32 ft (9.75 m).
1862 Sent out to Suez-Mauritius service.
1868 Transport during Abyssinian War.
1869 May 31: Sold Yokohama, Aspinall
Corner & Co (China Navigation Co) for
£5,719. Still afloat as a hulk in 1902.

30-31

30 **POTTINGER**

Bt 1846 W. Fairbairn & Sons, Millwall,
London; *T*: 1,401 g. **Dim** 205 ft 7 in
(62.66 m) × 34 ft (10.36 m) × 21 ft 7 in
(6.58 m). **Eng** Pad, direct acting
oscillating; *Cyl*: 75 in (190.5 cm); *Stroke*:
84 in (213.36 cm); 450 IHP; *Stm P*: 7 lb; 10
kts; By Miller Ravenhill & Co, Blackwall,
London. **H** Iron; *Coal*: 450 tons; *Cargo*: 350
tons; *Pass*: 90 1st.

1846 Mar 28: Launched.
Sept 15: Registered. Built for India service
but maiden voyage was to Black Sea.
Nov: Grounded in fog Thorness Bay, Isle of
Wight. Salvaged.
1847 Feb 16: First voyage to Galle
(Ceylon). Then Galle-Bombay-Hong Kong
run.
1850 Southampton-Malta-Constantinople
after re-engining and lengthening by
Wigram's at Blackwall to 220 ft 3 in (67.13
m); *T*: 1,850 g. Re-registered Dec 31 1849.
1852 Calcutta-Suez run.
1858 Troops of the 92nd Regiment
mutinied, refusing to sail on her from Suez
because they would have to berth on deck.
1862 Store ship at Bombay.
1867 July: Sold for scrap to Hajee Cassum
Joosub.

31 **HADDINGTON**

Bt 1846 Thomas Vernon & Co, Liverpool;
T: 1,847 g. **Dim** 217 ft 3 in (66.22 m) ×
33 ft (10.06 m) × 29 ft 6 in (8.99 m). **Eng**
Pad, oscillating; *Cyls*: 76 in (193.04 cm);
Stroke: 70 in (177.8 cm); 450 IHP; *Stm P*:
10 lb; 10 kts; By Bury, Curtis & Kennedy.
H Iron.

1846 Sister of *Pottinger* (*30*) for
Suez-Calcutta service.
Nov 17: Registered and left builders.

Dec 5: Maiden voyage Southampton-
Calcutta (arrived Mar 13 1847).
1854 Converted to sail at Blackwall, re-
registered Aug 12. Used as a supply ship
for replenishing P&O base stores in the
East. Cadet training ship.
1871 Mar 26: Sold Haviside & Co, London,
£8,696.
1888 Burnt out off Iquique after many
owners.

32

32 **RIPON**

Bt 1846 Money Wigram, Blackwall,
London; *T*: 1,508 g. **Dim** 217 ft 3 in
(66.22 m) × 33 ft 9 in (10.29 m) × 21 ft
1 in (6.43 m). **Eng** Pad, 2 cyls, direct acting
oscillating; *Cyls*: 75 in (190.5 cm); *Stroke*:
84 in (213.36 cm); 900 IHP; *Stm P*: 23 lb;
10 kts; By Miller Ravenhill & Co,
Blackwall, London. **H** Iron; *Pass*: 131 1st,
22 2nd, 1,000 troops on deck.

1846 June 27: Launched.
Oct 12: Southampton-Malta-Alexandria
service. Maiden voyage abandoned after
gale damage necessitating putting into Tor
Bay.
1848 Lengthened to 231 ft (70.41 m); *T*:
1,626 g.
1850 May: Carried HRH Prince Jung
Bahadur, Prime Minister of Nepal, to
Britain. He brought with him a large
collection of animals, including the first
hippopotamus seen in England.
1858 Dec: Carried crews Southampton-Le
Havre to take over the purchased vessels
Behar (*71*), *Ellora* (*72*), *Orissa* (*73*) and
China (*74*).
1862 Apr: Re-entered service after
lengthening to 276 ft 8 in (84.37 m) by
Wigram's. Engine now 2,000 IHP; 12 kts.
1864 Carried Garibaldi to England.
1870 Oct 28: Sold to Caird & Co,
Greenock, in part payment for *Pekin*
(*122*)—valued at £15,000. Converted to
sailing brig.
1880 Hulk at Trinidad, owners Gregor
Turnbull. Later scuttled at sea.

33-34

33 INDUS (I)

Bt 1847 Money Wigram, Blackwall, London; *T*: 1,386 g. **Dim** 208 ft (63.4 m) × 33 ft 9 in (10.29 m) × 21 ft 1 in (6.43 m). **Eng** Pad, 2 cyls, direct acting oscillating; *Cyls*: 75 in (190.5 cm); *Stroke*: 84 in (213.36 cm); 430 IHP; *Stm P*: 8 lb; 10 kts. **H** Iron; *Coal*: 450 tons; *Cargo*: 300 tons.

1847 Laid down as *Madras* (I).
Jan 2: Launched.
June: Registered.
June 20: Maiden voyage Southampton-Alexandria.
1852 Lengthened by Wigram's at Blackwall to 241 ft (73.46 m); *T*: 1,950 g. Re-boilered. Re-registered Dec 30.
1854 Broken shaft in Mediterranean. Towed Malta-Constantinople with troops by *Candia* (*63*), and back to Malta again.
1856 Carried Dowager Queen of Oudh and her suite from Alexandria to the UK, causing a lot of difficulties with accommodation owing to caste differences.
1863 Converted to sail and used as overseas base coal supply ship. Re-registered Nov 23.
1869 Nov 2: Sold to Mackay & Sons for £7,920 for Australia trade. Ended career as supply ship for the Eastern and South African Telegraph Co.

34 MALTA (I)

Bt 1848 Caird & Co, Greenock; *T*: 1,218 g. **Dim** 205 ft 9 in (62.71 m) × 33 ft 5 in (10.18 m) × 20 ft 6 in (6.25 m). **Eng** Pad, 2 cyls, oscillating; *Cyls*: 78 in (198.12 cm); *Stroke*: 72 in (182.88 cm); 1,217 IHP; *Stm P*: 7 lb; 10 kts; By Fawcett Preston & Co, Liverpool. **H** Iron.

1848 Mar 13: Registered.
Sept 6: Placed on Bombay-Far East service.
1858 Aug: re-registered after conversion to single screw direct acting horizontal trunk drive, by Robert Napier; *Cyls*: 72 in (182.88 cm); *Stroke*: 42 in (106.68 cm); 2,189 IHP; *Stm P*: 22 lb. Lengthened by John Laird, Birkenhead, to 285 ft 8 in (87.07 m); beam 39 ft (11.89 m).

1859 Apr 17: Opened Suez-Sydney service, via Mauritius though went via Cape on first southward voyage.
1878 Mar 24: Sold to J. McBryde for £6,502.
1882 Broken up.

35

35 EUXINE

Bt 1847 Caird & Co, Greenock; *T*: 1,164 g. **Dim** 229 ft 7 in (69.98 m) × 29 ft 8 in (9.04 m) × 18 ft (5.49 m). **Eng** Pad, 2 cyls, direct acting oscillating; *Cyls*: 74 ⅜ in (188.91 cm); *Stroke*: 84 in (213.36 cm); 1,069 IHP; *Stm P*: 6 lb; 9 kts. **H** Iron; *Coal*: 290 tons; *Cargo*: 440 tons; *Pass*: 80 1st, 18 2nd.

1847 Aug 30: Launched.
Dec 17: Delivered.
1848 Jan 3: Maiden voyage. On London-Constantinople service.
1853 First P&O ship to call at Marseilles on new Malta service, later extended to Alexandria.
1868 Nov: Disposed of to E. Bates, Liverpool, for £4,275. Rebuilt as a sailing ship.
1874 Aug: Burned at sea.

36 VECTIS (I)

Bt 1848 Thomas & Robert White, Cowes, Isle of Wight; *T*: 794 g. **Dim** 191 ft 8 in (58.42 m) × 29 ft 5 in (8.97 m) × 19 ft 3 in (5.87 m). **Eng** Pad, sgl cyl, side lever; 150 IHP; 9 kts; By John Penn & Co, Greenwich. **H** Wood; *Coal*: 275 tons.

1848 Intended for Marseilles-Malta service but when almost ready for sea she was purchased by the Sicilian Government for conversion into a gun-boat. Her success prompted the Sicilian authorities to acquire *Bombay* (*37*) and *Ganges* (*38*). *Vectis* did not enter P&O service.

37 BOMBAY (I)

Bt 1848 William Pitcher, Northfleet, London; *T*: 1,195 g. **Dim** 205 ft 6 in

(62.64 m) × 32 ft 2 in (9.8 m) × 21 ft 8 in (6.6 m). **Eng** Pad, sgl cyl, side lever; 150 IHP; 9 kts. **H** Wood.

1848 Intended for the Indian service via the Cape but purchased by the Sicilian Government for conversion into a gun-boat. Did not enter P&O service.

38 GANGES (I)

Details as *Bombay* (*37*) except: **Bt** 1849; *T*: 1,190 g.

1849 Intended for the Southampton-Malta-Alexandria service but purchased with her twin sister *Bombay* (*37*) by the Sicilian Government for conversion into a gun-boat. Did not enter P&O service.

39

39 CANTON (I)

Bt 1848 Tod & McGregor, Partick, Glasgow; *T*: 348 g. **Dim** 172 ft 7 in (52.6 m) × 21 ft 4 in (6.5 m) × 10 ft 7 in (3.23 m). **Eng** Pad, sgl cyl, side lever; *Cyl*: 66 in (169.23 cm); *Stroke*: 60 in (153.85 cm); 150 IHP, 8 kts. **H** Iron.

1848 May 26: Delivered for Canton river feeder service. Carried 2 × 32 lb guns for protection against pirates.
June 25: Sailed for East.
1849 Sept: Came upon the sailing warship HMS *Columbine* pursuing Chinese pirate junks. *Canton* towed the becalmed *Columbine* into action and assisted in the destruction of the pirates.
1851 Aground on an uncharted rock for eight weeks before refloated.
1859 Oct 4: Driven ashore at Macao in a typhoon. Captain J. D. Almond. Total wreck but no lives lost.

40-41

40 GANGES (II)

Bt 1850 Tod & McGregor, Partick, Glasgow; *T*: 1,187 g. **Dim** 235 ft 3 in

(71.7 m) × 29 ft 4 in (8.94 m) × 18 ft 4 in (5.59 in). **Eng** Pad, 2 cyls, direct acting; *Cyls*: 77 in (195.58 cm); *Stroke*: 78 in (198.12 cm); 1,162 IHP; *Stm P*: 11 lb; 11 kts. **H** Iron; *Coal*: 600 tons; *Pass*: 16 1st, 14 2nd.

1850 Dec 14: Registered. Built as replacement for *Ganges* (*38*).
1851 Feb 27: Maiden voyage to Constantinople; reached Malta in a record 8 days 4 hours.
Nov 18: Sent out to Bombay. Passage to the Cape, with troops, was in a record 37 days 22 hours.
1871 June 1: Sold for £4,533 to Rennie & Co, Shanghai. Broken up soon afterwards.

41 SINGAPORE (I)

Details as *Ganges* (*40*) except: **Bt** 1850; *T*: 1,190 g. **Eng** Oscillating; 1,122 IHP; *Stm P*: 13 lb. *Coal*: 750 tons.

1850 Sept 24: Launched.
Dec 14: Registered.
Dec 29: Maiden voyage Liverpool-Constantinople-Southampton.
1851 Placed on Bombay-Galle (Ceylon)-Hong Kong-Shanghai route.
1867 Mar: Inaugurated Shanghai-Yokohama service.
Aug 20: Struck uncharted rock eight miles off Hakodate inbound from Yokohama and sank without loss of life in about five minutes. Captain C. J. Wilkinson.

42-44

42 VALETTA (I)

Bt 1853 C.J. Mare, Poplar, London; *T*: 769 g. **Dim** 225 ft (68.58 m) × 27 ft 6 in (8.38 m) × 17 ft (5.18 m). **Eng** Pad, 2 cyls, oscillating; *Cyls*: 62 in (157.48 cm); *Stroke*: 54 in (137.16 cm); 1,027 IHP; Lamb's patent boilers; *Stm P*: 20½ lb; 13 kts; By John Penn & Co, Greenwich. **H** Wood, diagonal planking; *Coal*: 74 tons per day.

1853 June 8: Registered. First trial run to Cherbourg and back. Marseilles-Malta-Constantinople route plus branch service Malta-Corfu. Although *Valetta* broke all records her engine was so uneconomical

that a new 260 IHP engine by Penn was installed at Deptford in 1858, thereby saving 42 tons of coal per day. *Valetta*'s hull was wood because she was on the subsidised mail route and the Admiralty required wooden hulls. Later service Marseilles-Alexandria.
1859 Dismantled engine re-used in *Delta* (*88*).
1865 June: Sold to Egyptian Government, renamed *Chabrhiek*.

43 VECTIS (II)

Bt 1853 Thomas & Robert White, Cowes, Isle of Wight; *T*: 786 g. **Dim** 228 ft (69.49 m) × 29 ft 1 in (8.86 m) × 17 ft 2 in (5.23 m). **Eng** Details as *Valetta* (*42*) except: 1,058 IHP; *Stm P*: 21½ lb. **H** First ship to use White's diagonal planking.
1853 Jan 11: Launched.
June 8: Registered. Marseilles-Malta-Alexandria route.
1859 Re-engined with 260 IHP engine by John Penn & Co, Greenwich. Old engine used in *Massilia* (89).
1865 June: Sold to Egyptian Government, renamed *Kalwad*.

44 CADIZ

Bt 1853 Tod & McGregor, Partick, Glasgow; *T*: 816 g. **Dim** 226 ft 4 in (68.99 m) × 28 ft 4 in (8.64 m) × 18 ft 6 in (5.64 m). **Eng** Sgl scr, 2 cyls, trunk geared; *Cyls*: 56 in (142.24 cm); *Stroke*: 48 in (121.92 cm); 450 IHP; *Stm P*: 12 lb; 10 kts; By John Penn & Co, Greenwich. **H** Iron; *Coal*: 650 tons.

1853 Apr 9: Launched.
June 8: Registered. A screw version, with iron hull, of *Valetta* (*42*) and *Vectis* (*43*).
1854 Jan 2: Placed on Bombay-Hong Kong route but not as an official mail contract vessel. P&O's second screw driven ship. Originally fitted with Griffiths patent screw, but replacing this with a conventional screw improved the speed by one knot.
1870 July 25: Sold to Tector & Co, Yokohama, for £4,442. Later sold to Chinese, hulked at Shanghai.

45 SHANGHAI (I)

Bt 1851 Miller Ravenhill & Co, Blackwall, London; *T*: 546 g. **Dim** 182 ft 5 in

(55.6 m) × 25 ft 8 in (7.82 m) × 15 ft 5 in (4.7 m). **Eng** Sgl scr, sgl cyl, direct acting; *Cyl*: 39 in (99.06 cm); *Stroke*: 24 in (60.96 cm); 100 IHP; *Stm P*: 8 lb; 10 kts. **H** Iron; *Pass*: 40.

1851 Sept 22: Registered.
Oct 22: Left Southampton on maiden voyage. The first screw driven vessel for P&O, apart from the Mahmoudieh Canal tug *Atfeh* (*18*) (*Cadiz* (*44*) was only built in 1853). Purchased on the stocks, she was placed on the Hong Kong-Shanghai run.
1862 June 17: Too small for the route and sold to William Dickenson, Shanghai.

46 BOULAC

Bt 1850 Money Wigram, Blackwall, London; *T*: 272 g. **Dim** 169 ft 7 in (51.69 m) × 21 ft 2 in (6.45 m) × 7 ft 7 in (2.31 m). **Eng** Pad, sgl cyl. **H** Iron.

1850 June 17: Registered. Nile River service. Built by P&O on behalf of the Pasha's Government; presumed handed over on arrival in Egypt.

47 SIR JAMSETJEE JEEJEBHOY

Bt 1848 Dhunjibhoy Rustomjee, Bombay; *T*: 126 g. **Dim** 119 ft 3 in (36.35 m) × 15 ft 6 in (4.72 m) × 8 ft 8 in (2.64 m). **Eng** Pad, sgl cyl; 36 IHP; 6 kts. **H** Wood.

1848 Owned by Bombay SN Co.
1855 June 2: Purchased by P&O for Canton River service.
1856 Sale to Hong Kong Government announced. Intended for use in erecting Red Sea lighthouses, but due to breakdowns en route *Sir Jamsetjee Jeejebhoy* never reached further west than Ceylon and another vessel was used.
1859 Sold.

48 FAID RABANY

Bt 1852 Tod & McGregor, Partick, Glasgow; *T*: 274 g. **Dim** 174 ft 2 in (53.09 m) × 19 ft 6 in (5.94 m) × 7 ft 9 in (2.36 m). **Eng** Pad, sgl cyl. **H** Iron.

1852 Sept 4: Registered. P&O's use of her is not clear but a sister, *Faid Gahaad*, was owned by Pedro de Zulueta, a P&O director, and seems to have operated a secondary service between the UK and Egypt. *Faid Rabany* was presumably similarly employed. Her fate is unknown.

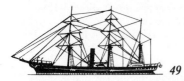

49

49 CHUSAN (I)

Bt 1852 Miller Ravenhill & Salkeld, Low Walker, Newcastle; *T*: 699 g. **Dim** 190 ft (57.91 m) × 29 ft 5 in (8.97 m) × 16 ft 1 in (4.9 m). **Eng** Sgl scr, 2 cyls, direct oscillating; *Cyls*: 39 in (99.06 cm); *Stroke*: 24 in (60.96 cm); 80 IHP; 8 kts. **H** Iron; *Coal*: 125 tons.

1852 Mar 24: Registered. Built for China feeder service to augment *Canton* (*39*). Equipped with steam hoses to repel pirates. May 15: Maiden voyage Southampton-Cape Verde (for coal)-Capetown-Melbourne-Sydney, where she arrived Aug 3.
Aug 31: Sydney-Melbourne-Singapore mail run inaugurated.
1854 Placed on Calcutta-Straits Settlements-Singapore-Hong Kong service.
1858 Based Hong Kong for Manila or Shanghai service.
June 3: Sold in Shanghai to David Sassoon & Sons.
1866 Sold to Feudatory of Matsuyama.
1868 Sold to Choshu Dan, renamed *Kayo Maru* and converted into a warship.
1870 Broken up.

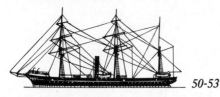

50-53

50 MADRAS (II)

Bt 1852 Tod & McGregor, Partick, Glasgow; *T*: 1,185 g. **Dim** 232 ft 9 in (70.94 m) × 31 ft 6 in (9.6 m) × 21 ft 2 in

(6.45 m). **Eng** Sgl scr, 2 cyls, beam geared; *Cyls*: 62 in (157.48 cm); *Stroke*: 60 in (152.4 cm); 750 IHP; *Stm P*: 10 lb; 9½ kts; By Robert Napier, Govan, Glasgow. **H** Iron; *Coal*: 300 tons; *Cargo*: 600 tons; *Pass*: 80 1st.

1852 Mar 24: Registered. For Singapore-Melbourne-Sydney service, to replace *Chusan* (*49*) which was too small. Four voyages to Constantinople before going out to Calcutta.
1858 Suez-Bombay route.
1862 Bombay-Sydney.
1873 Stranded on reef at Swatow Bar. Salvaged.
1874 Aug: Sold in Yokohama for £18,468 to Mitsubishi Co, renamed *Kunayanamurin Maru*. Later sold to NYK as *Kanagawa Maru*.
1896 Reported laid up at Nagasaki, later wrecked.

51 BOMBAY (II)

Details as for *Madras* (*50*) except: **Bt** 1852 Tod & McGregor, Partick, Glasgow; *T*: 1,186 g. **Dim** 234 ft (71.33 m) × 31 ft 4 in (9.55 m) × 21 ft 2 in (6.45 m).

1852 May 20: Launched.
July 21: Registered.
1853 Suez-Calcutta route.
1862 Galle-Sydney.
1869 Transferred to China trade.
1870 Sank USS *Oneida* in Yokohama harbour with heavy loss of life.
1878 Jan 25: Sold to Kwok Acheong, Hong Kong, for £5,726. Same name.
1880 Dec 24: Destroyed by fire off Woosung Bar.

52 NORNA

Bt 1853 Tod & McGregor, Partick, Glasgow; *T*: 970 g. **Dim** 242 ft 4 in (73.86 m) × 28 ft 4 in (8.64 m) × 18 ft 7 in (5.66 m). **Eng** Sgl scr, 2 cyls, steeple geared; *Cyls*: 56 in (142.24 cm); *Stroke*: 48 in (121.92 cm); 624 IHP; *Stm P*: 11 lb; 10 kts. **H** Iron; *Cargo*: 600 tons.

1853 Oct 28: Registered. Mostly Bombay-Hong Kong service. During Crimean War trooped Bombay-Suez.
1861-6 Suez-Mauritius.
1871 Mar 21: Sold Kwok Acheong, Hong Kong, for £7,122.

53 COLOMBO

Bt 1853 Robert Napier, Govan, Glasgow; *T*: 1,865 g. **Dim** 286 ft 6 in (87.33 m) × 36 ft (10.97 m) × 26 ft 8 in (8.13 m). **Eng** Sgl scr, 2 cyls, beam geared; *Cyls*: 72 in (182.88 cm); *Stroke*: 66 in (167.64 cm); 1,538 IHP; *Stm P*: 14 lb; 10 kts. **H** Iron; *Cargo*: 850 tons.

1853 Dec 9: Registered.
Dec 20: Maiden voyage Southampton-Alexandria.
1855 Crimean War transport. The troops nicknamed her 'Santa Claus' because she took the Christmas mail and provisions out to Balaclava.
1859 Lengthened in Liverpool to 317 ft 4 in (96.72 m), second funnel added. *T*: 2,127 g; *Stm P*: 18¼ lb.
May 9: Re-registered. Sent out to Suez-Calcutta run.
1862 Nov 19: Wrecked on Minicoy Island, Laccadives, Indian Ocean. Captain Farquhar. No casualties. Passengers taken off island by *Ottawa* (*62*), crew by *Nemesis* (*79*) and *Azof* (*77*).

54

54 FORMOSA (I)

Bt 1852 Smith & Rogers, Govan, Glasgow; *T*: 672 g. **Dim** 203 ft 6 in (62.03 m) × 25 ft 7 in (7.8 m) × 16 ft 7 in (5.05 m). **Eng** Sgl scr, 2 cyls, vertical acting with 4 piston rods; *Cyls*: 48 in (121.92 cm); *Stroke*: 42 in (106.68 cm); 800 IHP; *Stm P*: 12 lb; 8 kts. **H** Iron.

1852 July 1: Purchased.
July 31: Registered. Initially joined *Chusan* (*49*) on Australian run from Singapore (sailed from Southampton Aug 7) pending the arrival of *Bombay* (*51*).
1853 Transferred to Calcutta-Hong Kong-Shanghai service.
1856 Based on Hong Kong, various Far East services.
1867 Mar 25: Hit rock off Ocksen Island, beached at Amoy for repairs.
1870 Dec 2: Sold to China Navigation Co, Hong Kong, for £4,312. Same name.
1891 Converted to coal hulk at Hong Kong.

55-56

55 BENGAL (I)

Bt 1853 Tod & McGregor, Partick, Glasgow; *T*: 2,185 g. **Dim** 295 ft 9 in (90.14 m) × 38 ft 2 in (11.63 m) × 25 ft 4 in (7.72 m). **Eng** Sgl scr, 2 cyls, beam geared; *Cyls*: 80 in (203.2 cm); *Stroke*: 60 in (152.4 cm); 1,084 IHP; *Stm P*: 12 lb; 9 kts. **H** Iron; *Coal*: 45 tons per day; *Pass*: 135 1st.

1852 Oct 30: Launched.
1853 Feb 5: Registered. *Bengal*, at the time of her construction, was the largest steamer in the world and cost £70,000. She had a speaking tube between the bridge and engine room.
Aug: After a few Mediterranean voyages was placed on the Calcutta-Suez route. During Crimean War captured a Russian barque and towed it to Madras; the legality of this was doubtful.
1859 June: Driven ashore in a gale at Galle Point, Ceylon. Salvaged.
1863 Dec 12: Propeller shaft snapped in Indian Ocean. Towed to Aden by P&O's *Sultan* (*29*).
1864 Blown ashore near Calcutta by a cyclone and left high and dry in the garden of Bishop's College, Garden Reach. Refloated only after a channel was cut around her.
1868 Troopship during the Abyssinian Campaign.
1870 July 19: Sold for £8,738 to the New York, London & China Steam Ship Co of E. Bates, London. Same name.
1884 Sold to Gellatly, Hankey, Sewell & Co, London.
1885 Mar 2: Wrecked on Milton Reef, Java.

56 DOURO

Bt 1853 Tod & McGregor, Partick, Glasgow; *T*: 810 g. **Dim** 226 ft 4 in (68.99 m) × 28 ft 3 in (8.61 m) × 18 ft 6 in (5.64 m). **Eng** Sgl scr, 2 cyls, steeple geared; *Cyls*: 56 in (142.24 cm); *Stroke*: 48 in (121.92 cm); 554 IHP; *Stm P*: 11 lb; 10 kts. **H** Iron; *Coal*: 450 tons.

1853 June 25: Launched.

Aug 23: Registered. A smaller version of *Bengal* (55), built in the adjoining berth, for the Bombay-Singapore-Hong Kong service.
1854 May 24: Wrecked during a typhoon on the Paracels Shoal, Hong Kong, while under sail following damage to engines. Captain G. M. Hederstedt. Bulk of cargo lost, but no lives. Jolly boat under command of 2nd Officer went for assistance. *Tartar* (57) took off mails and passengers.
June 10: Abandoned as total loss.

57 TARTAR

Bt 1853 Thomas & Robert White, Cowes, Isle of Wight; *T*: 303 g. **Dim** 172 ft 8 in (52.63 m) × 22 ft 4 in (6.81 m) × 11 ft 6 in (3.51 m). **Eng** Pad, 2 cyls, trunk geared; *Cyls*: 50⅜ in (127.95 cm); *Stroke*: 39 in (99.06 cm); 557 IHP; *Stm P*: 16 lb; 8 kts. **H** Reinforced wood, iron scantlings.

1853 Sept 24: Registered. *Tartar* was specially built for the Canton-Shanghai coastal feeder service with Hong Kong as her home port. Ports of call included Swatow-Amoy-Foochow-Wenchow. To meet the shallows and hazards of the route the vessel was given a reinforced wood hull and a shallow draft. She was sailed out to the East.
1855 Aug 28: Sold to HM Government, as HM Gunboat *Coromandel*.
1856 Action against Chinese pirates.
1859 Sunk during attack on Peiho Forts.

58

58 HIMALAYA (I)

Bt 1853 C.J. Mare, Blackwall, London; *T*: 3,438 g, 4,690 dwt. **Dim** 372 ft (113.39 m) oa, 340 ft 5 in (103.76 m) × 44 ft 4 in (13.51 m) × 31 ft 4 in (9.55 m); *Dft*: 21 ft 4 in (6.5 m). **Eng** Sgl scr, 2 cyls, direct acting, horizontal trunk; 2,050 IHP; 4 Lamb's rectangular boilers; *Stm P*: 14 lb; 12 kts; By John Penn & Co, Greenwich; 2-bladed propeller, diam 18 ft (5.49 m).

H Iron, 3 decks, hull divided into six watertight compartments, saloon 100 ft (30.49 m) long with 170 seats; *Coal*: 1,200 tons, 17 tons per day; *Cargo*: 1,000 tons; *Pass*: 200 1st; *Crew*: 213.

Designed as a paddler but altered on stocks.

1853 May 24: Launched. The world's largest ship, designed by Mr T. Waterman. Dec 9: Registered.
1854 Jan 20: Maiden voyage Southampton-Alexandria. Captain A. Kellock. *Himalaya* made only one round voyage for P&O before the outbreak of the Crimean War increased coal prices to a point at which it became uneconomic to operate her.
July: Sold for £130,000, her cost price, to the British Government for use as a Crimean troopship. Retained P&O crew until Jan 1855. With the cessation of hostilities *Himalaya* was retained for trooping duties to India.
1894 Converted into a coal hulk. Renamed *HM Hulk C.60*.
1910 Based at Chatham, River Medway.
1920 Sold to private owners at Portland Harbour.
1940 June: Bombed and sunk by German air attack at Portland Harbour.

59-60

59 RAJAH

Bt 1853 C.J. Mare, Poplar, London; *T*: 537 g. **Dim** 163 ft 6 in (49.83 m) × 24 ft (7.31 m) × 16 ft 7 in (5.05 m). **Eng** Sgl scr, 2 cyls, trunk geared; *Cyls*: 39 in (99.06 cm); *Stroke*: 27 in (68.58 cm); 120 IHP; *Stm P*: 20 lb; 8 kts. **H** Iron, one pair of sheer legs.

1853 Jan 1: Launched.
June 8: Registered. Auxiliary steam collier intended for Far East. Carried special facilities for engine spares and acted as repair ship on the India Station.
1854-6 Crimean War duties included period as storeship for Baltic Fleet, and as a bakery.
1856 Oct: Southampton-Bombay.
1861 May 22: Sold to Sassoon & Sons, Shanghai.

60 MANILLA

Bt 1853 C.J. Mare, Poplar, London; *T*: 646 g. **Dim** 178 ft (54.25 m) × 26 ft (7.92 m) × 18 ft 6 in (5.64 m). **Eng** Sgl scr, 2 cyls, trunk geared; *Cyls*: 30 in (76.2 cm); *Stroke*· 27 in (68.58 cm); 290 IHP; *Stm P*: 16 lb; 9 kts. **H** Iron.

1854 Feb 14: Registered. An enlarged version of *Rajah* (*59*), built at the same yard, for use as a coal and stores supply ship in the Far East. Special storage facilities were included for the carriage of ammunition. This was used to re-stock P&O vessels on the China Station, all of which were armed against pirate junks.
1855 Ammunition carrier to Crimea. June: Caught fire in Balaclava Roadstead, Crimea. The vessel was saved and repaired.
1856 Aug: Southampton-Singapore.
1859 Sept 22: Rescued passengers and crew of SS *Italien* off Amoy.
1861 May 26: Sold to Messrs Gibb Livingstone & Co, Whampoa.
1881 Wrecked near Halifax, as sailing ship *Lancefield*.

61

61 SIMLA (I)

Bt 1854 Tod & McGregor, Partick, Glasgow; *T*: 2,441 g. **Dim** 330 ft 4 in (100.69 m) × 37 ft 9 in (11.51 m) × 27 ft 8 in (8.43 m). **Eng** Sgl scr, 2 cyls, steeple geared; *Cyls*: 90 in (228.6 cm); *Stroke*: 72 in (182.88 cm); 1,766 IHP; *Stm P*: 16 lbs; 11 kts. **H** Iron.

1854 May 4: Registered. Upon completion *Simla* was requisitioned by the British Government as a Crimean War transport.
1857 Feb 11: The British Admiralty awarded the Australian mail contract to the European & Australian Royal Mail Co and *Simla* was chartered by them for the service. Three round voyages Suez-Sydney.
1858 May: Returned to P&O. Placed on Suez-Calcutta route.
1871 Home via Suez Canal, Southampton-Alexandria service.

1875 Nov 12: Sold to Howdens of Glasgow in part payment (£15,000) for *Tanjore*'s engines (*104*). Converted by them into a four-masted sailing ship.
1884 Jan: Collided with *City of Lucknow*. Taken in tow but foundered with the loss of 20 lives.

62

62 OTTAWA (I)

Bt 1853 John Laird, Birkenhead; *T*: 1,275 g. **Dim** 238 ft 8 in (72.75 m) × 29 ft 2 in (8.89 m) × 23 ft 8 in (7.21 m); *Dft*: 16 ft 5 in (5 m). **Eng** Sgl scr, 2 cyls, oscillating geared; *Cyls*: 54 in (137.16 cm); *Stroke*: 48 in (121.92 cm); 700 IHP; *Stm P*: 17 lb; 10 kts; By Fawcett Preston & Co, Liverpool.

1853 Ordered as *Northern Light* for African SS Co. Launched November. Purchased by Canadian Steam Nav Co. Renamed *Ottawa*. 100 passengers.
1854 Feb 28: Maiden voyage Liverpool-Portland, Maine. Then placed on the Liverpool-Quebec-Montreal service. Sept: Requisitioned as Crimean War transport. Florence Nightingale was a frequent passenger between Scutari and Balaclava.
1857 Jan 26: Purchased for £21,000 by P&O. Based on Bombay, Hong Kong or Suez routes.
1868 Abyssinian War trooping.
1869 Hong Kong-Shanghai.
1873 Nov 6: Sold to Captain Hutchinson for £9,526.

63-64

63 CANDIA (I)

Bt 1854 C.J. Mare, Poplar, London; *T*: 1,961 g. **Dim** 281 ft (85.65 m) × 38 ft 9 in (11.81 m) × 26 ft 2 in (7.98 m). **Eng** Sgl scr, 2 cyls, trunk geared; *Cyls*: 71 in

(180.34 cm); *Stroke*: 48 in (121.92 cm); 1,490 IHP; *Stm P*: 20 lb; 12 kts. **H** Iron.

1853 Sept 19: Launched.
1854 Apr 15: Registered. Cost £69,200. After three voyages became Crimean War transport. Had collision with a Sardinian frigate in the Black Sea.
1857 Lengthened by Laird & Co to 317 ft 4 in (96.72 m); beam 40 ft 5 in (12.32 m); *T*: 1,982 g.
July 23: Re-registered. Suez-Calcutta service.
1860 Propeller shaft broke in Red Sea and *Candia* was towed back to Suez. There her fore-part was filled with sand ballast until the stern was clear of the water. A new shaft was inserted and a propeller fitted. The voyage then continued.
1864 Met cyclone between Aden and Calcutta; almost all rigging and two masts lost.
1871 Southampton-Alexandria.
1874 Acted as a troopship during Ashanti War. Did not return to P&O service.
Oct: Sold to James Howden for £11,708, and tonnage raised to 2,125 g. Later sold to NYK as *Wakanoura Maru*.
1898 Store ship at Hakodate.

64 NUBIA (I)

Bt 1854 John Laird, Birkenhead; *T*: 2,096 g. **Dim** 289 ft 3 in (88.16 m) × 38 ft (11.58 m) × 27 ft 4 in (8.33 m). **Eng** Details as *Candia* (*63*) except: oscillating type; *Cyls*: 78 in (198.12 cm); *Stroke*: 60 in (152.4 cm); 1,422 IHP.

1854 Aug 15: Registered. Southampton-Alexandria service. After leaving Malta *Nubia* experienced crew trouble which resulted in five men being placed in irons, and the ship had to return to Malta.
1855 Crimean War service.
1856 Calcutta-Suez.
1871 Galle-Australia route. Later based in Mediterranean.
1877 Dec 4: Sold to the London Schools Board for £8,253 for use as a boys' training ship. Renamed *Shaftesbury* after £40,000 conversion.
1906 Sold for scrap, leaving outstanding bills of £12,000.

65 EMEU

Bt 1854 Robert Napier, Govan, Glasgow;

65

T: 1,538 g, 4,320 dwt. **Dim** 266 ft 3 in (81.15 m) × 36 ft 3 in (11.05 m) × 19 ft 3 in (5.87 m). **Eng** Sgl scr, 2 cyls, beam geared; *Cyls*: 64 in (162.56 cm); *Stroke*: 48 in (121.92 cm); 300 IHP; 4 boilers; *Stm P*: 12 lb. **H** Iron; *Coal*: 950 tons; *Cargo:* 300 tons; *Pass*: 80 1st.

1854 Built as *Emeu* for Australasian Pacific Mail Stm Packet Co. Sisters were *Black Swan*, *Dinorwis*, *Kangaroo* and *Minura*.
1855 Sold to Cunard. Same name.
1857 Chartered to European and Australian Royal Mail Co. Ran ashore in Red Sea.
1858 Oct 9: Purchased by P&O for delivery at Sydney the following February. Placed on Sydney-Mauritius-Suez route.
1860 Bombay-Hong Kong service.
1873 Nov 5: Sold to W. MacArthur, London, for £6,508 and converted to full rigged sailing ship. Renamed *Winchester*.
1880 July 14: Wrecked on Straits of Magellan. Salvaged, and was a hulk in Chile in 1898.

66 UNION

Bt 1854 Charles Lungley, Rotherhithe, London; *T*: 237 g. **Dim** 157 ft 8 in (48.06 m) × 21 ft (6.4 m) × 14 ft 1 in (4.29 m). **Eng** Sgl scr, 2 cyls, direct acting, beam geared; *Cyls*: 24½ in (62.23 cm); *Stroke*: 36 in (91.44 cm); 227 IHP; *Stm P*: 12 lb; 8 kts. **H** Composite, wood with iron frames.

1854 Built as *Union* for Union Steam Collier Co, Southampton.
1858 Dec 30: Registered.
1859-60 Mauritius-Bourbon mail service.
1861-2 Attended lighthouse building at Ashrafi and Daedalus, Gulf of Suez.
1863 Feb 20: Sold Hong Kong.

67 ALMA

Bt 1854 John Laird, Birkenhead; *T*: 2,165 g. **Dim** 288 ft 1 in (87.81 m) × 37 ft 3 in (11.35 m) × 27 ft 3 in (8.31 m). **Eng** Sgl scr, 2 cyls, oscillating geared; *Cyls*: 78 in

(198.12 cm); *Stroke*: 60 in (152.4 cm);
1,445 IHP; *Stm P*: 16 lb; 11 kts; By Fawcett
& Preston. **H** Iron; *Coal*: 800 tons; *Cargo*:
750 tons.

Originally to have been named Pera (*I*) *but
renamed following the Battle of the Alma in
the Crimea.*

1854 The first Laird ship for P&O (the
Ottawa (*62*) was not purchased until 1858).
1855 Mar 19: Entered P&O service.
Crimea trooping.
1856 Suez-Calcutta service.
1859 June 12: Lost. Hit coral reef in Red
Sea one day out from Aden bound
Calcutta-Suez. The master, Captain
Henry, was sick at the time and her chief
officer was in command. His certificate was
suspended for 12 months. Baggage and
cargo lost but no casualties. Complement
taken off by *Nemesis* (*79*) and HMS
Cyclops.

68

68 ALHAMBRA

Bt 1855 Samuda Bros, Millwall, London;
T: 642 g. **Dim** 209 ft 3 in (63.78 m) × 27 ft
1 in (8.26 m) × 16 ft 3 in (4.95 m). **Eng** Sgl
scr, sgl cyl with 2 piston rods, geared; *Cyls*:
50¼ in (127.64 cm); *Stroke*: 36 in (91.44
cm); 454 IHP; *Stm P*: 18 lb; 10 kts. **H** Iron.

1855 June 29: Registered. Was originally
to have been named *Braganza* (II).
Employed almost exclusively on Peninsular
run.
1862 July 1: Sold to Joshua Bros, London,
on behalf of Blackwood & Co, Melbourne,
who put her on their Melbourne-Otago
(New Zealand) route.
1888 Foundered after hitting wreckage
while en route from Newcastle, New South
Wales, to Sydney.

69 PERA (II)

Bt 1855 C.J. Mare, Blackwall, London; *T*:
2,014 g. **Dim** 303 ft 5 in (92.48 m) × 42 ft
1 in (12.83 m) × 27 ft 1 in (8.26 m). **Eng** Sgl
scr, 2 cyls, vertical trunk geared, 33 rpm;
1,373 IHP; *Stm P*: 19½ lb; 12 kts; By

69

Rennie & Co. **H** Iron, main deck 7 ft
(2.13 m) high; *Coal*: 44 tons per day.

1855 Oct 9: Registered. Designed by James
Ash. *Pera* had to be hurriedly launched
ahead of schedule because of the
impending bankruptcy of the builder, C.J.
Mare.
1856 Jan 4: Southampton-Alexandria
service.
1859 Mar: Inaugurated the European end
of the UK-Australia mail route.
1865 Southampton-Alexandria-
Marseilles-Alexandria-Southampton
service.
1872 Re-engined.
1874 Bombay-Galle-Melbourne.
1876 Venice-Bombay.
1880 Oct: Sold at auction for £8,402 to
William Ross & Co, but not registered as
owned by them.
1882 June 11: Foundered off Cape Race,
Newfoundland, after colliding with an
iceberg.

70-73, 75-76

70 AVA

Bt 1855 Tod & McGregor, Partick,
Glasgow; *T*: 1,373 g. **Dim** 267 ft 8 in
(81.58 m) × 35 ft 2 in (10.72 m) × 16 ft 2 in
(4.93 m). **Eng** Sgl scr, 2 cyls, trunk geared;
Cyls: 70 in (177.8 cm); *Stroke*: 48 in
(121.92 cm); 1,056 IHP; *Stm P*: 17 lb; 12
kts. **H** Iron; *Pass*: 97 1st, 30 2nd.
*Fitted with a steam operated cargo winch,
quite an innovation.*

*Three builders constructed seven very
similar vessels which P&O assembled to
commence to standardise their fleet. These
were* Ava, Behar (*71*), Ellora (*72*), Orissa
(*73*), China (*74*), Aden (*75*) and Northam

47

(76). Four of the sisters were purchased from a single owner.

1855 June 29: Registered. Southampton-Alexandria run.
1857 Calcutta-Suez.
1888 Feb 16: Lost on Pigeon's Island off Trincomalee, bound Calcutta to Suez. Captain Kirton. Mails and cargo lost but nearly all £250,000 of specie saved. A new shaft intended for *Alma (67)* was recovered by divers.

71 BEHAR (I)

Bt 1855 John Laird, Birkenhead; *T*: 1,603 g. **Dim** 265 ft (80.77 m) × 36 ft 1 in (11 m) × 25 ft 5 in (7.75 m). **Eng** Sgl scr, 2 cyls, horizontal direct acting; *Cyls*: 56 in (142.24 cm); *Stroke*: 30 in (76.2 cm); 900 IHP; *Stm P*: 20 lb; 12 kts; By Humphrys & Co.

1855 Laid down as *Erie* for Canadian Steam Navigation Co but did not enter their service. She was sold to the Spanish company Vapores Correos Espanoles Trasatlanticos and renamed *Barcelona*.
1856 Resold to Gauthier Freres Compagnie Franco-Americaine and her name changed to *Barcelone*.
1858 Nov: Purchased by P&O for their Indian and Far East route network and renamed *Behar*.
Dec 21: Registered. Six voyages to Alexandria before sent out to Bombay.
1874 Nov 6: Sold in Yokohama for £19,564. Handed over Nov 19. Renamed *Niigata Maru*.
1878 New engines and boilers.
1897 Broken up.

72 ELLORA

Details as *Behar (71)* except: **Bt** 1855; *T*: 1,607 g. **Dim** 261 ft 2 in (79.6 m) × 36 ft 2 in (11.02 m) × 25 ft 8 in (7.82 m). **Eng** 1,055 IHP; By Rennie & Sons.

1855 Laid down as *Ontario* for the Canadian Steam Navigation Co. Sister to *Erie*. Sold, before commissioning, to Compagnie Franco-Americaine and renamed *Cadix*.
1858 Nov: Purchased. Towed by *Ripon (32)* from Brest to Southampton.
1859 Jan 31: Registered by P&O and renamed *Ellora*. Until 1865 on

Southampton-Alexandria run, then in the East.
1876 Feb 15: Sold at Melbourne for £9,191. Converted to sail. A hulk at Panama in 1899.

73 ORISSA (I)

Details as *Behar (71)* except: **Bt** 1856; *T*: 1,647 g. **Dim** 264 ft 6 in (80.62 m) × 35 ft 9 in (10.9 m) × 26 ft 6 in (8.08 m). **Eng** 950 IHP.

1856 Compagnie Franco-Americaine ordered her to join her sister, *Barcelone*, on the North Atlantic service. They named the ship *Franche-Comtois*.
1858 Nov: Purchased by P&O she was renamed *Orissa*.
Dec 30: Registered and placed on the Southampton-Malta-Alexandria run.
1860 Sent out to Bombay.
1878 Sept 24: Sold for £6,135 to J. Matheson & Co, Hong Kong. Converted to sail.

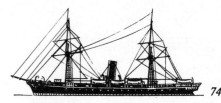

74

74 CHINA (I)

Details as *Behar (71)* except: **Bt** 1856; *T*: 2,016 g. **Dim** 269 ft 5 in (82.12 m) × 36 ft 5 in (11.1 m) × 23 ft (7.01 m). **Eng** Vertical direct acting; *Cyls*: 64 in (162.56 cm); *Stroke*: 32 in (81.28 cm); 1,488 IHP; By Humphrys & Tennant, Deptford, London.

1856 Built as *Alma* for Compagnie Franco-Americaine.
Apr: Maiden voyage Le Havre-New York.
1858 Nov: Purchased by P&O.
1859 Nov 16: Registered and renamed *China*. Lengthened to 279 ft (85.04 m) oa at Blackwall; *T*: 2,010 g. Most of career based in Bombay.
1865 Compound 2 cyl engine fitted.
1882 June 7: Sold for breaking up to S. Hartman, London. Fetched £6,775.

75 ADEN (I)

Bt 1856 Day Summers & Co, Northam, Southampton (Register: Summers & Day);

T: 812 g. **Dim** 225 ft 6 in (68.73 m) × 29 ft 5 in (8.97 m) × 18 ft 6 in (5.64 m). **Eng** Sgl scr, 2 cyls, direct acting, trunk geared; *Cyls*: 44½ in (113.03 cm); *Stroke*: 48 in (121.92 cm); 954 IHP; *Stm P*: 21 lb; 12 kts. *Cargo*: 600 tons; *Pass*: 112 1st, 22 2nd.

1856 Aug 21: Registered. Constructed with an experimental economy engine. Originally to have been named *Delta* (II). Far Eastern services.
1872 Sold to Chinese Merchants SN Co, Shanghai, for £15,029.

76 NORTHAM

Bt 1858 Day Summers & Co, Northam, Southampton (Register: Summers & Day); *T*: 1,330 g. **Dim** 274 ft (83.52 m) × 34 ft 7 in (10.54 m) × 26 ft (7.92 m). **Eng** Sgl scr, 2 cyls, inverted, direct acting; *Cyls*: 70 in (177.8 cm); *Stroke*: 36 in (91.44 cm); 1,514 IHP; *Stm P*: 20 lb; 13 kts. **H** Iron; *Pass*: 97 1st, 30 2nd.

1858 Mar 31: Launched.
June 11: Registered by P&O. The last of the class. *Northam* had fewer but better cabins than her sisters. Upon completion she positioned to Bombay via the Cape.
1859 Apr 28: Entered Suez-Ceylon-Sydney service.
1866 Suez-Bombay route.
1868 Sold to Day Summers as part payment for *Hindostan* (*117*) which these builders delivered to P&O in 1869.
1869 Sold to Union Steamship Co (now Union Castle) for £16,500 for their South African service. Same name.
1876 Sold and converted to a sailing ship. Renamed *Stars and Stripes*.
1878 Dec 21: Burnt at sea.

77 AZOF

Bt 1855 John Bourne & Co, Port Glasgow; *T*: 700 g. **Dim** 214 ft 1 in (65.25 m) × 27 ft 6 in (8.38 m) × 18 ft 6 in (5.64 m). **Eng** Sgl scr, 2 cyls, horizontal direct acting; *Cyls*: 21½ in (54.5 cm) and 42 in (106.68 cm); *Stroke*: 42 in (106.68 cm); 348 IHP; *Stm P*: 20 lb; 10 kts; By J. & G. Rennie, Blackfriars, London. Engine compounded at later date. **H** Iron; Cargo vessel.

1855 Built for James Hartley, London. (Hartley was a P&O director, who died in 1857.) Black Sea service.

1856 Nov 5: Purchased by P&O.
1857 Sent out to Aden-Mauritius-Bourbon service.
1859 To Bombay, later Far East routes.
1871 Jan 1: Sold to D. Gillers, Hong Kong, for £5,416.

78 COLUMBIAN

Bt 1855 W. Simons & Co, Whiteinch, Glasgow; *T*: 2,112 g. **Dim** 307 ft 4 in (93.68 m) × 38 ft 4 in (11.68 m) × 19 ft 6 in (5.94 m). **Eng** Sgl scr, 2 cyls, 4 pistons, horizontal direct acting; *Cyls*: 72 in (182.88 cm); *Stroke*: 36 in (91.44 cm); 2,116 IHP; *Stm P*: 25 lb. **H** Iron; *Pass*: 150. *Sister ship was* European.

1855 Ordered for the European and Australian Royal Mail Co.
1857 The mail contract to Australia was awarded to her owners but due to unserviceability the initial voyage under the contract was taken by P&O's *Simla* (*61*) in place of *Columbian*, and Cunard's *Emeu* (*65*) was also chartered.
1859 Dec 3: Registered by P&O, delivered in Sydney, and placed on the Suez-Mauritius-Australia route.
1864 June: Sold to Scott's in part payment for *Mongolia* (*102*). Re-engined with a 2 cyl, vertical direct acting type.
1867 Re-purchased (registered Oct 4). Bombay-Hong Kong or Bombay-Suez.
1877 Sold Bombay for £10,000 to Hajee Cassum Joosub.

79

79 NEMESIS

Bt 1857 Tod & McGregor, Partick, Glasgow; *T*: 2,018 g. **Dim** 312 ft (95.1 m) oa, 301 ft (91.74 m) × 41 ft 3 in (12.57 m) × 19 ft 5 in (5.92 m). **Eng** Sgl scr, 2 cyls, trunk geared; *Cyls*: 81 in (205.74 cm); *Stroke*: 54 in (137.16 cm); 1,894 IHP; *Stm P*: 18 lb; 13½ kts. **H** Iron, extra strong construction, 5 holds, 3 decks.

1857 Laid down as *Delhi* (I) but before completion the vessel was renamed

Nemesis to celebrate the collapse of the Indian Mutiny.

Nov 11: Delivered for Indian services.

1859 Mar 23: Collided with and sank pioneer British Indian SN Co ship *Cape of Good Hope* in Hughli.

1860 Sept: Grounded at Ras de Seine, France. All the passengers and crew were taken off safely and the ship salvaged.

1869 Apr 6: Sold to William Denny, Dumbarton, in part payment for *Sumatra* (*111*), delivered in 1867. Re-engined and lengthened to 352 ft (107.29 m); *T*: 2,717 g, 2,203 n; *Cyls*: 57 in (144.78 cm) and 95 in (241.3 cm); *Stroke*: 45 in (114.3 cm); 500 HP.

1871 Chartered to the Inman Line for six months at £1,500 per month. sold to P. Denny.

1883 Sold to Huntley, Berner & Co. Renamed *Perusia*.

1891 Broken up.

80 GRANADA

Bt 1857 Day Summers & Co, Northam, Southampton (Register: Summers & Day); *T*: 571 g. **Dim** 186 ft 3 in (56.77 m) × 26 ft 8 in (8.13 m) × 16 ft 7 in (5.05 m). **Eng** Sgl scr, 2 cyls, inverted, direct acting; *Cyls*: 45 in (114.3 cm); *Stroke*: 30 in (76.2 cm); 721 IHP; *Stm P*: 18 lb; 12 kts. **H** Iron.

1857 Sept 28: Registered. Eastern station.

1866 Sept 14: Sold in Yokohama to Prince Hijo.

81 MALABAR

Bt 1858 William Denny & Bros, Dumbarton; *T*: 917 g. **Dim** 224 ft 8 in (68.48 m) × 31 ft 2 in (9.5 m) × 20 ft 2 in (6.15 m). **Eng** Sgl scr, 2 cyls, inverted, direct acting; *Cyls*: 48 in (121.92 cm); *Stroke*: 42 in (106.68 cm); 724 IHP; *Stm P*: 12 lb; 11 kts; By Tulloch and Denny. **H** Iron; *Pass:* 100 1st.

1858 Feb 22: Registered. Bombay-Hong Kong route.

1860 May 22: Lost. Hit reef during squall in Galle harbour, bottom stove in, beached but broken up by gale. Passengers and crew saved, plus some cargo, and more recovered by divers.

82 BENARES

Bt 1858 Tod & McGregor, Partick,

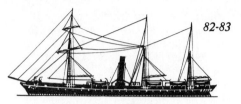

82-83

Glasgow; *T*: 1,491 g. **Dim** 293 ft 7 in (89.48 m) × 38 ft 5 in (11.71 m) × 26 ft 6 in (8.08 m). **Eng** Sgl scr, 2 cyls, inverted, direct acting; *Cyls*: 70 in (177.8 cm); *Stroke*: 36 in (91.44 cm); 1,373 IHP; *Stm P*: 16½ lb; 12 kts; By builders. **H** Iron.

Lifeboats were varnished mahogany instead of the usual white. This new colouring only became standard to P&O vessels around 1865 and lasted until 1888, when white lifeboats again appeared.

1858 Feb 1: Launched.

Mar 29: Registered.

Apr 9: Maiden voyage Gravesend-Alexandria.

1859 Suez-Mauritius-Australia service.

1862 Suez-Bombay route.

1865 Ceylon-Hong Kong-Shanghai connection.

1868 May 23: Wrecked near Shanghai. On voyage Shanghai-Hong Kong hit uncharted rock in Fisherman's Islands. Captain MacCulloch. No lives lost, specie and mails recovered by divers.

83 SALSETTE (I)

Details as *Benares* (*82*) except: **Bt** 1858 Tod & McGregor, Partick, Glasgow; *T*: 1,491 g. **Eng** 1,550 IHP.

1858 Feb 29: Launched.

May 17: Registered.

1859 Feb 12: Maiden voyage Sydney-Mauritius-Suez route.

1861 Placed on the Suez-Bombay route.

1871 May 25: Sold to J. Mathewson for £13,000. Renamed *Sumatra* and lengthened to 363 ft (110.64 m); *T*: 2,408 g.

1879 Sold to Adamson & Ronaldson Line. Same name. Used on London-Cardiff (Barry Docks)-Boston service, the call at Cardiff being for bunkering purposes only.

1881 Oct 12: Final voyage London-Boston before being put up for sale.

1882 Sold to London owners.

1898 Norwegian owners.

1900 Broken up.

84

⌐. *Fcsle*

86

84 CEYLON (I)

Bt 1858 Samuda Bros, Poplar, London; *T*: 2,021 g. **Dim** 306 ft 1 in (93.29 m) × 40 ft 9 in (12.42 m) × 26 ft 1 in (7.95 m). **Eng** Sgl scr, 2 cyls, inverted, direct acting; *Cyls*: 72 in (182.88 cm); *Stroke*: 36 in (91.44 cm); 2,054 IHP; *Stm P*: 20 lb; 13 kts; By Humphrys, Tennant & Dykes. **H** Iron; *Pass*: 130 1st, 30 2nd.

1858 June 12: Launched fully rigged. Aug 26: Registered. Placed on the Southampton-Malta-Alexandria service under the command of Captain R. W. Evans.
1863 Jan: Collided with the brig *Ridesdale* off Calshot Castle, Isle of Wight, sinking her.
1865-6 Re-engined at Deptford.
1874-5 Bombay-Melbourne.
1876 Venice-Alexandria ferry.
1881 Sold to John L. Clark for £9,235 for cruising out of Southampton. The first ship to cruise round the world. Transferred to the Polytechnic Touring Association 1892. Owned by Ocean Steam Yachting Co Ltd.
1907 Broken up.

85 NEPAUL (I)

Bt 1858 Thames Iron Ship Building Co, Blackwall, London; *T*: 769 g. **Dim** 244 ft (74.37 m) × 29 ft 7 in (9.02 m) × 18 ft (5.49 m). **Eng** Sgl scr, 2 cyls, inverted, direct acting; *Cyls*: 48 in (121.92 cm); *Stroke*: 30 in (76.2 cm); 960 IHP; *Stm P*: 21 lb; 10 kts. **H** Iron.

1858 Jan 17: Registered. Alexandria-Malta-Alexandria service. Captain R. Roberts.
1860 Suez-Mauritius.
1864 Based on Shanghai and Hong Kong.
1867 July 19: Sold at Shanghai to Japanese Government.

86 JEDDO

Bt 1859 John Laird, Birkenhead; *T*: 1,632 g. **Dim** 277 ft 3 in (84.51 m) × 35 ft 8 in (10.87 m) × 25 ft (7.62 m). **Eng** Sgl scr, 2 cyls, horizontal trunk, direct acting; *Cyls*: 70 in (177.8 cm); *Stroke*: 36 in (91.44 cm); 2,059 IHP; *Stm P*: 18 lb; 12 kts; By Robert Napier, Govan, Glasgow. **H** Iron.

1858 Dec 22: Launched.
1859 Feb 24: Registered. Her positioning voyage Southampton-Bombay (57 days) was P&O's fastest to date.
1860 July: Placed on the Bombay-Sydney run, after two voyages Bombay-Suez.
1866 Feb 2: Grounded on the Choul Cader reef 30 miles out of Bombay. All of the passengers and crew were safely taken off by P&O's *Salsette* (*83*) but *Jeddo* was lost. Her master, Captain Granger, had been in command of *Malabar* (*81*) when she was lost six years earlier.

87 IBERIA (II)

Bt 1859 Smith & Rogers, Govan, Glasgow.

1859 Registered as being owned by Malcolmsons. P&O does not normally include this vessel in its fleet lists.

88-89

88 DELTA (III)

Bt 1859 Thames Iron Ship Building Co, Blackwall, London; *T*: 1,618 g. **Dim** 324 ft 3 in (98.83 m) oa, 298 ft (90.38 m) × 35 ft 3 in (10.74 m) × 24 ft 6 in (7.47 m). **Eng** Pad, 2 cyls, oscillating; *Cyls*: 72 in (182.88 cm); *Stroke*: 84 in (213.36 cm); 1,612 IHP; *Stm P*: 20 lb; 10 kts; By John Penn & Co, Greenwich, originally from *Valetta* (*42*). **H** Iron; *Pass*: 126 1st, 50 2nd.

This vessel and Massilia (*89*) *were the final attempt by the British Admiralty to retain an interest in paddle propulsion. P&O agreed to build the vessels for the mail service only because the engines of* Valetta *(42) and* Vectis *(43) were available. In service the vessels were extremely steady but far too slow by comparison with contemporary screw driven vessels.*

1859 Sept 23: Registered.
Oct 12: Maiden voyage Southampton-Gibraltar-Malta-Alexandria.
1869 Nov 17: *Delta* was present at the opening of the Suez Canal and joined the procession of 67 vessels led by the French Royal Yacht *Aigle*, as far as Lake Timsah.
1874 May: Sold at Yokohama to the Japanese Government for £19,703.
Renamed *Takasago Maru*. Later operated by Nippon Yusen Kaisha.
1879 Sold to United States owners for use in the Gold Rush trade along the Californian and Alaskan coasts. Renamed *Centennial*.
1903 Used as a cargo vessel in the Russo-Japanese war.
1906 Went missing on a voyage from Muroran to San Francisco.
1913 A Russian arctic expedition reported having sighted the lost vessel encrusted in ice and locked deep in the centre of a vast ice field north of Saghalien. She was never seen again.

89 MASSILIA (I)

Details as *Delta* (*88*) except: **Bt** 1860 Samuda & Co, Millwall, London; *T*: 1,640 g. **Eng** 1,730 IHP; Originally from *Vectis* (*43*).

1860 Jan 9: Launched.
Apr 9: Registered.
Apr 12: Maiden voyage Southampton-Alexandria. Later Marseilles-Alexandria.
1877 July: Sold to Mitsubishi Co for £8,151. Renamed *Atago Maru*.
1896 Laid up at Nagasaki.
1898 Bought by Butterfield & Swire to be storeship at Cheefoo.

90 MOOLTAN (I)

Bt 1860 Thames Iron Ship Building Co, Blackwall, London; *T*: 2,257 g. **Dim** 370 ft (112.78 m) oa, 348 ft 8 in (106.27 m) × 39 ft 1 in (11.91 m) × 28 ft 7 in (8.71 m).
Eng Sgl scr, 2 cyls, compound inverted, tandem; *Cyls*: 43 in (109.22 cm) and 96 in (243.84 cm); *Stroke*: 36 in (91.44 cm); 1,734 IHP; 4 boilers; *Stm P*: 27½ lb; 12

90

kts; By Humphrys & Tennant, Deptford, London. **H** Iron, narrow build (length to beam ratio 9:1); *Coal*: 650 tons; *Pass*: 112 1st, 37 2nd.

Designed by James Ash as P&O's most luxurious vessel so far, Mooltan *was expensively decorated throughout. Her engines were the company's first compound type and were designed to reduce the consumption of coal by half. To assist in attaining a reliable service speed the vessel was also designed with a narrow beam. Unfortunately this produced severe rolling in a cross sea.* Mooltan *was never a successful ship.*

1861 Mar 8: Registered.
July 20: Entered service on the Southampton-Alexandria route. Later Calcutta-Suez.
1866 Despite the economy of the new type of engine it was found to be unreliable and a new engine and four improved boilers were installed.
1874 Nov 15: Prematurely laid up at London.
1880 Dec 14: Sold for £9,850 to Elles & Co, Liverpool. Fitted as four-masted barque, renamed *Eleanor Margaret*.
1891 Posted missing.

91

91 POONAH

Bt 1863 Thames Iron Ship Building Co, Blackwall, London; *T*: 2,152 g, 1,770 n.
Dim 334 ft 9 in (102.03 m) × 40 ft 9 in (12.42 m) × 27 ft 7 in (8.41 m). **Eng** Sgl scr, 2 cyls, compound inverted, tandem; *Cyls*: 48 in (121.92 cm) and 102 in (259.08 cm); *Stroke*: 27 in (68.58 cm); 2,356 IHP; *Stm P*:

25 lb; 12 kts; By Humphrys & Tennant, Deptford, London. **H** Iron, fcsle 68 ft (20.73 m).

1862 Nov 8: Launched. Was originally to have been named *Maharajah*.
1863 Feb 23: Registered. Southampton-Alexandria service. Blondin walked a tightrope between her main and mizzen masts while she was at sea.
1875 Aug 18: Re-registered after lengthening to 413 ft 9 in (126.11 m) by James Laing, Sunderland. New compound inverted engine by R. & W. Hawthorne, Newcastle; *Cyls*: 56 in (142.24 cm) and 97 in (246.38 cm); *Stroke*: 54 in (137.16 cm); 2,590 IHP, 550 HP; *Stm P*: 65 lb. Calcutta-Suez service.

1889 July: Sold at auction for breaking up. Fetched £5,231.
1892-3 Broken up at Sunderland.

92-93

92 CARNATIC

Bt 1862 Samuda Bros, Poplar, London; *T*: 1,776 g. **Dim** 294 ft 7 in (89.79 m) × 38 ft 1 in (11.61 m) × 25 ft 4 in (7.72 m). **Eng** Sgl scr, 4 cyls, compound inverted, tandem; *Cyls*: 43 in (109.22 cm) and 96 in (243.84 cm); *Stroke*: 36 in (91.44 cm); 2,442 IHP; *Stm P*: 27 lb; 12 kts; By Humphrys & Tennant, Deptford, London. **H** Iron.

1862 Dec 6: Launched. Was to have been named *Mysore*.
1863 Mar 24: Registered by P&O.
June 27: Sailed for Calcutta.
1869 Sept 13: Wrecked on coral reef off Shadwan at mouth of the Gulf of Suez, after leaving Suez for Bombay. Captain P.B. Jones. Before salvage was possible the ship broke in two and slipped off the ledge into deep water becoming a total loss, with the loss of five passengers and 21 crew. P&O's *Sumatra* (*111*) rescued the survivors and took them to Port Suez.

93 RANGOON

Details as *Carnatic* (*92*) except: **Bt** 1863.

Dim 2 in (5.08 cm) longer. **Eng** 1,870 IHP; *Stm P*: 25½ lb.
1863 Apr: Launched.
July 4: Registered. Calcutta (later Bombay)-Suez route.
1871 Placed on Ceylon-Australia route. Rated as a mail ship.
Nov 1: Foundered on Kadir Rock, Point de Galle, Ceylon. *Rangoon* had stopped, and was waiting for the arrival of the pilot launch to disembark the pilot who was in charge of the ship. A five knot current put her across the rock amidships and she was holed several times below the waterline. Within six hours the heeling ship had slipped sideways off the rocks into deep water and was lost. Her master at the time was Captain Scottowe, on his last trip before retirement after a faultless career; he was fully exonerated.

94 GOLCONDA (I)

Bt 1863 Thames Iron Ship Building Co, Blackwall, London; *T*: 1,909 g. **Dim** 314 ft 5 in (95.83 m) × 38 ft 3 in (11.66 m) × 26 ft 6 in (8.08 m). **Eng** Sgl scr, 4 cyls, compound inverted, tandem; *Cyls*: 43 in (109.22 cm) and 96 in (243.84 cm); *Stroke*: 36 in (91.44 cm); 2,112 IHP; *Stm P*: 25½ lb; 10 kts; By Humphrys & Tennant, Deptford, London. **H** Iron.

1863 Aug 29: Launched.
Dec 2: Registered.
1864 Jan 23: Sailed Southampton for Calcutta.
1865 Engine breakdown between Suez and Galle. Towed back to Suez by *Ansari* (*97*).
1874 New compound engines.
1881 May 17: Sold at Bombay for £5,311 to B. Mahomed Habdue Rayman.

95

95 SYRIA (I)

Bt 1863 Day Summers & Co, Northam, Southampton; *T*: 1,932 g. **Dim** 312 ft 5 in (95.22 m) × 36 ft (10.97 m) × 18 ft 5 in (5.61 m). **Eng** Pad, 2 cyls, oscillating, direct acting; *Cyls*: 76 in (193.04 cm);

Stroke: 54 in (137.16 cm); 2,602 IHP; *Stm P*: 27½ lb; 10 kts. **H** Iron.

1863 Aug 15: Launched. It had been originally proposed to name her *Scindia*. Nov 27: Registered.
1864 Jan 12: Maiden voyage Southampton-Alexandria. Spent career on services to Egypt.
1870 Sept 2: Sold to Caird & Co in part payment for *Mirzapore* (*118*); valued at £30,000. Sold to Union Line and converted to screw.
1877 Sold to Laing's, Sunderland.
1880 Apr: Foundered in Atlantic.

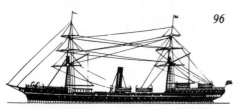

96

96 **DELHI** (II)

Bt 1864 Money Wigram, Blackwall, London; *T*: 1,899 g, 1,293 n. **Dim** 313 ft 3 in (95.48 m) × 38 ft (11.58 m) × 26 ft 3 in (8 m). **Eng** Sgl scr, 4 cyls, compound horizontal, tandem, direct acting; *Cyls*: 43 in (109.22 cm) and 90 in (228.6 cm); *Stroke*: 36 in (91.44 cm); 2,286 IHP; *Stm P*: 25 lb (superheated steam with surface condensers); 13.4 kts; By Ravenhill, Salkeld & Co. **H** Iron; *Pass*: 12.

Essentially a cargo carrier, but without the capacity to be really profitable.

1863 Sept 16: Launched.
1864 Jan 23: Commissioned. A screw driven version of *Syria* (*95*) with fore funnel omitted. Maiden voyage Southampton-Alexandria, later Bombay-Suez and Bombay-Hong Kong.
1870 Jan: The first P&O vessel to pass commercially through the Suez Canal, *Delta* (*88*) having only attended the opening ceremony.
1879 Laid up at Victoria Docks, London, and used as crew accommodation.
1881 March: Sold to Raeburn Verel & Co, Glasgow, for £5,350 and used as a cargo vessel only.
1882 Re-engined by Hutson & Corbett, Glasgow. Compound inverted; *Cyls*: 35 in (88.9 cm) and 60 in (152.4 cm); *Stroke*:

39 in (99.06 cm); 200 HP.
1895 Broken up in Holland.

97 **ANSARI**

Bt 1864 Stewart & Co; *T*: 146 g. **Eng** Pad; 40 HP. **H** Iron.

1864 Acquired. Cost £265. Tug at Suez, later at Alexandria.
1885 Sold for £265.

98 **CALABAH**

Details as *Ansari* (*97*) except: **Eng** 60 HP.

1864 Acquired. Initially at Calcutta, later Bombay.
1882 Engines removed, converted into a lighter.

99

99 **BARODA**

Bt 1864 Millwall Iron Works & Shipbuilding Co, Millwall, London; *T*: 1,874 g. **Dim** 309 ft 3 in (94.26 m) × 38 ft 1 in (11.61 m) × 26 ft 5 in (8.05 m). **Eng** Sgl scr, 4 cyls, compound inverted, tandem, direct acting; *Cyls*: 43 in (109.22 cm) and 96 in (243.84 cm); *Stroke*: 36 in (91.44 cm); 2,486 IHP; *Stm P*: 27 lb; 12 kts; By Humphrys & Tennant, Deptford, London, 'Economic' type. **H** Iron; *Pass*: 150 1st, 40 2nd.

The only vessel built for P&O by these builders. A comfortable 'tubby' ship, but by 1870 she was too small for P&O services.

1863 Aug 29: Launched.
1864 Jan 23: Registered. Mediterranean and then Suez-Bombay service.
1872 Bombay-Sydney.
1874 Venice-Alexandria service.
1876 Laid up at Victoria Docks, London, and used as crew accommodation.
1881 Mar: Sold for £5,360 to H. Castle & Sons Ltd for breaking up.

100 **NYANZA** (I)

Bt 1864 Thames Iron Works, London; *T*: 2,082 g. **Dim** 327 ft 3 in (99.75 m) × 36 ft

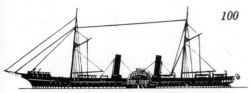

100

2 in (11.02 m) × 27 ft 6 in (8.38 m). **Eng** Pad, 2 cyls, oscillating; *Cyls*: 78½ in (199.39 cm); *Stroke*: 84 in (213.36 cm); 2,304 IHP; *Stm P*: 25 lb (with surface condensers); 12 kts; By J. & G. Rennie, Blackfriars, London. **H** Iron; *Pass*: 143 1st, 34 2nd.
Ordered as Rhoda.

1864 Nov 3: Registered.
Dec 12: Entered service. P&O's last paddle vessel, sleeker than *Syria* (*95*) and two kts faster. Unfortunately *Nyanza* was extravagant on fuel which led to only a short career with P&O, on the Southampton-Alexandria run.
1873 Jan 3: Sold to Union SS Co, Southampton, for £26,000. Lengthened and converted to screw.
1880 Sold to Sultan of Zanzibar.

101 COREA

Bt 1864 Gourlay Bros & Co, Dundee; *T*: 610 g. **Dim** 226 ft 8 in (69.09 m) × 27 ft (8.23 m) × 15 ft 4 in (4.67 m). **Eng** Sgl scr, 2 cyls, inverted, direct acting; *Cyls*: 51 in (129.54 cm); *Stroke*: 31 in (78.74 cm); 1,044 IHP; *Stm P*: 24 lb; 10 kts. **H** Iron; *Pass*: 40 1st.

1864 Apr 15: Purchased ready for sea for £26,000. Previous name *Cohen*.
Apr 30: Shanghai-Yokohama passenger and mail feeder service.
1865 June 29: Lost. Left Hong Kong for Swatow, Amoy and Foochow as a typhoon was breaking, and was never seen again. Captain J. W. Bird.

102

102 MONGOLIA (I)

Bt 1865 John Scott & Sons, Cartsdyke, Greenock; *T*: 2,999 g, 1,585 n. **Dim** 319 ft

4 in (97.33 m) × 40 ft 2 in (12.24 m) × 32 ft 7 in (9.93 m). **Eng** Sgl scr, 2 cyls, oscillating, geared; *Cyls*: 74 in (187.96 cm); *Stroke*: 66 in (167.64 cm); 1,705 IHP; *Stm P*: 22¾ lb; 10 kts; By Greenock Foundry Co. **H** Iron; *Pass*: 120 1st.

1865 July 5: Registered. Mainly employed on the Calcutta-Suez service.
1873-4 New compound engine fitted at Southampton by Day Summers & Co. *Cyls*: 48 in (121.92 cm) and 96 in (243.84 cm); *Stroke*: 54 in (137.16 cm). Funnel heightened to increase draught. The drawing illustrates the taller funnel. London-Bombay or Calcutta service, also Australia.
1878 Venice-Bombay.
1888 May: Sold for £3,788 in Bombay to agent of the Sultan of Zanzibar for breaking up.

103 NIPHON

Bt 1865 John Key, Kirkcaldy, Fife; *T*: 695 g. **Dim** 223 ft 7 in (68.15 m) × 26 ft 6 in (8.08 m) × 16 ft 1 in (4.9 m). **Eng** Sgl scr, 2 cyls, horizontal, direct acting; *Cyls*: 42¼ in (107.32 cm); *Stroke*: 24 in (60.96 cm); 750 IHP; *Stm P*: 20 lb; 10 kts. **H** Iron.

1865 Sept 22: Registered.
Sept 26: Ran aground en route from builders to Southampton.
Nov 1: Maiden voyage Southampton-Alexandria, then sent out to Hong Kong station.
1868 Jan 23: Lost. Struck a reef off House Hill near Amoy and broke in two the next day. Captain A. Peake. Eight passengers and five crew lost, and all cargo and mails except for one bag.

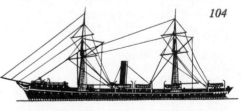

104

104 TANJORE

Bt 1865 Thames Iron Works, London; *T*: 1,971 g, 1,403 n. **Dim** 321 ft 2 in (97.89 m) × 38 ft 1 in (11.61 m) × 26 ft 4 in (8.03 m). **Eng** Sgl scr, 4 cyls, 'improved' compound horizontal, tandem, direct acting;

Cyls: 43 in (109.22 cm) and 90 in (228.6 cm); *Stroke*: 36 in (91.44 cm); 2,090 IHP; *Stm P*: 25 lb; 14 kts; By Miller Ravenhill & Co, Blackwall, London. **H** Iron, fcsle 51 ft (15.54 m), poop 93 ft (28.35 m).

1865 Aug 15: Commissioned for Southampton-Alexandria-Marseilles-Alexandria-Southampton service. On her trials *Tanjore* covered the measured mile at an astonishing 17 kts. Further tests showed that her improved engine was not only speedy but economical. As a result four P&O vessels were re-engined, viz *Ceylon* (*84*), *Columbian* (*78*), *China* (*74*) and *Pera* (*69*).
1870 New boilers and poop.
1873 Transferred to Suez-Bombay run.
1876 Re-engined by J. Howden & Co, Glasgow, who took *Simla* (*61*) in part payment. Compound inverted; *Cyls*: 52 in (132.08 cm) and 90 in (228.6 cm); *Stroke*: 48 in (121.92 cm).
1882 During the Arabi Pasha troubles in Egypt *Tanjore* was used as a refugee ship in Alexandria harbour.
1888 May 28: Withdrawn from service. Laid up at Bombay.
1890 Aug: Sold to Hajee Cassum Joosub, Bombay, for £6,794. Used on the Mecca pilgrimage trade to Jeddah.

105

105 **GEELONG** (I)

Bt 1866 William Denny & Bros, Dumbarton; *T*: 1,835 g, 1,139 n. **Dim** 275 ft (83.82 m) × 34 ft 3 in (10.46 m) × 25 ft (7.62 m). **Eng** Sgl scr, 2 cyls, inverted, direct acting; *Cyls*: 54 in (137.16 cm); *Stroke*: 36 in (91.44 cm); 1,200 IHP; *Stm P*: 20 lb; 11 kts. **H** Iron.

1866 Laid down as *Thomas Powell*. Purchased on the stocks.
Mar 5: Registered.
1867 Oct 22: Entered Ceylon-Australia service. Later service mostly in Far East.
1874 Engine converted to 2 cyl, compound inverted type by builders. *Cyls*: 44 in

(111.76 cm) and 70 in (177.8 cm); *Stroke*: 36 in (91.44 cm); 1,200 IHP; *Stm P*: 25 lb; 11 kts.
1887 Oct: Sold at Hiogo to Reynell & Co for £4,631. Renamed *Irhizaki Maru No 1*.
1891 June: Lost at sea.

106

106 **AVOCA**

Bt 1866 William Denny & Bros, Dumbarton; *T*: 1,480 g, 905 n. **Dim** 257 ft (78.33 m) × 32 ft 2 in (9.8 m) × 25 ft 5 in (7.75 m). **Eng** Sgl scr, 2 cyls, inverted, direct acting; *Cyls*: 54 in (137.16 cm); *Stroke:* 36 in (91.44 cm); 1,014 IHP; *Stm P*: 23 lb; 11 kts. **H** Iron.

1866 May 28: Registered. P&O were so satisfied with the performance of *Geelong* (*105*) that they bid for and obtained *Avoca* whilst she was still on the stocks.
Nov 23: Placed on the Ceylon-Australia service alongside *Geelong*.
1874 Engine converted by builders to 2 cyl, compound inverted type; *Cyls*: 44 in (111.76 cm) and 70 in (177.8 cm); *Stroke*: 36 in (91.44 cm); 250 HP.
1876 Served on Melbourne-Sydney feeder run.
1882 Oct 29: Sold at Bombay to agent of Sultan of Zanzibar for £12,943. Later bought by Hajee Cassum Joosub.
1900 Broken up.

107 **MALACCA** (I)

Bt 1866 Denton Gray & Co, Hartlepool; *T*: 1,709 g. **Dim** 284 ft (86.56 m) × 34 ft 1 in (10.39 m) × 25 ft 2 in (7.67 m). **Eng** Sgl scr, 2 cyls, horizontal, direct acting; *Cyls*: 55 in (139.7 cm); *Stroke*: 36 in (91.44 cm); 1,380 IHP; *Stm P*: 28 lb; 11 kts; By J. Richardson & Sons. **H** Iron; 1 deck and spar deck.

1866 May 23: Registered. Bought on the stocks.
1871 Rescued crew of HMS *Megaera* from St Paul's Island, Indian Ocean.
1874 Compound inverted engine fitted by T. Richardson, Hartlepool; *Cyls*: 42 in (106.68 cm) and 78 in (198.12 cm); *Stroke*:

39 in (99.06 cm).
1882 June: Sold at Bombay to agent of
Sultan of Zanzibar for £14,916.
1895 Sold to Dutch owners.

110-111

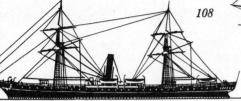

108

108 SURAT (I)

Bt 1866 Day Summers & Co, Northam,
Southampton; *T*: 2,578 g, 1,677 n. **Dim**
316 ft 2 in (96.37 m) × 41 ft 3 in (12.57 m)
× 30 ft 3 in (9.22 m). **Eng** Sgl scr, 2 cyls,
horizontal, direct acting; *Cyls*: 80 in
(203.2 cm); *Stroke*: 42 in (106.68 cm);
2,516 IHP; *Stm P*: 26 lb; 12 kts. **H** Iron.

1866 Mar 17: Launched.
Aug 2: Registered. India-Suez mail service.
1874 Sept 24: Lengthened to 356 ft 6 in
(108.68 m) by builders and re-engined. 2
cyls, compound inverted; *Cyls*: 52 in
(132.08 cm) and 90 in (228.6 cm); *Stroke*:
54 in (137.16 cm); 2,855 IHP; New boilers;
Stm P: 71 lb.
1876 Bombay-Venice route.
1882 Present with *Tanjore* (*104*) at
Alexandria during the Abrabi Pasha
bombardment. Used as a refugee ship.
1894 Sold Kobe for £10,043. Renamed
Shinyu Maru. Broken up soon afterwards.

109 SUNDA (I)

Bt 1866 Backhouse & Dixon,
Middlesbrough; *T*: 1,682 g, 1,030 n. **Dim m**
270 ft (82.3 m) × 33 ft 9 in (10.29 m) ×
26 ft 8 in (8.13 m). **Eng** Sgl scr, 2 cyls,
inverted, direct acting; *Cyls*: 55 in
(139.7 cm); *Stroke*: 36 in (91.44 cm); 1,342
IHP; *Stm P*: 26½ lb; 12 kts. **H** Iron;
spar deck, 5 holds.

1866 Built for Thomas Richardson & Sons,
Hartlepool.
Aug 2: Purchased by P&O on the stocks.
1867 Hong Kong-Shanghai or Yokohama.
1875 Beached between Hong Kong and
Yokohama after running onto reef.
1882 Aug: Sold at Bombay to agent of
Sultan of Zanzibar for £14,901.

110 BANGALORE (I)

Bt 1867 William Denny & Bros.
Dumbarton; *T*: 2,342 g, 1,310 n, 1,474
dwt. **Dim** 318 ft 4 in (97.03 m) × 38 ft 4 in
(11.68 m) × 26 ft 4 in (8.03 m). **Eng** Sgl scr,
2 cyls, inverted, direct acting; *Cyls*: 72 in
(182.88 cm); *Stroke:* 45 in (114.3 cm);
2,255 IHP; *Stm P*: 22 lb; 13 kts. **H** Iron.

1867 June 10: Commissioned for
Southampton-Marseilles-Alexandria
service.
1871 Transferred to Bombay-Australia
service.
1875 Compound, inverted engine installed
by builders; *Cyls*: 57 in (144.78 cm) and 95
in (241.3 cm); *Stroke*: 45 in (114.3 cm).
1878 Carried Indian troops to Malta.
1886 Feb 23: Sold to Hajee Cassum Joosub,
Bombay, for £5,052 for Mecca pilgrimage
trade to Jeddah.
1891 Sold to Wilhelm Wilhelmsen,
Norway. Renamed *Coringa*.
1905 Mar 18: Foundered in heavy seas near
the Azores.

111 SUMATRA (I)

Details as *Bangalore* (*110*) except: *T*:
2,488 g, 1,406 n. **Eng** 2,277 IHP; *Stm P*:
25 lb.

1867 Sept 13: Commissioned for general
Far East service. Cost £108,800.
1874 Compound inverted engine installed
by builders. As *Bangalore*.
1886 May 7: Sold to Hajee Cassum Joosub,
Bombay, for Mecca pilgrimage trade.
1889 Mar 4: Burnt at sea.

112 BANDORA

Bt 1866 Laird Bros, Birkenhead; *T*: 128 g.
Dim 85 ft (25.91 m) × 18 ft (5.49 m) × 6 ft
4 in (1.93 m). **Eng** Tw scr, 2 cyls; *Cyls*: 8 in
(20.32 cm); *Stroke*: 6 in (15.24 cm); 20
HP. **H** Iron.

1866 Jan 12: Registered. Lighter at
Bombay.

1915 Transferred to P&O subsidiary Mazagon Dock Co.

113 SEWREE

Details as *Bandora* (*112*).

1866 Oct: Registered.
1911 Dec 2: Sold.

114 FILIPINO

Bt 1866; *T*: 515 g. **H** Iron.

Although sometimes listed as P&O this ship was never actually owned by the company. She is included only for reference purposes.

1866 Feeder service Hong Kong-Manila.

115

115 TRAVANCORE

Bt 1868 John Key, Kirkcaldy, Fife; *T*: 1,889 g, 1,185 n. **Dim** 281 ft 6 in (85.8 m) × 35 ft 5 in (10.8 m) × 27 ft 8 in (8.43 m). **Eng** Sgl scr, 2 cyls, horizontal, direct acting; *Cyls*: 64 in (162.56 cm); *Stroke*: 36 in (91.44 cm); 1,428 IHP; *Stm P*: 24 lb; 12 kts; By Humphrys & Tennant, Deptford, London. **H** Iron.

1868 Purchased on the stocks for £76,000.
May 14: Placed on the Southampton-Gibraltar-Malta-Alexandria service under the command of Captain Methven.
1875 Compound engines installed.
1880 Mar 8: Wrecked on a flat rock near Cape Otranto, Southern Italy, whilst on the Brindisi-Alexandria run. All passengers and crew saved together with the mail and some cargo, but *Travancore* became a total loss.

116 DECCAN

Bt 1868 William Denny & Bros, Dumbarton; *T*: 3,128 g. **Dim** 368 ft 3 in (112.24 m) × 42 ft 5 in (12.93 m) × 30 ft 3 in (9.22 m). **Eng** Sgl scr, 2 cyls, inverted, direct acting; *Cyls*: 76 in (193.04 cm); *Stroke*: 48 in (121.92 cm); *Stm P*: 23 lb; 13 kts; 52 rpm; 4-bladed propeller, diam 18 ft 10 in (5.74 m), pitch 27 ft 6 in (8.38 m). **H**

116-117

Iron; *Coal*: 800 tons; *Cargo*: 1,400 tons; *Pass*: 175 1st, 52 2nd.

1868 Laid down as *Magdala*.
Nov 26: Purchased by P&O; cost £125,900. First named *Lahore* (I) then *Deccan*. Placed on Suez-Calcutta route. Commanded by Captain J.R. Kellock.
1875 Compound engines installed by Palmers at Jarrow.
1879 Dec 26: London-Capetown-Australia service. One voyage only.
1889 Sold to Hajee Cassum Joosub, Bombay, for Mecca pilgrimage trade to Jeddah.

117 HINDOSTAN (II)

Bt 1869 Day Summers & Co, Northam, Southampton; *T*: 3,113 g. **Dim** 353 ft 9 in (107.82 m) × 43 ft (13.11 m) × 30 ft 2 in (9.19 m). Other details as *Deccan* (*116*) except that steel was used above the waterline in the construction of *Hindostan*'s hull.

1869 Oct 2: Handed over.
Nov 3: Maiden voyage out to Calcutta, then placed on the Bombay-Suez route. This was the last delivery voyage via the Cape.
1872 UK-India via Suez Canal service. Then Venice-Suez Canal-India service.
1876 Re-engined by builders.
1879 Oct 21: At 0300 hours ran on to a reef 30 miles south of Madras. This was the first P&O loss in service since *Carnatic* (*92*) ten years earlier.

118

118 AUSTRALIA (I)

Bt 1870 Caird & Co, Greenock; *T*: 3,664 g. **Dim** 381 ft 9 in (116.36 m) × 44 ft 7 in

(13.59 m) × 33 ft (10.06 m). **Eng** Sgl scr, 2 cyls, compound inverted; *Cyls*: 62 in (157.48 cm) and 96 in (243.84 cm); *Stroke*: 54 in (137.16 cm); 2,626 IHP; *Stm P*: 40 lb; 11 kts; By builders. **H** Iron; *Pass*: 180 1st, 75 2nd.

The vessel was so heavily built that she was nicknamed the 'P&O Ironclad'. P&O's last clipper bow and their largest and longest vessel to date.

1870 Laid down as *Mirzapore* (I). Renamed before launching on Apr 5. Cost £118,600.
June 23: Registered. On her maiden voyage to India *Australia* was the first P&O ship to sail southbound through the Suez Canal.
1876 Re-engined with compound inverted type; 3,300 IHP; 13 kts.
1879 Outbound her propeller shaft snapped. The tug *Trusty* and HMS *Valorous* towed her back to Southampton.
1889 July: Sold by auction to the Union Steamship Co for £14,831. Renamed *Dane*. Placed on their intermediate service, but she proved to be too slow and was an unsuccessful ship.
1893 Laid up and then broken up on the Thames.

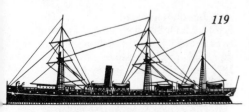

119

119 **INDUS** (II)

Bt 1871 William Denny & Bros, Dumbarton; *T*: 3,462 g, 2,089 n. **Dim** 360 ft 4 in (109.83 m) × 40 ft 4 in (12.29 m) × 34 ft 1 in (10.39 m); *Dft*: 24 ft 5 in (7.44 m). **Eng** Sgl scr, 2 cyls, compound inverted; 2,368 IHP; *Stm P*: 65 ¾ lb; 13 kts; By builders. **H** Iron, P&O's first straight stem; *Pass*: 129 1st, 50 2nd.

1871 The high steam pressure initially gave cause for comment on the grounds of safety. *Indus* was purchased on the stocks before being given a name. Cost £106,100.
Apr 22: Registered and placed on the Indian service.
June 3: Maiden voyage to Bombay via Suez.
1878 Re-engined by J. Howden & Co,

Glasgow. Compound inverted; 535 HP; *Cyls*: 54 in (137.16 cm) and 97 in (246.38 cm); *Stroke*: 60 in (152.4 cm).
1885 Nov 8: Wrecked on Muliavattu shoal 60 miles north of Trincomalee, Ceylon, en route Calcutta-London. All aboard were saved but the cargo was lost.

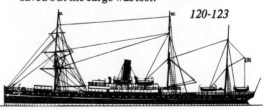

120-123

120 **KHEDIVE**

Bt 1871 Caird & Co, Greenock; *T*: 3,742 g, 2,123 n. **Dim** 377 ft 6 in (115.06 m) × 42 ft 4 in (12.9 m) × 33 ft (10.06 m). **Eng** Sgl scr, compound; *Cyls*: 68 in (172.72 cm) and 96 in (243.84 cm); *Stroke*: 54 in (137.16 cm); 2,695 IHP; *Stm P*: 68 lb; 12 kts; By builders. **H** Iron; *Pass*: 168 1st, 50 2nd.

Khedive, Mirzapore (121), *Pekin* (122) *and Peshawur* (123) *were P&O's largest vessels to date, all built by Caird & Co in 1871. They established a style which dominated the company's passenger design for the ensuing ten years and, despite a group of two funnelled vessels, was not outdated before the advent of* Caledonia (191) *in 1894. The ships were built to take advantage of the Suez Canal route to India.*

1869 Dec 18: Ordered.
1871 Apr 22: Handed over for service on the Suez Canal route to India.
1897 Jan 1: Sold to Duda, Abdullah & Co, Bombay, for £7,999.
Jan 11: Stranded off Portander, India, and became a total loss.

121 **MIRZAPORE** (II)

Details as *Khedive* (*120*) except: *T*: 3,763 g, 2,164 n. **Dim** 380 ft 3 in (115.9 m) × 42 ft 6 in (12.95 m) × 33 ft 1 in (10.08 m). **Eng** 3,182 IHP.

1871 May 20: Launched.
Aug 9: Handed over to P&O.
Sept 2: Maiden voyage Southampton-Alexandria and back. Thereafter *Mirzapore* spent most of her career on the London-Suez-Bombay-Ceylon-Calcutta-Singapore route. Her builders took *Syria*

(*95*) towards £15,000 of cost.
1898 Sold to Hajee Cassum Jossub for
Mecca pilgrimage trade between Bombay
and Jeddah.
1899 Broken up.

122 PEKIN (II)

Details as *Khedive* (*120*) except: *T*: 3,777 g,
2,125 n. **Dim** 378 ft 1 in (115.24 m) × 42 ft
5 in (12.93 m) × 33 ft 2 in (10.11 m). *Cyls*:
62 in (157.48 cm) and 104 in (264.16 cm).

1871 Oct 27: Registered. London-Suez-
Bombay service. Cost £119,500, of which
£15,000 was the value of *Ripon* (*32*).
1897 Sold to Hajee Cassum Jossub for
Mecca pilgrimage trade between Bombay
and Jeddah. Renamed *Jubedu*.
1900 Sept: Sprang a leak in River Hughli;
beached and broke her back.

123 PESHAWUR (I)

Details as *Pekin* (*122*) except: *T*: 3,749 g,
2,131 n.

1871 Oct 30: Launched.
Dec 22: Completed cost £113,500. This
ship was ordered as *Agra*. Joined *Pekin* on
the London-Suez-Bombay service.
1896 Used for Indian trooping duties.
1899 June: Sold to Hajee Cassum Jossub.
Renamed *Ashruf*. Price £7,600.
1905 Wrecked near Tamatave,
Madagascar.

124-127

124 HYDASPES

Bt William Denny & Bros, Dumbarton; *T*:
2,984 g, 1,891 n. **Dim** 361 ft 5 in (110.16 m)
× 39 ft 4 in (11.99 m) × 29 ft 4 in (8.94 m);
Dft: 21 ft 7 in (6.58 m). **Eng** Sgl scr, 2 cyls,
compound inverted; *Cyls*: 50 in (127 cm)
and 86 in (218.44 cm); *Stroke*: 54 in
(137.16 cm); 2,052 IHP, 500 HP; *Stm P*:
70 lb; 12 kts; By builders. **H** Iron; *Pass*: 126
1st, 41 2nd.

1872 Aug 23: Maiden voyage
Southampton-Bombay.

1882 Placed on Bombay-Ceylon-Australia
service.
1898 Sold to F. Gore, Shanghai, for
£5,850.

125 CATHAY (I)

Details as *Hydaspes* (*124*) except: *T*:
2,983 g, 1,884 n. **Dim** Length 360 ft 8 in
(109.93 m). Thinner funnel. Cost £93,000.

1872 June 27: Maiden voyage
Southampton-Suez-Bombay. Whilst
passing through the Canal the vessel went
aground for 24 hours.
1880 Re-boilered. Served on Adriatic,
Indian and Chinese routes.
1890 Sold to Nippon Yusen Kaisha, Japan.
Renamed *Ikai Maru*.
1903 Broken up in Japan.

126 MALWA (I)

Bt 1873 Caird & Co, Greenock; *T*: 2,933 g,
1,868 n. **Dim** 361 ft 5 in (110.16 m) × 39 ft
(11.89 m) × 29 ft (8.84 m); *Dft*: 21 ft 7 in
(6.58 m). **Eng** Details as *Hydaspes* (*124*)
except: By Caird & Co, Greenock. *Pass*:
143 1st, 42 2nd.

*Three yards on foremast, no wheel house.
Cost £90,900.*

1873 Jan 23: Registered.
Feb 12: Maiden voyage London-Calcutta.
1874 Brought home the body of the
explorer David Livingstone.
1875 Venice-Bombay-Sydney service.
1879 Re-boilered.
1884 Nov 25: Collided with Clan Lines'
Clan Forbes near Suez. *Malwa* had to be
beached but was successfully salvaged.
1894 Oct 10: Sold to Nippon Yusen
Kaisha, Japan, for £11,635. Renamed
Yamoto Maru. During the Sino-Japanese
war she was operated by Tetsu Yemosuki.
1900 Broken up in Japan.

127 BOKHARA

Details as *Malwa* (*126*) except: *T*: 2,944 g,
1,700 n. Cost £90,600.

1873 Mar 17: Registered.
June 21: Stranded near Kowloon but safely
refloated. Repaired in Hong Kong
dry dock.
1880 Re-boilered and refitted and then
placed on India-Australia route.
1884 Feb: Used as an Egyptian war

transport between Suez and Suakin.
1892 Oct 8: After leaving Shanghai for
Hong Kong under Captain C. D. Sams
Bokhara was struck by a typhoon which
gradually swamped her boilers. The
helpless vessel then drifted onto Sand
Island in the Pescadores off Formosa and
was completely wrecked. Out of 148 on
board only seven Europeans and 16 Lascars
survived.

128 TIMSAH

Bt 1873 Day Summers & Co, Northam,
Southampton; *T*: 191 g, 30 n. **Dim** 110 ft
1 in (33.55 m) × 23 ft 1 in (7.04 m) × 12 ft
7 in (3.84 m). **Eng** Sgl scr, 2 cyls,
compound, 120 NHP; *Cyls*: 26 in
(66.04 cm) and 52 in (132.08 cm); *Stroke*:
36 in (91.44 cm); By builders. **H** Iron.

1872 Mar 26: Ordered.
1873 May 16: Registered. Tug in Egypt,
but moved to Bombay 1877. Cost £13,200.
1885 Assisted at wreck of *Indus* (*119*) on
coast of Ceylon.
1910 Sold for £995.

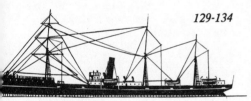

129-134

129 VENETIA

Bt 1873 William Denny & Bros,
Dumbarton; *T*: 2,726 g, 1,728 n. **Dim**
351 ft 7 in (107.16 m) × 38 ft 3 in (11.66 m)
× 27 ft 8 in (8.43 m); *Dft*: 21 ft 7 in
(6.58 m). **Eng** Sgl scr, 2 cyls, compound
inverted; *Cyls*: 49 in (124.46 cm) and 86 in
(218.44 cm); *Stroke*: 54 in (137.16 cm);
1,944 IHP, 500 HP; *Stm P*: 71¾ lb; 12 kts;
By builders. **H** Iron, fcsle 48 ft (14.63 m);
Pass: 80 1st, 36 2nd.

*A class of six vessels were built by two
shipyards, Denny and Caird, the Caird pair
being for Norddeutsch Lloyd. These were
Venetia, Lombardy (130), Gwalior (131),
Nizam (132), Assam (133) and Siam (134).
Of an intermediate type they saw service
almost entirely on the Indian and
Australian routes. They were another
example of the P&O rebuilding*
*programme which followed the opening of
the Suez Canal.*

1873 Feb 19: Commissioned. Maiden
voyage London-Shanghai. Returned with
fresh tea.
1875 Placed on the Venice-Brindisi-Suez-
Bombay route.
1878 London-Bombay-Melbourne-Sydney
route.
1879 Placed on Bombay-Galle (Ceylon)-
Sydney service.
1882 Reverted to original route from
Venice.
1885 Troop transport London-Ceylon-
China.
1893 Sept: Sold for £4,692 for breaking up
by B. Dunjeebhoy, Bombay.

130 LOMBARDY

Details as *Venetia* (*129*) except: *T*: 2,723 g,
1,571 n. **Dim** 2 in (5.08 cm) longer. Cost
£500 less.

1873 May 1: Registered. Indian trades; a
useful all round vessel.
1893 Sold at Bombay to Hajee Cassum
Joosub for £5,683. Renamed *Jubedu*.
1896 Broken up.

131 GWALIOR

Details as *Venetia* (*129*) except: *T*: 2,733 g,
1,629 n. Cost £98,200.

1873 May 9: Launched.
June 26: Registered. Mostly London-
Bombay and Bombay-Shanghai services.
1883 Vice-Bombay, also Venice-
Alexandria ferry.
1894 Aug 21: Sold to Kishimoto Gohio,
Osaka, for £7,290. Renamed *Shinahu
Maru*.
1904 Mar: Wrecked at Chemulpo while on
transport duties in Russo-Japanese war.

132 NIZAM

Details as *Venetia* (*129*) except: *T*: 2,726 g,
1,606 n. **Dim** 351 ft 3 in (107.06 m) × 38 ft
2 in (11.63 m) × 27 ft 8 in (8.43 m). Cost
£101,400.

1873 Aug 19: Registered. Indian services.
1884 Venice-Bombay.
1893 Broken up at Bombay by Essaji
Tabjhoy for £4,500.

133 ASSAM

Details as *Venetia* (*129*) except: **Bt** 1873
Caird & Co, Greenock; *T*: 3,033 g, 1,597 n.
Dim 350 ft (106.68 m) × 39 ft 4 in
(11.99 m) × 30 ft 8 in (9.35 m) **Eng** High
pressure cyl: 50 in (127 cm).

1873 Built as *Feldmarschal Moltke* for
Norddeutscher Lloyd's West Indian
service.
1875 Sept 7: Purchased by P&O for
£73,056 for Indian services and renamed
Assam.
1876-80 Bombay-Melbourne run.
1885 Venice-Bombay.
1895 Sold to Nippon Yusen Kaisha, Japan.
Renamed *Kaijo Maru*. Price £14,174.
1898 Broken up.

134 SIAM

Details as *Assam* (*133*) except: *T*: 3,026 g,
1,562 n. **Eng** Low pressure cyl: 85½ in
(217.17 cm).

1873 Built as *Minister Roon* for
Norddeutscher Lloyd.
1875 Sept 7: Purchased by P&O for
£72,877 and renamed *Siam*.
1876 Bombay-Melbourne run.
1881 London-Calcutta service, alternating
with London-Colombo from 1882 when
Colombo replaced Galle as the port of call
for Ceylon.
1895 Sold to Nippon Yusen Kaisha, Japan.
Renamed *Yorihime Maru*. Price £8,260.
1903 Condemned and scrapped.

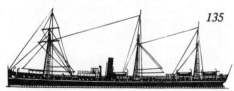

135

135 ZAMBESI

Bt 1873 Barclay Curle, Glasgow; *T*:
2,431 g. **Dim** 330 ft 6 in (100.74 m) × 36 ft
7 in (11.15 m) × 27 ft 5 in (8.36 m). **Eng** Sgl
scr, 2 cyls, compound inverted; *Cyls*: 45 in
(114.3 cm) and 78 in (198.12 cm); *Stroke*:
48 in (121.92 cm); 1,550 IHP, 310 HP; *Stm
P*: 60 lb; 11 kts. **H** Iron, 2 decks.

1873 May 12: Purchased on stocks. Cost
£76,100.
1888 Mar 23: Sold at Hiogo to F. Upton for
£6,960.

136 ADRIA

Bt 1873 John Blumer & Co, North Dock,
Sunderland; *T*: 1,225 g, 781 n. **Dim** 237 ft
6 in (72.39 m) × 30 ft 3 in (9.22 m) × 21 ft
6 in (6.55 m). **Eng** Sgl scr, 2 cyls, compound
inverted; *Cyls*: 27 in (68.58 cm) and 54 in
(137.16 cm); *Stroke*: 30 in (76.2 cm); 487
IHP, 120 HP; *Stm P*: 65 lb; 11 kts; By
Simpson & Co, London. **H** Iron.

1873 Dec 1: Registered. Cost £26,500. Coal
and stores vessel. Also Venice-Alexandria
run.
1881 Dec: Sold to Hajee Cassum Joosub,
Bombay, for £3,337.
1886 Lost.

137-138

137 KHIVA (I)

Bt 1873 James Laing, Sunderland; *T*:
2,609 g, 1,419 n. **Dim** 361 ft 4 in (110.13 m)
× 36 ft 8 in (11.17 m) × 27 ft 4 in (8.33 m).
Eng Sgl scr, 2 cyls, compound inverted;
Cyls: 50 in (127 cm) and 86 in (218.44 cm);
Stroke: 51 in (129.54 cm); 2,100 IHP, 450
HP; *Stm P*: 70 lb; 11 kts. **H** Iron, 2 decks,
raised fore deck 29 ft (8.84 m).

1873 Built for Ryde Line's South American
service. Named *Antwerpen*.
1874 Mar 3: Acquired for £86,400 before
she left her builders. Eastern services.
1885 Passenger accommodation reduced
to eight berths.
1890 Sold Bombay to Hajee Cassum
Joosub for £10,000.
1893 Caught fire in Red Sea with 900
pilgrims aboard; beached to save life but
the ship was destroyed.

138 KASHGAR (I)

Details as *Khiva* (*137*) except: **Bt** 1874; *T*:
2,621 g, 1,515 n. **Dim** 362 ft 5 in
(110.46 m).

1874 Laid down as *Brabant* for Ryde Line's
South American service. Purchased on the
stocks for £87,022 and renamed *Kashgar*.
June 6: Registered. Mostly Indian service
with one or two Australian voyages.

1886 Passenger accommodation reduced to eight berths.
1890 May: Sold at Yokohama, through Adamson & Co, London, for £10,749. Ran on local Japanese services or a few years and then broken up.

141

139

139 TEHERAN

Bt 1874 Gourlay Bros & Co, Dundee; *T*: 2,589 g, 1,671 n. **Dim** 360 ft (109.73 m) × 36 ft 2 in (11.02 m) × 26 ft 9 in (8.15 m). **Eng** Sgl scr, 2 cyls, compound inverted; *Cyls*: 48 in (121.92 cm) and 84 in (213.36 cm); *Stroke*: 48 in (121.92 cm); 2,016 IHP, 400 HP; *Stm P*: 70 lb; 11 kts; By builders. **H** Iron, fcsle 49 ft (14.94 m); *Pass*: 59 1st, 24 2nd.

1874 Mar 20: Launched.
May 2: Registered. Cost £94,100. London-India, India-Far East, Italy-India services.
1894 Sold Hiogo to Chingsten KKK for £9,497. Renamed *Toyei Maru*.
1905 Nov: Wrecked in Japanese waters.

2 cyls, compound inverted; *Cyls*: 60 in (152.4 cm) and 106 in (269.24 cm); *Stroke*: 54 in (137.16 cm); 2,870 IHP, 600 HP; *Stm P*: 56¼ lb; 12 kts. **H** Iron, 3 decks; *Pass*: 117 1st, 38 2nd.

Originally ordered as transatlantic liner for German owners.

1876 May 1: Delivered. Regarded as a very handsome ship. Cost £94,291.
1887 Jan 20: Collided with and sank Chinese transport *Wan Nien Ching*. 100 drowned.
1890 Dec 12: Wrecked on Shagstone Reef off Plymouth en route Calcutta-London.

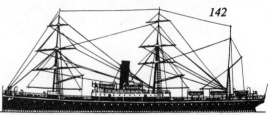

142

140

140 THIBET

Details as *Teheran* (*139*) except: *T*: 2,593 g, 1,671 n. Cost £200 less.

1874 Aug 29: Launched.
Oct 1: Registered.
1890 Altered to cargo ship for £8,500. Renamed *Cashmere*. Owned by Hajee Cassum Joosub.
1899 Broken up.

141 NEPAUL (II)

Bt 1876 Alex Stephen & Sons Ltd, Linthouse, Glasgow; *T*: 3,536 g, 1,988 n. **Dim** 375 ft 6 in (114.45 m) × 40 ft 1 in (12.22 m) × 32 ft 1 in (9.78 m). **Eng** Sgl scr,

142 KAISAR-I-HIND (I)

Bt 1878 Caird & Co, Greenock; *T*: 4,023 g, 2,401 n. **Dim** 400 ft 9 in (122.15 m) × 42 ft 3 in (12.88 m) × 31 ft 8 in (9.65 m). **Eng** Sgl scr, 2 cyls, compound inverted; *Cyls*: 60 in (152.4 cm) and 104 in (264.16 cm); *Stroke*: 60 in (152.4 cm); 3,808 IHP, 700 HP; *Stm P*: 70 lb; 15 kts; By builders. **H** Iron, 2 decks, 8 holds; *Pass*: 176 1st, 64 2nd.

1878 May 4: Launched.
July 24: Registered. P&O's largest, longest and fastest vessel to date. Cost £114,293. Placed on London-India route.
1880 The Indian voyages were extended to Australia during the spring and autumn peak travel periods.
1897 Broken up by Hajee Cassum Joosub at Bombay.

143 ANCONA

Bt 1879 Caird & Co, Greenock; *T*: 3,081 g,

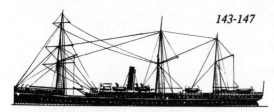

143-147

1,874 n. **Dim** 380 ft 9 in (116.05 m) × 38 ft
3 in (11.66 m) × 26 ft (7.92 m). **Eng** Sgl scr,
2 cyls, compound inverted; *Cyls*: 54 in
(137.16 cm) and 94 in (238.76 cm); *Stroke*:
60 in (152.4 cm); 3,202 IHP, 600 HP; *Stm
P*: 70 lb; 14 kts; By builders. **H** Iron, 3
decks, fcsle 48 ft (14.63 m), poop 112 ft
(34.14 m); *Pass*: 130 1st, 54 2nd.

Ancona, Verona (144), Rohilla (145),
Rosetta (146) *and* Ravenna (147)
*comprised a class of five sister ships built
for the Australian Mail service, setting out
from Southampton every two weeks.
Identification note: only* Ancona *of this
class had a well deck aft with a short poop.*

1879 July 25: Commissioned.
1882 Present at Alexandria during the
Arabi Pasha bombardment.

144 VERONA

Details as *Ancona* (*143*) except: *T*: 3,116 g,
1,862 n; **H** Poop 257 ft (78.33 m).

1879 Aug 30: Registered. Cost £86,304.
Nov 25: Maiden voyage London-Calcutta.
1899 Broken up in Holland.

145 ROHILLA

Details as *Ancona* (*143*) except: **Bt** 1880; *T*:
3,500 g, 2,252 n. **Dim** 386 ft 4 in (117.75 m)
× 40 ft 4 in (12.29 m) × 26 ft 9 in (8.15 m).
Eng 3,386 IHP; *Stm P*: 80 lb. **H** Poop
260 ft (79.25 m).

1880 June 2: Delivered. Worked up in
Mediterranean. Cost £86,937.
Dec 1: First voyage Southampton-
Colombo-Melbourne-Sydney. Later India
service.
1895 Rammed by SS *Hector* while
anchored at Shanghai.
1900 Sold to Toyo Kisen Kabusiki Kaisha,
Japan, for £10,791.
1905 July: Wrecked near Ujina.

146 ROSETTA

Bt 1880 Harland & Wolff, Belfast; *T*:

3,502 g, 2,136 n. **Dim** 390 ft 8 in (119.07 m)
× 40 ft 2 in (12.24 m) × 26 ft 8 in (8.13 m).
Eng Details as *Ancona* (*143*) except: 700
HP; By J. Howden & Co, Glasgow.

1880 P&O's first ship built in Ireland.
Sept 8: Maiden voyage from Southampton
to Australia.
1885 Converted to an armed merchant
cruiser at Hong Kong during diplomatic
tension with Russia.
1900 Sold to Nippon Yusen Kaisha, Japan.
Renamed *Rosetta Maru*.

147 RAVENNA

Bt 1880 William Denny & Bros,
Dumbarton; *T*: 3,372 g, 2,035 n. **Dim**
380 ft 2 in (115.88 m) × 40 ft 4 in (12.29 m)
× 25 ft 10 in (7.87 m). **Eng** Details as
Ancona (*143*) except: By builders. **H** Steel
(the company's first).

1880 Apr 24: Delivered. Cost £88,241.
Maiden voyage London-Bombay.
1898 Sold to G.P. Walford. Same name.
Price £11,679.
1892 Collided with and sank Japanese
cruiser *Chishima*.
1898 Found abandoned at sea by a United
States warship. Handed over to US
Government. Renamed *Scipio*.
1900 Sold Italy.
1902 Abandoned on fire at sea. Crew
landed at Lisbon.

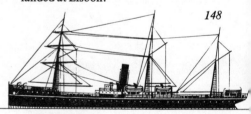

148

148 BRINDISI

Bt 1880 William Doxford, Pallion Yard,
Sunderland; *T*: 3,542 g, 2,143 n. **Dim** 360 ft
2 in (109.78 m) × 40 ft (12.19 m) × 31 ft
(9.45 m). **Eng** Sgl scr, 2 cyls, compound
inverted; *Cyls*: 48 in (121.92 cm) and 84 in
(213.36 cm); *Stroke*: 54 in (137.16 cm);
2,742 IHP, 550 HP; *Stm P*: 75 lb; 12 kts; By
builders. **H** Iron, 2 decks, 5 holds; *Pass*: 94
1st, 48 2nd.

1880 Laid down as *Maxima*. Purchased on
the stocks and renamed *Brindisi*. Cost
£80,989.

Dec 3: Commissioned.
1881 Jan: Placed on London-Australia service.
1889 Sold to Russian Government. Renamed *Dalny Vostock*.
1907 Broken up Japan.

149-150

149 **ROME**

Bt 1881 Caird & Co, Greenock; *T*: 5,013 g, 2,558 n. **Dim** 430 ft 1 in (131.09 m) × 44 ft 4 in (13.51 m) × 33 ft 6 in (10.21 m). **Eng** Sgl scr, 4 cyls, tandem compound inverted; *Cyls*: 2 × 44 in (111.76 cm) and 2 × 82 in (208.28 cm); *Stroke*: 66 in (167.64 cm); 4,677 IHP, 850 HP; 2 sgl ended boilers; *Stm P*: 90 lb; 15 kts. **H** Iron, fcsle 68 ft (20.73 cm), poop 49 ft (14.94 m), refrigerated space; *Pass*: 187 1st, 46 2nd.

Rome and Carthage (150) *were P&O's largest vessels to date and the first pair to exceed 5,000 gross tons. Designed to have steel hulls, they were built of iron because of steel shortages at the time.*

1881 Sept 12: Delivered. London-Bombay. First P&O ship to use Gravesend.
1892 Lengthened to 449 ft (136.86 m). *T*: 5,545 g. Triple expansion engine fitted. *Cyls*: 2 × 29 in (73.66 cm), 63½ in (161.29 cm) and 100 in (254 cm); *Stroke*: 60 in (152.4 cm); 6,000 IHP; 4 boilers; *Stm P*: 160 lb; By builders.
1904 May 10: Renamed *Vectis* (III) and used as a cruising ship.
1912 Oct: Sold to the French Government. Same name. Price £11,040.
1913 Broken up in Italy.

150 **CARTHAGE** (I)

Details as *Rome* (*149*) except: **Bt** 1881 Caird & Co, Greenock; *T*: 5,013 g. **H** Poop 40 ft (12.19 m).

1881 Oct 26: Maiden voyage to Australia.
1882 Hospital ship during Alexandria operations.
1892 Transferred to the Southampton-Bombay route but not re-engined.
1897 Took part in Queen Victoria's Diamond Jubilee fleet review at Spithead. *Carthage* was used as the Foreign dignitaries guest ship.
1903 Broken up at Bombay by Esafji Tajbhoy Borah. Price £10,749.

151 **CLYDE**

Bt 1881 William Denny & Bros, Dumbarton; *T*: 4,124 g, 2,442 n. **Dim** 390 ft (118.87 m) × 42 ft 1 in (12.83 m) × 32 ft 5 in (9.88 m). **Eng** Sgl scr, 2 cyls, compound inverted; *Cyls*: 58 in (147.32 cm) and 100 in (254 cm); *Stroke*: 63 in (160.02 cm); 5,240 IHP, 780 HP; *Stm P*: 88 lb; 15 kts; By builders. **H** Steel; *Coal*: 1,100 tons; *Cargo*: 3,500 tons; *Pass*: 120 1st, 48 2nd, 500 troops berthed between decks.

Clyde, Shannon (152), Thames (153), Ganges (154) *and* Sutlej (155) *were a group of five ships built for the Indian and Australian routes. Known as the River Class.*

1881 Sept 8: Registered. Cost £125,937.
1901 Sold to Shah SN Co (Esafji Tajbhoy Borah). Renamed *Shah Noor*. Mecca pilgrimage trade. Price £11,270.
1905 Broken up at Bombay.

151-155

152 **SHANNON**

Bt 1881 Harland & Wolff, Belfast; *T*: 4,189 g, 2,162 n. **Dim** 400 ft 1 in (121.95 m) × 42 ft 7 in (12.98 m) × 32 ft 8 in (9.95 m). **Eng** Sgl scr, 4 cyls, compound tandem; *Cyls*: 2 × 38 in (96.52 cm) and 2 × 76 in (193.04 cm); *Stroke*: 60 in (152.4 cm); 4,400 IHP, 750 HP; *Stm P*: 90 lb; 15 kts. **H** Iron.

No mainmast fitted. 10 ft (3.05 m) longer than her sister ships.

1881 P&O's last iron built ship. Dec 31: Registered. Cost £129,345.
1901 Sold to Esafji Tajbhoy Borah, Bombay, and broken up.

153 THAMES

Bt 1882 J. & G. Thomson, Clydebank, Glasgow; *T*: 4,101 g. **Dim** 390 ft 3 in (118.95 m) × 42 ft 2 in (12.85 m) × 32 ft 6 in (9.91 m). **Eng** Details as *Clyde* (*151*) except: 800 HP; *Stm P*: 85 lb; By builders. *Pass*: 120 1st, 46 2nd, plus troops between decks.

1882 The only J. & G. Thomson ship for P&O; as the John Brown shipyard the next P&O ship ordered from them was not until *Singapore* (*333*) of 1951, a gap of 69 years.
Feb 25: Registered.
Mar 29: Maiden voyage to Calcutta. Cost £119,363.
1886 Stranded whilst leaving Hong Kong.
1895 Inaugurated the Venice-Bombay service.
1898 Laid up at Victoria Dock, London.
1901 Sold by auction. Fetched £8,753. Broken up in France by Victor Amalbert, Marseilles.

154 GANGES (III)

Bt 1882 Barrow Shipbuilding Co, Barrow-in-Furness; *T*: 4,196 g. **Dim** Details as *Thames* (*153*). **Eng** Details as *Clyde* (*151*) except: 800 HP; By builders.

1882 Feb 8: Registered. Maiden voyage to Calcutta.
1896 Venice-Alexandria run.
1898 July 1: Caught fire and destroyed at Bombay whilst unladen. Broken up by Esafji Tajbjoy Borah.

155 SUTLEJ

Details as *Ganges* (*154*) except: *T*: 4,194 g, 2,157 n. Cost £117,026.

1882 Apr 4: Registered. Indian service, mainly Calcutta.
1899-1900 Troopship during Transvaal and Boer wars.
1900 Sold to Victor Amalbert, Marseilles, and broken up.

156 BALLAARAT

Bt 1882 Caird & Co, Greenock; *T*: 4,752 g, 2,667 n. **Dim** 420 ft 3 in (128.09 m) × 43 ft (13.11 m) × 34 ft 6 in (10.52 m). **Eng** Sgl scr, 2 cyls, compound inverted; *Cyls*: 56 in (142.24 cm) and 100 in (254 cm); *Stroke*: 66 in (167.64 cm); 4,312 IHP, 800 HP; 4 dbl ended boilers; *Stm P*: 90 lb; 15 kts; By builders. **H** Steel, 2 decks; *Pass*: 160 1st, 48 2nd. Patent iron beds substituted for bunks in first class accommodation.

Ballaarat, Parramatta (157), Valetta (158) *and* Massilia (159) *were four sisters all built for the Australian Mail service by Caird & Co, Greenock. Note spelling of* Ballaarat*'s name with four a's; all later* Ballarat*'s had only three.*

1882 Oct 25: Delivered.
Nov 9: Maiden voyage Southampton-Colombo-Melbourne-Sydney. Cost £133,608.
1893 Yards removed from the masts.
1900 Used for trooping to China at the time of the Boxer Rebellion.
1904 Sold to N. Pittaluga, Genoa, for £9,326. Renamed *Laarat* for delivery voyage and broken up in December.

157 PARRAMATTA

Details at *Ballaarat* (*156*) except: *T*: 4,759 g, 2,684 n. Cost £134,641.

1882 Dec 20: Registered. Australian service; available for armed cruiser duties.
1897 London-Calcutta.
1898 Bombay-Shanghai.
1903 Sold for £10,749 and broken up at Bombay by Moosa Hajee Cassum.

158 VALETTA (II)

Details as *Ballaarat* (*156*) except: **Bt** 1883; *T*: 4,911 g, 2,974 n. Cost £137,081.

1884 The first P&O ship with electric lighting installed (in first class saloons only).
Jan 3: Handed over.
1900 Munitions ship during Boxer Rebellion, China.
1903 Sold to Esafji Tajbhoy Borah's Shah SN Co and renamed *Alavia*. £12,199.
1906 Broken up.

159 MASSILIA (II)

Details as *Ballaarat* (*156*) except: **Bt** 1884; *T*: 4,908 g, 2,909 n. Cost £135,080.

156-159

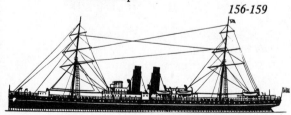

1884 Mar 21: Registered. P&O's first vessel to be fitted with hydraulic winches.
1885 During the diplomatic crisis with Russia *Massilia* was taken over at Sydney and converted into an armed merchant cruiser. *Rosetta* (*146*) was similarly converted at Hong Kong. Neither vessel saw Naval service.
1897 Calcutta service.
1903 Broken up at Genoa. Sold for £8,996.

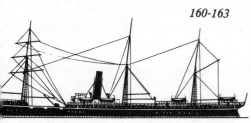

160-163

160 **TASMANIA**

Bt 1884 Caird & Co, Greenock; *T*: 4,488 g, 2,848 n. **Dim** 400 ft 4 in (122.02 m) × 45 ft 2 in (13.77 m) × 28 ft 9 in (8.76 m). **Eng** Sgl scr, 2 cyls, compound inverted; *Cyls*: 52 in (132.08 cm) and 96 in (243.84 cm); *Stroke*: 66 in (167.64 cm); 4,195 IHP, 624 NHP; *Stm P*: 90 lb; 14½ kts; By builders. **H** Steel, fcsle 79 ft (24.08 m), poop 260 ft (79.25 m); *Pass*: 107 1st, 44 2nd.

Tasmania, Chusan (161), Coromandel (162) and Bengal (163) *were four more Caird sisters, built at a cost of about £120,000 each for P&O's Indian services but capable of acting as relief steamers on the Australian route. They were also constructed so that they could serve as troopships or be speedily converted into armed merchant cruisers for use in the Pacific.*

1884 June 21: Delivered for Calcutta service.
1887 Apr 17: Wrecked on Monachi Rocks, Corsica. All passengers saved but 35 crew lost.

161 **CHUSAN** (II)

Details at *Tasmania* (*160*) except: *T*: 4,490 g, 2,852 n.

1884 Sept 30: Registered. Placed on Calcutta service.
1892 Rammed by a Swedish steamer as she left the Royal Albert Dock, London.

1905 Sold with *Coromandel* (*162*) and *Bengal* (*163*) to Esafji Tajbhoy Borah's Shah SN Co. Renamed *Shah Najaf*. Used on Mecca pilgrimage trade, Indian ports to Jeddah.
1908 Broken up in Bombay.

162 **COROMANDEL** (I)

Details as *Tasmania* (*160*) except: **Bt** 1885; *T*: 4,359 g, 2,783 n. **Eng** Sgl scr, tpl exp; *Cyls*: 35 in (88.9 cm), 56 in (142.24 cm) and 89 in (226.06 cm); *Stroke*: 66 in (167.64 cm); 4,200 IHP, 643 NHP; *Stm P*: 140 lb; 14½ kts.

1885 The first P&O vessel to be built with a triple expansion engine.
July 27: Maiden voyage Southampton-Colombo-Calcutta. Later Australia and Far East runs.
1895 Used as a troopship and then as a hospital ship during the Ashanti War. Collided with steamer *Cycle* off Eddystone Light.
1905 Sold to Shah SN Co with *Chusan* (*161*). Renamed *Shah Noor* (II) and used for the pilgrimage trade to Jeddah.
1908 Broken up at Bombay.

163 **BENGAL** (II)

Details as *Coromandel* (*162*) except: *T*: 4,344 g, 2,642 n.

1886 Jan 2: Maiden voyage London-Sydney.
1887 Took up normal station on the Calcutta route. Later Bombay-Shanghai.
1905 Sold to Shah SN Co and renamed *Shah Najam*. Employed on Indian pilgrimage trade. Price £12,505.
1908 Broken up at Bombay.

164 **GUTZLAFF**

Bt 1886 Boyd & Co, Shanghai; *T*: 136 g. **Dim** 105 ft 6 in (32.16 m) × 19 ft 5 in (5.92 m) × 9 ft 2 in (2.79 m). **Eng** Sgl scr, 2 cyls; *Cyls*: 20 in (50.8 cm) and 38 in (96.52 cm); *Stroke*: 42 in (106.68 cm); 65 NHP; By D. Rowan, Glasgow. **H** Iron, 1 deck.

1886 Sept 30: Registered. Tug at Shanghai. Cost £6,655.
1942 Taken over by Japanese. In 1946 was reported 'not yet repossessed, believed blown up.' Register closed 1949.

165-168

165 VICTORIA

Bt 1887 Caird & Co, Greenock; *T*: 6,522 g, 3,454 n. **Dim** 465 ft 9 in (141.96 m) × 52 ft (15.85 m) × 34 ft 1 in (10.39 m). **Eng** Sgl scr, tpl exp; *Cyls*: 40 in (101.6 cm), 63 in (160.02 cm) and 100 in (254 cm); *Stroke*: 72 in (182.88 cm); 7,000 IHP, 849 NHP; 4 dbl ended boilers; *Stm P*: 150 lb; 15 kts (the contract speed was 16½ kts); By builders. **H** Steel, 2 decks and spar deck, hydraulic deck cranes, fcsle 91 ft (27.74 m), poop 44 ft (13.41 m); *Coal*: 110 tons per day; *Cargo*: 4,000 tons; *Pass*: 250 1st, 160 2nd.

Victoria, Britannia (166), Oceana (167) and Arcadia (168) constituted P&O's famous Jubilee class, built at a cost approaching £200,000 each with names selected to commemorate Queen Victoria's Golden Jubilee. The sisters were also then the company's largest, longest, fastest and most expensive ships, a distinction which they held for only four years.

1887 Oct 1: Maiden voyage to Bombay. Cost £190,374.
Dec 31: First voyage London-Colombo-Melbourne-Sydney.
1894-5 Chartered to the British Government for six months with *Britannia* (*166*) for use as a troopship. Diverted to Cape to bring home participants in the Jameson Raid.
1909 Aug: Broken up at Genoa by Cerruti Bros. Price £11,520.

166 BRITANNIA

Details as *Victoria* (*165*) except: *T*: 6,525 g, 3,413 n. **Eng** High pressure cyl: 41 in (104.14 cm).

1887 Oct 18: Ran aground for 12 hours in the River Thames during delivery voyage. Undamaged. Cost £187,278.
Nov 5: Maiden voyage London-Colombo-Melbourne-Sydney.
1894 Ran aground, this time in the Suez Canal.

1894-5 Chartered for six months to British Government for trooping.
1907 Carried Prince Fushimi of Japan on state visit to Britain.
1909 Broken up at Genoa for Cerruti Bros.

167 OCEANA

Details as *Victoria* (*165*) except: **Bt** 1888 Harland & Wolff, Belfast; *T*: 6,610 g, 3,574 n. **Dim** 468 ft 4 in (142.75 m) × 52 ft 1 in (15.88 m) × 34 ft 7 in (10.54 m). **Eng** HP and MP cyls ½ in (1.27 cm) smaller. **H** Poop 47 ft (14.33 m).

1888 Mar: London-Colombo-Melbourne-Sydney service. *Oceana* remained on this route until 1905, when she was replaced by *Mooltan* (*235*).
1906 London-Bombay service.
1912 Mar 16: In collision with the German sailing barque *Pisagua*. Though critically damaged, *Oceana* stayed afloat for six hours before sinking off Beachy Head, two miles from the Sovereign lightship. 14 lives were lost when a lifeboat overturned whilst being launched. £750,000 of bullion was recovered from the wrecked ship, whose masts were visible above water. The court of enquiry placed blame for the accident with *Oceana*. The wreck was blown up.

168 ARCADIA (I)

Details as *Oceana* (*167*) except: *T*: 6,603 g, 3,574 n.

1888 May 9: Registered.
June 1: Maiden voyage London-Colombo-Melbourne-Sydney. Because of the loss of *Tasmania* (*160*), *Arcadia* spent much of her career on the Bombay route.
1911 Bombay-Far East service.
1914 Nov: Laid up at Southampton.
1915 Jan: Broken up at Bombay by Esafji Tajbhoy Borah. Price £13,000.

169 HEREWARD

Bt 1888 Cook, Welton & Gemmell, Hull; *T*: 108 g, 16 n. **Dim** 98 ft 2 in (29.92 m) × 20 ft

8 in (6.3 m) × 10 ft (3.05 m). **Eng** Sgl scr, tpl exp; *Cyls*; 12½ in (31.75 cm), 19½ in (49.53 cm) and 31½ in (80.01 cm); *Stroke*: 22½ in (57.15 cm); 60 HP; 1 sgl ended boiler; By C. D. Holmes & Co, Hull. **H** Steel, 1 deck.

1888 Sept 4: Registered. Tug at Bombay. Cost £5,264.
1915 Transferred to Mazagon Dock Co, a P&O subsidiary.
1918 Nov 28: Sold for breaking up.

170-171

170 ORIENTAL (II)

Bt 1888 Caird & Co, Greenock; *T*: 5,284 g, 3,085 n. **Dim** 410 ft 6 in (125.12 m) × 48 ft (14.63 m) × 34 ft 4 in (10.46 m). **Eng** Sgl scr, tpl exp; *Cyls*: 38 in (96.52 cm), 59½ in (151.13 cm) and 96 in (243.84 cm); *Stroke*: 66 in (167.64 cm); 6,000 IHP, 749 NHP; 3 dbl and 2 sgl ended boilers; *Stm P*: 150 lb; 15 kts; By builders. **H** Steel, 2 decks and spar deck; *Pass*: 170 1st, 96 2nd.

1888 Jan 21: Registered. Placed on Far East route. Cost £133,078.
1893 Delivered the mails to Hong Kong in a record 48 days.
1914 Collided with and sank Japanese steamer *Hokuse Maru*.
1915 Sold to the Hong Kong Steamship Co and renamed *Kong Kheng*. Price £39,096.
1922 Renamed *Song Hoi*.
1923 Refugee ship during Yokohama earthquake.
1924 Broken up at Hong Kong.

171 PENINSULAR

Details as *Oriental* (*170*) except: *T*: 5,294 g, 3,048 n.

Supposedly haunted by footsteps that walked round the hurricane deck, but an investigation by the Bombay Psychical Society discovered nothing.

1888 Oct 6: Launched.
1888 Nov 17: Registered. Cost £132,558. Placed on Bombay run but also served on

the Far East station.
1904 Aden-Bombay shuttle.
1909 Sold for £9,312 and broken up in Italy by Buzzo Bros, Genoa.

172-175

172 BOMBAY (III)

T: 3,319 g, 2,048 n. **Dim** 349 ft 5 in (106.5 m) × 42 ft 1 in (12.83 m) × 26 ft 6 in (8.08 cm). **Eng** Sgl scr, tpl exp; *Cyls*: 24 in (60.96 cm), 40 in (101.6 cm) and 62 in (157.48 cm); *Stroke*: 54 in (137.16 cm); 2,500 IHP, 282 NHP; 2 dbl ended boilers; *Stm P*: 160 lb; 12 kts; By Caird & Co, Greenock. **H** Steel, 2 decks, fcsle 49 ft (14.94 m), bridge 104 ft (31.7 m), poop 35 ft (10.67 m); *Pass*: 30.

1889 Jan 29: Launched.
Mar 12: Delivered. Cost £44,575.
1900 Mar: Caught fire in Royal Albert Dock.
1903 Sold to Messageries Maritimes for £13,500. Renamed *Danube* for Mediterranean service.
1920 Hit mine on Turkish run.
1924 Broken up.

173 HONG KONG

Details as *Bombay* (*172*) except: *T*: 3,174 g, 2,050 n. Cost £46,231.

1889 Apr 15: Launched.
May 10: Delivered. East India and China trades.
1890 Dec 1: Lost on Azalea Reef, Perim. All hands and most of the cargo saved. Captain Watkins.

174 SHANGHAI (II)

Details as *Bombay* (*172*) except: *T*: 3,323 g, 2,163 n. Cost £46,331.

1889 June 26: Registered.
1903 Sold to Messageries Maritimes for £13,500. Mediterranean services. Renamed *Crimée*.
1923 Scrapped.

175 CANTON (II)

Details as *Bombay* (*172*) except: *T*: 3,333 g, 2,164 n. Cost £46,146.

1889 Sept 26: Launched.
Oct 31: Registered. China trade.
1900 Transport during Boxer Rebellion.
1903 Oct 28: Sold to Messageries Maritimes for £13,162. Renamed *Bospheré*.
1922 Broken up in Italy.

176 CUMBALLA

Bt 1891 P&O, Bombay; *T*: 152 g, 113 n. **Dim** 98 ft (29.87 m) × 20 ft 7 in (6.27 m) × 7 ft 9 in (2.36 m). **Eng** Tw scr, compound; *Cyls*: 9 in (22.86 cm) and 16½ in (41.91 cm); *Stroke*: 14 in (35.56 cm); 50 NHP. **H** Steel.

1891 Dec 2: Built. Tender and water-boat at Bombay. Cost £5,630.
Broken up during the First World War.

177 ADEN (II)

Bt 1892 Sir Raylton Dixon & Co, Middlesbrough; *T*: 3,925 g, 2,517 n. **Dim** 366 ft (111.56 m) × 46 ft 1 in (14.05 m) × 27 ft 7 in (8.41 m). **Eng** Sgl scr, tpl exp; *Cyls*: 28 in (71.12 cm), 46 in (116.84 cm) and 77 in (195.58 cm); *Stroke*: 48 in (121.92 cm); 3,000 IHP; *Stm P*: 160 lb; 12 kts. **H** Steel; *Coal*: 470 tons; *Pass*: 36, plus troops carried between decks; *Crew*: 83.

1892 Jan 30: Entered service.
'Intermediate' type of vessel. Cost £66,744.
1897 Apr 23: Left Yokohama homeward bound with 34 passengers and 83 crew. Captain R. E. Hill.
June 9: Grounded and wrecked on Socotra Island in the Gulf of Aden. Only nine of the passengers survived. 78 lives lost. The survivors spent 18 days on the wreck before being rescued by SS *Mayo*.

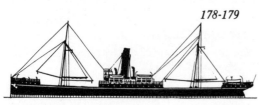

178-179

178 MALACCA (II)

Bt 1892 Naval Construction & Armaments

Co Ltd, Barrow-in-Furness; *T*: 4,045 g, 2,616 n. **Dim** 385 ft (117.35 m) × 45 ft 2 in (13.77 m) × 28 ft (8.53 m). **Eng** Sgl scr, tpl exp; *Cyls*: 28 in (71.12 cm), 46 in (116.84 cm) and 77 in (195.58 cm); *Stroke*: 54 in (137.16 cm); 3,000 IHP, 439 NHP; 2 dbl ended boilers; *Stm P*: 170 lb; 12 kts; By builders. **H** Steel, 2 decks, fcsle 58 ft (17.68 m), bridge 105 ft (32 m), poop 39 ft (11.89 m); *Pass*: 30 1st.

Malacca *and* Formosa (179) *were improved versions of the Jubilee Class of 1888 and the first P&O vessels to cost over £200,000.*

1892 Feb 15: Registered. Cost £70,750.
1904 Seized by Russian Volunteer Cruiser in Red Sea and taken to Suez. After a Government protest she was released but P&O received no compensation.
1909 Sold Forth Shipbreaking Co for £6,336.

179 FORMOSA (II)

Details as *Malacca* (*178*).

1892 Apr 7: Registered.
1909 Aug: Sold to Forth Shipbreaking Co for £6,336.

180 HIMALAYA (II)

Bt 1892 Caird & Co, Greenock; *T*: 6,898 g, 3,700 n. **Dim** 465 ft 7 in (141.91 m) × 52 ft 2 in (15.9 m) × 34 ft 7 in (10.54 m); *Dft*: 25 ft 11 in (7.9 m) (the maximum permitted for the Suez Canal). **Eng** Sgl scr, tpl exp; *Cyls*: 42 in (106.68 cm), 67 in (170.18 cm) and 108 in (274.32 cm); *Stroke*: 72 in (182.88 cm), 10,000 IHP, 1,356 NHP; 3 dbl and 3 sgl ended boilers; *Stm P*: 160 lb; 18 kts; By builders. **H** Steel, 2 decks and spar deck; *Pass*: 250 1st, 200 2nd; *Crew*: 320.

1892 June 3: Registered. P&O's largest and fastest ship with the largest low pressure cylinder in the fleet.
1893 Jan 6: First voyage London-Colombo-Melbourne-Sydney, a record.
1908 Indian service plus occasional runs to Far East.
1914 Aug: Commissioned at Penang as an armed merchant cruiser for Red Sea duties. Suez Canal guard ship.
1916 June: Purchased by British Admiralty, although manned by P&O personnel. Fitted with an aircraft deck and

180-181

a squadron of seaplanes. Based East
Africa.
1919 Re-purchased by P&O. Used as a
troopship.
1922 Broken up.

181 AUSTRALIA (II)

Details as *Himalaya* (*180*) except: *T*:
6,901 g, 3,590 n.

1892 Nov 25: Maiden voyage London-
Colombo-Melbourne-Sydney. Remained
on the Australian Mail service.
1904 June 20: Stranded at the entrance to
Port Philip Bay. Captain Cole. Later
caught fire, and was sold for £350 to a
Melbourne draper, who realised £180,000
for the wreck which remained on the shoal
for some years. Captain Cole was
exonerated from blame.

182 JAVA

Bt 1892 Caird & Co, Greenock; *T*: 4,093 g,
2,632 n. **Dim** 384 ft 7 in (117.22 m) × 45 ft
1 in (13.74 m) × 27 ft 10 in (8.48 m). **Eng**
Sgl scr, tpl exp; *Cyls*: 28 in (71.12 cm), 46 in
(116.84 cm) and 77 in (195.58 cm); *Stroke*:
54 in (137.16 cm); 3,000 IHP, 439 NHP; 2
dbl ended boilers; *Stm P*: 170 lb; 12 kts; By
builders. **H** Steel, fscle 59 ft (17.98 m),
bridge 104 ft (31.7 m), poop 38 ft (11.58 m);
Pass: 48 1st, 48 2nd.

*Java, Manila (183) and Japan (184) were
three intermediate vessels built by Caird &
Co. The short fcsle distinguishes them from
the Mazagon (186) class.*

1892 Sept 15: Registered. Cost £72,104.
Eastern services.
1900 Carried casualties home from Boxer
Rebellion.

1910 Sold Yokohama to Mr Hasada, for
£7,383. Renamed *Ume Maru*.
1926 Broken up, having passed through
many owners.

183 MANILA

Details as *Java* (*182*) except: *T*: 4,201 g,
2,711 n.

1892 Oct 28: Registered. Cost £72,295.
Bengal and Far East services.
1895 Transport for the Gold Coast
campaign. Also troopship and prison ship
during Transvaal War.
1904 Last P&O cargo sailing to Japan
before service suspended.
1910 June 20: Sold for breaking up for
£5,758 but was reprieved. Name changed to
Maria C. Four more owners before broken
up in 1925 as *Bracciano*.

184 JAPAN

Details as *Java* (*182*) except: **Bt** 1893; *T*:
4,319 g. **Dim** Length 397 ft 3 in (121.08 m).

1893 Sept 12: Registered. Cost £70,022.
Largely cargo services, had a history of
minor bangs and scrapes.
1910 Nov: Sold Kobe to Mr Kishimoto of
Osaka for £8,497. Renamed *Shimpo Maru*.
Sold Germany post-war, renamed *Walter
Holken*.
1924 Broken up.

185 GIUCOWAR

Bt 1893 P&O, Bombay; *T*: 249 builder's
measure. **Dim** 110 ft (33.53 m) × 22 ft
(6.71 m) × 8 ft (2.44 m). **Eng** Tw scr,
compound; 143 NHP; By builders. **H** Steel.
Tug at Bombay. Cost £5,697.

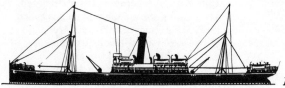

182-184

1915 Sold to Mazagon Dock Co (P&O subsidiary).

186-190

186 **MAZAGON**

Bt 1894 Alex Stephen & Sons Ltd, Linthouse, Glasgow; *T*: 4,997 g, 3,280 n. **Dim** 400 ft (121.92 m) × 48 ft (14.63 m) × 28 ft 9 in (8.76 m). **Eng** Sgl scr, tpl exp; *Cyls*: 27 in (68.58 cm), 45 in (114.3 cm) and 72 in (182.88 cm); *Stroke*: 48 in (121.92 cm); 3,500 IHP, 418 NHP; *Stm P*: 160 lb; 12 kts. **H** Steel, fcsle 42 ft (12.8 m), bridge 84 ft (25.6 m), poop 28 ft (8.53 m); *Pass*: 49 1st, 49 2nd.

1894 July 16: Registered. Cost £51,377. Short fcsle and short bridge deck. Calcutta-Colombo collier service.
1907 Sold to British India SN Co for £12,100. East Indian service.
1912 Resold to Japanese, renamed *Teikoku Maru*. Later French Naval auxiliary *Saint Nicholas*.
1922 Stranded. Salvaged but broken up.

187 **SUMATRA** (II)

Details as *Mazagon* (*186*) except: **Bt** 1895; *T*: 4,607 g, 2,976 n. **Dim** Beam 46 ft 7 in (14.2 m). **H** Fcsle 84 ft (25.6 m), bridge 140 ft (42.67 m).

1895 Aug 6: Registered. Cost £78,843. Intermediate services.
1914 Feb: Sold Bombay to Arab SS Co for £17,279.
1916 Sold to Portuguese, renamed *Mossamedes*.
1923 Wrecked, False Cape Frio.

188 **BORNEO**

Details as *Sumatra* (*187*) except: **Bt** 1895 Palmer Bros & Co, Jarrow, Hebburn-on-Tyne; *T*: 4,573 g, 2,944 n. **Dim** Length 401 ft 4 in (122.33 m).

1895 Aug 1: Registered. Cost £78,341.
1896 Transport service.
1914 Sold Kobe to Kishimoto KK, Osaka.

Fetched £12,716. Renamed *Harima Maru*.
1922 Sold to Spain and China Company, renamed *New China*.
1924 Sold to Mexican Government, renamed *Anahuac*.

189 **SUNDA** (II)

Details as *Borneo* (*188*) except: **Bt** 1895 Caird & Co, Greenock; *T*: 4,674 g, 2,987 n. **Eng** HP and MP cyl 1 in (2.54 cm) larger.

1895 Aug 19: Registered. Cost £77,566. Intended to be named *Madras* (III).
1914 Sold Kobe for £12,484 to Kishimoto KK, Osaka. Renamed *Hokokuo Maru*.
1915 Dec: Reported missing at sea.

190 **PALAWAN**

Details as *Sunda* (*189*) except: *T*: 4,686 g, 2,996 n.

1895 Oct 8: Registered. Cost £78,317. Usually on Calcutta intermediate service.
1914 Sold Bombay to Arab SS Co for £17,279. Renamed *Jeddah*.
1923 Bought by Bombay & Persia SS Co.
1924 Broken up in Italy.

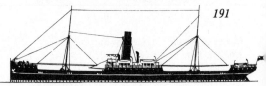

191

191 **CEYLON** (II)

Bt 1894 Sir Raylton Dixon & Co, Middlesbrough; *T*: 4,094 g, 2,637 n. **Dim** 375 ft (114.3 m) × 47 ft (14.33 m) × 28 ft (8.53 m). **Eng** Sgl scr, tpl exp; *Cyls*: 30 in (76.2 cm), 49 in (124.46 cm) and 77 in (195.58 cm); *Stroke*: 48 in (121.92 cm); 3,000 IHP, 470 NHP; *Stm P*: 160 lb; 12 kts. **H** Steel, fcsle 55 ft (16.76 m), bridge 110 ft (33.53 m), poop 48 ft (14.63 m); *Pass*: 20; *Crew*: 51.

1894 July 18: Entered service. Purchased for £62,341 after being on the stocks for a year.
1908 Passenger accommodation removed.
1913 Sold Kobe to Kishimoto KK, Osaka, for £15,314. Renamed *Yamato Maru*.
1916 Dec: Sold to French Government, renamed *Depute Pierre Goujon*.
1917 Sunk by submarine in the Bay of Biscay.

192

192 CALEDONIA

Bt 1894 Caird & Co, Greenock; *T*: 7,558 g,
3,529 n. **Dim** 486 ft (148.13 m) × 54 ft 2 in
(16.51 m) × 34 ft 6 in (10.52 m). **Eng** Sgl
scr, tpl exp, 5 cyls with 3 cranks in tandem;
Cyls: 2 × 33 in (83.82 cm), 69 in
(175.26 cm) and 2 × 84 in (213.36 cm);
Stroke: 72 in (182.88 cm); 11,000 IHP;
1,610 NHP; 3 dbl and 4 sgl ended boilers;
Stm P: 165 lb; 18 kts; By builders. **H** Steel,
fcsle 76 ft (23.16 m), bridge 255 ft
(77.72 m), poop 46 ft (14.02 m).

1894 July 18: Entered service with yellow
funnels and a white hull which was retained
for two years. Cost £233,729. P&O's largest
vessel to date.
1896 Reverted to P&O livery.
1903 First P&O ship to use Tilbury Dock.
1916 Dec: Mined off Marseilles but
reached port. Overhauled. Returned to
Bombay run.
1925 July 25: Sold, Bombay, to Goolam
Hossein Essaji and scrapped.

193 SIMLA (II)

Bt 1895 Caird & Co, Greenock; *T*: 5,884 g,
3,828 n. **Dim** 430 ft (131.06 m) × 49 ft 4 in
(15.04 m) × 29 ft 9 in (9.07 m). **Eng** Sgl scr,
tpl exp; *Cyls*: 31 in (78.74 cm), 50 in
(127 cm) and 82 in (208.28 cm); *Stroke*:
60 in (152.4 cm); 4,500 IHP, 662 NHP; 4 sgl
ended boilers; *Stm P*: 170 lb; 14 kts; By
builders. **H** Steel, fcsle 85 ft (25.91 m),
bridge 167 ft (50.9 m), poop 86 ft (26.21 m);
Pass: 90 1st, 62 2nd.

1894 Dec 11: Entered service. *Simla*,
Nubia (*194*) and *Malta* (*195*) were used as
troopships on many occasions. The

drawing illustrates *Simla* as *Troop
Transport No 2*.
1916 Apr 2: Torpedoed in the
Mediterranean 45 miles west of Malta.

194 NUBIA (II)

Details as *Simla* (*193*) except: *T*: 5,914 g,
3,824 n.

Was to have been called Singapore (*II*).

1895 Feb 5: Registered. Calcutta service.
1897 Cholera among Indian troops
aboard. Boer War transport and hospital
ship.
1915 June 20: Lost outside Colombo,
Ceylon, en route Bombay-Shanghai, while
waiting for the pilot.

195 MALTA (II)

Details as *Simla* (*193*) except: *T*: 6,064 g,
3,900 n. **Dim** Beam 50 ft 4 in (15.34 m).

1895 June 15: Registered. Initially placed
on Calcutta service.
1896 Troopship.
1900-2 Boer War transport.
1903 Placed on the Far East Mail route.
1908 Calcutta-Japan intermediate service.
1915 Jan 28: Shelled by German
submarine, which was driven off by
escorting destroyers.
1917 Requisitioned as a troopship.
1920 Demobilised. Laid up at Falmouth.
1922 June 30: Sold for breaking up in Italy
by Luigi Cehio.

196 HARLINGTON (I)

Bt 1895 J. P. Austin & Son, Wear Dock
Yard, Sunderland; *T*: 1,032 g, 627 n. **Dim**

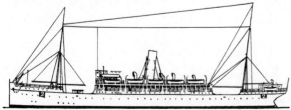

193-195

196

220 ft (67.06 m) × 31 ft 6 in (9.6 m) × 13 ft 7 in (4.14 m). **Eng** Sgl scr, tpl exp; *Cyls*: 17½ in (44.45 cm), 29 in (73.66 cm) and 47 in (119.38 cm); *Stroke*: 33 in (83.82 cm); 138 NHP; 1 sgl ended boiler; *Stm P*: 160 lb; 9 kts; By W. Allan & Co, Sunderland. **H** Steel, 1 deck, forward well deck and quarter deck aft.

1895 Built for the East Coast feeder service for J. & C. Harrison. Saved crew of pioneer turbine destroyer HMS *Cobra*, which had broken its back.
1896 Jan 23: Purchased for £14,272.
1914 Dec 2: Wrecked on West Sunk Sand, off Clacton, en route from the Tees to London. All saved.

197 INDIA (II)

Bt 1896 Caird & Co, Greenock; *T*: 7,911 g, 4,185 n. **Dim** 499 ft 10 in (152.35 m) × 54 ft 4 in (16.56 m) × 32 ft 10 in (10.01 m). **Eng** Sgl scr, tpl exp, 4 cyls; *Cyls*: 42½ in (107.95 cm), 68 in (172.72 cm) and 2 × 74½ in (189.23 cm); *Stroke*: 72 in (182.88 cm); 11,000 IHP; 3 sgl and 3 dbl ended boilers; *Stm P*: 170 lb; 16½ kts; By builders. **H** Steel, 5 decks, fcsle 78 ft (23.77 m), bridge 268 ft (81.69 m), poop 46 ft (14.02 m); *Pass*: 314 1st, 212 2nd, 2,500 troops; *Crew*: 400.

India, China (198), Egypt (199), Arabia (200) *and* Persia (201) *constituted a class of five vessels, four by Caird and one by Harland & Wolff, which all exceeded 7,900 grt and became P&O's largest ships to date. With a capacity for over 500 passengers and five decks they were an advance on their predecessors and cost nearly £240,000 each.*

1896 Sept 3: Registered. Placed on Indian service. Cost £234,597.

1898 Jan 28: First voyage to Melbourne and Sydney.
1914 Converted into an armed merchant cruiser.
1915 Aug 8: Torpedoed by *U-22* six miles off Bodo, Norway, whilst serving with the 10th Cruiser Squadron. *India* had halted to examine a suspected blockade runner. 160 lost. 141 survivors were picked up by SS *Gotaland* and taken into Narvik assisted by HM Armed Trawler *Saxon*.

198 CHINA (II)

Details as *India* (*197*) except: **Bt** Harland & Wolff, Belfast; *T*: 7,912 g, 4,165 n. **Dim** 500 ft 6 in (152.55 m) × 54 ft 2 in (16.51 m) × 33 ft 5 in (10.19 m). **Eng** By builders.

1896 Dec 18: Maiden voyage London-Suez-Colombo-Melbourne-Sydney.
1898 Grounded on Perim Island, Red Sea. *China* was underwater for three months before being salvaged and towed back to Britain where she had to be rebuilt.
1902 Broke Fremantle-Colombo record.
1914-18 Served as Naval hospital ship.
1916 June: Visited by King George V.
1928 June: Sold for £24,000 and broken up in Japan.

199 EGYPT

Details as *India* (*197*) except: **Bt** 1897; *T*: 7,912 g, 4,207 n.

1897 Aug 13: Registered. Indian and Australian services. Cost £239,492.
1910 Carried HRH the Princess Royal home from Egypt.
1915 Served as Hospital Ship No 52, principally in the Mediterranean.
1922 May 20: In dense fog off Ushant, France, *Egypt* sank in 20 minutes after a collision with the French ship *Seine*. 71 crew and 15 passengers were lost and gold bullion valued at £1,054,000 went down with the ship.
1930 The Italian salvage vessel *Artiglio* raised over half the lost bullion.

197-198

199-201

200 ARABIA

Details as *India* (*197*) except: **Bt** 1898; *T*: 7,930 g.

1897 Nov: Launched.
1898 Mar 12: Entered service as P&O's last single screw passenger liner for the Indian routes. Cost £250,000.
1905 Collided with and damaged steamer *Riverdale*, owned by J. Little & Co.
1912 *Arabia* was in collision with the British battleship HMS *Powerful*. Both ships were damaged.
1916 Nov 6: Torpedoed, en route from Australia, 112 miles south west of Cape Matapan by a German submarine. Although the ship sank in 20 minutes 721 persons were saved, of which 437 were passengers. 11 crew members were killed by the explosion. Also serious was the loss of the Australian mail. Following the sinking there was a sharp exchange of diplomatic notes between the USA and Germany.

201 PERSIA

Details as *India* (*197*) except: **Bt** 1900; *T*: 7,951 g, 4,198 n.

1900 Oct 10: Registered. P&O's largest vessel to date. Cost £260,920.
1904 Stopped by Russian warships in the Red Sea and searched. This was at the time of the Russo-Japanese war.
1912 *Persia* went ashore at Marseilles but on soft mud, and she came off undamaged.
1915 Dec 30: Torpedoed by *U-38* 70 miles south of Crete with the loss of 335 lives. Commander Valentiner of *U-38* was

branded as a war criminal. Following on from the loss, in May 1915, of Cunard's *Lusitania* the torpedoeing of *Persia* inflamed neutral opinion against Germany.

202 CANDIA (II)

Bt 1896 Caird & Co, Greenock; *T*: 6,482 g, 4,195 n. **Dim** 450 ft 7 in (137.34 m) × 52 ft 4 in (15.95 m) × 30 ft 7 in (9.32 m). **Eng** Tw scr, overlapping, 2 tpl exp; *Cyls*: 22½ in (57.15 cm), 36½ in (92.71 cm) and 60 in (152.4 cm); *Stroke*: 48 in (121.92 cm); 4,500 IHP, 679 NHP; 2 dbl ended boilers; *Stm P*: 170 lb; 12½ kts; By builders. **H** Steel, 2 decks, fcsle 59 ft (17.98 m), bridge 98 ft (29.87 m), poop 46 ft (14.02 m).

1896 Dec 9: Placed on Australian service. P&O's first true cargo vessel and first deep sea twin screw designed ship. *Candia* was also the largest steamer to be able to go up the Adelaide River. (Note: The P&O Mahmoudieh Canal tug *Atfeh* of 1842 (*18*) had twin screws.)
1902 Caught fire in the Suez Canal. The blaze was put out at Port Suez.
1909 Took out the first aeroplane, a Bleriot, to Australia.
1917 July 26: 3.58 am. Torpedoed, inbound for London with 9,000 tons of grain and food, off the Owers Lightship. One Lascar killed. All the remainder picked up in four lifeboats.

203 SOCOTRA (I)

Details as *Candia* (*202*) except: **Bt** 1897 Palmers & Co (ex-Palmer Bros), Jarrow,

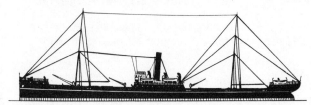

202-203

Hebburn-on-Tyne; *T*: 6,009 g, 3,896 n.
Eng By builders. **H** Fcsle 61 ft (18.59 m).

1897 Feb 11: Registered. Cost £80,549.
Maiden voyage to China.
1903 Collided with SS *Dallington* off
Belgian coast.
1915 Nov 26: Stranded by error on Paris-
Plage Le Touquet, France. Shortly
afterwards heavy weather broke her back.

204-206

204 TIENTSIN

Bt 1888 Palmer Bros, Jarrow, Hebburn-
on-Tyne; *T*: 3,950 g, 2,555 n. **Dim** 380 ft
(115.82 m) × 45 ft 4 in (13.82 m) × 27 ft
5 in (8.36 m). **Eng** Sgl scr, tpl exp; *Cyls*:
29 in (73.66 cm), 47 in (119.38 cm) and
76 in (193.04 cm); *Stroke*: 51 in
(129.54 cm); 3,000 IHP, 424 NHP; 2 dbl
ended boilers; *Stm P*: 150 lb; 14 kts; By
builders. **H** Steel, 2 decks; *Pass*: 70 1st, 46
2nd.

*The expansion of passenger traffic to the
Far East required not larger vessels but a
more frequent service. In order to step up
their sailings P&O purchased three Hall
Line sister ships,* Tientsin, Nankin (205)
and Pekin (206)*, and thereby were able to
provide fortnightly sailings in place of
monthly departures.*

1888 Built as *Branksome Hall* for Hall
Line.
1898 Dec: Purchased by P&O for £32,802.
Renamed *Tientsin*. Cargo routes east of
Suez.
1906 July: Sold Bombay Esafji Tajbhoy
Borah, for £7,435. Renamed *Shah Mazir*.
1909 Sold Hajaz SN Co, Bombay.
Renamed *Fakhri*.
1911 Wrecked Perim, no casualties.

205 NANKIN (I)

Details as *Tientsin* (*204*) except: *T*: 3,950 g,
2,557 n.

1888 Built as *Rufford Hall* for Hall Line.
1898 Dec 9: Purchased by P&O for
£33,523. Renamed *Nankin*. Hired as

transport for Transvaal War.
1904 Sold Kobe to M. Y. Kawasaki for
£20,996. Renamed *Motohira Maru No II*.
1907 Wrecked Soya Strait, broke up
during salvage.

206 PEKIN (III)

Details as *Tientsin* (*204*) except: **Bt** 1887;
T: 3,957 g, 2,523 n.

1887 Built as *Locksley Hall* for Hall Line.
1899 Jan: Purchased by P&O for £33,531.
Renamed *Pekin*. Boer War transport.
1906 Sold Bombay Esafji Tajbhoy Borah
for £7,446. Renamed *Shah Nawaz*.
1909 Resold, Hajaz SN Co, Bombay.
Renamed *Najmi*.
1911 Broken up at Bombay.

207-208

207 ISIS

Bt 1898 Caird & Co, Greenock; *T*: 1,728 g,
123 n. **Dim** 300 ft 2 in (91.49 m) × 37 ft
1 in (11.3 m) × 17 ft 6 in (5.33 m). **Eng** Tw
scr, 2 tpl exp, 4 cyls; *Cyls*: 24½ in
(62.23 cm), 39 in (99.06 cm) and 2 × 42 in
(106.68 cm); *Stroke*: 36 in (91.44 cm);
6,500 IHP, 755 NHP; 2 dbl and 2 sgl ended
boilers; *Stm P*: 160 lb; 19 kts; By builders.
H Steel; *Cargo*: 123 tons mail; *Pass*: 78 1st.

Isis *and* Osiris (208) *were sisters built for
the express service from Brindisi to Egypt.
Fast vessels known as the 'P&O
submarines' because they were reputed to
submerge at the beginning of each voyage
and only surface again when approaching
their destination!*

1898 June 8: Delivered at cost of £86,636
for the express service between Brindisi-
Alexandria-Port Said. Italian seamen and
firemen under British officers.
1914 Taken over as fleet messenger HMS
Isonzo.
1920 Sold to Bland Line. Renamed *Gibel
Sarsar*. Gibraltar-Morocco mail service.
1926 Broken up in Italy.

208 OSIRIS

Details as *Isis* (*207*) except: *T*: 1,738 g,

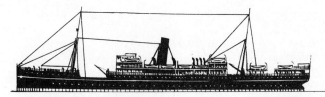

209-211

123 n. **Dim** 3 in (7.62 cm) longer.

1898 Built for the express service between Brindisi-Alexandria-Port Said. Cost £578 more than her sister.
1922 July 21: Sold for breaking up to J. Bagley & Co.

209 ASSAYE

Bt 1899 Caird & Co, Greenock; *T*: 7,376 g, 4,539 n. **Dim** 450 ft (137.16 m) × 54 ft 2 in (16.51 m) × 31 ft 7 in (9.63 m). **Eng** Tw scr, 2 tpl exp; *Cyls*: 28½ in (72.39 cm), 46 in (116.84 cm) and 76 in (193.04 cm); *Stroke*: 48 in (121.92 cm); 1,055 NHP; 3 dbl and 1 sgl ended boilers; By builders. **H** Steel, 3 decks, fcsle 94 ft (28.65 m), bridge 245 ft (74.68 m), poop 28 ft (8.53 m).

1899 Nov 28: Completed. Built for use as a troopship as and when required. Cost £160,860.
1914-18 Hospital ship.
1928 May 9: Sold for scrap. Broken up at Stavanger.

210 SOBRAON

Details as *Assaye (209)* except: **Bt** 1900; *T*: 7,382 g, 4,544 n.

1900 Mar 29: Delivered. Cost £160,515. Maiden voyage to Bombay.
1901 Apr 21: Lost on Tung Ying Island off Foochow at 3 am in dense fog. The ship was en route Shanghai to London on her third voyage.

211 PLASSY

Details as *Assaye (209)* except: *T*: 7,405 g, 4,412 n.

1900 Dec 28: Delivered. Cost £150,865.

Served almost exclusively on Government work.
1924 July 24: Sold for breaking up in Italy.

212 BANCA

Bt 1900 William Doxford, Pallion Yard, Sunderland; *T*: 5,995 g, 3,794 n. **Dim** 439 ft 9 in (134.04 m) × 51 ft 8 in (15.75 m) × 28 ft 10 in (8.79 m). **Eng** Sgl scr, tpl exp; *Cyls*: 27½ in (69.85 cm), 45½ in (115.57 cm) and 75 in (190.5 cm); *Stroke*: 54 in (137.16 cm); 3,500 IHP, 413 NHP; *Stm P*: 180 lb; 10 kts; By builders. **H** Steel, turret decker, 2 decks.

1900 Apr 20: P&O's only turret decked ship.
1923 Aug 9: Sold to Hinode KKK, Dairen. Renamed *Taiyu Maru*.
1930 Broken up.

213 SICILIA

Bt 1901 Barclay Curle, Glasgow; *T*: 6,696 g, 4,174 n. **Dim** 450 ft 4 in (137.26 m) × 52 ft 3 in (15.93 m) × 30 ft 4 in (9.24 m). **Eng** Tw scr, 2 tpl exp; *Cyls*: 22½ in (57.15 cm), 37½ in (95.25 cm) and 60 in (152.4 cm); *Stroke*: 48 in (121.92 cm); 4,500 IHP, 670 NHP; 2 dbl ended boilers; *Stm P*: 170 lb; 14 kts; By builders. **H** Steel, 3 decks, fcsle 90 ft (27.43 m), bridge 177 ft (53.95 m), poop 84 ft (25.6 m); *Pass*: 90 1st, 70 2nd.

Sicilia, Syria (214), Somali (215), Soudan (216) *and* Sardinia (217) *constituted a class of five 'S' class ships, which was followed by an almost identical group of eight Caird-built 'N' class vessels (218-225) which were delivered between 1901 and 1913. During the same twelve years P&O*

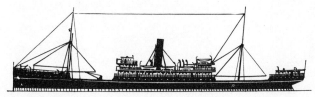

213-217

also added the five 'P' class ships (226-230), the ten 'M' class (231-240) and their four 'D' class ships (241-244). Despite this massive programme of new building the five Lund replacement 'B' class vessels (252-256) were all also in service by 1914. In all thirty-eight ships in six P&O designed classes for India, Australia and the Far East routes.

1901 Feb 5: Registered. Cost £152,088. Maiden voyage to Calcutta.
1926 Jan: Sold to Kishimoto KKK, Osaka, and broken up.

214 SYRIA (II)

Details as *Sicilia* (*213*) except: **Bt** Alex Stephen & Sons, Linthouse, Glasgow; *T*: 6,660 g, 4,191 n. **Eng** MP cyl 36 in (91.44 cm); By builders. **H** Fcsle 89 ft (27.13 m), bridge 176 ft (53.64 m), poop 83 ft (25.3 m).

1901 June 12: Registered. Used on charter for trooping.
1924 June 26: Sold for breaking up to John Cashmore partnership.

215 SOMALI (I)

Details as *Sicilia* (*213*) except: **Bt** Caird & Co, Greenock; *T*: 6,780 g, 4,225 n. **Eng** MP cyl 36 in (91.44 cm); 642 NHP; By builders. **H** Bridge 171 ft (52.12 m), poop 85 ft (25.9 m).

1901 June 17: Registered. Cost £153,242. Calcutta and China services.
1914-18 Hospital ship and trooping.
1923 Laid up at Truro.
Dec 10: Sold to Petersen & Albeck, Copenhagen.

216 SOUDAN (I)

Details as *Somali* (*215*) except: *T*: 6,680 g, 4,207 n. Cost £152,270.

1901 Constant charter for Indian trooping.
1914-18 Hospital ship.

1925 Dec: Sold to Kishimoto KKK, Osaka.
1926 Broken up.

217 SARDINIA

Details as *Sicilia* (*213*) except: **Bt** 1902; *T*: 6,574 g, 4,126 n. **H** Bridge 174 ft (53.04 m). Cost £130,917.

1902 Maiden voyage South African trooping.
1919 Repatriated Australian troops.
1925 July 23: Sold to Kishimoto KKK, Osaka, for £15,000. Scrapped.

218 NILE

Bt 1906 Caird & Co, Greenock; *T*: 6,694 g, 4,179 n. **Dim** 449 ft 9 in (137.08 m) × 52 ft 2 in (15.9 m) × 30 ft 7 in (9.32 m). **Eng** Tw scr, 2 quad exp, 8 cyls; *Cyls*: 19 in (48.26 cm), 27 in (68.58 cm), 38¼ in (97.16 cm) and 54 in (137.16 cm); *Stroke*: 48 in (121.92 cm); 4,500 IHP, 707 NHP; *Stm P*: 215 lb; 14 kts. **H** Steel, 2 decks, fcsle 85 ft (25.91 cm), bridge 149 ft (45.42 m), poop 78 ft (23.77 m); *Pass*: 54 1st, 40 2nd.

1906 June 27: Registered. Cost £105,057.
1909 Rammed by cable steamer *Teleconia* while at anchor below Gravesend.
1915 Jan 11: Struck Hojiro Rock in the Inland Sea of Japan and became a total loss. Captain Powell.

219 NAMUR

Details as *Nile* (*218*).

1906 Sept 3: Registered. Cost £104,871. Japanese service.
1917 Oct 29: Torpedoed when homeward bound in convoy in the Mediterranean, 55 miles east of Gibraltar. Sank in 40 minutes. One life lost.

220 NYANZA (II)

Details as *Nile* (*218*) except: **Bt** 1907; *T*: 6,695 g, 4,180 n. **Eng** 675 NHP.

1907 Jan 31: Registered. Cost £104,680.

218-225

Japanese service.
1916 Beat off submarine attack with gunfire.
1917 Dec: Torpedoed in Channel, but reached port.
1918 Feb: Torpedoed. Beached at Falmouth with loss of four lives. Returned to Indian and Eastern service after war.
1927 Sept 16: Sold for breaking up in Japan.

221 NORE

Details as *Nile* (*218*) except: **Bt** 1907; *T*: 6,696 g, 4,180 n. **Eng** 625 NHP.

1907 Jan 18: Registered.
1925 Nov 23: Sold to Thos. W. Ward Ltd, Sheffield, for £14,400.

222 NANKIN (II)

Details as *Nile* (*218*) except: **Bt** 1912; *T*: 6,846 g, 4,251 n.

1912 July 2: Entered service. Cost £115,127, a rise of over 10% compared with earlier ships in the class.
1917 Missed by submarine torpedo.
1919 Caught fire while at Devonport with ammunition cargo.
1932 Sept 14: Sold to Eastern & Australian SS Co.
1942 May 10: Captured by German raider No 10 *Thor* in the South Indian Ocean 1,000 miles from Australia. Taken to Yokohama and became German supply ship *Leuthen*.
Nov 20: Destroyed at Yokohama together with *Thor* and the tanker *Uckermark* by fire and explosion.

223 NOVARA

Details as *Nile* (*218*) except: **Bt** 1912; *T*: 6,875 g, 4,250 n.

1912 July 27: Launched. Cost £115,056.
Sept 11: Entered service.
Oct 10: Maiden voyage.
1914 Transport at beginning of war.
1918 Transatlantic service.
1932 June 21: Sold for breaking up.

224 NAGOYA

Details as *Nile* (*218*) except: **Bt** 1913; *T*: 6,874 g, 4,250 n.

1913 Apr 19: Entered service. Cost £120,741. Far Eastern service.

1918 Hospital ship, North Russia, until endangered by advancing Bolsheviks.
1932 July 11: Sold for breaking up, Amakasu Gomei Kaisha, Yokohama. £7,250.

225 NELLORE

Details as *Nile* (*218*) except: **Bt** 1913; *T*: 6,856 g, 4,250 n. Thinner funnel.

1913 May 5: Launched.
June 25: Entered service. Cost £120,433.
1916 Caught fire at Malta. Scuttled and beached.
1929 Sold to Eastern & Australian SS Co.
1944 June 29: Torpedoed in the Indian Ocean en route Bombay-Australia. 47 survivors began a 28-day, 2,500 mile open boat voyage to Madagascar; only nine survived.

226 PALERMO

Bt 1903 Barclay Curle, Glasgow; *T*: 7,597 g, 4,909 n. **Dim** 479 ft 6 in (146.15 m) × 57 ft 2 in (17.42 m) × 32 ft 6 in (9.91 m). **Eng** Tw scr, 2 tpl exp; *Cyls*: 22½ in (57.15 cm), 37 in (93.98 cm) and 60½ in (153.67 cm); *Stroke*: 48 in (121.92 cm); 5,000 IHP, 506 NHP; *Stm P*: 185 lb; 14 kts; By builders. **H** Steel, 2 decks, fcsle 54 ft (16.46 m), bridge 98 ft (29.87 m), poop 43 ft (13.11 m).

The 'P' class ships (226-230) were similar to the 'S' class in profile but had an open promenade in the after half of the bridge deck.

1903 June 25: Delivered for Indian and Far East services.
1915-17 Australian transport.
1924 Oct 22: Sold for breaking up to Societa Italiana Produtti Metallice.

227 PERA (III)

Details as *Palermo* (*226*) except: **Bt** Workman Clark & Co, Belfast; *T*: 7,635 g, 4,916 n. **Eng** *Cyls*: MP 36½ in (92.71 cm), LP 61 in (154.94 cm); 516 NHP; By builders. **H** Fcsle 52 ft (15.85 m), poop 44 ft (13.41 m).

1903 July 8: Delivered for Indian and Far East services.
1917 Oct 19: Torpedoed in the Mediterranean 60 miles off Ras el Tin en

route Liverpool to Calcutta. *Pera* was the left hand vessel in a convoy row of ten abreast. The crew were rescued by HMS *Clematis* but one life was lost.

228 **PALMA**

Details as *Pera* (*227*) except: *T*: 7,632 g, 4,913 n. **H** Poop 45 ft (13.72 m).

1903 Oct 7: Registered. Cost £107,110.
1920 Towed the disabled Australian Government steamer *Australmead* 1,200 miles to Mauritius.
1924 Nov 19: Sold for breaking up to Attilio Ardito Genoa.

229 **POONA**

Details as *Palermo* (*226*) except: **Bt** 1905 Barclay Curle, Glasgow; *T*: 7,625 g, 4,878 n. **H** Fcsle 53 ft (16.15 m).

1905 Jan 30: Registered.
1924 Oct 8: Sold to Italian breakers.

230 **PESHAWUR** (II)

Details as *Palermo* (*226*) except: **Bt** 1905; *T*: 7,634 g, 4,885 n. **Eng** 550 NHP. **H** Fcsle 53 ft (16.15 m).

1905 Apr 30: Entered service on the Far East and Australian route.
1910 Transferred to the Branch Line service with Lund's Blue Anchor vessels. Released *Narrung* (*249*) and *Wakool* (*250*), and they were sold in 1912.
1916 Damaged by drifting steamer at Newport.
1917 Oct 9: As HM Transport E.8210 *Peshawur* was torpedoed twice one mile off the South Rock Lighthouse, Northern Ireland, inbound from Sydney, Nova Scotia. She had safely crossed the Atlantic and was sunk after the convoy had dispersed. 13 out of the 125 aboard were lost.

231 **MOLDAVIA** (I)

Bt 1903 Caird & Co, Greenock; *T*: 9,505 g,

4,928 n. **Dim** 545 ft (166.12 m) oa, 520 ft 10 in (158.75 m) × 58 ft 4 in (17.78 m) × 33 ft 3 in (10.13 m). **Eng** Tw scr, overlapping, 2 tpl exp; *Cyls*: 33 in (83.82 cm), 52½ in (133.35 cm) and 84 in (213.36 cm); *Stroke*: 54 in (137.16 cm); 12,000 IHP, 1,588 NHP; 3 dbl and 4 sgl ended boilers; *Stm P*: 185 lb; 17 kts; By builders; 90 rpm; Propeller diam 18 ft (5.49 m), pitch 23 ft (7.01 m). **H** Steel, 3 decks, 6 holds, 10 hydraulic cranes, fcsle 93 ft (28.35 m), bridge 263 ft (80.16 m), poop 46 ft (14.02 m); *Coal*: 122 tons per day; *Cargo*: 90,000 cu ft refrig, 19,000 tons; *Pass*: 348 1st, 166 2nd; *Crew*: 370.

The celebrated 'M' class of ten ships (231-240) were strange sisters because they increased in size and sophistication progressively between Moldavia, *which began the series at 9,505 g, and* Medina, *which ended it at 12,358 g.*

1903 Built for the Australian route, but *Moldavia*'s maiden voyage was a shake-down run to Bombay. Cost £336,178.
Dec 11: First sailing London-Colombo-Melbourne-Sydney.
1907 Ran aground on the Goodwin Sands, but floated off safely before being held in the mud.
1911 Auckland added to the Sydney service.
1915 Commissioned by the British Admiralty and converted into an armed merchant cruiser.
1918 May 23: Torpedoed in the English Channel off Beachy Head whilst carrying American troops. *Moldavia* continued to steam for 15 minutes but then began to sink. 56 died in the explosion but all the remainder were taken off by the escorting destroyers.

232 **MONGOLIA** (II)

Details as *Moldavia* (*231*) except: *T*:

231-232,235

233-234,236-240

9,505 g, 4,936 n.

1903 Oct 16: Completed for the Australian route. Cost £336,024.

1904 Stopped by Russian cruisers in the Red Sea and searched. *Persia* (*201*) was also stopped.

1908 Severely damaged by fire.

1914 Remained on P&O passenger service to Australia.

1917 June 28: Sunk 58 miles off Bombay by a mine laid by the German raider *Wolf*. Although *Mongolia* sank in 13 minutes all the lifeboats were launched and reached the shore. 23 lives were lost.

233 MARMORA

Bt 1903 Harland & Wolff, Belfast; *T*: 10,509 g, 5,239 n. **Dim** 530 ft 5 in (161.67 m) × 60 ft 4 in (18.39 m) × 25 ft 6 in (7.77 m). **Eng** Tw scr, 2 quad exp; *Cyls*: 29 in (73.66 cm), 42 in (106.68 cm), 60 in (152.4 cm) and 85 in (215.9 cm); *Stroke*: 54 in (137.16 cm); 13,000 IHP, 1,799 NHP; 5 dbl and 2 sgl ended boilers; *Stm P*: 185 lb; 15 kts; By builders. **H** Steel, 3 decks, fcsle 88 ft (26.82 m), bridge 278 ft (84.73 m), poop 105 ft (32 m).

1903 Nov 13: Delivered for Australian service. Cost £344,084.

1914 Commissioned as an armed merchant cruiser. 10th Cruiser Squadron, Cape Verde Division.

1916 Nov: Sold to the British Admiralty but re-purchased in 1917.

1918 July 23: Torpedoed and sunk off the south coast of Ireland with the loss of ten crew.

234 MACEDONIA

Details as *Marmora* (*233*) except: **Bt** 1904; *T*: 10,512 g, 5,244 n. **H** 2 decks and spar deck; *Pass*: 377 1st, 187 2nd.

1904 Feb 12: Maiden voyage Tilbury (London)-Bombay. Cost £344,296.
April: Placed on the Australian run.

1907 Placed on the experimental

China-London route.

1914 Aug: Converted in nine days into an armed merchant cruiser with 8 × 4.7 in (12.06 cm) guns.
Dec: *Macedonia* and HMS *Bristol* were support ships at the Battle of the Falkland Islands and between them they sank Admiral Von Spee's supply ships *Baden* and *Santa Isabel*.

1916 Purchased for four years by the Admiralty.

1921 Refitted and placed on the Far Eastern run.

1931 June: Broken up in Japan.

235 MOOLTAN (II)

Details as *Moldavia* (*231*) except: **Bt** 1905; *T*: 9,621 g, 4,828 n. *Cyls*: 30 in (76.2 cm), 43 in (109.22 cm), 61 in (154.94 cm) and 87 in (220.98 cm). **H** Fcsle 94 ft (28.65 m), bridge 268 ft (81.69 m), poop 86 ft (26.21 m).

Identification note: Mooltan *had no ports forward on bridge deck.*

1905 Oct 4: Registered. Made her maiden voyage to Bombay.

1906 Replaced *Oceana* (*167*) on the Australian route.

1908 Carried the Empress Eugenie to Ceylon and back.

1911 P&O guest ship at the Spithead Coronation Naval Review of King George V.

1917 July 26: 7.15 am. Torpedoed and sunk off the coast of Sardinia en route for Marseilles. *Mooltan* was in convoy with *Lotus* of Messageries Maritimes and escorted by the Japanese destroyers *Ume* and *Kusonoki*. Although all 554 aboard, and her mail, were saved the ship had to be abandoned to protect *Lotus* from the prowling submarine.

236 MOREA

Bt 1908 Barclay Curle, Glasgow: *T*: 10,895 g, 5,965 n. **Dim** 562 ft (171.3 m) oa,

540 ft (164.59 m) × 61 ft 2 in (18.64 m) ×
24 ft 7 in (7.49 m). **Eng** Tw scr, 2 quad exp;
Cyls: 30½ in (77.47 cm), 44 in (111.76 cm),
61 in (154.94 cm) and 87 in (220.98 cm);
Stroke: 54 in (137.16 cm); 13,000 IHP,
1,842 NHP; 4 sgl and 4 dbl ended boilers;
Stm P: 215 lb; By builders. **H** Steel, 2
decks, fcsle 92 ft (28.04 m), bridge 277 ft
(84.43 m), poop 108 ft (32.92 m); *Pass*: 407
1st, 200 2nd.

1908 Dec 4: Maiden voyage
Tilbury-Colombo-Melbourne.
1915 Converted into a hospital ship.
1916 May: Transport for part of the
Australian Expeditionary Force.
1918 Apr: Converted into an armed
merchant cruiser. Served as HMS *Morea*
with 7 × 6 in (15.24 cm) guns.
1919 Oct: Returned to Australian route
and later served on the Far East service.
1930 June: Arrived in Japan for breaking
up.

237 **MALWA** (II)

Details as *Morea* (*236*) except: **Bt** 1908
Caird & Co, Greenock; *T*: 10,883 g,
5,900 n.

1908 Oct 10: Launched.
1909 Jan 29: Maiden voyage Tilbury-
Colombo-Melbourne-Sydney.
1910 Collided with *Nairn* (J. B. Murray &
Co) off Colombo.
1917 Requisitioned for use as a troopship.
1920 Sept 24: Resumed service on the
Australian route.
1932 Dec 16: Sold and broken up in Japan.

238 **MANTUA** (I)

Details as *Morea* (*236*) except: **Bt** 1909
Caird & Co, Greenock; *T*: 10,946 g,
5,980 n. **H** Fcsle 91 ft (27.74 m), bridge 272
ft (82.91 m), poop 107 ft (32.61 m).

1909 June 4: Maiden voyage to Australia.
Cost £308,053.
1913-14 Cruise ship.
1914 Aug 2: Because of the imminence of
war *Mantua* was hurriedly recalled from a
Baltic cruise. On arrival back in Britain she
was converted into an armed merchant
cruiser in only nine days and armed with 8
× 4.7 in (11.94 cm) guns.
1915 Used as a troopship.
1920 Refitted by Vickers Armstrong and

returned to the Australian service with a
call at Bombay.
1935 May: Sold for scrapping for £32,000
and broken up at Shanghai; she was the last
survivor of the famous 'M' class.

239 **MALOJA** (I)

Details as *Marmora* (*233*) except: **Bt** 1911;
T: 12,431 g, 6,078 n. **Dim** 550 ft 5 in
(167.77 m) × 62 ft 10 in (19.15 m) × 34 ft
5 in (10.49 m). *Pass*: 450 1st, 220 2nd.

1911 *Maloja*'s maiden voyage was a cruise
to the Western Isles. Then she joined
Medina (*240*) to carry guests to Bombay for
the Delhi Durbar. P&O's largest vessel to
date.
1912 Feb 9: Placed on the Australian
service via Colombo.
1916 Feb 27: *Maloja* left Tilbury on Feb 26,
with 121 passengers and a crew of 121.
Next day she struck a mine off Dover. The
engines were put astern to take way off the
ship but could not then be stopped as a 75°
list developed, and *Maloja* went down still
moving astern. 122 lives were lost. The ship
which stood by, the Canadian *Empress of
Fort William*, was also mined. The wreck
of *Maloja* was blown up in 1964.

240 **MEDINA**

Details as *Morea* (*236*) except: **Bt** 1911
Caird & Co, Greenock; *T*: 12,358 g,
6,879 n. Cost £332,377.

1911 Prior to entering service *Medina* was
used as the Royal Yacht for King George
V's journey to India. To carry the Royal
standard a third mast was borrowed from
Nankin (*205*) and installed as a mainmast.
For the voyage out and home the ship
served as HMS *Medina*.
1912 Feb 9: Returned to P&O service.
June 28: First voyage to Australia.
1917 Apr 28: Shortly after sailing from
Plymouth the vessel was torpedoed at 4 pm
off Start Point. Six crew were killed. She
sank in three and a half hours.

241 **DELTA** (IV)

Bt 1905 Workman Clark & Co, Belfast; *T*:
8,053 g, 4,780 n. **Dim** 470 ft 2 in (143.31 m)
× 56 ft 5 in (17.2 m) × 31 ft 6 in (9.6 m).
Eng Tw scr, 2 quad exp; *Cyls*: 25½ in
(64.77 cm), 36½ in (92.71 cm), 52 in
(132.08 cm) and 74 in (187.96 cm); *Stroke*:

241-244

51 in (129.54 cm); 8,000 IHP, 1,251 NHP; 2 dbl and 4 sgl ended boilers; *Stm P*: 215 lb; 15½ kts; By builders. **H** Steel, 3 decks, fcsle 103 ft (31.39 m), bridge 182 ft (55.47 m), poop 96 ft (29.26 m); *Pass*: 160 1st, 80 2nd.

1905 Sept: Registered. Cost £159,783. Far Eastern service.
1914 Naval hospital ship at Tsingtau.
1919 Repatriated Australian troops before refitting and returning to Far East service.
1929 Aug 28: Sold to Japanese breakers.

242 DONGOLA (I)

Details as *Delta* (*241*) except: **Bt** 1905 Barclay Curle, Whiteinch, Glasgow; *T*: 8,038 g, 4,723 n. **Dim** Length 470 ft (143.25 m). **H** Fcsle 102 ft (31.09 m), poop 95 ft (28.95 m).

1905 Nov 10: Registered. Used for India trooping. Cost £160,167.
1907 Made a record run Southampton-Bombay in 18 days 7 hours.
1911 Attended the Coronation Naval Review.
1915 Used as hospital ship in the Dardanelles.
1920 Had to be beached in River Thames after colliding with *Wimbledon*.
1922 Collided with *Kumano Maru*, which was found to blame.
1923 Undertook relief work after the Yokohama earthquake.
1926 June 28: Sold for £16,000 and broken up.

243 DELHI (III)

Details as *Delta* (*241*) except: **Bt** 1905 Caird & Co, Greenock; *T*: 8,090 g, 4,784 n. **Dim** Length 470 ft (143.26 m). **Eng** 1,257 NHP.

1905 Nov 23: Registered.
1911 Dec 13: Lost. Went ashore in a gale off Cape Spartel, Tangiers. The 85 passengers included the Princess Royal and her family. Three crewmen were lost.

244 DEVANHA (I)

Details as *Delhi* (*243*) except: **Bt** 1906; *T*: 8,092 g, 4,785 n. **Dim** Length 470 ft (143.26 m).

1906 Jan 31: Registered. Placed on the intermediate service to India and the Far East.
1915 Landed the 12th Australian Battalion at Anzac Beach, Gallipoli. Remained there as a hospital ship in the company of her sister *Dongola* (*242*). *Devanha* was the last vessel to leave the beach area.
1916 Apr 5: Picked up the survivors of British India's torpedoed *Chantala* and landed them at Malta.
1919 Returned to the Far East run with occasional Australian voyage.
1928 Mar 21: Sold for £21,000 and broken up in Japan.

245 SALSETTE (II)

Bt 1908 Caird & Co, Greenock; *T*: 5,842 g, 2,392 n. **Dim** 440 ft (134.11 m) × 53 ft 2 in (16.21 m) × 28 ft (8.53 m). **Eng** Tw scr, 2 quad exp; *Cyls*: 28 in (71.12 cm), 40 in (101.6 cm), 57 in (144.78 cm) and 82 in (208.28 cm); *Stroke*: 48 in (121.92 cm); 10,000 IHP, 1,535 NHP; *Stm P*: 215 lb; 20 kts; By builders. **H** Steel; Carried practically no cargo; *Pass*: 100 1st, 120 2nd.

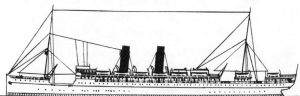

245

1908 June 22: Delivered with white hull and yellow funnels. *Salsette* was built for the Aden-Bombay express service connecting with the weekly Australian steamer. She was P&O's fastest ship and had a reputation for being a heavy roller. When travelling at full speed *Salsette* was also a wet ship.
1916-17 Served on the London (Tilbury)-Bombay-Colombo-Melbourne-Sydney route.
1917 July 20: Torpedoed in the English Channel close to Portland Bill and sank in 50 minutes. 15 were killed by the explosion. The remaining passengers and crew were rescued and landed at Weymouth.

 246

246 DEWAN

Bt 1909 J. P. Rennoldson & Sons, South Shields; *T*: 282 g, 6 n. **Dim** 120 ft (36.57 m) × 26 ft 2 in (7.98 m) × 11 ft 10 in (3.61 m). **Eng** Tw scr, 2 tpl exp; *Cyls*: 13½ in (34.29 cm), 22 in (55.88 cm) and 36 in (91.44 cm); *Stroke*: 27 in (68.58 cm); 183 NHP; *Stm P*: 170 lb; 8 kts. **H** Steel, 1 deck.

1909 Dec 9: Tug. Purchased on the stocks for use at Bombay.
1915 Transferred to P&O subsidiary Mazagon Dock Co. Broken up about 1945.

247 COMMONWEALTH

Bt 1902 Barclay Curle, Whiteinch, Glasgow; *T*: 6,616 g, 4,172 n. **Dim** 450 ft 2 in (137.21 m) × 52 ft 2 in (15.9 m) × 30 ft 7 in (9.32 m). **Eng** Tw scr, 2 tpl exp; *Cyls*: 24 in (60.96 cm), 40 in (101.6 cm) and 64 in (162.56 cm); *Stroke*: 48 in (121.92 cm); 4,000 IHP, 843 NHP; *Stm P*: 180 lb; 13½ kts. **H** Steel, 2 decks, fcsle 90 ft (27.43 m), bridge 164 ft (49.99 m), poop 70 ft (21.34 m); *Pass*: 75 1st, 300 3rd.

1902 Built for Lund's Blue Anchor Line, for the Australian service via Capetown.
1910 Apr 6: Acquired with the Blue Anchor Line fleet of five vessels. Her passenger accommodation was modified to 450 3rd class only.
Sept 15: Inaugurated P&O's new service to Australia via the Cape of Good Hope route. The traffic was mainly emigrant. P&O called this the 'Branch Service'.
1923 Broken up at Spezia by Stabilimento Metallurgico Ligure Societa.

248 GEELONG (II)

Bt 1904 Barclay Curle, Whiteinch, Glasgow; *T*: 7,954 g, 5,134 n. **Dim** 450 ft 2 in (137.21 m) × 54 ft 6 in (16.61 m) × 35 ft 7 in (10.85 m). **Eng** Tw scr, 2 tpl exp; *Cyls*: 23 in (58.42 cm), 40 in (101.6 cm) and 65 in (165.1 cm); *Stroke*: 48 in (121.92 cm); 4,150 IHP, 803 NHP; 2 dbl and 2 sgl ended boilers; *Stm P*: 200 lb; 13½ kts; By builders. **H** Steel, 1 deck, fcsle 92 ft (28.04 m), bridge 168 ft (51.21 m), poop 88 ft (26.82 m); *Pass*: 90 1st, 450 3rd.

1904 Entered Blue Anchor service as *Australia*, but because of confusion with P&O's ship of the same name (*181*) she was renamed *Geelong*.
1910 May 10: Entered P&O service. Her passenger accommodation was changed to 700 3rd class for the Australian Branch

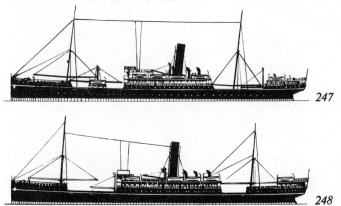

247

248

249-251

Service via the Cape.
1915 Used as an Australian Expeditionary
Force transport.
1916 Jan 1: Collided in convoy with the
steamer *Bonvilston* (2,866 g), owned by E.
Thomas Radcliffe of Cardiff, and sank 100
miles NW of Alexandria. Neither vessel
carried lights. All saved.

249 NARRUNG

Bt 1896 William Doxford, Pallion Yard,
Sunderland; *T*: 5,078 g, 3,179 n. **Dim**
400 ft (121.92 m) × 47 ft 7 in (14.5 m) ×
28 ft 5 in (8.66 m). **Eng** Sgl scr, quad exp;
Cyls: 30½ in (77.47 cm), 44 in (111.76 cm),
60 in (152.4 cm) and 89 in (226.06 cm);
Stroke: 54 in (137.16 cm); 3,000 IHP, 516
NHP; *Stm P*: 200 lb; 13 kts; By Wigham
Richardson, Newcastle. **H** Steel; *Pass*: 50
1st.

1896 Built for the Blue Anchor Line's
Australian service via the Cape.
1902 Came upon Howard Smith & Co's
Boveric, which had been drifting for 37
days after losing her screw. Towed *Boveric*
to Fremantle.
1910 June 22: Entered P&O service
together with the other Blue Anchor ships.
A replacement for *Narrung* was
immediately ordered.
1912 Sold to Eng Hok Fong SS Co, Hong
Kong, for £23,633—and she cost P&O
£21,317!
1913 Transferred to the Mexico SS Co.
Renamed *Mexico City*.
1917 Feb 5: Torpedoed and sunk off
Holyhead, N Wales. 29 lives lost.

250 WAKOOL

Details as *Narrung* (*249*) except: **Bt** 1898
Sunderland SB Co, Sunderland; *T*:
5,004 g, 3,147 n. **Eng** Tpl exp; *Cyls*: 28 in
(71.12 cm), 47 in (119.38 cm) and 78 in
(198.12 cm); *Stroke*: 54 in (137.16 cm); 580
NHP; 4 sgl ended boilers; *Stm P*: 180 lb. **H**
Fcsle 50 ft (15.24 m), bridge 186 ft
(56.69 m), poop 35 ft (10.67 m).

1898 Built for Lund's Blue Anchor Line
service to Australia.
1910 Jan 26: Acquired by P&O with the
remainder of the fleet.
July 20: First voyage for P&O to Australia
via the Cape.
1912 Sold to Goshi Kaisha Kisimoto
Shokwa, Dairen, and renamed *Kwanto
Maru*.
1917 Sold to the French Government.
Renamed *Le Myre de Villers*.
1919 Re-sold to Brabant & Provost,
Marseilles. Same name.
1923 Sold to S. Bertorelli, Spezia, and
broken up in 1925.

251 WILCANNIA

Details as *Wakool* (*250*) except: **Bt** 1899; *T*:
4,953 g, 3,129 n. **Eng** 594 NHP. **H** Fcsle
40 ft (12.19 m), poop 39 ft (11.89 m).

1899 Built for Lund's Blue Anchor Line
service to Australia via the Cape.
1910 Mar 23: Transferred to P&O
following the purchase of Lunds. Cost
£35,152.
Aug 17: First sailing for P&O to Australia
via the Cape.
1913 Mar: Followed *Wakool* (*250*) into the
service of Goshi Kaisha Kisimoto and
renamed *Shinkoku Maru*. Price £17,277.
1917 Sold, with her sister ship, to the
French Government. Renamed *Dumont
d'Urville*.
1919 Sold to Messageries Maritimes and
renamed *Andre Chenier*.
1926 Broken up at Spezia.

252 BALLARAT (I)

Bt 1911 Caird & Co, Greenock; *T*: 11,120 g.
6,890 n. **Dim** 500 ft 1 in (152.43 m) × 62 ft
9 in (19.13 m) × 37 ft 9 in (11.51 m). **Eng**
Tw scr, 2 quad exp; *Cyls*: 23½ in
(59.69 cm), 34½ in (87.63 cm), 48½ in
(123.19 cm) and 70 in (177.8 cm); *Stroke*:
54 in (137.16 cm); 9,000 IHP, 1,200 NHP; 2
dbl and 2 sgl ended boilers; *Stm P*: 215 lb;
15 kts; By builders. **H** Steel, 3 decks, fcsle

252-256

82 ft (24.99 m), bridge 205 ft (62.48 m), poop 21 ft (6.4 m); *Pass*: 1,100 3rd (350 permanent berths and 750 seasonal).

Caird built all five of the P&O Branch Line replacement vessels (252-256). Their design was simple but sturdy, and so successful that their five post-war successors were remarkably similar.

1911 Sept 23: Launched.
Nov 1: Maiden voyage to Australia via the Cape. Established a record of 37½ days. Cost £176,109.
1914 Requisitioned for trooping from India and Australia, then served as HM Ambulance Transport *A 70 Ballarat*.
1917 Apr 25: Torpedoed by *U-32* in the English Channel. Taken in tow but finally sank at 4.30 am on Apr 26, seven and a half miles off the Lizard. All 1,750 aboard were saved. She was carrying Australian troops to Britain.

253 BELTANA

Details as *Ballarat* (*252*) except: **Bt** 1912; *T*: 11,167 g, 6,975 n.

1911 Laid down as *Bendigo* (I).
1912 Jan 24: Launched.
Apr 5: Registered. Cost £179,365.
1914 Used as a troopship for Indian and Australian forces.
1917 North Atlantic troopship.
1919 Resumed service on the Australian route but via Suez not the Cape.
1930 May: Sold to Toyo Hoyei KK for £27,000. Due to the depression she was not converted into a whale factory ship as proposed but was laid up.
1933 Broken up.

254 BENALLA

Details as *Ballarat* (*252*) except: **Bt** 1913; *T*: 11,118 g, 6,988 n.

1912 Oct 27: Launched.
1913 Feb 7: Registered.
Mar: Maiden voyage to Australia.
1914 Australian Expeditionary Force

troopship.
1915 July: Caught fire off Durban but the blaze was extinguished in port.
1917 Placed on the North Atlantic service under the Liner Requisition Scheme.
1921 May: Back in P&O service. Collided with *Patella* and had to be beached at Pevensey.
1927 Transported the first consignment of steel for Sydney Harbour Bridge.
1931 Jan: Broken up in Japan.

255 BERRIMA

Details as *Ballarat* (*252*) except: **Bt** 1914; *T*: 11,137 g, 7,037 n. **Dim** Beam 62 ft 3 in (18.97 m).

1913 Sept 13: Launched.
Dec 5: Handed over for Australian route.
1914 Aug: Armed Merchant Cruiser.
Oct: Converted to troopship.
1917 Saw North Atlantic service under the Liner Requisition Scheme.
Feb 18: 8 pm. Struck a mine off Portland Bill inward bound for London.
1920 Resumed P&O service. Stranded off Margate but refloated.
1929 Following the closure of the service via the Cape of Good Hope *Berrima* was transferred to the Australian service via the Suez Canal.
1930 Sept: Sold to Japanese ship breakers.

256 BORDA

Details as *Ballarat* (*252*) except: **Bt** 1914; *T*: 11,136 g, 7,036 n. **Dim** Beam 62 ft 3 in (18.97 m).

1913 Dec 17: Launched.
1914 Mar 27: Maiden voyage to Australia via the Cape. Cost £208,977.
Aug 4: Taken over for trooping duties.
1920 Resumed her P&O service to Australia via the Cape.
1928 Laid up.
1930 Apr: Broken up in Japan.

257 KHIVA (II)

Bt 1913 Cammell Laird, Birkenhead; *T*:

9,135 g, 5,590 n. **Dim** 480 ft 6 in (146.46 m) × 58 ft 2 in (17.73 m) × 37 ft 7 in (11.46 m). **Eng** Tw scr, 2 quad exp; *Cyls*: 23½ in (59.69 cm), 34½ in (87.63 cm), 48½ in (123.19 cm) and 70 in (177.8 cm); *Stroke*: 54 in (137.16 cm); 7,000 IHP, 1,204 NHP; 2 dbl and 2 sgl ended boilers; *Stm P*: 215 lb; 14 kts; By builders. **H** Steel, 3 decks, fcsle 88 ft (26.82 m), bridge 176 ft (53.64 m), poop 93 ft (28.35 m); *Pass*: 80 1st, 68 2nd.

1913 Sept 19: Launched.
1914 Jan 7: Handed over. Cost £197,658. Maiden voyage to China and Japan.
1914-18 Remained on Indian and Australian passenger services.
1919 Jan: One of the first P&O ships released by Government. London-Bombay service.
1931 May 5: Sold for £15,500 for breaking up in Japan.

258 KHYBER (I)

Details as *Khiva* (*257*) except: **Bt** 1914; *T*: 9,114 g, 5,674 n. **Dim** Length 480 ft 5 in (146.43 m).

1914 Mar 17: Delivered. Cost £196,346.
Apr: Maiden voyage London-Yokohama.
1915 Aug: Fire in cargo in Tilbury Docks.
1918 Nov: Repatriation of POWs and refugees.
1919 Sept: Returned to Bombay service.
1922 Damaged by fire at Marseilles.
1926 Laid up off Southend.
1931 Oct: Sold Japanese breakers for £16,250.

259 KASHGAR (II)

Details as *Khiva* (*257*) except: **Bt** 1914 Caird & Co, Greenock; *T*: 9,005 g, 5,551 n.

1914 Dec 15: Placed on Far East service.
1917 Requisitioned for trooping to the Mediterranean.
1919 Oct: Returned to P&O Far East service.

1932 Mar 31: Sold for £16,400 to T. Okushoji for breaking up in Japan.

260 KARMALA (I)

Details as *Khiva* (*257*) except: *T*: 9,128 g, 5,680 n.

1914 June 22: Delivered. Cost £196,274. HQ ship for Indian Expeditionary Force during Tanga operations.
1915 Returned to merchant service.
1917 Requisitioned; mostly transatlantic runs with foodstuffs.
1932 Apr: Sold for breaking up.

261 KASHMIR

Details as *Khiva* (*257*) except: **Bt** 1915 Caird & Co, Greenock; *T*: 8,985 g, 5,551 n. **Dim** 479 ft 10 in (146.25 m) × 58 ft 2 in (17.73 m) × 37 ft 7 in (11.46 m).

1914 Apr 2: Delivered. Far East service, occasionally to Australia.
1916 Dec: Requisitioned for trooping in the Mediterranean.
1918 Used on the North Atlantic to carry United States troops and stores to Britain. Oct 6: Collided off Islay with Orient Line's *Otranto*, which was wrecked with the loss of 431 lives.
1919 Mar: Returned to P&O service. Southampton-Capetown-Australia; then Far East run.
1932 Sold with *Kashgar* (*259*) to T. Okushoji for breaking up.

262 KALYAN

Details as *Khiva* (*257*) except: **Bt** 1914; *T*: 9,118 g, 5,680 n. **H** Poop 83 ft (25.3 m).

1914 Sept 24: Launched. Originally to have been named *Khorassan*. Cost £199,012.
1915 Apr 28: Delivered after a completion delay due to the War.
Took part in the Gallipoli campaign. Hove in close to the beach and landed two batteries of guns.
1918-19 Hospital ship in White Sea

257-262

operations against Bolsheviks.
1919 Dec: Maiden commercial sailing.
1932 Feb 12: Sold for breaking up in
Japan. £16,750.

263-264

263 HARLINGTON (II)

Bt 1913 Osbourne Graham & Co, Hylton,
Sunderland; *T*: 1,089 g, 568 n. **Dim** 210 ft
(64.01 m) × 32 ft (9.75 m) × 15 ft 5 in
(4.7 m). **Eng** Sgl scr, tpl exp; *Cyls*: 17 in
(43.18 cm), 28 in (71.12 cm) and 46 in
(116.84 cm); *Stroke*: 30 in (76.2 cm); 142
NHP; *Stm P*: 180 lb; 9 kts. **H** Steel, 1 deck,
fcsle 20 ft (6.1 m), bridge 10 ft (3.05 m),
quarter deck 108 ft (32.92 m).

1913 Built for Societé Francaise
d'Armements, France, as *Figulina*.
1915 Jan 20: Acquired by P&O to replace
Harlington (*196*) lost in 1914. Renamed
Harlington (II).
1916 Dec 9: Mined near the Shipwash
Light vessel off Harwich and sank in four
minutes. The crew were saved by the collier
Hartyn which then immediately hit another
mine. Seven of *Harlington*'s crew and two
from *Hartyn* were drowned.

264 FRODINGHAM

Details as *Harlington* (*263*) except: *T*:
1,081 g, 561 n.

1913 Built as *Gyula* for the same company
as her sister.
1915 Jan 21: Acquired by P&O and
renamed *Frodingham*.
1923 May 17: Sold to Neville Shipping Co,
Cardiff.
1927 Foundered off Land's End.

265 KAISAR-I-HIND (II)

Bt 1914 Caird & Co, Greenock; *T*:

11,518 g, 6,014 n. **Dim** 520 ft (158.5 m) ×
61 ft 2 in (18.64 m) × 33 ft 1 in (10.08 m).
Eng Tw scr, 2 inverted quad exp; *Cyls*:
30½ in (77.47 cm), 44 in (111.76 cm), 61 in
(154.94 cm) and 84 in (213.36 cm); *Stroke*:
54 in (137.16 cm); 14,000 IHP, 1,964 NHP;
4 dbl and 4 sgl ended boilers; *Stm P*: 215 lb;
18½ kts; By builders. **H** Steel, 4 decks,
fcsle 40 ft (12.19 m), bridge deck 261 ft
(79.55 m); *Pass*: 315 1st, 333 2nd.

1914 June 27: Launched.
Oct 1: Maiden voyage London-Bombay in a
record 17 days 20 hours and 52 minutes.
Cost £363,176. P&O's most expensive ship
to date.
1916 Her Bombay service was extended to
Australia.
1917 Trooping. *Kaisar-I-Hind* escaped
four torpedo attacks due to her speed. The
fourth dented her hull but failed to
explode. The lucky plates were thereafter
painted green and remained so until
replaced years later.
1921 Chartered to Cunard Line and
temporarily renamed *Emperor of India*
(but note that 'Kaisar' means Empress).
1922 Resumed P&O service.
1938 Apr 29: Arrived at Blyth to be broken
up by Hughes Bolkow & Co.

266

266 MATA HARI

Bt 1915 Chas Rennoldson, South Shields;
T: 1,020 g, 511 n. **Dim** 220 ft (67.06 m) ×
35 ft 2 in (10.72 m) × 13 ft (3.96 m). **Eng**
Sgl scr, tpl exp; *Cyls*: 17½ in (44.45 cm),
29 in (73.66 cm) and 47 in (119.38 cm);
Stroke: 30 in (76.2 cm); 1,650 IHP, 165
NHP; 2 sgl ended boilers; *Stm P*: 180 lb; 9
kts; By Shields Engineering Co, North
Shields. **H** Steel.

The name is Malaysian for 'Moon'.

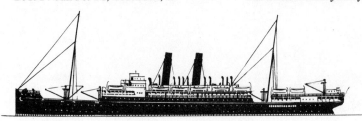

265

267-268

1915 Built. Ordered for P&O but, damaged on launching, she was sold before completion to the British India SN Co, a P&O subsidiary, for Malayan feeder service.
1924 Aug 26: Purchased by P&O.
1942 Feb 28: Captured by the Japanese in Banka Strait, Dutch East Indies, en route Singapore-Batavia with refugees. Subsequently became a war casualty.

267 NALDERA

Bt 1918 Caird & Co, Greenock (the builders now became known as Harland & Wolff, Greenock); *T*: 16,088 g, 8,936 n. **Dim** 600 ft (182.88 m) oa, 580 ft 10 in (177.04 m) × 67 ft 2 in (20.47 m) × 49 ft 2 in (14.99 m); *Dft*: 29 ft 7 in (9.02 m). **Eng** Tw scr, 2 quad exp; *Cyls*: 32½ in (82.55 cm), 46½ in (118.11 cm), 69 in (175.26 cm) and 96 in (243.84 cm); *Stroke*: 60 in (152.4 cm); 18,000 IHP, 1,430 NHP; *Stm P*: 215 lb; 17 kts; By builders. **H** Steel, 4 decks and hurricane deck; *Coal*: 2,943 tons (later 2,460 tons oil); *Cargo*: 253,000 cu ft (7,164 cu m); *Pass*: 426 1st, 247 2nd; *Crew*: 462.

Naldera *and* Narkunda (268) *were P&O's first ships with three funnels and with cruiser sterns,* Narkunda *being recognised by a short forecastle to the foremost deck crane. Their completion was delayed by Government indecision.*

1913 Nov 3: Ordered and commenced but work was suspended during the war.
1917 Dec 29: Launched.
1918 Completion was ordered as an armed merchant cruiser but was delayed by her conversion into a troopship. Completed in May.
1920 Mar 24: Entered service on the Australian route. *Naldera* was the 83rd, final and largest vessel built for P&O by Caird & Co.
1931 Transferred to London-Bombay-Far East route.
1938 Nov: Sold for scrapping at Bo'ness, Firth of Forth, by P. & W. Maclellan Ltd.

268 NARKUNDA

Bt 1920 Harland & Wolff, Belfast; *T*: 16,118 g, 9,424 n. **Dim** 581 ft 5 in (177.22 m) × 69 ft 5 in (21.16 m) × 27 ft 8 in (8.43 m). **Eng** Tw scr, 2 quad exp; *Cyls*: 33 in (83.82 cm), 47 in (199.38 cm), 67½ in (171.45 cm) and 97 in (246.38 cm); *Stroke*: 60 in (152.4 cm); 15,300 IHP, 1,428 NHP; 17 kts. **H** Details as *Naldera* (*267*).

Identification note: short fcsle to foremost crane.

1920 Mar 30: Entered service on the Australian run. P&O's largest ship.
1931 Transferred to the Far East routes after the entry into service of *Strathnaver* (*307*) and *Strathaird* (*308*).
1935 Second class converted to tourist class.
1940 Requisitioned for use as a troopship.
1942 Nov 14: During the North African landings *Narkunda* was bombed and sunk off Bougie, Algeria, en route to Algiers after unloading troops, with the loss of 31 lives.

269 PESHAWUR (III)

Bt 1919 Barclay Curle & Co, Glasgow; *T*: 7,934 g, 4,935 n. **Dim** 449 ft 6 in (137.01 m) × 58 ft 2 in (17.73 m) × 37 ft 1 in (11.3 m);

269

Dft: 29 ft 6 in (8.99 m). **Eng** Tw scr, 2 tpl exp; *Cyls*: 26½ in (67.31 cm), 44 in (111.76 cm) and 73 in (185.42 cm); *Stroke*: 48 in (121.92 cm); 7,000 IHP, 1,162 NHP; 2 dbl and 2 sgl ended boilers; *Stm P*: 215 lb; 13 kts; By builders. **H** Steel, 2 decks and shelter deck, fcsle 43 ft (13.11 m), poop 31 ft (9.45 m); *Coal*: 1,108 tons; *Cargo*: 460,000 cu ft (13,026 cu m); *Pass*: 12.

1918 Oct 7: Laid down as *War Diana*, a wartime standard 'G' type vessel.
1919 Sept 26: Launched.
Dec 18: Acquired by P&O. Renamed *Peshawur*.
1943 Dec 23: Sunk by an acoustic homing torpedo near Madras (11.11N, 80.11E) en route Swansea-Calcutta. All aboard were saved although the ship's three cats were drowned.

270-271

270 **ESTON**

Bt 1919 Goole Shipbuilding & Repairing Co, Goole, Yorks; *T*: 1,487 g, 806 n. **Dim** 240 ft 2 in (73.2 m) × 36 ft 1 in (11 m) × 19 ft 1 in (5.82 m). **Eng** Sgl scr, tpl exp; *Cyls*: 18 in (45.72 cm), 30 in (76.2 cm) and 50 in (127 cm); *Stroke*: 33 in (83.82 cm); 172 NHP; 2 sgl ended boilers; *Stm P*: 180 lb; 10 kts; By Earles Co, Hull. **H** Steel, 1 deck; *Cargo*: 102,940 cu ft (2,915 cu m) (grain); *Crew*: 21.

1919 Dec 8: Acquired. Coastal feeder and collier service.
1940 Jan 28: Presumed mined off Blyth, Northumberland. Left Hull for Blyth on Jan 26 and disappeared. Two lifeboats and one body were washed ashore.

271 **REDCAR**

Details as *Eston* (*270*) except: **Bt** 1920; *T*: 1,475 g, 794 n.

1920 Apr 8: Acquired.
1946 Apr 2: Sold to H. R. Rilson, Southampton.

272 **NAGPORE**

Bt 1920 Earles Shipbuilding & Engineering Co, Hull; *T*: 5,283 g, 3,226 n. **Dim** 400 ft

5 in (122.05 m) × 52 ft 2 in (15.9 m) × 32 ft (9.75 m). **Eng** Sgl scr, tpl exp; *Cyls*: 27 in (68.58 cm), 44 in (111.76 cm) and 73 in (185.42 cm); *Stroke*: 48 in (121.92 cm); 2,800 IHP, 517 NHP; 3 sgl ended boilers; *Stm P*: 180 lb; 10½ kts; By Richardsons, Westgarth, Middlesbrough. **H** Steel, fcsle 39 ft (11.89 m), bridge 113 ft (34.44 m), poop 49 ft (14.94 m).

1920 Sept 1: A wartime standard 'B' type ship adapted for P&O service. The only Earles-built ship for P&O. India-Far East route.
1942 Oct 28: Torpedoed in convoy en route for Britain off the Canary Islands. Broke in two and sank.

272-276

273 **LAHORE** (II)

Details as *Nagpore* (*272*) except: **Bt** R. Thompson & Sons, Sunderland; *T*: 5,304 g, 3,161 n. **Eng** By North East Marine, Sunderland.

1920 Apr 17: Delivered. The only ship built for P&O by R. Thompson.
1941 Mar 8: Torpedoed off Freetown whilst acting as vice-commodore ship in a convoy of 54 vessels. *Lahore* was the fifth vessel to be hit, and caught fire because the hold where the torpedo struck contained 50 tons of matches.

274 **KIDDERPORE**

Details as *Nagpore* (*272*) except: **Bt** Swan Hunter & Wigham Richardson, Wallsend-on-Tyne; *T*: 5,334 g, 3,263 n. **Eng** By builders. **H** Fcsle 40 ft (12.19 m).

1920 Feb 14: Delivered. India-Japan cargo routes.

275 **ALIPORE**

Details as *Nagpore* (*272*) except: **Bt** Palmers, Jarrow; *T*: 5,273 g, 3,241 n. **Eng** By builders.

1920 July 15: Delivered. India-Far East service.

1940 Two outbreaks of fire in cotton cargo. Sabotage suspected.
1942 Sept 30: Torpedoed off British Guiana. *Alipore* was missed by the first torpedo but as she turned away from the track of the first she was struck by the second. Sunk by incendiary shells from her attacker. Eight lives lost.

276 JEYPORE

Details as *Nagpore* (272) except: **Bt** Wm Gray & Co, Weir Shipyard, Sunderland; *T*: 5,318 g, 3,209 n.

1920 May 15: Acquired. The first P&O ship built by Wm Gray.
1942 Nov 3: Torpedoed in mid-Atlantic en route from America to Britain and sank within 20 minutes burning fiercely.

277 PADUA

Bt 1912 J. C. Tecklenborg, Geestemunde, Germany; *T*: 5,907 g, 4,922 n. **Dim** 450 ft 9 in (137.39 m) × 57 ft 2 in (17.42 m) × 26 ft 11 in (8.2 m). **Eng** Sgl scr, tpl exp; *Cyls*: 28 in (71.12 cm), 47 in (119.38 cm) and 78¾ in (200.03 cm); *Stroke*: 54 in (137.16 cm); 3,600 IHP, 734 NHP; *Stm P*: 206 lb; 10 kts. **H** Steel, 2 decks, fcsle 50 ft (15.24 m), bridge and poop 381 ft (116.13 m).

1912 Built as *Luneberg* for Deutsch-Australische line.
1920 Oct 15: Acquired as a war loss replacement. Renamed *Padua*. Spent much of her time laid up.
1933 May: Sold for breaking up.

278 PERIM (I)

Bt 1916 J. C. Tecklenborg, Geestemunde, Germany; *T*: 7,648 g, 4,779 n. **Dim** 469 ft 6 in (143.1 m) × 58 ft 6 in (17.83 m) × 32 ft 2 in (9.8 m). **Eng** Sgl scr, tpl exp; *Cyls*: 31½ in (80.01 cm), 51 in (129.54 cm) and 82¾ in (210.19 cm); *Stroke*: 55 in (139.7 cm); 3,500 IHP, 504 NHP; *Stm P*: 200 lb; 11 kts. **H** Steel, 2 decks.

1916 Built as *Treuenfels* for Hansa Line, Germany.
1920 Oct 15: Bought as a war loss replacement. Renamed *Perim*.
1935 Feb 26: Sold for breaking up.

279 BEGUM

Bt 1913 P&O Workshops, Mazagon, Bombay; *T*: 194 g, 131 n. **Dim** 110 ft 9 in (33.76 m) × 23 ft (7.01 m) × 8 ft 8 in (2.64 m). **Eng** Compound; *Cyls*: 9 in (22.86 cm) and 16½ in (41.91 cm); *Stroke*: 14 in (35.56 cm); 160 HP; *Stm P*: 110 lb; 8 kts.

1913 May 8: Registered at Bombay. Passenger tender and water boat; 250 passengers, ten crew, 144 tons of water.
1915 Transferred to Mazagon Dock Co (a P&O subsidiary).

280 MIRZAPORE (III)

Bt 1921 Sir W. A. Armstrong Whitworth & Co, Newcastle; *T*: 6,715 g, 4,135 n. **Dim** 412 ft 2 in (125.63 m) × 55 ft 9 in (16.99 m) × 34 ft 7 in (10.54 m). **Eng** Sgl scr, 2 stm turb, double reduction geared; 2,300 SHP, 600 NHP; 3 sgl ended boilers; *Stm P*: 200 lb; 12 kts; By C. A. Parsons & Co, Newcastle. **H** Steel, 1 deck and shelter deck, fcsle 36 ft (10.97 m), poop 42 ft (12.8 m); *Pass*: 4; *Crew*: 104.

1921 Feb 22: Launched.
Oct 6: Delivered. Indian and Far Eastern

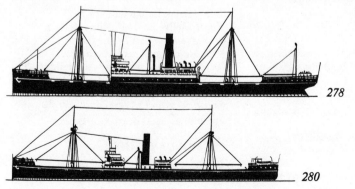

278

280

281-285

services, but laid up at Bombay for considerable periods.
1939 Mar: Sold to Belgian shipbreakers.

281 BALLARAT (II)

Bt 1921 Harland & Wolff, Greenock; *T*: 13,033 g, 7,950 n. **Dim** 519 ft 9 in (158.42 m) × 64 ft 2 in (19.56 m) × 42 ft (12.8 m); *Dft*: 30 ft (9.14 m). **Eng** Tw scr, 2 quad exp; *Cyls*: 23½ in (59.69 cm), 34½ in (87.63 cm), 48½ in (123.19 cm) and 70 in (177.8 cm); *Stroke*: 54 in (137.16 cm); 9,500 IHP, 1,341 NHP; 2 dbl and 3 sgl ended boilers; *Stm P*: 214 lb; 13½ kts; By J. G. Kincaid, Greenock. **H** Steel, 3 decks, fcsle 58 ft (17.68 m); *Cargo*: 16, 424 cu m (580,004 cu ft); *Pass*: 491 3rd plus 743 temporary berths; *Crew*: 288.

Ballarat, Baradine (282), Barrabool (283), Balranald (284) *and* Bendigo (285) *were five sister ships built by the Harland & Wolff Group for the Branch Line service and destined to have short service careers.*

1920 Sept 4: Launched.
1921 Dec 14: Delivered.
1922 Jan 27: Maiden voyage to Australia via the Cape.
1929 Fitted with Bauer-Wach exhaust turbines and oil fuel; 15 kts; *Pass*: 586.
June 7: Resumed service London-Malta-Suez-Australia.
1935 May 27: Broken up by Thos W. Ward at Briton Ferry, South Wales. Price £23,500.

282 BARADINE (I)

Details as *Ballarat* (*281*) except: **Bt** Belfast; *T*: 13,144 g, 7,990 n. **Dim** Beam 64 ft 5 in (19.63 m).

1920 Nov 28: Launched.
1921 Sept 21: Maiden voyage to Australia via the Cape.
1929 Re-engined, as *Ballarat* (*281*).
Apr 12: Placed on Malta-Suez-Australia route.
1936 Mar 13: Last departure for Sydney.

June 30: Sold for breaking up by W. H. Arnott Young at Dalmuir.

283 BARRABOOL

Details as *Ballarat* (*281*) except: **Bt** 1923 Belfast; *T*: 13,148 g, 7,996 n. **Dim** Beam 64 ft 5 in (19.63 m). **Eng** By builders.

1923 Mar 30: Delivered for Australia via the Cape service.
1926 Quarantined at Adelaide with 1,200 passengers aboard.
1929 Re-engined, as *Ballarat* (*281*).
1930 Mar 9: Resumed service on the Malta-Suez-Australia route.
1936 July 31: Broken up by Douglas at Bo'ness, Firth of Forth.

284 BALRANALD (I)

Details as *Ballarat* (*281*) except: **Bt** 1922; *T*: 13,039 g, 7,938 n.

1922 Apr 5: Delivered. Maiden voyage London-Australia via the Cape.
1929 Re-engined, as *Ballarat* (*281*).
May 10: Resumed service Malta-Colombo-Australia run.
1936 Feb 14: Final sailing for Australia.
June 2: Sold for £26,000 to Douglas & Ramsey. Broken up at Troon.

285 BENDIGO (II)

Details as *Ballarat* (*281*) except: **Bt** 1922; *T*: 13,039 g, 7,939 n.

1922 Jan 26: Launched.
Aug 9: Delivered for the Branch Line service to Australia via the Cape.
1929 Re-engined, as *Ballarat* (*281*).
July 5: Resumed service to Australia via Malta and Colombo.
1936 Jan 17: Final sailing to Australia.
May 6: Sold for £26,000 to Thos W. Ward and broken up at Barrow-in-Furness.

286 MOLDAVIA (II)

Bt 1922 Cammell Laird, Birkenhead; *T*: 16,436 g, 10,115 n. **Dim** 573 ft (174.65 m)

286

oa, 552 ft 5 in (168.38 m) × 71 ft 7 in (21.82 m) × 38 ft 5 in (11.71 m); *Dft*: 33 ft 10 in (10.31 m). **Eng** Tw scr, dbl reduction geared turbine; 13,250 IHP, 2,602 NHP; 3 dbl and 4 sgl ended boilers; *Stm P*: 215 lb; 16 kts; By C. A. Parsons. Each shaft had three gearings at 90 rpm. **H** Steel, 4 decks, 7 holds, 10 watertight divisions; the hull was built from steel warship plates left over from the war; *Coal*: 1,850 tons; *Pass*: 222 1st, 175 2nd; *Crew*: 337.

1921 Oct 1: Launched.
1922 Sept 19: Delivered with only one funnel, which was criticised as being so insignificant that it marred her profile.
Oct 13: Maiden voyage Tilbury-Bombay.
1923 Feb: Transferred to the Australian intermediate route Tilbury-Marseilles-Port Said-Colombo-Fremantle-Adelaide-Melbourne-Sydney.
1928 Second class accommodation re-designated third, and a dummy second funnel added which unbalanced *Moldavia*'s looks by being too far aft.
1930 Third class only, 840 passengers.
1934 Steam superheaters fitted together with new propellers to give 17 kts.
1937 Sept 17: Final Australian voyage. Laid up.
1938 Apr 18: Sold to John Cashmore Ltd to be broken up. Handed over at Tilbury.

287 **MONGOLIA** (III)

Bt 1923 Armstrong Whitworth, Walker-on-Tyne; *T*: 16,385 g, 10,333 n. **Dim** 551 ft 7 in (168.12 m) × 72 ft (81.95 m) × 38 ft 6 in (11.73 m). **Eng** Tw scr, dbl

reduction geared turbines; 13,250 IHP, 2,567 NHP; 3 dbl and 4 sgl ended cylindrical boilers; *Stm P*: 215 lb; 16 kts; By builders. **H** Steel, 5 passenger decks; *Cargo*: 14,158 cu m (499,982 cu ft); *Pass*: 231 1st, 180 2nd; *Crew*: 337.

1923 Apr 26: Delivered.
May 11: Maiden voyage to Australia via Suez Canal.
1930 Passenger accommodation converted to 840 tourist class.
1938 May 7: Chartered to the New Zealand Shipping Co and renamed *Rimutaka*. Passengers reduced to 272 tourist class.
1944 Carried the Duke of Gloucester to Australia, where he was to be Governor General.
1950 Jan 10: Sold to Cia de Nav Incres Panama for £95,000. Renamed *Europa*.
1952 Transferred to the Liberian flag by her owners and renamed *Nassau*. Caribbean cruising.
1961 Sold to Nav Turisticana Mexicana and renamed *Acapulco*. Her new owners modernised the ship and her profile.
1965 Broken up in Japan.

288 **MOOLTAN** (III)

Bt 1923 Harland & Wolff, Belfast; *T*: 20,847 g, 12,836 n. **Dim** 600 ft 9 in (183.11 m) × 73 ft 5 in (22.38 m) × 48 ft 7 in (14.81 m). **Eng** Tw scr, 2 quad exp; *Cyls*: 33 in (83.82 cm), 47 in (119.38 cm), 67½ in (171.45 cm) and 97 in (246.38 cm); *Stroke*: 60 in (152.4 cm); 16,000 IHP, 2,632 NHP; 6 dbl and 2 sgl ended boilers; *Stm P*: 215 lb; 16 kts; By builders. **H** Steel, 3

287

decks, fcsle 111 ft (33.83 m), bridge 351 ft
(106.99 mm); *Pass*: 327 1st, 329 2nd; *Crew*:
422.

The two beautiful sister ships Mooltan *and*
Maloja *(289) were designed to be the largest
ships capable of transmitting the Suez
Canal. They were also the first P&O vessels
to exceed 20,000 tons.*

1923 Feb 15: Launched.
Sept 21: Delivered.
Dec 21: Maiden voyage London-Colombo-
Melbourne-Sydney.
1929 Routed via Bombay. Re-engined with
Bauer-Wach exhaust geared turbines; 17
kts.
1939 Oct: Converted to armed merchant
cruiser, based Freetown. Rearmost funnel
reduced by half to improve the arc of fire for
the anti-aircraft guns.
1941 Troopship to Bombay.
1942 Nov 11: Present at the North African
landings at Arzeu.
1948 Returned to service with 1,030 tourist
class berths. *T*: 21,039 g.
Aug 26: Returned to the Australian route.
1954 Jan 22: Sold to British Iron & Steel
Corporation and broken up at Faslane.

289 **MALOJA** (II)

Details as *Mooltan (288)* except: *T*:
20,837 g, 12,830 n.

1923 Apr 19: Launched.
Oct 25: Handed over.
1924 Jan 18: Maiden voyage London-
Colombo-Melbourne-Sydney.
1930 Re-engined, as *Mooltan (288)*.
1939 Oct: Converted at Bombay to armed
merchant cruiser.
1941 Troopship. Became the largest
troopship to enter Bone, N. Africa.
1948 June 10: Resumed Australian service.
1,030 tourist class only.
1954 Apr 2: Sold for £170,000 to British
Iron & Steel Corporation and broken up at
Inverkeithing, Scotland.

290 **BULAN**

Bt 1924 Alex Stephen & Sons, Linthouse,
Glasgow; *T*: 1,048 g, 442 n. **Dim** 220 ft 4 in
(67.16 m) × 35 ft 1 in (10.69 m) × 13 ft 1 in
(3.99 m); *Dft*: 13 ft 5 in (4.09 m). **Eng** Sgl
scr, tpl exp; *Cyls*: 17½ in (44.45 cm), 29 in
(73.66 cm) and 47 in (119.38 cm); *Stroke*:
30 in (76.2 cm); 165 NHP; 2 sgl ended
boilers; *Stm P*: 170 lb; 10 kts; By builders.
H Steel.

290

1924 Malayan feeder services. Manned by
British India SN Co; *Crew*: 29, plus pilot.
1939 Patrol duties as unit of Malayan
Auxiliary fleet.
1941 Dec: Rescued crew of SS *Pinna*, dive-
bombed by Japanese.
1942 Feb: Evacuated refugees Singapore-
Batavia and then to Ceylon.
1952 June 1: Sold to Wo Fat Sing Ltd,
Hong Kong, for £43,500.

291 **RAZMAK**

Bt 1925 Harland & Wolff, Greenock; *T*:
10,602 g, 4,900 n. **Dim** 519 ft (158.19 m)
oa, 500 ft 5 in (152.53 m) × 63 ft 2 in
(19.25 m) × 34 ft (10.36 m); *Dft*: 26 ft 1 in
(7.95 m). **Eng** Tw scr, 2 quad exp; *Cyls*:
30½ in (77.47 cm), 44 in (111.76 cm), 63 in
(160.02 cm) and 89 in (226.06 cm);
Stroke: 54 in (137.16 cm) with LP dbl
reduction geared Bauer-Wach turbines
and a hydraulic coupling; 12,000 IHP,
1,949 NHP; *Stm P*: 215 lb; 16 kts; By
Harland & Wolff, Belfast. **H** Steel, 2 decks,
fcsle 73 ft (22.25 m), bridge and poop 396 ft
(120.7 m); *Pass*: 142 1st, 142 2nd; *Crew*:
252.

1925 Built to replace *Salsette (245)* on the
Aden-Bombay shuttle.
Feb 26: Trials.
Mar 13: Maiden voyage Aden-Bombay.

291

1927-30 The new vessels for the Australian route had the speed to call at Bombay. *Razmak* was used on various routes.
1930 Nov: Following the loss of their *Tahiti* in the Pacific *Razmak* was transferred to the P&O subsidiary Union SS Co of New Zealand. Renamed *Monowai*. *Pass*: 430 one class. Lowered the Sydney-San Francisco record.
Placed on the New Zealand-Australian service.
1960 June: Sold for £165,000 to Far East Metal Industry and Shipping Co for breaking up.

292 CATHAY (II)

Bt 1925 Barclay Curle, Glasgow; *T*: 15,104 g, 8,746 n. **Dim** 523 ft 4 in (159.51 m) × 70 ft 2 in (21.39 m) × 46 ft (14.02 m). **Eng** Tw scr, 2 quad exp; *Cyls*: 29½ in (75.93 cm), 42¼ in (107.32 cm), 60¾ in (154.31 cm) and 87 in (220.98 cm); *Stroke*: 54 in (137.16 cm); 13,000 IHP, 2,075 NHP; 3 dbl and 4 sgl ended boilers; *Stm P*: 215 lb; 16 kts; By builders. **H** Steel, fcsle 92 ft (28.04 m), bridge 255 ft (77.72 m); *Cargo*: 12,810 cu m (452,378 cu ft); *Pass*: 203 1st, 103 2nd; *Crew*: 278.

1924 Oct 31: Launched by Lady Inchcape, wife of P&O's chairman.
1925 Mar 27: Maiden voyage London-Colombo-Australia.
1932 Bombay added to the route.
1933 Dec: Lost a screw whilst trying to make up time between Colombo and Fremantle.
1939 Oct: Converted into an armed

merchant cruiser. Used on the Bombay-Durban patrol.
1942 Converted to a troopship.
Nov 11: Bombed at Bougie, N Africa. Caught fire, then a delayed action bomb set off her ammunition which blew off the stern, and *Cathay* sank.

293 COMORIN (I)

Details as *Cathay* (*292*) except: *T*: 15,116 g, 8,744 n.

1924 Oct 31: Launched.
1925 Apr 11: Delivered.
Apr 24: Maiden voyage London-Colombo-Melbourne-Sydney. Bombay added in 1929. Far East route after the arrival of the 'Straths'.
1930 Engines modified by the addition of a low pressure exhaust turbine; 17½ kts.
1939 Commissioned for the Northern Patrol as an armed merchant cruiser.
1941 Apr 6: Whilst serving as HMS *Comorin* the ship caught fire, off Sierra Leone, in heavy seas and gale force winds. The crew of 450 were taken off by *Glenartney* and the destroyers HMS *Lincoln* and HMS *Broke* which repeatedly came right alongside. Only 20 men were lost. Next day HMS *Broke* torpedoed the blazing hulk.

294 CHITRAL (I)

Details as *Cathay* (*292*) except: **Bt** 1925 Alex Stephen & Sons, Linthouse, Glasgow; *T*: 15,248 g, 8,773 n. **Dim** Length 526 ft 4 in (160.43 m). **Eng** By builders.

1925 Jan 27: Launched.

292-294

July 3: Maiden voyage to Australia.
1930 Engine modified, as *Comorin* (*293*).
1932 Bombay added as a port of call.
1939 Oct: Commissioned as armed merchant cruiser.
Nov 23: Rescued the survivors of HMS *Rawalpindi* (*297*).
1943 Converted to troopship.
1946 Twin posts replaced main mast.
1948 Dec 30: Resumed the Australian service. 740 emigrants outward.
1953 Apr 2: Sold for £167,500 to British Iron & Steel Corporation and broken up at Dalmuir.

295 **RANPURA**

Bt 1925 R. & W. Hawthorn Leslie & Co, Newcastle; *T*: 16,688 g, 9,331 n. **Dim** 548 ft 4 in (167.13 m) × 71 ft 4 in (21.74 m) × 47 ft (14.33 m). **Eng** Tw scr, 2 quad exp; *Cyls*: 32½ in (82.55 cm), 46½ in (118.11 cm), 67 in (170.18 cm) and 96 in (243.84 cm); *Stroke*: 60 in (152.4 cm); 15,000 IHP, 2,403 NHP; 6 dbl ended cylindrical boilers with forced draft; *Stm P*: 215 lb; 16 kts; By builders. **H** Steel, 6 passenger decks, fcsle 84 ft (25.6 m), bridge 305 ft (92.86 m); *Cargo*: 4,200 tons (9,745 cu m); *Pass*: 310 1st, 290 2nd; *Crew*: 357.

1924 Sept 13: Launched.
1925 Apr 8: Delivered for the Bombay direct service.
1930 Bauer-Wach exhaust turbines fitted.
1936 Apr 6: Went aground in a fierce gale at Gibraltar outward bound whilst carrying Chinese art treasures from the London exhibition of Chinese art. Safely re-floated.
1939 Aug 27: Reached Aden then directed to Calcutta and converted into an armed merchant cruiser. Served in the Eastern Mediterranean based at Port Said. One funnel.
1944 Purchased by the Admiralty and converted into a fleet repair ship and depot ship.
1961 Broken up at Spezia.

296 **RANCHI**

Details as *Ranpura* (*295*) except: *T*: 16,738 g, 8,850 n.

1925 July 29: Placed on Bombay direct service.
1930 Engines modified, as *Ranpura* (*295*).
1939 Aug 27: Requisitioned as armed merchant cruiser.
1943 Mar: Converted to a troopship. Mediterranean, Middle East and Indian service.
1948 June 17: Refitted at Belfast and returned to service without her second funnel. Used on the Australian emigrant service. 950 berths.
1952 Oct 6: Final sailing to Australia.
1953 Jan 19: Broken up at Newport, S Wales, by British Iron & Steel Corporation. Price £200,000.

297 **RAWALPINDI**

Details as *Ranpura* (*295*) except: **Bt** Harland & Wolff, Greenock; *T*: 16,697 g, 9,459 n. **Eng** By Harland & Wolff, Belfast.

1925 Sept 3: Handed over. Placed firstly on the Indian route and then Far East service.
1930 Engine modified, as *Ranpura* (*295*).
1939 Aug 24: Converted to an armed merchant cruiser with 8 × 6 in (15.24 cm) guns.
Nov 23: Engaged the German battleships *Scharnhorst* and *Gneisenau* for 40 minutes off Iceland before breaking in two and sinking with the loss of 265 crew and her captain, E. C. Kennedy RN. The convoy scattered safely.

298 **RAJPUTANA**

Details as *Ranpura* (*295*) except: **Bt** Harland & Wolff, Greenock; *T*: 16,644 g,

295-298

9,456 n. **Eng** By Harland & Wolff, Belfast.

1925 Aug 6: Launched.
Dec 30: Delivered. Maiden voyage on the
Bombay direct route. Later transferred to
the Japan service.
1930 Engine modified, as *Ranpura* (*295*).
1939 Sept: At the outbreak of war
Rajputana was at Yokohoma. She was sent
to Esquimault, British Columbia, for
conversion into an armed merchant
cruiser. Used for convoy duties and
escorted 700 vessels without loss. One
funnel.
1941 Apr 13: Twice torpedoed at dawn by
U-108 west of Ireland. 41 killed, 283
survivors.

cu ft); *Pass*: 415 1st, 258 2nd; *Crew*: 417.

1927 Apr: Ordered as *Taj Mahal*.
1928 Sept 15: Launched.
1929 Mar 7: Delivered for India direct
service.
1932 Sept: Established a London-Bombay
record of 16 days 1 hour 42 minutes.
1938 Permanent swimming pool added.
1940 Converted for trooping.
1942 Nov 11: Torpedoed by *U-407* off
Oran, Algeria. *Viceroy of India* was
withdrawing from the port after landing
her troops and their vehicles when she was
attacked. Four were lost out of 454 aboard.
The survivors were rescued by HMS
Boadicea.

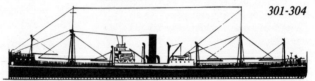

301-304

299

299 LAHEJ

Bt 1927 Harland & Wolff, Greenock; *T*:
283 g, 93 n. **Dim** 120 ft (36.58 m) × 27 ft
(8.23 m) × 12 ft 2 in (3.71 m). **Eng** Tw scr,
2 tpl exp; *Cyls*: 13½ in (34.29 cm), 23½ in
(59.69 cm) and 36 in (91.44 cm); *Stroke*:
27 in (68.58 cm). **H** Steel, 1 deck.

1927 Sept 5: Delivered. P&O's tug at
Aden.
1961 Apr 12: Sold for breaking up to
Mohamed Ali Hussein, Aden.

300 VICEROY OF INDIA

Bt 1929 Alex Stephen & Sons, Linthouse,
Glasgow; *T*: 19,648 g, 10,087 n. **Dim** 612 ft
(186.54 m) oa, 586 ft 1 in (178.64 m) ×
76 ft 2 in (23.22 m) × 41 ft 6 in (12.65 m).
Eng Tw scr, 2 turbo-electric engines; 17,000
SHP; 6 water-tube boilers; *Stm P*: 350 lb;
19 kts; By builders; Electric motors by
British Thomson-Houston. **H** Steel, 4
decks, fcsle 82 ft (24.99 m), bridge 354 ft
(107.9 m); *Cargo*: 6,166 cu m (217,749

301 BANGALORE (II)

Bt 1928 Barclay Curle & Co, Glasgow; *T*:
6,067 g, 2,875 n. **Dim** 436 ft (132.89 m) ×
57 ft 6 in (17.53 m) × 29 ft 9 in (9.07 m).
Eng Sgl scr, quad exp; *Cyls*: 30½ in
(77.47 cm), 44 in (111.76 cm), 63½ in
(161.29 cm) and 91 in (231.14 cm); *Stroke*:
57 in (144.78 cm) plus one low pressure
turbine, dbl reduction geared by
hydraulic coupling to the shaft; 1,236
NHP; *Stm P*: 230 lb; 10 kts; By builders. **H**
Steel, 1 deck, fcsle 34 ft (10.36 m).

The four sister ships Bangalore, Burdwan
(302), Behar (303) *and* Bhutan (304) *were
given P&O type names and operated by
P&O but actually owned by Hain.*

1928 Built for Hain SS Co but given P&O
nomenclature and operated by them.

302 BURDWAN

Details as *Bangalore* (*301*) except: *T*:

300

6,069 g, 2,879 n.

1928 Built for Hain SS Co. Operated by P&O on general cargo services.
1942 June 15: Bombed, and finally sank off Pantellaria Island, Mediterranean.

303 **BEHAR** (II)

Details as *Bangalore* (*301*) except: **Bt** 1928 Harland & Wolff, Greenock; *T*: 6,100 g, 2,910 n. **Eng** By builders.

1928 Built for Hain SS Co. Operated by P&O.
1944 Nov 24: The Japanese cruiser *Tone* sank *Behar* by gunfire. Her commander rescued the crew of 80, but his orders were to take no prisoners and 65 were killed before the order was rescinded. The captain of *Tone* was later imprisoned as a war criminal.

304 **BHUTAN**

Details as *Bangalore* (*301*) except: **Bt** 1929 Harland & Wolff, Greenock; *T*: 6,104 g, 2,912 n. **Eng** By builders.

1929 Built for Hain SS Co. Operated by P&O.
1942 June 14: Bombed and sunk in a Malta convoy.

305 **SOMALI** (II)

Bt 1930 Harland & Wolff, Greenock; *T*: 6,809 g, 3,522 n. **Dim** 459 ft (139.9 m) × 60 ft 7 in (18.47 m) × 29 ft 9 in (9.07 m); *Dft*: 27 ft 11 in (8.51 m). **Eng** Sgl scr, quad exp and Bauer-Wach exhaust turbine;

Cyls: 30½ in (77.47 cm), 44 in (111.76 cm), 63½ in (161.29 cm) and 91 in (231.14 cm); *Stroke*: 60 in (152.4 cm) with low pressure turbine and hydraulic coupling; 7,000 IHP, 1,384 NHP; By J. G. Kincaid, Glasgow. **H** Steel, 2 decks and shelter deck; *Cargo*: 582,000 cu ft (16,480 cu m), 68,000 cu ft (1,926 cu m) refrig in 4 chambers.

1930 Dec 18: Delivered.
1941 Mar 26: Bombed and sunk off Blyth, Northumberland.

306 **SOUDAN** (II)

Details as *Somali* (*305*) except: **Bt** 1931 Barclay Curle, Glasgow; *T*: 6,677 g, 3,477 n. **Eng** By builders.

1931 Jan 22: Delivered.
1942 May 15: Mined off Capetown.

307 **STRATHNAVER** (I)

Bt 1931 Vickers-Armstrong, Barrow-in-Furness; *T*: 22,270 g, 13,431 n. **Dim** 638 ft 7 in (194.64 m) × 80 ft 2 in (24.43 m) × 33 ft 1 in (10.08 m); *Dft*: 26 ft 5 in (8.05 m). **Eng** Tw scr, turbo electric, 28,000 SHP; 4 main water tube boilers and auxiliary water tube boilers; *Stm P*: 425 lb; 21 kts; Electric motors by British Thomson-Houston, Rugby. **H** Steel, 1st and 3rd funnels dummies; *Pass*: 500 1st, 670 tst; *Crew*: 500.

1931 Feb 5: Launched.
Oct 2: Maiden voyage London-Bombay-Colombo-Melbourne-Sydney.
1939 Converted to a troopship.
1943 Was used in the Red Sea as training ship for invasion of Italy.

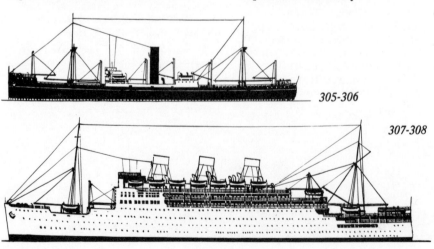

305-306

307-308

309-310

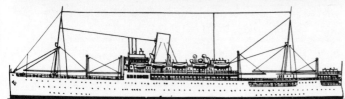

309a

1948-9 Reconditioned at Belfast. Emerged with centre funnel only.
1950 Jan 5: Resumed Australian service.
1954 Converted to one class; *Pass*: 1,252. Bombay call omitted.
1961 Dec 7: Final voyage to Australia.
1962 Apr: Sold to Shun Fung Ironworks, Hong Kong, for breaking up.

308 STRATHAIRD (I)

Details as *Strathnaver* (*307*) except: **Bt** 1932; *T*: 22,544 g, 13,485 n.

1932 Feb 12: Maiden voyage London-Bombay-Colombo-Australia.
1939-45 Served as a troopship. Carried 128,961 personnel.
1946-7 Reconditioned. Emerged with centre funnel only.
1948 Jan: Resumed Australian service.
1954 Converted to one class; *Pass*: 1,200. Bombay call omitted.
1961 Mar 28: Last voyage to Australia.
1967 July 21: Sold to Shun Fung Ironworks, Hong Kong, for scrap.

309 CARTHAGE (II)

Bt 1931 Alex Stephen & Sons, Linthouse, Glasgow; *T*: 14,304 g, 7,665 n. **Dim** 522 ft 6 in (159.26 m) × 71 ft 5 in (21.77 m) × 42 ft 1 in (12.83 m). **Eng** Tw scr, 6 geared turbines; 14,000 SHP; *Stm P*: 425 lb; 18 kts. **H** Steel, swimming pool; *Pass*: 175 1st, 196 2nd.

1930 Laid down as *Canton* (III) for Far East route.
1931 Aug 18: Launched.
Nov 28: Delivered. Far East route.
1932 Apr 22: Placed on Australian service.
1939 Converted at Calcutta into an armed

merchant cruiser.
1943 Converted in the USA to a troopship. Based at Calcutta.
1948 Rebuilt with forward funnel only (*309a*). Resumed P&O service.
1961 Feb 13: Sold to Mitsui Bussan KK, Osaka, for scrap. Broken up in Japan. Delivered as *Carthage Maru*.

310 CORFU

Details as *Carthage* (*309*) except: *T*: 14,251 g, 7,665 n.

1930 Laid down as *Cheefoo* for Far East service.
1931 May 20: Launched.
Sept 26: Commissioned for Far East services.
1939 Requisitioned for use as an armed merchant cruiser.
1940 Damaged in collision by the aircraft carrier HMS *Hermes* off Freetown. Repaired there.
1944 Converted at Mobile, Alabama, into a troopship for Far East.
1945 *Corfu* was in the first convoy to re-enter Singapore.
1949 Feb: Resumed P&O services to the Far East.
1961 Sold to Mitsui Bussan KK, Osaka, and broken up there. Renamed *Corfu Maru* for delivery voyage.

311 STRATHMORE (I)

Bt 1935 Vickers-Armstrong, Barrow-in-Furness; *T*: 23,580 g, 13,993 n. **Dim** 665 ft (202.69 m) oa, 640 ft 4 in (195.17 m) × 82 ft 2 in (25.04 m) × 33 ft 7 in (10.24 m). **Eng** Tw scr, 6 sgl reduction geared turbines; 4,912 NHP; 4 water tube boilers; *Stm P*:

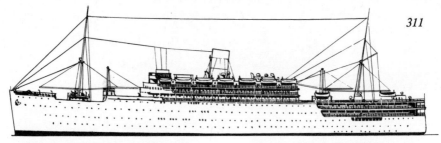

311

450 lb; 20 kts; By builders. **H** Steel, 3 decks, fcsle 81 ft (24.69 m), bridge 319 ft (97.23 m); *Pass*: 525 1st, 500 tst.

1935 Apr 4: Launched.
Oct 4: Maiden voyage was a cruise.
Nov: Placed on the London-Australia express service.
1939-45 Served as a troopship.
1948-9 Reconditioned by builders.
1949 Oct 27: Resumed P&O service to Sydney via Bombay.
1961 Converted to one class ship; *Pass*: 1,250. Bombay call omitted.
1963 June 20: Last voyage to Australia, then sold to John S. Latsis, Piraeus. Renamed *Marianna Latsis*. Used on the Mecca pilgrimage run from Karachi.
1966 Renamed *Henrietta Latsis*.
1969 Broken up at Spezia.

312 **STRATHEDEN**

Bt 1937 Vickers-Armstrong, Barrow-in-Furness; *T*: 23,732 g, 14,127 n. **Dim** 664 ft 6 in (202.54 m) oa, 639 ft 6 in (194.92 m) × 82 ft 2 in (25.04 m) × 35 ft 7 in (10.85 m). **Eng** Tw scr, 6 sgl reduction geared turbines; 24,000 SHP, 4,112 NHP; 4 water tube boilers; *Stm P*: 450 lb; 20 kts; By builders. **H** Steel, 3 decks, fcsle 81 ft (24.69 m), bridge 316 ft (96.32 m); *Pass*: 530 1st, 450 tst.

1937 June 10: Launched.
Dec 24: Maiden voyage to Australia.

1939-45 Served as a troopship.
1946-47 Reconditioned by builders.
1947 June: Resumed her original P&O service.
1950 Made four round voyages to New York on charter to Cunard.
1961 Apr: Converted to a one class ship. Bombay call omitted.
1963 Aug 7: Final Australian voyage, then chartered to the Travel Savings Association for cruises.
1964 Sold to John S. Latsis, Piraeus. Renamed *Henrietta Latsis*.
1966 Renamed *Marianna Latsis*.
1969 Broken up at Spezia.

313 **STRATHALLAN**

Details as *Stratheden* (*312*) except: *T*: 23,722 g, 14,134 n.

1937 Sept 23: Launched.
1938 Mar 18: Maiden voyage to Australia.
1939 Requisitioned for use as a troopship.
1942 Dec 12: Took part in the North African landings. Left the Clyde as commodore ship of her convoy en route for Oran with 4,000 troops and 250 nurses aboard.
Dec 21: 2.25 am. Torpedoed by *U-562* off Oran, Algeria. Four killed by explosion. The ship's lifeboats took off all the nurses and 1,000 troops. *Strathallan* was taken in tow but between 10 am and 2 pm the list continued to develop. The remaining

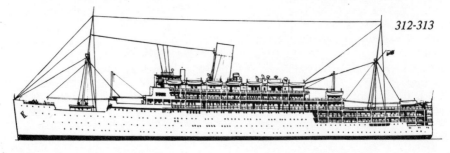

312-313

troops were then taken off. The fire aboard her had by now reached the ammunition store, so the crew were evacuated. *Strathallan* finally rolled over and sank only 19 miles short of her destination.

314 ETTRICK

Bt 1938 Barclay Curle, Glasgow; *T*: 11,279 g, 6,709 n. **Dim** 516 ft 9 in (157.51 m) oa, 496 ft 6 in (151.33 m) × 63 ft 2 in (19.25 m) × 31 ft (9.45 m); *Dft*: 23 ft 3 in (7.09 m). **Eng** Tw scr motorship, 2 Doxford diesels, 2 stroke sgl acting, 10 cyls; *Cyls*: 22 in (55.88 cm); *Stroke*: 66 in (167.64 cm); 1,510 NHP; 2 dbl ended boilers; 20 kts; By builders. **H** Steel, 3 decks, fcsle 61 ft (18.59 m); *Pass*: 1,150 troops.

1938 Aug 25: Launched as a consort to the British India and Bibby Line troopships. P&O's only permanent troopship.
1939 Jan 16: Maiden voyage with troops to West Indies.
1940 May 17: Left Gibraltar for Bordeaux to rescue 250 refugees.
June 14: Arrived at Brest but driven off by bombing; proceeded to St Nazaire where she found the Germans had taken the port.
June 22: Went on to Bayonne and took aboard 2,000 refugees for England, including King Zog of Albania and his retinue.
1942 Nov 8: Took part in the North African landings at the port of Azeu.
Nov 15: Torpedoed on her homeward

voyage 120 miles NW of Gibraltar. 24 lives lost.

315 CANTON (IV)

Bt 1938 Alex Stephen & Sons, Linthouse, Glasgow; *T*: 15,784 g, 9,255 n. **Dim** 568 ft 4 in (173.23 m) oa, 541 ft 7 in (165.07 m) × 73 ft 5 in (22.38 m) × 41 ft 9 in (12.73 m); *Dft*: 29 ft 6 in (8.99 m). **Eng** Tw scr, 2 sets of 3 Parsons steam turbines, sgl reduction geared; 18,500 SHP, 4,032 NHP; *Stm P*: 435 lb; 18 kts; By builders. **H** Steel, 2 decks, open air swimming pool, fcsle 91 ft (27.74 m), bridge 287 ft (87.48 m); *Pass*: 302 1st, 244 tst; *Crew*: 350.

1938 Apr 14: Launched.
Oct 7: Maiden voyage Tilbury-Suez-Far East in P&O traditional colours.
1939 White hull and buff funnel.
Sept: Converted into an armed merchant cruiser. Later converted, at Capetown, into a troopship; as such *Canton* steamed 220,830 miles.
1946 Refitted and re-entered service to Far East in white livery.
1962 Oct 3: Sold for breaking up to Leung Yan Shipbreaking Co, Hong Kong.

316 SURAT (II)

Bt 1938 Alex Stephen & Sons, Linthouse, Glasgow; *T*: 5,529 g. **Dim** 445 ft (135.64 cm) × 58 ft 8 in (17.88 m) × 28 ft 5 in (8.66 m). **Eng** Sgl scr motorship; 12 kts; By builders. **H** Steel, 1 deck, fcsle 38 ft (11.58 m).

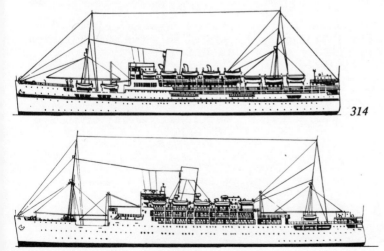

314

315

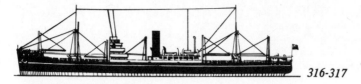

316-317

318

1938 Dec 1: Delivered.
1941 May 6: Torpedoed west of Freetown.

317 SHILLONG (I)

Details as *Surat (316)* except: *T*: 5,528 g.

1939 Feb 14: Delivered.
1943 Apr 5: Torpedoed in North Atlantic.

318 SOCOTRA (II)

Bt 1943 Barclay Curle, Glasgow; *T*:
7,754 g, 3,851 n. **Dim** 485 ft 6 in (147.98 m)
oa, 465 ft 7 in (141.91 m) × 62 ft (18.9 m)
× 38 ft 4 in (11.68 m). **Eng** Tw scr, oil
engine, 8 cyls; *Cyls*: 26 in (66.04 cm);
Stroke: 91½ in (232.41 cm); 1,721 NHP; 16
kts; By builders. **H** Steel, 1 deck and shelter
deck, fcsle 48 ft (14.63 m).

1943 Built for the Ministry of War
Transport; P&O as managers.
1946 July 3: Purchased by P&O.
1965 June 18: Sold for scrap.

319 PARINGA

Bt 1936 John Brown, Clydebank; *T*:
11,063 g, 6,521 n. **Dim** 532 ft 2 in (162.2 m)
× 70 ft 5 in (21.46 m) × 34 ft 7 in
(10.54 m). **Eng** Tw scr, Doxford opposed
diesels, 10 cyls; *Cyls*: 28 in (71.12 cm);
Stroke: 88 in (223.52 cm); 13,250 SHP,
2,528 NHP; 19½ kts. **H** Steel, 2 decks and
shelter deck; *Cargo*: 517,000 cu ft (14,640
cu m).

1936 Built as *Essex* for Federal Steam
Nav Co.
1947 Feb 7: Transferred to P&O.
Renamed *Paringa*.
1955 Returned to Federal Line. Renamed
Norfolk.
1962 Sold for breaking up.

320 PALANA

Details as *Paringa (319)* except: *T*:
11,063 g, 6,516 n.

1936 Nov 17: Launched as *Sussex* for
Federal Steam Nav Co.
1937 Feb 11: Maiden voyage to Australia.
1946 Nov 26: Transferred to P&O.
Renamed *Palana*.
1951 Jan 3: Struck a reef off Mackay,
Australia. Repairs took 18 months.
1954 Returned to Federal. Renamed
Cambridge.
1962 Sold to Mitsubishi, Japan, and
broken up at Niigata.

321 PINJARRA

Bt 1944 James Laing, Sunderland; *T*:
9,888 g, 7,087 n. **Dim** 500 ft 4 in (152.5 m)
oa, 475 ft 5 in (144.91 m) × 64 ft 1 in
(19.53 m) × 40 ft (12.19 m). **Eng** Sgl scr, 3
steam turbines; 1,388 HP; 2 water tube
boilers; *Stm P*: 440 lb; 16 kts; By
Richardsons, Westgarth, Hartlepool. **H**
Steel, 2 decks, fcsle 40 ft (12.19 m), poop
34 ft (10.36 m).

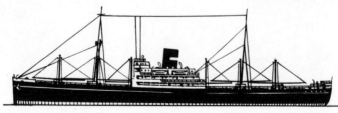

319-320

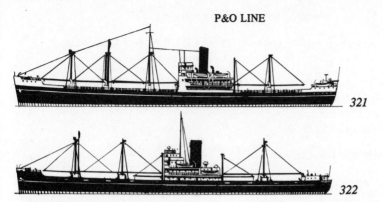

321

322

1944 Built for the Ministry of War Transport as *Empire Paragon*.
1946 July: Acquired by P&O. The first James Laing-built vessel for 70 years, since *Kashgar* (*138*).
1962 Sold. Renamed *Hong Kong Importer* of International Import Lines, Nassau.
1970 Broken up at Taiwan.

322 **PERIM** (II)

Bt 1945 Barclay Curle, Glasgow; *T*: 9,550 g, 5,639 n. **Dim** 499 ft 6 in (152.25 m) oa, 480 ft 2 in (146.36 m) × 64 ft 9 in (19.74 m) × 38 ft 6 in (11.73 m). **Eng** Sgl scr, 3 steam turbines, dbl reduction geared; 1,547 HP; 2 water tube boilers; *Stm P*: 440 lb; 15 kts; By builders. **H** Steel, 3 decks, fcsle 46 ft (14.02 m).

1945 Nov 29: Handed over.
1967 May 23: Sold for breaking up.

323 **ADEN** (III)

Bt 1946 Alex Stephen & Sons, Linthouse, Glasgow; *T*: 9,943 g, 5,870 n. **Dim** 495 ft 4 in (150.98 m) oa, 477 ft (145.39 m) × 64 ft 9 in (19.74 m) × 39 ft (11.89 m). **Eng** Sgl scr, 3 steam turbines, dbl reduction geared; 1,819 HP; 2 water tube boilers; *Stm P*:

460 lb; 15 kts; By builders. **H** Steel, 2 decks, fcsle 39 ft (11.89 m).

1946 Built as *Somerset* for Federal Steam Nav Co.
1954 Renamed *Aden* and transferred to P&O management but not actually to their ownership.

324 **DONGOLA** (II)

Bt 1946 Westcoast Shipbuilders Ltd, Vancouver, British Columbia; *T*: 7,371 g, 4,397 n. **Dim** 441 ft 6 in (134.57 m) oa, 424 ft 7 in (129.41 m) × 57 ft 2 in (17.42 m) × 34 ft 10 in (10.62 m). **Eng** Sgl scr, tpl exp; *Cyls*: 24½ in (62.23 cm), 37 in (93.98 cm) and 70 in (177.8 cm); *Stroke*: 48 in (121.92 cm); *Stm P*: 230 lb; 9½ kts; By Dominion Engineering Co, Latching, Quebec. **H** Steel, 2 decks; *Cargo*: 13,585 cu m (479,747 cu ft) (grain).

1946 Laid down as 'Ocean' type standard ship *Orford Ness*. Completed as *Rabaul* for W. R. Carpenter of Sydney.
1947 Dec: Acquired by P&O. Renamed *Dongola*. Australia-Calcutta-Chittagong service.
1949-52 Under British India management.

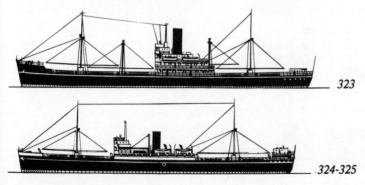

323

324-325

103

1961 May 8: Sold to Surrendra (Overseas) Ltd, Calcutta.

325 DEVANHA (II)

Details as *Dongola* (*324*) except: **Bt** 1947; *T*: 7,367 g, 4,387 n.

1947 Jan: Built as *Lautoka* for W. R. Carpenter, Sydney.
Sept 3: Purchased by P&O. Renamed *Devanha*.
1953-61 UK-Karachi-Bombay-Calcutta route.
1961 Apr 11: Sold to Fraternity Shipping Co, Hong Kong.

326 KARMALA (II)

Bt 1945 Bethlehem Fairfield Shipyard Inc, Baltimore, Maryland; *T*: 7,673 g, 4,583 n. **Dim** 441 ft 4 in (134.52 m) × 62 ft 1 in (18.92 m) × 34 ft 6 in (10.52 m). **Eng** Sgl scr, 2 steam turbines, dbl reduction geared; 6,000 SHP at 90 rpm; *Stm P*: 479 lb; 15 kts; By Westinghouse Electric & Mfg Co, Pittsburg. **H** Steel, 2 decks, fcsle 89 ft (27.13 m); *Cargo*: 524,000 cu ft (14,838 cu m).

1945 Built as *Sheepshead Bay Victory*.
1947 Purchased by Billmeir's Stanhope SS Co. Renamed *Stanholme*.
1947 Oct 6: Acquired by P&O. Renamed *Karmala*.
1967 Aug: Broken up at Kaohsiung.

327 KHYBER (II)

Details as *Karmala* (*326*) except: *T*: 7,675 g, 4,592 n.

1945 Built as *Mahanoy City Victory*.
1946 Purchased by Billmeir's Stanhope SS Co. Renamed *Stanmore*.
1947 Sept 9: Sold to P&O. Renamed *Khyber*.

1964 Sold. Renamed *Comet Victory*. Dragon SS Co, Liberia.
1968 Aug 12: Renamed *Ocean Comet*. Owned by Republic SS Co, Monrovia, Liberia.
1969 Dec: Arrived at Kaohsiung for breaking up.

328 SOUDAN (III)

Bt 1948 Barclay Curle, Glasgow; *T*: 9,080 g, 4,387 n. **Dim** 523 ft 10 in (159.66 m) oa, 501 ft 10 in (152.96 m) × 67 ft (20.42 m) × 43 ft (13.11 m); *Dft*: 29 ft 6 in (8.99 m). **Eng** Tw scr, 2 oil engines, 6 cyls; *Cyls*: 26 in (66.04 cm); *Stroke*: 91 in (231.14 cm); 13,600 BHP; 16 kts; Doxford engines by builders. **H** Steel; *Cargo*: 580,540 cu ft (16,439 cu m) bulk, 93,270 cu ft (2,641 cu m) refrig; *Pass*: 12; *Crew*: 87 (later 101).

Identification note: single post on fcsle.

1947 Oct 7: Launched.
1949 Apr 1: Maiden voyage on Far East route.
1970 Feb 24: Sold to Mitsui KK for breaking up at Kaohsiung, Taiwan.

329 SOMALI (III)

Details as *Soudan* (*328*) except: *T*: 4,389 n.

1948 Apr 22: Launched.
Dec 15: Delivered. Placed on UK-Malaya-Singapore-Hong Kong-Shanghai-Japan route.
1969 Oct 1: Sold to Happy Cia Nav, Panama. Renamed *Happyland*.

330 HIMALAYA (III)

Bt 1949 Vickers-Armstrong, Barrow-in-Furness; *T*: 27,955 g, 15,443 n. **Dim** 709 ft (216.1 m) oa, 668 ft (203.61 m) × 90 ft 6 in

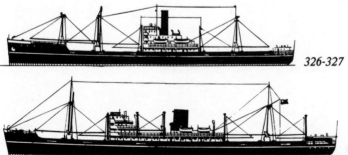

326-327

328-329

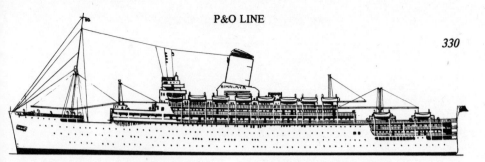

(27.58 m) × 50 ft (15.24 m); *Dft*: 31 ft (9.45 m). **Eng** Tw scr, 6 reduction geared turbines, high pressure turbine dbl reduction, remainder sgl reduction geared; 42,500 SHP; 4 water tube boilers, fitted with first Weir water distilling plant; 22½ kts; By builders. **H** Steel, 2 decks, fcsle 95 ft (28.96 m), bridge 394 ft (120.09 m); *Pass*: 760 1st, 410 tst; *Crew*: 640.

1948 Oct 5: Launched. Interior design by MacInnes, Gardner & Partners.
1949 Oct 6: Maiden voyage Tilbury-Bombay (15 days)-Melbourne (28 days)-Sydney (30 days).
1958 Sydney-Auckland-Vancouver-San Francisco route.
1959 Placed on the London-Sydney-Trans-pacific service.
1963 Nov: Converted to one class after the withdrawal of the last of the 'Straths'. UK-Australia route.
1974 Oct: Last voyage was UK-Hong Kong.
Nov 30: Sold to Mitsui for breaking up at Taiwan.

331 SURAT (III)

Bt 1948 Vickers-Armstrong, Naval Yard, Walker-on-Tyne; *T*: 8,925 g, 4,808 n. **Dim** 522 ft (159.11 m) oa, 497 ft 7 in (151.66 m) × 67 ft 4 in (20.52 m) × 30 ft 5 in (9.27 m); *Dft*: 29 ft 7 in (9.02 m). **Eng** Sgl scr, 3 reduction geared turbines, high pressure turbine dbl reduction geared, remainder sgl reduction geared; 13,000 SHP; *Stm P*: 585 lb; 17 kts. **H** Steel, shelter deck and 2 lower decks, fcsle 52 ft (15.85 m); *Cargo*: 586,646 cu ft (16,612 cu m) in 5

holds; *Pass*: 12; *Crew*: 90.

1947 Nov 28: Launched. Four single and four double cabins.
1948 Oct 22: Registered. Operated on the Far East service.
1968 Sept 10: Renamed *Pando Head*.
1972 Apr 10: Sold to Thos W. Ward and broken up at Inverkeithing, Scotland.

332 SHILLONG (II)

Details as *Surat* (*331*) except: **Bt** 1949; *T*: 8,934 g, 4,816 n.

1948 June 10: Launched.
1949 Mar 5: Delivered.
1957 Oct 23: Sank in the Red Sea after a collision with Purfina's tanker *Purfina Congo*. Two crew died in the collision. Six passengers and 84 crew were rescued by the Danish tanker *Shotland*, owned by Danske-Fransk.

333 SINGAPORE (III)

Details as *Surat* (*331*) except: **Bt** 1951 John Brown, Clydebank; *T*: 9,236 g, 5,010 n. **Dim** 522 ft 10 in (159.36 m) oa, 498 ft 9 in (152.02 m) × 69 ft 2 in (21.08 m) × 30 ft 4 in (9.24 m); *Dft*: 29 ft 6 in (8.99 m). **Eng** 18 kts.

1951 May 5: Maiden voyage Tilbury-Rotterdam-Southampton-Genoa-Singapore-Hong Kong.
1964 Renamed *Comorin* (II). Remained on Far East services.
1968 Renamed *Pando Cove*.
1972 Mar 22: Sold to Ferrobuques, Bilbao, for breaking up.

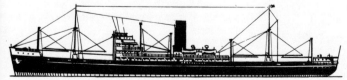

331-334

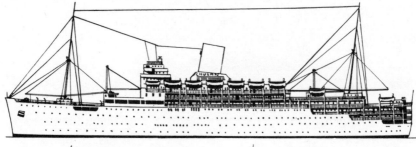

335

336-337

334 SUNDA (III)

Details as *Singapore* (*333*) except: **Bt** 1952;
T: 9,235 g, 4,965 n.
Identification note: only Sunda *had fcsle
derrick post.*

1952 June 11: Launched.
Oct 23: Maiden voyage to Malaya and Far
East.
1968 Nov: Renamed *Pando Strait*.
1972 June 26: Sold for breaking up.

335 CHUSAN (III)

Bt 1950 Vickers-Armstrong, Barrow-in-
Furness; *T*: 24,215 g, 13,445 n. **Dim** 672 ft
6 in (204.98 m) oa, 646 ft 6 in (197.05 m) ×
85 ft 2 in (25.96 m) × 36 ft 2 in (11.02 m);
Dft: 29 ft (8.84 m). **Eng** Tw scr, 6 dbl
reduction geared steam turbines, high
pressure turbine dbl reduction, remainder
sgl reduction geared; 42,500 SHP; 4 water
tube boilers; *Stm P*: 535 lb; 23 kts; By
builders. **H** Steel, 2 decks, upper fcsle
110 ft (33.53 m), fcsle and bridge 550 ft
(167.64 m); *Pass*: 474 1st, 514 tst.

*Fitted with Denny-Brown stabilisers 12 ft
(3.66 m) × 6 ft 6 in (1.98 m) which damp a
40° roll down to 4°. This was the first to be
fitted in a major passenger liner.*

1949 June 29: Launched.
1950 July 14: Delivered. Commenced her
career with a series of cruises.
Sept: First voyage to Bombay, thereafter on
the Far East service.
1951 Thornycroft cowl added to funnel.
1959 Used for world cruises.

1963 Australia-Hong Kong-Yokohama
service.
1970 Jan: Last passenger sailing to
Bombay.
1973 July: Sold to Mitsui and broken up at
Kaohsiung, Taiwan.

336 COROMANDEL (II)

Bt 1949 Barclay Curle, Glasgow; *T*:
7,065 g, 4,026 n. **Dim** 484 ft 6 in (147.68 m)
oa, 465 ft 5 in (141.86 m) × 62 ft 10 in
(19.15 m) × 27 ft 8 in (8.43 m). **Eng** Sgl scr,
oil engine, 6 cyls; *Cyls*: 26 in (66.04 cm);
Stroke: 91 in (231.14 cm); By builders. **H**
Steel, 1 deck and shelter deck; *Cargo*:
15,882 cu m (560,864 cu ft), 571 cu m
(20,164 cu ft) refrig; *Crew*: 69.

1949 Oct 20: Delivered.
1969 Oct 16: Sold. Renamed *Shun Ming*.

337 CANNANORE

Details as *Coromandel* (*336*) except: *T*:
7,065 g, 4,026 n.

1948 Oct 7: Launched.
1949 July 5: Delivered for UK-India
service.
1960 Transferred to Far East route.
1962 Returned to Indian service and
operated by British India SN Co.
1971 Oct: Transferred to P&O General
Cargo Division.
1972 Mar 1: Sold to Pac-Trade Nav Co,
Liberia.

338 PATONGA

Bt 1953 Alex Stephen & Sons, Linthouse,

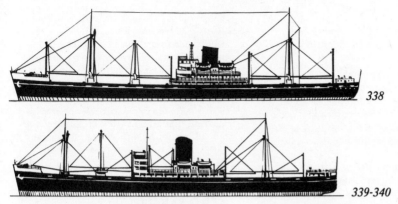

338

339-340

Glasgow; *T*: 10,071 g, 5,898 n. **Dim** 482 ft 4 in (147.01 m) × 64 ft 7 in (19.69 m) × 39 ft 2 in (11.94 m); *Dft*: 27 ft 5 in (8.36 m). **Eng** Sgl scr, 3 dbl reduction geared turbines; 8,000 BHP; *Stm P*: 570 lb; 15½ kts; By builders. **H** Steel, 1 deck and shelter deck; *Cargo*: 390,000 cu ft (11,044 cu m) insulated, 116,000 cu ft (3,285 cu m) dry cargo.

1953 Aug 7: Launched.
Dec 7: Delivered for use on the Australian services.
1975 May 28: Renamed *Strathlauder*.
1977 Sept 9: Arrived at Karachi for breaking up.

339 **BALLARAT** (III)

Bt 1954 Alex Stephen & Sons, Linthouse, Glasgow; *T*: 8,792 g, 4,894 n. **Dim** 490 ft 9 in (149.58 m) × 69 ft (21.03 m) × 40 ft 3 in (12.27 m). **Eng** Sgl scr, 3 steam turbines, high pressure dbl reduction, remainder sgl reduction geared; 13,000 SHP; 2 water tube boilers; *Stm P*: 585 lb; By builders. **H** Steel, 2 decks and shelter deck, 6 holds, fcsle 43 ft (13.11 m); *Cargo*: 19,162 cu m (676,695 cu ft) (bale); *Crew*: 80.

1954 Apr 6: Launched.
July 16: Delivered for the Australian trade.
1968 July: Renamed *Pando Cape* and transferred to Far East service.
1972 Nov 11: Sold to the Ben Line. Renamed *Benledi*.

340 **BENDIGO** (III)

Details as *Ballarat* (*339*) except: *T*: 8,782 g, 4,856 n.

1954 Aug 12: Launched.
Nov 25: Entered UK-Australia service.
1968 Oct: Renamed *Pando Sound* and transferred to Far East route.
1972 May 11: Sold for scrap. Broken up by Thos W. Ward at Neath.

341 **ARCADIA** (II)

Bt 1954 John Brown, Clydebank; *T*: 29,664 g, 16,077 n. **Dim** 721 ft 4 in (219.86 m) oa, 668 ft (203.61 m) × 90 ft 8 in (27.63 m) × 40 ft (12.19 m); *Dft*: 31 ft (9.45 m). **Eng** Tw scr, 6 dbl and sgl reduction geared steam turbines, high pressure only dbl reduction geared: 42,500 IHP; 3 water tube boilers; *Stm P*: 620 lb; 22 kts; By builders. **H** Steel, 8 decks, 545 cabins, upper fcsle 125 ft (38.1 m), fcsle

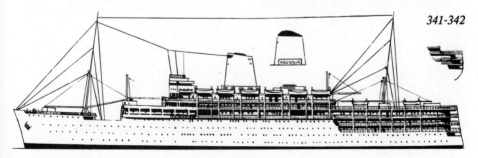

341-342

107

and bridge 511 ft (155.75 m); *Cargo*:
166,979 cu ft (4,728 cu m) bulk and
110,781 cu ft (3,137 cu m) refrig; *Pass*: 679
1st, 735 tst; *Crew*: 711.

1953 May 14: Launched.
1954 Feb 22: Maiden voyage London-
Bombay-Colombo-Melbourne-Sydney.
1959 Fitted with air conditioning
throughout. Then placed on the London-
Australia-transpacific-San Francisco
service.
1974 Based on the West Coast of USA for
cruises to Alaska and Mexico.
1975 Replaced *Himalaya* (*330*) on
Australian route; then based in Australia.
1978 Present fleet.

342 IBERIA (III)

Details as *Arcadia* (*341*) except: **Bt**
Harland & Wolff, Belfast; *T*: 29,614 g,
15,885 n. **Dim** 718 ft 8 in (219.05 m) oa.
Eng By builders. *Pass*: 697 1st.

1954 Jan 21: Launched.
Sept 28: Maiden voyage London-Bombay-
Colombo-Melbourne-Sydney.
1956 Mar 27: Badly damaged in a collision
with the tanker *Stanvac Pretoria* off
Colombo.
1959 Placed on the transpacific service.
1961 Modernised, air conditioned
throughout and stabilisers fitted.
1972 June 3: Last voyage to UK and then
used for cruising.
1973 Feb 7: Broken up at Kaohsiung by
Nan Feng Steel.

343 EMPIRE FOWEY

Bt 1935 Blohm & Voss, Hamburg; *T*:
19,121 g, 10,779 n. **Dim** 633 ft 10 in
(193.19 m) × 74 ft 2 in (22.61 m) × 27 ft
5 in (8.36 m). **Eng** Tw scr, 6 steam turbines
dbl reduction geared; *Stm P*: 585 lb; 17½
kts; 1945 engine by Alex Stephen & Sons,
Linthouse, Glasgow. **H** Steel, 3 decks;
Pass: 155 1st, 104 2nd, 80 3rd.

1935 Built as *Potsdam* for Norddeutscher
Lloyd's Far East service.
1945 Ceded to Britain. Placed in P&O
management. Converted into a troopship;
102 sergeants and 1,206 troops.
Re-engined and re-boilered by Alex
Stephen & Co.
1961 Sold to the Pan-Islamic Co, Karachi,
Pakistan. Renamed *Safina-el-Hujjaj*. Used
on the Karachi-Jeddah Mecca pilgrimage
traffic. Made five voyages in the 66 day
Hadj period. *Pass*: 166 1st, 295 2nd, 2,141
pilgrims.

344 BALRANALD (II)

Bt 1956 Scotts SB & E Co, Greenock; *T*:
8,513 g, 3,906 n, 10,140 dwt. **Dim** 514 ft
(156.67 m) oa, 480 ft (146.3 m) × 67 ft 6 in
(20.57 m) × 41 ft 8 in (12.7 m); *Dft*: 27 ft
8 in (8.43 m). **Eng** Sgl scr, 3 Pametrada
turbines, high pressure dbl, remainder sgl
reduction geared; 11,275 SHP; 2 water
tube boilers; *Stm P*: 525 lb; 17 kts; By
builders. **H** Steel, 1 deck and shelter deck,
fcsle 42 ft (12.8 m); *Crew*: 112.

1956 Nov: Built as *Nyanza* for British India
SN Co.
1964 Nov 17: Transferred to P&O.
Renamed *Balranald* for UK-Australian
route.
1968 July 23: Returned to British India SN
Co. Renamed *Nyanza*.
1971 Became a part of the P&O General
Cargo Division.
1974 Mar 6: Sold to Arya National
Shipping Co, Teheran. Renamed *Arya
Gol*.

345 BARADINE (II)

Details as *Balranald* (*344*) except: *T*:
8,511 g, 3,876 n, 10,140 dwt.

1956 Nov 2: Built as *Nardana* for British
India SN Co for UK-Australia service.
1963 Oct 3: Transferred to P&O. Renamed
Baradine.

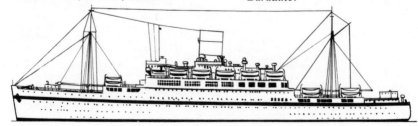

343

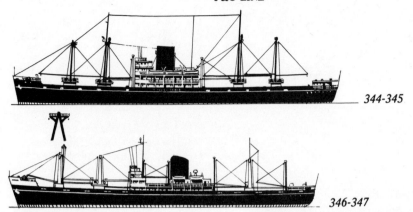

344-345

346-347

1968 Aug 30: Reverted to *Nardana* and British India SN Co.
1971 Oct: Transferred to P&O General Cargo Division.
1973 Dec 7: Sold to Arya National Shipping Co, Teheran. Renamed *Arya Pan*.

346 SALMARA

Bt 1956 John Brown (Clydebank) Ltd, Glasgow; *T*: 8,199 g, 4,438 n, 11,292 dwt. **Dim** 499 ft 8 in (148.98 m) oa, 470 ft (143.26 m) × 64 ft 6 in (19.66 m) × 42 ft (12.8 m); *Dft*: 28 ft 10 in (8.79 m). **Eng** Sgl scr, Brown-Doxford, 6 cyl diesel; *Cyls*: 750 mm (29.53 in); *Stroke*: 2,500 mm (98.43 in); 8,000 BHP; 15½ kts. **H** Steel, 2 decks, 50 ton derrick, fcsle 45 ft (13.72 m); *Cargo*: 526,000 cu ft (14,895 cu m); *Crew*: 84.

1956 July 9: Built for Far East service.
1966 Sold to the P&O subsidiary company Eastern & Australian SS Co. Renamed *Arakawa*.
1973 Apr 19: Transferred to British India SN. Renamed *Teesta*.
1975 Transferred to P&O General Cargo Division. Renamed *Strathloyal*.
1977 Broken up.

347 SALSETTE (III)

Details as *Salmara* (*346*) except: *T*: 8,199 g, 4,438 n, 11,302 dwt.

1956 July 9: Maiden voyage London-Rotterdam-Genoa-Port Swettenham-Singapore-Manila-Hong Kong-Tientsin-Tsingtao.
1966 Sept: Sold to Eastern & Australian SS Co. Renamed *Aradina*.
1970 Mar: Transferred to British India SN Co. Renamed *Tairea*.
1971 Returned to P&O management.
1975 Apr 17: Renamed *Strathlomond*.
1977 Nov 14: Arrived Karachi for breaking up. Became *United Viscount*, Lenton Shipping Co. Still in service.

348 MALOJA (III)

Bt 1959 Smith's Dock Co, Middlesbrough; *T*: 12,987 g, 7,303 n, 19,119 dwt. **Dim** 559 ft 3 in (170.46 m) oa, 534 ft (162.76 m) × 71 ft 3 in (21.72 m) × 39 ft 2 in (11.94 m); *Dft*: 30 ft 1 in (9.17 m). **Eng** Sgl scr, 2 steam turbines dbl reduction geared; 8,250 BHP; *Stm P*: 645 lb; 14½ kts; By Hawthorn Leslie (Eng), Newcastle. **H** Steel, 1 deck, fcsle 53 ft (16.15 m), bridge 56 ft (17.07 m), poop 113 ft (34.44 m); *Oil*: 922,926 cu ft (26,135 cu m).

1959 Oil tanker. Built for Charter Shipping Co, Bermuda, a P&O subsidiary, and operated by Trident Tankers Ltd, London.

349 MANTUA (II)

Details as *Maloja* (*348*) except: **Bt** 1960; *T*:

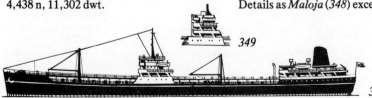

349

348-349

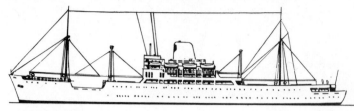

350-351

12,899 g, 7,293 n, 19,016 dwt.

1960 Oil tanker.
1974 Aug 24: Broken up by Gulf Trading
Agency at Gadani.

350 **CHITRAL** (II)

Bt 1956 Soc Anon des Chantiers et Ateliers
de Saint Nazaire; *T*: 13,821 g, 7,230 n. **Dim**
557 ft 8 in (169.98 m) oa, 511 ft 10 in
(156.01 m) × 70 ft (21.34 m) × 40 ft 7 in
(12.37 m); *Dft*: 28 ft 1½ in (8.57 m). **Eng**
Sgl scr, dbl reduction geared Parsons
turbine; 12,500 BHP; 3 water tube boilers;
Stm P: 670 lb; 16½ kts; By builders. **H**
Steel, 2 decks, fcsle 73 ft (22.25 m), bridge
309 ft (94.18 m); *Cargo*: 11,390 cu m
(402,232 cu ft); *Pass*: 274 1st; *Crew*: 214.

1956 Built for Compagnie Maritime Belge,
Antwerp, as *Jadotville* for service to the
Belgian Congo.
1961 Feb 9: Acquired by P&O. Renamed
Chitral (II) to replace *Carthage* (*309*).
Mar 2: First voyage to Far East.
1970 Oct 13: Following the closure of the
Suez Canal *Chitral* and her sister *Cathay*
(*351*) were transferred to the Eastern &
Australian SS Co for service between
Australia and Japan.
1975 Dec 3: Withdrawn, with *Cathay*, and
broken up by Chou's Iron & Steel Co,
Taiwan.

351 **CATHAY** (III)

Details as *Chitral* (*350*) except: **Bt** 1957
Anon Cockerill-Ougrée, Hoboken,

Antwerp; *T*: 13,531 g, 7,628 n.

1957 Built for Compagnie Maritime Belge,
Antwerp, as *Baudouinville*, for service to
the Belgian Congo.
1961 Feb 28: Acquired by P&O. Renamed
Cathay.
1970 Oct 13: *Cathay* was transferred to the
Eastern & Australian SS Co for service
between Australia and Japan.
1975 Withdrawn from service. *Cathay* and
Chitral were built with extensive cargo
space and relatively few passenger berths.
The lack of cargo on the route made the
ships uneconomic for further operation.
1976 *Cathay* sold to Republic of China as a
merchant seaman's training ship.

352 **CANBERRA**

Bt 1961 Harland & Wolff, Belfast; *T*:
45,270 g, 23,672 n. **Dim** 818 ft 6 in
(249.48 m) oa, 740 ft (225.55 m) × 102 ft
(31.09 m) × 41 ft 6 in (12.65 m); *Dft*: 32 ft
8 in (9.95 m). **Eng** Tw scr, 2 steam turbines;
88,200 BHP driving 2 generators, 32,200
kilowatts, 6,000 volt alternating current
connected to 2 electric motors 42,500 SHP
each; 3 water tube boilers; *Stm P*: 940 lb;
27½ kts; Thrust propeller forward; By
builders and Associated Electrical
Industries, Rugby. **H** Steel, 2 decks, 855
cabins, 14 public rooms; *Pass*: 548 1st,
1,690 tst; *Crew*: 938.

1960 Mar 16: Launched. Designer: John
West. Interior design: Sir Hugh Casson.
1961 June 2: Maiden voyage Southampton-

352

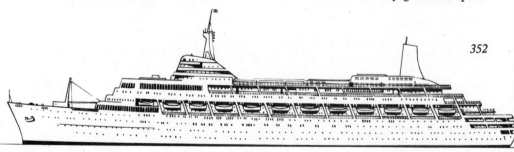

353-354

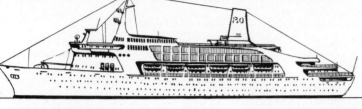

355

Colombo-Melbourne-Sydney. Then placed on the transpacific service.
1975 Cruising and round the world voyages. Present fleet.

353 PANDO GULF

Bt 1957 Barclay Curle, Glasgow; *T*: 8,753 g, 4,056 n. **Dim** 520 ft (158.5 m) oa, 485 ft 3 in (147.9 m) × 68 ft 3 in (20.8 m) × 42 ft 3 in (12.88 m). **Eng** Sgl scr, 2 steam turbines dbl reduction geared; 12,100 SHP; 2 water tube boilers; *Stm P*: 565 lb; 17½ kts; By builders. **H** Steel, 1 deck and shelter deck, fcsle 43 ft (13.11 m); *Pass*: 12.

1957 Built for British India SN Co as *Woodarra*.
1968 Aug 22: Transferred to P&O. Renamed *Pando Gulf*.
1974 Aug 9: Sold to Ben Line. Renamed *Benalbanach*.

354 PANDO POINT

Details as *Pando Gulf (353)* except: **Dim** 520 ft 3 in (158.57 m) oa.

1957 Built as *Waroonga* for British India SN Co.
1968 Sept 9: Transferred to P&O and renamed *Pando Point*.
1974 Aug 9: Sold to Ben Line. Renamed *Benwyris*.

There were seven ships renamed into the 'P-and-O' nomenclature. They were:
Pando Cape *ex* Ballarat (339)
Pando Cove *ex* Singapore (333)
Pando Gulf (353) *ex* Woodarra
Pando Head *ex* Surat (331)

Pando Point (354) *ex* Waroonga
Pando Sound *ex* Bendigo (340)
Pando Strait *ex* Sunda (334)

355 SPIRIT OF LONDON

Bt 1972 Cantieri Navali del Tirreno e Riuniti, Riva Trigoso, Italy; *T*: 17,370 g. **Dim** 535 ft 7 in (163.25 m) × 62 ft 5 in (19.02 m) × 25 ft 6 in (7.77 m). **Eng** Tw scr, 4 medium speed geared Fiat diesels; 18,000 BHP; 20½ kts; Installed by builders; Equipped with forward bow thruster. **H** Steel, 3 decks, fully air conditioned; *Pass:* 874 1st; *Crew:* 322.

1972 Ordered by Lauritz Kloster, Norway. Purchased on the stocks.
Apr 29: Named *Spirit of London* but due to bad weather the launching had to be delayed until May 9.
Oct 11: Delivered.
Nov 11: Maiden voyage.
1974 Oct: Following the acquisition of Princess Cruises Inc renamed *Sun Princess*. Operated on cruises from the West Coast of North America to Alaska or Mexico according to season.

P&O General Cargo Division

Following the establishment of the P&O General Cargo Division the process of renaming ships with the 'Strath' prefix began. Ships registered with Avenue Shipping Co, Asiatic SNC, Federal SN Co and Frank Strick & Co were transferred

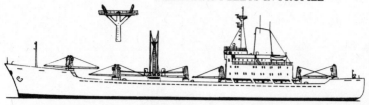

356-358

and renamed. In the following section (356-395) the 'Straths' are depicted in the order that they were transferred to the General Cargo Division, and not in the order of their renaming.

356 STRATHARDLE

Bt 1967 Mitsui Zosen, Tamano; *T*: 9,863 g, 4,740 n. **Dim** 563 ft (171.6 m) oa including bulbous bow, 523 ft 3 in (159.49 m) × 79 ft 6 in (24.23 m) × 45 ft 10 in (13.97 m). **Eng** Sgl scr, oil engine, 9 cyls; *Cyls*: 840 mm (33.07 in); *Stroke*: 1,800 mm (70.87 in); 207,000 BHP; 21 kts; By builders, Burmeister & Wain type. **H** Steel, 2 decks, fcsle 82 ft (24.99 m), poop 32 ft (9.75 m); *Cargo*: 20,954 cu m (739,979 cu ft).

1966 Sept 19: Launched.
1967 Jan 20: Delivered.
Mar 7: Arrived London.
Mar 23: Maiden voyage to Far East via Panama (due to closure of Suez Canal).
1971 Transferred to P&O General Cargo Division. Blue funnel with P&O logo.
1972 Placed on Japan-Pakistan-Persian Gulf route. Present fleet.

357 STRATHBRORA

Details as *Strathardle* (*356*).

1967 Mar 31: Handed over.
1971 Transferred to P&O General Cargo Division. Blue funnel and logo. Present fleet.

358 STRATHCONAN

Details as *Strathardle* (*356*).

1967 June 15: Handed over.
1971 Transferred to P&O General Cargo

Division. Blue funnel and logo. Present fleet.

359 STRATHIRVINE

Bt 1957 Alex Stephen & Sons, Linthouse, Glasgow; *T*: 6,270 g, 3,554 n. **Dim** 460 ft 3 in (140.28 m) oa, 432 ft (131.67 m) × 58 ft 9 in (17.91 m) × 39 ft 6 in (12.04 m). **Eng** Sgl scr, oil engine, 5 cyls; *Cyls*: 670 mm (26.38 in); *Stroke*: 2,320 mm (91.34 in); 5,500 BHP; 14 kts; By Doxford, installed by builders. **H** Steel, 1 deck and shelter deck, fcsle 42 ft (12.8 m).

1957 Built as *Donegal* for Avenue Shipping Co (Trinder Anderson, Managers).
1972 Mar 29: Transferred to P&O.
1975 June 13: Renamed *Strathirvine*.
1978 Sold to Triton Nav Corp, Panama. Renamed *Athina*.

360 STRATHINCH

Details as *Strathirvine* (*359*) except: *T*: 6,305 g, 3,530 n.

1962 Built as *Antrim* for Avenue Shipping Co.
1972 Mar 29: Transferred to P&O.
1975 Mar 2: Renamed *Strathinch*.
1977 Sold to Triton Nav Corp, Maldives. Renamed *Athina*.

361 STRATHINVER

Details as *Strathirvine* (*359*) except: **Bt** 1959 Smiths Dock Co, Middlesbrough; *T*: 7,167 g, 4,141 n. **Dim** 525 ft 3 in (160.1 m) oa, 496 ft 8 in (151.38 m) × 60 ft 3 in (18.36 m) × 38 ft 10 in (11.84 m).

1959 Built as *Galway* for Avenue Shipping Co.
1972 Mar 29: Transferred to P&O.
1975 June 19: Renamed *Strathinver*.

359-361

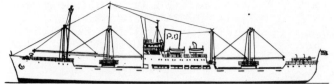

362-363

362 STRATHNEWTON

Bt 1959 Lithgows Ltd, Port Glasgow; *T*: 6,024 g, 3,389 n. **Dim** 481 ft 9 in (146.84 m) oa, 450 ft 6 in (137.31 m) × 62 ft 3 in (18.97 m) × 37 ft 11 in (11.56 m). **Eng** Sgl scr, oil engine, 6 cyls; *Cyls*: 620 mm (24.41 in); *Stroke*: 1,400 mm (55.12 in); 5,500 BHP; 14 kts; By J. G. Kincaid, Burmeister & Wain type. **H** Steel, 2 decks, fcsle 100 ft (30.48 m), poop 42 ft (12.8 m).

Ports along bridge deck. Funnel had a slightly sloping top.

1959 June: Built as *Nurmahal* for Asiatic Steam Nav.
1971 Transferred to British India SN Co. Later managed by Hain-Nourse.
1972 May 11: Transferred to P&O ownership.
1975 Mar 17: Renamed *Strathnewton*.
1977 Nov: Broken up at Karachi.

363 STRATHNEVIS

Details as *Strathnewton* (*362*) except: *T*: 6,099 g, 3,319 n.

Windows on bridge deck. No sloping top to funnel.

1963 Apr: Built as *Nurjehan* for Asiatic Steam Nav. Later managed by Hain-Nourse.
1972 Chartered to T. & J. Harrison. Renamed *Advocate*.

1973 Jan 30: Reverted to *Nurjehan*, owned by P&O.
1975 Renamed *Strathnevis*.
1978 Sold to Unimed Shipping Co, Greece. Renamed *Ioannis*.

364 STRATHNAIRN

Bt 1963 Chas Connell & Co, Glasgow; *T*: 7,109 g, 3,788 n. **Dim** 508 ft 3 in (154.91 m) oa, 470 ft (143.26 m) × 65 ft 3 in (19.89 m) × 40 ft (12.19 m). **Eng** Sgl scr, oil engine, 5 cyls; *Cyls:* 760 mm (29.92 in); *Stroke*: 1,550 mm (61.02 in); 7,500 BHP; 14 kts; Sulzer diesel by Barclay Curle. **H** Steel, 2 decks, fcsle 40 ft (12.19 m), poop 40 ft (12.19 m).

1963 Mar: Built as *Kohinur* for Asiatic Steam Nav.
1972 May 11: Transferred to P&O ownership.
1975 Apr 17: Renamed *Strathnairn*.
1978 Sold to British Bay Shipping Co, Singapore. Renamed *Silvergate*.

365 STRATHTEVIOT

Bt 1962 John Readhead & Sons, South Shields; *T*: 7,277 g, 3,905 n. **Dim** 508 ft 3 in (154.91 m) oa, 470 ft 11 in (143.54 m) × 65 ft 3 in (19.89 m) × 40 ft 1 in (12.22 m). **Eng** Sgl scr, oil engine, 5 cyls; *Cyls*: 760 mm (29.92 in); *Stroke*: 1,550 mm (61.02 in); 7,500 BHP; Sulzer diesel by Wallsend

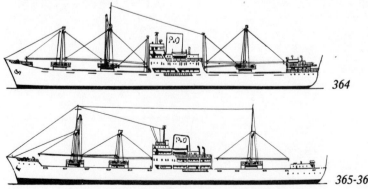

364

365-366

Slipway & Eng Co. **H** Steel, 2 decks, fcsle 39 ft (11.89 m).

1962 Dec: Built as *Trefusis* for Hain SS Co.
1972 May 11: Transferred to P&O ownership.
1975 July 11: Renamed *Strathteviot*.
1978 Sold to Kodros Shipping Corp, Monrovia. Renamed *Evia*.

366 STRATHTAY

Details as *Strathteviot* (*365*).

1962 May: Built as *Trebartha* for Hain SS Co.
1972 May 11: Transferred to P&O ownership.
1975 July 7: Renamed *Strathtay*.
1978 Sold to Marikog Shipping Co, Panama. Renamed *Zak*.

367 STRATHTRUIM

Bt 1963 William Hamilton & Co, Port Glasgow; *T*: 6,875 g, 3,682 n. **Dim** 505 ft 3 in (154 m) oa, 470 ft (143.26 m) × 65 ft 3 in (19.89 m) × 40 ft (12.19 m); *Dft*: 30 ft 9 in (9.37 m). **Eng** Sgl scr, Sulzer diesel, 5 cyls; *Cyls*: 760 mm (29.92 in); *Stroke*: 1,550 mm (61.02 in); 7,500 BHP; 17 kts; By Fairfield-Rowan, Glasgow. **H** Steel, 2 decks, fcsle 38 ft (11.58 m), poop 40 ft (12.19 m).

1963 Aug: Built as *Treneglos* for Hain SS Co.
1972 May 11: Transferred to P&O General Cargo Division.
1974 Nov 28: Renamed *Strathtruim*.
1978 Sold to Torenia Maritime Inc, Monrovia. Renamed *Siam Bay*.

368 STRATHNAVER (II)

Bt 1962 Chas Connell & Co, Glasgow; *T*:

9,890 g, 5,628 n. **Dim** 508 ft 3 in (154.91 m) oa, 470 ft (143.26 m) × 65 ft 3 in (19.89 m) × 40 ft (12.19 m). **Eng** Sgl scr, Sulzer diesel, 5 cyls; *Cyls*: 760 mm (29.92 in); *Stroke*: 1,550 mm (61.02 in); 7,500 BHP; By Barclay Curle, Glasgow. **H** Steel, 2 decks, fcsle 40 ft (12.19 m), poop 40 ft (12.19 m).

1962 Nov: Built as *Jumna* for Nourse SS Co.
1972 May 11: Transferred to P&O General Cargo Division.
1975 Mar 20: Renamed *Strathnaver*.
1978 Sold to Proteas Maritime Inc, Singapore. Renamed *Singapore Progress*.

369 STRATHLEVEN

Bt 1953 Alex Stephen & Sons, Linthouse, Glasgow; *T*: 7,432 g, 4,032 n. **Dim** 499 ft 3 in (152.17 m) oa, 470 ft 3 in (143.33 m) × 64 ft 8 in (19.71 m) × 42 ft (12.8 m). **Eng** Sgl scr, Sulzer diesel, 10 cyls; *Cyls*: 580 mm (22.83 in); *Stroke*: 760 mm (29.92 in), sgl reduction geared via electro-magnetic coupling; 900 BHP; 16 kts; By Sulzer Bros, Winterthur, installed by builders. **H** Steel, 2 decks, fcsle 49 ft (14.94 m).

1953 Built as *Middlesex* for Federal SN Co.
1965 Renamed *Jelunga* and operated by Nourse.
1972 May 11: Transferred to P&O General Cargo Division.
1975 Mar 20: Renamed *Strathleven*.
1978 Broken up.

370 STRATHLAIRG

Bt 1951 Swan Hunter & Wigham Richardson, Newcastle; *T*: 7,267 g, 4,107 n. **Dim** 484 ft 4 in (147.68 m) oa, 455 ft 7 in (138.86 m) × 62 ft 7 in (19.08 m) × 40 ft 8 in (12.39 m). **Eng** Sgl scr, Doxford

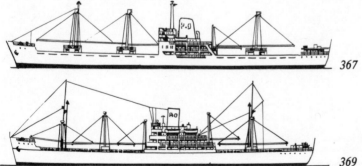

367

369

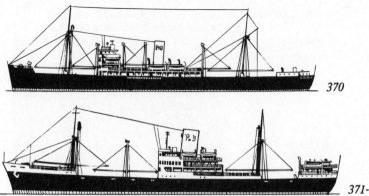

370

371-372

diesel, 6 cyls; *Cyls*: 670 mm (26.38 in); *Stroke*: 2,320 mm (91.34 in); 14½ kts; By builders. **H** Steel, 1 deck and shelter deck, fcsle 42 ft (12.8 m).

1951 Sept: Built as *Chakdina* for British India SN Co.
1973 Apr 19: Transferred to P&O General Cargo Division.
1975 Oct 25: Renamed *Strathlairg*.
1977 Sept 3: Arrived at Kaohsiung for breaking up by Lien Hung Steel Co.

371 STRATHAIRLIE

Bt 1956 John Readhead & Sons, South Shields; *T*: 8,345 g, 4,439 n. **Dim** 510 ft 4 in (155.56 m) oa, 465 ft 10 in (141.99 m) × 62 ft 6 in (19.05 m) × 33 ft 4 in (10.16 m); *Dft*: 26 ft 7 in (8.1 m). **Eng** Sgl scr, Doxford diesel, 6 cyls; *Cyls*: 670 mm (26.38 in); *Stroke*: 2,320 mm (91.34 in); 6,800 BHP; By Hawthorn Leslie, Newcastle. **H** Steel, 2 decks, fcsle 98 ft (29.88 m), bridge 177 ft (53.95 m), poop 41 ft (12.5 m).

'Straths' with endings commencing in 'A' are ex-Strick vessels.

1956 Built as *Baluchistan* for F. C. Strick & Co.
1973 Apr 19: Transferred to P&O General Cargo Division.
1975 Renamed *Strathairlie*.
1977 Aug 26: Arrived at Kaohsiung for breaking up by Tien Cheng Steel.

372 STRATHAROS

Details as *Strathairlie* (*371*) except: **Bt** 1959 Caledon SB & Eng Co, Dundee; *T*: 8,121 g, 4,632 n.

1959 Built as *Baharistan* for F. C. Strick & Co.
1973 Apr 19: Transferred to P&O General Cargo Division.
1975 Apr 4: Renamed *Stratharos*.
1978 Sold to Chi Kong Nav Co, Panama. Renamed *Chi Kong*.

373 STRATHADDIE

Bt 1960 John Readhead & Sons, South Shields; *T*: 9,633 g, 5,373 n. **Dim** 500 ft 6 in (155.56 m) oa, 466 ft (142.04 m) × 63 ft 6 in (19.35 m) × 40 ft 4 in (12.29 m). **Eng** Sgl scr, Doxford diesel, 6 cyls; *Cyls*: 670 mm (26.38 in); *Stroke*: 2,320 mm (91.34 in); 6,600 BHP; 17 kts; By Hawthorn Leslie, Newcastle. **H** Steel, 2 decks, fcsle 106 ft (32.31 m), poop 47 ft (14.33 m).

1960 Built as *Farsistan* for F. C. Strick & Co.
1973 Apr 19: Transferred to P&O General Cargo Division.
1975 Jan 27: Renamed *Strathaddie*.
1978 Sold to Cori Shipping Corp, Liberia. Renamed *Sophocles*.

374 STRATHATLOW

Details as *Strathaddie* (*373*) except: *T*:

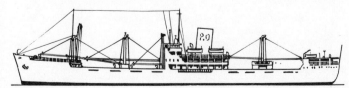

373-375

9,449 g, 5,297 n. **Eng** By William Doxford & Sons, Sunderland.

1959 Built as *Gorjistan*, F. C. Strick & Co.
1973 Apr 19: Transferred to P&O General Cargo Division.
1975 Feb 25: Renamed *Strathatlow*. Present fleet.

375 **STRATHASLAK**

Details as *Strathaddie* (*373*) except: **Bt** 1960; *T*: 7,457 g, 3,780 n.

1960 Nov: Built as *Kohistan* for F. C. Strick & Co.
1972 Transferred to P&O General Cargo Division.
1975 Feb 21: Renamed *Strathaslak*.

376 **STRATHASSYNT**

Bt 1963 John Readhead & Sons, South Shields; *T*: 9,270 g, 5,188 n. **Dim** 503 ft 3 in (153.39 m) oa, 470 ft (143.26 m) × 65 ft 9 in (20.04 m) × 39 ft 1 in (11.91 m). **Eng** Sgl scr, Doxford diesel, 6 cyls; *Cyls*: 670 mm (26.38 in); *Stroke*: 2,100 mm (82.68 in); 10,000 BHP; 17 kts; By William Doxford & Sons, Sunderland. **H** Steel, 2 decks, fcsle 97 ft (29.57 m), poop 45 ft (13.72 m).

1963 Built as *Turkistan* for F. C. Strick & Co for Arabian Gulf service.
1972 Mar 24: Transferred to P&O General Cargo Division.

1975 Feb 21: Renamed *Strathassynt*.
June: First P&O vessel to transit the re-opened Suez Canal northbound. Present fleet.

377 **STRATHAVOCH**

Bt 1965 Hawthorn Leslie (Ship Builders), Newcastle; *T*: 8,531 g, 4,542 n. **Dim** 485 ft 5 in (147.96 m) oa, 452 ft 4 in (137.87 m) × 63 ft 2 in (19.25 m) × 38 ft 11 in (11.86 m). **Eng** Sgl scr, diesel, 6 cyls; *Cyls*: 750 mm (29.53 in); *Stroke*: 1,600 mm (62.99 in); 9,000 BHP; 16¼ kts; By Fairfield-Rowan, Glasgow. **H** Steel, 2 decks, fcsle 43 ft (13.11 m).

1965 Mar: Built as *Elysia* for Anchor Line's Indian service.
1968 Sold to F. C. Strick and renamed *Armanistan*.
1973 Apr 19: Transferred to P&O General Cargo Division.
1975 Renamed *Strathavoch*. Present fleet.

378 **STRATHCARRON**

Bt 1969 Swan Hunter Shipbuilders, South Shields; *T*: 10,031 g, 4,981 n. **Dim** 504 ft 10 in (153.87 m) oa including bulbous bow, 469 ft 10 in (143.21 m) × 70 ft 2 in (21.39 m) × 40 ft 6 in (12.34 m). **Eng** Sgl scr, Burmeister & Wain diesel, 6 cyls; *Cyls*: 740 mm (29.13 in); *Stroke*: 1,600 mm (62.99 in); 11,600 BHP; 17 kts; By Harland

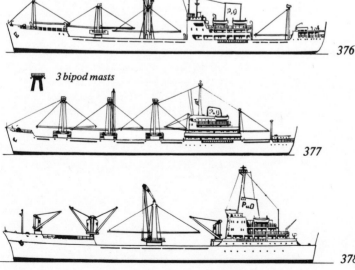

376

3 bipod masts

377

378-379

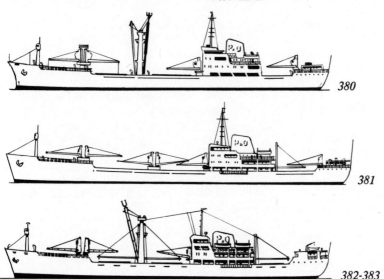

380

381

382-383

& Wolff, Belfast. **H** Steel, 2 decks, fcsle
48 ft 2 in (14.63 m), 1 300 ton Stulcken
derrick.

*'Straths' with endings commencing with
'C' and 'M' are ex-British India vessels
built in the 1960s. Earlier ships had 'L' or
'N' endings.*

1969 June 30: Launched for British India
as *Amra*.
Nov 14: Commenced service Japan-Persian
Gulf.
1973 Apr 19: Transferred to P&O General
Cargo Division.
1975 June 4: Holed in collision with the
Norwegian *Fernspring* (Fearnley & Eger) at
Kobe, Japan.
1976 Jan 9: Renamed *Strathcarron*.
Present fleet.

379 STRATHCARROL

Details as *Strathcarron* (*378*).

1969 Built as *Aska* for British India.
1973 Apr 19: Transferred to P&O registry.
1976 Renamed *Strathcarrol*. Present fleet.

380 STRATHARLICK

Bt 1969 Swan Hunter Shipbuilders, South
Shields; *T*: 9,627 g, 5,475 n. **Dim** 475 ft
(144.78 m) × 69 ft 9 in (21.26 m) × 40 ft
(12.19 m). **Eng** Sgl scr, Doxford diesel, 6
cyls; *Cyls*: 670 mm (26.38 in); *Stroke*:
2,140 mm (84.25 in); 12,000 BHP; 17 kts;
By Doxford & Sunderland SB & Eng Co,

Sunderland. **H** Steel, 2 decks, fcsle 102 ft
(31.09 m), poop 44 ft (13.41 m).

1969 Jan 17: Launched as *Tabaristan* for
F. C. Strick & Co.
May 7: Delivered seven weeks ahead of
schedule. Cost £2 million.
Placed on UK-Arabian Gulf service.
1972 Mar 24: Transferred to P&O General
Cargo Division.
1975 Apr 22: Renamed *Stratharlick*.
Present fleet.

381 STRATHAIRD (II)

Details as *Stratharlick* (*380*) except: **Bt**
1970 Swan Hunter Shipbuilders, South
Shields; *T*: 9,778 g, 5,526 n. **H** Deck cranes
amidships.

1970 Nov: Built as *Nigaristan* for F. C.
Strick & Co.
1974 Feb 14: Transferred to P&O General
Cargo Division.
1975 Jan 27: Renamed *Strathaird*. Present
fleet.

382 STRATHAPPIN

Bt 1965 John Readhead & Sons, South
Shields; *T*: 9,280 g, 5,212 n. **Dim** 503 ft 2 in
(153.4 m) oa, 469 ft 10 in (143.21 m) ×
67 ft 7 in (20.6 m) × 38 ft 10 in (11.84 m).
Eng Sgl scr, Doxford diesel, 6 cyls; *Cyls*:
670 mm (26.38 in); *Stroke*: 2,100 mm
(82.68 in); 10,000 BHP; 17 kts; By William
Doxford & Sons, Sunderland. **H** Steel, 2

decks, fcsle 108 ft (32.92 m), poop 45 ft
(13.72 m).

1965 Jan: Built as *Sharistan* for F. C.
Strick & Co.
1973 Apr 19: Transferred to P&O General
Cargo Division.
1975 Jan 31: Renamed *Strathappin*.
Present fleet.

383 STRATHALVIE

Details as *Strathappin* (*382*) except: **Bt**
1966; *T*: 9,296 g, 5,118 n.

1966 Built as *Floristan* for F. C. Strick &
Co.
1973 Apr 19: Transferred to P&O General
Cargo Division.
1975 Feb 25: Renamed *Strathalvie*.
Present fleet.

384 STRATHANGUS

Bt 1966 John Readhead & Sons, South
Shields; *T*: 8,700 g, 4,800 n. **Dim** 503 ft 2 in
(153.37 m) oa, 469 ft 10 in (143.21 m) ×
63 ft 10 in (19.46 m) × 37 ft 6 in (11.43 m).
Eng Sgl scr, diesel, 6 cyls; *Cyls*: 670 mm
(26.38 in); *Stroke*: 2,100 mm (82.68 in);
10,000 BHP; 17¼ kts; By William Doxford
& Sons, Sunderland. **H** Steel, 2 decks, fcsle
108 ft 3 in (32.99 m), poop 45 ft 3 in
(13.79 m).

1966 Built as *Serbistan* for F. C. Strick &
Co.
1973 Apr 19: Transferred to P&O General
Cargo Division.
1975 Jan 6: Renamed *Strathangus*. Present
fleet.

385 STRATHANNA

Details as *Strathangus* (*384*) except: *T*:
8,819 g, 5,212 n.

1966 Built as *Registan* for F. C. Strick &
Co.
1972 Mar: Transferred to P&O General
Cargo Division.
1975 Mar 7: Renamed *Strathanna*. Present
fleet.

386 STRATHMAY

Bt 1970 Swan Hunter Shipbuilders,
Wallsend-on-Tyne; *T*: 11,208 g, 6,004 n.
Dim 514 ft 9 in (156.9 m) oa including
bulbous bow, 474 ft 11 in (144.75 m) ×
76 ft 3 in (23.24 m) × 42 ft 6 in (12.95 m).
Eng Sgl scr, Sulzer diesel, 6 cyls; *Cyls*:
900 mm (35.43 in); *Stroke*: 1,550 mm
(61.02 in); 17,400 BHP; 19 kts; By Barclay
Curle, Glasgow. **H** Steel, 2 decks, fcsle 95 ft
2 in (29 m), poop 127 ft 4 in (38.8 m).

1970 Mar 9: Launched as *Manora* for
British India SS Co.
Sept 15: Entered service. General cargo
carrier.
1971 Transferred to P&O General Cargo
Division.
1973 Apr 19: Ownership changed to P&O
from British India.
1975 May 9: Renamed *Strathmay*.
Operated on the Australian-Persian Gulf
route. Present fleet.

387 STRATHMEIGLE

Details as *Strathmay* (*386*) except: **Bt** 1971;
T: 11,143 g, 5,947 n.

1971 Mar 10: Delivered as *Merkara* for
British India's Japan-Persian Gulf route.

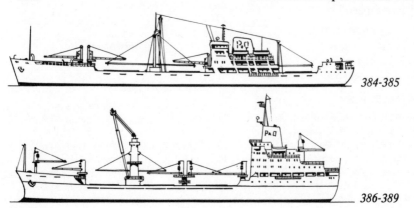

384-385

386-389

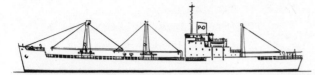

390-395

General cargo carrier.
Oct: Transferred to P&O General Cargo Division.
1973 Ownership changed from British India to P&O.
1975 Apr: Renamed *Strathmeigle*. Present fleet.

388 STRATHMORE (II)

Details as *Strathmay* (*386*) except: *T*: 11,143 g, 5,947 n.

1971 Built as *Morvada* for British India's Japan-Persian Gulf service. Pallet carrier; fitted with side doors. Present fleet.

389 STRATHMUIR

Details as *Strathmay* (*386*) except: *T*: 11,143 g, 5,947 n.

1971 Built as *Mulbera* for British India's Japan-Persian Gulf service. Pallet carrier; fitted with side doors. Present fleet.

390 STRATHDARE

Bt 1974 Austin & Pickersgill, Sunderland; *T*: 9,014 g, 6,383 n. **Dim** 440 ft 1 in (134.14 m) × 67 ft 2 in (20.47 m) × 38 ft 6 in (11.73 m). **Eng** Sgl scr, Sulzer diesel, 5 cyls; *Cyls*: 680 mm (26.77 in); *Stroke*: 1,250 mm (49.21 in); 7,500 BHP; 15 kts; By G. Clark & North East Marine Ltd, Wallsend. **H** Steel, 1 deck, fcsle 43 ft 3 in (13.18 m).

First of a class of six standard SD-14 type ships by Austin & Pickersgill.

1974 Built for P&O General Cargo Division.
1976 Transferred to the P&O-Ellerman joint service. Renamed *City of Exeter*, Ellerman Lines Ltd. General cargo carrier.

391 STRATHDEVON

Details as *Strathdare* (*390*) except: *T*: 9,214 g, 6,264 n.

1975 Jan: General cargo carrier. Present fleet.

392 STRATHDIRK

Details as *Strathdare* (*390*) except: *T*: 9,230 g, 6,103 n.

1976 Aug 27: Launched. General cargo carrier. Present fleet.

393 STRATHDOON

Details as *Strathdare* (*390*) except: *T*: 9,230 g, 6,103 n.

1976 Oct: General cargo carrier. Present fleet.

394 STRATHDUNS

Details as *Strathdare* (*390*) except: *T*: 9,230 g, 6,103 n.

1977 Jan: General cargo carrier. Present fleet.

395 STRATHDYCE

Details as *Strathdare* (*390*) except: *T*: 9,230 g, 6,103 n.

1977 Mar: General cargo carrier. Present fleet.

396 VENDEE

Bt 1972 Swan Hunter Shipbuilders (Readhead Division), South Shields; *T*: 6,088 g, 2,478 n. **Dim** 433 ft 10 in (132.23 m) oa including bulbous bow, 402 ft (122.53 m) × 64 ft 1 in (19.53 m) × 38 ft 6 in (11.73 m). **Eng** Sgl scr, Doxford diesel, 6 cyls; *Cyls*: 670 mm (26.38 in);

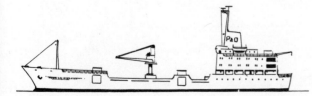

396-397

Stroke: 2,140 mm (84.25 in); 12,000 BHP; 18 kts; By Doxford & Sunderland, Sunderland. **H** Steel; *Cargo*: 7,629 cu m (269,414 cu ft), 2,310 pallets and 56 on deck.

Vendee *and* Vosges (397) *were two British India ships given Moss-Hutchison names.*

1972 Built as *Zaida* for British India's Australia-Japan service. When delivered placed on the P&O-managed Crusader Shipping Co's Australia-Japan route.
1973 Apr 19: Transferred to P&O ownership.
1975 Oct 15: Renamed *Vendee*.

397 **VOSGES**

Details as *Vendee* (*396*) except: *T*: 6,088 g, 2,536 n.

1972 Built as *Zeila*.
1975 Oct 15: Renamed *Vosges*. Present fleet.

398-399

398 **MELITA**

Bt 1971 Hall, Russell & Co, Aberdeen; *T*: 2,686 g, 1,197 n. **Dim** 344 ft 11 in (105.13 m) oa, 309 ft 11 in (94.46 m) × 53 ft 3 in (16.23 m) × 31 ft 6 in (9.6 m). **Eng** Sgl scr, Vee Pielstick diesel, 14 cyls; *Cyls*: 400 mm (15.75 in); *Stroke*: 460 mm (18.11 in); 5,670 BHP; 15½ kts; By Crossley Premier (England), Manchester; Controlled pitch propeller. **H** Steel, 2 decks, fcsle 45 ft 3 in (13.79 m), 1 × 30 ton Stulcken derrick, 2 × 5 ton electro-hydraulic Brissoneau & Lotz deck cranes.

1971 Built for Moss-Hutchison's Mediterranean service.
1973 Sept 29: Transferred to P&O General Cargo Division. Present fleet.

399 **MAKARIA**

Details as *Melita* (*398*) except: **Bt** 1972.

1972 Built for Moss-Hutchison UK-Mediterranean service.
1973 Sept 29: Transferred to P&O General Cargo Division. Present fleet.

P&O Bulk Shipping Division

In 1972 the Bulk Shipping Division was formed and all the group's tanker fleet and liquified gas carriers were transferred. The tankers came from Charter Shipping Co, Trident Tankers, Orient SN Co, and Hain-Nourse.

400 **MALWA** (III)

Bt 1961 Vickers-Armstrong, Barrow-in-Furness; *T*: 23,900 g, 14,245 n, 39,233 dwt. **Dim** 690 ft 6 in (210.46 m) oa, 661 ft 2 in (201.52m) × 90 ft 5 in (27.56 m) × 48 ft (14.63 m). **Eng** Sgl scr, 2 steam turbines, dbl reduction geared; 17,600 SHP; 2 water tube boilers; Stm *P*: 700 lb; 16 kts. **H** Steel, oil tanker, 1 deck, fcsle 84 ft (25.6 m), poop 152 ft (46.33 m).

1961 Nov: Delivered to Charter Shipping Co, Bermuda, operated in P&O colours.
1972 Sept 27: Transferred to P&O Bulk Shipping Division. Managed by Trident Tankers Ltd.
1975 Oct 12: Disposed of.

401 **GARONNE**

See Orient SN Co entry 31.

402 **ERNE**

Bt Chas Connell & Co, Glasgow; *T*: 13,728 g, 7,908 n. **Dim** 559 ft 7 in (170.56 m) oa, 535 ft 9 in (163.3 m) × 71 ft 9 in (21.87 m) × 40 ft 2 in (12.24 m). **Eng** Sgl scr, 2 steam turbines dbl reduction

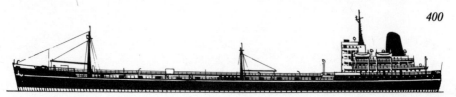

400

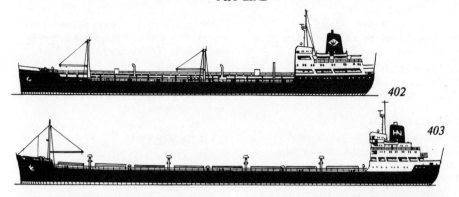

402

403

geared; 8,800 BHP; 14½ kts; By Barclay Curle & Co, Glasgow. **H** Steel, oil tanker, 1 deck, fcsle 65 ft (19.81 m), poop 116 ft (35.36 m).

1962 Feb: The first tanker to be built for the new P&O subsidiary company Trident Tankers.
1972 Transferred to P&O Bulk Shipping Division. Present fleet.

403 ATHERSTONE

Bt 1965 Hitachi Zosen, Innoshima; *T*: 25,991 g, 17,713 n, 43,965 dwt. **Dim** 675 ft 11 in (205.77 m) oa, 639 ft 9 in (195 m) × 90 ft 2 in (27.48 m) × 54 ft 7 in (16.64 m). **Eng** Sgl scr, Burmeister & Wain diesel, 7 cyls; *Cyls*: 840 mm (33.07 in); *Stroke*: 1,800 mm (70.87 in); 16,100 BHP; 15 kts; By builders. **H** Steel, bulk carrier, 1 deck, fcsle 58 ft (17.68 m), poop 113 ft (34.42 m).

1965 Apr: Built for Hain-Nourse Ltd.
1972 Transferred to P&O Bulk Shipping Division. Managers Hain-Nourse. Present fleet.

404 ERIDGE

Bt 1966 Mitsui Zosen, Tamano; *T*: 42,825 g, 27,303 n, 72,692 dwt. **Dim** 823 ft (250.85 m) oa, 794 ft 2 in (242.06 m) × 104 ft 3 in (31.78 m) × 61 ft 10 in (18.85 m). **Eng** Sgl scr, Burmeister & Wain diesel, 9 cyls; *Cyls*; 840 mm (33.07 in); *Stroke*:

1,800 mm (70.87 in); 20,700 BHP; 16 kts; By builders. **H** Steel, bulk/oil carrier, 1 deck, fcsle 61 ft (18.59 m).

1966 Oct 1: Built for Trident Tankers.
1972 Transferred to P&O Bulk Shipping Division. Present fleet.

405 GRAFTON

Details as *Eridge* (*404*) except: **Bt** 1967 Hitachi Zosen, Sakai; *T*: 43,330 g, 27,004 n, 73,829 dwt.

1967 Apr 26: Built for Trident Tankers.
1972 Transferred to P&O Bulk Shipping Division. Present fleet.

406 HEYTHROP

Details as *Eridge* (*404*) except: **Bt** 1967 Hitachi Zosen, Sakai; *T*: 43,330 g, 27,029 n, 73,800 dwt. **Dim** 798 ft (243.23 m). **H** Fcsle 70 ft (21.34 m).

1967 June 30: Built for Trident Tankers.
1972 Transferred to P&O Bulk Shipping Division. Present fleet.

407 FERNIE

Bt 1967 Mitsui Zosen, Tamano; *T*: 42,446 g, 28,872 n, 74,422 dwt. **Dim** 825 ft 1 in (251.48 m) oa, 796 ft (242.62 m) × 105 ft 8 in (32.21 m) × 61 ft (18.59 m). **Eng** Sgl scr, Burmeister & Wain diesel, 9 cyls; *Cyls*: 840 mm (33.07 in); *Stroke*: 1,800 mm

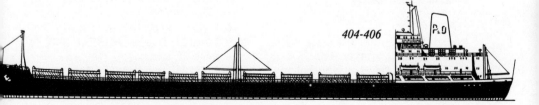

404-406

(70.87 in); 20,700 BHP; 16 kts; By builders. **H** Steel, bulk carrier, 1 deck, fcsle 74 ft (22.56 m).

1967 June 21: Built for Trident Tankers. **1972** Transferred to P&O Bulk Shipping Division. Present fleet.

408 ARDTARAIG

Bt 1963 Mitsui SB & Eng Co, Chiba; *T*: 119,666 g, 78,942 n, 214,218 dwt. **Dim** 1,063 ft 11 in (324.28 m) oa including bulbous bow, 1,018 ft (310.29 m) × 157 ft 11 in (48.13 m) × 89 ft (27.13 m) **Eng** Sgl scr, 2 steam turbines dbl reduction geared; 28,000 SHP; 16 kts; By Ishikawajima-Harima Heavy Industries, Tokyo. **H** Steel, oil tanker, 1 deck.

1963 Mar: Built for Trident Tankers. **1972** Transferred to P&O Bulk Shipping Division. Present fleet.

409 ARDSHIEL

Details as *Ardtaraig* (*408*) except: **Bt** 1969; *T*: 119,678 g, 78,956 n, 214,085 dwt.

1969 Dec: Built for Trident Tankers. **1972** Transferred to P&O Bulk Shipping Division.
1977 Feb 23: Sold. Renamed *Marakanda*, United Petroleum Shipping, Andros, Greece.

410 ARDLUI

Details as *Ardtaraig* (*408*) except: **Bt** 1970; *T*: 119,728 g, 78,873 n, 214,180 dwt.

1970 Mar 28: Delivered to Trident Tankers.
1972 Transferred to P&O Bulk Shipping Division. Present fleet.

411 ARDVAR

Details as *Ardtaraig* (*408*) except: **Bt** 1970; *T*: 119,730 g, 78,871 n, 214,029 dwt.

1970 June: Delivered to Trident Tankers. **1972** Transferred to P&O Bulk Shipping Division. Present fleet.

412 IRFON

Bt 1971 Howaldtswerke-Deutsche Werft, Kiel; *T*: 82,206 g, 61,481 n, 152,509 dwt. **Dim** 946 ft 3 in (288.42 m) oa including bulbous bow, 902 ft 3 in (275.01 m) × 142 ft 6 in (43.43 m) × 77 ft 8 in (23.67 m).

Eng Sgl scr, 2 steam turbines dbl reduction geared; 15¾ kts; By AEG, West Berlin. **H** Steel, ore/bulk/oil carrier, 1 deck, fcsle 72 ft (21.95 m).

1971 May 11: Built for Trident Tankers. **1972** Transferred to P&O Bulk Shipping Division. Present fleet.

413 JEDFOREST

Details as *Irfon* (*412*) except: **Bt** 1972 Eriksbergs M/V Lindholmen Div, Gothenburg, Sweden; *T*: 83,714 g, 64,441 n, 154,900 dwt. **Dim** 956 ft 8 in (291.59 m) oa. **H** Fcsle 63 ft (19.2 m).

1972 May 25: Delivered to P&O Bulk Shipping Division. Present fleet.

414 KILDARE

Details as *Jedforest* (*413*) except: **Bt** 1973; *T*: 154,450 dwt.

1973 Oct 17: Delivered to P&O Bulk Shipping Division. Present fleet.

415 ORAMA

Bt 1964 Lithgows Ltd, Port Glasgow; *T*: 38,767 g, 23,097 n, 65,972 dwt. **Dim** 775 ft (236.22 m) oa, 746 ft 3 in (227.46 m) × 106 ft (32.31 m) × 56 ft (17.07 m). **Eng** Sgl scr, Burmeister & Wain diesel, 10 cyls; *Cyls*: 840 mm (33.07 in); *Stroke*: 1,800 mm (70.87 in); 20,700 BHP; 16¾ kts; By J. G. Kincaid, Greenock. **H** Steel, oil tanker, 1 deck, fcsle 76 ft (23.16 m), poop 140 ft (42.67 m).

1964 June: Delivered to Trident Tankers. **1972** Transferred to P&O Bulk Shipping Division.
1974 Mar 9: Sold. Renamed *Ioannis Angelicoussis*, owned by Brotherhood Cia Naviera, Piraeus, Greece.

416 ORISSA (II)

Details as *Orama* (*415*) except: **Bt** 1965; *T*: 39,035 g, 23,716 n, 66,048 dwt. **Dim** 779 ft 9 in (237.67 m) oa.

1965 Apr: Built for Trident Tankers. **1972** Sept 27: Transferred to P&O Bulk Shipping Division.
1974 Mar 24: Sold. Renamed *Anangel Prudence* of Fronisis Shipping Co, Piraeus, Greece (Agelef Shipping Group).

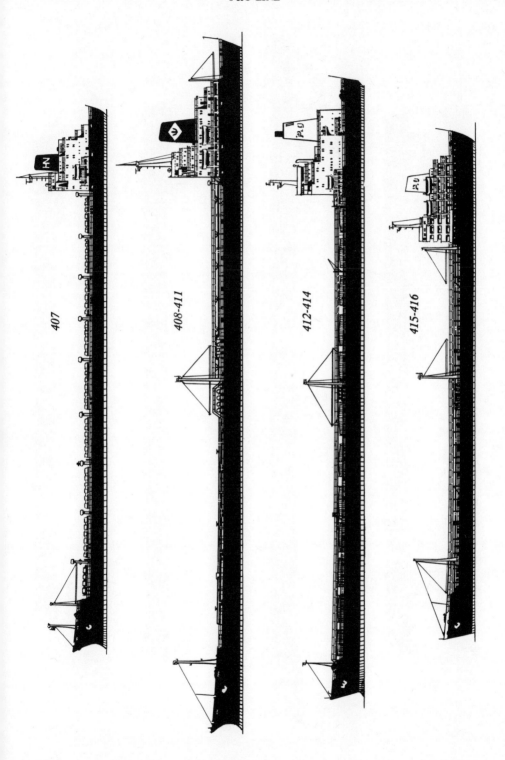

407

408-411

412-414

415-416

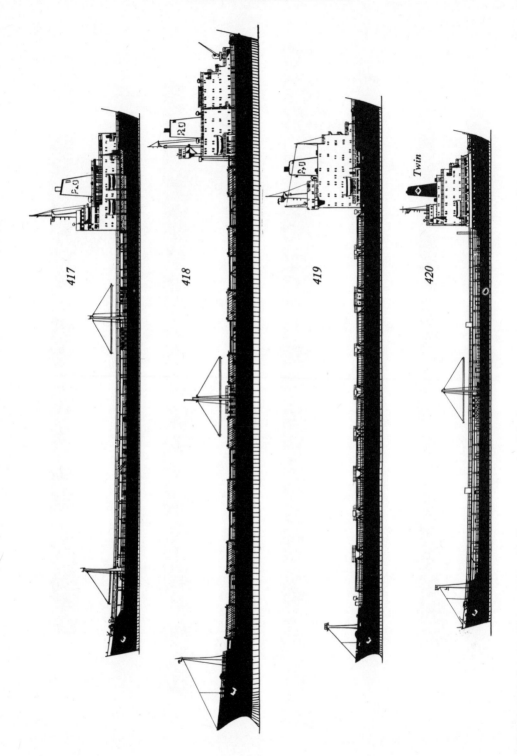

417

418

419

420

Twin

417 **OTTAWA** (II)

Bt 1964 Swan Hunter & Wigham Richardson, Wallsend; *T*: 51,756 g, 32,805 n, 93,072 dwt. **Dim** 851 ft 3 in (259.46 m) oa, 816 ft (248.72 m) × 125 ft 3 in (38.18 m) × 62 ft (18.9 m). **Eng** Sgl scr, 2 steam turbines dbl reduction geared; 27,100 SHP; 2 water tube boilers; *Stm P*: 830 lb; 16½ kts; By Wallsend Slipway & Engineering Co, Wallsend. **H** Steel, oil tanker, 1 deck, fcsle 78 ft (23.77 m).

1964 Dec: Delivered to Trident Tankers.
1972 Sept 27: Transferred to P&O Bulk Shipping Division. Present fleet.

418 **LAUDERDALE**

Bt 1972 Mitsubishi Heavy Industry, Nagasaki; *T*: 143,959 g, 111,557 n, 264,591 dwt. **Dim** 1,100 ft 10 in (335.53 m) oa including bulbous bow, 1,049 ft 7 in (319.91 m) × 176 ft (53.64 m) × 90 ft 3 in (27.51 m). **Eng** Sgl scr, 2 steam turbines dbl reduction geared; 32,000 BHP; 2 water tube boilers; *Stm P*: 900 lb; 16 kts; By builders. **H** Steel, ore/oil carrier, 1 deck, fcsle 90 ft (27.43 m).

1972 Dec: Built for P&O Bulk Shipping Division. The largest vessel yet owned by the P&O SN Co. Present fleet.

419 **MEYNELL**

Bt 1973 Mitsubishi Heavy Industry, Hiroshima; *T*: 69,911 g, 44,419 n, 129,390 dwt. **Dim** 856 ft 2 in (260.96 m) oa including bulbous bow, 810 ft 1 in (246.91 m) × 133 ft 3 in (40.61 m) × 78 ft 7 in (23.95 m). **Eng** Sgl scr, diesel, 8 cyls; *Cyls*: 900 mm (35.43 in); *Stroke*: 1,550 mm (61.02 in); 22,883 BHP; 15½ kts; By builders. **H** Steel, bulk carrier, 1 deck, poop 85 ft (25.91 m).

1973 Built for P&O Bulk Shipping Division. Present fleet.

420 **TALAMBA**

Bt Swan Hunter & Wigham Richardson,

Wallsend; *T*: 34,709 g, 19,893 n, 59,697 dwt. **Dim** 764 ft 10 in (233.12 m) oa, 735 ft (224.02 m) × 106 ft 10 in (32.56 m) × 53 ft (16.15 m). **Eng** Sgl scr, 2 steam turbines dbl reduction geared; 17,600 SHP; 2 water tube boilers; *Stm P*: 675 lb; 16¼ kts; By Wallsend Slipway & Engineering Co, Wallsend. **H** Steel, oil tanker, 1 deck, fcsle 69 ft (21.03 m), poop 141 ft (42.98 m).

1964 Feb: Delivered to Trident Tankers.
1972 Sept 27: Transferred to P&O Bulk Shipping Division.
1976 Jan 3: Engine room flooded 32.48N 30.19W en route from Zuetina to Houston. Towed to Azores then to Brest.
Feb 17: Left Brest in tow for Hamburg to be broken up.

421 **OPAWA**

Bt 1965 Barclay Curle, Glasgow; *T*: 38,996 g, 23,948 n, 65,819 dwt. **Dim** 775 ft 9 in (236.45 m) oa, 746 ft 3 in (227.46 m) × 106 ft (32.31 m) × 56 ft (17.07 m). **Eng** Sgl scr, Burmeister & Wain diesel, 10 cyls; *Cyls*: 840 mm (33.07 in); *Stroke*: 1,800 mm (70.87 in); 20,700 BHP; 16¼ kts; By J. G. Kincaid & Co, Greenock. **H** Steel, oil tanker, 1 deck, fcsle 75 ft (22.86 m), poop 146 ft (44.5 m).

1965 Delivered to Trident Tankers.
1972 Sept 27: Transferred to P&O Bulk Shipping Division.
1974 Apr 22: Sold. Renamed *Anangel Friendship*, Agelef Shipping Co, London.

422 **ARDMAY**

Bt 1975 A/S Horten Verft, Horten, Norway; *T*: 19,144 g, 11,958 n, 31,600 dwt. **Dim** 553 ft 3 in (168.63 m) oa including bulbous bow, 529 ft 7 in (161.42 m) × 85 ft (25.91 m) × 48 ft (14.63 m). **Eng** Sgl scr, Sulzer diesel, 6 cyls; *Cyls*: 760 mm (29.92 in); *Stroke*: 1,550 mm (61.02 in); 12,000 BHP; 16 kts; By builders. **H** Steel, oil tanker, 1 deck, fcsle 56 ft (17.07 m), poop 111 ft (33.83 m).

421

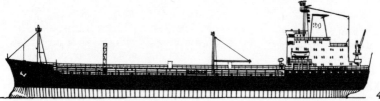

422-423

1975 June: Built for P&O Lines Ltd and managed by the P&O Bulk Shipping Division, London. Present fleet.

423 **ARDMORE**

Details as *Ardmay (422)*.

1975 Oct: Built for P&O Lines Ltd and managed by the P&O Bulk Shipping Division. Port of registry is Southampton. Present fleet.

Liquified petroleum gas carriers

A fleet of seven vessels operated by the P&O Bulk Shipping Division (the seventh being Orient Line's Garinda).

424 **GAMBHIRA**

Bt 1969 Astilleros de Cadiz SA, Seville; *T*: 11,083 g, 6,045 n. **Dim** 502 ft 8 in (153.21 m) oa including bulbous bow, 458 ft 7 in (139.78 m) × 69 ft 11 in (21.31 m) × 40 ft 6 in (12.34 m). **Eng** Sgl scr, Sulzer diesel, 6 cyls; *Cyls*: 760 mm (29.92 in); *Stroke*: 1,550 mm (61.02 in); 9,600 BHP; 15 kts; By builders. **H** Steel, liquified gas carrier, 1 deck, fcsle 62 ft (18.9 m), poop 104 ft (31.7 m).

1969 Apr: Built as *Butanueve* for Butano

SA Madrid.

1971 Renamed *Butanaval* by Arcadia Reedeerei GmbH.

1973 Feb 20: Purchased by P&O Bulk Shipping division. Renamed *Gambhira*. Present fleet.

425 **GAZANA**

Bt 1972 Cammell Laird, Birkenhead; *T*: 21,357 g, 11,528 n. **Dim** 583 ft 4 in (177.8 m) oa including bulbous bow, 541 ft 2 in (164.95 m) × 85 ft 5 in (26.04 m) × 55 ft 8 in (16.97 m). **Eng** Sgl scr, diesel, 8 cyls; *Cyls*: 740 mm (29.14 in); *Stroke*: 1,600 mm (63 in); 15,000 BHP; 16¼ kts; By J. G. Kincaid. **H** Steel, 1 deck.

1972 Feb 28: Delivered to P&O Bulk Shipping Division. Present fleet.

426 **GAMBADA**

Details as *Gazana (425)* except: **Bt** 1973.

1973 Mar 2: Delivered to P&O Bulk Shipping Division. Chartered to Mundogas SA, Panama, in which P&O has a 43% interest. Present fleet.

427 **GARMULA**

Bt 1972 Rosenberg Verft A/S, Stavanger; *T*: 32,213 g, 21,515 n, 38,928 dwt. **Dim** 679 ft 2 in (207.01 m) oa, 649 ft 6 in (197.97 m) × 103 ft 2 in (31.45 m) × 61 ft

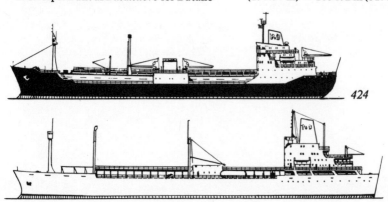

424

425-426

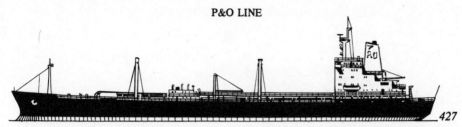

427

(18.59 m). **Eng** Sgl scr, Sulzer diesel, 7 cyls; *Cyls*: 900 mm (35.43 in); *Stroke*: 1,550 mm (61.02 in); 20,300 BHP; 17½ kts; By Sulzer Bros, Winterthur, Switzerland. **H** Steel, 1 deck, ice strengthened.

1972 Built for P&O Bulk Shipping Division. Present fleet.

428 GARBETA

Bt 1975 Moss Verft A/S, Moss, Norway; *T*: 15,481 g, 8,530 n, 18,165 dwt. **Dim** 544 ft 8 in (166.01 m) oa, 501 ft 7 in (152.89 m) × 75 ft 6 in (23.01 m) × 50 ft 10 in (15.49 m). **Eng** Sgl scr, Burmeister & Wain diesel, 7 cyls; *Cyls*: 740 mm (29.14 in); *Stroke*: 1,600 mm (63 in); 14,600 BHP; 16½ kts; By Nylands Verkstad. **H** Steel, liquid gas carrier, 1 deck, fcsle 70 ft (21.34 m), poop 87 ft (26.52 m).

1975 P&O Bulk Shipping Division. Present fleet.

429 GANDARA

Bt 1976 Swan Hunter Shipbuilders, Hebburn-on-Tyne; *T*: 15,611 g, 9,205 n, 17,650 dwt. **Dim** 526 ft 5 in (160.45 m) oa, 498 ft 5 in (151.92 m) × 78 ft 9 in (24 m) × 53 ft 2 in (16.21 m). **Eng** Sgl scr, Burmeister & Wain diesel, 7 cyls; *Cyls*: 740 mm (29.13 in); *Stroke*: 1,600 mm (63 in); 14,600 BHP; 17 kts; By J. G. Kincaid &

Co, Greenock. **H** Steel, liquid gas carrier, 1 deck.

1976 P&O Bulk Shipping Division. Present fleet.

Princess Cruises Incorporated

Under the name of Princess Cruises Incorporated P&O Lines operate three cruise liners (Pacific Princess, Island Princess, *and* Sun Princess) *from the West Coast of the United States of America. For* Sun Princess *see* Spirit of London (355).

430 PACIFIC PRINCESS

Bt 1971 Rheinstahl Nordseewerke, Emden; *T*: 19,903 g, 11,163 n. **Dim** 553 ft 6 in (168.71 m) oa including bulbous bow, 473 ft 3 in (144.25 m) × 80 ft 9 in (24.61 m) × 49 ft 7 in (15.11 m). **Eng** Tw scr, 4 Fiat diesels geared, each paired to each shaft by independent couplings, 10 cyls; *Cyls*: 420 mm (16.54 in); *Stroke*: 500 mm (19.69 in); 18,000 BHP; 21½ kts; By Fiat SGM, Turin; Controllable pitch propellers and bow thruster. **H** Steel, 3 decks with 4th and 5th clear of machinery space; *Pass*: 650 one class, 749 berths in peak season; *Crew*: 301.

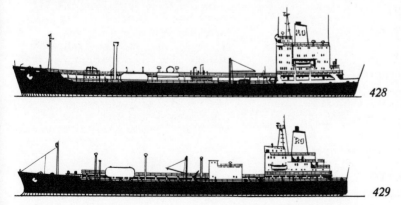

428

429

127

430-431

1968 Ordered.
1971 Built as *Sea Venture* for Norwegian Cruise Ships A/S, Oslo. A joint company formed by Oivind Lorentzen and Fearnley & Eger. *Sea Venture* cost £7½ million and her builders are said to have lost £2 million on the order for her and her sister *Island Venture*. A third ship was cancelled.
1972 Inaugurated New York-Bermuda service.
1974 Pacific Cruises Inc purchased by P&O.
1975 Renamed *Pacific Princess*. Based at Los Angeles. Present fleet.

431 ISLAND PRINCESS

Details as *Pacific Princess* (*430*) except: **Bt** 1972; *T*: 19,907 g, 11,165 n.

1974 Company acquired by P&O.
1975 Renamed *Island Princess*. Present fleet.

New ships on order

For P&O Bulk Shipping Division

432 GALPARA

Delivery: 1978; *Cargo*: 54,000 cu m (1,906,980 cu ft).

433 GOLCONDA (II)

Details as *Galpara* (*432*).

434 GARALA

Details as *Galpara* (*432*) except: *Delivery*: 1979.

432-434 are sisters of Garinda (*33 in the Orient Line illustrated fleet list*).

For P&O Strath Services Limited

435 STRATHESK

Delivery: 1978; *T*: 16,632 dwt.

436 STRATHEWE

Details as *Strathesk* (*435*) except: *T*: 16,760 dwt.

437 STRATHELGIN

Details as *Strathewe* (*436*).

438 STRATHERROL

Details as *Strathewe* (*436*).

439 STRATHETTRICK

Details as *Strathewe* (*436*) except: *Delivery*: 1979.

440 STRATHFIFE

Details as *Strathesk* (*435*) except: *T*: 17,000 dwt.

441 STRATHFYNE

Details as *Strathfife* (*440*).

P&O Australia Ltd

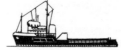

442-443

442 LADY LORNA

Bt 1970 Carrington Slipways Pty, Newcastle, New South Wales; *T*: 545 g, 240 n. **Dim** 161 ft 6 in (49.23 m) oa × 34 ft 1 in (10.39 m) × 11 ft (3.35 m). **Eng** Tw scr, 2 Vee oil engines, 8 cyls; *Cyls*: 10 in (25.4 cm); *Stroke*: 12 in (30.48 cm); 3,200 BHP; 12½ kts; By English Electric Diesels, Stafford. **H** Steel, 1 deck, fcsle 64 ft (19.51 m).

1970 Feb 13: Registered at Sydney. Offshore supply ship.
1974 Mar 8: Transferred to P&O Australia Ltd.

443 LADY LAURIE

Details as *Lady Lorna* (*442*) except: *T*: 535 g, 292 n.

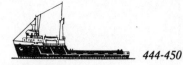
444-450

444 LADY SARAH

Bt 1972 Carrington Slipways Pty, Newcastle, New South Wales; *T*: 932 g, 484 n. **Dim** 169 ft 8 in (51.71 m) × 43 ft 6 in (13.26 m) × 16 ft (4.88 m). **Eng** Tw scr, 4 sets diesel, reverse reduction geared, 8 cyls; *Cyls*: 260 mm (10.24 in); *Stroke*: 320 mm (12.6 in); 13½ kts; By Daihatsu Diesel Mfg Co, Osaka, Japan. **H** Steel, 1 deck.

1972 Nov 9: Delivered.
1977 Mar 31: Transferred to P&O Australia Ltd. Present fleet.

445 LADY VILMA

Details as *Lady Sarah* (*444*) except: **Bt** 1973; *T*: 987 g, 484 n.

1973 Feb: Delivered. Present fleet.

446 LADY RACHEL

Details as *Lady Sarah* (*444*) except: *T*: 987 g, 484 n.

1973 Aug 22: Delivered. Present fleet.

447 LADY CYNTHIA

Details as *Lady Sarah* (*444*) except: *T*: 987 g, 484 n.

448 LADY VERA

Details as *Lady Sarah* (*444*) except: *T*: 987 g, 484 n.

1974 May 17: Delivered. Present fleet.

449 LADY GAY

Details as *Lady Sarah* (*444*) except: *T*: 987 g, 484 n.

1974 Nov 29: Delivered. Present fleet.

450 LADY JANE

Details as *Lady Sarah* (*444*) except: *T*: 987 g, 484 n.

1975 Sept 4: Delivered. Present fleet.

451-452

451 COCKBURN

Bt 1959 Evans Deakin & Co, Brisbane; *T*: 419 g. **Dim** 139 ft (42.37 m) oa, 125 ft 2 in (38.15 m) × 32 ft 7 in (9.93 m) × 14 ft 6 in (4.42 m). **Eng** Sgl scr, diesel, 8 cyls; *Cyls*: 368 mm (14.49 in); *Stroke*: 483 mm (19.02 in); By Crossley Bros, Manchester. **H** Steel, 1 deck.

1959 Nov: Built as a fire fighting tug for British Petroleum as *BP Cockburn*.
1975 Aug 1: Acquired by P&O Australia Ltd. Managed by Kwinana Towage Services. Present fleet.

452 PARMELIA

Details as *Cockburn* (*451*).

1959 Dec: Built for British Petroleum as *BP Parmelia*.
1975 Aug 1: Acquired. Present fleet.

453

453 LADY ANN

Bt 1976 Carrington Slipways Pty, Newcastle, New South Wales; *T*: 1,160 g, 628 n. **Dim** 177 ft 6 in (54.1 m) × 45 ft 3 in (13.79 m) × 18 ft 1 in (5.51 m). **Eng** Tw scr, 2 diesels, 8 cyls; *Cyls*: 260 mm (10.24 in); *Stroke*: 320 mm (12.6 in); By Daihatsu Diesel Mfg, Osaka, Japan. **H** Steel, 1 deck.

1976 Oct 18: Delivered. Present fleet.

P&O Offshore Services Ltd

454

454 LADY ALISON

Bt 1965 Hall Russell & Co, Aberdeen. **Dim** 188 ft (57.3 m) oa × 37 ft 7 in (11.46 m) × 10 ft 9 in (3.28 m). **Eng** Tw scr, 2 × 8 cyl motors; 1,600 BHP; 12 kts; By Blackstone & Co, Stamford; Cross thrust propeller fitted forward, flexible couplings. **H** Steel, 1 deck, fcsle 83 ft (25.3 m).

1965 Nov: Delivered.
1970 Oct 1: Sold to International Offshore Services Ltd, Hamilton, Bermuda.

455

455 **LADY BRIGID**

Bt 1966 J. Bolson & Co, Poole. **Dim** 158 ft
(48.16 m) oa, × 37 ft 10 in (11.53 m) ×
12 ft (3.66 m). **Eng** Tw scr, 2 × 8 cyl sgl
acting motors; 1,600 BHP; 12 kts; By
Blackstone & Co, Stamford. **H** Steel, 1
deck, fcsle 50 ft (15.2 m).

1966 Apr: Delivered.
1970 Sold to International Offshore
Services Ltd, Hamilton, Bermuda.

456

456 **LADY EDWINA**

Bt 1966 J. Lewis & Sons, Aberdeen; *T*:
247 g, 87 n. **Dim** 105 ft 3 in (32.08 m) oa ×
25 ft 8 in (7.82 m) × 9 ft 3 in (2.82 m). **Eng**
Tw scr, 2 × 6 cyl reverse reduction geared
motors; 674 BHP; By Davey, Paxman,
Colchester. **H** Steel, 1 deck.

1966 Apr: Delivered.
1970 Sold to International Offshore
Services Ltd, Hamilton, Bermuda.
Renamed *Spurn Haven*. Owned by Spurn
Shipping Co. Converted at a cost of £40,000
for handling giant monobuoys at the mouth
of the River Humber. Based Immingham.

457

457 **LADY CLAUDINE**

Bt 1966 Brooke Marine, Lowestoft; *T*:
620 g, 236 n. **Dim** 158 ft 3 in (48.23 m) oa ×
36 ft 9 in (11.2 m) × 12 ft (3.66 m). **Eng** Tw
scr, machinery aft, 2 oil engines 4 stroke sgl
acting, 8 cyls; *Cyls*: 8¾ in (22.23 cm);
Stroke: 11½ in (29.21 cm); 1,600 BHP;
11½ kts; By Blackstone & Co, Stamford;
Forward thrust propeller. **H** Steel, 1 deck,
fcsle 52 ft (15.85 m).

1966 May: Delivered.
1970 Oct 1: Sold to International Offshore
Services Ltd, Hamilton, Bermuda.

458 **LADY DELIA**

Bt 1966 Brooke Marine, Lowestoft; *T*:

458-459

773 g, 337 n. **Dim** 170 ft (51.82 m) oa ×
37 ft 9 in (11.51 m) × 12 ft 6 in (3.81 m).
Eng Tw scr, 2 oil engines 4 stroke sgl
acting, 8 cyls; *Cyls*: 8¾ in (22.23 cm);
Stroke: 11½ in (29.21 cm); 1,600 BHP;
11½ kts; By Blackstone & Co, Stamford.
H Steel, 1 deck.

1966 July 30: Delivered.
1970 Oct 1: Sold to International Offshore
Services Ltd, Hamilton, Bermuda.

459 **LADY FIONA**

Details as *Lady Delia* (*458*).

1966 Sept 30: Delivered.
1970 Oct 1: Sold to International Offshore
Services Ltd, Hamilton, Bermuda.

P&O Subsea (UK) Ltd

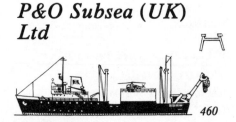

460

460 **SUBSEA I**

Bt 1964 Seebeckwerft, Bremerhaven; *T*:
1,514 g, 436 n. **Dim** 245 ft 8 in (74.88 m) oa,
229 ft 5 in (69.93 m) × 41 ft 5 in (12.62 m)
× 17 ft 1 in (5.21 m). **Eng** Tw scr, 3 diesels,
8 cyls; *Cyls*: 870 mm (34.25 in); *Stroke*:
360 mm (14.17 in) driving 3 electric
generators, connected to 2 drive motors;
2,700 BHP; 13 kts; By Klockner-
Humboldt-Deutz, Cologne. **H** Steel, 2
decks, fcsle 109 ft (36.22 m).

1964 Built as the stern trawler fish factory
Erich Ollenhauer for
Gemeinwirtschaftliche Hockseefischerei,
Bremerhaven; *T*: 1,845 g, 800 n.
1975 Widened and renamed *Northsea
Hunter*.
1976 Sold to P&O Energy Division and
converted into a depot ship for
submersibles. Renamed *Subsea I*. 261 ft
4 in (79.65 m) × 52 ft 6 in (16 m) × 25 ft
6 in (7.77 m). Present fleet.

130

Orient Line

History

1797 The London shipbroking business of James Thompson & Co was founded.
1815 The company was listed as owning 15 small sailing vessels.
1828 James Anderson, born 1811 in Peterhead, Scotland, joined the firm at its office in Billiter Square, London.
1842 James Anderson, aged 31, became a partner in the organisation.
1853 James Thompson & Co operated a number of sailing ships on tramping voyages to all parts of the world. In this year they launched at Rotherhithe the 1,033 gross ton, three-masted barque *Orient*, with the intention of using her for the Australian Gold Rush trade. But the Crimean War began in 1854 and *Orient* was used as a tranport.
1863 The title of the company was changed to Anderson, Thompson & Co. James Anderson's nephew James G. K. Anderson, who entered the firm in 1854, was also a partner and the Andersons actually ran the business.
1866 *Orient* made her first voyage on a regular basis to Australia and the company's Australian business became known as the Orient Line of Packets to Australia which was quickly shortened to Orient Line.
1869 When the last of the Thompson family retired the company's name was again changed, this time to Anderson, Anderson & Co. However this period was the hey-day of the large sailing ship and the Orient Line made no attempt to change from sail to steam.
1870 A. G. Anderson & W. R. Anderson, nephews of James G. K. Anderson, were made partners in the company.

1874 March 28: Orient's first excursion into steamer ownership occurred when they chartered the auxiliary steamer *Easby* from Frederick Green & Co, which left London for Port Philip via the Cape. Frederick Green & Co were mainly interested in India, and to secure a second steamer for the berth *St Osyth* of Watts Milburn was chartered. Her passage from London, via Plymouth and the Cape, to Melbourne took 42 days.
In the same year the Pacific Steam Navigation Co was forced by heavy losses to reduce its weekly service from Liverpool to the Pacific coast of South America down to twice-monthly. As a result no fewer than five of their steamships were laid up at Liverpool. Two were sold to the Royal Mail SP Co but the remainder were left idle, reputedly at a cost of £6,000 per annum each.
1877 Anderson, Anderson & Co, in conjunction with Frederick Green & Co, offered to charter four vessels for a voyage each to Australia, with an option to purchase them if the venture was successful.
June 26: *Lusitania* left Gravesend via Plymouth and the Cape (no stop) for Melbourne, and did the passage in just over 40 days. *Chimborazo* and *Cuzco* followed, but for the Oct 24 sailing the Royal Netherlands Steamship Co's *Stad Amsterdam* had to be substituted for *Garonne* (I).
1878 The voyages were profitable and the two partner firms decided to exercise their option to acquire the four ships. To do so they formed the Orient Steam Navigation Co with a capital of £44,642 and they, with

the Pacific Steam Navigation Co, were the major subscribers. The first sailing after the formation of the company was taken by the delayed *Garonne* (I) and she, in reality, took the first Orient Line sailing.

The service to Australia was to be monthly and in order to provide reliability of service PSNC's *Acongagua*, sister of *Lusitania*, was chartered both as a standby vessel and to cover the maintenance periods of the other ships on the route. She carried out this role for four years, being manned by a PSNC crew. From March 1878 calls at Capetown were added to the route to increase business.

1879 The Orient Line decided upon a policy of having ships superior to those of their competitors. Solid though the ex-PSNC liners were, they were not custom-built for the Australian route, especially the long crossing from the Cape to Australia where high capacity coal bunkers were a necessity. To mark the emergence of the new epoch Orient's first designed ship was named *Orient*, after the barque of 1853. She was the largest vessel on the route and was, incidentally, the first steamer built to meet British Admiralty requirements for wartime service as an armed merchant cruiser.

Nov 3: *Orient* left London for Adelaide and established a 37 days 22 hours record.

Late in 1879 P&O advertised that fortnightly sailings to Australia would commence in January 1880. The Orient shareholders, the Andersons, Frederick Green and PSNC, decided to match the competition by transferring to the Australian service four PSNC ships, thereby bringing the fleet up to a total of ten. The four PSNC vessels placed on the berth were *Cotopaxi*, *Liguria*, *Potosi* and *Sorata*. The arrangement was simple. The Andersons and Green, together, would manage the ships on the usual broking terms and PSNC would retain any and all voyage profits.

Dec 29: *Garonne* (I), by coincidence, repeated her debut of 1878 and took the first sailing, and by so doing introduced the fortnightly service ahead of P&O. It was perhaps fortunate that the Orient Line, in using PSNC ships to start the original service in 1878, retained the PSNC livery and their own *Orient* perpetuated this.

Thus to the onlooker the five additional ships maintained the same house style and even their names presented no problem.

1881 Oct: In an attempt to stimulate trade the company began to route alternate sailings via the Suez Canal instead of the Cape.

Dec: *Austral* joined the fleet.

1883 The first mail subsidy was secured from the Government of New South Wales, but the contract called for direct passages via the Suez Canal to Melbourne in 39 days and rail onwards to Sydney. This ruled out the voyage via the Cape. The Orient Line thereafter despatched only occasional extra steamers via Capetown. One problem of the new route was coal beyond Suez; P&O used and controlled supplies at Aden, and the Orient Line eventually established their coaling station at Diego Garcia, 2,000 miles south of the Red Sea.

1885 *Lusitania* was chartered for six months as an armed merchant cruiser during the Russian crisis.

1886 *Ormuz* (I) joined the Orient SN fleet and, for the same service, PSNC completed *Oroya* and *Orizaba*. These three twin-funnelled ships began the custom of having all Australian service ships use names beginning with 'O'.

1887 Orient moved their London terminal down to the new Tilbury docks.

1888 The re-negotiated mail contracts for both Orient and P&O placed upon them a joint responsibility for bunkering and provisioning. This led to an increase in general co-operation which was eventually, in 1919, to lead to virtual amalgamation. It also spelled the end of Diego Garcia as a coaling station.

1889 Aug 3: *Ormuz* (I) represented the company at the Spithead Naval Review.

1890 Two more PSNC 'O's were seconded for the Australian service, *Orotava* and *Oruba*. They actually made a few voyages to Valparaiso first but were transferred to replace *Liguria* and *Iberia*, the latter being the replacement standby for *Acongagua*.

1891 Nov 6: *Ophir* entered service. Her appearance led to the belief that a third, centre funnel had been omitted. In fact her engine room was placed between the two boiler rooms with the idea of minimising shell damage if she was used as an armed merchant cruiser. Her profile was 'modern' compared with her Victorian consorts. *Ophir* was a heavy coal consumer throughout her 30 years and this reduced her cargo capacity.

1894 Trade with Australia was poor and in this year, for the first time, no dividend was paid.

1897 Sept: James Anderson died at the age of 87.

1897-8 *Orient* was refitted and was remodelled with a single tall funnel.

1898 P&O, with Orient, again shared the new mail contract, but the journey time stipulation was now reduced to 31¼ days.

1899 Orient took delivery of *Omrah* and PSNC contributed *Ortona*.

Oct: The Boer War commenced. *Austral*, *Orient*, *Orotava* and *Ortona* were all used as troopships between 1899 and 1903.

1901 The linkage with PSNC became closer. The company adopted the marketing name of Orient-Pacific Line.

Mar: *Ophir* was used as the Royal Yacht for the opening of the Commonwealth Parliament and carried the Duke (later King George V) and Duchess of York to Australia. For the voyage she was given a white hull with blue band and buff funnels.

1902 *Orontes* (I) was completed and with her commissioning the aged *Cuzco* was sold for breaking up.

1906 The Royal Mail SP Co acquired the Pacific Steam Navigation Co and therefore their four Australian steamers, *Oroya*, *Orotava*, *Oruba* and *Ortona*, together with PSNC's Australian interests. The service now became known as the Orient-Royal Mail Line. But the most important effect of the change came when Royal Mail gave their four steamers buff-coloured funnels instead of black. Within a short time the Orient Line followed suit.

The relationship between the new partners was not good, with Royal Mail wishing to withdraw the management of its vessels from both Anderson and Green so that they might operate them on their own account.

1907 Royal Mail bid, alongside P&O and Orient, for the mail contract but failed. They also competitively dispatched their own new *Asturias* to Australia as an extra sailing.

July: Royal Mail gave notice of their wish to terminate the Orient-Royal Mail Line relationship and to withdraw their four ships at the end of the present contract in 1909. To counter the effects of this move, and to restore confidence in their Australian strength, Orient ordered five 12,000 ton ships designed to outclass all comers.

1909 April 30: *Ortona* took the last sailing from London for the Orient-Royal Mail Line.

June 25: *Orsova* (I), the first of Orient's new class of vessel, left Tilbury on her maiden voyage to Australia. P&O's 'M' class, now coming into service, were only 10,000 tons and were a trifle slower. *Orsova* was given the company's first Admiralty cowl-topped funnels, which were still standard even when *Garonne* (II), an oil tanker, was built in 1959. *Orsova* was followed by *Otway*, *Osterley*, *Otranto* (I) and *Orvieto* (although this ship was a transition to the following group, commencing with *Orama* (I) in 1911).

1911 *Orama* (I) replaced *Ormuz* (I).

1913 *Ormonde* was laid down as a replacement for *Ophir*. However because of the war she was not completed until 1917, and *Ophir* survived until 1922.

1914 Aug 4: The First World War began. *Orvieto*, *Otranto* (I) and *Orama* (I) were all taken up for military duties, as a minelayer and two armed merchant cruisers respectively.

1915 Jan: *Ophir* was requisitioned for use as an armed merchant cruiser, to be followed by *Otway*.

July: *Orsova* (I) was taken over for trooping, but this time on charter to the Australian Government.

1916 Oct: *Orontes* (I) also became a troopship.

1917 Next *Omrah* and *Osterley* went for trooping service, leaving Orient without a single ship with which to maintain their services.

1917 July 22: *Otway* was torpedoed and lost in the Minches.

Oct 19: *Orama* (I) was sunk by a submarine off Southern Ireland. Because of the war losses *Ormonde* was hurriedly completed for trooping service.

1918 May 5: *Omrah* fell victim to a torpedo off Sardinia.

Oct 6: *Otranto* (I) was very badly damaged in collision with P&O's *Kashmir* and, out of control, drifted ashore on the Isle of Islay where she became a total loss. Tragically 431 lives were lost.

Nov 11: First World War ended.

1919 A few sailings took place, but it was not until September that Government control of shipping ceased. *Orontes* (I), *Orsova* (I), *Orvieto*, *Osterley* and *Ormonde* were returned to the Orient Line. *Ophir*, now owned by the Admiralty, was laid up. To overcome the shortage *Indarra* of the Australasian United SN Co was chartered in December. When she proved to be too slow the ex-Norddeutsch Lloyd *Konigin Luise* took her place and eventually, in 1921, became *Omar*.

In this year P&O acquired 51% of Orient Line through their shipbroking firm of Gray Dawes & Co.

1919-20 Orient acquired from the Shipping Controller the ex-Norddeutsch Lloyd *Zeppelin*, which became *Ormuz* (II); *Prinz Ludwig* was, at the same time, renamed *Orcades* (I).

1924-25 The postwar spate of cargo building had died down sufficiently to see the larger passenger companies resume construction. The queue was long and Orient had wisely ordered their new class of ships a full two years earlier.

1924 A class of five 20,000 ton vessels had been ordered and *Orama* (II) was the first to be delivered. She replaced *Omar*, which was sold to the London Greek Byron SS Co.

1925 *Oronsay* (I) and *Otranto* (II) joined the fleet and their arrival released *Orcades* (I), which was broken up in Germany.

1927 *Ormuz* (II) went back to her original Norddeutsch Lloyd ownership and re-appeared on the North Atlantic as *Dresden*.

1928 Oct: *Orford* was delivered.

1929 Sept: *Orontes* (I), the final ship of the series, set a more modern trend. She had a graceful raking stem and her deck stanchions were reduced to those beneath her gravity lifeboat davits. With the arrival of *Orontes* (II) the 20 year old *Osterley* was sold for breaking up.

1930 Nov: *Orvieto* was withdrawn and broken up in early 1931.

1931 The world depression severely affected many companies, especially those on the North Atlantic. Orient, however, had a well balanced fleet and although

profits fell no disposals took place.

1935 Sept: The single-funnelled, single-masted version of the *Orama* (II) class, *Orion* was delivered with Orient's new colour scheme of a corn-coloured hull. The colour had been used experimentally in early 1935 on *Orama* (II), but her livery reverted to a black hull before the arrival of *Orion*. Slightly surprisingly *Orion* reverted to an increase in the number of deck stanchions and this was the main way in which she could be identified from her sister ship, *Orcades* (II).

1936 Oct: *Orsova* (I) ended her career with the company.

1937 Oct: *Orcades* (II), sister of *Orion*, was delivered. She had reduced numbers of deck stanchions, similar to *Orontes* (II).

1938 The Australian service was extended to New Zealand.

1939 Sept 3: The Second World War began. The Orient fleet comprised eight ships, *Ormonde*, *Orama* (II), *Oronsay* (I), *Otranto* (II), *Orford*, *Orontes* (II), *Orion* and *Orcades* (II), and within a few weeks every one was taken over for Government service.

1940 June 1: *Orford* became the first casualty when she was lost by bombing at Marseilles.

June 6: *Orama* (II) sunk off Norway by the German trio *Scharnhorst*, *Gneisenau* and *Admiral Hipper*, with *Hipper* gallantly picking up all the survivors.

1942 Oct 9: *Oronsay* (I) went down off the West Coast of Africa.

Oct 10: *Orcades* (II) fell victim to *U-172* in the South Atlantic.

1945 *Empire Orwell*, formerly *Pretoria*, of the German East Africa Line was allocated to Orient management but not ownership.

1947 Only in February of this year did Orient re-commence sailings on its own account. All four surviving vessels, *Ormonde*, *Otranto* (II), *Orontes* (II) and *Orion* needed substantial refitting and overhaul. Thus the first post-war sailing took place on Feb 25, by *Orion*. The ageing *Ormonde* returned as an emigrant ship, operated by the company for the Ministry of Transport. At the age of thirty it was clear that *Ormonde* would not see service for very much longer, though in fact she did perform her duties for another five years.

1948 Dec: Orient's first replacement ship,

Orcades (III), entered service with a new vertical profile atop a conventional Orient (and P&O) type hull. Faster than any of her predecessors, she was scheduled to complete the voyage to Australia in four weeks.

1951 May: *Oronsay* (II) arrived. Her appearance was a derivation of *Orcades* (II) with a pepper-pot funnel topped by Orient's familiar cowl.

1954 The third replacement vessel, *Orsova* (II), entered service in March. Slightly larger than her consorts she had the odd distinction of being without masts altogether. The fleet now comprised six ships: *Otranto* (II), *Orontes* (I), *Orion*, *Orcades* (III), *Oronsay* (II) and *Orsova*. Between them, and in conjunction with P&O's *Arcadia*, *Himalaya* and *Iberia*, a twice-monthly service was maintained. This enabled *Oronsay* to undertake a transpacific service Sydney-Auckland-Suva-Honolulu-Victoria, British Columbia-Vancouver-San Francisco, replacing the *Aorangi* of the Canadian Australasian Line.

1957 *Otranto* (II) was sold for breaking up.

1958 The transpacific service sailings were increased by the addition of P&O vessels and was named the Orient and Pacific Line.

1959 The company entered tanker ownership by building *Garonne* (II).

1960 Dec 3: *Oriana*, the company's largest passenger ship, entered service on a London-Australia-San Francisco service. May 2: P&O-Orient Lines (Passenger Services) Ltd was formed to operate all the passenger vessels of both concerns. Initially no outward sign of the new organisation occurred.

Orontes (II) was withdrawn and sold for breaking up.

1962 The operation of *Garonne* (II) was transferred to P&O's Trident Tankers Ltd.

1963 May: *Orion* made her final voyage to Australia and was then withdrawn for scrapping.

1964 The Orient corn-coloured hull was changed for the P&O white. *Orcades* (III), *Oronsay* (II), *Orsova* and *Oriana* were repainted, with the first two ships being transferred to P&O ownership. *Garonne* (II) was also transferred at this time although Trident Tankers remained the operating company.

1965 P&O acquired the outstanding minority shareholding in Orient SN Co and the concern became a wholly owned subsidiary. *Oriana* and *Orsova* were transferred to the P&O registry.

1966 The P&O-Orient Line's name was dropped and the Orient name thereafter disappeared. Thus ended the separate history of a company which specialised in the Australian trade, and which for most of its career led its competitors in the standard of service offered.

Routes

1877 London (Gravesend)-Plymouth-via the Cape (no call)-Melbourne-Sydney-Adelaide-Suez Canal-London.

1878 Calls at Capetown introduced.

1881 Outward sailings to Australia were alternately via the Suez Canal and the Cape of Good Hope.

1883 The route via the Cape was dropped and the regular voyages became: London-Gibraltar-Port Said-Suez-Colombo-Albany-Adelaide-Melbourne-Sydney.

1887 Tilbury became the London base for Orient sailings.

1890 Naples was added as a port of call.

1919 Some sailings were extended to Brisbane.

1933 Palma de Majorca and Toulon were added to the Mediterranean call pattern, but not for every sailing.

1938 Auckland was added beyond Sydney.

1954 The transpacific route was inaugurated: Sydney-Auckland-Suva-Honolulu-Victoria, British Columbia-San Francisco.

1958 Joint P&O-Orient services were introduced to Australia and transpacific.

Livery

Funnel 1877 Black, 1906 Buff yellow.
Hull 1877 Black with green waterline, 1935 Corn cream with green waterline, 1964 White for passenger ships.
Uppers White.
Masts Biscuit.
Lifeboats White.

Fleet index

This index includes Pacific Steam Navigation Co vessels which served under Orient management.

Illustrated fleet list

1 LUSITANIA

Bt 1871 Laird Bros, Birkenhead; *T*: 3,877 g, 2,494 n. **Dim** 379 ft 10 in (115.77 m) × 41 ft 4 in (12.6 m) × 35 ft 3 in (10.74 m). **Eng** Sgl scr, 2 cyls, compound; *Cyls*: 60 in (152.4 cm) and 104 in (264.16 cm); *Stroke*: 48 in (121.92 cm); 550 NHP; *Stm P*: 65 lb; 13 kts; By builders. **H** Iron, 3 complete decks, 5 steam winches; *Pass*: 84 1st, 100 2nd, 270 emigrants.

1871 Built for Pacific Steam Navigation Co for Liverpool-South America service. Cost £91,852.
1877 Feb: Chartered, with guaranteed profits, to Anderson & Anderson's Orient-Pacific Line.
June 28: First voyage owned by Orient-Pacific Line. Plymouth-Melbourne Australian service. Voyage in 40 days 6 hours.
1886 Re-engined. Triple expansion.
1900 Mar 31: Acquired by Elder Dempster for the Liverpool-Halifax-St John service of the Beaver Line.
1901 June 26: Wrecked on Cape Race whilst chartered to the Allen Line.

2 GARONNE (I)

Details as *Lusitania* (*1*) except: **Bt** 1871 Robert Napier & Sons, Glasgow; *T*: 3,876 g, 2,468 n. **Dim** 382 ft 1 in (116.46 m) × 41 ft 5 in (12.62 m) × 35 ft 8 in (10.87 m). **Eng** By builders.

1871 Built for PSNC's South American service.
1877 June: Sold to Orient-Pacific Line service to Australia.
1878 Apr 17: First voyage to Australia for Orient SN Co.
1889 July 6: Final voyage to Australia. Then used for cruising.
1897 Acquired by F. Waterhouse, Seattle, and used for the Alaska goldrush trade. Same name.
1905 Broken up at Genoa.

3 CUZCO

Details as *Garonne* (*2*) except: **Bt** 1871 John Elder & Co, Glasgow; *T*: 3,898 g, 2,439 n. **Eng** By builders.

1871 Built for PSNC's South American service.
1877 Chartered to Anderson & Anderson for Orient-Pacific Line service.
Sept 29: First voyage for new owners, London-Suez-Sydney.
1878 Acquired by Orient SN Co.
1888 Triple expansion engines fitted; 15 kts.
1902 May 23: Last voyage to Australia.
1905 Broken up at Genoa.

1-4,34-36,39

4 CHIMBORAZO

Details as *Cuzco* (*3*) except: *T*: 3,847 g.
Dim 384 ft (117.04 m) × 41 ft 4 in
(12.6 m) × 35 ft 4 in (10.67 m).

In addition to Lusitania, Garonne (I),
Cuzco *and* Chimborazo *two further Pacific
Steam Navigation sisters,* Aconcagua *and*
John Elder, *were also used on the
Australian run but were not owned by
Orient SN.*

1871 Built for PSNC's South American
service.
1877 Chartered to Anderson & Anderson.
1878 Purchased by Orient SN Co.
1887 May 12: Final voyage London-Suez-
Sydney.
1889 Cruise ship to the Norwegian Fjords.
1894 Sold to P. J. Pitcher of Liverpool.
Renamed *Cleopatra*. Used for cruising by
the Polytechnic Touring Association.
1895 Owned by the Ocean Cruising &
Yachting Co.
1897 Broken up at Preston, Lancs.

5 ORIENT

Bt 1879 John Elder, Glasgow; *T*: 5,386 g,
3,231 n. **Dim** 460 ft (140.21 m) oa, 455 ft
6 in (138.84 m) × 46 ft 4 in (14.12 m) ×
35 ft (10.67 m). **Eng** Sgl scr, 3 cyls,
compound; *Cyls*: 60 in (152.4 cm) and 2 ×
85 in (215.9 cm); *Stroke*: 60 in (152.4 cm);
5,400 IHP, 1,000 NHP; 60 rpm; 4 dbl
ended boilers; *Stm P*: 74 lb; 17 kts; By
builders. **H** Iron; *Coal*: 3,000 tons; *Pass*:
120 1st, 130 2nd, 300 steerage, 1,500
troops.

1879 June 5: Launched. Cost £150,000.
Nov 3: Maiden voyage London-Melbourne-
Sydney via the Cape, and inbound via
Suez.
1884 Electric light installed.
1898 Triple expansion engines installed;
Cyls: 40 in (101.6 cm), 66 in (167.64 cm)
and 109 in (276.86 cm); *Stroke*: 60 in
(152.4 cm); *Stm P*: 180 lb; 17 kts.
Modernised. *T*: 5,453 g. Single funnel (*5a*).
1899 Nov: Troopship during the Boer War.
1903 July 17: Resumed service to Sydney.
1909 July 23: final voyage to Australia.
1910 Sold for £12,500 and broken up in
Italy. Renamed *Oric* for the voyage.

6 AUSTRAL

Bt 1881 John Elder & Co, Glasgow; *T*:
5,524 g, 3,214 n. **Dim** 456 ft (138.99 m) ×
48 ft 3 in (14.71 m) × 33 ft 10 in (10.31 m).
Eng Sgl scr, 3 cyls, compound; *Cyls*: 62 in
(157.48 cm) and 2 × 86 in (218.44 cm);
Stroke: 60 in (152.4 cm); 1,000 NHP; 4 dbl
ended boilers; *Stm P*: 75 lb; 17 kts; By
builders. **H** Steel (their first), 2 decks; *Pass*:
120 1st, 130 2nd, 300 3rd.

1882 Jan 18: Maiden voyage London-Suez-
Melbourne-Sydney.
Nov 11: Sank whilst re-coaling at Sydney.
Four drowned.
1883 Mar 28: Refloated. Temporary
repairs effected at the Cockatoo yard.
Returned to builders for refitting. Salvage
cost was £50,000. Funnels heightened.
1884 Apr: Chartered to the Anchor Line,
Glasgow, for their Liverpool-New York
service, to run with the *City of Rome* being

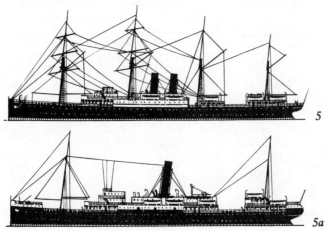

5

5a

6

managed by them.
Nov 12: Returned to Orient Line service to
Australia.
1900 Used as a Boer War troopship.
1902 Broken up at Genoa.

7 ORMUZ (I)

Bt 1886 Fairfield SB & E Co, Glasgow; *T*:
6,031 g, 3,225 n. **Dim** 482 ft (146.91 m) oa,
465 ft 6 in (141.88 m) × 52 ft 1 in (15.88 m)
× 19 ft 1 in (5.82 m). **Eng** Sgl scr, tpl exp;
Cyls: 45½ in (115.57 cm), 73 in (185.42 cm)
and 112 in (284.48 cm); *Stroke*: 72 in
(182.88 cm); 9,000 IHP, 1,400 NHP; 6 dbl
ended boilers; *Stm P*: 150 lb; 18 kts; By
builders. **H** Steel, 2 decks; *Pass*: 106 1st,
170 2nd, 120 steerage.

1886 Sept 29: Launched. LP cylinder one
of the largest ever at 112 in (284.48 cm).
1887 Feb 3: Maiden voyage London-Suez-
Melbourne-Sydney.
1911 Aug 18: Final voyage for Orient.
1912 Sold to Compagnie de Navigation
Sud-Atlantique. Renamed *Divona*.
1922 Sold to Lefevre-Despeaux for scrap.

8 OPHIR

Bt 1891 Robert Napier & Sons, Glasgow;

T: 6,814 g, 2,920 n. **Dim** 465 ft (141.73 m)
× 53 ft 5 in (16.29 m) × 34 ft 1 in
(10.39 m). **Eng** Tw scr, 2 tpl exp; *Cyls*: 34 in
(86.36 cm), 51½ in (130.81 cm) and 85 in
(215.9 cm); *Stroke*: 54 in (137.16 cm);
1,398 NHP; 5 dbl and 2 sgl ended boilers;
Stm P: 160 lb; 18 kts; By builders. **H** Steel,
4 decks, fcsle 59 ft (17.98 m), bridge 252 ft
(76.81 m), poop 42 ft (12.8 m).

1891 Nov 6: Maiden voyage London-Suez
Canal-Melbourne-Sydney.
1915 Jan: Commissioned as an armed
merchant cruiser.
1918 Purchased by the British Admiralty
and converted into a hospital ship.
1919 Feb: Laid up in the River Clyde with
other surplus ships.
1922 Broken up at Troon, Scotland.

9 OMRAH

Bt 1899 Fairfield SB & E Co, Glasgow; *T*:
8,130 g, 4,419 n. **Dim** 490 ft 7 in (149.53 m)
× 56 ft 7 in (17.25 m) × 26 ft (7.92 m). **Eng**
Tw scr, 2 tpl exp; *Cyls*: 33 in (83.82 cm),
54½ in (138.43 cm) and 89 in (226.06 cm);
Stroke: 57 in (144.78 cm); 1,772 NHP; 3
dbl and 2 sgl ended boilers; *Stm P*: 180 lb.
H Steel, 2 decks, fcsle 66 ft (20.12 m),

7

8

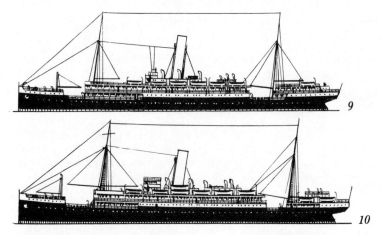

bridge 260 ft (79.25 m), poop 77 ft (23.47 m).

1899 Feb 3: Maiden voyage London-Suez Canal-Melbourne-Sydney.
1916 Nov 3: Final voyage to Australia. Converted into a troopship.
1918 May 12: Torpedoed 40 miles south west of Cape Spartivento. *Omrah* had left Alexandria for Marseilles on May 1 with six other transports, carrying troops of the 52nd and 74th Divisions. She was on her return journey from Marseilles when lost, fortunately without serious loss of life.

10 **ORONTES** (I)

Bt 1902 Fairfield SB & E Co, Glasgow; *T*: 9,028 g, 4,622 n. **Dim** 513 ft 7 in (156.54 m) × 58 ft 2 in (17.73 m) × 34 ft 5 in (10.49 m). **Eng** Tw scr, quad exp; *Cyls*: 27¼ in (69.22 cm), 39 in (99.06 cm), 56 in (142.24 cm) and 80 in (203.2 cm); *Stroke*: 60 in (152.4 cm); 1,700 NHP; *Stm P*: 215 lb; 18 kts. **H** Steel, 3 decks, fcsle 74 ft (22.56 m), bridge 267 ft (81.38 m), poop 74 ft (22.56 m).

1902 Oct 24: Maiden voyage London-Suez-Melbourne-Sydney.
1916 Oct: Troopship.

1919 Oct 25: Resumed her Australian service but with an extension up to Brisbane.
1921 Laid up in the River Thames at Southend.
1922 Mar: Sold for conversion into an exhibition ship. Renamed *British Trade*. Aug: Re-possessed by Orient Line and renamed *Orontes*.
1926 Broken up.

11 **OTWAY**

Bt 1909 Fairfield SB & E Co, Glasgow; *T*: 12,077 g, 6,690 n. **Dim** 535 ft 10 in (163.32 m) × 63 ft 2 in (19.25 m) × 34 ft 2 in (10.41 m). **Eng** Tw scr, 2 quad exp; *Cyls*: 28¾ in (73.03 cm), 41 in (104.14 cm), 58½ in (148.59 cm) and 84 in (213.36 cm); *Stroke*: 60 in (152.4 cm); 2,000 NHP; 4 dbl and 2 sgl ended boilers; *Stm P*: 215 lb; 18 kts; By builders. **H** Steel, 3 decks, bridge 60 ft (18.29 m); *Pass*: 280 1st, 130 2nd, 900 3rd; *Crew*: 350.

1909 July 9: Maiden voyage London-Suez-Melbourne-Sydney-Brisbane.
1915 Converted into an armed merchant cruiser.
1917 July 22: Torpedoed and sunk in the

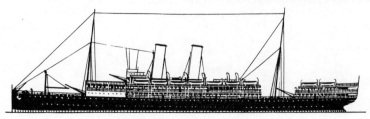

Minches whilst serving as a unit of the Northern Patrol. 10 killed.

12 OSTERLEY

Details as *Otway* (*11*) except: **Bt** 1909 London & Glasgow Ship Building Co, Glasgow; *T*: 12,129 g, 6,781 n. **Dim** Length 535 ft (163.07 m). **Eng** 1,973 NHP. **H** Bridge 57 ft (17.37 m).

1909 Aug 6: Maiden voyage to Australia terminating at Brisbane.
1917 June: Troopship.
1919 Jan: Returned to Orient's Australian service.
1930 Broken up.

13 ORSOVA (I)

Details as *Otway* (*11*) except: **Bt** John Brown, Clydebank; *T*: 12,026 g, 6,831 n. **Dim** Length 536 ft 2 in (163.42 m).

1909 June 25: Maiden voyage London-Suez-Melbourne-Sydney-Brisbane.
1915 May: Converted to a troopship.
1917 Mar 14: Torpedoed near to Eddystone Lighthouse. Beached in Cawsand Bay and then towed to Devonport Dockyard for repairs.
1919 Nov 22: Resumed Orient Line service.
1933 Converted to a one class vessel.
1936 Oct: Scrapped at Bo'ness, Firth of Forth.

14 OTRANTO (I)

Details as *Otway* (*11*) except: **Bt** 1909 Workman Clark, Belfast; *T*: 12,124 g,

7,433 n. **Dim** 535 ft 4 in (163.17 m) × 64 ft (19.51 m) × 38 ft 7 in (11.76 m).

1909 Oct 1: Maiden voyage London-Suez-Melbourne-Sydney-Brisbane.
1914 Converted into an armed merchant cruiser.
1918 Oct 6: Wrecked at Islay after colliding with P&O's *Kashmir*.

15 ORVIETO

Details as *Otranto* (*14*) except: *T*: 12,133 g, 7,421 n. **H** Bridge 305 ft (92.96 m); *Pass*: 235 1st, 186 2nd, 696 3rd.

1909 Nov 26: Maiden voyage to Australia.
1914 Converted into the mine layer HMS *Orvieto*. Later became an armed merchant cruiser.
1919 Nov 1: Returned to Orient's Australian service.
1931 Broken up.

16 ORAMA (I)

Bt 1911 John Brown, Clydebank; *T*: 12,927 g, 8,179 n. **Dim** 551 ft (167.95 m) × 64 ft 2 in (19.56 m) × 39 ft (11.89 m). **Eng** Tpl scr, 8 cyls and low pressure turbine; *Cyls*: 2 × 27½ in (69.85 cm), 2 × 42 in (106.68 cm) and 4 × 47 in (119.38 cm); *Stroke*: 54 in (137.16 cm); 1,970 NHP; 2 dbl and 5 sgl ended boilers with forced draught; *Stm P*: 215 lb; 18 kts; By builders. **H** Steel, 3 decks, fcsle 54 ft (16.46 m), bridge 288 ft (87.78 m).

1911 Nov 10: Maiden voyage to Australia.
1914 Converted into an armed merchant cruiser.

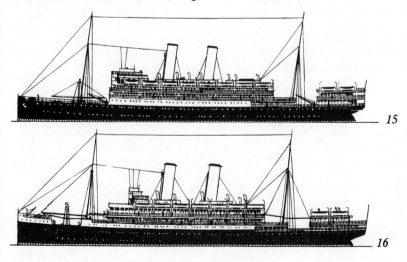

15

16

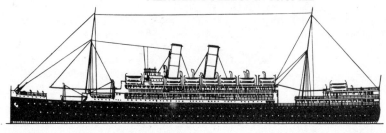

17

1917 Oct 19: In company with eight US destroyers *Orama* was escorting a 17-vessel convoy when she was torpedoed by *U-62*. She took four hours to sink. The USS *Conynham* attempted unsuccessfully to ram the submarine.

17 ORMONDE

Bt 1917 John Brown, Clydebank; *T*: 14,982 g, 9,021 n. **Dim** 580 ft 5 in (176.92 m) × 66 ft 7 in (20.29 m) × 40 ft 5 in (12.32 m). **Eng** Tw scr, 4 geared stm turbines; 2,120 NHP; 4 dbl and 2 sgl ended boilers; *Stm P*: 215 lb; 18 kts; By builders. **H** Steel, 2 decks and shelter deck, fcsle 59 ft (17.98 m), bridge 303 ft (92.35 m); *Coal*: 1,586 tons; *Pass*: 278 1st, 195 2nd, 1,000 3rd; *Crew*: 380.

1918 June: Completed as a troopship.
1919 Nov 15: Maiden voyage to Australia.
1923 Converted from coal to oil burning.
1933 Refitted with one class accommodation.
1939 Requisitioned as a troopship. Took part in the evacuations from Norway and France.
1942 Nov: Present at the North African landings, then Sicily and Italy.
1944 Based Bombay for Far East trooping.
1947 Returned to the Australian route as an emigrant vessel.
1952 Dec: Sold for breaking up at Dalmuir, Scotland.

18 OMAR

Bt 1896 A. G. 'Vulkan', Stettin, Germany;

T: 11,103 g, 6,790 n. **Dim** 523 ft 1 in (159.44 m) × 60 ft 1 in (18.31 m) × 34 ft 10 in (10.62 m). **Eng** Tw scr, 2 quad exp; *Cyls*: 25¼ in (64.14 cm), 38¼ in (97.16 cm), 52¾ in (133.99 cm) and 75¾ in (192.41 cm); *Stroke*: 55 in (139.7 cm); 846 NHP; By builders. **H** Steel, 4 decks, fcsle 67 ft (20.42 m), bridge 257 ft (78.33 m), poop 82 ft (24.99 m); *Pass*: 170 1st, 757 3rd.

1896 Constructed as *Konigin Luise* for Norddeutscher Lloyd. North Atlantic or Australian routes.
1904-10 Served on the New York-Trieste route via Gibraltar or Tangier.
1919 Surrendered to Great Britain as war reparations. Managed by Orient Line.
1921 Refitted and renamed *Omar*.
Jan 29: First voyage as *Omar* to Australia.
1924 Sold to Byron SS Co (British but Greek owned; Embericos Brothers). Renamed *Edison*.
1929 Sold to the National SN Co of Greece. Same name.
1935 Broken up in Italy.

19 ORCADES (I)

Bt 1903 A. G. 'Vulkan', Stettin, Germany; *T*: 9,764 g, 5,704 n. **Dim** 492 ft (149.96 m) × 57 ft 7 in (17.55 m) × 35 ft (10.67 m). **Eng** Tw scr, 2 quad exp; *Cyls*: 25 in (63.5 cm), 36 in (91.44 cm), 52 in (132.08 cm) and 75 in (190.5 cm); *Stroke*: 55 in (139.7 cm); 831 NHP; By builders. **H** Steel, 2 decks; *Pass*: 123 1st, 476 3rd.

1903 Built as *Prinz Ludwig* for Norddeutscher Lloyd's Far East service.

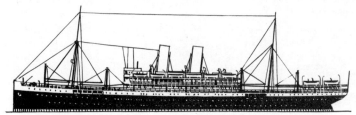

18

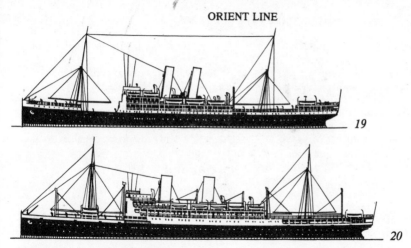

19

20

1919 Surrendered to Great Britain and placed under P&O management.
1921 Sold by the Shipping Controller to Orient Line. Renamed *Orcades*.
Oct 8: First Orient voyage to Australia.
1925 Broken up in Germany by M. Stern, Bremerhaven.

20 ORMUZ (II)

Bt 1914 Bremer Vulkan Vegesack, Bremen; *T*: 14,588 g, 8,082 n. **Dim** 550 ft (167.64 m) × 67 ft 4 in (20.52 m) × 35 ft 1 in (10.69 m). **Eng** Tw scr, 2 quad exp, 1,100 NHP; *Cyls*: 28¾ in (73.03 cm), 43¼ in (109.86 cm), 60⅓ in (153.25 cm) and 84¾ in (215.27 cm); *Stroke*: 59 in (149.86 cm); *Stm P*: 215 lb; 16 kts. **H** Steel, 4 decks, fcsle 113 ft (34.44 m), bridge and poop 403 ft (122.83 m); *Pass*: 292 1st, 882 3rd; *Crew*: 300.

1914 Built as *Zeppelin* for Norddeutscher Lloyd.
1919 Surrendered to Great Britain. Managed by Orient Line.
1920 Purchased and renamed *Ormuz*. Renovated throughout.
1921 Dec 11: First voyage to Australia for new owners.

1927 Sold back to Norddeutscher Lloyd, renamed *Dresden*.
1934 June 20: Wrecked on the coast of Norway whilst cruising. At 4 pm she struck a rock at Klepp on Boku Island but was safely refloated. As a precaution she was beached near Blikshavn, Karmoy Island. At 2.45 am next day she commenced to list and by 8 am lay on her side as a total loss. Only one passenger was lost but three more died during the transfer of the survivors.

21 ORAMA (II)

Bt 1924 Vickers-Armstrong, Barrow-in-Furness; *T*: 19,777 g, 11,896 n. **Dim** 632 ft (192.63 m) × 75 ft 2 in (22.91 m) × 32 ft 10 in (10.01 m). **Eng** Tw scr, 6 turbines sgl reduction geared to 2 shafts; 3,836 NHP; 6 dbl and 4 sgl ended boilers with forced draught; *Stm P*: 215 lb; 18 kts; By builders. **H** Steel, 3 decks and part 4th, fcsle 74 ft (22.56 m), bridge 349 ft (106.38 m), upper bridge 300 ft (91.44 m); *Oil*: 90 tons per day at 16 kts; *Cargo*: 294,000 cu ft (8,325 cu m) (bulk); *Pass*: 1,700; *Crew*: 420.

1924 Nov 15: Maiden voyage London-Melbourne-Sydney-Brisbane. At one stage *Orama* had a cream-coloured hull.

25, 21-24

1940 Converted into a troopship. Used to transport the British Expeditionary Force to Norway following the German invasion. June 8: The *Orama*, together with the aircraft carrier *Glorious*, the destroyers *Acasta* and *Ardent* and the oil tanker *Oil Pioneer*, were all some 300 miles west of Narvik when the German high seas force comprised of *Scharnhorst*, *Gneisenau* and the heavy cruiser *Admiral Hipper* swept the area using scouting aircraft. All five allied vessels were sunk. *Orama* lost 19 killed and 280 were taken prisoner by *Admiral Hipper*. Fortunately she was not carrying troops at the time of her sinking.

22 ORONSAY (I)

Details as *Orama (21)* except: **Bt** 1925 John Brown, Clydebank; *T*: 20,001 g, 11,441 n. **Dim** Length 633 ft 7 in (193.12 m). **Eng** By builders. **H** Fcsle 71 ft (21.64 m), bridge 344 ft (104.85 m).

1925 Feb 7: Maiden voyage to Australia.
1939 Requisitioned for use as a troopship. Used between Australia and Canada.
1940 June: *Oronsay*, together with *Otranto (23)* and *Ormonde (17)*, took part in the evacuation of British troops from Bay of Biscay French ports. *Oronsay* was at St Nazaire on June 17. The embarking of troops took five hours during which the ship was hit several times, and nearby Cunard's *Lancastria* was sunk with the loss of about 2,800 lives. Due to severe damage *Otranto* had to sail home to Plymouth by the use of an atlas and a 12 in (30.48 cm) school ruler.
1942 Oct 9: Torpedoed twice 800 miles west-south-west of Monrovia, Liberia. Five drowned. 288 crew were rescued by a British warship and 30 more by the French sloop *Dumont d'Urville*; the latter were interned at Dakar. The ship was returning from taking Free French troops to occupy Madagascar.

23 OTRANTO (II)

Details as *Orama (21)* except: **Bt** 1925; *T*: 20,026 g, 12,031 n. **Eng** 3,722 NHP; 6 dbl and 2 sgl ended boilers. **H** Bridge 342 ft (104.24 m), upper bridge 312 ft (95.1 m).

1926 Jan 9: Maiden voyage to Australia.
1939 Converted into a troopship.
1942 Nov: Fitted out as an assault ship.

Present at the North African, Sicilian and Italian landings.
1948-9 Refitted as a one-class ship by Cammell Laird, Birkenhead.
1949 July 14: Resumed service to Australia.
1957 Feb 13: Final sailing to Sydney was via Capetown.
June: Sold and broken up at Faslane, Scotland.

24 ORFORD

Details as *Orama (21)* except: **Bt** 1928; *T*: 19,941 g, 12,027 n. **Dim** Length 632 ft 2 in (192.68 m), depth 33 ft 1 in (10.08 m). **Eng** 6 dbl and 2 sgl ended boilers. **H** Bridge 361 ft (110.03 m).

1928 Oct 13: Maiden voyage to Australia.
1939 Requisitioned as a troop transport. Allocated to the French Government for bringing troops from Madagascar.
1940 June 1: During the evacuation of the British forces from France *Orford*, anchored in the roadstead at Marseilles, was bombed and destroyed by fire. 14 dead. The ship was beached and abandoned.
1947 Refloated and towed to Savona, Italy, for breaking up.

25 ORONTES (II)

Details as *Orama (21)* except: **Bt** 1929; *T*: 20,097 g, 12,010 n. **Dim** Length 638 ft 2 in (194.51 m) because of her raking stem, depth 33 ft 1 in (10.08 m). **Eng** 3,825 NHP; 6 dbl and 2 sgl ended boilers. *Pass*: 1,600; *Crew*: 420.

1929 Oct 26: Maiden voyage London-Melbourne-Sydney-Brisbane.
1940 Converted to troopship.
1942 Nov: Took part in the North African landings.
1943 Present at the Sicilian landings at Avola. 4,000 troops went ashore by her landing barges in less than two hours. *Orontes* returned with a fresh load of troops and put these ashore at Salerno, Italy.
1945 Trooping to Far Eastern areas in preparation for the invasion of Japan. When she berthed at Sydney in June she was the first Orient liner to visit the port in almost three years.
1947-8 Reconditioned at Southampton as a one class ship.
1948 June 17: Resumed Australian service.
1962 Mar: Arrived at Valencia, Spain, for breaking up.

26-27

26 ORION

Bt 1935 Vickers-Armstrong, Barrow-in-
Furness; *T*: 23,371 g, 14,032 n. **Dim** 665 ft
(202.69 m) oa, 640 ft 4 in (195.17 m) × 82 ft
2 in (25.04 m) × 33 ft 7 in (10.24 m). **Eng**
Tw scr, 6 steam turbines sgl reduction
geared to 2 shafts; 4,912 NHP; *Stm P*:
450 lb; 4 water tube boilers; 20 kts; By
builders. **H** Steel, 3 decks, fcsle 81 ft
(24.69 m), lower fcsle and bridge 622 ft
(189.59 m), upper fcsle and bridge 499 ft
(152.1 m); *Pass*: 1,139; *Crew*: 466.

1935 Sept 28: Maiden voyage to Australia.
The ship was launched from Australia by
wireless by the Governor General, the
Duke of Gloucester.
1939 Requisitioned for use as a troopship.
1941 Sept: Collided with the battleship
HMS *Revenge*.
1946-7 Reconditioned by builders.
1947 Feb 25: Resumed Australian service.
1954 Sept 17: Placed on the transpacific
service Sydney-Auckland-Vancouver-
San Francisco.
1963 June: Used as a hotel ship at
Hamburg.
Nov: Broken up in Belgium.

27 ORCADES (II)

Details as *Orion* (*26*) except: **Bt** 1937; *T*:
23,456 g, 14,029 n.

*Orcades had a taller funnel and fewer
stanchions on the promenade decks than
Orion.*

1937 Oct 9: Maiden voyage to Australia.
1939 Converted into a troopship.
1942 Oct 10: Torpedoed by *U-172* 300
miles west-south-west of the Cape of Good
Hope with 1,000 aboard. 48 were killed by
the two torpedoes but the remainder were
rescued by the Polish steamer *Narwick*. At
first, manned by 55 volunteers, *Orcades*
managed to steam at five knots, but she
became increasingly unmanageable and
was finally abandoned, to sink shortly
afterwards.

28 ORCADES (III)

Bt 1948 Vickers-Armstrong, Barrow-in-
Furness; *T*: 28,472 g, 11,140 n. **Dim** 711 ft
(216.71 m) oa, 708 ft 8 in (216 m) × 93 ft
6 in (28.5 m) × 31 ft (9.45 m). **Eng** Tw scr, 6
steam turbines, high pressure turbine
double reduction geared, intermediate and
low pressure turbines sgl reduction geared
to 2 shafts; 42,500 SHP; 4 Foster Wheeler
water tube boilers; *Stm P*: 590 lb; 23 kts; By
builders. **H** Steel, 2 decks, 3rd in hold
spaces, 8 passenger decks; *Cargo*:
163,200 cu ft (4,621 cu m) refrig; *Pass*: 780
1st, 780 tst; *Crew*: 608.

1948 Dec 14: Maiden voyage to Australia.
Cost £3 million. Passage time 28 days
(pre-war 36 days). Four round voyages a
year.
1955 Aug 22: London-Panama-San
Francisco-Vancouver-Auckland-Sydney-
Suez-London cruise.
1958 Placed on Australia-Transpacific

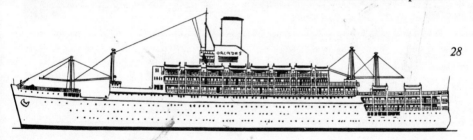

28

145

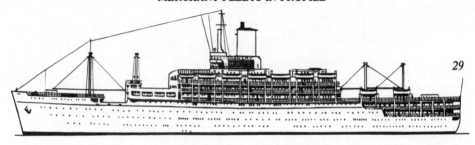

29

service-San Francisco-Vancouver route.
1962 Sept 21: Transferred to P&O
ownership. White hull, red waterline.
1964 May: Converted to one-class vessel.
1973 Feb 7: Sold for breaking up.

29 ORONSAY (II)

Details as *Orcades* (*28*) except: **Bt** 1951; *T*:
28,136 g. *Pass*: 668 1st, 830 tst; *Crew*: 622.

1951 Caught fire whilst fitting out. The
blaze was confined to Number Two hold
but as the ship continued to list holes were
burned in her hull to release the water from
the fire pumps.
May 16: Maiden voyage to Australia.
1954 Jan 1: Made her first transpacific
voyage, Sydney-San Francisco.
1958 Placed on transpacific service.
1962 Sept 21: Transferred to P&O
ownership. White hull and red waterline.
1975 Oct 9: Sold for breaking up.

30 ORSOVA (II)

Bt 1954 Vickers-Armstrong, Barrow-in-
Furness; *T*: 29,091 g, 11,940 n. **Dim** 722 ft
10 in (220.32 m) × 90 ft 7 in (27.61 m) ×

30 ft 11 in (9.42 m). **Eng** Tw scr, 6 steam
turbines, with the high pressure dbl
reduction geared and the intermediate and
low pressure sgl reduction geared; 3 water
tube boilers; *Stm P*: 630 lb; 22 kts; By
builders. **H** Steel, 2 decks, 3rd in hold
spaces; *Pass*: 1,500.
1954 Mar 17: Maiden voyage to Australia.
1958 Placed on transpacific route
Australia-USA.
1965 Mar 31: Transferred to P&O
ownership. White hull and red waterline.
1974 Feb 12: Sold for breaking up.

31 GARONNE (II)

Bt 1959 Vickers-Armstrong, Barrow-in-
Furness; *T*: 24,097 g, 40,057 dwt. **Dim**
690 ft 3 in (210.39 m) oa × 90 ft 5 in
(27.56 m) × 36 ft 4¾ in (11.09 m). **Eng** Sgl
scr, 2 steam turbines dbl reduction geared;
2 water tube boilers; *Stm P*: 700 lb; 15 kts;
By builders. **H** Steel, oil tanker, 1 deck.

1959 In company with other P&O group
companies Orient entered the tanker
owning field.
1962 Dec: Transferred to Trident Tankers,

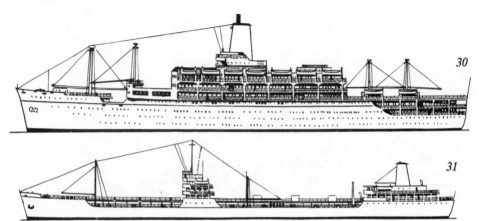

30

31

146

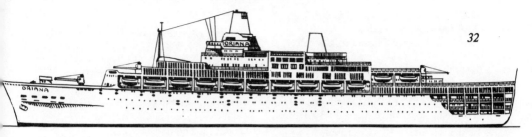

32

the operators of all the P&O-owned tankers.
1965 Mar 31: Transferred to P&O ownership but retained the Orient name.

32 ORIANA

Bt 1960 Vickers-Armstrong, Barrow-in-Furness; *T*: 41,910 g, 12,835 n. **Dim** 804 ft (245.06 m) oa × 97 ft 2 in (29.62 m) × 32 ft (9.75 m). **Eng** Tw scr, 6 dbl reduction geared steam turbines; 4 water tube boilers; *Stm P*: 905 lb; 23 kts; By builders. **H** Steel, 2 full decks and 2 part decks; *Pass*: 1,500.

1960 Nov: Maiden voyage was to Lisbon with the Association of British Travel Agents' Convention aboard.
Dec 3: First voyage to Australia, then on to the transpacific service Sydney-Auckland-Vancouver-San Francisco.
1978 Present fleet.

33 GARINDA

Bt 1977 Thyssen Nordseewerke GmbH, Emden; *T*: 34,895 g, 22,916 n, 41,683 dwt. **Dim** 719 ft 11 in (219.43 m) oa, 682 ft 3 in (207.95 m) × 93 ft 6 in (28.5 m) × 65 ft 7 in (19.99 m). **Eng** Sgl scr, MAN diesel, 6 cyls; *Cyls*: 900 mm (35.43 in); *Stroke*: 1,600 mm (62.99 in); 19,920 BHP; 16¾ kts; By Masch Augsburg-Nurnberg, Augsburg. **H** Steel, liquid gas carrier, 1 deck.

1977 Built for Orient Steam Navigation Co. Managed by P&O Bulk Shipping Division. Present fleet.

Pacific Steam Navigation Co ships under Orient management

34 ACONGAGUA

Bt 1872 John Elder, Glasgow; *T*: 4,105 g, 2,639 n. **Dim** 404 ft 9 in (123.37 m) × 41 ft 5 in (12.62 m) × 35 ft 4 in (10.77 m). **Eng** Sgl scr, compound inverted; *Cyls*: 61 in (154.94 cm) and 112 in (284.48 cm); *Stroke*: 48 in (121.92 cm); 600 HP; *Stm P*: 65 lb; By builders. **H** Iron, 1 deck.

1872 Built for PSNC's South American service.
1878 Used by Orient as a standby vessel. Never actually purchased from PSNC.
1881 Reverted to Liverpool-Valparaiso service.
1895 Sold to Verdeau & Compagnie, Bordeaux, renamed *Egypte*.
1896 Broken up.

35 SORATA

Details as *Acongagua* (*34*) except: *T*: 4,014 g, 2,573 n. **Dim** Length 401 ft 4 in (122.33 m), beam 42 ft 9 in (13.03 m).

1872 Built for PSNC's South American service Liverpool-Valparaiso.
1879 *Sorata* was one of the four PSNC ships transferred to Orient management.
1880 Feb 13: First voyage London-Australia.

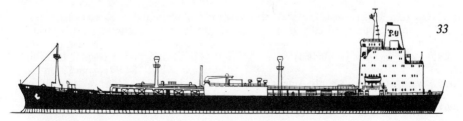

33

1886 Apr 29: Last voyage to Australia. Reverted to PSNC service.
1895 Broken up at Tranmere, Cheshire.

36 **COTOPAXI**

Details as *Acongagua* (*34*) except: **Bt** 1873; *T*: 4,022 g, 2,583 n. **Dim** Length 402 ft 2 in (122.58 m), beam 42 ft 9 in (13.03 m).

1873 Built for PSNC's Liverpool-Valparaiso service.
1880 Apr 14: First voyage London-Australia.
1882 Dec 28: Final voyage for Orient. Reverted to PSNC services to Valparaiso.
1889 May 15: Wrecked Magellan Strait. Collided with the German steamer *Olympia* and beached. *Cotopaxi* was careened and replated on the spot. After refloating safely she struck another reef of rocks and sank. All 202 aboard were saved by *Setos* of the Kosmos Line, Germany.

37 **LIGURIA**

Bt 1874 John Elder, Glasgow; **T**: 4,666 g, 2,980 n. **Dim** 433 ft 5 in (132.11 m) × 45 ft (13.72 m) × 35 ft 4 in (10.77 m). **Eng** Sgl scr, 2 cyls compound inverted; *Cyls*: 56 in (142.24 cm) and 78 in (198.12 cm); *Stroke*: 60 in (152.4 cm); 750 HP; *Stm P*: 70 lb; By builders. **H** Iron, 1 deck.

1874 Built for PSNC's South American service.
1880 One of four vessels transferred to Orient management.
May 12: First voyage London-Suez-Melbourne-Sydney.
1890 May 9: Last Australian voyage. Thereafter reverted to Valparaiso route.
1903 Broken up at Genoa.

38 **IBERIA**

Details as *Liguria* (*37*) except: **Bt** 1873; *T*: 4,689 g, 2,982 n.

1873 Built for PSNC Liverpool-Valparaiso service.
1881 Replaced *Acongagua* (*37*) as standby vessel on the London-Suez-Melbourne-Sydney run.
1883 Jan 25: Placed on regular service to Australia.
1890 Reverted to PSNC's South American route.
1903 May: Broken up at Genoa.

39 **POTOSI**

Details as *Acongagua* (*34*) except: **Bt** 1873; *T*: 4,218 g, 2,704 n. **Dim** 421 ft 7 in (128.5 m) × 43 ft 4 in (13.21 m) × 33 ft 6 in (10.21 m). *Cyls*: 58 in (147.32 cm) and 101 in (256.54 cm).

1873 Entered PSNC service to Valparaiso.
1880 One of four vessels transferred to Orient Line management.
July 7: First voyage to Australia.
1887 May 26: Final voyage to Australia. Thereafter Liverpool-Valparaiso.
1897 Broken up at Genoa.

40 **ORIZABA**

Bt 1886 Barrow SB Co, Barrow-in-Furness; *T*: 6,077 g, 3,410 n. **Dim** 460 ft (140.21 m) × 49 ft 4 in (15.04 m) × 19 ft 5 in (5.92 m). **Eng** Sgl scr, tpl exp: *Cyls*: 40 in (101.6 cm), 60 in (152.4 cm) and 100 in (254 cm); *Stroke*: 72 in (182.88 cm); 1,200 HP; *Stm P*: 160 lb; 12 kts; By builders. **H** Steel, 3 decks, fcsle 47 ft (14.33 m), poop 35 ft (10.67 m).

1886 Built for PSNC but placed on the Orient-managed Australian route.
Sept 30: Maiden voyage to Australia via Suez.
1905 Feb 17: Wrecked on Garden Island near Fremantle.

41 **OROYA**

Details as *Orizaba* (*40*) except: *T*: 6,057 g, 3,394 n.

1887 Feb 17: PSNC-owned but placed in Orient service. Maiden voyage London-Suez-Melbourne-Sydney.
1906 Feb: Transferred with PSNC fleet to Royal Mail SP Co ownership. Continued on Australian route. Yellow funnels.
1909 Apr 16: Last sailing from London to Australia. Thereafter broken up at Genoa.

42 **OROTAVA**

Bt 1889 Barrow SB Co, Barrow-in-Furness; *T*: 5,857 g, 3,364 n. **Dim** 430 ft (131.06 m) × 49 ft 3 in (15.01 m) × 34 ft 2 in (10.41 m). **Eng** Sgl scr, tpl exp; *Cyls*: 39 in (99.06 cm), 61 in (154.94 cm) and 97 in (246.38 cm); *Stroke*: 66 in (167.64 cm); 764 NHP; *Stm P*: 160 lb; 14 kts; By Naval Construction & Armament Co, Barrow. **H**

Steel, 2 decks, fcsle 66 ft (20.12 m), poop 48 ft (14.63 m).

1889 Built for PSNC. Liverpool-Valparaiso service. Made two voyages before being transferred to Orient management.
1890 June 6: First voyage London-Suez-Melbourne-Sydney.
1896 Capsized and sank at Tilbury whilst being coaled. Four lives lost. Raised and refitted.
1897 Feb: Resumed service to Australia.
1899 Requisitioned as a troopship for the Boer War.
1903 Mar 13: Resumed service to Australia.
1906 Feb: Ownership passed to Royal Mail with the purchase by them of PSNC. Remained on the Australian route. Yellow funnels.
1909 March 5: Final voyage to Australia.
1914 Became an armed merchant cruiser.
1919 Broken up.

43 ORUBA

Details as *Orotava* (*42*) except: *T*: 5,852 g, 3,351 n.

1889 Built, like *Orotava*, for PSNC's Valparaiso route.
1890 Transferred to Orient Line service. July 4: First voyage to Australia.
1906 Feb: Transferred, with PSNC fleet, to Royal Mail. Remained on the Australian run. Yellow funnels.

1908 Oct 16: Final service to Australia. Placed on the Royal Mail South American berth.
1914 Purchased by British Admiralty and rebuilt to represent the battleship HMS *Orion*.
1915 Scuttled at Mudros Harbour, Lemnos Island, Greece, as a breakwater.

44 ORTONA

Bt 1899 Vickers Armstrong, Barrow-in-Furness; *T*: 7,945 g, 4,115 n. **Dim** 500 ft (152.4 m) × 55 ft 4 in (16.86 m) × 33 ft 7 in (10.24 m). **Eng** Tw scr, 2 tpl exp; *Cyls*: 30 in (76.2 cm), 50 in (127 cm) and 83 in (210.82 cm); *Stroke*: 66 in (167.64 cm); 764 NHP; *Stm P*: 160 lb; 14 kts; By Naval Construction & Armament Co, Barrow. **H** Steel, 2 decks, fcsle 66 ft (20.12 m).

1899 Nov 24: Maiden voyage to Australia under the joint Orient-PSNC service.
1902 June: Trooping duties to South Africa.
1903 Oct 9: Returned to the Australian route.
1906 Feb: Acquired by Royal Mail together with remainder of PSNC fleet.
1909 Apr 30: Last Australian voyage.
1910 Renamed *Arcadian* and converted into a cruise ship.
1915 Troopship.
1917 Apr 15: Torpedoed in Eastern Mediterranean.

Blue Anchor Line

History

The company which carried the well-loved name of the Blue Anchor Line only lasted for forty-one years from its inception until the acquisition of its fleet of five steamers by the Peninsular & Oriental Steam Navigation Group in 1910. Ironically the seeds of its demise were sown in the very year of the company's foundation.

1837 Sept 21: Wilhelm Lund was born at Aabenraa, Denmark. At the time of his birth the town was called Apenrade and formed a part of the German Duchy of Schleswig, although the Duchy was under the suzerainty of the Danish king.

1848 German forces invaded Schleswig but failed to annexe the province. Lund, aged 11, was a toll collector at the time and to complete his education his father, Captain Wilhelm Lund, sent him to Altona, Hamburg. Here he was apprenticed as a shipwright and sailmaker.

1857 At the age of 20 he went to sea and voyaged to Australia and his experiences fired in him an ambition to develop his connections with the country. On his return to Europe in 1858 he went to Christiania (Oslo) as manager of a small shipowning firm.

1860 Because of the links between England and the Australasian world Wilhelm Lund decided to go to London. Travelling in one of the vessels which he had managed, he arrived without a job or friends and with only half a sovereign in his pocket. To get started he obtained temporary work with a Danish firm but quickly moved to an English company. He lived frugally and left his savings in the company. However, during a short visit home to Aabenraa the firm went into liquidation and Wilhelm

Lund returned to find himself penniless again.

1861 This time he decided to start up on his own, at his trade of sailmaking, in Limehouse. He was undoubtedly good at his job; during his time in Oslo he had even invented a new rig and sail for Scandinavian coastal schooners which enabled fewer men to set or reef the sails. Thus it was that William Walker, of Rotherhithe, contracted with Lund to rig and fit the sails of the China clippers which he was at that time building.

1866 Lund was ambitious to enter into shipowning, and his chance came when Walker launched a vessel on his own account and Lund's share for supplying the sails and rigging was 8/64 shares. The vessel, the *Jeddo*, was profitable and when the partners sold their ship in 1868 Lund promptly ordered himself a vessel twice the size.

1869 Thus in 1869 *Ambassador*, the first vessel to fly Lund's Blue Anchor house flag, entered service. She was composite built, iron framed and wooden planked. This was a fairly new innovation at that time. *Ambassador* inaugurated Lund's 'Triangular Trading' route. The outbound voyage was with passengers and cargo to Australia. North in ballast to China and home in the China Clipper races loaded with tea.

1874 Lund purchased *Mikado* from William Walker. She was similar to, but slightly smaller than, his own *Ambassador*, having been built a year earlier. By now the Suez Canal, which had opened in 1869, was making the China route less attractive to the Cape sailing ships and Lund decided to concentrate on the direct Australia routes. He left the China trade to the steamers now streaming through Suez.

1876 Still only 30 Wilhelm Lund took delivery of the iron hulled *Serapis* from Scotts of Greenock. She was over 1,000 tons, ship-rigged and capable of competing with any trader on the route. He now had a fleet of three.

1880 Like all farsighted owners Lund was keen on steam. Thus, with the financial backing of friends, he bought his first steamer, *Delcomyn*, the first designed wool-carrier on the Australian route. She was a fast 10 knot vessel with the accent on cargo, not passengers. And to differentiate her from P&O's black funnel ships Lund added his house flag to her funnel, thereby introducing the familiar marking. Her coming saw the need for the appointment of handling agents in British and Australian ports. Wilhelm Lund asked Houlder Brothers and their associated concern Trinder Anderson to be berthing agents.

Delcomyn was immediately successful and Lund promptly ordered a consort, the slightly larger *Yeoman*, which was delivered in 1882. She was one of the few ships built at the Tyneside yard of Campbell, MacIntosh & Bowstead. In the same year Lund added the small sailing vessels *Eleanor* and *Talavera* for general tramping.

1884 *Mikado* was sold to J. M. Way of London.

1885 She was replaced, however, by the *Ella*, a Canadian-built barque. In the same year *Harland* was delivered by Richardson Duck of Stockton-on-Tees. She was the largest and last sailing ship for Lund. Iron hulled and almost twice as large as *Serapis* she was rather overshadowed by Lund's pre-occupation with steamers. Nevertheless, she remained in the fleet for five years before being sold.

1886 *Hubbuck* commissioned. She set a three-masted pattern which lasted for the next ten ships to enter service.

1887 *Riverina* delivered, followed by *Murrumbidgee*, both sisters of *Hubbuck*.

1888 *Wilcannia* (I) and *Echuca* joined their sisters. The fleet now consisted of seven workmanlike vessels and was noted for its unobtrusive regularity of service. By now the name Blue Anchor Line was becoming

well known in Australia, although in Britain it still carried the name Wilhelm Lund & Co.

1889 A fleet replacement plan was introduced to take advantage of the enormous strides in engine efficiency which had taken place during the previous ten years. *Delcomyn* possessed only a two cylinder compound inverted engine compared with the triple expansion installed in all the later vessels, and when *Bungaree* was delivered *Delcomyn* was sold. This year also saw the decision to end the connection with sail at the conclusion of the existing wool contracts.

1890 *Culgoa*, the seventh steamer in four years, was delivered, and by now the concentration on regular steam sailings made sail an outmoded part of the company's activities. Accordingly all the remaining sailing ships were sold. *Ambassador*, Lund's first ship, went to Burgess & Co and lasted another five years; *Serapis* went to Norway (P. N. Winther of Nordby); the old *Talavera* and *Eleanor* were broken up; and the newest of them, *Harland*, set off on another 33 years of life, until she was broken up in 1923. By January 1890 Lund had seven steamers with more on order.

Jan 26: *Riverina* went aground on Ram Head, en route from Melbourne to Sydney, within days of the delivery of *Culgoa*, thereby reducing the fleet to six. The intended sale of *Yeoman* had to be deferred.

1891 Continuing the three-masted tradition *Wallarah* was delivered in June, but misfortune struck again when, on Aug 2 during her maiden outbound voyage to Australia, she grounded on Dassen Island, near Cape Town, and became a total loss. Fortunately all the crew and passengers were safely rescued.

In July her sister *Woolloomooloo* was delivered.

1892 The third sister, *Yarrawonga*, entered service in October 1892. Her arrival finally released *Yeoman* which was sold to Linea Vapores Serra of Bilbao, for the ore trade, as the *Rita*.

1893 *Warrigal* was the first quadruple expansion ship in the fleet. *Murrumbidgee* was sold to Bensaude & Co of Lisbon. She remained under the Portuguese flag for the

151

last 30 years of her life retaining her second name, *Peninsular*, for the whole of the period.

1894 The company moved from 18 Jermyn Street to 3 East India Avenue.

Woolloomooloo and *Warrnambool* were each fitted with refrigerated space. This came at a time when the demand for general cargoes, specifically wool, was dropping and freight rates were under pressure. Such was the demand for the carrying of fruit and meat, however, that Lund also had *Yarrawonga*, *Culgoa* and *Bungaree* fitted with refrigerated holds.

1895 The demand for emigrant berths, sparked off by the Australian gold rush, persuaded Wilhelm Lund to move into the passenger business. He initially ordered three sister ships with plans to increase the total as the need arose.

1896 Oct 6: *Narrung* was commissioned. Her profile heralded the modern look; two pole masts without yards and, in addition to the emigrant space aft, she had passenger accommodation for 50 first class amidships.

Warrigal was given 100,000 cu ft (2,815 cu m) of refrigerated space and she set the pattern for all later Lund ships.

1897 *Wilcannia* (I) was sold to Alfred Holt and renamed *Anchises*. *Echuca* went to Robert Sloman as *Catania*.

1898 Following Wilhelm Lund's practice of building sister ships based upon a successful design the *Wakool* was delivered in October. Her advent released both *Culgoa*, sold to the US Navy as a Spanish-American War storeship, and *Hubbuck*, the originator of her large class of three-masters, sold to the Egypt & Levant SS Co.

1899 July: The third of the passenger ships entered service. Lund named her *Wilcannia* (II) after the vessel sold to Alfred Holt. It was the only time during the history of his company that this occurred. By the turn of the century the company operated three passenger ships and four cargo vessels on their monthly service.

When the Boer War commenced Lund ships were used to transport troops and horses from England to Capetown and horses and supplies from Australia on the inbound leg. Regular sailings had to be suspended.

1900 R. P. Houston & Co opened a service

from South America to South Africa, spurred on by the needs of the Boer War. To operate the service they needed additional tonnage and Lund sold them *Woolloomooloo* and *Warrnambool*; they were renamed *Harmonides* and *Harmodius*.

1901 Following the return to Blue Anchor of *Narrung* and *Warrigal* passenger services to Australia were re-introduced.

1902 Lund's next vessel was yet another step forward. She was larger, faster and had more passenger accommodation than any previous ship owned. Her name, *Commonwealth*, departed from the habit of using Aboriginal words; she was named to celebrate the formation of the Commonwealth of Australia.

May: *Narrung*, with a full complement of passengers bound for the coronation of King Edward VII, found Howard Smith's disabled *Boveric*, which had been drifting without a propeller for 37 days. Despite the coronation commitment her master took *Boveric* in tow and reached Fremantle five days later. As it happened King Edward went down with appendicitis and the coronation was postponed.

It was in this year too that *Harmonides*, ex *Woolloomooloo*, collided with and sank Red Star Line's *Waesland* off Anglesey in Liverpool Bay.

1903 June saw the release from service of *Wakool* as she rejoined her sisters on the passenger route.

Yarrawonga joined her two sisters in the R. P. Houston fleet and was renamed *Hermione*, whilst *Bungaree* went to the Quebec SS Co and, after being renamed *Parima*, went into the Quebec-West Indies service.

1904 Blue Anchor ordered another passenger liner which they intended to name *Australia*, but it was pointed out that this would cause confusion with P&O's ship of the same name which had been built in 1892. Accordingly Blue Anchor named their new vessel *Geelong* and she left on her maiden voyage via the Cape on May 27. Ironically barely a month later, on June 29 whilst *Geelong* was still on her maiden voyage, P&O's *Australia* was stranded at the entrance to Port Philip Bay and a few days later was destroyed by fire. But for *Geelong* the die was cast and no move was made by Wilhelm Lund to change her name.

With the advent of *Geelong* Blue Anchor had a passenger fleet of five ships and one remaining cargo vessel, *Warrigal*. Their monthly passenger service alternated with those of George Thompson's Aberdeen Line so that between them the two concerns offered fortnightly sailings. Aberdeen's contribution to the joint service were *Moravian*, *Salamis*, *Sophocles*, *Miltiades* and *Marathon*.

Nov 2: The business was incorporated into a limited company which recognised the popular name by which Wilhelm Lund's fleet was universally known: the Blue Anchor Line Ltd. The new company acquired the fleet's six ships, *Warrigal*, *Narrung*, *Wakool*, *Wilcannia* (II), *Commonwealth* and *Geelong*, and Wilhelm Lund & sons were managers of the company. Wilhelm's two sons F. W. and A. E. Lund were joint managing directors. Blue Anchor Line and George Thompson's Aberdeen Line agreed to operate between them a fortnightly passenger service from London to Australia via Cape Town and South African ports, with passage tickets interchangeable between the two.

1906 *Warrigal* was sold to W. Thomson & Sons of Dundee and renamed *Latona*. She was the last of the three-mast class.

1908 Oct: Barclay Curle delivered the company's largest vessel, *Waratah*, which was soon to become one of the most celebrated names in the annals of shipping disasters. Her debut was hailed with acclaim on the Australian run. Her first class was excellent and the emigrant accommodation aft was spacious and comfortable. During her maiden voyage to Australia she was visited by hundreds at each port of call. Her commander was Captain J. E. Ilbery, Commodore of the Line.

1909 July 7: *Waratah* left Adelaide on the homeward leg of her second round voyage, arriving at Durban on July 25. She left Durban for Cape Town on July 26 with 92 passengers and 119 crew, passing *Clan MacIntyre* early on July 27. This was the last ever to be heard of *Waratah*. Not a trace of wreckage has ever come to light. All that is known is that a severe south-westerly gale, said by some to be the worst in living

memory, crossed her forecast route on July 29 and it has to be assumed that she capsized and sank. A search vessel, specially chartered by the Australian Government, spent an unsuccessful month looking for traces or even survivors. One can only assume that any debris would have been carried south into Antarctica by the Agulhas current.

1910 An official court of enquiry was held in London. The point before the court was the question of *Waratah*'s stability. Former passengers claimed that she was top heavy and one passenger, a Mr Claud Sawyer, is said to have left the ship at Durban for this reason. However her officers and Captain, J. E. Ilbery, had all re-signed for the fateful voyage without any comments on this aspect. In addition Captain Ilbery had made more voyages to Australia than any other master on the route. There was a report that without ballast *Waratah* was a little 'tender', but at Durban she had coaled and watered for the full voyage home and was therefore well down to her marks.

1910 Jan: P&O acquired, for £275,000, Blue Anchor Line's goodwill and the five passenger ships which they owned. For years P&O had wished to secure a foothold on the emigrant route to Australia via the Cape and in 1899 had even attempted, unsuccessfully, to break into the business with sailings by *Ravenna* and *Brindisi*. P&O named their new group the P&O Branch Service to Australia.

Following the transfer of the ships the Blue Anchor Line Ltd went into voluntary liquidation in July. The Lund fleet of five (*Narrung*, *Wakool*, *Wilcannia* (II), *Commonwealth* and *Geelong*) was operated as a separate entity by P&O, retaining the Lund funnel and flying the Lund house flag at the foremast, but P&O's white band was added to the hull. The fleet was also converted to third class only. The offices of the new P&O venture stayed at East India Avenue. Plans to improve the service were at once put in hand and in November orders were placed for five new, larger steamers destined to replace the Lund vessels. The new ships kept to the Lund colours and were called after Australian place names commencing with B, the initial letter indicating 'Branch' Line vessels.

1911 *Ballarat* (I) was the first ship delivered.

1912 May: *Beltana* followed, and *Wakool* went to Kishimoto KKK as *Kwanto Maru*.

1913 March: *Benalla* was the third delivery and with her arrival *Narrung* was sold to Hong Kong owners and renamed *Mexico City*, whilst Kishimoto purchased *Wilcannia* (II) to join their *Kwanto Maru*, renaming their new acquisition *Shinkoko Maru*. Both these ships were ultimately sold to the French Government to replace war losses.

Dec: *Berrima*, fourth of the class, was commissioned.

1914 March saw the final member of the quintet delivered. She was the *Borda*. P&O plain black funnels were given to the seven Branch Service vessels and all signs of the Blue Anchor Line thereby disappeared.

Routes

London-Tenerife-Capetown-Adelaide-Melbourne-Hobart-Launceston-Sydney. Sydney-Suva-Levula (Fiji Islands). Albany added as a port of call in 1904.

Livery

Funnel Plain black. White band and diagonal chained anchor in blue.
Hull Black with pale pink waterline.
Uppers Brown.
Masts Brown.
Lifeboats White, 1910 Brown.

Fleet index

Illustrated fleet list

1 JEDDO

Bt 1865 William Walker, Rotherhithe; *T*: 327 g. **Dim** 123 ft (37.49 m) × 27 ft (8.23 m) × 14 ft 8 in (4.47 m). SV; Barque. **H** Wood.

1865 Built for builder.
1866 Lund purchased 8/64 share.
1868 Sold to Samuel Cocking & T. A. Singleton, London.
1871 Sold to F. D. Walker, Yokohama.
1872 Sold to Japanese at Kanagawa.

2 AMBASSADOR

Bt 1869 William Walker, Rotherhithe; *T*: 714 g. **Dim** 176 ft (53.64 m) × 31 ft 3 in (9.53 m) × 19 ft 1 in (5.82 m). SV; Barque. **H** Composite, iron frames wooden planking.

1869 Built for Wilhelm Lund.
1890 Sold to Burgess & Co, London.
1894 Sold to Ole J. Olsen, Christiansand (Oslo).
1895 Condemned and broken up.

3 MIKADO

Bt 1868 William Walker, Rotherhithe; *T*: 666 g. **Dim** 166 ft (50.6 m) × 31 ft (9.45 m) × 18 ft 9 in (5.72 m). SV; Ship.

1868 Built for builder. The Captain was J. E. Ilbery (lost with *Waratah* in 1909).
1874 Acquired by Wilhelm Lund.
1884 Sold to J. M. Way, London.
1886 Sold to E. F. Angel, London.
1888 Sold to S. Fegan, London.
1890 Sold to W. M. Ayre, London.
1891 Sold to R. Y. Ffitch and then Union SS Co, NZ, as hulk.

4 SERAPIS

Bt 1876 Scott & Co, Greenock; *T*: 1,027 g. **Dim** 224 ft (68.28 m) × 35 ft 6 in (10.82 m) × 20 ft 1 in (6.12 m). SV; Ship. **H** Iron.

1876 Built for W. Lund. Designed for Australian wool trade.
1890 Sold to P. N. Winther, Nordby.
1906 Sold to A. B. Massa, Genoa.
1912 Broken up at Genoa.

5 ELEANOR

Bt 1867 R. Lewis, Milford; *T*: 429 g. **Dim** 136 ft (41.45 m) × 27 ft 6 in (8.38 m) × 17 ft 1 in (5.21 m). SV; Barque. **H** Wood.

1867 Built for J. J. Holdsworth, London.
1882 Acquired by Lund.
1890 Broken up.

6 TALAVERA

Bt 1853 (builder's name not in Lloyds Register), Sunderland; *T*: 384 g. **Dim** 127 ft 6 in (38.86 m) × 25 ft 5 in (7.75 m) × 17 ft 2 in (5.23 m). SV; Barque. **H** Wood.

1853 Built for Duff & Co, Liverpool.
1855 Sold to A. Smith & Co.
1860 Sold to Neave & Co, London.
1870 Sold to Mannering & Co, London.
1876 Firm became Mannering & Anderson.
1881 Sold to J. F. Gibb, London.
1882 Acquired by Wilhelm Lund.
1890 Broken up.

7 ELLA

Bt 1873 P. V. Valin, Quebec; *T*: 1,011 g. **Dim** 178 ft (54.25 m) × 36 ft (10.97 m) × 21 ft 3 in (6.48 m). SV; Barque.

1873 Built for builder.
1885 Acquired by Lund.
1890 Broken up.

8 HARLAND

Bt 1885 Richardson Duck & Co, Stockton-on-Tees; *T*: 1,742 g. **Dim** 250 ft 9 in (76.43 m) × 39 ft (11.89 m) × 24 ft 1 in (7.34 m). SV; Ship. **H** Iron.

1885 Built for Lund.
1890 Sold to Stuart Bros, London.
1899 Sold to H. H. Schmidt, Hamburg. Renamed *Wilhelmine*.
1912 Sold to G. C. Brovig. Renamed *Bennestvet*.
1917 Transferred to Th Brovig.
1923 Broken up.

9

9 DELCOMYN

Bt 1880 Wigham Richardson, Newcastle; *T*: 1,817 g, 1,184 n. **Dim** 280 ft (84.34 m) × 35 ft 4 in (10.77 m) × 22 ft 7 in (6.88 m). **Eng** Sgl scr, 2 cyls, compound inverted; *Cyls*: 31 in (78.74 cm) and 62 in (157.48 cm); *Stroke*: 48 in (121.92 cm); 260 HP; *Stm P*: 90 lb; 9 kts; By builders. **H** Iron, 2 decks, fcsle 30 ft (9.14 m), bridge 16 ft (4.88 m), poop 26 ft (7.92 m).

1880 Oct: Built for London-Australia service. *Delcomyn* was commanded on her maiden voyage by Captain J. E. Ilbery, who was to be lost aboard *Waratah* in 1909.
1889 Sold to Bucknall Brothers, who in 1891 became British & Colonial SN Co.
1897 Sold to J. B. Lussich, Buenos Aires. Renamed *Felipe Lussich*. Sold to F. Francioni, Buenos Aires. Renamed *Corcega*. Sold to Cia Argentina de Navegacion (Mihanovich). Renamed *Patagonia*.
1916 Broken up.

10 YEOMAN

Bt 1882 Campbell, MacIntosh & Bowstead, Newcastle; *T*: 2,194 g, 1,427 n. **Dim** 285 ft 2 in (86.92 m) × 36 ft 7 in (11.15 m) × 26 ft (79.2 m). **Eng** Sgl scr, 2

10

cyls, compound inverted; *Cyls*: 35 in (88.9 cm) and 68 in (172.72 cm); *Stroke*: 48 in (121.92 cm); 300 HP; *Stm P*: 85 lb; 9 kts; By T. Clark, Newcastle. **H** Iron, 1 deck and spar deck.

1882 Mar: Entered service, London-Cape-Australia.
1887 Triple expansion engines installed; *Cyls*: 25 in (63.5 cm), 38½ in (97.79 cm) and 63 in (160.02 m); *Stroke*: 48 in (121.92 cm); 300 HP; *Stm P*: 50 lb; 10 kts; By Wigham Richardson, Newcastle.

1891 Sold to Vapores Serra, Bilbao, Spain. Renamed *Rita*.
1898 Seized by USS *Yale* off Puerto Rico during the Spanish-American War and renamed *Burnside*. Operated by the War Department of the US Government.
1923 Broken up in USA.

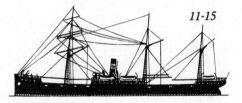

11-15

11 HUBBUCK

Bt 1886 J. L. Thompson & Sons, Sunderland; *T*: 2,749 g, 1,775 n. **Dim** 325 ft (99.06 m) × 40 ft (12.19 m) × 25 ft 10 in (7.87 m). **Eng** Sgl scr, tpl exp; *Cyls*: 27 in (68.58 cm), 42 in (106.68 cm) and 69 in (175.26 cm); *Stroke*: 45 in (114.3 cm); 400 HP; *Stm P*: 150 lb; 10 kts; By T. Richardson & Son, Hartlepool. **H** Steel, 2 decks, fcsle 40 ft (12.19 m), bridge 90 ft (27.43 m), poop 37 ft (11.28 m); *Pass*: 40 1st, located in the poop.

1886 The company's first steel hull. Introduced the three-mast silhouette of all the company's cargo vessels.
1898 Sold to Talbot SS Co (T. Bowen Rees) later transferred to their Egypt & Levant SS Co.
1910 Sold to Franco-British SS Co (Oliver & Co).

157

1914 Acquired by British Admiralty. Used as boom defence vessel at the mouth of the River Humber.
1919 Sold to Dutrus y Carsi, Valencia. Renamed *Eugenio Dutrus*.
1924 Apr 26: Wrecked near Tarifa, Southern Spain, en route Gijon-Cartagena.

12 RIVERINA

Details as *Hubbuck (11)* except: **Bt** 1887 Wigham Richardson, Newcastle; *T*: 2,883 g, 1,865 n. *Cyls*: 27 in (68.58 cm), 43 in (109.22 cm) and 71 in (180.34 cm). **H** Fcsle 39 ft (11.89 m), poop 39 ft (11.89 m).

1887 The first of the company's vessels to carry an Australian Aborigine name.
1890 Jan 27: Wrecked at Ram Head near Gabo Island, Victoria, en route Melbourne-Sydney.

13 MURRUMBIDGEE

Details as *Hubbuck (11)* except: **Bt** J. L. Thompson & Sons, Sunderland; *T*: 2,836 g, 1,836 n. **Eng** By T. Richardson & Sons, Hartlepool. **H** Fcsle 41 ft (12.5 m).

1887 Entered service.
1893 Sold to Bensaude & Co, Lisbon. Renamed *Peninsular*.
1901 Sold to Empresa Nacional de Navegacao para Africa-Portugueza.
1918 Owners retitled Companhia Nacional de Navegacao.
1923 Broken up.

14 WILCANNIA (I)

Details as *Hubbuck (11)* except: **Bt** 1888 Wigham Richardson, Newcastle; *T*: 2,718 g, 1,841 n. **Eng** By builders. **H** Fcsle 43 ft (13.11 m).

1888 Entered service.
1897 Sold to Alfred Holt, Ocean SS Co. Renamed *Anchises*.
1898 Transferred to Holt's Dutch subsidiary Nederlandsche Stoomboot Maatschappij Oceaan.
1906 Reverted to Ocean SS Co.
1910 Broken up at Briton Ferry.

15 ECHUCA

Details as *Hubbuck (11)* except: **Bt** 1889 Raylton Dixon, Middlesbrough; *T*: 2,826 g, 1,822 n.

1889 Entered service.
1898 Sold to Robert Sloman, Hamburg. Renamed *Catania*.
1906 Sold to Furness Withy & Co, West Hartlepool. Renamed *Almeriana*.
1914 Broken up at Briton Ferry.

16-18

16 BUNGAREE

Bt 1889 Wigham Richardson, Newcastle; *T*: 2,893 g, 1,875 n. **Dim** 335 ft (102.11 m) × 42 ft 1 in (12.83 m) × 24 ft (7.32 m). **Eng** Sgl scr, tpl exp; *Cyls*: 28 in (71.12 cm), 45 in (114.3 cm) and 73 in (185.42 cm); *Stroke*: 48 in (121.92 cm); 420 NHP; 2 dbl ended boilers; *Stm P*: 150 lb; 10 kts; By builders. **H** Steel, 2 decks and spar deck, fcsle 41 ft (12.5 m), poop 214 ft (65.23 m).

1889 Delivered for Australian service.
1903 Sold to Quebec SS Co. Renamed *Parima*.
1920 Transferred to Bermuda & West India SS Co, Hamilton, Bermuda. Same name.
1925 Broken up in Italy.

17 CULGOA

Details as *Bungaree (16)* except: **Bt** 1890 J. L. Thompson & Sons, Sunderland; *T*: 3,325 g, 1,980 n.

1890 Entered service.
1895 Refrigerated space installed.
1898 Sold to US Government for use in the Spanish-American War as a store ship.
1922 Sold to L. H. Stewart, New York. Renamed *Champlain*.
1924 Broken up at New York.

18 YARRAWONGA

Bt 1891 J. L. Thompson & Sons, Sunderland; *T*: 4,011 g, 2,555 n. **Dim** 360 ft (109.73 m) × 44 ft 6 in (13.56 m) × 24 ft 3 in (7.39 m). **Eng** Sgl scr, tpl exp; *Cyls*: 28 in (71.12 cm), 45 in (114.3 cm) and 73 in (185.42 cm); *Stroke*: 54 in (137.16 cm); 445 NHP; *Stm P*: 115 lb; 10

kts; By Wigham Richardson, Newcastle. **H**
Steel, 2 decks, fcsle 43 ft (13.11 m), poop
233 ft (71.02 m).

1891 Entered service.
1903 Dec: Sold to R. P. Houston,
Liverpool. Renamed *Hermione*.
1917 Apr 14: Mined off Coningsbey
Lightship. Towed into Dunmore Bay,
Waterford, but condemned as she lay and
broken up.

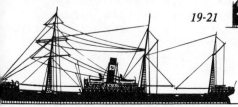

19-21

19 WOOLLOOMOOLOO

Bt 1891 Wigham Richardson, Newcastle-
upon-Tyne; *T*. 3,521 g, 2,221 n. **Dim** 360 ft
(109.73 m) × 44 ft 5 in (13.54 m) × 26 ft
(7.92 m). **Eng** Sgl scr, tpl exp; *Cyls*: 28 in
(71.12 cm), 45 in (114.3 cm) and 73 in
(185.42 cm); *Stroke*: 54 in (137.16 cm); 445
NHP; *Stm P*: 155 lb; 10 kts. **H** Steel, 2
decks, fcsle 38 ft (11.58 m), bridge 98 ft
(29.87 m), poop 36 ft (10.97 m).

1891 Entered service.
1901 Mar: Sold to R. P. Houston & Co.
Renamed *Harmonides*.
1902 Rammed and sank the Red Star
vessel *Waesland* off Anglesey.
1919 Sold to Kaye Son & Co. Renamed
Khartoum.
1926 Broken up at Genoa.

20 WALLARAH

Details as *Woolloomooloo* (*19*) except: **Bt**
1891 Sunderland Ship Building Co,
Sunderland; *T*: 3,505 g, 2,203 n.

1891 Entered service.
Aug 2: Wrecked on maiden voyage on
Dassen Island, Cape Coast, South Africa.

21 WARRNAMBOOL

Details as *Woolloomooloo* (*19*) except: **Bt**
1892 Sunderland Ship Building Co,
Sunderland; *T*: 3,515 g, 2,213 n. **H** Fcsle
39 ft (11.89 m), bridge 96 ft (29.26 m), poop
40 ft (12.19 m).

1892 Entered service.
1900 Dec: Sold to R. P. Houston & Co.
Renamed *Harmodius*.
1919 Sold with *Harmonides* (*19*) to Kaye
Son & Co. Renamed *Kut*.
1926 Broken up at Briton Ferry.

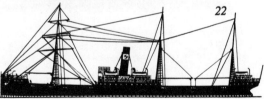

22

22 WARRIGAL

Bt 1893 Sunderland Ship Building Co,
Sunderland; *T*: 4,387 g, 2,778 n. **Dim**
400 ft (121.92 m) × 47 ft 7 in (14.5 m) ×
26 ft 7 in (8.1 m). **Eng** Sgl scr, quad exp;
Cyls: 25½ in (64.77 cm), 36½ in
(92.71 cm), 52 in (132.08 cm) and 78 in
(198.12 cm); *Stroke*: 54 in (137.16 cm); 552
NHP; *Stm P*: 200 lb; 11 kts; By Wigham
Richardson, Newcastle. **H** Steel, 2 decks,
fcsle 46 ft (14.02 m), bridge 100 ft
(30.48 m), poop 44 ft (13.41 m).

1893 Entered service. An enlarged version
of *Woolloomooloo* (*19*) class and without
sisters of her size.
1906 Mar: Sold to W. Thomson,
Dundee. Renamed *Latona*.
1908 Sold to Cairns, Noble & Co.
May 20: Sank off Wolf's Rock Lighthouse
following a collision.

23 NARRUNG

See P&O section for details of this ship.

24 WAKOOL

See P&O section for details of this ship.

25 WILCANNIA (II)

See P&O section for details of this ship.

26 COMMONWEALTH

See P&O section for details of this ship.

27 GEELONG

See P&O section for details of this ship.

28 WARATAH

Bt 1908 Barclay Curle, Glasgow; *T*:
9,339 g, 6,004 n. **Dim** 465 ft (141.73 m) ×
59 ft 5 in (18.11 m) × 27 ft (8.23 m). **Eng**

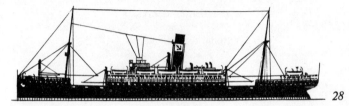

28

Tw scr, 2 quad exp; *Cyls*: 23 in (58.42 cm), 32½ in (82.55 cm), 46½ in (118.11 cm) and 67 in (170.18 cm); *Stroke*: 48 in (121.92 cm); 1,003 NHP; 5 sgl ended boilers; *Stm P*: 215 lb; 14 kts; By builders. **H** Steel, 2 decks and spar deck, fcsle 85 ft (25.91 m), bridge 176 ft (53.64 m), poop 100 ft (30.48 m); *Pass*: 100 1st, 750 emigrants.

1908 Nov 6: Maiden voyage London-Capetown-Adelaide-Melbourne-Sydney. **1909** July 26: Left Durban for Capetown on the inbound leg of her second voyage. Reported next day by *Clan MacIntyre* but thereafter disappeared without trace, to become one of the greatest unsolved mysteries of the sea. 92 passengers and 119 crew lost.